Theoleptos of Philadelpheia

THE MONASTIC DISCOURSES

A Critical Edition, Translation and Study
by Robert E. Sinkewicz, C.S.B.

The *Monastic Discourses* constitute the largest part of the surviving
literary corpus of Theoleptos of Philadelpheia. They cover a variety of
genres ranging from counsels of spiritual direction to exhortations on
monastic discipline and liturgical homilies. Written between the years
1307 and 1322, they are prime-of importance for the study of Byzantine
spirituality just prior to the outbreak of the Hesychast and Palamite
controversies; they in fact contain evidence indicating that negative
criticisms of certain tendencies in spirituality were already emerging. Only
the writings of St. Gregorios of Sinai are comparable in importance
for this period. These texts are almost unique in that they are for the
most part addressed to women, namely, to the princess Eirene-Eulogia
Choumnaina and the nuns under her direction at the monastery of
Philanthropos Soter in Constantinople. As such they offer some valuable
insights into the life of an aristocratic religious community in the capital.

Born in 1250, Theoleptos of Philadelpheia emerged on the scene as
a prominent churchman after the demise of the ill-fated Union of the
Churches concluded at the Council of Lyon in 1274. Already well known
for his opposition to the unionist policy of the emperor, Michael VII
Palaiologos, Theoleptos was elevated to the Metropolitan see of Philadelpheia in 1283. Subsequently, he played a major role in the opposition
to the Arsenite schism. His two *Philadelpheian Discourses*, written sometime between 1285 and 1310, demonstrate the solicitude of his pastoral
ministry among the people of Philadelpheia during these troubled years.
These texts also offer important insights into Byzantine ecclesiology. The
letters addressed by Theoleptos to Eirene-Eulogia during the years 1307
till his death at the end of 1322 provide many details regarding the
complex personality of this Byzantine princess prior to her involvement
with the anti-Palamite cause and the less sympathetic opinions of her
held by the members of the opposing camp. Along with the *Monastic
Discourses*, these works form one of the most important (and least
known) dossiers in the corpus of Late Byzantine religious literature.

The *Monastic Discourses* are here edited, most for the first time, and
provided with an English translation and an accompanying study. The
Greek text is based on the fourteenth century manuscript, Ottobonianus
graecus 405 in the Vatican Library. A full set of indices is provided
to assist in the study of the text.

STUDIES AND TEXTS 111

Theoleptos of Philadelpheia

THE MONASTIC DISCOURSES

A Critical Edition, Translation and Study

by

ROBERT E. SINKEWICZ, C.S.B.

PONTIFICAL INSTITUTE OF MEDIAEVAL STUDIES

Acknowledgment

This book has been published with the help of a grant
from the Canadian Federation for the Humanities, using
funds provided by the Social Sciences and Humanities
Research Council of Canada

CANADIAN CATALOGUING IN PUBLICATION DATA

Theoleptos, Metropolitan of Philadelpheia, ca. 1250-ca. 1326
   Theoleptos of Philadelpheia : the Monastic discourses

(Studies and texts, ISSN 0082-5328 ; 111)
Text in English and Greek.
Includes bibliographical references and index.
ISBN 0-88844-111-8

1. Monastic and religious life of women - History - Middle Ages, 600-1500 -
Sources.   2. Monastic and religious life - History - Middle Ages, 600-1500 -
Sources.   3. Monasticism and religious orders, Orthodox Eastern - Lydia.
4. Monasticism and religious orders, Orthodox Eastern - Turkey - Istanbul.
I. Sinkewicz, Robert E. (Robert Edward), 1948- . II. Title.   III. Series:
Studies and texts (Pontifical Institute of Mediaeval Studies) ; 111.

BX385.A1T43 1992   271'.98'0949618   C92-094711-5

PRINTED BY UNIVERSA, WETTEREN, BELGIUM

Contents

Preface VII

Abbreviations VIII

1. Life and Works of Theoleptos 1

    A. Sources 1
    B. Early Life 2
    C. Early Episcopate 6
    D. Later Ecclesiastical and Political Involvements 9
    E. The Arsenite Schism 11
    F. Eirene-Eulogia Choumnaina 18
    G. The Writings of Theoleptos 20
        1. The Letters and the *Monastic Discourses* 20
        2. Liturgical Compositions 24

2. The Teaching of Theoleptos 26

    A. Introduction 26
    B. Monastic Life 26
    C. From Asceticism to Contemplation 32
    D. The Ecclesial Dimension 47
        1. Integration of Liturgical and Monastic Spirituality 47
        2. The Church 56
    E. Conclusion 63

3. The Text 67

    A. Manuscripts of the *Monastic Discourses* 67
    B. The Contents 69
    C. Remaining Manuscripts 74
    D. Printed Editions 76
        1. The *Philokalia* Edition 76
        2. Recent Editions 76
    E. The Remaining Manuscripts and the *Philokalia* Edition ... 77
    F. Constitution of the Text 77
    G. Sigla and Abbreviations 78

Theoleptos of Philadelpheia, *Monastic Discourses*

Text and Translation 80/81

Bibliography 385
Index of Biblical Citations 391
Index of References to Classical, Patristic and Byzantine Texts 399
Index of Images of Daily Life 401
General Index 403

Preface

During the latter part of his career Sévérien Salaville of the Institut Français des Études Byzantines was preparing a critical edition of the works of Theoleptos of Philadelpheia. Apart from the brief studies and editions of individual texts noted in the bibliography below, Fr. Salaville was unable to complete this work before his death. He did however prepare a French translation of the *Monastic Discourses*, which Albert Failler graciously loaned to me and from which I profited greatly in preparing my own translation. I hope that the fine work of this French translation will not be lost to the public but will find its way into print someday soon.

I would also like to express my thanks to Jean Hoff of the Department of Publications of the Pontifical Institute for her careful reading of the text and translation and for the numerous valuable suggestions and improvements which she was able to offer.

The research for this edition, translation and study was assisted by a grant from the Social Sciences and Humanities Research Council of Canada.

Abbreviations

AG — *Anecdota Graeca*
BZ — *Byzantinische Zeitschrift*
CFHB — *Corpus fontium historiae byzantinae*
DS — *Dictionnaire de spiritualité*
EO — *Échos d'Orient*
EP — *Epistula*
EPP — *Epistulae*
GCS — *Die griechischen christlichen Schriftsteller*
JÖB — *Jahrbuch der Österreichischen Byzantinistik*
MD — *Monastic Discourses*
PD — *Philadelpheian Discourses*
PG — *Patrologia graeca*
REB — *Revue des études byzantines*
RSBN — *Revista di studi Bizantini e neoellenici*, n.s.
SC — *Sources chrétiennes*

Abbreviations for the books of the Bible follow the norms of the *Revised Standard Version*. Personal names are given in the standard anglicized or latinized form for Patristic authors, but in the transcribed Greek form for Byzantine authors.

1

Life and Works of Theoleptos

A. Sources

Given the prominence he held in the eyes of his contemporaries, it is perhaps surprising that so little information has come down to us about the life and ecclesiastical career of Theoleptos of Philadelpheia. He was eulogized by his great friend, Nikephoros Choumnos, the imperial chancellor under Andronikos II, but in the tradition of that literary form the laudatory verbiage took precedence over the facts.[1] Three historians of the period, all of whom were well acquainted with the bishop, wrote of his ecclesiastical and political involvements, offering at least a chronological framework and some of the more significant details of his career.[2] As one would expect, his friends and colleagues either wrote to him or often spoke of him in their letters but here too the literary genre was not given to a presentation of abundant details.[3] Unlike his less modest contemporaries, Theoleptos

---

[1] Nikephoros Choumnos, *Epitaphios*, ed. J.F. Boissonade, *Anecdota graeca*, 5 vols. (Paris, 1829-1833; repr. Hildesheim, 1962) 5:183-239. Cf. J. Verpeaux, *Nicéphore Choumnos, Homme d'état et humaniste byzantin (ca 1250/1255-1327)* (Paris, 1959), pp. 97-99.

[2] Georgios Pachymeres, *Georges Pachymérès, Relations Historiques*, ed. A. Failler, 2 vols. (CFHB 24.1-2; Paris, 1984); *Georgii Pachymeris de Michaele et Andronico Paleologis libri tredecim*, ed. I. Bekker, 2 vols. (Bonn, 1835): in the following notes the older Bonn edition is cited only for those sections that have not yet appeared in the Failler edition. Ioannes Kantakouzenos, *Ioannis Cantacuzeni eximperatoris Historiarum libri IV*, ed. L. Schopen, 3 vols. (Bonn, 1828-1832). Nikephoras Gregoras, *Nicephori Gregorae Byzantina Historia*, ed. L. Schopen and I. Bekker, 3 vols. (Bonn, 1829-1845).

[3] Especially Nikephoros Choumnos; letters edited by J.F. Boissonade, *Anecdota nova* (Paris, 1844; repr. Hildesheim, 1962) EPP 88-89 (117-125), 91 (126-127), 94-97 (128-135), 128 (148-149). Cf. also Nikephoros Gregoras, EP 61, *Nicephori Gregorae Epistulae*, ed. P.A.M. Leone, 2 vols. (Matino, 1982-1983) 2:183-185. Unfortunately there is no surviving letter collection from Theoleptos' other great friend, Theodoros Mouzalon.

himself apparently saw no reason to bequeath his correspondence to posterity.[4] For some of the surviving letter collections, their loss would have left history no poorer, but in the case of Theoleptos the few letters preserved by his spiritual daughter, the princess Eirene-Eulogia Choumnaina, suggest that the bishop's humility may have deprived history of a source of great value.[5] The bishop's own writings say almost nothing about his career, but they do speak eloquently of the pastoral care he devoted to his people in Philadelpheia and of the spiritual teaching he offered to the monastery of Philanthropos Soter in Constantinople.[6] With these sources and a few minor notices history must be content.

B. EARLY LIFE

According to Nikephoros Choumnos, Theoleptos was born in Nikaia in 1250.[7] Nothing is known of his family or of this early period of his life. His own writings witness to the fact that he must have enjoyed a higher education and his contemporaries commented on his erudition, which included even the profane sciences.[8] By the year 1275 Theoleptos was already married and a deacon in Nikaia.[9] It seems that he was not comfortable with the married vocation, for he would often retire into the countryside around the city in order to practise asceticism. Choumnos' account is rather vague at this point, but it may be that Theoleptos was in fact spending his time in nearby monasteries.[10] On

---

[4] A very large number of letter collections have survived from this period. If Theoleptos had 'published' his letters, they would almost certainly have been circulated in enough copies to guarantee their survival.

[5] One of these letters was edited many years ago by S. Salaville, "Une lettre et un discours inédits de Théolepte de Philadelphie," REB 5 (1947) 105-106; the remainder are being edited by A.C. Hero, "The Unpublished Letters of Theoleptos, Metropolitan of Philadelphia (1283-1322)," *Journal of Modern Hellenism* 3 (1986) 1-31; idem, 4 (1987) 1-17; the remaining two letters will be published shortly.

[6] For the pastoral care he exercised in Philadelpheia see R.E. Sinkewicz, "A Critical Edition of the Anti-Arsenite Discourses of Theoleptos of Phildelpheia," *Mediaeval Studies* 50 (1988) 46-95.

[7] *Epitaphios* 188 (Nikaia), 200 (Theoleptos was 25 in 1275 when Patriarch Ioannes Bekkos [1275-1282] ordered the strict enforcement of the Union of Lyon). The Union was promulgated in Constantinople on 16 Jan. 1275 according to Pachymeres, 5.22 (508-511).

[8] Kantakouzenos 1.14 (1:67). As was often the case, study of the profane sciences may not have extended much beyond rhetoric which included an acquaintance with a restricted corpus of the Greek Classics.

[9] Choumnos, *Epitaphios* 200.

[10] *Epitaphios* 201. R. Janin, *Les églises et les monastères des grands centres byzantins* (Paris, 1975), pp. 105-125.

these occasions Satan tempted him with lustful memories of his beautiful wife, who was much attached to her husband. The young deacon redoubled his ascetic efforts but without success. Finally, Theoleptos submitted himself to the direction of a monk renowned for his holiness and revealed to him the temptation that was troubling him. Through the prayers of this monk the devil withdrew and harassed him no longer. The same monk then began to instruct him in the ways of asceticism, contemplation and vigilance of the mind.[11]

On 16 January 1275 the Union of the Churches established at the Council Lyon in the previous year was solemnly proclaimed in Constantinople.[12] Theoleptos together with the monks in the vicinity of Nikaia were apparently vocal in their opposition to the unionist policy of Michael VIII Palaiologos. Theoleptos was arrested and brought before the emperor in Constantinople. According to the interview reported by Choumnos, Theoleptos was quite blunt in stating his opposition to Church Union and in accusing the emperor of perverting the sacred scriptures. This did not sit well with Michael VIII and with his attendants who administered a beating to the deacon.[13] The patriarch of Alexandria, Athanasios II, was among the bishops present there and attempted to persuade Theoleptos to adopt a more conciliatory attitude toward the imperial policy. Since he persisted in his recalcitrance, he was thrown into prison. However, his imprisonment turned out to be a brief one and he was soon allowed to return to Nikaia.[14]

Back in Nikaia, Theoleptos retired to a hermitage where he could converse with God in solitude.[15] There was still, however, the problem posed by his wife. In his *Epitaphios*, Choumnos explained that the devil had persuaded her that she was being wronged by her husband. She went to him and upbraided him for abandoning the marriage which he had freely chosen. The woman was under the influence of the devil's deception and could not be persuaded to love the ways of God and

---

[11] Καὶ οὗτος τὸν κατὰ θεὸν βίον, πρᾶξιν ὁμοῦ καὶ θεωρίαν καὶ νῆψιν νοὸς παρ' ἐκείνου, εὖ μάλα καὶ καλῶς καὶ οἰονεὶ κατ' ἐπιστήμην εἰδότος, διδάσκεται, Choumnos, *Epitaphios* 201.

[12] Pachymeres 5.22 (508-511).

[13] *Epitaphios* 204-205.

[14] *Epitaphios* 206. On the activities of Athanasios II see A. Failler, "Le séjour d'Athanase II d'Alexandrie à Constantinople," REB 35 (1977) 43-71. Athanasios II may have interceded with the emperor to have Theoleptos released, just as he did later for Ioannes Kosmas, the future patriarch. See Failler, p. 47.

[15] Choumnos, *Epitaphios* 209.

turn away from the affairs of the world for the benefit of her soul. Only after a full year did the devil give up the contest and withdraw.[16]

This episode recounted by Nikephoros Choumnos should be understood not so much as a devaluation of the married state in itself but as an indication of the higher value given to the monastic vocation. In harmony with the hagiographical tradition, Choumnos understood that the special call of God granted to Theoleptos took precedence over all other human commitments including that of the marriage bond. In this context opposition to God's plan could only be understood as the work of the enemy.[17]

Even in his eremitical retirement Theoleptos was sought out by many both as a defender of Orthodoxy and as a spiritual counsellor. Choumnos noted that this was taking place at a time when he was not yet in priestly orders and had no power to administer sacramental confession.[18] Theoleptos' withdrawal from the world lasted for a total of eight years.[19] During that time he came under the influence of at least two and perhaps three spiritual directors. First, there was the monk, already mentioned, who initiated him into the spiritual life.[20] Then, there was Nikephoros the Hesychast. In the second of his *Triads in Defence of the Holy Hesychasts* Gregorios Palamas mentions that Theoleptos was among those instructed in divine things by Nikephoros during the time of the latter's exile from Mount Athos.[21] If the witness of Palamas is taken seriously, this contact between Nikephoros and Theoleptos poses a problem. The imperial police brought Nikephoros and his companions to Constantinople sometime early in 1276. Nikephoros was imprisoned there for some five and a half months. He was then taken by the Venetians by sea to St. John of Acre to appear before a Latin tribunal. This would mean that the contact between the two men would have to be placed at the time when both were in prison in the capital during the spring of 1276. At some later date it seems that Nikephoros returned to Mount Athos. Conceivably, he could have met Theoleptos on his return journey, but such an

---

[16] *Epitaphios* 209-212.

[17] Choumnos, of course, was also speaking from the vantage point of hindsight.

[18] *Epitaphios* 212.

[19] See Eulogia, EP 15.83-86, and Director, EP 16.20-32, *A Woman's Quest for Spiritual Guidance. The Correspondence of Princess Irene Eulogia Choumnaina Palaiologina*, ed. A. Hero (Brookline, MA, 1986).

[20] Choumnos, *Epitaphios* 201.

[21] *Triad* 2.2.3 (323), *Grégoire Palamas. Défense des saints hésychastes*, ed. J. Meyendorff, 2 vols., 2nd edition (Spicilegium sacrum lovaniense, Études et documents 30; Louvain, 1973).

alternative is rather unlikely. It would seem therefore that the witness of Palamas should be treated with some caution.[22]

When the patriarch Philotheos Kokkinos wrote his *Encomium* for Gregorios Palamas, he stated that Theoleptos was on Mount Athos when he was called to the leadership of the church of Philadelpheia.[23] Philotheos had himself been a monk on the Holy Mountain and could have learned of Theoleptos' sojourn there from monks who had known him.[24] Nevertheless, it is strange that Choumnos makes no reference to such an episode in his *Epitaphios*.[25]

Theoleptos' third spiritual relationship was with the monk Neilos, whom Choumnos referred to in highly laudatory terms.[26] According to the *Epitaphios*, Theoleptos sought out Neilos for fear that he might be running the race in vain, while thinking to himself that he was running well.[27] When Neilos fell ill and was on the point of death, Theoleptos was inconsolable over their impending separation. However, three days after Neilos' death he appeared to Theoleptos in a dream. It was through this experience that Theoleptos received the gifts of the Spirit that enabled him to write about vigilance and watchfulness of the mind.[28] This account in the *Epitaphios* would suggest that the relationship with Neilos was one of spiritual friendship which had a decisive influence on the life of Theoleptos.[29]

---

[22] I am assuming that Nikephoros the Hesychast is identical with the Nikephoros of the *Dialexis of Clement and Nikephoros* in *Dossier grec de l'Union de Lyon (1273-1277)*, ed. V. Laurent and J. Darrouzès (Archives de l'Orient chrétien 16; Paris, 1976), pp. 486-507 (text), 82-88 (discussion). Cf. D. Stiernon, "Nicéphore l'Hésychaste," DS 11 (1982) 198-203. A. Rigo adduces further reasons for doubting the testimony of Palamas in this case. See "Nota sulla dottrina ascetico-spirituale de Teoleptos Metropolita de Filadelfia (1250/51-1322)," RSBN 24 (1987) 170-172.

[23] "Gregorios received these and other teachings from Theoleptos, that truly famous luminary of Philadelpheia, who moved on, or rather went up from the sacred hesychia and community of the Holy Mountain to assume the leadership of the Church [of Philadelpheia]," *Encomium Gregorii Palamae*, PG 151:561A.

[24] Cf. A. Solignac, "Philothée Kokkinos," DS 12 (1984) 1389-1392.

[25] Rigo takes this as sufficient reason to reject the possibility of a stay on Athos ("Nota," p. 170), but he fails to take into account the text from Philotheos Kokkinos which clearly places Theoleptos on the Holy Mountain, which can only mean Mount Athos.

[26] Καὶ προσλαμβάνει Νεῖλον ἐκεῖνον τὸν μέγαν, πάντων, ὧν ἡμεῖς ἴσμεν ἐπὶ τοῖς τοιούτοις σπουδάσμασι λαμπρὰν δόξαν ἐσχηκότων τὰ πρῶτα φέροντα, *Epitaphios* 217-218.

[27] ... μή ποτε λάθοι τρέχων εἰς κενόν, ἑαυτῷ δοκῶν ὀρθῶς τρέχειν, ibid. 217.

[28] Ibid. 217-220.

[29] Meyendorff, on the contrary, has taken Neilos to be "un des maîtres de Théolepte" in his *Introduction*, p. 41.

John Meyendorff has suggested the identification of the Neilos of the *Epitaphios* with Neilos the Italian mentioned by Gregorios Palamas in his *Triads* and by Theoktistos in his life of Patriarch Athanasios I, and also with Neilos of Sicily whom Pachymeres referred to in disparaging terms because of the monk's views on appropriate and inappropriate almsgiving.[30] Neilos would then have been a monk associated with one of the monasteries of Mount Saint-Auxentios on the Asian side of the Bosphoros not far from Chalcedon. This would place him well within the region of the monasteries and hermitages frequented by Theoleptos prior to his call to the episcopacy in 1283.

C. EARLY EPISCOPATE

The feeble Union of the Churches established at the Council of Lyon in 1274 effectively came to an end when Michael VIII died on 11 December 1282 and was succeeded by his son Andronikos II who two weeks later deposed the unionist patriarch Ioannes Bekkos. The elderly and ailing Joseph I was restored to the patriarchal throne on 31 December only to die a few months later on 23 March 1283. Gregorios II of Cyprus was raised to the throne as Joseph's successor on 11 April 1283. Two weeks later the removal of all the bishops who had supported the unionist cause was formally proclaimed in the capital.[31] It would have been not long after this that Theoleptos was elevated to the metropolitan see of Philadelpheia at the young age of only thirty-three years.[32]

Although deposed from the patriarchate and imprisoned in Brusa, Bekkos had not yet given up the fight. He immediately undertook a campaign for the vindication of his theology. The council that Bekkos so much wanted was finally convoked on 5 February 1285 in the palace

---

[30] Meyendorff, *Introduction*, pp. 40-41. See also Rigo, RSBN 24 (1987) 171-174.

[31] On the deposition of the bishops see V. Laurent, *Les Regestes des actes du patriarcat de Constantinople*, Vol 1: *Les actes des patriarches*, Fasc. 4: *Les Regestes de 1208 à 1309* (Le patriarcat byzantin, Série 1; Paris, 1971), N. 1463.

[32] Eulogia, EP 15.83-86 (ed. Hero): "My master, the bishop, became even more enlightened at the age of thirty-three (eight years after he retired from the world) through the help of those who benefited from him." Director, EP 16.20-32 (ed. Hero): "And even if he assumed the episcopal office eight years after he retired from the world, and thirty-three years after he was born, and rushed to help many people, bear in mind and consider the power which is bestowed by divine grace upon those who have been called to this task and have well obeyed the call. Remember also that before he was called, that God-loving man did not devote himself to such a task nor did he dare to do so, but he lived in deserted places free of crowds, until he was given the word through the holy ordination."

of Blachernai. Two further sessions were held but Bekkos would not yield to the Orthodox arguments on the procession of the Holy Spirit. Finally, a further session in August requested Patriarch Gregorios to draw up a *Tomos* that would provide a detailed refutation of the unionist theology of the procession. The *Tomos* was signed and the Council of Blachernai was brought to a close.[33]

In the *Tomos* Gregorios of Cyprus had expounded the theology of the procession of the Holy Spirit in a form that departed from the traditional stock arguments. The Fathers had spoken of a procession of the Holy Spirit from the Father *through* the Son. The Latin Church insisted that the Spirit proceeded from the Father and from the Son (but *tanquam ex uno principio*).[34] Patriarch Gregorios, in an effort to allow for an eternal relationship between the Son and the Spirit, proposed an eternal *manifestation* of the Spirit through the Son. This was the problematic doctrine expounded in the *Tomos* of Blachernai. It was problematic for two reasons: it departed from the precise wording of the statements of the Fathers and it sounded like a concession to Latin theology.[35]

Opposition to the *Tomos* was not long in coming. The initial adversaries came from the ranks of the lower clergy, from the unionists, from the Arsenite party and from Georgios Moschabar's circle. It seems that the hierarchy originally stayed somewhat aloof from this opposition movement. It was not until April 1287 that Gregorios sought assistance from his bishops. At that point the bishop of Ephesus, Ioannes Cheilas,

[33] Theoleptos of Philadelpheia was among the signatories of the *Tomos*. There is some confusion regarding the form of his name in the document. See V. Laurent, "Les signataires du second synode des Blakhernes (été 1285)," EO 26 (1927) 129-149. According to Laurent, two fifteenth-century manuscripts (one closely dependent on the other) give his name in the form, Theopemptos. A third manuscript, dated to the fourteenth century, reports the usual form, Theoleptos. Laurent apparently took Theopemptos to be the correct reading and suggested that this form was the bishop's monastic name which he used here, perhaps because of some hesitation regarding the patriarch's theological position. This explanation is unconvincing. The Theopemptos reading is based effectively on only one manuscript witness which could well be erroneous. Even if Theopemptos were correct, the bishop could hardly deny that he had signed the *Tomos* and thus endorsed the theological positions contained therein.

[34] Cf. the definition of the Council of Lyon in 1274: "Fideli ac devota professione fatemur, quod Spiritus Sanctus aeternaliter ex Patre et Filio, non tanquam ex duobus principiis, sed tanquam ex uno principio ... procedit.", *Enchiridion symbolorum definitionum et declarationum de rebus fidei et morum*, ed. H. Denzinger and A. Schönmetzer, 32nd edition (Rome, 1965), no. 850.

[35] A more detailed exposition of the theology of the *Tomos* can be found in A. Papadakis, *Crisis in Byzantium. The 'Filioque' Controversy in the Patriarchate of Gregory II of Cyprus (1283-1289)* (New York, 1983), pp. 86-96.

may already have had doubts about the patriarch's theology, for a year later (February-March 1288) he still had not replied to Gregorios' request of the previous year. At about this time Theoleptos left the capital and returned to Philadelpheia. Before very long he would join Ioannes of Ephesus and Daniel of Kyzikos as leaders of the opposition.[36]

The situation was made much worse when a former student of the patriarch, a monk by the name of Mark, decided that he could clear up the controversy by publishing his own commentary on the *Tomos*. This would have been shortly before autumn 1288. When the metropolitan of Philadelpheia received a copy of the commentary just after its publication, he went off to discuss it with his great friend the Logothete Theodoros Mouzalon. They quickly came to the conclusion that Mark's commentary contained serious dogmatic errors and that these were in fact the same opinions held by Gregorios II in his *Tomos*.[37]

Sometime in the second half of 1288 Patriarch Gregorios retired to the monastery of the Hodegoi but he continued to fulfil his administrative responsibilities.[38] Pressure to secure his removal was mounting rapidly. The opposition was now divided into two groups. One group led by Ioannes of Ephesus and Daniel of Kyzikos wanted to have the problematic theology of the *Tomos* formally condemned and the patriarch removed from office. The other group was led by Theoleptos, who had changed his mind on the whole affair and had come to see that it was really Mark and not the patriarch who was responsible for the controversy. Theoleptos counted on his side both the emperor Andronikos II and Theodoros Mouzalon, and even Georgios Moschabar, one of Gregorios' former opponents.

The affair was finally settled in June 1289 at an assembly in the imperial palace. Theoleptos pronounced publicly on the patriarch's orthodoxy and attributed the cause of all the troubles to Mark. As he had agreed to do, for the sake of the peace of the church, Gregorios offered his script of resignation on the next day — but without his signature. This provoked a certain amount of consternation but the metropolitan of Philadelpheia managed to quell the objections and the patriarch dutifully retired.[39]

---

[36] Cf. Papadakis, pp. 102-112; Laurent, *Regestes*, NN. 1505, 1506, 1509; S. Eustratiades, Γρηγορίου τοῦ Κυπρίου οἰκουμενικοῦ πατριάρχου Ἐπιστολαὶ καὶ Μῦθοι (Alexandria, 1910), ep 179, pp. 185-186; Pachymeres 2.3 (2:115-117).

[37] Pachymeres 2.4 (2:117-120).

[38] Pachymeres 2.6 (2:121-122)

[39] Pachymeres 2.8-9 (2:127-133). Cf. Papadakis, *Crisis*, pp. 132-137.

D. Later Ecclesiastical and Political Involvements

During the first patriarchate of Athanasios I (1289-1293) the sources say little about the ecclesiastical involvements of Theoleptos. There are no surviving documents indicating his participation in the Standing Synod of the capital. In 1294 Theodoros Mouzalon died and Nikephoros Choumnos, another close friend of Theoleptos, assumed his functions in the imperial administration.[40] From the letters that Choumnos wrote to him, it seems that the bishop may have served as his spiritual father.[41] In addition Choumnos often sought the advice of Theoleptos on his writings.[42]

In 1297 Theoleptos was in Constantinople for a synodal deliberation under Patriarch Ioannes XII Kosmas (1294-1303) to determine whether the emperor could treat with the sultan of Babylon (Cairo) as his brother. Opinion was divided but with the support of Theoleptos the decision was made to sanction the emperor's proposal.[43]

About the same time or not long afterwards the metropolitan of Philadelpheia was involved in a much more serious affair. Andronikos II was faced with problems on the empire's frontiers — with the Tatars in the North, with Serbia in the West and with the aftermath of a revolt in Asia Minor that had been led by Alexios Philanthropenos. In need of a loyal and able general, the emperor decided to appoint Ioannes Tarchaneiotes commander of the East. He did so in spite of the fact that Tarchaneiotes was the acknowledged leader of one of the Arsenite factions. Needless to say, Patriarch Ioannes Kosmas was not pleased and he communicated his displeasure to the emperor.[44] Andronikos II for his part refused to entertain any criticisms of his new general. Tarchaneiotes proceeded to organize the defence of Asia Minor against Turkish encroachments. In so doing he deprived many of the soldiers of their οἰκονομίαι. Unwilling to accept this situation, the malcontents went to Theoleptos and insinuated that Tarchaneiotes was disloyal to the emperor and. was in fact plotting a rebellion. Theoleptos was already on hostile terms with the general and opposed his championing of the Arsenite cause. Theoleptos and the dissidents met up with Tarchaneiotes at Pyrgion, where he had taken refuge in

---

[40] Verpeaux, p. 39.

[41] E.g., EP 88, AG 117-119.

[42] Choumnos addressed a least two of his religious compositions to Theoleptos. See Verpeaux, pp. 18, 146-147.

[43] Pachymeres 3.23 (2:246-249). Cf. Laurent, *Regestes*, N. 1569.

[44] Cf. Laurent, *Regestes*, N. 1573.

a monastery. From outside the walls they presented their accusations, which were met only with denials from the general. In the final outcome Tarchaneiotes was forced to retire from Asia Minor, thus depriving the beleaguered region of one of the few capable military commanders left to that Byzantine province.[45]

Several years later in 1301 Theoleptos was in Constantinople supporting the patriarch Ioannes XII Kosmas in opposition to most of the Standing Synod on the question of restoring Ioannes Cheilas to the see of Ephesus from which he had been removed in 1289 for refusing to recognize Gregorios II's orthodoxy.[46] In July 1302 Theoleptos again supported the patriarch in a synodal action to condemn Hilarion, the metropolitan of Selymbria, for a calumny that he had instigated.[47]

In 1304 Philadelpheia underwent a prolonged siege at the hands of the Turks. The historian Pachymeres described in some detail the severe hardships endured by the people of the city especially as their food supplies dwindled.[48] Choumnos naturally gave prominence to the role played by Theoleptos, but Pachymeres passed over him in silence and attributed the lifting of the siege to the arrival of the Catalan Company.[49] A Catalan chronicle gives the following account.

> The people of Philadelpheia, freed by the valor of Catalan arms from the siege that had so distressed them, went out to meet the army. Their administrators and Theoleptus, their bishop, a man of rare sanctity, whose prayers had done more to defend the city than had the arms of the people who guarded it, headed their people.[50]

During the second patriarchate of Athanasios I (1303-1309) it seems that Theoleptos was seldom mentioned in the patriarchal records, preferring to spend most of the time in his diocese, unlike many of his episcopal colleagues who preferred the life and intrigue of the capital.[51]

---

[45] Pachymeres 3.25 (2:257-262).

[46] Pachymeres 4.10 (2:299). Cf. Laurent, *Regestes*, N. 1579.

[47] Laurent, *Regestes*, N. 1584.

[48] Pachymeres 5.21 (2:421).

[49] Choumnos, *Epitaphios* 229-234.

[50] *Francisco de Moncada, Expedición de los Catalanes y Aragoneses contra Turcos y Griegos*, ed. S. Gili y Gaya (Madrid, 1954), p. 53; *The Catalan Chronicle of Francisco de Moncada*, trans. F. Hermandez and J.M. Sharp (El Paso, 1975), pp. 44-45.

[51] See Athanasios I, EP 25 To the Emperor, *The Correspondence of Athanasius I Patriarch of Constantinople*, ed. A.-M. Talbot, (CFHB 7; Washington, 1965), pp. 57, 333-334. This letter, written ca. 1304-1305, indicates that Theoleptos was in Philadelpheia at the time.

Both Philotheos Kokkinos in his *Encomium* of Gregorios Palamas and Palamas himself in his *Triads* claim that Theoleptos was Gregorios' first mentor in the spiritual life.[52] This could only have taken place when the bishop was in Constantinople during 1307-1308. Since Palamas was born in 1296, he would have been only eleven or twelve years old at the time when he met Theoleptos. It is possible that the saintly bishop made a deep impression on the young man and may even have offered him some spiritual counsel. However, since the period of contact was brief and at such a young age, the direct influence of Theoleptos on the spiritual and theological formation of Palamas must have been negligible.[53]

E. THE ARSENITE SCHISM

The problem of the Arsenite schism dates back to the time when Michael vııı blinded Ioannes Laskaris, the legitimate heir to the throne, and assumed the supreme power himself. The emperor was immediately excommunicated by the patriarch Arsenios, who would allow no concession to the political realities of the situation. His opposition won him removal from office shortly afterwards in 1265. The new patriarch, Germanos, was opposed by those who considered his election uncanonical and he was forced to abdicate in 1266. Joseph, who was next on the patriarchal throne, absolved the emperor of the excommunication in the following year. As a defender of the Laskarid dynasty, Patriarch Arsenios had many followers in Asia Minor and they quickly rose to support his cause. Thus began a schism between Arsenites and

---

[52] "Gregorios received these and other teachings from Theoleptos, that truly famous luminary of Philadelpheia, who moved on, or rather went up from the sacred hesychia and community of the Holy Mountain to assume the leadership of the Church [of Philadelpheia]. Theoleptos served Gregorios as the very best of spiritual fathers and guides, and from him Gregorios received an excellent initiation in sacred vigilance and intellectual prayer. In a marvelous way, Gregorios attained the habitual practice of this prayer even while he was still living in the midst of the tumults of the world," Philotheos, *Encomium*, PG 151:561A. "Certain men, who have born witness shortly before our time and who have been recognized as possessing the power of the Holy Spirit, have passed these teachings on to us *by word of mouth*; in particular, this theologian, this veritable theologian and surest visionary of the true mysteries of God, who was famous in our day; I refer to the well-named Theoleptos, bishop of Philadelpheia, or rather, one who from there illumined the world as from a lampstand (cf. Rev 1:20, 3:7-13)," Palamas, *Triad* 1.2.12 (99.11-13).

[53] Palamas left Constantinople for Athos about 1316 and did not return for more than twenty years, long after the death of Theoleptos. See. J. Meyendorff, *Introduction à l'étude de Grégoire Palamas* (Patristica sorbonensia 3; Paris, 1959), p. 50.

Josephites that plagued the empire into the first decade of the next century.[54]

Apart from its political aspects, the affair involved serious ecclesiastical ramifications. While a validly appointed patriarch is still alive, he cannot be legitimately deposed even by the emperor (except, of course, in a situation involving heresy). Nevertheless, the church had in fact tolerated such situations in the past. A further pretext for the controversy was found in a rumour being circulated, to the effect that Joseph had been excommunicated by Arsenios.[55] If this were true, Joseph's election would certainly be invalid. This in turn would mean the invalidity of all jurisdictional acts performed by him. Thus, all ordinations approved or done by him would be null and void. Any priests or bishops accepting communion with the patriarch would likewise incur excommunication. Even an emperor crowned by an illegitimate patriarch would find his claim to the throne jeopardized. This was precisely the situation that faced Andronikos II (1282-1328), who had been crowned by the patriarch Joseph.

Theoleptos delivered two lengthy discourses to the people of Philadelpheia in which he addressed the local state of affairs that resulted from the agitations of the Arsenites.[56] Unfortunately, it is not possible to date these discourses more precisely within the twenty-five years from 1285 to 1310. The Arsenites were causing trouble in the church of Philadelpheia by advocating that the people break off communion from the bishops, disregard the clergy and their counsels, and cease attending church. The bishops in question are those who succeeded Arsenios or those who accepted communion with these patriarchs. Such bishops and any priests ordained by them would have been considered by the Arsenites as illegitimate.

These two discourses are significant because they provide information regarding the various interests that motivated the schismatics or at

[54] The major works on the Arsenite schism are as follows. J. Sykoutres, "Περὶ τοῦ σχίσματος τῶν Ἀρσενιατῶν," Ἑλληνικά 2 (1929) 257-332; idem, 3 (1930) 15-44; ibid., 5 (1932) 107-126. V. Laurent, "La question des Arsénites," Ἑλληνικά 3 (1930) 463-470; idem, "Les grandes crises religieuses à Byzance: La fin du schisme arsénite," Académie roumaine, Bulletin de la section historique 26 (1945) 225-313. J. Darrouzès, Documents inédits d'ecclésiologie byzantine (Archives de l'Orient chrétien 11; Paris, 1970), pp. 86-106, 340-413 (with further bibliography).

[55] On this question see V. Laurent, "L'excommunication du patriarche Joseph Ier par son prédécesseur Arsène," BZ 30 (1929-1930) 489-496.

[56] Ed. R.E. Sinkewicz, "A Critical Edition of the Anti-Arsenite Discourses of Theoleptos of Philadelpheia," Mediaeval Studies 50 (1988) 46-95. The two discourses will subsequently be referred to as PD 1 and PD 2.

least certain factions among them. First of all, Theoleptos attributed base motives to many of the dissidents. They are wolves in sheep's clothing, deceitful men and false teachers who feign piety. Disguising themselves with an outward show of poverty (σχῆμα πτωχείας, in other words, as monks), they penetrate city and countryside, and instruct the people of God to stay away from church, to flee the sacred rites and to refuse obedience to bishops. They break up families, counselling them not even to take food and drink together. Notwithstanding their supposedly pious motives, they go about extorting money from people and they themselves spend their time in the markets, the theatres, fairs, taverns and other such places of ill repute.[57]

This description of the situation is corroborated by the historian Georgios Pachymeres:

> In truth the schism in the church at that time continued to grow to such a point that even within households families were divided, the father adopting one position and a son another, and similarly with mother and daughter, daughter-in-law and mother-in-law. The most numerous [among the schismatics] were the monks in Hyacinth's party, an unstable lot who wandered from place to place, agitating on behalf of the exiled patriarch [Arsenios].[58]

Ioannes Cheilas, the bishop of Ephesus, also had harsh words to say about the dissidents. According to him, they were using the faith and doctrine merely as pretexts, while their true motives were jealousy, hatred, lust for power and love of money.[59] In the texts just mentioned, both Theoleptos and Pachymeres noted that the schismatics were wont to appeal to theological principles. While there was undoubtedly some element of rhetorical polemic in the attribution of base motives to the Arsenites, there are many texts that confirm their theological, or more precisely, canonical interests. Writing about the year 1275, the monk Methodios (later metropolitan of Kyzikos) commented on those who pursue a rigorously conservative position at the expense of the concord and peace of the church.

> One who, for the sake of a rigorist application of some canon, causes trouble, creates factions and schism within the body of the church which is preserved by its religious orthodoxy, even if he thinks he is motivated by piety, such a person has forgotten himself. On the outside he is like

[57] PD 2.25; cf. PD 1.5.
[58] Pachymeres 4.28 (406-409).
[59] *On the Arsenite Schism* i.11 in *Documents inédits d'ecclésiologie byzantine*, ed. J. Darrouzès, p. 358.

a wolf that comes along in sheep's clothing and on the inside he is filled with deceit and rapacity.[60]

Theoleptos spoke of the Arsenites in almost identical terms. He further contrasted their current destructive conservatism with their laudable opposition to the policy of seeking union with the Latin Church advocated by the emperor Michael Palaiologos. That situation involved heretical doctrine. The current instance was a matter of ecclesiastical law, not heresy. Therefore, οἰκονομία should take precedence over ἀκρίβεια for the sake of the unity of the church.[61]

There was yet a further separatist motivation, at least among some of the Arsenites. Immediately after referring to the monks of Hyacinth's party, Pachymeres added: "But there were others, too, renowned for their virtue, who came from Galesios and other monasteries."[62] Galesios was an important monastic centre just north of Ephesus and thus not very far from Philadelpheia.[63] Several times in these discourses Theoleptos made reference to certain groups of dissidents who had severed communion from bishops or priests for reasons of moral laxity or merely mediocre practice of virtue.[64] The bishop of Ephesus had to respond to a similar situation in which Arsenite priests and even unordained monks were exercising the ministry of spiritual direction (which may have included sacramental confession) without the necessary episcopal authorization. Some even claimed they had received this authorization from the monk Hyacinth who in turn had received the jurisdiction to bestow such authorization from Patriarch Arsenios.[65]

Within Byzantine Christianity there was a latent sectarian element that would surface from time to time in the form of a movement of religious enthusiasm advocating the highest ideals of spirituality and holiness. Such movements frequently succumbed to the temptation of breaking away from the church of the impure to form a parallel church of the holy. In this context it is not uncommon to find much attention focused on the criticism of the moral laxity of the church hierarchy and the large, usually urban, monastic institutions.

Theoleptos, therefore, together with some of his contemporaries, recognized the great danger of the threat posed to the church by the

[60] *De schismate vitando* 14 (PG 140:797AB).
[61] Theoleptos expressed these views in PD 2.11 and 18.
[62] Pachymeres 4.28 (408-409).
[63] R. Janin, *Les églises*, pp. 241-250.
[64] PD 1.10, 2.25.
[65] *On the Arsenite Schism* II.8, IV.16-19 (and marginal note 10), IV.20-28, pp. 364, 388-390, 390-391.

schism between the Arsenites and the Josephites both in the directly ecclesiastical context and also on the social level.[66] Nevertheless, when it came time to formulate a reconciliation with the Arsenites, it was the metropolitan of Philadelpheia who went into schism with the church of Constantinople.

For the peace of the church the patriarch Niphon I on 14 September 1310 finally lifted the excommunications pronounced against the Arsenites. The proclamation read from the ambo of Hagia Sophia was then circulated by encyclical letter.[67] Theoleptos had not been in the capital when the decision was taken but upon hearing of it he immediately broke off communion with the patriarch, complaining that he had neither been informed nor consulted at the time. Arsenios of Tyre described the situation in his *Appeal to Ioannes Kantakouzenos*.[68]

> You have heard of the most holy Theoleptos, who was greatly renowned for that virtue of God-befitting bishops and for his experience, so to speak, in divine and human affairs. For a period of almost ten years this metropolitan of Philadelpheia broke communion with two of the patriarchs who lived in his time, refusing all concelebration and any mention in the Sacred Liturgy, even though the occasion did not involve any doctrinal error, nor was it a pretext for other canonical questions; rather it was a case of economy which, voted by the Synod, brought a very great peace to the church. Having affirmed the church, which had been torn by the Latin heresy, the emperor was most zealous in approving this act.

It is an indication of the prestige held by Theoleptos that his rupture with Constantinople provoked neither his excommunication nor even a censure. However, back in Philadelpheia Theoleptos had difficulties with some of his clergy and in particular with the protonotarios Manouel Gabalas, who favoured the reconciliation with the Arsenites and considered his bishop's action to be a source of scandal.[69] This

---

[66] For further details on the social aspects see R.E. Sinkewicz, "Church and Society in Asia Minor in the Late Thirteenth Century: the Case of Theoleptos of Philadelpheia" in *Conversion and Continuity: Indigenous Christian Communities in Islamic Lands, Eighth to Eighteenth Centuries*, ed. M. Gervers and R.J. Bikhazi (Toronto, 1990), pp. 355-364.

[67] J. Darrouzès, *Les Regestes des actes du patriarcat de Constantinople*, Vol 1: *Les actes des patriarches*, Fasc. 4: *Les Regestes de 1310 à 1376* (Le patriarcat byzantin, Série 1; Paris, 1977), NN. 2003 and 2004.

[68] See the citation of the Greek text in S.I. Kourouses, Μανουὴλ Γαβαλᾶς, εἶτα Ματθαῖος Μητροπολίτης Ἐφέσου (1271/2-1355/60), vol. 1: Τὰ βιογραφικά (Athens, 1972), pp. 137-138.

[69] The opposition to Theoleptos is reflected in the letters of Pseudo-Ioannes Cheilas (= Manouel Gabalas) published by J. Gouillard, "Après le schisme Arsénite. La

roused the anger of Theoleptos and he put Gabalas under canonical censure. At one point (probably in 1313) the emperor invited Theoleptos to come to the capital to defend his actions but again there was no mention of any sanctions. Gabalas then had recourse to the patriarch Niphon for the righting of the injustice that had been done to him, but apparently without success.[70]

A little later, at the end of 1315 or the beginning of 1316, Manouel Gabalas was involved in the affair of Theoleptos' nephew. According to Gabalas, this nephew had become a monk but turned out to be a rather scurrilous character who caused trouble in the local church, incited the army to civil war and embezzled the money destined for the poor which had been placed under his administration by the metropolitan. Later caught in adultery, excommunicated and sent into exile, the wily monk went off to Constantinople and took refuge in the monastery of Kanikleiou (probably, Μονὴ τῆς Θεοτόκου τῆς Γορ-γοεπηκόου) but was soon expelled. He then proceeded to curry favour with the emperor and fraudulently obtained an exarchal mandate from the patriarch for the administration of patriarchal rights in Philadel-pheia.[71] The final outcome is not known. During this same period, beginning at least in 1309-1310, it seems that Theoleptos was also involved in a sort of power struggle with the governor (strategos) of Philadelpheia, Manouel Tagaris. The precise nature of the disagreement and its causes remain obscure, but the fact alone indicates once again the significance of the role played by Theoleptos even in civil affairs.[72]

Sometime between September 1317 and August 1318 the presence of Philadelpheia's metropolitan was again recorded in the acts of the Standing Synod of Constantinople. He continued to attend the synodal meetings up to a point between November 1318 and February 1319.[73] Apparently a reconciliation had taken place but the circumstances are not known.

It is indeed unfortunate that no documents survive from the pen of Theoleptos to illuminate the motives for his apparent schism.

---

correspondance inédite du Pseudo-Jean Chilas," *Académie roumaine. Bulletin de la section historique* 25 (1944), pp. 194-211. See also the discussion in Kourouses, pp. 316-330.

[70] Kourouses, pp. 319-322.

[71] Gouillard, pp. 203-207. Kourouses, pp. 322-326.

[72] See Kourouses, pp. 129-130.

[73] On the documents in question see Darrouzès, *Regestes* NN. 2082, 2083, 2085, 2086, 2087, 2093.

Arsenios of Tyre claimed that the venerable bishop was piqued because he had not been consulted on the proposed reconciliation of the Arsenites, but for such a man as Theoleptos mere pique seems out of character and hardly constitutes a sufficient reason for schism.[74] Arsenios also considered Theoleptos obdurate in his insistence on ἀκρίβεια in the face of the οἰκονομία exercised by the patriarch.[75] That however would be a complete reversal of the principles expressed by Theoleptos in his anti-Arsenite discourses. Perhaps the real reasons for the bishop's schism lie in the particular circumstances of the church of Philadelpheia, about which so little is known. His anti-Arsenite discourses witness to the seriousness of the difficulties created by the Arsenites and their sympathizers in Philadelpheia. A reconciliation worked out in Constantinople may have been seen in Philadelpheia as a muted justification of the Arsenite cause and more than a mere οἰκονομία. Theoleptos suffered no serious sanction for his 'schism', which may in itself be an indication that Constantinople had some understanding and sympathy for the difficult position of Philadelpheia's metropolitan. It would thus be hazardous to assume an inconsistency between the views expressed in the Philadelpheian discourses and the course of action Theoleptos chose after the reconciliation of the Arsenites in 1310.

The last recorded intervention of Theoleptos in public affairs took place in 1321. On 5 April the bishop together with Patriarch Gerasimos, Theodoros Metochites, Nikephoros Choumnos and Konstantinos Akropolites were present as witnesses when Andronikos II proposed to pass judgement on the rebellious activities of his grandson.[76] Then shortly before Pentecost of the same year Theoleptos together with Kallikrenites was sent on the mission to meet with the younger emperor, Andronikos III, in Adrianople.[77] This is still another instance of the great public prestige and respect enjoyed by the metropolitan of Philadelpheia.

---

[74] Ὁ καὶ τὴν εὐσέβειαν ἅμα καὶ τὴν πολυειδῆ φρόνησιν ἀπαράμιλλος, τοσούτου δὴ χρόνου τῶν πατριαρχῶν ἀποδιεστὼς ὁ Φιλαδελφείας, ᾗπερ ἔφημεν, ἄλλα τε πλεῖστα καὶ αὐτονομίαν ἐπεγκαλῶν τοῖς διαπραξαμένοις, καὶ ἐμβριθῶς καταιτιώμενος ὅτι μὴ καὶ αὐτὸς παρελήφθη συνίστωρ καὶ σύμψηφος, τί τοιοῦτο δεινὸν διὰ τοῦτο πεπόνθει; Arsenios of Tyre, *Appeal to Kantakouzenos*, Kourouses, p. 138.

[75] Kourouses, pp. 137-138.

[76] Kantakouzenos 1.14 (1:67-71).

[77] Kantakouzenos 1.19 (1:93-97); Gregoras 8.6 (1:320-321). On the controversy surrounding the interpretation of these texts see G. Fatouros and T. Krischer, *Johannes Kantakouzenos, Geschichte* (Bibliothek der griechischen Literatur 17; Stuttgart, 1982), pp. 241-243.; J.L. van Dieten, *Nikephoros Gregoras, Rhomäische Geschichte* (Bibliothek der griechischen Literatur 24; Stuttgart, 1988), pp. 23-26.

F. Eirene-Eulogia Choumnaina

Eirene was born to Nikephoros Choumnos and his wife in 1291.[78] In 1303 at the age of twelve she was married to the Despot Ioannes Palaiologos, the son of Andronikos II and Yolanda-Eirene of Mont-ferrat. When her husband died in 1307, Eirene was left inconsolable. Theoleptos had been a friend of the family for many years and he intervened on this occasion to persuade the young widow to forsake the vanities of the world for the sake of spiritual marriage with Christ in the monastic life. In the face of her father's vehement protests Eirene chose to accept the bishop's counsel and received the tonsure from him under the monastic name Eulogia.[79] At this point there is some difficulty with the chronology. Theoleptos' first letter to Eulogia indicates that she entered monastic life shortly after her husband's death, that is, in the summer or fall of 1307. After distributing a portion of her fortune for the poor and for the ransom of captives, she devoted the rest to the restoration of the monastery of the Philanthropos Soter in Constantinople.[80] It seems unlikely that the restorations could have been completed before the end of 1307. They must then have been undertaken after she had already assumed the monastic habit. However, Eirene-Eulogia was not the sole benefactor of the monastery. Her father in his will declared that he wanted to be buried in the monastery that he had built together with his wife.[81] In this case the restorations may have been well under way when the young princess decided to make her contribution to the work and enter the monastery as its abbess.

---

[78] On Eirene Choumnaina see V. Laurent, "Une princesse byzantine au cloître. Irène Eulogie Choumnos Paléologine, fondatrice du couvent de femmes Philanthropos Soter," EO 29 (1930) 29-60 and "La direction spirituelle à Byzance. La correspondance d'Irène-Eulogie Choumnaina Paléologine avec son second directeur," REB 14 (1956) 49-86. For the most recent discussion and a sound chronology of her life see A.C. Hero, "Irene-Eulogia Choumnaina Palaiologina, Abbess of the Convent of Philan-thropos Soter in Constantinople," *Byzantinische Forschungen* 9 (1985) 119-147.

[79] For the protests of her father see I. Ševčenko, "Le sens et la date du traité 'Anepigraphos' de Nicéphore Choumnos," *Académie royale de Belgique. Bulletin de la classe des lettres et des sciences morales et politiques*, 5ème série, t. 35 (1949) 472-488. The first letter that introduces the collection of the *Monastic Discourses* in Ottob. gr. 405 dates from the spring or summer of 1307 and offers some insights into Eirene's state of mind just prior to her tonsure. For the edition of the letter see below, pp. 80-83.

[80] Gregoras 29.22 (3:238).

[81] PG 140:1481C. This is further confirmed by the title of the typikon of the monastery which states that the monastery was restored both by Eirene-Eulogia and by her parents. See Ph. Meyer, "Bruchstücke zweier τυπικὰ κτητορικά," BZ 4 (1895) 48.

The Philanthropos Soter was, at least in a loose sense, a double monastery. Shortly before his death Theoleptos gave permission to Nikephoros Choumnos to enter the adjacent men's monastery under the monastic name Nathanael. At the same time his wife entered the women's monastery under the direction of her daughter. The discourses of Theoleptos add only a few pieces of information on the character of this institution as a double monastery. Only one discourse is addressed to the monks (called 'brothers') of the adjacent men's monastery.[82] MD 17 is a spiritual instruction given on Easter but which also treats of the death of Leo Monomachos. This Brother Leo was in all likelihood a hieromonk from the men's monastery who provided for the nuns both liturgical services and perhaps also spiritual direction in the absence of Theoleptos.[83] The extent to which Theoleptos served as a spiritual director to the men's monastery is unclear. The fact that he was absent from Constantinople for most of the time suggests that there was probably a second director/confessor for both the monks and the nuns.

Laurent and others have puzzled over a passage in MD 9.5 which seems to suggest almost a mixed monastery rather than a double one.[84] This is the passage in question.

> This is the grace of the common life; such is the assistance provided by the fellowship: a single enclosure for the cells, the same chapel for the sacred hymns, the same table for meals. All things are held in common and the same things belong to all, so that interior goods as well as external goods are common property, and all the more so in the case of interior goods.

The problem phrase is ἡ περιοχὴ τῶν μονῶν μία, which Laurent translated "l'enclos des monastères est unique," which would mean that the men's and women's monasteries were contained in a single enclosure. Either this must be taken as an enclosure in a very loose sense or, better, the word μονή should be taken in its secondary sense as referring to an individual cell. MD 9 is a general instruction on monastic disciple without any indication of whether it was addressed to Eulogia's community or to that of the nearby monastery or to both.

---

[82] MD 10.1.

[83] "You know, my sisters, you saw him with your own eyes and had him as a guest at table and as a fellow traveller on the way; together you plied the sea of this life," MD 17.2. On the role of the priest and spiritual director in women's monasteries see C. Galatariotou, "Byzantine Women's Monastic Communities: The Evidence of the Typika," JÖB 38 (1988) 286-287.

[84] V. Laurent, "Une princesse," pp. 29-60

The administration of the monastery's endowment and properties probably remained largely in the hands of Eulogia or at least within the Choumnos family.[85] However, beyond that, Eulogia's authority as abbess was restricted to the women's community. Many of the discourses bear the address "Sisters and Mothers," which corresponds, it seems, to two distinct ranks of nuns. The division into choir nuns and serving sisters is found also in the typika for women's monasteries.[86]

As for the location of the monastery of Philanthropos Soter, the common opinion now holds for a position some sixty metres north-east of Incili Kiöşk. Some remains of the buildings are still visible in the maritime wall.[87]

G. THE WRITINGS OF THEOLEPTOS

1. *The Letters and the* Monastic Discourses

The manuscript Ottobonianus graecus 405 contains five letters and twenty-three *Monastic Discourses*. Three of the letters have been edited and the remaining two are soon to follow.[88] They have all now been dated with some degree of certitude.[89] The first letter introduces this corpus of Theoleptos' works and dates from the late spring to summer of 1307. The next three letters were written between December 1321 and the spring of 1322. Theoleptos wrote the last letter from his deathbed near the end of 1322. The other chronological reference points have already been mentioned. The bishop was in Constantinople from some point in 1307 when he tonsured Eulogia but was back in Philadelpheia in 1309 when he sent Manouel Gabalas on a mission to Constantinople.[90] As far as the sources indicate, Theoleptos did not return to the capital until sometime between September 1317 and August 1318. He stayed there for six months to one year, returning

---

[85] Laurent, "Une princesse," p. 49-50.

[86] Cf. Gregoras 29.22 (3:238-239). See also Galatariotou, "Byzantine Women's Monastic Communities," pp. 271-273.

[87] See R. Janin, *La géographie ecclésiastique de l'Empire Byzantin*, Pt. 1: *Le siège de Constantinople et le patriarcat oecuménique*, T. 3: *Les églises et les monastères*, 2nd edition (Paris, 1969), pp. 527-529.

[88] The first letter was edited by S. Salaville, "Une lettre et un discours inédits de Théolepte de Philadelphie," REB 5 (1947) 105-106; I have produced a new edition and translation of this letter below, pp. 80-83. The remaining letters are being edited by A.C. Hero, "The Unpublished Letters of Theoleptos, Metropolitan of Philadelphia (1283-1322)," *Journal of Modern Hellenism* 3 (1986) 1-31, and 4 (1987) 1-17.

[89] For the dating see Kourouses, pp. 336-339.

[90] Kourouses, p. 68.

to Philadelpheia between November 1318 to February 1319. He was back in the capital again by April of 1321 to mediate between the elder and younger emperors and returned to his diocese by November of the same year. This is the chronological framework in which the *Monastic Discourses* have to be situated.

The term *Monastic Discourses* is taken as a convenient general title for the twenty-three works distinct from the letters in the manuscript Ottob. gr. 405. The dating of these texts is difficult and in most cases can only be described as tentative. There are however a few chronological anchors or hints. Twelve of the discourses are either homilies or instructions associated with specific points in the liturgical cycle. MD 18-22 constitute a series of homilies for the third to the sixth Sunday of Easter and for Pentecost. MD 17 is a spiritual instruction associated with Easter Sunday and MD 15 is another instruction which quotes the troparion of the Bridegroom which is sung during Holy Week. MD 15 also contains one of the few autobiographical references found in the non-epistolary writings of Theoleptos. The bishop expressed the strength of his solicitude and love for the nuns under his direction and described how this flame of charity has sustained him through the rigours of travel between Philadelpheia and Constantinople during the winter.[91] If these do in fact represent a series of homilies and instructions given by Theoleptos during one of his stays in Constantinople, the scope of the search is narrowed to three possibilities, namely, the spring of 1308, 1318, or 1321. As I will show in a moment, the discourses appear to be arranged for the most part in chronological order. If this is so, the series should probably be placed in the spring of 1321. It would also mean that Theoleptos arrived back in the capital sometime during the winter months of 1320-1321.

There are five other discourses with liturgical associations. MD 4 is a homily for the Tenth Sunday of Luke. Because of its position in the corpus, it might be located in the year 1307 on the 26th of November. MD 5 is an instruction for the feast of the Transfiguration, which could then be placed on 6 August 1308. MD 11 is a homily for Cheesefare Sunday which discusses the practice of Lenten abstinence. It is followed by MD 12, which gives a brief summary of the meaning of fasting. The next available chronological slot for these two discourses, assuming that they were given in Constantinople, would be 5 March 1318 and shortly afterwards in the same month. MD 13 is a spiritual instruction comparing the mystery of Christ's birth to the monastic

[91] MD 15.7.

life. It was offered on an occasion when Theoleptos was absent from Constantinople (presumably in Philadelpheia) and from its position in the collection it can be dated to Christmas of 1318, 1319 or 1320.

The dating of the corpus' introductory letter to spring-summer of 1307 has already been discussed. The first discourse followed shortly afterwards, for it is clearly addressed to Eirene-Eulogia, recently "a princess in the world" but who had now chosen "to become the bride of Christ" by entering the monastic life. The newly professed Eulogia had requested of Theoleptos this brief outline of Christian asceticism.[92] In MD 3 Eulogia's name is not mentioned directly, but there can be little doubt that this simple spiritual instruction on the ascetic life is also addressed to her and written at her request. It is also likely that this discourse was written not long after her monastic profession. Theoleptos exhorted Eulogia to hold fast to the ideals of monastic life and compared her retreat from the world to the monastery to the Israelites' departure from Egypt and sojourn in the desert. He also stressed the importance of detachment from personal associations with parents, relations, friends and acquaintances. These emphases all suggest that Eulogia's entrance into monastic life was a recent event. These two discourses were then written sometime in the second half of 1307 or the early part of 1308. If position in the collection is an indication of date, the second discourse should also be situated within the same time frame as MD 1 and 3.

The last discourse in the collection is addressed both to the Abbess Eulogia and to the nun Agathonike. It is designated as a partial reminder of what Theoleptos had said to the two women on various occasions. In his third letter to Eulogia, dated to the early part of 1322, Theoleptos said, "I sent to you three quaternia containing a partial reminder of what I said to you. Read them carefully. Show them also to Agathonike and let her, too, have a copy." MD 23 was the text written on these three quires.[93] The two letters edited by Hero suggest that there had been some sort of quarrel or disagreement between Eulogia and Agathonike in which the latter appealed to Theoleptos

---

[92] MD 1.1-2.

[93] Τετραδόπουλα τρία ἔστειλά σοι μερικὴν ὑπόμνησιν διαλαμβάνοντα τῶν λα-ληθέντων πρὸς ὑμᾶς καὶ ἀναγίνωσκε ταῦτα ἐπιμελῶς, δεῖξον δὲ ταῦτα καὶ τῇ Ἀγαθονίκῃ καὶ κτησάσθω καὶ αὐτὴ τὰ ἴσα, ed. Hero, ΕΡ 2.236-239. Compare this with the title of MD 23: Μερικὴ διατράνωσις πρὸς ὑπόμνησιν ἄγουσα τῶν παρὰ τοῦ ταπεινοῦ Φιλαδελφείας Θεολήπτου διαφόρως λαληθέντων τῇ σεβασμιωτάτῃ βασιλίσσῃ Εὐλογίᾳ μοναχῇ καὶ τῇ μετ' αὐτῆς καὶ ὑπ' αὐτὴν Ἀγαθονίκῃ μοναχῇ. In Ottob. gr. 405 MD 23 covers 21 folios: in other words it would fill 3 quaternia with 3 folios left blank.

for counsel. The bishop did in fact intercede and the two were reconciled.[94]

Thus MD 23 has the surest dating of all the discourses while MD 1 and 3 can be placed with some certainty at the beginning of Theoleptos' association with Eirene-Eulogia. The collection in Ottob. gr. 405 was very likely compiled by the abbess of the Philanthropos Soter.[95] Since there is no other apparent rationale in the ordering of the discourses, it is tempting to take their arrangement as a chronological one.[96] The dating can thus be laid out in the following table.[97]

MD	Short Title	Date
1.	Hidden Activity in Christ	1307
2.	Vigilance and Prayer	1307
3.	Deliverance from Egypt	1307
4.	Tenth Sunday of Luke	November 26, 1307
5.	Transfiguration	August 6, 1308
6.	Hesychia and Prayer	
7.	Discernment of Passions	
8.	Submission to the Superior	
9.	Monastic Community	
10.	Silence	
11.	Cheesefare Sunday	March 5, 1318
12.	Fasting	March 1318
13.	Christ's Birth	December 1319/1320
14.	Humility	
15.	Spiritual Love	April 13-15, 1321
16.	Untitled	
17.	Easter Sunday	April 19, 1321
18.	3rd Sunday after Easter:	May 3, 1321 Myrrophores
19.	4th Sunday after Easter:	May 17, 1321 Paralytic
20.	5th Sunday after Easter:	May 17, 1321 Samaritan
21.	6th Sunday after Easter:	May 24, 1321 Man Blind from Birth
22.	Pentecost	June 7, 1321
23.	Spiritual Testament	Early 1322

[94] Hero, EP 1.222-224 indicates that the repentant nun wrote herself to Theoleptos, and EP 1.404 refers to his reply. However, in EP 2.6-14 Theoleptos refers to a letter recently sent to Eulogia (presumably EP 1) in addition to a letter sent to Agathonike at the same time. Eulogia is also to read this letter sent to Agathonike (EP 2.223-225.).

[95] See the codicological discussion below, pp. 67-68.

[96] Cf. Kourouses, p. 339; Rigo, RSBN 24 (1987) 178-180.

[97] Note that in the case of MD 19, the Fourth Sunday of Easter actually fell on May 10 but the homily was not actually given by Theoleptos until the following Sunday due to a brief absence from the capital. This may have been the occasion of Theoleptos' mission to Andronikos III in Adrianople.

The discourses can be classified in three categories: treatises of spiritual instruction (MD 1-3, 6, 10, 12-17 and 23), instructions on monastic discipline (MD 7-9) and homilies (MD 4-5, 11, 18-22). The first and third discourses were addressed to Eulogia and the last was addressed both to her and to Agathonike. Eleven are addressed to the nuns of the Philanthropos Soter (MD 7-8, 13, 15-22). Eight have no specific address (MD 2, 4-6, 9, 11-12, 14). Only MD 10 is addressed to the monks of the adjacent monastery under the same name.

Reference has already been made to the letters, and the historical circumstances of the Philadelpheian discourses have been examined above. Their doctrinal significance will be treated later.

2. *Liturgical Compositions*

The liturgical prayers and hymns composed by Theoleptos are perhaps the least known aspect of his literary corpus. A special study will be required to isolate the ones that can be genuinely attributed to him. In the meantime I offer a list of the compositions that are attributed to him in the manuscripts.

1. **Canon in dulcissimum Iesum**: inc. Ἰησοῦ γλυκύτατε Χριστέ, Ἰησοῦ μακρόθυμε. This work consists of a canon followed by 4 stichera. It is printed in the Greek Horologion, where it is ascribed to Theoktistos the Studite.[98] The work is attributed to Theoleptos in at least 3 manuscripts: Mone Vatopediou 1034, fols. 207r-221r; Jerusalem [Athens], Metochion Panagiou Taphou 386, fols. 232r-235v; Athens, Ethnike Bibliotheke 684, fols. 138r-141v.

2. **Canon Compunctionis**: inc. Ἀπωσαμένη φροντίδας βιωτικάς. Ed. R. Romano, "Un canone inedito di Teolepto di Filadelfia sulla fine

---

[98] Ὡρολόγιον τὸ μέγα (Rome, 1876), pp. 324-328; Ὡρολόγιον τὸ μέγα, 8th edition (Venice, 1895), pp. 481-486; Παρακλητικὴ ἤτοι Ὀκτώηχος ἡ μεγάλη (Rome, 1885), pp. 732-736; Παρακλητικὴ ἤτοι Ὀκτώηχος ἡ μεγάλη (Venice, 1871), pp. 362-363. For Theoktistos see PLP 7498. On the ascription of this canon to Theoktistos see A.-M. Talbot, *Faith Healing in Late Byzantium* (The Archbishop Iakovos Library of Ecclesiastical and Historical Sources 8; Brookline, MA, 1983), p. 152, nos. 9-10 (no. 10 is the same work as 9; the incipit given in 10 is that of the eirmos to the canon). Of the 3 manuscripts cited by Talbot only one actually attributes the work to Theoktistos (Vat. gr. 778). The work is found in 5 other manuscripts but, according to the catalogues, without any author attribution: Jerusalem, Βιβλιοθήκη τοῦ Οἰκουμενικοῦ Πατριαρχείου, Saba 162, fols. 355-359; Moscow, Gosudarstvenniy Istoricheskiy Musey, Sinodalnoe Sobranie 305 (269/CCLVI), fols. 240r-243v; Odessa, Ἑλληνικὴ Σχολή Δ 1, fols. 276-287; Sinaiticus graecus 319 (1627); Venice, Biblioteca Nazionale Marciana, Appendice Cl. II 191 (coll. 1279), fols. 1v-6v.

del mondo," *Bolletino della Badia Greca di Grottaferrata* 31 (1977) 15-29; corrected by E. Follieri in ʙᴢ 71 (1978) 174; Latin translation in ᴘɢ 143:404-408. This work is found in 4 manuscripts: Venice, Biblioteca Nazionale Marciana, Append. gr. ɪɪ 191 (coll. 1279), fols. 44v-48v; El Escorial, Real Biblioteca de San Lorenzo X-IV-16 (De Andrés 411), fols. 249v-256v; Vienna, Österreichische Nationalbibliothek, Theologicus graecus 76, fols. 37r-51r; Padua, Biblioteca Universitaria 1722 (Mioni 158), fols. 78r-83r. Only the last manuscript was used by Romano.

3. **In sanctum Iohannem Damascenum**: inc. ῾Η μὲν χεὶρ τοῦ βαπτιστοῦ δεσποτικῆς κορυφῆς. Ed. M. Velimirović, "The Musical Works of Theoleptos, Metropolitan of Philadelpheia," *Studies in Eastern Chant* 2 (1971) 155-165. In addition to the 2 manuscripts he used there is one other: Athens, Bibliotheke tes Boules 58, fols. 7v-8r.

4. **Ad regem caelestem**: inc. Οὐράνιε βασιλεῦ, φιλάνθρωπε κύριε, μακρόθυμε. Ed. J. Goar, *Euchologion sive Rituale Graecorum* (Venice, 1730; repr. Graz, 1960), p. 623; ed. Velimirović, as above, no. 3; Italian translation in A. Garzya, "Preghiere di un vescovo bizantino del xɪɪɪ secolo" in *Convivium Dominicum, Studi sull' Eucarestia nei padri della Chiesa antica e miscellanea patristica* (Catania, 1959), pp. 331-336. Garzya bases his translation on the text in Milan, Ambrosianus graecus A 139 sup (44), fols. 317r-319v.

5. **In monachos defunctos**: inc. Τὴν πολυτάραχον θάλασσαν. Ed. ῾Ωρολόγιον (Rome, 1677), p. 110; Italian translation in Garzya, as above, no. 4, based also on the text of the Ambrosianus manuscript.

2

The Teaching of Theoleptos

A. Introduction

As noted in the preceding chapter, the *Monastic Discourses* of Theoleptos of Philadelpheia can be assigned to three general categories, namely, instructions on monastic discipline, spiritual discourses and homilies. However, when it comes to treating the teaching of Theoleptos, such categories become blurred and cannot be taken in an absolute sense. Monastic discipline must of course be interior as well as exterior and thus involves the struggle for virtue in confrontation with the opposition of the passions. The asceticism of the virtuous life in turn can only be supported by the contemplative remembrance of God rooted in the practice of unceasing prayer of the heart. Finally, the 'place' of man's healing and transfiguration is to be found only in the Church, the Body of Christ. This sacramental locus of salvation is best described by Theoleptos in his homilies and in the two pastoral discourses which he delivered in Philadelpheia to counter the activities of the Arsenites. From the external praxis of the Christian or the monastic life inward to its spiritual illumination in the Divine Light and then outward to its ecclesial dimension in the Body of Christ, Theoleptos views the whole process against the reflecting foil of a full and integrated theology. His teaching is thus very much a theological spirituality. There cannot of course be any authentic Christian spirituality which is not theological, i.e., rooted in God and his Christ, birthed by the Holy Spirit and come to life in the Church. While all expressions of Christian spirituality are truly theological, some are so explicitly while others must be taken as implicit. The teaching of Theoleptos is a fully expressed and explicit theological spirituality.

B. Monastic Life

Probably at the very beginning of her monastic career (i.e., in 1307), Theoleptos wrote for Eirene-Eulogia Choumnaina a simple treatise on

the practices of asceticism such as would be suitable for one who had recently made the passage from the lay to the monastic state (MD 3). He explained that this passage involves a separation from material things, from personal associations with family and friends, from the passions of the flesh, and lastly from vainglory and pride. Of course the separation must go beyond the merely physical context to include all thoughts and memories of such things which might give rise to the passions and become occasions of sin.[1] Sin has a threefold locus in the human person: first in the mind, which is the seat of pride, second in the will, which is the ground of the irrational passions, and third in the senses, which give access to bodily pleasures. In another vein, he referred to the ten ways of sin that find their origin in the five senses, in the spoken word and in the four created elements. These ten ways of sin must be countered by the ten commandments of Christ (which Theoleptos enumerated in detail).[2]

The struggle of the ascetic life is made possible only by the cross of Christ. The passions are put to death by means of the cross, and dispassion is attained through the strength of Christ. The virtues attained by this means must always be accompanied by deep humility, or else all will be lost. If the virtues form the vertical beam of the cross, it is humility which provides the horizontal beam.[3] "Humility completes the cross which illumines you and which you have chosen."[4]

In keeping with the Christocentric emphasis which permeates his spiritual doctrine, Theoleptos recommended to Eulogia the imitation of Christ. The disciple must walk in the footsteps of the master and above all remember the humility of the Lord Jesus. Faithful to the Pauline terminology, the bishop stressed that it is the lot of the Christian to be crucified with Christ, buried with Christ, raised with Christ and glorified with Christ.[5] He also drew out, much as St. Paul did, the parallels between the Old Law and the new dispensation of grace: the one spoke of Moses and the deliverance from bondage in Egypt, the other proclaims Christ, the New Moses, and the deliverance from the slavery of sin.[6] To complete the doctrinal framework for his ascetic teaching, Theoleptos referred at the end of his discourse to the goal of the ascetic struggle, namely, the restoration of the original beauty

[1] MD 3.2-5.
[2] MD 3.11-12.
[3] MD 3.8-10.
[4] MD 3.9.
[5] MD 3.7.
[6] MD 3.15-16.

of the Image and Likeness of God in man and the union of the tripartite soul with the Holy Trinity. In this union the soul enjoys an ineffable pleasure.[7]

There are three discourses that treat more directly questions of external monastic discipline. The first instruction, on discernment of the passions (MD 7), is the most specific and may have been occasioned by a serious quarrel between two nuns of the monastery or a situation in which bitterness among the nuns was becoming common.[8] The case which Theoleptos described is one where a serious quarrel would arise between two sisters and degenerate into mutual hatred with neither sister willing to take the first step towards reconciliation. When either one is reproached and counselled by her spiritual father, she quickly denies all blame on her part and claims to be practising charity. Theoleptos warned of the great harm that is done both to one's own soul and to others when one causes hurt to another either by a reproach or an angry word and then shows no sensitivity towards the other person. There is danger here of self-deceit or demonic deception. The presence of an uncharitable disposition can render worthless the works of asceticism and virtue.

Like the preceding discourse, MD 8 also treats of a matter of monastic discipline; namely, the importance of submission to the authority of the superior. Here too it must be asked whether Theoleptos was addressing himself to a particular situation in the monastery of the Philanthropos Soter. Was Mother Eulogia having difficulties exercising her authority as abbess? In order to draw out the theological significance of monastic obedience Theoleptos developed an allegorical, moral exegesis of the Gospel story of the two foundations, one of sand, the other of rock.[9] It is of course in the sacrament of baptism that the Christian is formed into the house of Christ. This house must be continually preserved and restored by the diligent observance of the commandments. If the commandments are not kept, Christ will not dwell within such a house and the Christian will be subject to all those dispositions which follow upon a will that has become addicted to pleasure: namely, idiorrhythmy, insubordination, disobedience, contrariness, contentiousness and self-satisfaction.[10] The house of Christ

---

[7] MD 3.18.

[8] Note the statement in MD 7.2: "This is precisely what I often see happening among you."

[9] Mt 7:24-27 and Lk 6:46-49.

[10] MD 8.2-3. Idiorrhythmy in this context seems to include any sort of singularity adopted by an individual in the practice of the monastic life.

consists of purity of heart and sanctification of the body. It must be firmly set on the solid foundation of submission and obedience to the superior. The building can then proceed from the ground up, stone upon stone, i.e., virtue upon virtue. In order for it to be complete and of any value a building must have a roof, which for the house of Christ is formed by humility. The indwelling of Christ in the soul is then assured. No storm or disturbance whatsoever can prevail against this house founded on rock.[11]

In the third discourse on monastic discipline (MD 9) Theoleptos spoke in a more general way about the ideals of cenobitic monasticism. His emphasis falls clearly on the common and communal character of a religious life lived under the bonds of fraternal charity and obedience to the superior. Great danger would follow upon the rupture of these bonds. Even a single monk who fails in charity or develops a self-willed and contentious disposition can give to the devil sufficient foothold to destroy the common life of the monastery.[12] To illustrate the ideal Theoleptos drew upon his own monastic experiences. These accounts are presented in a manner very similar to some of those given by Ioannes Climacus in the fifth step of *The Ladder*.[13] Having presented the ideal of the common life, he lamented that its actual state had of late degenerated to a deplorable level. As these three instructions have already indicated, discussion of external praxis passes quickly to consideration of interior dispositions. Thus, to avoid occasions of malicious gossip or exchanges of angry words the virtue of silence must be pursued in both its exterior and interior aspects. In MD 10, where Theoleptos treated this topic, he began with a discussion of the necessity of exterior silence understood as the avoidance of all sins of speech that offend against charity. He had already dealt with this problem in the three preceding discourses and so here he passed over it quickly in order to move on to a treatment of the blessings of interior silence, which is understood as the means for attaining freedom from the passions and as the necessary prerequisite for the higher gifts of the spiritual life.[14]

In his little work on spiritual love (MD 15) Theoleptos took the discussion of charity to a new level. He wrote this as an exhortation to the nuns to preserve the garment of love granted by God to the first parents in paradise and restored to humanity by the incarnation

---

[11] MD 8.5-6.

[12] MD 9.3.

[13] Ioannes Climacus, *Scala Paradisi* 4 (PG 88:677-728).

[14] MD 10.1-2 (external praxis) and 3-13 (interior dispositions).

of Christ. This restoration involves the return of the soul from the disunity of material and sinful attractions to the simplicity and unity of divine love.[15] Only then can the soul hope to find refuge in the fortress of God's help. At the end he interjected a personal note in expressing the strength of his solicitude and love for the nuns under his direction and described how this flame of charity had sustained him through the rigours of travel between Philadelpheia and Constantinople during the winter months.[16]

In a number of his discourses Theoleptos discussed the importance of the virtue of humility both in the praxis of the monastic life and in the monk's personal stance before God.[17] However in MD 14 he dealt with the subject in a more detailed manner, setting it within the context of the two interrelated moments of the Christian life, namely, the ascetic and the contemplative. The devil lays for man the two traps of pleasure and false honour. By the former trap one becomes fixed to the transitory things of this world and by the latter the achievements of virtue are destroyed. The goal of the ascetic struggle then is to separate the soul from attachment to the world, the flesh and pleasure, and in achieving this to avoid the onslaught of vainglory and pride. The observance of the commandments and the practice of the virtues reestablish the freedom of the individual in the pursuit of the good (always, of course, with God's assistance) and gradually rebuild the house of the knowledge of God.

Humility plays a special role above and beyond that of the other virtues. Theoleptos called it the indissoluble mortar of virtue's edifice.[18] Humility is the counter to vainglory and pride, which are capable of destroying the entire enterprise of the spiritual life. Both the just man and the sinner must look to humility for their salvation: the just man, lest he fall into vainglory and pride over his achievements; the sinner, to find relief from the burden of sin through acknowledgement of his wrongdoing.[19]

To illustrate the works of humility, Theoleptos turned to the Gospel account of the tax collector and the Pharisee and also to the story of Israel's deliverance from Egypt.[20] In the former he underlined the application of humility to both the just man and the sinner; in the

---

[15] MD 15.5.
[16] MD 15.7.
[17] E.g. MD 2.23, 3.7-8, 18.7-8, 21.4.
[18] MD 14.3.
[19] MD 14.9-10.
[20] MD 14.15-18 and 19-24.

latter he pointed to humility as the passage through which the Christian escapes from the pursuit of vainglory and pride. Upon the Christian who practises the holy dyad of virtue and humility Christ bestows the gift of dispassion. In this life of deep calm in Christ, love takes possession of the mind and unites it with God, where it finds its joy and peace.[21] In the end, humility is simply a recognition of the poverty of the human condition and an acknowledgement of the divine wealth in which man is given to share only by God's loving condescension.

The ordinary Christian, and the monk or nun in a special way, engage in the struggle for virtue and for liberation from evil. In the short untitled instruction of MD 16 Theoleptos treated the subject of sin in terms of man's wilful subjection to the tyranny of the devil. Through sin man borrows from Satan, the money-lender, the currency of wicked desires and evil thoughts.[22] Through his incarnation and death on the cross Christ has ransomed mankind from the devil's tyranny. To appropriate the saving grace of the redemption the Christian must imitate the life of Christ and observe faithfully his commandments.[23] Meditation on the sufferings of Christ supports the soul in its struggle to attain freedom from the passions and lead a life of virtue.[24]

Theological reflections were sometimes occasioned by significant events in the monastery of the Philanthropos Soter. This was the case with MD 17, which is a spiritual instruction delivered on or for Easter Sunday but which deals with the death of Leo Monomachos. In all likelihood the latter was a hieromonk from the adjacent men's monastery who provided for the nuns both liturgical services and perhaps also spiritual direction in the absence of Theoleptos. The death of Leo Monomachos was apparently sudden and unexpected. The event prompted Theoleptos to speak (or write?) to the nuns on the practice of remembrance of death. This of course is a stock topic of monastic literature and Theoleptos did in fact reflect some of the ideas expressed in the discussion of the subject by Ioannes Climacus. The thought of

[21] MD 14.20.

[22] The depiction of Satan as a money-lender surely reflects something of the popular perception of this profession. Even though this is a topos that appears early in Christian literature, its use here is accompanied by far more graphic and detailed description than is normal. N. Oikonomides has noted the proliferation of usurious practices in the late Byzantine period in his *Hommes d'affaires grecs et latins à Constantinople (xiiie-xve siècles)* (Montreal, 1979), especially pp. 53-63. Theoleptos used the imagery of the money-lender several times in his works. See MD 14.27 and 19.17-18. All this suggests that we have here more than a mere literary topos.

[23] MD 16.4.

[24] MD 16.4-5. This emphasis on the importance of meditation on the sufferings of Christ is somewhat unusual in Byzantine spirituality.

death instils compunction and a spirit of repentance, while at the same time it grants freedom from cares and an attitude of prayer and vigilance. "Those who hold death at the center of their being ... freely withdraw from everything and they renounce their own will."[25] Remembrance of death then prompts one to live in a continual attitude of repentance, to confess one's sins, to practise almsgiving and to be assiduous in one's attendance at liturgical services.[26]

In his treatment of the monastic life Theoleptos demonstrated a sense of practicality that took into account the basic failings of human nature and the simple means required to overcome these failings, but at the same time he was always concerned to point beyond the day-to-day living of monasticism (or of Christianity, plain and simple) to the deeper theological meaning of human existence that can only find its fulfilment in the contemplation of God.

C. From Asceticism to Contemplation

Theoleptos devoted four treatises to a more direct examination of the two dimensions of the spiritual life, namely, the ascetic and the contemplative. In response to Eirene-Eulogia's request for a brief outline of the practice of Christian asceticism, the metropolitan wrote the first of the *Monastic Discourses*. In the first section of the treatise he dealt with the *praxis* of ascetic discipline, but then went on to discuss *theoria*, or contemplative prayer, and concluded with a treatment of various matters pertaining to monastic life.

According to the section concerned with the discipline of asceticism,[27] this moment or aspect of the spiritual life involves a fundamental conversion from sin and a determined struggle to acquire the virtues. The conversion required is that demanded by the Gospel (or "by the commandments of Christ" in Byzantine terminology). It calls for freedom from all forms of attachment to the world and the things of the world. It means rooting out the passions or the eight deadly sins.[28] The flight from the world moves towards refuge in Christ and the voluntary acceptance of his poverty and humility.

---

[25] Ioannes Climacus, *Scala Paradisi* 6 (PG 88:793c); C. Luibheid and N. Russell, *John Climacus, The Ladder of Divine Ascent* (New York, 1982), p. 132.

[26] MD 17.6.

[27] MD 1.1-15.

[28] The tradition of the eight deadly sins goes back to Evagrius Ponticus, who described them in great detail in his *Praktikos*, *Évagre le Pontique, Traité Pratique ou le Moine*, ed. A. and C. Guillaumont, 2 vols. (SC 170-171; Paris, 1971). Note the extensive doctrinal discussion in the first volume.

Theoleptos was quick to point out that this passage from sin to grace is rooted in the sacrament of baptism, which restores the individual to the state of original righteousness enjoyed in paradise prior to the fall. Monastic profession serves as a second baptism in which the Christian conforms his or her life to Christ anew through repentance. The renunciation required by repentance must be both exterior and interior: not only must material goods and worldly affairs be abandoned, but even thoughts of such things should be set aside. Thinking back with sadness to what one has renounced is a clear indication of imperfect detachment.[29] On several occasions Theoleptos mentioned specifically the importance of separation from family, relatives and friends. These pointed remarks were undoubtedly made for Eulogia's benefit, for throughout her monastic career she had great difficulty in avoiding involvements with her family and with the public affairs of the capital. The attachments and sinful preoccupations of one's past life leave memories imprinted in the discursive intellect, where they can continue to trouble the nun or the monk. These memories can be eradicated only by prayer and tears of repentance, which open the heart to the grace of Christ.

Ascetic praxis and contemplative prayer are not distinct or separate stages of the spiritual life. Theoleptos makes it quite clear that one cannot exist without the other, and so he devotes the next section of his treatise to a discussion of *theoria*.[30] In the opening words of this section Theoleptos places himself squarely in the tradition of Nikephoros the Hesychast and the *Methodos* of Pseudo-Symeon: "Seated in your cell, set your remembrance on God, raising the mind from all things and casting it soundlessly towards God, pouring out the entire disposition of your heart before him, while binding yourself to him in love."[31] Theoleptos did not treat the exterior practices of the Jesus Prayer, nor does he quote any formula for the prayer but the context and the references to the "Invocation of the Name" or the "Invocation of Christ" leave no doubt that the spirituality of the Jesus Prayer is here in question.[32]

---

[29] This is referred to as the passion of dejection or mourning (λύπη). As one who had once been destined to become empress, had her husband not died, Eirene had lost much and was given to occasional fits of depression over this fact.

[30] MD 1.16-28.

[31] Cf. Pseudo-Symeon, *Methodos. La méthode d'oraison hésychaste*, ed. I. Hausherr (Orientalia Christiana 9.2, no. 36; Rome, 1927), pp. 164-165; Nikephoros the Hesychast, *De vigilantia et custodia cordis* 4 (PG 147:963B).

[32] Theoleptos uses the following terms in MD 1 to refer to the Jesus Prayer: "repeating the Name of the Lord (17)," "Invocation of the Divine Name (17)," "Invocation (18),"

In the opening paragraph of this section Theoleptos set before his reader the ultimate goal and highest state of contemplative prayer. In contemplation it is God himself who draws the vision and longing of the mind to himself and illumines it with a divine Light. All worldly preoccupations now cease completely and the mind turns towards God and begins to see in a manner free of form and by means of a transcendent unknowing. The mind attains to no knowledge because God's glory remains unapproachable and incomprehensible in his transcendent being. Nevertheless, goodness overflows from the divine transcendence and nurtures the mind with love, increases its capacity and makes it worthy of eternal rest. These terms are very similar to those that Gregorios Palamas would later use to describe the highest experience of God when he set out his defence of the holy hesychasts.[33]

In the paragraphs that follow, Theoleptos described in greater detail the workings of prayer both with regard to its external practice and the interior disposition that accompanies it. He first defined prayer as "a dialogue of the discursive intellect (διάνοια) with the Lord, in which the discursive intellect runs through the words of supplication with the mind's gaze fixed entirely on God." Then the Light of the knowledge of God will overshadow the soul like a luminous cloud. The mention of the luminous cloud is clearly a reference to the Light of the Transfiguration.[34]

Theoleptos then proceeded to examine further the human side of the process of prayer. The entire human person is involved in the practice of the Jesus Prayer. The first moment calls for the activity of the body. As suppliants before the Emperor must present themselves at court in person in order to make a petition, so too Christians at prayer present themselves before God and address to him the words of their supplication. Such words must of course be accompanied by the activity of the discursive intellect. It is the διάνοια which speaks the words interiorly. When one's thoughts are continually occupied with prayer before God, they are freed from the encumbrance of the passions. Beyond the mere words of the invocation, the mind (νοῦς) is called upon to interiorize the prayer through its attentiveness. The work of the mind is the remembrance of God whereby it clings to

---

"the short words of the Prayer (21)," "the silent repetition of the Divine Name (23)," "pronouncing the Name of God (25)," "repeating the words of the Prayer again and again (25)," "the mental Invocation of Christ (29)."

[33] Cf. *Triads* 1.3.17 and 28 (145-147 and 171) and 2.3.41 (469-471).
[34] Mt 17:5.

him "in the silence of an utterly simple mental act."[35] In its attentiveness the mind is accompanied by the work of the spirit or soul, namely, compunction and love. Thus the mind is said to gaze fixedly upon God in a fervent disposition of repentance and love.[36] These three activities of prayer, corresponding to the three parts of the soul, are not really distinct, but rather flow into one another. Thus Theoleptos noted that prayer "calls the powers of the soul back from the dispersion caused by the passions, binds them to one another and to itself, uniting the tripartite soul to the one God in three hypostases."[37] Here Theoleptos only hinted at the intimate relationship between the soul and the Trinity established by man's creation in the Image and Likeness of God, but he treated of this elsewhere in greater detail.[38] At this stage of contemplative prayer the inner self becomes more and more grounded in the unceasing remembrance of God. This for Theoleptos and for the Eastern tradition is the state of communion with the divine enjoyed by Adam and Eve in paradise.

Theoleptos by no means neglected the practical aspects and the difficulties of prayer.[39] When the discursive intellect becomes tired and can no longer focus its attention on the words of the prayer, it is best to find a suitable book and read, but taking care that one absorbs the meaning of what is read. This should rekindle one's fervour, bringing sweetness, gladness and joy. Reading and meditation are given special prominence in the spiritual teaching of the metropolitan of Philadelpheia. They constitute an essential source of spiritual nourishment and of instruction in the Christian life, and in this context they have much the same meaning as that of *lectio divina* and *meditatio* in Benedictine monasticism.[40] Reading accompanied by meditation is

---

[35] MD 1.20.

[36] In this context Theoleptos alternated between the two terms ἀγάπη and ἔρως. Even though he does not mention this specifically, it should also be noted that the dispositions of love and compunction correspond to the two parts of the formula of the Jesus Prayer: "Lord Jesus Christ, (Son of God), / have mercy on me, (a sinner)." For the formulaic variations see K. Ware, "The Jesus Prayer in St Gregory of Sinai," *Eastern Churches Review* 4 (1972) 3-22; A. Rigo, "Le formule per la preghiera di Gesù nell'Esicasmo athonita," *Cristianesimo nella storia* 6 (1985) 1-18.

[37] MD 1.24.

[38] See R. Sinkewicz, "St. Gregory Palamas and the Doctrine of God's Image in Man According to the Capita 150," Θεολογία 57 (1986) 857-881; idem, *St. Gregory Palamas, The One Hundred and Fifty Chapters* (Toronto, 1988), pp. 16-34.

[39] MD 1.27-28.

[40] Cf. J. Leclercq, *The Love of Learning and the Desire for God. A Study of Monastic Culture* (New York, 1985), pp. 15-17; and also the discussion of meditation in I. Hausherr, *Noms du Christ et voies d'oraison* (Orientalia Christiana Analecta 157; Rome, 1960), pp. 167-175.

compared with food that must be chewed by the teeth before it can give pleasure to the taste. Thus only when the words of the reading have been turned about in the soul, will gladness and joy arise in the discursive intellect. The religious is urged to commit to memory brief passages of the Gospels or sayings from the Desert Fathers or the lives of the saints. The Psalms are another favoured source for meditation. Such reading should be done out loud but in a quiet voice.[41] The mind must grasp the meaning of the words and to this end a single verse may be read over and over again. As the Psalm is read or the verse repeated, the gaze of the mind must be fixed upon God through remembrance. Here we see the close alliance between reading, meditation and prayer. It is also clear that Theoleptos did not restrict the practice of prayer to the Jesus Prayer alone.[42]

The final section of this little treatise discusses a variety of topics related to general monastic discipline. Many of these matters would be taken up again and examined at greater length. The practice of making genuflections accompanied by the Jesus Prayer is mentioned briefly as a method of rousing oneself to a spirit of repentance.[43] Manual labour that can be done while praying is useful for warding off sleep and laziness and will also help in the struggle against the passion of acedia. A similar disposition towards remembrance of God at all times should be upheld especially in chapel but also in the monastery refectory and in private as one follows the assigned cell rule.[44] The bishop concluded his discourse with an exhortation on the necessity of confession of thoughts as an essential weapon in the struggle against the passions.

[41] This reading is thus distinct from the readings or Psalms of the liturgical office.

[42] S. Salaville devoted a section of his article on this text to the meaning of meditation in these passages. See "Formes ou méthodes de prière d'après un Byzantin du XIVᵉ siècle, Théolepte de Philadelphie," EO 39 (1940) 20-23. His comparison with the type of discursive meditation associated with the practice of 'mental prayer' or *oraison mentale* in the post-Reformation schools of French spirituality is not really appropriate for Theoleptos. The *lectio divina* of the Benedictine tradition is a much more apt parallel.

[43] MD 1.29

[44] MD 1.30-31. Theoleptos refers to the cell rule in the phrase, τοῦ τυπωθέντος σοι κανόνος ἐξέχου (30). MD 1.32 mentions the mortification set by the rule: τῆς κατὰ τὸν κανόνα κακοπαθείας. This is not the formal rule or typikon of the monastery, but the individual practices and counsels given to each nun or monk by their spiritual father to be carried out privately or in their cell. This sort of cell rule goes back to the origins of Byzantine tradition of spiritual direction in the Egyptian desert: cf. *Apophthegmata patrum*, Makarios 3 (456), Synkletike 15 (906) (PG 65:261A-264B, 425C-D). This entire treatise can be considered as the cell rule that Eulogia requested of Theoleptos.

The second of the *Monastic Discourses* was written in reply to a group of critics who were attacking those who devote their lives to vigilance and prayer.[45] It would seem that Gregorios Palamas was not the first to write in defence of the holy hesychasts. Who were the people under attack? From what Theoleptos said, it seems that there were more than just ordinary Christians or simple monks involved; some exercised the role of teaching and guiding others in the spiritual life. These teachers proclaimed the riches of spiritual activity in word and in deed. They taught the workings of holy knowledge for the benefit of others. They were considered as heralds of this way.[46] Such a description clearly indicates that those under attack included leading figures in a contemporary spiritual renewal.

Little is know about the prominent monastic teachers in the early years of the fourteenth century. During the second half of the preceding century Nikephoros the Hesychast had become a noted spiritual teacher on Mount Athos and Theoleptos himself was supposedly one of his disciples. According to Palamas, Barlaam the Calabrian directed his attacks in part at least against the writings of Nikephoros.[47] Gregorios of Sinai, who has left a more extensive literary corpus, lived into the first half of the fourteenth century (1255-1346) and became one of the leaders of the contemporary monastic renewal. Beyond these two prominent personages we have little more than a list of several names left to us by Palamas: Neilos of Italy, Seliotes, Elias, Gabriel and Athanasios.[48] This text of Theoleptos thus confirms the existence of at least a small group of spiritual teachers active already at the beginning of the fourteenth century. They were prominent enough to draw criticism and the matter of spiritual experience was of sufficient note in Constantinople that Theoleptos deemed it necessary to address a treatise on the subject to the abbess of the Philanthropos Soter. Ironically, the same abbess later became a zealous anti-Palamite.

---

[45] Note the title: "Discourse on vigilance and prayer, the holy dyad and mother of virtues, to dissuade those who out of ignorance wag the tongue against those who cultivate this, and to persuade every Christian to learn this dyad, which raises up, as with a pair of wings, the one borne aloft by it and guides him upwards to the love of the blessed Trinity."

[46] MD 2.2 and 7.

[47] *Triad* 2.2.2-3 (321-323). On Nikephoros see D. Stiernon, "Nicéphore l'Hésychaste," DS 11 (1982) 198-203.

[48] *Triad* 1.2.12 (99-101). Palamas refers here both to Patriarch Athanasios, who was an ecclesiastical reformer, and also to a second Athanasios, who was a spiritual teacher.

The metropolitan described the criticisms only in general terms. The critics were insisting that the advocates of spiritual activity were making impossible claims and that their teachings were merely mental constructs and not mystical realities. These detractors disparage spiritual activity as a delusion and believe those who teach it to be deranged. They have no experience of the good they are maligning and slander those who strive to learn this art. They treat the subject of prayer contemptuously and disdain those who have acquired experience of prayer through their poverty. For them spiritual knowledge or science (τὴν πνευματικὴν ἐπιστήμην) is nothing more than ignorance and delusion.[49] Later, in another section of his treatise, Theoleptos made reference to "those who devote all their attention to profane wisdom."[50] This profane knowledge is by its nature transitory and begets irrational desires. Those who place all their trust in it imagine that they know everything and will inevitably be caught up in the passions of vainglory, arrogance, conceit, anger, jealousy, rivalry and garrulity. Those who have loved the world's wisdom are strangers to prayer, for they have found their contentment in the knowledge they have acquired through their own erudition.[51] Thus, because of the reference here to prayer, it seems clear that Theoleptos is identifying the devotees of profane wisdom with the adversaries of spiritual experience mentioned earlier. Almost thirty years later Gregorios Palamas would resume this debate over profane wisdom and spiritual experience in his *Triads*.

It should also be mentioned that Theoleptos made frequent reference in this treatise to the contemplative vision as an experience of the Divine Light. The critics of spiritual experience are of course unable to gaze upon this Light because of their inner blindness. The Light of Divinity shines only in pure minds. Prayer is called the art that bestows Light or the activity that begets Light.[52] However, even though he referred to it frequently, Theoleptos did not make the Divine Light a separate subject of discussion, as Palamas did later in his exchanges with Barlaam the Calabrian.

In reply to the adversaries of spiritual experience and to affirm the nuns of the Philanthropos Soter in the high ideal of their chosen vocation, Theoleptos set out an exposition of the spiritual life under the terms of vigilance and prayer. Behind these two terms stands the

---

[49] MD 2.2, 6-7 and 51-52.

[50] ... οἱ θύραθεν σοφίᾳ ἐπερειδόμενοι, MD 2.42; the discussion continues through 42-45.

[51] MD 2.41.

[52] MD 2.1-2, 6, 8 and also 11, 14, 43 (the Light of divine knowledge).

older Evagrian distinction between the practical and theoretic or the ascetic and the contemplative aspects of the Christian life. The replacement of the more traditional term πρᾶξις by νῆψις is not too surprising but its extensive and almost exclusive use in this treatise is perhaps significant, for it suggests a similar usage by an earlier author, namely, Hesychios of Batos (eighth-tenth century) who wrote a work entitled *On Vigilance and Virtue*.[53] For both Theoleptos and Hesychios 'vigilance' covers the entire gamut of ascetic labours that prepare the human person for communion with God. Earlier tradition had used the term in a much more restricted sense: viz. the virtue of the sober and watchful mind that guards its thoughts against the attacks of the passions that would destroy its remembrance of God.[54]

Before treating the specifics of the subjects of vigilance and prayer, Theoleptos described the goal of all spiritual activity. The end of true watchfulness and unceasing prayer is the formation of the inner, heavenly self. This is a movement initiated by God which draws the human person away from all self-centred and worldly attachments towards the contemplation of God in love.[55] The source of this grace that makes the ascent to God possible is found in the incarnation of the Word.

> The descent of God the Word to man has this purpose, namely, to free the rational faculty of the soul from irrational servitude to the passions and to bestow upon man once again the power taken from him by the enemy so that he may stand valiantly against sin and serve the living God in purity. And so I make my ascent through the incarnation of the Son of God to the denial of carnal pleasures and I am released from the bonds of pleasure.[56]

In the next paragraph Theoleptos spoke of the incarnation in a way that clearly indicates its central importance in his spiritual doctrine. He may in fact have been referring to his own experience of a special mystical grace.

---

[53] *Philokalia* 1:141-173; PG 93:1479-1544. On Hesychios see J. Kirchmeyer, DS 7 (1969) 408-410.

[54] Nikephoros the Hesychast follows the same idea as Hesychios and Theoleptos but shows no predilection for a particular term. He in fact places 'vigilance' in a list of other terms which he says all mean the same thing. *On Guarding of the Heart* in *Philokalia* 4:26 (PG 147:961B). The equivalent terms are προσοχή, νοὸς τήρησις, καρδιακὴ φυλακή, νῆψις, νοερὰ ἡσυχία.

[55] MD 2.8-11.

[56] MD 2.19.

> If, when I heard mystically a voice telling me of the divine incarnation,
> I was struck with fear because of the unbearable power of the Godhead,
> I, in turn, fell into ecstasy over the boundless riches of the divine goodness,
> when I considered the works of this saving economy.[57]

The statement is brief and the translation is a little more explicit than the Greek, and so some caution should be exercised in interpreting it as an extraordinary mystical experience. There can however be no doubt about the statement's emphasis on the centrality of the incarnation in Theoleptos' own spiritual life.

When he moved to the subject of vigilance in itself, Theoleptos noted its role in awakening the power of discernment. As the self becomes less controlled by its attachments to the pleasures of the senses and to the affairs of the world, it can then be guided more by reason. Thus it is better able to distinguish good from evil and to recognize the initial impulses of temptation.[58] Discernment or right judgement, as he sometimes calls it, can only become fully operative when vigilance is joined to prayer. The discernment discovered in prayer works to purify bodily nature so that it may become an instrument in the service of the virtues. Discernment was lost in the fall of the first parents and rational nature became enslaved to irrational desires; it is restored by Christ in his incarnation.[59]

Vigilance plays its most active role in the discursive intellect, for this is the principal battleground for the conflict between sin and grace. The διάνοια is the locus for all active thinking and discursive reasoning. It is influenced by the senses through the imagination which in turn is the route whereby temptation and sin gain access to the inner person. The discursive intellect is capable of giving assent to thoughts and when it does so, the images of the thoughts leave their imprint for good or ill. Under the pale of sin the discursive intellect becomes a region void of all light, but under grace it is in the thought world of the faculty that the inner, heavenly self is formed.[60] As already noted in the discussion of MD 1, the discursive intellect plays an active role in the practice of the Jesus Prayer. Thus, through the vigilant guarding of its thoughts with particular attention to the activity of the imagination and with the assistance of prayer, the discursive intellect comes to share in the grace of divine illumination.[61]

---

[57] MD 2.20.
[58] MD 2.12 and 14-15.
[59] MD 2.34-35 and 46-48.
[60] MD 2.5, 9, 16, 25, 27.
[61] MD 2.9, 26, 34, 54. Theoleptos attributes to the διάνοια a role very similar to

Another way in which Theoleptos considered the workings of vigilance was in terms of the re-unification of the powers of the soul which had become dispersed by sin. Once the soul has fallen under the domination of the passions, its powers are dispersed and can only be gathered together again when the soul takes upon itself the impressions of the different virtues and finds its unity in the single thought of the love of God. With vigilance established in the mind and *hesychia* in the discursive intellect, the faculties of the soul attain an uttermost simplicity and absence of form. Then the knowledge of ineffable realities is revealed to the soul by God.[62]

When he passed on to the subject of prayer, Theoleptos insisted that prayer and vigilance are mutually dependent. The ascetic labours of fasting, self-discipline, poverty, vigils, genuflections and so forth are practised as a preparation for prayer and must be accompanied by prayer lest their purpose be diverted by the deceptive devices of the enemy. There is always a danger that one will put too much confidence in one's own efforts or fall into thinking that one has already acquired perfection merely through these outward accomplishments. This warning is a traditional one and can be found, for example, in Hesychios of Batos:

> Vigilance and the Jesus Prayer, as I have said, mutually reinforce each
> other; for close attentiveness goes with constant prayer, while prayer goes
> with close vigilance and attentiveness.[63]

As is already evident from MD 1, any discussion on prayer for Theoleptos revolves around the Jesus Prayer. Except for one occasion he does not refer directly either to the formula or to the physical technique sometimes associated with it. Instead he uses a small range of similar terms that come very close to those used by Hesychios. The most favoured term is "the Invocation" (ἐπίκλησις) usually followed by some further qualification.[64]

---

that given it by Hesychios of Batos, although the latter, unlike Theoleptos, frequently speaks of the heart with much the same import. Cf. Hesychios, *On Vigilance and Virtue* 8, 14, 52, 54, 90, 118-119, 121, 146, 174-175 (*Philokalia* 1:141-173).

    [62] MD 2.17-18, 21-22.
    [63] *On Vigilance and Virtue* 94 (*Philokalia* 1:155).
    [64] For example, "equipping the mind with the Invocation of his Glorious Name" — τὴν ἐπίκλησιν τοῦ ἐνδόξου ὀνόματος αὐτοῦ (9); "engrave upon your discursive intellect the Name of Christ" — τὸ τοῦ Χριστοῦ ὄνομα (26); "ceaselessly uttering the Jesus Prayer in the depths of the soul" — τὸ γὰρ Κύριε Ἰησοῦ ἀνενδότως φθεγγομένη ἐν τῷ βάθει τῆς ψυχῆς (31, apparently a reference to the actual formula); "I work at the Invocation of his much loved Name" — τὴν ἐπίκλησιν ἐνεργοῦσα τοῦ πολυποθήτου ὀνόματος αὐτοῦ (32); "utter spiritually and soberly in your discursive

As the highest faculty of the soul, the mind is the ultimate locus of contemplation and prayer where God communicates with the human person both in knowledge and love. Theoleptos insisted quite emphatically on both these aspects of higher spiritual experience. Prayer teaches the knowledge of Christ and bestows the knowledge of God through his Holy Spirit.[65] When the soul approaches the love of God it is joined not only to its own powers but also to other human persons and so comes to love both God and neighbour. Thus, here as elsewhere, Theoleptos was careful to note that the individual's ascent to God always has a dimension that is open towards his neighbour.

A much shorter but nonetheless important treatise *On Hesychia and Prayer* (MD 6) was also devoted to a discussion of the soul's transformation in the love and knowledge of God, a subject which had been touched upon near the end of the second discourse. Although the term *hesychia* is used in the title of the treatise, it is not mentioned again, but the topic itself is treated in some detail. According to this text Theoleptos understood *hesychia* as the state or grace of freedom from the passions and all attachments. As such it is closely allied with dispassion or impassibility. It is an essential prerequisite for pure prayer and union with God. Theoleptos' account of the original blessings enjoyed by Adam and Eve is in fact also a description of the gift of *hesychia*. This graced state is attained by a variety of means such as the practice of ascetic exercises, meditation on Sacred Scripture which enables the mind to abide in the discursive intellect, and, most important of all, dedication to steadfast prayer. By these means the religious attains *hesychia* and purity of heart.[66]

The discussion of prayer in this little treatise is especially significant since it offers one of the few references to the mystical wound of love that occur in Byzantine theological literature. Theoleptos explains that attentive prayer leads to the dawning of the knowledge of God; divine

---

intellect the Name of the Lord your God" — φθέγγου νοερῶς καὶ νηφαλέως ἐν τῇ διανοίᾳ τὸ ὄνομα τοῦ θεοῦ σου (34); "the continuous Invocation of the Lord Jesus — τῇ συνεχεῖ ἐπικλήσει τοῦ κυρίου 'Ιησοῦ (45); "our heart calls upon the Name of the Living God" — ἐπικαλουμένη τὸ ὄνομα τοῦ ζῶντος θεοῦ (53). There are numerous similar references in Hesychios' centuries *On Vigilance and Virtue* in *Philokalia* 1:141-173: ἐπίκλησις 5, 143; ἐπίκλησις τοῦ 'Ιησοῦ Χριστοῦ 24, 28, 29, 42, 46, 90, 103, 105, 142; συνεχὴς ἐπίκλησις τοῦ κυρίου ἡμῶν 'Ιησοῦ Χριστοῦ 32, 97, 98; 'Ιησοῦ εὐχή 7, 11, 94, 102, 116, 120, 122, 137, 182, 183, 188, 196; 'Ιησοῦ Χριστοῦ εὐχή 10, 42, 143, 168; εὐχὴ πρὸς Χριστὸν 'Ιησοῦν τὸν θεὸν ἡμῶν 39; τὸ προσκυνητὸν ὄνομα τοῦ 'Ιησοῦ 20, 152, 169; τὸ ἅγιον ὄνομα τοῦ Χριστοῦ 41; τὸ γλυκὺ πρᾶγμα καὶ ὄνομα 'Ιησοῦ 122.

[65] MD 2.29, 40, 44, 48.

[66] MD 6.8-9.

knowledge in turn attracts to itself the love of the soul and unites the soul to God. When the human heart is joined to God in love, the mind's contemplation can no longer be alienated from the knowledge of God. In other words, the knowledge and love of God are inseparable. At this point the soul is wounded with the arrow of love and the mind enjoys an ineffable, divine pleasure. In this wounding the mind is immersed in the knowledge of God and the soul withdraws from all beings. It then passes from a dialogue of sweetness to a profound silence, wherein the mind enjoys a union with God at a level beyond all knowledge.[67] Earlier, in MD 1.5 Theoleptos had spoken of being "wounded by the arrow of love attained in tranquillity," but in that context the reference is apparently to an initial gift of grace enabling the necessary detachment from worldly things. Still, some progress in *hesychia* is required before the gift is granted.

The biblical source for the *vulnus amoris* is found in Cant 2:5, "I am wounded with love" (τετρωμένη ἀγάπης ἐγώ). Origen commented extensively on this verse both in the prologue to his *Commentary on the Canticle of Canticles* and also in his second homily.[68] Much of what Origen has to say was repeated (or plagiarized) by Theodoret of Cyr.[69] Finally, Gregory of Nyssa expounded at some length on the subject in his own commentary.[70] After that the sources are largely silent until the time of Metropolitan Theoleptos.

At the end of his life the bishop of Philadelpheia left Eirene-Eulogia and another nun, Agathonike, with a sort of spiritual testament summarizing much of his teaching but presenting it at a new level of profundity (i.e., MD 23). Towards the end of this treatise there is a brief summary of its contents:

> In these writings you will discover the powers of the soul, the differences between them, their natural movements, the leadings of the Spirit and his mystical workings, and you may see the new day of which the Prophet speaks in his rejoicing: "This is the day which the Lord has made. Let us be glad and rejoice in it (Ps 117:24)."[71]

---

[67] MD 6.5.

[68] *Libri x In Canticum Canticorum, Prologus*, ed. W.A. Baehrens (GCS 33; Leipzig, 1925), pp. 66-67, cf. also p. 194; *In Canticum Canticorum Homilia* 2.8, *Origène, Homélies sur le Cantique des Cantiques*, ed. O. Rousseau, (SC 37bis; Paris, 1966), pp. 132-135.

[69] Theodoret, PG 81:90D.

[70] Gregory of Nyssa, *In Canticum Canticorum Homilia* 4, PG 44:852A-853A (ed. Jaeger, *Opera* 6:127-129).

[71] MD 23.59.

The work thus begins with an analysis of the inner reality of the human person. The three powers of the inner self are described as mind, word and love (νοῦς, λόγος, ἔρως) with the latter two subordinate to the first. In the domain of knowledge the power of reason concerns itself with the examination of beings, discerning the truth in them and through that truth ascending to a knowledge of God. In the moral domain it serves in the struggle for virtue by discriminating between good and evil. Finally, by its meditation on the Word of God and on theological considerations it seeks and finds God. However, it is only through the power of love that the mind is united with God and attains the joy of contemplation. In the mind's ascent to God there is thus both an active and a passive moment. The mind begins by seeking God actively (ἐνεργεῖ ὁ νοῦς) through its reasoning power, but when it has attained union with God through its power of love the process of reasoning ceases and the mind contemplates God beyond knowledge; then the mind is passively acted upon by God (ἐνεργεῖται). The experience is one of delight, of fervent love, an illumination from the most sweet and ineffable Light.[72] The prominence of affective terms both here and elsewhere in the discourse is noteworthy. The importance of this discussion of the three powers of the soul is worth noting, for to the usual members, mind and reason (or equivalent terms) Theoleptos has added the affective dimension of the human person in such a way as to give it a value and a role that it never had in Platonism. The use of the term ἔρως with its more emotional and affective connotations rather than ἀγάπη makes this all the more striking.

Order or disorder in the interior life of the human person depends largely on the activity of the senses. Theoleptos distinguished three sorts of such activity. The activity of the senses can be considered morally neutral when the mind is simply involved in sense perception for the apprehension of the sensible world. The activity of the senses becomes morally good when the mind employs its faculty of reason to govern the senses and use them properly in the ascent to God. Moral evil enters in when the mind descends to the level of sensible desires no longer governed by reason and thus falls prey to the passions.[73]

Attachment to the attractions offered by the senses is a slippery path that leads to the formation of a habitus of sin. Theoleptos described this as a gradual process. First, the mind is enticed by the desire for sensible objects and then seeks out the pleasures to be found in the

---

[72] MD 23.1-2.
[73] MD 23.3.

body through the enjoyment of sensibles. Even if there is no opportunity for a desire to be satisfied through the body, the fulfilment of the pleasure may be realized in the discursive intellect by means of the imaginative faculty. When desire enters the soul in this fashion, it expels discernment from the reasoning faculty, wresting control of the faculties from it. Finally, when desire finds its realization in a pleasure of the body, the memory of that act is imprinted in the imagination, where its promptings will inevitably lead to further such acts of the body. In this way a habit or sinful disposition is formed.[74]

The downward slide can of course be reversed. This return is effected by the introversion of the mind and its ascent to God, which Theoleptos describes in terms that have many patristic echoes.[75] The mind must flee the externals which have lured it from its proper pursuit. Only then will it be able to gather itself inwards, returning to itself where it can hold converse with its own natural word hidden within the discursive intellect. Through its essential word the mind joins itself to prayer and through prayer it ascends to the knowledge of God using all its power and disposition of love.[76] The mind's detachment from sensibles and all memory of them brings it to a state of simplicity, where it can raise its thoughts to God, "giving voice to the Name of the Lord in the depth of continuous remembrance."[77]

In order to pursue further the theological anthropology he was developing Theoleptos turned to the Genesis account of man's creation in the Image and Likeness of God and of the sleep or 'ecstasy' of Adam at the moment of Eve's creation. Although Theoleptos was following the path of a typical allegorical exegesis, reading a spiritual interpretation into each element of the biblical account, there lies behind his choice of the creation narrative for this purpose a clear sense of the divine dimension and spiritual orientation of human existence. These belong to man by virtue of his creation in God's Image and Likeness and only by living in accord with them can he find true life; the alternative is truly death.

The divine Logos created the human mind endowed with *logos* and *eros*. The interior, intellectual word which issues naturally from the mind was thus created in the image of God the Word. Through the

---

[74] MD 23.4-5.

[75] Cf. for example Basil, EP 2.2 in *Saint Basile. Lettres*, ed. Y. Courtonne (Paris, 1957) 1:6-8.

[76] MD 23.6-11. Theoleptos explained the role of the mind, its word and its power of love in the practice of the Jesus Prayer in MD 1.16-21.

[77] ... τὸ ὄνομα κυρίου διὰ τῆς συνεχοῦς μνήμης βαθέως ὑποφωνῶν, MD 23.11.

knowledge of beings the natural logos guides the mind to God as the cause of beings, returning it as an image to its archetype. In the service of virtue this inner word employs the longing (πόθος) of the soul to do good works. The divine Likeness is restored to the soul by the power of love, which affixes the virtues to the soul and guides the mind towards union with the divine by preserving it in the remembrance of God and preparing it for contemplation. Thus through knowledge the mind learns to gaze always upon the one to whom it is bound and through love the soul surrenders its faculties to God that he may sanctify them for his service.[78]

The sleep of Adam at the moment of Eve's creation from his rib[79] was taken by Theoleptos as symbolic of the withdrawal from all things of the world and the mortification of one's carnal attitudes which must precede divine illumination and the bestowal of the gifts of the Spirit. Adam's 'ecstasy' points to the Christian's death to the world and life in Christ, while the fashioning of Eve points to the redemption of mankind by Christ on the cross.[80]

After this lengthy disquisition on theological anthropology Theoleptos turned to the everyday concerns of the practice of psalmody. Ever aware of the realities of monastic life, he knew that there was always a temptation to avoid the real meaning of the exercise by paying more attention to the singing itself or to other distractions, or by considering it a burden and merely rushing through it to get to the end. Meditation on the Scriptures and the prayer of the psalter were of the utmost importance in the mind of Theoleptos. Vocal psalmody must always be accompanied by the mind's attention to the meaning of the words. The fruit is understanding and the dawning of wisdom that is manifest in the practice of the virtues. This psalmody of the soul is nothing less than conversation with God and requires a fervent disposition, mental awareness and a humble attitude. Meditation on the scriptures prepares the mind to grasp something of the mystery of the Lord's incarnation. The voluntary poverty or *kenosis* of Christ in assuming humanity redeems man from the poverty of his sinfulness and raises him to the grace of divinization. This meditation leads not to a purely intellectual understanding but to an interior illumination that enables the Christian to enter fully into the *imitatio Christi*.[81] Thus it would

---

[78] MD 23.12-19.
[79] Gen 2:21-22.
[80] MD 23.20-32.
[81] MD 23.33-50.

seem that for Theoleptos meditation and *lectio divina* held a place of equal importance with the practice of the Jesus Prayer.

The last section of the treatise is devoted to a theological exegesis of the Baptism of Christ.[82] The immersion in the Jordan waters symbolizes the praxis of the moral virtues; the vision of the heavens split asunder indicates the natural contemplation of beings; and the descent of the dove of the Spirit accompanied by the Father's voice points to true Theology (i.e., the Trinity).[83] Christ is himself the perfection of virtue, he provides the knowledge of beings and is the supreme interpreter of Theology. The descent of the Spirit on the Son (in his Baptism) indicates the hypostatic procession of the Spirit from the Father, the Spirit's natural relationship to the Son, and the Father as cause of the Son and the Spirit. Further, the Spirit proceeds from the Father, rests in the Son as his Spirit, while he is not separated from the Father nor divided from the Son.

Theological truth and personal salvation were intimately related for the Byzantine Christian. At a moment in history where there was a heightened awareness of the dangers of Latin trinitarian doctrine, it is not then surprising to see Theoleptos concluding a discourse on spirituality with a brief summary of the orthodox doctrine of the Trinity and the words, "Eschew and reject the Italian appendage (i.e., the *filioque*) with all your will and strength, for it troubles the pure stream of Theology."[84]

D. The Ecclesial Dimension

1. *Integration of Liturgical and Monastic Spirituality*

In the collections of writings of monastic spirituality that have come down to us from Byzantium the subjects treated revolve almost exclusively around matters of spiritual teaching and monastic discipline. References to the liturgical life of the church and the manner in which it may have been integrated into monastic spirituality are rare. Gregorios Palamas, for example, left a corpus of sixty-three homilies.[85] While these constitute an important (though little studied) part of Palamas' writings, they were addressed, at least for the most part, to a non-monastic audience. They can thus tell us little about the

---

[82] MD 23.51-56.

[83] This is the well known Evagrian triad. Cf. Evagrius, *Praktikos* 1 (SC 171; Paris, 1971), p. 498.

[84] MD 23.56.

[85] J. Meyendorff, *Introduction*, pp. 389-397.

integration of monastic and liturgical spirituality other than for Palamas himself. Gregorios of Sinai wrote at least one liturgical discourse (on the feast of the Transfiguration), but the circumstances of its composition are unclear and the text did not circulate with his remaining monastic writings.[86] Although liturgical theology plays a major role in the teaching of Nikolaos Kabasilas, he was not himself a monk nor did he write for a clearly defined monastic audience.[87]

For the most part the works of Late Byzantine monastic writers deal with the spirituality of the individual standing before God. The treatises of Nikephoros the Hesychast, Gregorios of Sinai, Kallistos and Ignatios Xanthopoulos, and the *Methodos* of Pseudo-Symeon speak only briefly, if at all, of the liturgical prayer of the church. The absence or rarity of liturgical references in many monastic writings may be partially circumstantial. Such writings constitute a loose genre with its own stock of topics. The liturgical context, though seldom adverted to, should undoubtedly be assumed. However, the question of integration cannot be entirely avoided. John Meyendorff rightly pointed out that hesychast theologians such as Gregorios Palamas and Philotheos Kokkinos played an important role in liturgical renewal in the church at large.[88] But to what extent did such a renewal have an effect on the integration of monastic spirituality and liturgical theology? The *Monastic Discourses* of Theoleptos of Philadelpheia present a unique opportunity for addressing this question, for they contain not only treatises of spiritual instruction and monastic discipline but also homilies and discourses of liturgical inspiration. Furthermore, they are all addressed to a single defined monastic community.

One Christmas, perhaps in 1319 or 1320, Theoleptos wrote for the nuns of the Philanthropos Soter a spiritual instruction taking the mystery of the birth of Christ as an insight into the meaning of the monastic life (MD 13). One by one the bishop passed over each of the aspects of the feast and its liturgy inviting the sisters to meditate on its inner significance for illuminating their chosen vocation. Thus, paraphrasing a kontakion of Romanos the Melodist sung at Matins

---

[86] Ed. D. Balfour, "Saint Gregorios the Sinaite: Discourse on the Transfiguration," Θεολογία 52 (1981) 631-681.

[87] On Kabasilas see G.T. Dennis (ed.), *The Letters of Manuel II Palaeologus* (CFHB 8; Washington, 1977), pp. xxx-xxxiv. For his liturgical theology see the edition by S. Salaville, R. Bornert, J. Gouillard and P. Perichon, *Nicolas Cabasilas, Explication de la Divine Liturgie* (SC 4bis; Paris, 1967), pp. 9-46. See also M.-H. Congourdeau (ed.), *Nicolas Cabasilas, La vie en Christ*, 2 vols. (SC 355, 361; Paris, 1990), especially 1:11-47.

[88] Meyendorff, *Introduction*, pp. 59-60.

on December 26, Theoleptos said, "The only-begotten Son of God, begotten from the Father without a mother, is also born from his mother without a father." This salvific mystery, he explained, points in their case to the monastic renunciation of family relationships.[89] Further, just as "Christ was begotten of a virgin and has made the virgin a mother and the mother has remained a virgin," so too in the monastic life converse with the world is left behind and the marriage bond is renounced. Since monasticism requires a virginity of both body and spirit, not only is renunciation of marriage required but also all attachment to bodily pleasures and comforts as well as all concern for worldly goods.[90]

Other parallels between the feast of Christmas and monastic life are drawn out in great detail. Christ was born in a cave: the nuns receive a spiritual rebirth in their monastery.[91] Mary wrapped the newborn infant in swaddling clothes: from this the nuns must learn to be satisfied with simple monastic garb and avoid all interest or concern for extra clothing, variety of colours, quality linen, soft wool and silk garments.[92] Christ was laid in a manger for irrational animals: the nuns are to learn to suffer the abuses, slanders and trials which they may have to endure because of their virtue. But in so doing their patience will shine like the Star, people will abandon the world like another Persia, and turning towards a life in God they will come to the monastery like another Bethlehem.[93] As Christ was nourished with milk, so the nuns partake of the food of the Gospel teachings and the lives of the Fathers in order that they may be raised to the highest contemplations.[94] The flight from Herod is a warning to abandon the rebellions of the flesh and the unruliness of the passions through the practice of asceticism and the remembrance of hell.[95] Through such parallels that fall very much within the common liturgical and exegetical tradition the venerable metropolitan sought to teach the nuns under his direction to use the occasion of this feast of the church as a liturgical meditation directly related to their chosen way of life.

In a liturgical instruction for the feast of the Transfiguration (MD 5) Theoleptos employed an allegorical exegesis of the Gospel text for

---

[89] MD 13.3. Eirene-Eulogia found this renunciation particularly difficult.
[90] Ibid.
[91] MD 13.5.
[92] MD 13.6.
[93] MD 13.7.
[94] MD 13.9.
[95] MD 13.10.

the day[96] to produce a paradigm for progress in the spiritual life. The Christian is first faced with a basic option: take the easy way of worldly pleasures or accept the difficult ascent of the mountain of asceticism and virtue. Then, once a decision for the good has been taken, progress must be made in three areas, symbolized by the three apostles who were with Christ on Mount Tabor. The first two areas cover exterior (Peter) and interior (James) asceticism. The senses must be brought under control by a life of self-discipline and observance of the commandments of Christ. Interiorly, all worldly attitudes and impassioned thoughts must be laid aside; suffering must be borne for the sake of the Gospel and for the good of others. John represents the individual's ascent to God through meditation on the divine scriptures and consideration of the 'logoi' of nature (i.e., $\theta\epsilon\omega\rho\acute{\iota}\alpha$ $\varphi\upsilon\sigma\iota\kappa\acute{\eta}$). When the entire disposition of the body, the soul and the discursive intellect has become oriented towards the Lord, then the gift of pure and undistracted prayer is granted. This charism brings with it a more complete detachment from all things and a profound illumination of the mind with the divine Light. This is a foretaste of the full fruition of the divine Light to be enjoyed by the blessed in the future age. The apostle John is thus a symbol of the highest contemplation of God attainable in this life.

In his discourses Theoleptos did not speak at any great length about the divine Light and certainly not to the extent that Gregorios Palamas did. Nevertheless, Theoleptos was clearly aware of this tradition. He referred to "the Light of divinity which shines in pure minds," to Jesus Christ, who "illumines the discursive intellect with the Light of his divinity," and to the most sweet, ineffable Light that springs forth from the contemplation of God.[97] It is not surprising however that his homiletic text on the Transfiguration contains the most significant references to the divine Light. Through the practice of pure prayer the mind is illumined by the divine Light and becomes entirely luminous, but the mind is not alone in passing through this transformation. The whole person becomes coloured with the Light and even the members of the body are transfigured. According to Theoleptos this transformation is a moral one, at least in its perceptible effects: "words of understanding come forth from the mouth" and "the organs of sense clothe themselves with the adornment of sanctity and the members of the body labour in the service of good deeds."[98] The divine

---

[96] Lk 9:28-36 at Matins, Mt 17:1-9 at the Liturgy.
[97] MD 2.2, 11.19 and 23.2. Cf. also MD 2.14 and 21.1.
[98] MD 5.4.

Light also has an eschatological dimension. The Transfiguration on Mount Tabor is a prefiguration of the ineffable glory in which Christ will come to judge the world at the end of time. Furthermore, it is in this same Light of divine glory that all the faithful will share at the dawning of the new age of the heavenly kingdom.[99] These are doctrinal themes that would soon receive great attention in the polemic between Barlaam the Calabrian and Gregorios Palamas.[100]

In his homily on the Tenth Sunday of Luke (MD 4) Theoleptos commented on the two focal points of the Gospel text for the day, namely, the healing of the crippled woman on the Sabbath and the reaction of the Jews.[101] In the opening and closing sections (1-5 and 20-24) he treated the woman as a moral allegory for the conversion and healing of the sinner. The entire central section is devoted to discussing the woman as a type of the Jews who came to believe in Christ. The two themes are linked by the parallel between the woman's (i.e., the sinner's) attachment to the senses with the resulting ailment she suffered and the Jew's attachment to the corporeal aspect of the Law (viz., the letter of the Law) with their consequent blindness to faith.

When the soul is disposed towards the flesh and the body becomes attached to the pleasures of the senses, the mind is unable to maintain its heavenward gaze and in the end rebels against Christ, rejecting his commandments. In the case of the Jews their minds were darkened by their inability to look beyond the letter of the Law. When Christ came, he dispelled the shadows of the Old Law and revealed the spirit of the Law. And so those Jews who were not shackled by envy and whose vision was not clouded by the letter of the Law believed in Christ. The moral of the homily then lies in the necessity of rising above the merely corporeal, sense-oriented level of human existence in order to ready the mind for the contemplation of the spiritual.

At the beginning of Great Lent, perhaps in 1318, Theoleptos offered both a homily and a brief instruction laying down the proper attitudes and practices that the nuns (and the monks?) should adopt in order to derive the fullest spiritual benefit from this liturgical season. As the title indicates, MD 11 was a homily delivered on Cheesefare Sunday, which is the last of the pre-Lenten Sundays.[102] During the preceding

[99] MD 5.6.
[100] Meyendorff, *Introduction*, pp. 242-244, 267-269.
[101] Lk 13:10-17.
[102] For a discussion of the liturgy and practices of Lent see the introduction to *The Lenten Triodion*, translated by Mother Mary and Kallistos Ware (London, 1977), pp. 13-64. Note the bibliography on p. 28.

week abstinence from meat was prescribed but cheese and dairy products were still permitted. Great Lent began on the Monday following Cheesefare Sunday and subsequently the fast would exclude meat, fish, cheese, oil and wine.[103] There were of course considerable variations in the actual practice of the fast.[104]

The homily treats of several stock Lenten themes. Fasting must not be confined to a purely external abstinence from food: it must include an interior confrontation with the passions and it requires the accompaniment of prayer.[105] The passions that war against charity are given a special prominence. The Gospel read on this Sunday (Mt 6:14-21) emphasizes the theme of forgiveness in addition to the proper attitude to be adopted while fasting. Similarly both the liturgical office and the homily recall the fast imposed on Adam in paradise (not to eat of the forbidden tree) and his subsequent expulsion from the garden together with the penalty of death because he listened to Eve and failed to keep the fast. The failure of the first Adam was undone by Christ, the New Adam, who kept the fast in the desert, refusing the devil's suggestions and thereby showing us the weapons to be used in the struggle against the enemy.[106]

There is nothing in the homily that would necessitate a monastic audience and the gender references are unspecific, unlike other homilies where they are feminine. It may well be that this homily was actually delivered orally in Philadelpheia and then sent on to Constantinople for the edification of the nuns (and monks) of the monastery of the Philanthropos Soter.

The brief instruction of MD 12 on the Lenten fast appears in the collection almost as a sort of appendix to the preceding discourse for Cheesefare Sunday. However, it is difficult to say whether or not this was the original intention. It shares with MD 11 the scriptural (but not the liturgical) references to the Adamic transgression of the fast

---

[103] As mentioned in MD 11.7 and 9.

[104] For an example of monastic practice see P. Gautier, "Le Typikon de la Théotokos Evergetis," REB 40 (1982) 38-43.

[105] See for example the Sticheron of St. Theodore for Vespers of Sunday evening on Cheesefare Sunday (*Triodion*, p. 181): "Let us set out with joy upon the season of the Fast, and prepare ourselves for spiritual combat. Let us purify our soul and cleanse our flesh; and as we fast from food, let us abstain also from every passion. Rejoicing in the virtues of the Spirit may we persevere with love, and so be counted worthy to see the solemn Passion of Christ our God, and with great spiritual gladness to behold his holy Passover."

[106] MD 11.13 and 21. The office for Cheesefare Sunday commemorates the casting out of Adam from paradise. See *Triodion*, pp. 168-183.

and to the fast of Christ in the desert at the beginning of his public ministry (Mt 4:1-11).[107] As already noted, such references are characteristic of the first week of Great Lent. For the rest, MD 12 offers a six-point summary of the ascetic labours involved in the Fast.

In the spring of 1321 Theoleptos was in Constantinople and delivered a series of homilies at the Philanthropos Soter from the Third Sunday of Easter through to Pentecost. The liturgy for the Third Sunday of Easter celebrates both Christ's burial by Joseph of Arimathaea and the resurrection appearance to the Myrrh-bearing women. The Gospel for Matins (Lk 24:1-12) supplies the account for the latter and the Gospel for the Liturgy (Mk 15:43-16:8) the account for the former. In MD 18 Theoleptos chose to speak on the symbolism of Christ's burial by Joseph of Arimathaea. He developed this theme in such a way that the application seems to be addressed to both a general audience and perhaps also a monastic audience. The bishop exhorted his congregation to imitate Joseph's virtuous work by practising the corporal and spiritual works of mercy: visit the imprisoned, comfort the sick, ransom the captives, urge sinners to repentance. It is difficult to see how these first three works would be practised by the nuns of the Philanthropos Soter. In contrast, the second half of the homily seems more appropriate in a monastic context, though not exclusively. Here the audience is urged to flee all worldly attachments and beseech God for deliverance from the slavery of sin. Then through repentance and the practice of the virtues accompanied by sincere humility the Christian will preserve himself as a member of Christ's Body, guarding this treasure in the holy tomb of remembrance. Although the possibility is clearer in other homilies, Theoleptos seems on occasion to have taken a homily given elsewhere (in Philadelpheia most likely) and adapted it to his monastic audience.

The homily for the Fourth Sunday of Easter, which Theoleptos termed an instruction or a catechesis,[108] is an allegorical, moral exegesis of the Gospel of the Paralytic read at the Liturgy (Jn 5:1-15). He explained that the miracle can be taken as symbolic of the transition from the crippling sickness of sin to the health of virtue. The acquired habitus of sin induces a sickness in the three faculties of the soul (the rational, the irascible and the concupiscible) and leaves it open to the attacks of the eight passions. This of course is the traditional teaching, which goes back to Evagrius.[109]

---

[107] Note that these two themes also appear in EP 1.83-90.

[108] MD 19.1.

[109] Evagrius, *Praktikos* 15-33, pp. 536-577. On the association of the various passions

For a remedy of the sickness of sin the Christian must turn to the five means of repentance: namely, abstention from evil deeds, practice of good works, remembrance of one's sins, confession and perpetual mourning (κλαῦθμος) or weeping (πένθος). Here and elsewhere Theoleptos spoke frequently about remembrance of sins and confession. This remembrance of sins in one's heart involves meditation on the future judgement and the ensuing punishment for sinners; it instils a feeling of reproach, shame and fear of condemnation; in the end it issues forth in the form of tears of repentance. It seems that for Theoleptos there are two parallel forms of remembrance, the first directed at one's sins, the second directed towards God. The traditional formula of the Jesus Prayer brings together these two 'moments' of remembrance: "Lord Jesus Christ, Son of God, have mercy on me." Theoleptos insisted repeatedly that repentance must lead the sinner to confession of his sins. This fivefold process of repentance restores the soul to its original state. In the beginning God had sown the virtues in the soul: only later did the passions insinuate themselves among the human race. In other words the transformation from the state of sin to the state of grace involves a return to original righteousness. At two points in the homily Theoleptos appeared to be addressing a more general, non-monastic audience. In paragraph 2 he castigated the popular observance of religious holidays with drinking, dancing, singing and games to the neglect of the essential spiritual observance of the feasts of the saints. Then towards the end of the homily he warned of the danger of a repentance which is not carried through to completion. He gave four examples: failure to attend church regularly, lack of resolution in avoiding fornication, stealing from one's neighbour out of covetousness, and persistence in usurious practices.[110] This raises once again the question of the composition of the liturgical homilies. Since it is unlikely that Theoleptos was here addressing the nuns, it seems necessary to assume that this homily was given first on some other occasion and then repeated or partially adapted for the congregation of the Philanthropos Soter.[111]

---

with the three parts of the soul see John Cassian, *Conlatio* 24.15, ed. E. Pichery (sc 64; Paris, 1959), pp. 186-187.

[110] MD 19.13-17.

[111] In the opening paragraph Theoleptos had explained that having been absent from Constantinople on the previous Sunday he was unable to offer the nuns the benefit of his preaching but he would make up for the loss by offering them the homily for that day even though it was a week later. MD 19 may then have been an adaptation of the homily given elsewhere on the preceding Sunday.

The homily for the Sunday of the Samaritan Woman (MD 20) is somewhat less interesting than the preceding ones. It treats the simple theme of passage from the sensible water of worldly concerns and evil habits to the living water of spiritual grace received through repentance and confession of sins. In this case there is no evidence of a non-monastic audience. As an example of repentance, Theoleptos cites the reconciliation of two sisters who had been at odds because of anger and a rancorous attitude. Here as elsewhere the ecclesial emphasis of Theoleptos' spiritual teaching is clear, for he sees the church (in both a physical and spiritual sense) as the place of repentance and growth in faith. It is in the church, listening attentively to the words of the liturgy, that the Christian or the monk comes to the knowledge of the ways of God.

In MD 21, a homily for the Sixth Sunday of Easter, Theoleptos treated the theme of spiritual blindness. In the case of the man born blind Christ healed both the eyes of the body that they might see the light of day and also the eyes of the soul that they might see the Divine Light and recognize Christ's divinity. The bishop then moved quickly to another kind of spiritual blindness, that caused by an attachment to transitory things and the affairs of this world. Here too the healing of blindness is to be found in Christ. More specifically it requires imitation of Christ through meditation on his works and words; this will open the eyes of the soul and lead to true knowledge. The salvific effects of the incarnation are worked upon human nature first of all interiorly. Christ took upon himself human nature in the womb of the Theotokos filling our nature with divine goodness, anointing it with the oil of divinity; through the baptism he instituted he washes it clean and divinizes it. Secondly, salvation is appropriated personally by the Christian through meditation on Christ's descent among men in the flesh and on the humility and poverty of his life; the Christian learns to imitate such humility and to model his or her life on the life of Christ.

In this manner the Christian is introduced to what Theoleptos called the ways of mystical virtue. The soul now washed and anointed casts off the disability left by the passions and looks upon its Benefactor. The attitude of humility acquired through meditation on the life of Christ gradually softens the free will which had become hardened in irascibility and restores it to gentleness and the practice of good works. Imitation of Christ means also participation in his mission of proclaiming the Good News and thereby restoring sight to the blind. Theoleptos offered three examples. Someone who has fallen away from

regular church attendance might return to the grace of ecclesial observance if properly encouraged by a fellow Christian. Someone suffering from the oppression of poverty may easily turn to blasphemy, unless a more fortunate person should come forward in the spirit of almsgiving and offer to provide for his needs. Finally, in the case of a person who takes offence and gets angry with another, reconciliation can be quickly achieved if the other party assumes all blame (whether deserved or not) and asks forgiveness.

In documents of Byzantine spirituality the imitation of Christ rarely receives the same degree of emphasis that it does in the writings of Theoleptos. This *imitatio Christi* proceeds from the inner reality of divinization effected by Christ's assumption of human nature to a personal appropriation through the moral imitation of the example of Christ's life and finds its outward expression in the apostolic mission in which the Christian participates as a disciple of Christ sent forth to proclaim the Gospel and to continue Christ's saving works.

On the feast of Pentecost Theoleptos took the occasion as an opportunity to speak of the works of the Holy Spirit, but he did so first in relation to Christ's saving works and then in relation to the church.[112] Christ is the true mediator between God and man, who offers salvation first in the saving works of his incarnation, death and resurrection and then in the gift of his Spirit bestowed on the disciples in order that they might gather all peoples into the one church. The work of the Holy Spirit is to separate believers from unbelievers, the good from the bad. In us he establishes his abode, which we once possessed but lost. Here Theoleptos reiterated the patristic doctrine that redemption is a restoration to that communion with God once enjoyed by man in paradise.

2. *The Church*

Most late Byzantine hesychast writers do not display a developed theology of the church in their writings. Their immediate concerns were more narrowly focused on the process of a personal conversion from sin and transformation in grace. This does not necessarily mean that they were ignorant of ecclesiology or thought it of little importance; they simply did not write about it. During the course of his career Theoleptos had to confront two major ecclesiastical upheavals that threatened the very fabric of the Orthodox church in Byzantium,

---

[112] MD 22.

namely, the Unionism forced upon the Greeks by the Council of Lyon
and the Arsenite Schism. As a result, Theoleptos was probably more
conscious than most writers of the theological reality of the church.
Although his ecclesiology is most clearly expressed in his anti-Arsenite
Philadelpheian Discourses, this awareness in fact pervades all his
writings.

In these anti-Arsenite writings the metropolitan of Philadelpheia went
to great lengths to make it clear that the church is the one and only
place of salvation. *Extra ecclesiam nulla salus est*! The church is
identified with Christ, for it is his body. In stretching out his arms
on the cross, Christ gathered all into the unity of the church.[113] The
church is the paradise planted by Christ and watered by the blood
of the cross. Here the Christian stands like another Adam, seeking
to grow into the likeness of God.[114] Beginning with the sacrament of
Illumination (Baptism) the church offers each Christian all the means
needed to attain the fullness of salvation and life in Christ. Chief among
these means is the Eucharist, which as the Body and Blood of Christ
is fundamentally identified with the church. The sacred gifts of bread
and wine offered upon the altar are transformed into the Body and
Blood of Christ by the visitation (ἐπιφοίτησις) of the Holy Spirit and
through their consecration by faithful, orthodox priests. Thus anyone
who refuses communion (as the Arsenites were doing) is in fact rejecting
Christ himself, trampling upon the Body and Blood of the Lord as
mortal flesh and dead blood, treating the sacred gifts as ordinary bread
and wine offering no life.[115]

Also of prime importance for Theoleptos are the readings and
psalmody of the liturgical assemblies. Communion in the sacrament
means not only reception of the eucharistic species but also partaking
of the psalmody as one's food and imbibing the readings as one's drink.
Theoleptos encourages his people to fill their souls "from the Gospels
of the Saviour ... for the four Gospels of Christ are truly wellsprings,
watering with the knowledge of God the four bounds of creation held
in the thirst of unbelief."[116] Hearing and studying the Word of God
proclaimed in the churches grant life and illumination to the soul
enabling it to attain the knowledge of God and good moral conduct.[117]
In the paradise of the church planted by Christ the Christian is exhorted

---

[113] PD 2.13.
[114] PD 1.7.
[115] PD 2.7-8.
[116] PD 1.9.
[117] PD 2.5.

to eat the food of teaching, to accept counsel and to seek words of profit from other Christians who are assiduous in their church attendance and in their study of the sacred scriptures.[118] In other words, the metropolitan of Philadelpheia is rare among Byzantine theologians in making explicit the close relationship between Word and Sacrament in the articulation of his ecclesiology and in giving such a strong emphasis to the sacramental role of the Word of God in itself.[119]

In the church established by Christ the bishops and priests serve as mediators between God and man. Bishops must have a firm mastery of orthodox thought and adhere unswervingly to correct doctrine, for it is their responsibility to teach the commandments of Christ and strengthen every Christian in the faith. It is their zeal that will unite the members of Christ into the one body of the church. The bishop must also work for the reconciliation of sinners, admonishing and counselling evildoers and praying God to give them strength to return to the good.[120]

By the institution of the sacrament of orders and by the bestowal of the apostolic mission Christ entrusted his disciples with the office of pastor. In turn this office is passed on to the bishops of the church and so through the bishops and their priests the grace of Christ is passed on to the people. Through the bishops and the priests God cares for his people and through his ministers it is God himself who speaks. The orthodox priest duly recognized by his bishop serves and acts in the church as Christ himself. To accept the bishop and the priest is to receive Christ himself, and by receiving Christ the faithful receive also the Father and the Holy Spirit, thus entering into the fullness of the Trinitarian life manifest in the church.[121] The role of the layperson is to offer respectful obedience to the bishops and priests so as to benefit fully from the grace of God communicated through their ministry. The respect and honour shown to a priest or bishop is rendered ultimately to Christ.[122]

---

[118] PD 1.5.

[119] In his *Exposition of the Divine Liturgy* Nikolaos Kabasilas discussed the liturgy of the Word primarily as a preparation and purification of the Christian community prior to the great sanctification of the mysteries. The readings from the Apostolos and the Gospels present step by step the manifestation of Christ to mankind. Cf. *Exposition* 22.4-5, (SC 4bis; Paris, 1967), pp. 154-156. In contrast the writings of Theoleptos offer a much fuller valuation of the role of the Word of God in the liturgy.

[120] PD 1.6.

[121] PD 1.7-8. Here as elsewhere Theoleptos demonstrates his acute sense of the 'whole cloth' of theology. Cf. his Trinitarian understanding of the Jesus Prayer as described above, pp. 34-35.

[122] PD 1.7 and 9.

But what happens if the priest's life is mediocre, morally lax or even worse? Is the grace of God still mediated through the ministry of such a priest? The answer given by Theoleptos was an emphatic yes. Sin does not render grace ineffective. The priest's moral state is not the determinative element, for grace is operative by virtue of the office of the priesthood. As a man a priest is as weak as other men, but as a priest grace operates through him regardless of his moral state. The priestly ministry is God's and not man's. As God's work it is always effective.[123]

Theoleptos was quite realistic in recognizing that often enough a priest's life might fall short of holiness.[124] Even if a priest's life is imperfect, he may still be capable of offering sound teaching and profitable counsel. The existence of some imperfection is not sufficient reason to reject also all the good there may be in the man.[125]

> If by chance you notice someone who is negligent in his conduct but offers helpful and beneficial advice to his neighbours, or someone who possesses good works but as a human being shows certain faults, there is no profit in disregarding his numerous good qualities and maliciously focusing attention on his few faults, thereby rejecting even what is valuable because of matters that deserve to be overlooked.[126]

Apart from the common sense and practicality of such advice Theoleptos may have had in mind the particular circumstances of the Arsenite Schism, which apparently involved a group that advocated a sort spiritual idealism: anything less than perfect holiness just was not good enough.[127] This is confirmed by another passage from the *Philadelpheian Discourses* where Theoleptos spoke of the holiness of the individual Christian.

> Examine yourself and you will find that a part of your soul serves God and, in turn, a part of it serves evil. God does not reject that part of you which serves him because of that part which is indifferent. Nor, in turn, does he overlook your contempt, for the sake of obedience in

---

[123] PD 2.22-25.

[124] On the general state of the lower clergy see C. Cupane, "Una 'classe sociale' dimenticata: il basso clero metropolitano. Un tentativo di ricostruzione alla luce del Registro del Patriarcato Costantinopolitano (1315-1402)" in *Studien zum Patriarchatsregister von Konstantinopel I*, ed. H. Hunger (Österreichische Akademie der Wissenschaften, philosophisch-historische Klasse, Sitzungsberichte, 383. Band; Vienna, 1981), pp. 61-83.

[125] PD 1.10-12.

[126] PD 1.11.

[127] Cf. J. Darrouzès, *Documents inédits*, pp. 100-104.

the rest of you. Rather, to the extent that you offer God your free will, grace shall come to your assistance, granting you the reward for your service. And conversely, to the extent that you willingly turn from God, there shall be a parting from grace within you, for he punishes unbridled disobedience of thought.[128]

No Christian in this life is either wholly good or wholly evil. God's love is ever present to assist the individual in this ongoing conversion from sin and transformation in grace.

In the middle of the fourteenth century Nikolaos Kabasilas returned to the question of the unworthy minister and the communication of sacramental grace. He arrived at the same conclusion as the metropolitan of Philadelpheia. When the church is aware of the unworthiness of a minister, it excludes such a priest from the celebration of the liturgy. However, in most cases it is not possible for the church to know whether or not a particular minister is in the state of mortal sin. Thus there remains the problem of whether sanctification is still communicated to the faithful when the liturgy is celebrated by a sinful priest. Kabasilas insisted that the holy gifts offered in the liturgy always remain pure and acceptable to God even in the case where they may be presented by an unworthy priest. In the liturgy the celebrant is no more than the servant of grace; he offers nothing of his own. It is the grace of God alone that effects the sanctification of the gifts and this grace is ever operative. The gifts are therefore sanctified by the very act of their presentation.[129] Theoleptos was dealing with a somewhat larger context but in both cases the answer is the same.

It is interesting to contrast the position taken by Kabasilas and Theoleptos with that advocated by Symeon the New Theologian in the eleventh century. In the first of his letters Symeon addressed the question, "Whether it is permissible for men to confess their sins to certain monks who are not priests, since we hear that the power of binding and loosing is given to priests only."[130] According to Symeon the power to celebrate the sacred liturgy and to bind and loose sins was given by Christ to his apostles and they in turn passed on this ministry to the bishops and priests that succeeded them. However, the bishops and priests succumbed to heresies or were caught up in the pursuit of pleasures and honours. As a result the gift of the Holy Spirit

---

[128] PD 2.23.

[129] *Exposition of the Divine Liturgy* 28.1-5 (SC 4bis; Paris, 1967), pp. 176-178.

[130] Text in K. Holl, *Enthusiasmus und Bussgewalt im griechischen Mönchtum* (Leipzig, 1896), pp. 110-127; see also PG 95:284-304.

passed on to the monks, who strove to emulate the apostles by virtue of their deeds. Symeon in fact put it rather bluntly.

> The power to forgive sins is not given by God in any absolute sense solely by virtue of priestly ordination and the rank conferred thereby. This is true both for monks who wear the habit and for those who have been ordained and have acceded to the order of priesthood and for those who have been deemed worthy of the episcopal office, namely, patriarchs, metropolitans and bishops. Only the celebration of the Liturgy has been accorded to them, but I think that not even this has been given to many of them lest being chaff they be burned up thereby. Rather, this is granted solely to those priests, bishops and monks who through their holiness are numbered among the choruses of Christ's disciples.[131]

In the actual praxis of Byzantine Christians the ministry of the monk or the monk-priest was the most common recourse for the forgiveness of sins. The ministry of formal ecclesiastical penance was reserved for priests, who in practice were almost always monks.[132] Symeon expressed a rather singular opinion in taking the sacramental and extra-sacramental practice to a radical conclusion.[133] Certainly by the time of Theoleptos and Nikolaos Kabasilas the notion of sacramentality had become firmly attached to the sacerdotal and ultimately episcopal ministry in the church and to a more ecclesial understanding of the workings of sacramental grace.

This strongly ecclesial approach to the Christian life is also very evident in the homilies of Theoleptos. For example, Theoleptos was quite insistent that sinners who have been overcome by the attractions of the world and the temptations of the devil cut themselves off from the possibility of salvation by ceasing to attend church services. They suffer the affliction of the paralytic or of the man born blind.[134] In turn, the greatest act of charity is to guide sinners back to the path of salvation. This means primarily getting them to return to the church, not just in a general sense but more importantly in the specific, physical sense of getting them into the church building to attend the office and the liturgy through which they can receive healing and salvation.

---

[131] Symeon, EP 1.14 in *Enthusiasmus*, ed. Holl, p. 124.

[132] The evidence of the saints' lives has been examined in great detail by R.J. Barringer, "Ecclesiastical Penance in the Church of Constantinople: A Study of the Hagiographical Evidence to 983 A.D." (D.Phil. diss. Oxford University, 1979).

[133] There is in fact little evidence that Symeon's radical views received much support among his contemporaries.

[134] MD 19.13 and 21.8.

When the sinner is reproached by his conscience for doing wrong in spending his time outside the church, he repents, feels remorse and starts going to church. If then he enters the church and assists there with fear and listens to the psalmody, his soul finds healing and salvation, for he has an upright way of thinking, which like a man plunges him into the church as into a pool when his conscience reproves him. But if he is reproached by his conscience and apparently regrets his irregular attendance at church, yet does not go but says to himself, "I am going to do this errand and settle this business as well and after that I will go to the concluding part of the Vespers service. But if I do not get there, tomorrow I will attend Matins or the Liturgy" —, he remains unhealed and is deprived of his salvation. For while he apparently considered going to church, the cares of life and attachment to the world got the better of him and deprived him of the occasion of entering the church and hearing the divine scriptures and dispossessed him of healing for his soul.[135]

In other words, for Theoleptos who was himself a monk of profound spirituality the proper recourse for a Christian seeking salvation and spiritual guidance was not the holy man and the monk but the church with its liturgical services and sacramental ministry. The church then is the divinely constituted place of repentance, illumination and entry into eternal life.

Therefore, let us be earnest in attending church so that in entering the church we may be washed and purified from all the stains of sin and the eyes of our souls may be illumined and we may never fall asleep in death, but be deemed worthy of eternal life in Christ Jesus the Lord.[136]

In still another case, where Theoleptos was quite clearly addressing the nuns under his direction, he explained to them that the church is the place of converse with God and a source of spiritual nourishment not only for themselves but so that prepared in this way they might be able to proclaim the Gospel to others.[137] Here too he was speaking of the church both in the larger theological sense but without ever leaving the sense of the physical building and its importance as the sacramental space in which the Christian hears the Word of God and is nourished by the celebration of the sacred mysteries.

[135] MD 19.13.
[136] MD 21.10. Cf. MD 18.7 and 19.3.
[137] MD 20.8-9. Cf. MD 22.1.

E. CONCLUSION

In his spiritual teaching Theoleptos of Philadelpheia was very much a traditionalist. There is little in his writings that was not said at some time by someone else. As a theologian, his works reflect a profound meditation on the scriptures; he utters scarcely a phrase that is without a biblical allusion or a direct quotation. As a Byzantine, he looks back to the heritage of the past and above all to the writings of the Fathers of the Church and to the tradition of the great monastic teachers. It is striking however that, apart from the Bible, Theoleptos quotes directly from other writers only very rarely. This is an indication of how well he has assimilated his sources, although it makes it more difficult for the modern reader to discern the literary dependencies of his thought. Indeed it is easy enough to find parallels but parallels are not necessarily sources. Such a search for sources however must not obscure the fact that there is a genuine originality in the spiritual and theological doctrine of this Byzantine prelate. The originality lies precisely in the synthesis he crafted out of the diverse and numerous strands of preceding tradition. Perhaps the most striking characteristic of this synthesis is its struggle to achieve an integral and balanced theological framework within which to express and live out the spiritual life of the Christian, and more specifically of the monk or nun.

The above discussion of the theological spirituality of Theoleptos is intended as no more than an introductory guide to the reading of the *Monastic Discourses*. The subject can and should be pursued at much greater length. For example, it would be helpful to situate Theoleptos among his contemporaries, or near contemporaries, and his immediate successors in the monastic tradition. It has been more than sixty years since Fr. Irénée Hausherr completed his edition and study of the *Methodos* of Pseudo-Symeon. A renewed study of this late thirteenth century work is clearly warranted. Nikephoros the Hesychast, who may in fact be the author of the *Methodos*, also produced a short florilegium of texts drawn from the lives of the saints and a number of monastic authors. This suggests the possible existence of a common collection of spiritual texts that emerged at the end of the thirteenth century or the beginning of the fourteenth, viz., a late Byzantine *Philokalia*. Such a collection or collections certainly existed later (though their morphology has never been adequately studied), but it will be necessary to investigate the manuscript tradition in order to determine how early this phenomenon arose. A Philokalic collection, whether early or late, would attest to the emergence of a more unified

tradition of monastic spirituality. If early, it would accord well with
the synthetic quality of the theological spirituality of Theoleptos.

There are two major authors belonging to the late thirteenth and
early fourteenth centuries who would have to be brought into the
picture in order to ascertain the fuller significance of Theoleptos'
contribution. First, there is Gregorios of Sinai, for whom we will soon
have a proper critical edition and introductory study prepared by Hans-
Veit Beyer. Second, there is Gregorios Palamas. For the latter, it should
again be pointed out that the most fruitful area of investigation lies
in the corpus of his homilies which frequently exhibit what could be
called a 'hesychast' exegesis similar to that employed by Theoleptos.
It would not however be very productive to centre such a study around
the unlikely possibility of direct influence of Theoleptos on Palamas.
The parallels that do exist or that might be discovered are more likely
to be explained by the existence of a common body of monastic
teaching that was gradually emerging at the beginning of the fourteenth
century, particularly on Mount Athos but elsewhere as well.

Through the writings of Theoleptos, Gregorios of Sinai and Gregorios
Palamas it should also be possible to pursue further the origins of
the so-called hesychast controversy. Theoleptos witnesses to the fact
that the question of the validity of spiritual experience had been raised
several decades prior to the arrival of Barlaam the Calabrian in
Byzantium. Both Theoleptos and Gregorios of Sinai exhibit a tendency
towards the use of a highly affective language in their writings. It was
precisely this sort of thing that first attracted Barlaam's attention. The
third section of Palamas' first *Triad in Defence of the Holy Hesychasts*
is a rebuttal of Barlaam's attacks against the reality of mystical graces
and it is here that Palamas developed his notion of spiritual perception
(νοερὰ αἴσθησις). It appears that the matter was not settled by Palamas
because later authors believed it necessary to return to the question
in even greater detail. The subject was treated in the *Century* attributed
to Kallistos and Ignatios Xanthopoulos and, more importantly, in
several of the works of Kallistos Angelikoudes.

The appearance of a warmly affective spirituality in Byzantium,
which was so cool towards the spontaneous expression of the emotions,
suggests the presence of a cultural phenomenon of some significance.
The spiritual renewal which passed through the diminished Byzantine
empire of the fourteenth century failed to respect political borders and
rapidly spread into much wider spheres of influence. It is thus a cultural
and even social force that cannot be ignored in any consideration of
late Byzantine society. It is common enough now to look at late

Byzantine culture in terms of a Palaeologan Renaissance which saw a revival of interest in the learning of antiquity.[138] This is an important and recurring phenomenon throughout the history of Byzantine culture, but all the same such a model is too limited to allow for an adequate appreciation of what was happening during the two centuries that preceded the Ottoman conquest.

Another perspective worth exploring would be the conflict between freedom and formalism in Byzantine culture. In the religious domain the hesychast renewal broke free of some of the restraints that had encumbered the more formalistic orthopraxis of Byzantine Christianity. The enthusiastic and affective element that began to inspire the monastic renewal apparently shocked some people and provoked a reaction. The doctrine of the essence and energies in God expounded at great length by Palamas was ultimately a defence of the reality of grace as God's gracious gift of himself to the Christian. The vehemence of the anti-Palamites might become more easily understandable if it is seen as the reaction of an element within Byzantium that had become so formalistic in its practice of Christianity that it was unable to break free of the mold and accept a true renewal of the Gospel ideals to which it claimed to adhere so faithfully.

To determine the validity of this sort of analysis it would be necessary to explore the characteristics of formalistic orthopraxis in greater detail. Many of the writings associated with this element have either not been studied or have been too readily dismissed as rhetorical exercises. For example, the religious writings of Nikephoros Choumnos, Nikephoros Gregoras and even Theodoros Metochites would bear much closer scrutiny from this point of view. Perhaps 'formalistic orthopraxis' is too harsh a label (I suspect it is) and it may ultimately be possible to discern a spirituality and a lived Christianity within the group of the formalists which has a validity within its own terms but which was too much closed in upon itself to accept the revival of a more enthusiastic form of Christianity.

An examination of these questions should pay some attention to language, for it seems that the advocates of the renewal exhibit an unusual tendency to break free of the formal constraints of the late Byzantine 'Hochsprache.' In this context Theoleptos is a remarkable example. His writings are crafted with a great care for the rhetorical

---

[138] See for example I. Ševčenko, "The Palaeologan Renaissance" in *Renaissances before the Renaissance: Cultural Revivals of Late Antiquity and the Middle Ages*, ed. W. Treadgold (Stanford, CA, 1984), pp. 144-223.

art but they never lose their lucidity. The imagery of daily life that appears so frequently in his discourses gives them an immediacy and liveliness that is rare in late Byzantine literature. Other monastic writers of the fourteenth century similarly resort to a simpler style of expression, though most do not achieve quite the same level of artistry as that found in Theoleptos.[139] This of course makes their works more accessible to a larger number of people and hence to the possibility of a wider sphere of influence. Those who wrote in the 'Hochsprache' wrote for a limited and elite social group.[140] Many, at least of the middle class, may have aspired to become members of this closed circle but only a few attained such a distinction. It would not be surprising to find that the Christianity of such an inward oriented group was conservative and narrowly traditionalist. This along with the other suggestions made above on the subject of cultural freedom and formalism are perhaps in their present form over-simplifications. The nuances will only be revealed with further research.

The list of research desiderata is a long one. It is clearly not possible to pursue these avenues here in the context of a few brief introductory chapters of this critical edition. The task will have to be relegated to another book.

---

[139] It is interesting to observe Palamas employing a turgid and quite unartful form of the 'Hochsprache' when he is engaged in his polemics with the Barlaamites and Akindynists, but turning to a very much clearer and understandable language when writing his homilies or works of spirituality.

[140] See I. Ševčenko, "Society and Intellectual Life in the Fourteenth Century," *Actes du XIVᵉ Congrès international des études byzantines, Bucarest 1971* (Bucharest, 1974) 1:69-92.

3

The Text

The complete collection of Theoleptos' twenty-three discourses survives today in only two manuscripts, one in the Vatican Library and the other in the library of the Greek Orthodox Patriarchate in Alexandria.

O = Vatican City, Biblioteca Apostolica Vaticana, Ottobonianus graecus 405.[1] Fourteenth century, parchment, 230 x 160 mm.

Collation: 1x7(7), 9x8(79), 2x7(93), 8x8(157), 1x12(169), 9x8(240), 1x4(244), 1x1(245), 1x2(247).

There are a total of thirty-three gatherings. The first gathering (fols. 1-7) is not numbered but the remainder bear a number in the lower right corner on the recto side of the first folio in each gathering (e.g., fol. 8r marked ἕν, fol. 16r β′, fol. 24 τρία). When the volume was trimmed for its modern binding many of the gathering numbers were lost. The last visible mark is ΚΔ′ on fol. 193r. It should be noted that the first gathering, which is unnumbered, comprises the letter addressed by Theoleptos to Eirene-Eulogia at the beginning of her monastic vocation. The gathering numbers start with the first of the discourses on fol. 8. This may suggest that the placement of the letter at the beginning of the codex was an afterthought. At front and back the manuscript was joined to its binding with paper paste sheets.

The material throughout is good quality parchment with very few blemishes. Fols. 133 and 242 were replaced with blank sheets of paper. The original fol. 133 contained the conclusion of MD 11, now lost.

---

[1] E. Feron, F. Battaglini, *Codices manuscripti graeci Ottoboniani Bibliothecae Vaticanae* (Rome, 1893), p. 216.

The folios are numbered from beginning to end in pencil, i.e., 1-247. Fol. 178 is followed by 178a. The folios are also numbered in Greek in an older hand starting from fol. 6 where the introductory letter begins. In the lower margin at the beginning of each separate text the number of folios for that text is indicated in red ink. The number of lines per page varies from twenty-three to twenty-five (fols. 1-79 = 22 lines; fols. 80-161 = 25 lines; fols. 162-169 = 24 lines; fols. 170-247 = 23 lines). The codex was written by two copyists: the first did fols. 2r-79r and fols. 98r-247, the second fols. 80r-97v. The first copyist marked off paragraphs by capital (enlarged) letters and extension into the exterior margin; the second copyist did not divide the text in any way.

Annotations: The initial and final folios bear several annotations, given as follows.

Fol. 1r: + μιχαη[λ] (at top)

Γρηγόριος ἐκ τῶν πετρ ... (at bottom, scarcely legible)

Fol. 1v: + μιχαήλ τάχα καὶ ἱερωδῖἄκωνος (written several times)

Fol. 2r: ὦ χ(ριστ)έ μου φύλαττε, τὴν κεκτημένην (upper margin). This would indicate that the owner of the codex was a woman, probably Eirene-Eulogia herself.

τοῦ θρόνου ἀλεξανδρεί(ας) (bottom margin, apparently in the same ink and hand as the Greek foliation numbers)

Fol. 5r: κ(ύρι)ε δόξα σοι + δι᾿ εὐχῶν τὸν ἁγίον π(ατέ)ρων ἡμῶν κ(ύρι)ε Ι(ησο)ῦ χ(ριστ)ὲ ὁ θ(εὸ)ς ἡμὸν ἐλεησον ἡμᾶς αμὴν (at top)[2]

iosepph coragius (middle)

Fol. 247r: + αὕτη ἡ θεῖα καὶ ἱερα βίβλος ὑπάρχει τοῦ θεοφιλεστάτου ἐπισκόπου Στρουμνήτζης ᾿Ανανίου

Signature as above in monocotilydon (ink and hand same as Greek foliation numbers)

Fol. 247v: Several scarcely legible jottings. + μακαριος, + ἀνάστιτω ὁ θ(εὸ)ς, an illegible line, μακάριος.

---

[2] The formula of the Jesus Prayer with the ὁ θεὸς ἡμῶν inclusion is an old one. Barlaam criticized the monks in the circle of Gregorios Palamas for introducing a new formula with the inclusion replaced by υἱὲ τοῦ θεοῦ. See R. Sinkewicz, "An Early Byzantine Commentary on the Jesus Prayer: Introduction and Edition," *Mediaeval Studies* 49 (1987) 208-220.

A = Alexandria, Patriarchal Library, Alexandrinus graecus 131.[3] Fourteenth century, paper, 210 x 150 mm., 179 folios.[4]

Although Moschonas in his catalogue speaks of foliation, the microfilm copy available to me shows only pagination.[5] However, on certain pages the page number has been crossed out and the equivalent folio number added below. The first two folios of the manuscript are unnumbered and contain a πίναξ written in a later hand. The first part of the introductory letter has been lost (probably a single folio). The recto of the first surviving folio is numbered 2 with the number 1 partially erased, just to the left. The verso is numbered 4 and the pagination continues on to page 360. The text was written by a single copyist throughout in a neat, clearly legible hand. Unlike the Vatican manuscript, there are no paragraph divisions in the text.

Annotations: In the lower margin of page 2 (the recto of the folio containing the surviving portion of EP 1), there is the note in a late hand:

τοῦ πατριαρχικοῦ τῆς Ἀλεξανδρείας θρόνου.

On the last page (p. 360) there is another, lengthier note:

καὶ ταύτην τὴν ψυχωφελεστάτην βίβλον εὑρὼν διεσκορπισμένην ἐστάχωσα ἁπλούστατα, ἵνα μὴ ἀπολεσθῇ παντελῶς. ἐν ἔτει ‚αωξθ′ (1869)

✝Ὁ Πηλουσίου Ἀμφιλόχιος ἐκ τῆς νήσου Πάτμου

B. THE CONTENTS

Both of these manuscripts report the text of five letters and twenty-three discourses composed by Theoleptos. No other manuscripts are known to contain such a collection. The ordering of the works in the two manuscripts is significantly different. As noted above the order of Ottob. gr. 405 is roughly chronological.[6] Alex. gr. 131 however represents an attempt to order the liturgical discourses according to

---

[3] Th.D. Moschonas, *Πατριαρχεῖον Ἀλεξανδρείας. Κατάλογοι τῆς πατριαρχικῆς βιβλιοθήκης* (Alexandria, 1945) 1:117-127.

[4] A. Hero expressed some reservations about Moschonas' dating of the manuscript to the fourteenth century in her article, "The Unpublished Letters of Theoleptos, Metropolitan of Philadelphia (1283-1322)," *Journal of Modern Hellenism* 3 (1987) 2, n. 7. I can see no reason for doubt, as the hand of the manuscript clearly belongs to the first half of the fourteenth century.

[5] The microfilm was provided by the Μορφωτικὸν Ἵδρυμα Ἐθνικῆς Τραπέζης, Ἱστορικὸ καὶ Παλαιογραφικὸ Ἀρχεῖο, Ὑπηρεσία Μικροφωτογραφήσεως.

[6] See above, pp. 20-23.

their position in the liturgical cycle. The resulting arrangement appears as follows:

EP   1
MD   1.   Hidden Activity in Christ
MD   2.   Vigilance and Prayer
MD   3.   Deliverance from Egypt
MD   4.   Tenth Sunday of Luke
MD   6.   Hesychia and Prayer
MD 14.   Humility
MD   7.   Discernment of Passions
MD   8.   Submission to the Superior
MD 15.   Spiritual love
MD 16.   [Untitled]
MD 10.   Silence — monks
MD 12.   Fasting
MD   9.   Monastic Community
MD 13.   Christ's Birth
MD 11.   Cheesefare Sunday
MD 17.   Easter Sunday
MD 18.   Easter Sunday 3: Myrrophores
MD 19.   Easter Sunday 4: Paralytic
MD 20.   Easter Sunday 5: Samaritan
MD 21.   Easter Sunday 6: Bind Man
MD 22.   Pentecost Sunday
MD   5.   Transfiguration
MD 23.   Spiritual Testament
EP   2-5

The copyist of Ottob. gr. 405 mistakenly copied MD 7 a second time between MD 9 and 10. In Alex. gr. 131 MD 7 appears only once.

The Relationship of the Ottobonianus and the Alexandrinus Manuscripts

The collation of the two manuscripts that contain the entire series of letters and discourses reveals that Alexandrinus graecus 131 is a direct copy of Ottobonianus graecus 405.

1. Virtually all incorrections in O have been passed on to A:[7]

---

[7] The citations are all from the *Monastic Discourses*. In the text variants cited below, the number of the *Monastic Discourse* is followed by the line number in the edition (and not the paragraph number as elsewhere in the introductory chapters).

2.12 ἐμφωλεύουσα: ἐμφολεύουσα OA

2.116 φίλον: φίλων OA

2.142 ὀδύνης: ὀδύνης OA

2.207 τικτομένη: τυκτομένη OA

2.216 συλλαμβάνει: συλαμβάνει OA

2.218 ἐπτοήθη: ἐπτωήθη OA

2.235 ἐπτοήθη: ἐπτωήθη OA

2.251 πεφόβημαι: πεφόβημε OA

2.278 εὐωδίαν: εὐωδμίαν OA

2.311 ἀπηλλαγμένον: ἀπηλαγμένον OA

2.338 ἀπολίπετε: ἀπολίπεται OA

2.350 ἠσφαλισμένους: ἠσφαλιμένους OA

2.424 ἀνολιγώρως: ἀνολιγόρως OA

2.569 θηλυδριώδους: θηλυδρώδους OA

2.576 ἐπειγομένους: ἐπηγομένους OA

2.621 προσκαρτερεῖτε: προσκαρτερεῖται OA

2.623 ὄντος: ὄντως OA

2.637 τῷ: τὸ OA

2.660 ἐγγιεῖ: ἐγκιεῖ OA

2.678 διαβήτης: διαβίτης OA

2.681 γῦρον: γύρον OA

3.40 περιεπόλουν: περιεπώλουν OA

3.78 ἥνωσε: ἤνωσε OA

3.117-118 ὑψηλῇ ... ταπεινῇ, ὑψηλῇ ... ταπεινῇ OA

3.150 ἀνολιγώρως: ἀνολιγόρως OA

4.19 διατοῦτο OA

4.30 βρῖθον: βρίθον OA

4.62 ἀποκαλύπτον: ἀποκαλύπτων OA

4.83 πρὸς: πρὸ O, πρὸ A

4.132 ἀναπεπτωκὼς: ἀναπεπτωκὸς OA

5.65 προεμήνυσε: προεμύνησε OA

8.20 φιλονικεία OA [cf. 80 φιλονεικίας]

8.80 φιλονεικίας OA [cf. 20 φιλονικεία]

10.57 ἀνεζώωσεν: ἀνεζώοσεν OA

11.36 παχὺς: παχεῖς OA

11.130 βδελυρίας: βδελλυρίας OA

11.135 πύρωσιν: πήρωσιν OA

11.206 ἐνισχύει: ἐν ἰσχύει OA

11.210 ἀναψύχοντα: ἀνὰ ψύχοντα OA

11.216 ἐξυμνεῖ: ἐξ ὑμνεῖ OA

12.9 ἐλλείψεις: ἐλλείψις OA

12.18 λιπαρῶν: λυπαρῶν OA

12.29 γλωσσαλγίας: γλωσαλγείας OA

12.43 διηνεκεῖ: διηνεκῆ OA

13.8 ὁμογνωμοσύνης: ὁμογνομοσύνης ΟΑ
13.65 τούτῳ: τοῦτο ΟΑ
13.80 Βηθλεὲμ: Βιθλεὲμ ΟΑ
13.99 ἀνωτάτω: ἀνοτάτω ΟΑ
13.115 ἐπιτεταγμένη: ἐπιτεταμένη ΟΑ
14.11 ἐξαλλάσσοντα: ἐξαλάσσοντα ΟΑ
14.21 ἡρμοσμένης: εἱρμοσμένης ΟΑ (cf. 180)
14.21 ὁλοκληρίας: ὀλοκληρίας ΟΑ
14.89 ἐπιτηδείαν: ἐπιτηδίαν ΟΑ
14.180 ἡρμοσμένης: εἱρμοσμένης ΟΑ (cf. 21)
14.198 τῷ¹: τὸ ΟΑ
14.207 δυνηθείς: δυνηθῆς Ο, δηνηθῆς Α
14.249 παρεδρεύοντας: παραδρεύοντας ΟΑ
14.327 ἐξ ἀπορίας: ἐξαπορίας ΟΑ
14.331 διὰ παντὸς: διαπαντὸς ΟΑ
14.337 ἔξωθεν: ἔξοθεν ΟΑ
15.79-80 διεσκέδασεν: διεσκέδαζεν ΟΑ
17.91 ἔλαιον cum Sal.: ἔλεον ΟΑ
17.98 ἡμᾶς: ὑμᾶς ΟΑ
18.17 ἐκώλυσεν: ἐκώλησεν ΟΑ
18.85 σινδὼν: σινδὸν ΟΑ
19.118 κλαυθμόν: κλαθμόν ΟΑ
22.17 ἑωρτάσαμεν: ἑορτάσαμεν ΟΑ
22.33 γλῶσσαι: γλῶσαι ΟΑ
23.95 ὑπεράνω: ὑπὲρ ἄνω ΟΑ
23.101 ἐμφυσήματι: ἐν φυσήματι ΟΑ
23.126 ἄγνοιαν: ἄγνειαν ΟΑ
23.126 ἄγνοια: ἄγνεια ΟΑ
23.146 κατ' αἴσθησιν: καταίσθησιν Ο, κατταίσθησιν Α
23.197 τῷ: τὸ ΟΑ
23.237 ῥύθμιζε: ῥίθμιζε ΟΑ
23.337 ἀγαπᾶται: ἀγαπᾶτε ΟΑ
23.478 ἴδῃς: ἤδης ΟΑ
23.491 πιστωθήσομαι: πιστοθήσομε ΟΑ

2. Certain of the readings passed on from O to A are particularly significant in that they strongly suggest that A is a direct copy of O.

    1.13 ἐπιτέτραπται: ἐπιτέραπται Α. In O the τ is attached to the ε and could easily be missed.

    2.290 ὀπτευόμενος: ὀπταυόμενος Ο, ὀπτανόμενος Α. The υ could easily be mistaken for a ν.

    4.83 πρὸς: πρὸ Ο, πρὸ Α; and 6.57. πρὸς: πρὸ Ο, πρὸ Α. In both cases A misread O's abbreviation for πρὸς.

6.85 ἠσχύνοντο [-vo- with ink partially faded] O: ἠσχύντο A

19.20 συνδραμὸν Oᵖᶜ: συνδραμὼν OᵃᶜA. A failed to notice the correction
ʽ written above ω.

19.139 ψευδεῖς O: ψευδ ... A. Apparently, A could not read the
abbreviation -εῖς in O.

20.37 οὐκ αὐξάνει: οὐκαυξάνει OA; and 20.38 ὑπὸ δίψης: ὑποδίψης OA.
Frequently, O runs words together and is always followed in this
by A.

3. There are only three instances where O gives readings not reported
also by A. In each case A has provided an obvious correction to the
text in O.

2.88 τὴν bis O
20.105 τὴν ἡμετέραν ψυχήν A: τὴν ἡμετέρα ψυχήν O
22.38 ἡμετέραν A: ἡμέτερα O

4. Throughout the text of O there are frequent interlinear and marginal
corrections done by a second hand (O¹), all of which were incorporated
by A, with only one exception (MD 15.58).

1.159 ὕδατος OA: τος scripsit super ras. O¹ [15v]
1.375 καὶ add. supra O¹ [25v]: in textu A
2.354 ἀποκτέννω OA: v add. supra O¹ [42v]
2.632 παύσονται add. in marg. inf. O¹ [54r], in textu A
4.156 δεῖ in marg. add. O¹ [74r], in textu A
4.263 ἑαυτοὺς in marg. add. O¹ [79r], in textu A
11.106 ζωγραφῶν OA: v add. in marg. O¹ [127r]
11.111 γὰρ OA: add. supra O¹ [127v]
12.19 ἤ² inseruit supra O¹ [134v], in textu A
13.28 ἑαυτήν add. in marg. O¹ [138r], in textu A
14.65 φεύγειν OA: v add. supra O¹ [145v]
14.154 οὐ et μὴ add. in marg. vel supra O¹ [150r], in textu A
14.163 καὶ¹ add. supra O¹ [150v], in textu A
14.279 καὶ add. in marg. O¹ [156r], in textu A
14.300-301 τῶν καλῶν ... μὴ ... καὶ add. O¹ [157r], in textu A
15.58 ἥνπερ: v inseruit O¹: ἥπερ OᵃᶜA
18.33 περικαλύψαντες: v add. supra O¹ [171r], in textu A
18.55 κακῆς O¹ [172r], A: καλῆς Oᵃᶜ
18.56 λυτρωθῆναι: ναι add. supra O¹ [172r], in textu A
18.70 οὐχ add. supra O¹ [172v], in textu A
18.77 ἐλευθερωθεὶς: εἰς add. supra O¹ [173r], in textu A
18.110 ἀπολαύσει: σει in marg. add. O¹[174v], in textu A
19.8 εἴχετε: ει inseruit O¹ [175r], in textu A
19.123 καὶ² add. O¹ [179r], in textu A
19.146 ἐλεγχθῇ OA: γ add. supra O¹ [180r]

19.147 δοκεῖν OA: εἶν scripsit O¹ [180r]
19.173 φησίν: ν add. supra O¹ [181r], in textu A
20.13 φησίν: ν add. supra O¹ [183v], in textu A
20.31 νενεκρωμένους: νε add. supra O¹ [184v], in textu A
20.91 ὁ add. supra O¹ [187r], in textu A

5. While O was carefully copied, the execution of A can only be described as careless. Only a small sample can be listed.

2.54 ταῖς: τες A
2.162 ἀργὸς: ἀγγὸς A
2.229 ἔχθρας ... κατὰ τῆς om. A
2.355 αἰσχρὰ: ἐσχρὰ A
2.368 ὅσοι: ὅσι A
2.446 ῥαθυμίᾳ: θαθυμίᾳ A
2.598 ἀπὸ τῆς bis A
2.677 καὶ²: αἰ A
2.710 καὶ θεωρίαν: φυλωρίαν A
3.30 ῥαθυμίαν: ῥθυμίαν A
3.115 αὐτῆς: καὶ τῆς A
3.120 εἰπόντος: εἰτόντος A

C. Remaining Manuscripts

M = Venice, Biblioteca Nazionale Marciana, ms I 29 (coll. 949).[8]

This is a composite manuscript made up of gatherings of varying dates. Part ix containing two Theoleptos texts can be dated to the late fourteenth to early fifteenth century. The ordering of the folios has been badly disturbed and only recently restored correctly by A. Rigo as follows: MD 1, fols. 378r-385v, 400r-405v; MD 23 (complete), fols. 405r, 388, 394-399, 387-386, 372-377, 368-369v.[9] The folios have suffered seriously from water damage which has left a significant portion of the text illegible or nearly so.

K = Athos, Μονὴ Κωνσταμονίτου 25 (Lambros 461).[10] Fifteenth century, paper, 8vo., 384 folios.

---

  8 E. Mioni, *Bibliothecae divi Marci Venetiarum Codices graeci manuscripti*, pars prior (Rome, 1967) 1:34-39.
  9 A. Rigo, "Nota sulla dottrina ascetico-spirituale di Teolepto Metropolita di Filadelfia (1250/51-1322)," rsbn 24 (1987) 176-177, n. 53.
  10 Sp.P. Lambros, *Catalogue of the Greek Manuscripts on Mount Athos. Κατάλογος τῶν ἐν ταῖς βιβλιοθήκαις τοῦ Ἁγίου Ὄρους ἑλληνικῶν κωδίκων*, 2 vols. (Cambridge, MA, 1895, 1900), 1:38.

This manuscript contains a miscellany of ascetic literature, among which are found two of Theoleptos' *Monastic Discourses*: MD 1 on fols. 337r-345r and MD 23 on fols. 345r-354v.

T = Athos, Μονὴ Καρακάλλου 72 (Lambros 1585).[11] AD 1776, paper, 215 x 150 mm., 5 initial folios (unnumbered) 706 pages.

On initial fol. 5v there is the inscription: ἐγράφη εἰς τοὺς 1776 αὐγούστου 20 εἰς τὴν ὕδραν παρὰ κωνσταντίου μοναχοῦ. This is another ascetic miscellany, with Theoleptos' MD 1 found on pp. 587-603; MD 23 is absent.

B = Athos, Μονὴ Βατοπεδίου 214.[12] AD 1862, paper, 128 x 100 mm., α'-ιγ' + 714 pages.

On the first folio there is the inscription:

Ἐκλογὴ ἐκ πολλῶν Νηπτικῶν Ἁγίων Πατέρων, περιέχουσα τὸ ἄνθος τῶν περὶ καθαρᾶς καρδιακῆς προσευχῆς, καὶ τῶν τούτοις· ἀπάνθισμά τε περὶ ἡσυχίας, καθαρότητος νοός, καὶ προσευχῆς, ἐν κεφαλαίοις πολλοῖς, καὶ ἑτέρων λόγων πάνυ ὡραιοτάτων, καὶ πλεῖστα ὠφελιμωτάτων, πρὸς ὠφέλειαν τῶν Μοναχῶν, πρὸ πάντων τῶν Ἡσυχαστῶν. Ἐν ἔτει Σωτηρίῳ: ‚αωξβ'. ἐν Μηνὶ Νοεμβρίῳ.

MD 1 is found on pp. 221-263. A number of extracts from MD 23, divided into 9 capita, are found on pp. 264-274.

Turin, Biblioteca Nazionale, MS B.VII.11 (Pasini gr. 352).[13] Fourteenth century, paper, 269 folios.

According to the catalogue of Pasini this manuscript contained only two works, namely, the *Spiritual Century* of Kallistos and Ignatios Xanthopoulos (fols. 1-250/1) and MD 1 of Theoleptos (fols. 251-269). The manuscript survived the fire of 1945 in only very fragmentary form. None of the folios containing MD 1 were preserved. The incipit given by Pasini for MD 1 is as follows: Τὸ μοναδικὸν ἐπάγγελμα δένδρον ἐστὶν ὑψίκομόν τε καὶ γονιμώτατον (i.e., MD 1.3, ll. 31-32). There is no information regarding the presence or absence of MD 23 in the codex.

---

[11] Lambros, *Catalogue*, 1:137.

[12] S. Eustratiades and Arkadios Vatopedinos, *Catalogue of the Greek Manuscripts in the Library of the Monastery of Vatopedi on Mount Athos* (Harvard Theological Studies 11; Cambridge, MA, 1924), p. 46.

[13] J. Pasinus, A. Rivautella, F. Berta, *Codices manuscripti Bibliothecae Regiae Taurinensis Athenaei per linguas digesti et binas in partes distributi* (Turin, 1749) 1:481; F. Cosentini, *Inventari dei manoscritti delle biblioteche d'Italia* (Florence, 1922) 28:46.

D. Printed Editions

1. *The* Philokalia *Edition*

Ph = *ΦΙΛΟΚΑΛΙΑ ΤΩΝ ΙΕΡΩΝ ΝΗΠΤΙΚΩΝ* συνερανισθεῖσα παρὰ τῶν ἁγίων καὶ θεοφόρων πατέρων ἡμῶν ἐν ᾗ διὰ τῆς κατὰ τὴν πρᾶξιν καὶ θεωρίαν ἠθικῆς φιλοσοφίας ὁ νοῦς καθαίρεται, φωτίζεται, καὶ τελειοῦται ἐπιμελείᾳ μὲν ὅτι πλείστη διορθωθεῖσα, νῦν δὲ πρῶτον τύποις ἐκδοθεῖσα διὰ δαπάνης τοῦ τιμιωτάτου, καὶ θεοσεβεστάτου κυρίου Ἰωάννου Μαυρογορδάτου εἰς κοινὴν τῶν ὀρθοδόξων ὠφέλειαν (Venice, 1782), pp. 855-862 (MD 1), pp. 863-865 (MD 23, excerpts in 9 capita).

ΦΙΛΟΚΑΛΙΑ ΤΩΝ ΙΕΡΩΝ ΝΗΠΤΙΚΩΝ ... καὶ εἰς ἣν προσετέθησαν τὰ ἐκ τῆς ἐν Βενετίᾳ ἐκδόσεως ἐλλείποντα κεφάλαια τοῦ μακαρίου Πατριάρχου Καλλίστου (Athens, 1893).[14]

ΦΙΛΟΚΑΛΙΑ ΤΩΝ ΙΕΡΩΝ ΝΗΠΤΙΚΩΝ ... . 5 vols. (Athens, 1957-1963) 4:4-12 (MD 1), 4:13-15 (MD 23, excerpts in 9 capita).

Migne, J.P., ed. *Patrologia graeca* 143 (Paris, 1865; repr. Turnhout, 1978), cols. 379-399 (MD 1), 399-404 (MD 23, excerpts in 9 capita).[15]

2. *Recent Editions*

Beyer, H.-V. "Die Katechese des Theoleptos von Philadelpheia auf die Verklärung Christi." JÖB 34 (1984) 171-198 (pp. 188-194 = MD 5).

Salaville, S. "Un directeur spirituel à Byzance au début du xive siècle: Théolepte de Philadelphie. Homélie inédite sur Noël et la vie religieuse." In *Mélanges Joseph de Ghellinck* (Museum lessianum. Section historique 14; Gembloux, 1951) 2:877-887 (pp. 881-883 = MD 13).

——. "Formes ou méthodes de prière d'après un Byzantin du xive siècle." EO 39 (1940) 1-25 (pp. 3-4, MD 1.1-2).

——. "Une lettre et un discours inédits de Théolepte de Philadelphie." REB 5 (1947) 101-115 (pp. 105-106 = EP 1; pp. 112-115 = MD 17).

——. "La vie monastique grecque au début du xive siècle d'après un discours inédit de Théolepte de Philadelphie." REB 2 (1944) 119-125 (pp. 120-125 = MD 9, lengthy extracts).

---

[14] This edition was not available to me.
[15] Migne took the texts from the Venice edition of the *Philokalia*.

E. The Remaining Manuscripts and the *Philokalia* Edition

These witnesses are closely related in that for MD 1 they all omit the opening section (MD 1.1-2) and they all change the feminine references to masculine. The Venice and Turin manuscripts are of special interest because they show that the modified text of MD 1 was not the work of the compilers of the *Philokalia*, but of some anonymous late Byzantine editor. The Batopediou manuscript is a direct copy of the printed *Philokalia*. Neither for MD 1 nor for MD 23 does any of these remaining manuscripts report many readings of value, although they occasionally offer corrections to the text of O. The corrections appear to be conjectural emendations. Most of these involve mood changes.

1. Examples of gender change.

    1.51 καθηλώσασα: καθήλωσας MKTBPh
    1.62 παραβαλοῦσα: παραβαλὼν MKTBPh
    1.63 περιβαλομένη: περιβαλλόμενος MKTBPh
    1.64 ἐπαγγειλαμένη: ἐπαγγειλάμενος MKTBPh
    1.108 ἀποβαλομένη: ἀποβαλλόμενος MKTBPh
    1.183 ἐπιρρίπτουσα: ἐπιρρίπτων MKTBPh

2. Corrections to the text of O.[16]

    1.52 τὸν TBPh: τῶν OAK
    1.78 καὶ: καὶ εἰ TBPh
    1.87 ἀγαπήσεις: ἀγαπήσῃς KB
    1.92 παρέχει: παρέχῃ K
    1.112 καταπαύσεις: καταπαύσῃς KTBPh
    1.113 διαναστήσῃ: διαναστήσει K
    1.113 νικήσεις: νικήσῃς BPh
    1.139 εὑρήσεις: εὑρήσῃς MKT, εὕρῃς BPh
    1.149 ἀναλίσκηται: ἀναλίσκεται TBPh
    1.152 διανύηται: διανύεται KTBPh

F. Constitution of the Text

In light of the above evidence the text of the *Monastic Discourses* must be based on O. Orthographic errors have been corrected, but the readings of O and A are given in the apparatus. Deviance from

---

[16] Only a sample is given.

the Classical use of the moods has been retained in the text, because some or all of these cases could go back to Theoleptos himself and it is impossible to distinguish between his usage and readings introduced by copyists. Readings peculiar to A are normally not given in the apparatus. Likewise, there seems to be no reason to report the readings of the Athonite manuscripts and the *Philokalia* edition. Where my emendations of the text are supported by M, this has been noted in the apparatus.

G. Sigla and Abbreviations

O = Ottob. 405
A = Alex. 131
M = Marc. gr. II 29

add.   addidit
corr.   correxi
hab.   habet
in marg.   in margine
transp.   transposuit
Sal.   Salaville
sub ras.   sub rasuram

Theoleptos of Philadelpheia

THE MONASTIC DISCOURSES

Θεολήπτου Φιλαδελφείας

Ἐπιστολὴ πρὸς βασίλισσαν Εἰρήνην καὶ κτητόρισσαν τῆς σεβασμίας
καὶ βασιλικῆς μονῆς τοῦ σωτῆρος Χριστοῦ τοῦ Φιλανθρώπου, τὴν διὰ
τοῦ θείου καὶ ἀγγελικοῦ σχήματος μετονομασθεῖσαν Εὐλογίαν μοναχὴν
5 καὶ γνησίαν πνευματικὴν θυγατέρα αὐτοῦ χρηματίσασαν, ἣν καὶ
οἰκείαις χερσὶν ἀπεκείρατο

1. Τὸν κατὰ κόσμον νυμφίον ἀποβαλοῦσα διὰ θανάτου, τὰ τῆς
χηρείας τελεῖς καὶ τὰ τῆς συνηθείας τηρεῖς καὶ διαναπαύεις τὸν
λογισμὸν τὴν ἔξωθεν σεμνότητα περιποιουμένη. ἐπεὶ οὖν τὴν τοῦ
10 σώματος ἀπόλαυσιν ἀπώλεσας καὶ ἐν τῇ τῶν πενθούντων βαδίζεις
χώρᾳ σπούδασον τὴν λογικὴν ψυχὴν οἰκειῶσαι τῷ θεῷ λόγῳ καὶ
σεαυτὴν συνάψαι τῷ Χριστῷ καὶ τὸ κατὰ πνεῦμα συστήσασθαι
συνοικέσιον. κατάλειψον τὰς ἐν τῷ παλατίῳ πυκνὰς διατριβάς· ἔασον
τὸ πλῆθος τῶν ὑπηρετῶν· παράδραμε πάσης κολακείας τὴν ματαιό-
15 τητα. μνήσθητι ὅτι μετὰ βραχὺ μεμονωμένη καταβαίνεις εἰς Ἅιδην·
μεμονωμένη κατατίθεσαι τάφῳ· μεμονωμένη παρίστασαι τῷ φρικτῷ
κριτηρίῳ εἰ καὶ μετὰ πάντων ἀνίστασαι· μεμονωμένη τῆς κατὰ σὲ
πολιτείας τὴν ἀπολογίαν παρέχεις· οὐδένα συνήγορον ἔχεις, οὐ τῶν
τεκόντων, οὐ τῶν προσηκόντων, οὐ τῶν κολακευόντων, οὐ τῶν
20 προπεμπόντων ἢ τῶν ἑπομένων. αἱ ἀγαθαὶ δὲ πράξεις καὶ ἡ πεπαρ-
ρησιασμένη συνείδησις, αὗται μόναι συνήγοροί σου πεφύκασι.
τούτων τὴν κατανόησιν ἕξεις.

2. Εἰ τὸ σῶμα χρονίζει ἐν κελλίῳ καὶ ὁ νοῦς παραμένει ἐν καρδίᾳ,
λέγουσα καὶ αὐτή, *καταμόνας εἰμὶ ἐγὼ ἕως ἂν παρέλθω*, τότε καὶ
25 Χριστὸς οἰκισθήσεται ἐν σοί, ὡς τὸν οἶκον τῆς διανοίας κοσμούσῃ
καὶ Χριστὸν ἐπιβωμένῃ διὰ τῆς συνεχοῦς ἐπικλήσεως. *μνησθήσομαι,*
γὰρ φησίν, *τοῦ ὀνόματός σου ἐν πάσῃ γενεᾷ καὶ γενεᾷ.* ὅταν γὰρ τὰς

Theoleptos of Philadelpheia

LETTER TO PRINCESS EIRENE, THE FOUNDRESS OF THE AUGUST
IMPERIAL MONASTERY OF CHRIST PHILANTHROPOS SOTER, TO THE NUN
NOW NAMED EULOGIA BY HER RECEPTION OF THE DIVINE AND ANGELIC
HABIT, HIS TRUE SPIRITUAL DAUGHTER, WHOM HE TONSURED WITH HIS
OWN HANDS[1]

1.   Now that you have lost through death your bridegroom of this
world,[2] you perform the duties of widowhood and observe its customs;
you calm your thoughts by your preoccupation with external solemnity.
Since you have lost the pleasures of the body and walk in the land
of those who mourn, make haste to liken your rational soul to God
the Word, to join yourself to Christ and to form a spiritual marriage
with him. Forsake your frequent stays in the Palace. Dismiss your
flock of servants. Disdain the vanity of any flattery. Remember that
in but a little while you go all alone to Hades. All alone you will
be laid in the tomb. All alone you will present yourself to the dreadful
tribunal, even though you will rise again with everyone. All alone you
will have to present a defence for your way of life. You will have
no one to plead for you, not one of your parents, not one of your
relations, not one of your flatterers, nor one of your escort or your
attendants. Good works and a clear conscience, these alone are your
advocates. You should bear these things in mind.

2.   If your body stays in your cell and your mind abides in your
heart while you say, "I am alone until I pass away,"[3] then Christ will
make his abode in you, for you have adorned the house of your
discursive intellect and called upon Christ in continual supplication.[4]
For scripture says, "I shall remember your name in every generation."[5]

---

[1] This letter was first published by S. Salaville, "Une lettre et un discours inédits
de Théolepte de Philadelphie," REB 5 (1947) 101-115.

[2] Namely, Ioannes Palaiologos, son of Andronikos II and Yolanda-Eirene of
Montferrat. He had died in the early months of 1307. He was married to Princess
Eirene in 1303 (PLP 21475).

[3] Ps 140:10.

[4] For Theoleptos the term ἐπίκλησις is virtually synonymous with the Jesus Prayer.

[5] Ps 44:18.

αἰσθήσεις τοῦ σώματος τοῖς τῶν ἐντολῶν ὡραΐζῃς τρόποις, τὴν δὲ
γλῶσσαν τοῖς θείοις ὕμνοις κατασφαλίζῃς, τὰς δὲ δυνάμεις τῆς ψυχῆς
30 τῇ πυκνότητι τῆς προσευχῆς κατασεμνύνῃς, εὐφυῶς τότε λέγεις·
μνησθήσομαι τοῦ ὀνόματός σου ἐν πάσῃ γενεᾷ καὶ γενεᾷ, ὡς σώματι καὶ
πνεύματι τῷ κυρίῳ εὐαρεστοῦσα.

3. Βίαζε σεαυτὴν ἐν πᾶσι καὶ γυμνάζου πάντοτε πρὸς τὴν
στενότητα, κατὰ μικρὸν ἐλαττοῦσα τὸν πλατυσμόν, ἵνα καὶ τὴν ἰσχὺν
35 τῆς σαρκὸς ὑποχαλάσῃς καὶ τὴν ψυχὴν ἐνδυναμώσῃς· ἡ τῆς σαρκὸς
γὰρ ἧττα νίκην περιποιεῖται τῇ ψυχῇ, καὶ ἡ τοῦ σώματος εὔλογος
θλίψις ἀναβλύζειν οἶδε χαρὰν τῷ πνεύματι. θλίβε τοιγαροῦν σάρκα
τοῖς τῶν καλῶν πόνοις καὶ παρηγόρει πένητας ἐκ τῶν προσόντων
σοι, ἵνα ὅταν ὁ νυμφίος ἀποκαλύπτηται ἐξέλθῃς εἰς ἀπάντησιν,
40 καιομένην λαμπάδα κατέχουσα δαψιλὲς τὸ ἔλαιον φέρουσαν, πίστιν
φημὶ καὶ σώφρονα βίον καὶ τὴν ἐλεημοσύνην, μεθ᾽ ὧν καὶ τῆς εἰς
τὸν νυμφῶνα εἰσόδου ἀξιοῦσαι καὶ τῆς τοῦ κυρίου χαρᾶς ἀπολαύεις·
ἧς καὶ τύχοιμεν διὰ τῶν κατ᾽ ἀρετὴν πόνων καὶ τῆς ὑπομονῆς τῶν
ἐπερχομένων θλιβερῶν, πρεσβείαις τῆς ἁγίας Θεοτόκου καὶ πάντων
45 τῶν ἠγαπηκότων τὸν κύριον. Ἀμήν.

When you beautify the senses of your body with the ways of the commandments and fortify your tongue with the divine hymns and exalt the faculties of your soul with the intensity of your prayer, then you will say indeed, "I shall remember your name in every generation," since you will be pleasing to the Lord in body and spirit.

3.   Exert yourself in all these matters and train yourself at all times for the practice of frugality, gradually reducing the opulence of your lifestyle in order to diminish the strength of the flesh and to fortify the soul. The defeat of the flesh wins victory for the soul, and the reasonable affliction of the body can bring joy to burst forth for the spirit. Afflict your flesh then with the labours of good works and comfort the poor with your own possessions that, when the Bridegroom appears, you may go out to meet him holding your lamp lighted and supplied with abundant oil, I mean, with faith, with a chaste life and with almsgiving, whereby you will be deemed worthy to enter the bridal chamber and relish the joy of the Lord.[6] Through the intercession of the Holy Theotokos and all those who have loved the Lord may we attain this grace by the labours of virtue and by patient endurance of the sufferings that come upon us. Amen.

---

[6] Cf. Mt 25:1-13.

Λόγος τὴν ἐν Χριστῷ κρυπτὴν ἐργασίαν διασαφῶν καὶ δεικνὺς ὡς ἐν βραχεῖ τοῦ μοναδικοῦ ἐπαγγέλματος τὸν σκοπόν

1. Βασίλισσα χρηματίσασα κατὰ κόσμον, ἐσπούδασας καὶ κατὰ παθῶν βασιλεῦσαι καὶ τὴν ἀξίαν τοῦ σώματος εἰς τὴν τῆς ψυχῆς
5 εὐπρέπειαν μεθαρμόσασθαι καὶ διὰ τῆς κατὰ τὰς ἀρετὰς ἀληθείας τὴν κατὰ τὰ πράγματα φαντασίαν διακρούσασθαι καὶ δεῖξαι τὴν πτωχείαν ἀληθινὸν πλοῦτον καὶ τὴν εὐτέλειαν μεγαλειότητα καὶ τὴν κάκωσιν ἄνεσιν καὶ τὴν θλίψιν χαράν. τῆς ὄντως φιλοσοφίας τὰ κατορθώματα· οὗ χάριν καὶ ἀξίως τῆς ἐπαινουμένης μεταμφιάσεως
10 πρὸς ἡμᾶς τὴν ἐρώτησιν ἐποίησω καὶ διενοήσω τύπον μαθεῖν σύντομον ἀσκητικῷ βίῳ κατάλληλον. καὶ ἡμεῖς ἅμα μὲν ὑπακοὴν ἐκπεραίνοντες, ἅμα δὲ καὶ ὀφειλὴν ἀποτιννύντες (καὶ γὰρ παντὶ τῷ αἰτοῦντι παρέχειν ἡμῖν ἐπιτέτραπται κατὰ τὴν ἐνοῦσαν ἡμῖν μικρὰν δύναμιν, μᾶλλον δὲ κατὰ τὸ μέτρον τῆς δοθείσης ἡμῖν χάριτος),
15 ἀφάτῳ θεοῦ χρηστότητι τὸν παρόντα λόγον ἐκθέμενοί σοι ἐγχειρίζομεν, τὴν τρίβον τοῦ μονήρους βίου ἐξομαλίζοντες κατ-αντῶσαν εἰς τὴν ὁδὸν τὴν σωτήριον, αὐτὸν τὸν Χριστόν, τὴν ἀληθινὴν τῶν εἰς αὐτὸν ἠλπικότων παράκλησιν.

2. Ἐκ βάθους καρδίας ὀφείλεις ἐξυμνεῖν τὸν θεόν, ὅτι σοφίας
20 ἀκτῖνας εἰσδεξαμένη παρ' αὐτοῦ, τὸ τῆς νεότητος ἄνθος ἀσκητικοῖς πόνοις μαρᾶναι διενοήσω· ὅτι ἐν τῇ ἀκμῇ τῆς νεότητος διατελοῦσα, τῶν τῆς νεότητος κολακευμάτων κατεφρόνησας καὶ μονάζειν προέ-κρινας καὶ Χριστῷ νυμφευθῆναι ἠγάπησας. ἐπεὶ οὖν τὸν ἀχλυποιὸν κόσμον ἀφῆκας, πρὸς δὲ τὸν τῆς ἀρετῆς διαυγέστατον κόσμον

DISCOURSE EXPLAINING THE HIDDEN ACTIVITY IN CHRIST
AND SHOWING BRIEFLY THE GOAL OF MONASTIC PROFESSION[1]

1. Having once been a princess in the eyes of the world, you have earnestly endeavoured to reign over the passions, to bring the dignity of the body into harmony with the beauty of the soul, to rid yourself of the empty appearance of worldly affairs by the truth found in virtue, and to demonstrate that poverty is true wealth, that humility is greatness, that mortification is a release, and that suffering is joy. These are the attainments of true philosophy.[2] For this reason, in a manner worthy of your laudable change of vocation, you asked for and gave thought to learning from us a brief rule appropriate for the ascetic life.[3] We, by obediently complying, at the same time pay a debt, for it has been enjoined upon us to provide for every petitioner[4] according to what little ability we have, or rather, according to the measure of the grace given us.[5] By the indescribable goodness of God, we have composed the present treatise and entrust it to your hands, so as to smooth the path of the monastic life which leads to the road of salvation, namely, Christ himself, the true consolation of those who have placed their hope in him.

2. From the depths of your heart you ought to praise God because, having received from him rays of wisdom, you decided to wither the bloom of your youth with ascetic labours.[6] In the prime of your youth, you despised its flatteries and chose the monastic life, preferring to become the bride of Christ. Therefore, since you have abandoned this

---

[1] This text was first published in the *Philokalia* (Venice, 1782), pp. 855-862, but there the first two paragraphs are absent and the feminine gender references are all changed to masculine. S. Salaville supplied the missing paragraphs and commented extensively on the text in his article, "Formes ou méthodes de prière d'après un Byzantin du xive siècle, Théolepte de Philadelphie," EO 39 (1940) 1-25. For κρυπτὴ ἐργασία see "For you have died, and your life is hid with Christ in God (Col 3:3)"; also I. Hausherr, *Noms du Christ*, pp. 167-175.

[2] On this use of the term 'philosophy' see A.-M. Malingrey, *Philosophia. Étude d'un groupe de mots dans la littérature grecque, des présocratiques au ive siècle après J.-C.* (Paris, 1961), pp. 237-260.

[3] On τύπος as rule see *Apophthegmata patrum*, Makarios 3 (456) (PG 65:264B).

[4] Cf. Lk 6:30.

[5] Cf. Eph 4:7.

[6] Eirene entered monastic life in 1307 at the age of sixteen.

25 ἔδραμες καὶ τὸν καινοποιὸν βίον μετετάξω βιοῦν, χρεὼν πάντως καὶ
τὰ οἰκεῖα τῷ μοναδικῷ ἐπαγγέλματι φρονήματά τε καὶ πράγματα
κατασπάζεσθαι, ἀλλὰ μὴ νενοθευμένην ἐπιδείκνυσθαι τὴν τοῦ βίου
μεταβολήν, ἵνα μὴ τῆς κοσμικῆς συγχύσεως μίγμα ἐπιφερομένη, τὴν
καθαρὰν τῆς ἀρετῆς ἐπιταράττῃς ὄψιν, κἀντεῦθεν ἄκαρπος γένηται
30 ἡ ἀναχώρησίς σου.

3. Τὸ μοναδικὸν ἐπάγγελμα δένδρον ἐστὶν ὑψίκομόν τε καὶ
γονιμώτατον, οὗ ῥίζα μὲν ἡ τῶν σωματικῶν πάντων ἀλλοτρίωσις,
κλάδοι δὲ ἡ ἀπροσπάθεια τῆς ψυχῆς καὶ τὸ μηδεμίαν σχέσιν πρὸς
τὰ πράγματα, ὧν τὴν φυγὴν ἐποιήσατο, ἔχειν· καρπὸς δὲ τῶν ἀρετῶν
35 ἡ κτῆσις καὶ ἡ θεοποιὸς ἀγάπη καὶ ἡ ἐκ τούτων μὴ διακοπτομένη
εὐφροσύνη· *ὁ καρπός, γάρ φησι, τοῦ πνεύματός ἐστιν ἀγάπη, χαρά,
εἰρήνη.*
4. Ἡ τοῦ κόσμου φυγὴ τὴν πρὸς Χριστὸν καταφυγὴν χαρίζεται·
κόσμον δὲ λέγω τὴν φιλίαν τῶν αἰσθητῶν πραγμάτων καὶ τῆς σαρκός.
40 ὁ ἐκ τούτων ἀλλοτριούμενος ἐν ἐπιγνώσει τῆς ἀληθείας οἰκειοῦται
Χριστῷ. κτώμενος τὴν ἀγάπην αὐτοῦ, δι᾽ ἣν ἅπαντα τὰ τοῦ κόσμου
ἀποποιησάμενος, τὸν πολύτιμον μαργαρίτην, Χριστόν, ἐξωνήσατο.
Χριστὸν ἐνδέδυσαι διὰ τοῦ σωτηρίου βαπτίσματος· ἀπεβάλου τὸν
ῥύπον διὰ τοῦ θείου λουτροῦ· τῆς πνευματικῆς χάριτος τὴν λαμπρό-
45 τητα ἐκομίσω καὶ τὴν εὐγένειαν τῆς πλάσεως ἀπέλαβες διὰ τῆς
ἀναπλάσεως. ἀλλὰ τί γέγονε; μᾶλλον δὲ τί πέπονθεν ὁ ἄνθρωπος ἐξ
ἀβουλίας; διὰ τῆς πρὸς τὸν κόσμον φιλίας ἠλλοίωσε τοὺς θείους
χαρακτῆρας· διὰ τῆς πρὸς τὴν σάρκα συμπαθείας ἠχρείωσε τὴν
εἰκόνα, ἡ ἀχλὺς τῶν ἐμπαθῶν λογισμῶν ἠμαύρωσε τὸ τῆς ψυχῆς
50 ἔσοπτρον, δι᾽ οὗ Χριστός, ὁ νοητὸς ἥλιος, ἐμφανίζεται.

5. Σὺ τῷ τοῦ θεοῦ φόβῳ τὴν ψυχὴν καθηλώσασα, ἐπέγνως τὸν
σκοτασμὸν τῆς κοσμικῆς ἀνωμαλίας, συνῆκας τὸν ἐκ τῶν θορύβων
συναγόμενον τῆς διανοίας σκορπισμόν, ἑώρακας τὸν ἐκ τοῦ πολυτα-
ράχου βίου συναντῶντα τοῖς ἀνθρώποις μάταιον περισπασμόν,
55 ἐτρώθης τῷ βέλει τοῦ κατὰ τὴν ἡσυχίαν ἔρωτος, ἐζήτησας τὴν

51 σὺ Oac: σοὶ Opc   52 τὸν corr. (M): τῶν OA

mist-encumbered world to run off to the most radiant world of virtue and have made the change to a life of renewal, it is absolutely necessary that you embrace the ways both of thinking and of acting which are proper to the monastic profession. But you must also show that your change of vocation is not half-hearted, lest by bringing with you a mixture of worldly confusion you disturb the pure vision of virtue with the result that your withdrawal from the world bears no fruit.

3. Monastic profession is a towering and very fruitful tree whose roots consist of disassociation from all corporeal things and whose branches consist of the detachment of the soul and its refusal to have any relationship with those things from which it has fled. Its fruit is the acquisition of the virtues, divinizing love and the joy which cannot be severed from these. For scripture says, "The fruit of the Spirit is love, joy and peace."[7]

4. Flight from the world provides a refuge in Christ. By the world I mean attachment to sensible things and to the flesh. He who dissociates himself from these things in recognition of the truth attains to the likeness of Christ. In acquiring the love of Christ, for the sake of which he renounced all the things of this world, he purchased the pearl of great price, namely, Christ.[8] Through saving baptism you have clothed yourself in Christ;[9] you divested yourself of defilement through the divine bath, procured for yourself the radiance of spiritual grace and through this re-creation received the noble birth of our first creation. But what has happened? Or rather, what has man suffered as a result of his self-will? By his attachment to the world he altered the divine impress. By his association with the flesh he corrupted the Image; the mist of impassioned thoughts darkened the mirror of the soul in which Christ, the spiritual sun, is visible.

5. By fixing your soul upon the fear of God, you recognized the darkness inherent in the vicissitudes of this world; you realized the distracting effect of turmoil upon the discursive intellect; you have noted the empty distractions that befall people who lead an overly busied life; you have been wounded by the arrow of love attained in tranquillity;[10] you have sought peace from your thoughts (for you

---

[7] Gal 5:22.

[8] Mt 13:46.

[9] Cf. Gal 3:27.

[10] Or perhaps 'love for tranquillity.' The *vulnus amoris* is discussed in greater detail in MD 6.5. Here the reference is apparently to an initial gift of grace to enable the necessary detachment from worldly things. Still, some progress in *hesychia* is required before the gift is granted.

εἰρήνην τῶν λογισμῶν, ἔμαθες γάρ, *ζήτησον εἰρήνην καὶ δίωξον αὐτήν·*
ἐπόθησας τὴν ἐκεῖθεν ἀνάπαυσιν, ἐπειδὴ ἤκουσας, *ἐπίστρεψον, ψυχή*
μου, εἰς τὴν ἀνάπαυσίν σου. διὰ γοῦν ταῦτα καὶ διενοήσω τὴν εὐγένειαν,
ἣν ἀπέλαβες ἐν τῷ βαπτίσματι κατὰ χάριν, ἀπεβάλου δὲ κατὰ γνώμην
60 διὰ τῶν παθῶν ἐν τῷ κόσμῳ ἀνακαλέσασθαι.

6. Ἀμέλει καὶ τὴν ἀγαθὴν γνώμην εἰς ἔργον ἐξέβαλες, τῷ ἱερῷ
φροντιστηρίῳ παραβαλοῦσα καὶ τὰ τίμια τῆς μετανοίας ἄμφια
περιβαλομένη καὶ τὴν μέχρι θανάτου καταμονὴν ἐν τῷ μοναστηρίῳ
εὐψύχως ἐπαγγειλαμένη. δευτέραν ἤδη συνθήκην πρὸς θεὸν ἐποιήσω·
65 τὴν πρώτην εἰς τὸν παρόντα βίον εἰσερχομένη, τὴν δευτέραν πρὸς
τὸ τέλος τοῦ παρόντος βίου ἐπειγομένη. τότε διὰ τῆς εὐσεβείας τῷ
Χριστῷ προσελήφθης· νῦν διὰ τῆς μετανοίας τῷ Χριστῷ προσηρ-
μόσθης. ἐκεῖ χάριν εὗρες· ὧδε χρέος συνέθου. τότε νηπιάζουσα τοῦ
δοθέντος σοι ἀξιώματος οὐκ ἠδυνήθης, εἰ καὶ ὕστερον αὐξηθεῖσα
70 τὸ μέγεθος ἔγνως τῆς δωρεᾶς καὶ χαλινὸν ἐπὶ στόματος φέρεις· νῦν
ἐν τελείῳ φρονήματι διατελοῦσα, τὴν δύναμιν τῆς συνταγῆς
ἐπιγινώσκεις.

7. Ὅρα μὴ καὶ ταύτην ἀθετήσασα τὴν ὑπόσχεσιν, καθάπερ τι
σκεῦος συντριβέν, ὁλοκλήρως ἀπορριφῇς *εἰς σκότος τὸ ἐξώτερον, ἔνθα*
75 *ὁ κλαυθμὸς καὶ ὁ βρυγμὸς τῶν ὀδόντων.* δίχα γὰρ τῆς κατὰ τὴν
μετάνοιαν ὁδοῦ ἄλλη τρίβος ἐπανάγουσα πρὸς σωτηρίαν οὐ πέφυκεν.
ἄκουσον τί σοι Δαβὶδ ἐπαγγέλλεται· *τὸν ὕψιστον ἔθου καταφυγήν σου*
καὶ τὴν κατὰ Χριστὸν προείλου τεθλιμμένην ζωήν, *οὐ προσελεύσεται*
πρὸς σὲ κακὰ τὰ ἐκ τῆς πλατείας καὶ εὐρυχώρου τῆς κοσμικῆς
80 ἀναστροφῆς προσδοθέντα σοι. οὐχ ἕψεταί σοι μετανοεῖν αἱρουμένῃ
ἔρως χρημάτων, τρυφή, τιμή, καλλωπισμός, ἀκρασία αἰσθήσεων· οὐ
διαμενοῦσι παράνομοι κατέναντί σου, μετεωρισμὸς διανοίας,
αἰχμαλωσία νοός, χαύνωσις ἀλλεπαλλήλων λογισμῶν καὶ ἄλλη πᾶσα
ἑκούσιος παρατροπὴ καὶ σύγχυσις· οὐδὲ φιλία γεννητόρων, ἀδελφῶν,

learned, "Seek peace and follow after it").[11] You desired rest from all this because you heard, "Return, my soul, to your rest."[12] For the sake of these things, then, you took thought for the noble birth which you received by grace in baptism and in your resolution you refused to allow yourself to be called back to the world by the passions.

6.   And, of course, you have put your good purpose into action by entering the holy convent, by clothing yourself with the precious robes of repentance and by courageously promising to remain in the monastery until death. You have now made your second commitment to God. The first you made when you came into this present life and the second as you press on towards the end of this present life. At the former time you were bound to Christ in piety; now you have conformed yourself to Christ in repentance. There you found grace; here you have contracted a debt. At the former time, because you were a baby, you were incapable of appreciating the dignity that was given to you, though later, when you had grown older, you recognized the great value of the gift and hold the bit in your mouth;[13] now that you have attained complete maturity, you recognize the meaning of your promise.

7.   Beware lest, in rejecting this promise, like a broken pot, you be cast out entirely "into the outer darkness where there is weeping and gnashing of teeth."[14] For apart from the road of repentance there is no other path leading to salvation.[15] Listen to what David announces to you: "You have made the Most High your refuge"[16] and have chosen the life of suffering in Christ; "Evils shall not befall you,"[17] that is, those meted out to you by the flat and broad road of life in the world.[18] Love of possessions, pleasure, public esteem, adornment, lack of control over the senses shall not follow you, since you have chosen repentance. Lawless enemies shall not hold out against you,[19] namely, distractions of the discursive intellect, captivity of the mind, obfuscation caused by thoughts piled upon thoughts or any other willful deception and confusion; nor shall affection for parents, brothers and sisters, relatives,

---

[11] Ps 33:15.
[12] Ps 114:7.
[13] Cf. Is 37:29, Jas 3:3.
[14] Mt 8:12.
[15] Cf. Lk 13:3.
[16] Ps 90:9.
[17] Ps 90:10.
[18] Cf. Mt 7:13-14.
[19] Ps 5:6.

85 συγγενῶν, φίλων καὶ συνήθων συναντήσει σοι· οὐδὲ ἡ πρὸς τούτους
ἄκαιρος καὶ ἀσυντελὴς συντυχία καὶ ὁμιλία παροικήσει ἐν σοί.

8. Εἰ τούτων τὴν ἀποταγὴν ἀγαπήσεις σώματι καὶ ψυχῇ, μάστιξ
ὀδύνης οὐκ ἐγγιεῖ ἐν τῇ σῇ ψυχῇ καὶ λύπης βέλος οὐ τρώσει τὴν
σὴν καρδίαν, οὐδὲ σὸν σκυθρωπάσει πρόσωπον. ὁ γὰρ τῆς ἐνηδόνου
90 συνηθείας ἀποδιαστὰς καὶ τὴν πρὸς τὰ εἰρημένα πάντα προσπάθειαν
ἀπωσάμενος, τὰς ἀκίδας τῆς λύπης ἀμβλύνει. ὁ Χριστὸς γὰρ τῇ
ἀγωνιζομένῃ ψυχῇ ἐμφανίζεται καὶ χαρὰν ἀνεκλάλητον παρέχει τῇ
καρδίᾳ· καὶ τὴν πνευματικὴν χαρὰν οὐδὲν τῶν ἐκ τοῦ κόσμου τερπνῶν
ἢ δεινῶν αἴρειν ποτὲ δύναται. μελέται γὰρ ἀγαθαὶ καὶ σωτηριώδεις
95 μνῆμαι καὶ θεῖα διανοήματα καὶ λόγοι σοφίας διακονοῦντες τῷ
ἀγωνιστῇ, διαφυλάττουσιν αὐτὸν ἐν πάσαις ταῖς ὁδοῖς τῶν κατὰ θεὸν
ἔργων αὐτοῦ. ὅθεν καὶ ἐπιβαίνει ἐπὶ πᾶσαν ἄλογον ἐπιθυμίαν καὶ
θυμὸν προπετῆ, καθάπερ ἐπὶ ἀσπίδα καὶ βασιλίσκον, καὶ καταπατεῖ
ὡς λέοντα τὴν ὀργὴν καὶ τὴν ἡδονὴν ὡς δράκοντα.

100 **9.** Ἡ δὲ αἰτία, ὅτι πᾶσαν τὴν ἐλπίδα αὐτοῦ ἀπὸ τῶν ἀνθρώπων
καὶ τῶν εἰρημένων πραγμάτων ἀποστήσας τῷ θεῷ προσέδησε καὶ
γνῶσιν θεοῦ πλουτεῖ καὶ θεὸν ἀεὶ νοερῶς πρὸς τὴν ἑαυτοῦ βοήθειαν
ἐκκαλεῖται· *ὅτι ἐπ' ἐμέ*, φησίν, *ἤλπισε, καὶ ῥύσομαι αὐτόν· σκεπάσω
αὐτόν, ὅτι ἔγνω τὸ ὄνομά μου. κεκράξεται πρός με, καὶ ἐπακούσομαι,*
105 καὶ οὐ μόνον τῶν *θλιβόντων ἀπαλλάξω, ἀλλὰ καὶ δοξάσω αὐτόν.*

10. Ὁρᾷς τῶν κατὰ θεὸν ἀσκουμένων τοὺς ἀγῶνας καὶ τὰ ἐντεῦθεν
βραβεῖα; σπούδασον λοιπὸν τὴν κλῆσιν πρᾶξιν ποιήσασθαι· καὶ ὡς
ἐμονώθης τῷ σώματι ἀποβαλομένη τὰ πράγματα, οὕτω καὶ τῇ ψυχῇ
μονώθητι συναποβαλομένη καὶ τὰ νοήματα τῶν πραγμάτων. μετημ-
110 φίασω τὸ σχῆμα; ποίησον καὶ τὸ ἐπάγγελμα πρᾶγμα. ἀποδιέστης τῶν
πολλῶν καὶ τῶν ξένων; ἀπόθου καὶ τοὺς ὀλίγους καὶ τοὺς προσή-
κοντας κατὰ γένος. εἰ μὴ καταπαύσεις ἀπὸ τῆς τὰ ἔξω περιπλανήσεως,
οὐ διαναστήσῃ πρὸς τοὺς ἔσωθεν ἐνεδρεύοντας· εἰ μὴ νικήσεις τοὺς
διὰ τῶν φανερῶν πολεμοῦντας, οὐ τροπώσῃ τοὺς ἀφανεῖς ἐπιβούλους.
115 ὅταν δὲ τοὺς ἔξω περισπασμοὺς καταργήσῃς καὶ τοὺς ἔσω λογισμοὺς
καταλείψῃς, ἐγείρεται τότε ὁ νοῦς ἐν τοῖς ἔργοις καὶ τοῖς λόγοις

friends and acquaintances impinge upon you; nor shall untimely and unprofitable relationships with these people find a home with you.

8. If you love renunciation of these things with body and soul, the scourge of pain shall not come near your soul and the arrow of dejection shall not wound your heart[20] nor bring sadness to your face. One who has left behind habitual attachment to pleasure and has rejected the attractions of all the aforementioned passions blunts the darts of dejection. Christ reveals himself to the soul engaged in this struggle and grants to the heart an indescribable joy, and this spiritual joy none of the pleasures or sufferings of the world can ever take away. Meditation on good things, remembrance of saving realities, thoughts of God and words of wisdom, put to the service of the one engaged in struggle, guard him in all the paths of his works for God. And so he treads on every irrational desire and reckless irascibility, just as one would tread on an asp and a basilisk; he tramples down anger like a lion and pleasure like a dragon.[21]

9. The reason is that he has withdrawn all his hope from men and the things just mentioned and has fixed it upon God; he is rich in the knowledge of God and in his mind is ever calling God to his assistance. Scripture says, "Because he has placed his hope in me, I will rescue him; I will watch over him because he knew my name. He has cried out to me and I will answer him." Not only will I deliver him from his oppressors, "but also I will honour him."[22]

10. Do you see the struggles of those who practise asceticism in the ways of God and the rewards they obtain thereby? Hasten then to make your calling a reality. As you chose a monasticism of the body by abandoning material goods, so choose also the monasticism of the soul by abandoning even the thoughts of material goods. You have exchanged your clothes for the habit? Make also your profession a reality. You have taken leave of the many who are strangers? Leave behind also the few who are your relatives. If you do not put a stop to your dalliance with external things, you will not be able to stand up against those who lie in wait for you within. If you do not vanquish those who war against you by visible means, you shall not put to flight your invisible attackers. When you have annihilated external distractions and abandoned interior thoughts, then the mind awakens

---

[20] Cf. Ps 90:5,10. Dejection is one of the eight vices or evil thoughts first analyzed by Evagrius, *Praktikos* 15-33 (sc 171:536-577).

[21] Cf. Ps 90:11, 13.

[22] Ps 90:14-15.

τοῦ πνεύματος· καὶ ἀντὶ τῆς συντυχίας τῶν συγγενῶν καὶ συνήθων, τοὺς τρόπους τῶν ἀρετῶν ἐκτελεῖς· καὶ ἀντὶ τῶν ματαίων λόγων τῶν ἐκ τῆς κοσμικῆς ὁμιλίας τικτομένων, ἡ μελέτη καὶ ἡ δήλωσις τῶν 120 θείων λόγων τῶν κατὰ τὴν διάνοιαν κινουμένων φωτίζει καὶ συνετίζει τὴν ψυχήν.

11. Ἡ λύσις τῶν αἰσθήσεων δεσμὸς γίνεται τῆς ψυχῆς· καὶ ὁ δεσμὸς τῶν αἰσθήσεων ἐλευθερίαν βραβεύει τῇ ψυχῇ. ἡλίου δύσις νύκτα ποιεῖ· καὶ ὁ Χριστὸς ὑποχωρεῖ ἐκ τῆς ψυχῆς καὶ τῶν παθῶν 125 ὁ σκοτασμὸς αὐτὴν καταλαμβάνει καὶ οἱ νοητοὶ θῆρες αὐτὴν διασπαράττουσιν. ἀνέτειλεν ὁ αἰσθητὸς ἥλιος καὶ θῆρες μὲν συνάγονται εἰς τὰς καταδύσεις αὐτῶν· ἀνατέλλει καὶ ὁ Χριστὸς ἐν τῷ στερεώματι τῆς εὐχομένης διανοίας καὶ πᾶσα ἡ τοῦ κόσμου συνήθεια οἴχεται καὶ ἡ φιλία τῆς σαρκὸς παρέρχεται καὶ ὁ νοῦς διαπορεύεται 130 ἐπὶ τὸ ἔργον αὐτοῦ, ἤτοι τῶν θείων τὴν μελέτην, ἕως ἑσπέρας· οὐ καιρικῷ διαστήματι περιορίζων τοῦ πνευματικοῦ νόμου τὴν ἐργασίαν καὶ ἐν μέτρῳ ταύτην ποιούμενος, ἀλλὰ καὶ μέχρις ἂν τὸ πέρας τὴν παροῦσαν ζωὴν καταλαβόν, τὴν ἐκ τοῦ σώματος ἔξοδον τῆς ψυχῆς ἀπεργάσεται.

135 **12.** Ὃ δὴ καὶ δηλῶν ὁ προφήτης λέγει· *ὡς ἠγάπησα τὸν νόμον σου, κύριε· ὅλην τὴν ἡμέραν μελέτη μού ἐστιν·* ἡμέραν καλῶν ὅλον τὸν δίαυλον τῆς παρούσης ζωῆς ἑκάστου. στῆσον τοιγαροῦν τὰς ὁμιλίας τῶν ἔξω καὶ πύκτευσον πρὸς τοὺς ἔσω λογισμούς, μέχρις ἂν εὑρήσεις τὸν τόπον τῆς καθαρᾶς προσευχῆς καὶ τὸν οἶκον, ἐν ᾧ 140 Χριστὸς κατοικεῖ, φωτίζων καὶ γλυκαίνων σε τῇ ἐπιγνώσει καὶ τῇ ἐπισκέψει αὐτοῦ καὶ παρασκευάζων τὰς μὲν ὑπὲρ αὐτοῦ θλίψεις ἡγεῖσθαι χαράν, τὰς δὲ κοσμικὰς ἡδονάς, καθάπερ τι ἀψίνθιον, μὴ προσίεσθαι. τὰ πνεύματα τῆς θαλάσσης ἐγείρει τὰ κύματα καί, εἰ μὴ παύσονται οἱ ἄνεμοι, οὐ κοπάζει τὰ κύματα, οὐχ ἡμεροῦται ἡ 145 θάλασσα. καὶ τὰ πνεύματα τῆς πονηρίας ἀνακινοῦσιν ἐν τῇ ψυχῇ τοῦ ἀμελοῦς μνήμην γονέων, ἀδελφῶν, συγγενῶν, συνήθων, συμποσίων, πανηγύρεων, θεάτρων καὶ τῶν ἄλλων πάντων τῆς ἡδονῆς φαντασμάτων· καὶ ὑπαγορεύουσιν ὄψει καὶ γλώττῃ καὶ σώματι τὴν ἐντυχίαν ποιεῖσθαι, ἵνα καὶ ἡ ἐνεστῶσα ὥρα ἀναλίσκηται ματαίως, 150 καὶ ἡ ἐπιοῦσα, ἡνίκα μόνη μένῃς ἔνδον τοῦ κελλίου, δαπανᾶται ἐν ταῖς μνήμαις τῶν θεαθέντων καὶ λαληθέντων, καὶ οὕτως ἀσυντελὴς ἡ ζωὴ τοῦ μοναχοῦ διανύηται.

13. Αἱ κοσμικαὶ ἐργασίαι τὰς ἑαυτῶν μνήμας γλύφουσιν ἐν τῇ διανοίᾳ, καθάπερ πόδες ἀνθρώπου τὰ ἴδια ἴχνη ἐν χιόνι βαδίζοντες.

to the works and words of the Spirit. In place of meetings with your relatives and acquaintances you will achieve the ways of the virtues; in place of the empty words born of worldly conversations the study and elucidation of divine words active in your discursive intellect will illumine and instruct your soul.

11. The unleashing of the senses entails the chaining of the soul, and the chaining of the senses bestows freedom on the soul. The setting of the sun brings on the night; Christ withdraws from the soul, and the darkness of the passions overtakes it and the spiritual beasts rend it to pieces. The sensible sun rises and the beasts gather in their lairs; Christ rises in the firmament of the mind at prayer and all intercourse with the world vanishes, the attraction of the flesh passes away and the mind goes about its work, that is, meditation on divine things, till evening.[23] Without placing a temporal limit on the practice of the spiritual law or confining it to a given measure, but to the end of the present life, the mind will work to effect the liberation of the soul from the body.

12. This is what the prophet means when he says, "How have I loved your law, O Lord; it is my meditation all the day."[24] He calls "day" the entire course of the present life for each person. Therefore, put a stop to your dealings with the outside world and fight against your inner thoughts until you discover the place of pure prayer and the house where Christ dwells. There he will grant you the illumination and sweetness of knowing and considering him and he will make you regard the trials you endure for his sake as joy and reject worldly pleasures as you would absinth. The winds stir up the waves of the sea and, if the wind does not stop, the waves do not die down and the sea does not grow calm. The winds of evil rouse in the careless soul memories of parents, brothers and sisters, relations, acquaintances, banquets, festivals, theatrical spectacles and all sorts of other pleasureful phantasies. They suggest the collusion of sight, tongue and body so that the present hour is wasted, and the following hour when you are alone in your cell is spent on memories of what was seen and said, and so the entire life of the monk is used up without profit.

13. Worldly activities leave their memories inscribed upon the discursive intellect, just as a man's feet leave footprints when he walks

---

[23] Cf. Ps 103:19-23.
[24] Ps 118:97.

155 εἰ βρώματα τοῖς θηρίοις παρέχομεν, πότε θανατώσομεν αὐτά; καὶ
εἰ ἐν ἔργοις καὶ λογισμοῖς τῆς ἀλόγου φιλίας καὶ συνηθείας
ἀδολεσχοῦμεν, πότε τὸ τῆς σαρκὸς νεκρώσομεν φρόνημα; πότε ἢν
ἐπηγγειλάμεθα κατὰ Χριστὸν ζωὴν ζήσομεν; ὁ ἐν χιόνι τύπος τῶν
ποδῶν ἢ λάμψαντος ἡλίου λύεται ἢ καταρραγέντος ὕδατος οἴχεται.
160 καὶ αἱ κοιλανθεῖσαι μνῆμαι ἐν τῇ διανοίᾳ ἐκ φιληδόνου διαθέσεως
διὰ τῶν αἰσθήσεων καὶ τῶν πράξεων ὑπὸ Χριστοῦ τοῦ ἀνατέλλοντος
ἐν τῇ καρδίᾳ διὰ προσευχῆς καὶ τῆς εὐκατανύκτου βροχῆς τῶν
δακρύων ἐξαφανίζονται.

14. Ὁ γοῦν μὴ κατὰ λόγον πράττων μοναχός, πότε τὰς ἐν τῇ
165 διανοίᾳ προλήψεις ἀπαλείψει; τελεῖται πρᾶξις ἀρετῶν ἐν τῷ σώματι,
ἐὰν καταλείψῃς τὴν τοῦ κόσμου συνήθειαν. τυποῦνται μνῆμαι ἀγαθαὶ
καὶ θεῖοι λόγοι φιλοχωροῦσιν ἐν τῇ ψυχῇ, ἐὰν συνεχέσιν εὐχαῖς μετὰ
θερμῆς κατανύξεως ἀνυομέναις ἐν τῇ διανοίᾳ τὰς μνήμας τῶν
προτέρων πράξεων ἐξαλείψῃς. ὁ φωτισμὸς γὰρ τῆς ἐπιμόνου τοῦ θεοῦ
170 μνήμης καὶ ἡ συντριβὴ τῆς καρδίας δίκην ξυρίου τὰς πονηρὰς
ἀποξέουσι μνήμας.

15. Μιμήθητι τῶν μελισσῶν τὴν σοφίαν· ἐκεῖναι γὰρ ἰδοῦσαι τὸ
σμῆνος τῶν σφηκιῶν περὶ αὐτὰς τὴν πτῆσιν ποιούμενον, ἔνδον τοῦ
σίμβλου παραμένουσι καὶ τὴν ἐκ τῶν ἐπιβούλων βλάβην διαδιδρά-
175 σκουσι. σφηκίας νόει τὰς κοσμικὰς συντυχίας, ταύτας σπουδῇ πολλῇ
φεύγουσα· παράμενε ἐν τῷ ταμιείῳ τοῦ σεμνείου, κἀντεῦθεν πειρῶ
πάλιν εἰσέρχεσθαι ἐν τῷ ἐνδοτέρῳ τῆς ψυχῆς φρουρίῳ, ὅπερ οἶκος
Χριστοῦ ἐστιν, ἐν ᾧ εἰρήνη καὶ χαρὰ καὶ γαλήνη βεβαίως ὁρᾶται.
τοῦ νοητοῦ ἡλίου Χριστοῦ τὰ δῶρα ταῦτα, καθάπερ τινὰς ἀκτῖνας
180 παρ᾽ ἑαυτοῦ ἐκπέμποντος καὶ ὥσπερ τινὰ μισθὸν παρεχομένου τῇ
ὑποδεχομένῃ αὐτὸν ψυχῇ μετὰ πίστεως καὶ φιλοκαλίας.
16. Καθημένη γοῦν ἐν τῷ οἴκῳ μνημόνευε θεοῦ, ἐπαίρουσα τὸν
νοῦν ἀπὸ πάντων καὶ πρὸς τὸν θεὸν ἀφθόγγως ἐπιρρίπτουσα καὶ
πᾶσαν τῆς καρδίας διάθεσιν ἐκχέουσα ἐνώπιον αὐτοῦ καὶ διὰ τῆς
185 ἀγάπης αὐτῷ προσκολλωμένη. μνήμη γὰρ θεοῦ θεωρία θεοῦ ἐστιν,
ἕλκοντος τὴν ὅρασιν καὶ τὴν ἔφεσιν τοῦ νοῦ πρὸς ἑαυτὸν καὶ τῷ
παρ᾽ ἑαυτοῦ φωτὶ περιαυγάζοντος αὐτόν. ἐπιστρέφων γὰρ ὁ νοῦς πρὸς
τὸν θεὸν ἐν τῷ καταπαύειν πάσας τὰς εἰδοποιοὺς τῶν ὄντων ἐννοίας,
ἀνειδέως ὁρᾷ καὶ τῇ καθ᾽ ὑπεροχὴν ἀγνωσίᾳ διὰ τὸ τῆς δόξης

in the snow. If we give food to wild beasts, when will we put them to death? And if we waste our time in works and thoughts involving irrational affection and associations, when will we mortify the attitude of the flesh?[25] When will we live the life of Christ which we professed? The imprint of the feet in the snow either dissolves when the sun has begun to shine or disappears in a rainstorm. And the memories that have hollowed out a place in the discursive intellect as a result of the pleasureful disposition of our senses and acts are utterly dispelled by Christ when he dawns in the heart through prayer and the conscience-stricken rain of tears.

14. When will the monk who does not conduct his life according to reason expunge the preconceptions existing in his discursive intellect? The bodily practice of the virtues is accomplished, if you abandon your association with the world. Good memories leave their impress on the soul and divine words find a place there, if you expunge the memories of your former activities with continual prayers offered up in the discursive intellect with fervent compunction. For the illumination coming from the constant remembrance of God, along with contrition of heart, cuts off evil memories like a razor.

15. Imitate the wisdom of the bees. If they see there is a swarm of wasps flying around them, they stay inside the beehive and escape harm from their attackers. Think of worldly associations as wasps and flee them with great haste. Stay in the treasury of your monastery and from there try, in turn, to gain entrance to the inner citadel of the soul, which is the dwelling place of Christ where peace, joy and calm are clearly visible. These are the gifts of Christ, the spiritual sun, who sends them forth from himself like rays and who offers them as a kind of recompense to the soul that receives him in faith and love for the good.

16. Seated then in your cell, set your remembrance on God, raising the mind from all things and casting it soundlessly towards God, pouring out the entire disposition of your heart before him, while binding yourself to him in love.[26] For the remembrance of God is contemplation of God, who draws the seeing and the longing of the mind to himself, enveloping it with the radiance of his Light. When the mind turns to God by halting all form-encumbered considerations of beings, it sees without forms[27] and it illumines its vision by means of a transcendent unknowing on account of the inaccessibility of God's

[25] Cf. Rom 8:6-7.
[26] Cf. Pseudo-Symeon, *Methodos*, pp. 164-165.
[27] Cf. Maximus the Confessor, *De caritate* 2.61 (PG 90:1004D).

190 ἀπρόσιτον τὴν ἑαυτοῦ βλέψιν λαμπρύνει· καὶ μὴ γινώσκων διὰ τὴν
ἀκαταληψίαν τοῦ ὁρωμένου, γινώσκει διὰ τὴν ἀλήθειαν τοῦ κυρίως
ὄντος καὶ μόνου τὸ ὑπερεῖναι ἔχοντος· καὶ διὰ τὸ πλούσιον τῆς
ἐκεῖθεν ἐκβλυζούσης ἀγαθότητος τρέφων τὸν ἑαυτοῦ ἔρωτα καὶ τὴν
ἰδίαν ἐντρέχειαν πληροφορῶν, ἀναπαύσεως ἀλήκτου καὶ μακαρίας
195 καταξιοῦται. ταῦτα μὲν τὰ τῆς ἀκριβοῦς μνήμης γνωρίσματα.

17.   Προσευχὴ δέ ἐστι διαλογὴ διανοίας πρὸς κύριον, ῥήματα
δεήσεως διανύουσα μετὰ τῆς τοῦ νοῦ πρὸς τὸν θεὸν ὁλικῆς ἀτενίσεως·
τῆς διανοίας γὰρ συνεχῶς ὑπαγορευούσης τὸ τοῦ κυρίου ὄνομα καὶ
τοῦ νοῦ ἐναργῶς τῇ ἐπικλήσει τοῦ θείου ὀνόματος προσέχοντος, τῆς
200 τοῦ θεοῦ γνώσεως τὸ φῶς καθάπερ φωτεινὴ νεφέλη πᾶσαν ἐπισκιάζει
τὴν ψυχήν. ἕπεται δὲ τῇ μὲν ἀκριβεῖ μνήμῃ τοῦ θεοῦ ἀγάπη καὶ χαρά·
ἐμνήσθην, γάρ φησι, τοῦ θεοῦ καὶ ηὐφράνθην· τῇ δὲ καθαρᾷ προσευχῇ
γνῶσις καὶ κατάνυξις· ἐν ᾗ ἂν ἡμέρᾳ, γάρ φησιν, ἐπικαλέσομαί σε,
ἰδοὺ ἔγνων ὅτι θεός μου εἶ σύ· καὶ πάλιν, θυσία τῷ θεῷ πνεῦμα
205 συντετριμμένον.

18.   Νοὸς γὰρ καὶ διανοίας παρισταμένων τῷ θεῷ δι' ἐναργοῦς
ἀτενίσεως καὶ θερμῆς δεήσεως, καὶ τῆς ψυχῆς ἡ κατάνυξις ἀκολουθεῖ.
νοῦ δὲ καὶ λόγου καὶ πνεύματος προσπιπτόντων τῷ θεῷ, τοῦ μὲν διὰ
προσοχῆς, τοῦ δὲ δι' ἐπικλήσεως, τοῦ δὲ διὰ κατανύξεως καὶ ἀγάπης,
210 ὅλος ὁ ἔνδον ἄνθρωπος λειτουργεῖ τῷ κυρίῳ· ἀγαπήσεις, γάρ φησιν,
κύριον τὸν θεόν σου ἐξ ὅλης τῆς ἰσχύος σου καὶ ἐξ ὅλης τῆς καρδίας
σου καὶ ἐξ ὅλης τῆς διανοίας σου.
19.   Πλὴν εἰδέναι σε καὶ τοῦτο βούλομαι, μήπως προσεύχεσθαι
λογιζομένη μακρὰν τῆς εὐχῆς βαδίζῃς καὶ ἀκερδῶς κάμνῃς καὶ
215 διακενῆς τρέχῃς· ὅπερ ἐν τῇ τοῦ στόματος ψαλμῳδίᾳ τελεῖται, ὅτι
πολλάκις ἡ γλῶσσα τῶν στίχων τὰ ῥήματα λέγει, ὁ δὲ νοῦς ἀλλαχοῦ
φέρεται, εἰς πάθη καὶ πράγματα μεριζόμενος, ὡς ἐντεῦθεν καὶ τὴν
σύνεσιν τῆς ψαλμῳδίας λυμαίνεσθαι. τοῦτο γίνεται καὶ ἐν τῇ διανοίᾳ·

glory. Because of the incomprehensibility of the object of its vision, the mind knows without knowing on account of the truth of the one who truly is and who alone possesses transcendent being.[28] Because of the abundance of goodness that rushes forth from him, the mind nurtures its love and, growing in its capacity, is deemed worthy of blessed rest without end. These are the signs of true remembrance of God.

17. Prayer is a dialogue of the discursive intellect with the Lord,[29] in which the discursive intellect runs through the words of supplication with the mind's gaze fixed entirely on God. For when the discursive intellect is repeating the *Name of the Lord* without ceasing and the mind has its attention clearly fixed on the *Invocation of the Divine Name*, the Light of the knowledge of God overshadows the soul completely like a luminous cloud.[30] Love and joy follow upon true remembrance of God, for scripture says, "I remembered God and I rejoiced."[31] Knowledge and compunction follow upon pure prayer, for scripture says, "On the day when I call upon you, behold I know that you are my God";[32] and also, "A sacrifice to God is a contrite spirit."[33]

18. When the mind and the discursive intellect present themselves to God with a clear gaze and fervent supplication, there follows also compunction of soul. When mind, word and spirit are prostrate before God, the first by attention, the second by *Invocation*, and the third by compunction and love, then the entire inner man serves the Lord. For scripture says, "You shall love the Lord your God with all your strength, with all your heart and with all your mind."[34]

19. Moreover, I want you to know this too, lest thinking you are praying, you wander far from prayer, labour without profit and run the race in vain.[35] This can happen in the case of vocal psalmody, where often the tongue says the words of the verses, but the mind is carried elsewhere, distracted among passions and external things so that your understanding of the psalmody suffers as a result. This also

[28] Even though he is not alluding to any specific passage in the *Corpus Areopagiticum*, Theoleptos is here using terms which are strongly 'Dionysian' in character.

[29] Cf. Evagrius, *De oratione* 3 (PG 79:1168CD): ἡ προσευχὴ ὁμιλία ἐστὶ νοῦ πρὸς θεόν.

[30] Mt 17:5 (the Transfiguration).

[31] Ps 76:4.

[32] Ps 55:10.

[33] Ps 50:19.

[34] Mk 12:30 (Deut 6:5).

[35] Cf. Gal 2:2.

πολλάκις γὰρ αὐτῆς διερχομένης τὰ ῥήματα τῆς εὐχῆς, ὁ νοῦς οὐ
220 συνοδεύει, οὐδὲ ἐνατενίζει τῷ θεῷ, πρὸς ὃν καὶ ἡ κατὰ τὴν προσευχὴν
διαλογὴ γίνεται, ἐκτρέπεται δὲ ὑπό τινων ἐννοιῶν λεληθότως. καὶ
ἡ μὲν διάνοια λέγει συνήθως τὰ ῥήματα, ὁ δὲ νοῦς τῆς τοῦ θεοῦ
γνώσεως διολισθαίνει· ὅθεν καὶ τότε ἡ ψυχὴ ἀκατάνυκτος καὶ
ἀδιάθετος φαίνεται, ὡς τοῦ νοῦ σκορπιζομένου εἴς τινας φαντασίας
225 καὶ μετεωριζομένου ἢ πρὸς ἃ κλέπτεται ἢ βουλεύεται. εὐκτικῆς γὰρ
γνώσεως μὴ παρούσης, μηδὲ τοῦ δεομένου παρισταμένου τῷ δυναμένῳ
παρακαλεῖν, πῶς γλυκανθήσεται ἡ ψυχή; πῶς εὐφρανθήσεται καρδία
προσποιουμένη εὔχεσθαι, ἀλλ᾽ οὐκ ἀληθινὴν προσευχὴν περιποιουμένη; *εὐφρανθήσεται καρδία ζητούντων τὸν κύριον.* ζητεῖ δὲ τὸν κύριον
230 ὁ διανοίᾳ ὅλῃ καὶ διαθέσει θερμῇ προσπίπτων τῷ θεῷ καὶ πᾶν νόημα
τοῦ κόσμου διακρουόμενος διὰ τὴν τοῦ θεοῦ γνῶσιν καὶ ἀγάπην,
τὰς ἀναδιδομένας ἐκ τῆς συνεχοῦς καὶ καθαρᾶς προσευχῆς.

20. Ἐγὼ δέ, σαφηνείας ἕνεκα, τοῦ κατὰ τὴν θείαν μνήμην ἐν τῷ
235 νῷ θεωρήματος καὶ τοῦ κατὰ τὴν καθαρὰν προσευχὴν ἀξιώματος ἐν
τῇ διανοίᾳ τὸν σωματικὸν ὀφθαλμὸν καὶ τὴν γλῶσσαν εἰς εἰκόνας
προτίθημι. ὃ γάρ ἐστι κόρη τῷ ὀφθαλμῷ καὶ προφορὰ λόγου γλώσσῃ,
τοῦτο μνήμη τῷ νῷ καὶ προσευχὴ τῇ διανοίᾳ. ὡς γὰρ ὀφθαλμὸς τῇ
βλεπτικῇ αἰσθήσει τοῦ προκειμένου ὁρατοῦ ἀπολαύων, οὐδεμίαν
240 φωνὴν ποιεῖται, τῇ πείρᾳ δὲ τῆς ὁράσεως τὴν γνῶσιν τοῦ ὁρωμένου
δέχεται, οὕτω καὶ νοῦς διὰ τῆς μνήμης ἐρωτικῶς τῷ θεῷ προσχωρῶν
τῇ προσκολλήσει τῆς διαπύρου διαθέσεως καὶ τῇ σιγῇ τῆς ἁπλουστάτης νοήσεως ὑπὸ τῆς θείας ἐλλάμψεως καταυγάζεται, ἀρραβῶνα
τῆς μελλούσης λαμπρότητος κομιζόμενος.

245 **21.** Καὶ ὥσπερ πάλιν ἡ γλῶσσα ῥήματα λόγου προφέρουσα τὴν
ἄδηλον θέλησιν τοῦ νοῦ ἐμφανίζει τῷ ἀκούοντι, οὕτω καὶ διάνοια
τὰ βραχυσύλλαβα ῥήματα τῆς προσευχῆς πυκνῶς καὶ θερμῶς
ἀναγγέλλουσα, τὴν τῆς ψυχῆς αἴτησιν ἀνακαλύπτει τῷ πάντα εἰδότι
θεῷ, καὶ τῇ εὐκτικῇ προσεδρίᾳ καὶ ἐπιμόνῳ συντρίβει καρδίαν. καὶ
250 ἡ συντριβὴ ἀνοίγει τὰ φιλάνθρωπα σπλάγχνα τοῦ συμπαθοῦς καὶ
πλουσίαν τὴν σωτηρίαν εἰσδέχεται· *καρδίαν, γάρ φησι, συντετριμμένην
καὶ τεταπεινωμένην ὁ θεὸς οὐκ ἐξουδενώσει.*

occurs in the discursive intellect, for often, while it is going through the words of the prayer, the mind does not accompany it, nor does it have its gaze fixed on God to whom the dialogue of prayer is directed; rather, the mind is secretly diverted by certain considerations. The discursive intellect says the words as usual, but the mind slips away from the knowledge of God. As a result, then, the soul finds itself without compunction and confused, since the mind is scattered among various phantasies, where it is distracted, either caught by surprise or willingly. If the knowledge that accompanies prayer is absent and if the one offering supplication is not present before the one who is able to console, how will the soul receive sweetness? How will the heart that pretends to pray, but has not acquired true prayer, know joy? "The heart of those who seek the Lord shall rejoice."[36] He seeks the Lord who prostrates himself before God with all his discursive intellect and with a fervent disposition and drives away every worldly thought for the sake of the knowledge and love of God which arise from continuous and pure prayer.

20.   For the purpose of clarification I propose two images, representing respectively contemplation in the mind occupied in remembrance of God and the proper quality of the discursive intellect occupied in pure prayer: namely, the bodily eye and the tongue. The pupil is related to the eye and the utterance of a word to the tongue in the same way as remembrance is related to the mind and prayer to the discursive intellect. Just as the eye that enjoys the visible object through the sense of sight makes no sound and receives knowledge of the object seen by the experience of seeing, so too the mind that through remembrance approaches God in love by clinging to him with a fervent disposition and in the silence of an utterly simple mental act is illumined by the divine radiance and receives a pledge of the future splendour.

21.   And likewise, just as the tongue makes clear the hidden intention of the mind to the listener when it utters words in speech, so too with its intense and ardent proclamation of the short words of the *Prayer* the discursive intellect reveals the soul's petition to the God who knows all things, and by its steadfast perseverance in prayer it afflicts the heart with contrition. And contrition opens the benevolent heart of the Compassionate One and welcomes the riches of salvation. For scripture says, "A contrite and humbled heart, O God, you will not spurn."[37]

---

[36] Ps 104:3.
[37] Ps 50:19.

22.   Χειραγωγήσει σε εἰς καθαρὰν προσευχὴν καὶ τὸ τελούμενον
εἰς τὸν ἐπὶ γῆς βασιλέα· ὅταν γὰρ προσέλθῃς βασιλεῖ, καὶ σώματι
255 παρίστασαι καὶ γλώσσῃ καθικετεύεις καὶ ὀφθαλμῷ πρὸς αὐτὸν
ἐνατενίζεις καὶ οὕτω τὴν βασιλικὴν εὐμένειαν πρὸς ἑαυτὸν ἕλκεις.
τοῦτο καὶ σὺ ἐκτέλει, κἂν τῇ συνάξει τῆς ἐκκλησίας, κἂν τῇ μονώσει
τῆς οἰκίας· συναγομένη γὰρ ἐν ναῷ κυρίου μετὰ τῶν ἀδελφῶν, ὥσπερ
τὴν διὰ σώματος παράστασιν ποιεῖς τῷ κυρίῳ καὶ τὴν διὰ γλώσσης
260 ψαλμῳδίαν προσφέρεις αὐτῷ, οὕτως ἔχε καὶ τὸν νοῦν προσέχοντα
τοῖς λόγοις καὶ τῷ θεῷ καὶ εἰδότα τίνι διαλέγεται καὶ ἐντυγχάνει·
εὐτόνως γὰρ καὶ καθαρῶς τῆς διανοίας τῇ προσευχῇ σχολαζούσης,
χαρᾶς ἀναφαιρέτου καὶ εἰρήνης ἀνεκλαλήτου καταξιοῦται ἡ καρδία.
κατὰ μόνας δὲ αὖθις ἐν τῷ οἴκῳ προσεδρεύουσα, τῆς κατὰ διάνοιαν
265 προσευχῆς ἐξέχου, νήφοντι τῷ νῷ καὶ συντετριμμένῳ πνεύματι, καὶ
θεωρία ἐπισκιάσει σοι διὰ τῆς νήψεως καὶ γνῶσις κατασκηνώσει ἐν
σοὶ διὰ τῆς προσευχῆς, καὶ σοφία ἀνακλιθήσεται ἐν σοὶ διὰ τῆς
κατανύξεως, τὴν ἄλογον ἡδονὴν ἐξορίζουσα καὶ τὴν θείαν ἀγάπην
εἰσοικίζουσα.

270 **23.**   Πίστευσόν μοι τὴν ἀλήθειαν λέγοντι. εἰ ἐν πάσῃ σου τῇ
ἐργασίᾳ ἀχώριστον ἕξεις τὴν μητέρα τῶν καλῶν, τὴν προσευχήν,
οὐ νυστάξει ἕως ὑποδείξει σοι τὸν νυμφῶνα καὶ ἔνδον ἀγάγῃ σε καὶ
δόξης ἀρρήτου καὶ εὐφροσύνης πληρώσει σε· ἐπειδὴ πάντα τὰ
κωλύματα περιαίρουσα τὴν τρίβον τῆς ἀρετῆς ὁμαλίζει καὶ εὐχερῆ
275 τῷ ζητοῦντι καθίστησι. καὶ ὅρα τὸν τρόπον τῆς κατὰ διάνοιαν
προσευχῆς. ἡ διαλογὴ ἀναιρεῖ τοὺς ἐμπαθεῖς λογισμούς· ἡ τοῦ νοῦ
πρὸς τὸν θεὸν ἀποσκοπὴ φυγαδεύει τὰς ἐννοίας τοῦ κόσμου· ἡ
κατάνυξις τῆς ψυχῆς τὴν φιλίαν τῆς σαρκὸς ἀποσοβεῖ· καὶ ὁρᾶται
ἡ προσευχὴ ἐκ τοῦ ὑπαγορεύειν ἀσιγήτως τὸ θεῖον ὄνομα συμφωνία
280 καὶ ἕνωσις νοῦ καὶ λόγου καὶ ψυχῆς· *ὅπου γάρ, φησίν, εἰσὶ δύο ἢ*
τρεῖς ἐν τῷ ἐμῷ ὀνόματι, ἐκεῖ εἰμι ἐν μέσῳ αὐτῶν.

24.   Οὕτως οὖν ἡ προσευχὴ τὰς τῆς ψυχῆς δυνάμεις ἀπὸ τοῦ
διαμερισμοῦ τῶν παθῶν ἀνακαλουμένη καὶ πρὸς ἀλλήλας καὶ πρὸς
ἑαυτὴν συνδέουσα, τὴν τριμερῆ ψυχὴν τῷ ἐν τρισὶν ὑποστάσεσιν
285 ἑνὶ θεῷ οἰκειοῖ. πρῶτον γὰρ διὰ τῶν τῆς ἀρετῆς τρόπων τὸ τῆς
ἁμαρτίας αἶσχος ἐκ τῆς ψυχῆς ἀποξέσασα, εἶτα τὸ κάλλος τῶν θείων

22.   The conduct required before the earthly emperor can also serve as an example to guide you to pure prayer. When you approach an emperor, you present yourself in person and make earnest entreaty with your tongue and you fix your eyes upon him, and in this way you attract the imperial favour to yourself.[38] This is also what you should do, whether in the liturgical assemblies in church or in the solitude of your cell. When you are assembled in the Lord's temple together with your sisters, just as you present yourself bodily to the Lord and offer the psalmody to him with your tongue, so fix also the attention of your mind on the words and on God, aware of the one with whom you are speaking and conversing. For if the discursive intellect devotes its time to intense and pure prayer, the heart is deemed worthy of inalienable joy and indescribable peace. When next you are sitting alone in your cell, cling to prayer in your discursive intellect with your mind vigilant and your spirit contrite, and contemplation will overshadow you through your vigilance, knowledge will make its abode in you through prayer, and wisdom will bend repose in you through your compunction, banishing irrational pleasure and instilling divine love.

23.   Believe me, for I speak the truth. If in all your occupations you hold inseparably to the mother of good things, namely, prayer, she will not rest till she shows you the bridal chamber and, leading you within, grants you fullness of ineffable glory and joy. For removing all obstacles, she makes smooth the path of virtue and renders it easy for the one who is seeking it. Mark also the way of prayer for the discursive intellect. This dialogue removes thoughts encumbered by the passions. The mind's gaze toward God puts to flight worldly considerations. Compunction of soul chases away the attraction of the flesh. And prayer, which consists of the never silent repetition of the *Divine Name*, can be seen as the harmony and union of mind, word and soul, for scripture says, "Where two or three are gathered together in my name, there am I in the midst of them."[39]

24.   In this way, then, prayer calls the powers of the soul back from the dispersion caused by the passions, binds them to one another and to itself, uniting the tripartite soul to the one God in three hypostases. First, through the ways of the virtues it scrapes the shame of sin from the soul; then through its own sacred knowledge it restores

---

[38] Cf. Evagrius, *Rerum monachalium rationes* 11 (PG 40:1264C).
[39] Mt 18:20.

χαρακτήρων διὰ τῆς καθ᾽ ἑαυτὴν ἁγίας γνώσεως ἀναζωγραφήσασα, παρίστησιν τὴν ψυχὴν τῷ θεῷ. ἡ δὲ αὐτίκα γινώσκει τὸν ἑαυτῆς ποιητήν, *ἐν ᾗ, γάρ φησιν, ἡμέρᾳ ἐπικαλέσομαί σε, ἰδοὺ ἔγνων ὅτι θεός* 290 *μου εἶ σύ·* καὶ γινώσκεται ὑπ᾽ αὐτοῦ, *ἔγνω, γάρ φησιν, κύριος τοὺς ὄντας αὐτοῦ.* γινώσκει καὶ γινώσκεται· γινώσκει διὰ τὸ καθαρὸν τῆς εἰκόνος, πᾶσα γὰρ εἰκὼν ἐπὶ τὸ πρωτότυπον ἔχει τὴν ἀναφοράν· γινώσκεται διὰ τὴν κατὰ τὰς ἀρετὰς ὁμοίωσιν, δι᾽ ὧν καὶ γνῶσιν ἔχει θεοῦ καὶ ὑπὸ θεοῦ γινώσκεται.

295 **25.** Ὁ δεόμενος τυχεῖν βασιλικῆς εὐμενείας τριπλοῦν μεταχειρίζεται τρόπον· ἢ φωναῖς ἱκετεύει, ἢ σιγῶν παρίσταται, ἢ πρὸ ποδῶν τοῦ δυναμένου βοηθεῖν ἑαυτὸν ἐπιρρίπτει. καὶ ἡ καθαρὰ προσευχή, νοῦν καὶ λόγον καὶ πνεῦμα πρὸς ἑαυτὴν συνάπτουσα, διὰ μὲν τοῦ λόγου τὸ ὄνομα τοῦ θεοῦ ὑπαγορεύει καὶ τὴν δέησιν ἀναφέρει, διὰ 300 δὲ τοῦ νοῦ τῷ παρακαλουμένῳ θεῷ ἐνατενίζει ἀρεμβάστως, διὰ δὲ τοῦ πνεύματος τὴν κατάνυξιν, τὴν ταπείνωσιν καὶ τὴν ἀγάπην ἐμφανίζει, καὶ οὕτω δυσωπεῖ τὴν ἄναρχον τριάδα, τὸν πατέρα καὶ τὸν υἱὸν καὶ τὸ ἅγιον πνεῦμα, τὸν ἕνα θεόν. ὥσπερ ἡ ποικιλία τῶν ἐδεσμάτων διεγείρει τὴν ὄρεξιν εἰς μετάληψιν αὐτῶν, οὕτως αἱ 305 διάφοροι τῶν ἀρετῶν ἰδέαι τὴν ἐντρέχειαν τοῦ νοῦ ἐξυπνίζουσι. διὰ τοῦτο τὴν ὁδὸν τῆς διανοίας ὁδεύουσα, τὰ ῥήματα τῆς εὐχῆς ἀναλέγου καὶ διαλέγου, τῷ κυρίῳ ἀεὶ βοῶσα καὶ μὴ ἐκκακοῦσα, πυκνὰ δεομένη καὶ τὴν ἀναίδειαν μιμουμένη τῆς τὸν ἀμείλικτον κριτὴν δυσωπησάσης χήρας.

310 **26.** Τότε πνεύματι περιπατεῖς καὶ σαρκικαῖς ἐπιθυμίαις οὐ προσέχεις καὶ λογισμοῖς κοσμικοῖς οὐ διατέμνεις τῆς εὐχῆς τὴν συνέχειαν· ναὸς δὲ τοῦ θεοῦ χρηματίζεις, ἀπερισπάστως τὸν θεὸν ἐξυμνοῦσα. οὕτω κατὰ διάνοιαν εὐχομένη, ἀξιοῦσαι καὶ εἰς μνήμην θεοῦ διαβαίνειν καὶ ἐν τοῖς ἀδύτοις τοῦ νοῦ εἰσιέναι καὶ μυστικαῖς 315 θεωρίαις τὸν ἀόρατον κατοπτεύειν καὶ γνωστικαῖς ἐννοίαις καὶ ἀγαπητικαῖς ἐκχύσεσι, μόνη τῷ θεῷ μόνῳ κατὰ μόνας λειτουργεῖν.

27. Ὅταν οὖν ἴδῃς σεαυτὴν χαυνουμένην ἐν τῇ εὐχῇ, βιβλίον μεταχειρίζου καὶ τῇ ἀναγνώσει προσέχουσα τὴν γνῶσιν εἰσδέχου, μὴ παροδευτικῶς τοὺς λόγους διερχομένη, διανοητικῶς δὲ τούτους

the beauty of the divine impress and presents the soul to God. The soul immediately knows its creator, for scripture says, "On the day when I call upon you, behold I know that you are my God";[40] and the soul is known by him, for it says, "The Lord knew his beings."[41] It knows and is known:[42] it knows on account of the purity of the Image, for every image refers back to its model; it is known on account of the Likeness attained in the virtues, whereby the soul both possesses knowledge of God and is known by God.

25.   Someone who wants to gain the imperial favour can accomplish this in three ways: either he makes supplication in words, or he presents himself in silence, or he throws himself at the feet of the one who has the power to help him. So too pure prayer, which joins to itself mind, word and spirit, by means of the word pronounces the *Name of God* and offers up supplication, by means of the mind gazes without distraction towards God upon whom it calls, by means of the spirit manifests its compunction, humility and love, and thus importunes the one God and eternal Trinity, Father, Son and Holy Spirit. Just as a variety of foods rouses the desire to partake of them, so too the various notions of the virtues awaken the diligence of the mind. For this reason, in traveling the way of the discursive intellect, repeat the words of the *Prayer* again and again, ever crying out to the Lord without losing heart, making frequent supplications and imitating the persistence of the widow who importuned the harsh judge.[43]

26.   Then, you walk in the Spirit and pay no attention to the desires of the flesh;[44] you do not interrupt the continuity of your prayer with worldly thoughts, but in praising God without distraction you become a temple of God. Praying in this way with the discursive intellect, you become worthy to pass to the remembrance of God, to enter into the sanctuary of the mind, to behold the invisible in mystical contemplations, in considerations endowed with knowledge and in outpourings of love and to serve God alone in utter solitude.

27.   Therefore, when you notice yourself becoming lax in prayer, take a book in hand and, as you attend to the reading, penetrate to the sense; do not pass over the words in cursory fashion, but examine them thoroughly with your intelligence and store up their treasures

[40] Ps 55:10.
[41] Num 16:5, 2 Tim 2:19.
[42] Cf. 1 Cor 13:12.
[43] Lk 18:2-6.
[44] Gal 5:16.

320 διασκοπουμένη καὶ τὸν νοῦν θησαυρίζουσα. εἶτα μελέτην ποιοῦ τῶν
ἀναγνωσθέντων, ἵνα γλυκαίνηταί σου ἡ διάνοια ἐκ τῆς κατανοήσεως
καὶ ἀνεπίληστα διαμένη τὰ ἀναγνώσματα, κἀντεῦθεν προσανάπτηταί
σου ἡ θέρμη ἐν τοῖς θείοις διανοήμασιν· *ἐν τῇ μελέτῃ μου, γάρ φησιν,
ἐκκαυθήσεται πῦρ.* ὡς γὰρ τὸ βρῶμα ἡδύνει τὴν γεῦσιν ὑπὸ τῶν
325 ὀδόντων λεπτυνόμενον, οὕτω τὰ θεῖα λόγια στρεφόμενα ἐν τῇ ψυχῇ
πιαίνει τὴν διάνοιαν καὶ κατευφραίνει· *ὡς γλυκέα, γάρ φησι, τῷ
λάρυγγί μου τὰ λόγιά σου.*

28. Ἀποστήθιζε καὶ λόγους εὐαγγελικοὺς καὶ τῶν μακαρίων
πατέρων ἀποφθέγματα καὶ τοὺς βίους αὐτῶν ἀνίχνευε, ἵνα ἔχῃς ταῦτα
330 πάντα μελέτημα ἐν ταῖς νυξίν. ὅπως τὴν διάνοιαν ἐκ τῆς εὐχῆς
ἀκηδιάσασαν τῇ ἀναγνώσει καὶ τῇ μελέτῃ τῶν θείων λόγων
ἀνακαινίζῃς καὶ ἐντρεχεστέραν παρασκευάζῃς εἰς προσευχήν, τὴν
διὰ στόματος ψαλμῳδίαν ἐκτέλει, πλὴν ἡσύχῳ πάνυ φωνῇ καὶ μετ᾽
ἐπιστασίας τοῦ νοῦ, μὴ ἀνεχομένη ἀδιανόητόν τι τῶν λεγομένων
335 καταλιπεῖν· ἀλλ᾽ εἴ ποτέ τι διαδράσει τὸν νοῦν, ἐπαναλάμβανε τὸν
στίχον, ὁσάκις καὶ γένηται, μέχρις ἂν τὸν νοῦν ἐπακολουθοῦντα
ἕξεις τοῖς λεγομένοις. ἰσχύει γὰρ ὁ νοῦς καὶ ψάλλειν τῷ στόματι
καὶ θεοῦ μνημονεύειν· καὶ τοῦτο καταμάνθανε ἐκ τῆς φυσικῆς πείρας.
ὡς γὰρ ὁ συντυγχάνων τινὶ καὶ διαλεγόμενος, τούτῳ καὶ προσέχει
340 τοῖς ὀφθαλμοῖς, οὕτω καὶ ψάλλων χείλεσι καὶ θεῷ ἐνατενίζειν διὰ
τῆς μνήμης δύναται.

29. Κλίσεις γονάτων μὴ παραιτοῦ. ἐκ μὲν γὰρ τοῦ γόνυ κλίνειν
ἡ πτῶσις τῆς ἁμαρτίας εἰκονίζεται, ἔμφασιν ἐξαγορεύσεως παρεχο-
μένη· ἐκ δὲ τοῦ ἀνίστασθαι ἡ μετάνοια ὑποσημαίνεται, ἐπαγγελίαν
345 βίου τοῦ κατ᾽ ἀρετὴν αἰνιττομένη. ἑκάστη δὲ γονυκλισία τελείσθω
μετὰ τῆς νοερᾶς τοῦ Χριστοῦ ἐπικλήσεως, ἵνα ψυχῇ καὶ σώματι
προσπίπτουσα τῷ κυρίῳ τὸν τῶν ψυχῶν καὶ σωμάτων θεὸν
εὐδιάλλακτον ἀπεργάσῃ. εἰ δὲ καὶ ἔργον ἀθόρυβον ταῖς χερσὶ
παρέξεις μετὰ τῆς κατὰ διάνοιαν προσευχῆς εἰς τὸ ἀποκρούεσθαι
350 ὕπνον καὶ ῥαθυμίαν, καὶ τοῦτο τὸν ἀσκητικὸν ἀγῶνα συγκροτεῖ.
πᾶσαι γὰρ αἱ δηλωθεῖσαι ἐργασίαι μετ᾽ εὐχῆς ἀνυόμεναι, ἀκονοῦσι
τὸν νοῦν, ἀκηδίαν ἐξορίζουσι, νεαρωτέραν τὴν ψυχὴν παρασκευά-
ζουσι καὶ ὀξύτερον καὶ θερμότερον τὸν νοῦν εἰς τὴν κατὰ διάνοιαν
ἐργασίαν ἀπασχολεῖσθαι ποιοῦσι.

in the mind. Then, meditate on what you have read that your discursive intellect may receive sweetness from its understanding and your readings may not be forgotten; in this way, your fervour will be enkindled in these divine reflections, for scripture says, "In my meditation a fire will be kindled."[45] Just as food gives pleasure to the taste when it is chewed by the teeth, so when the divine words are turned about in the soul they bring gladness and joy to the discursive intellect, for scripture says, "How sweet are your sayings to my mouth."[46]

28. Learn by heart words taken from the Gospels and sayings of the blessed Fathers and search out their lives so that you may have all these to meditate upon in the night.[47] So that, when the discursive intellect wearies of prayer, you may refresh it with reading and meditation on divine words and ready it for prayer, perform your vocal psalmody, but in a very quiet voice and with the mind's attention, not allowing it to leave any of the words imperfectly understood; rather, if something gets past the mind, take up the verse again, as many times as necessary, until you get the mind to follow what is being said. The mind is capable of both vocal psalmody and remembrance of God. You can learn this from natural experience. For just as when you meet someone and talk to him you also pay attention to his eyes, so too when you say the psalms with your lips, it is possible to fix your gaze upon God by remembrance.

29. Do not shun the practice of making genuflexions, for in bending the knee is found the image of the fall into sin and a representation of confession; by standing up again repentance is indicated and this in turn suggests the promise of a life of virtue. Each genuflexion should be accompanied by the mental *Invocation of Christ* so that, by prostrating yourself before the Lord in soul and body, you may readily be reconciled with the one who is God over souls and bodies. If you can provide your hands with work of an undistracting nature and accompany it with prayer in the discursive intellect in order to ward off sleep and laziness, this too constitutes the ascetic struggle. All external activities that are associated with prayer sharpen the mind, banish acedia, rejuvenate the soul and leave the mind more intensely and fervently engrossed with the activity of the discursive intellect.

[45] Ps 38:4.
[46] Ps 118:103.
[47] Cf. Ps 76:6-7.

355 **30.** Κρούσαντος τοῦ ξύλου, προέρχου τῆς κέλλης, τοῖς μὲν ὀφθαλμοῖς τοῦ σώματος τῇ γῇ προσέχουσα, τὴν δὲ διάνοιαν τῇ τοῦ θεοῦ μνήμῃ προσερείδουσα· εἰσελθοῦσα ἐν τῷ ναῷ καὶ τὸν χορὸν συμπληροῦσα, μήτε τῇ γλώσσῃ ἀργολόγει μετὰ τῆς πλησιαζούσης μοναχῆς, μήτε τῷ νῷ μετεωρίζου εἰς ματαιότητας· ἀλλὰ τὴν μὲν 360 γλῶσσαν τῇ ψαλμῳδίᾳ μόνῃ, τὴν δὲ διάνοιαν ἀσφαλίζου τῇ προσευχῇ. ἀπολύσεως γεγενημένης, ἀπέρχου πρὸς τὸν σὸν οἶκον καὶ τοῦ τυπωθέντος σοι κανόνος ἐξέχου.

31. Εἰς τὴν τράπεζαν ἀπιοῦσα μὴ περισκόπει τὰς μερίδας τῶν ἀδελφῶν, μηδὲ μέριζε τὴν ψυχήν σου ὑπονοίαις οὐ καλαῖς. τὰ 365 παρακείμενα δὲ ἐνώπιόν σου βλέπουσα καὶ ἁπτομένη, τῷ μὲν στόματι τὴν τροφήν, τῇ ἀκοῇ δὲ τὴν ἀκρόασιν τῶν ἀναγινωσκομένων, τῇ δὲ ψυχῇ τὴν προσευχὴν δίδου, ἵνα σώματι καὶ πνεύματι τρεφομένη ὁλοκλήρως ἐξυμνῇς τὸν ἐμπιπλῶντα ἐν ἀγαθοῖς τὴν ἐπιθυμίαν σου. ἐκεῖθεν ἀναστᾶσα, μετὰ σεμνότητος καὶ σιγῆς εἰσέρχου εἰς τὸ 370 κελλίον σου καὶ ὡς φιλεργὸς μέλισσα φιλοπόνει τὰς ἀρετάς. ὅταν ἀνύῃς διακονίαν μετὰ τῶν ἀδελφῶν, αἱ χεῖρες ἐργαζέσθωσαν, σιωπάτω τὰ χείλη καὶ ὁ νοῦς μνημονευέτω θεοῦ. καὶ εἴ ποτέ τις κινηθείη ἀργολογεῖν, εἰς διακοπὴν τῆς ἀταξίας ἐγειρομένη ποίει μετάνοιαν. λογισμοὺς ἀποτρέπου καὶ μὴ παραχώρει τούτους διατρέχειν τὴν 375 καρδίαν καὶ ἐγχρονίζειν· ὁ χρονισμὸς γὰρ τῶν ἐμπαθῶν λογισμῶν, τὰ μὲν πάθη ζωογονεῖ, τὸν δὲ νοῦν θανατοῖ, ἀλλὰ προσβάλλοντας αὐτοὺς αὐτίκα ἐκ πρωτονοίας ἐπείγου τῷ βέλει τῆς προσευχῆς ἀναιρεῖν. εἰ δ' ἐπιμένοιεν κρούοντες καὶ συγχέοντες τὴν διάνοιαν καὶ ποτὲ μὲν ὑποχωροῦντες, ποτὲ δὲ ἐπερχόμενοι, ἴσθι ὅτι ἐκ 380 προλαβόντος θελήματός εἰσιν ὠχυρωμένοι. διὰ τοῦτο καὶ δίκαια ἔχοντες εἰς τὴν ψυχὴν διὰ τὴν ἧτταν τῆς προαιρέσεως, ταράττουσι καὶ ἐνοχλοῦσι. δεῖ οὖν αὐτοὺς στηλιτεύειν διὰ τῆς ἐξαγορεύσεως, θριαμβευόμενοι γὰρ οἱ πονηροὶ λογισμοὶ φυγαδεύονται.

32. Ὡς γὰρ φωτὸς φαίνοντος τὸ σκότος ὑποχωρεῖ, οὕτω καὶ τὸ 385 φῶς τῆς ἐξαγορείας ἀφανίζει τοὺς λογισμοὺς τῶν παθῶν, σκότος καὶ αὐτοὺς χρηματίζοντας· ἐπειδὴ ἡ κενοδοξία καὶ ἡ ἄνεσις, ἃς εἶχον τόπον οἱ λογισμοί, κατεστράφησαν διὰ τῆς κατὰ τὴν ἐξαγόρευσιν αἰσχύνης καὶ τῆς κατὰ τὸν κανόνα κακοπαθείας· ὅθεν καὶ τὴν διάνοιαν εὑρίσκοντες ἐλευθέραν ἤδη τῶν παθῶν γεγενημένην τῇ

30.   When the simandron sounds,[48] leave your cell with the eyes of the body on the ground while fixing the discursive intellect on the remembrance of God. Go into the church and fulfill your choir duties. Do not allow your tongue to indulge in idle chatter with the nun beside you nor allow your mind to engage in vain distractions. Rather, set your tongue firmly to psalmody alone and your discursive intellect to prayer. When the dismissal is given, go off to your cell and cling to the rule that has been set for you.

31.   When you are at table, do not look around at the portions your sisters got, nor allow your mind to be divided by nasty suspicions. As you look upon and touch what is set before you, give food to your mouth, attentiveness to the readings to your ears and prayer to your soul, so that nourished in body and spirit you may wholeheartedly praise the one who satisfies your desire with good things. When you rise up from the table, go to your cell in reverent silence and like a busy bee work industriously at the virtues. When you are performing a service in the company of your sisters, let your hands do the work, let your lips keep silence and let your mind be occupied with remembrance of God. And if anyone should ever be moved to idle chatter, make a prostration to urge her to cut off the impropriety. Turn away from thoughts and do not allow them to penetrate and dally in the heart, for dallying with passionate thoughts rouses the passions to life but brings death to the mind. With the arrow of prayer make haste to destroy the thoughts that attack you right from their first inception. But if they should remain to beat upon and confuse the discursive intellect, sometimes withdrawing, sometimes attacking, know that they have gotten their strength from a prior act of the will. For this reason, because they have claims on the soul due to their defeat of its free will, they trouble and disturb it. Therefore, it is necessary to expose them by confession, for evil thoughts are put to flight when they are trotted out in public.

32.   Just as when light appears darkness retreats, so too the light of confession obliterates thoughts encumbered by passions, for these are also darkness. Vainglory and presumption, to which our thoughts give pride of place, are subdued by the shame of confession and the mortifications set by the rule. Thus, when they find the discursive intellect already freed from the passions by continuous and contrite

---

[48] The simandron is a sort of wooden gong. Theoleptos uses the term τὸ ξύλον. Cf. MD 9.7.

390 συνεχεῖ καὶ εὐκατανύκτῳ προσευχῇ, μετ᾽ αἰσχύνης δραπετεύουσιν.
ὅτε γὰρ πειρᾶται ὁ ἀγωνιστὴς τέμνειν τῇ προσευχῇ τοὺς ταράττοντας
αὐτὸν λογισμούς, τέμνει μὲν πρὸς βραχὺ καὶ εἴργει τὴν πολύνοιαν
αὐτῶν, ὡς παλαίων καὶ ἁμιλλώμενος, οὐ λυτροῦται δὲ εἰς ἅπαν, ἐπειδὴ
τὰς αἰτίας τῶν ἐνοχλούντων λογισμῶν στέργει, τὴν ἀνάπαυσιν τῆς
395 σαρκὸς καὶ τὴν κοσμικὴν φιλοτιμίαν, δι᾽ ἃς καὶ πρὸς ἐξαγόρευσιν
ὁρμὴν οὐ ποιεῖται· ὅθεν καὶ εἰρήνην οὐκ ἄγει, διότι τὰ τῶν πολεμίων
κατέχει δίκαια. τίς δὲ κατέχων ἀλλότρια σκεύη, οὐκ ἀπαιτεῖται ταῦτα
παρὰ τῶν ἐχόντων; τίς δὲ ἀπαιτούμενος καὶ μὴ ἀπολύων ἃ κατέχει
κακῶς, λυτροῦται ἀπὸ τῶν ἀντιδίκων αὐτοῦ;

400   **33.** Ὅτε δὲ ὁ ἀγωνιζόμενος τῇ τοῦ θεοῦ μνήμῃ δυναμωθεὶς τὴν
ἐξουδένωσιν ἀγαπήσει καὶ τὴν κάκωσιν τῆς σαρκὸς καὶ τὴν
ἐξαγόρευσιν τῶν λογισμῶν ἀνεπαισχύντως ποιήσει, αὐτίκα οἱ μὲν
πολέμιοι ἀναχωροῦσιν, ἡ δὲ διάνοια ἐλευθέρα τυγχάνουσα, τὴν
συνέχειαν τῆς προσευχῆς καὶ τὴν τῶν θείων μελέτην ἀδιάκοπον ἔχει.
405 πᾶσαν ὑπόνοιαν κινουμένην ἐν τῇ καρδίᾳ κατά τινος παραιτοῦ
παντελῶς, ὡς καταλύουσαν ἀγάπην καὶ εἰρήνην. πᾶσαν δὲ συμφορὰν
ἔξωθεν ἐπερχομένην γενναίως καταδέχου, ὡς τὴν σωτήριον ὑπομονὴν
προξενοῦσαν, ὑπομονὴν τὴν μονὴν καὶ ἀνάπαυσιν χαριζομένην ἐν
τοῖς οὐρανοῖς. οὕτω τὰς ἡμέρας ἀνύουσα, ἐν μὲν τῇ παρούσῃ ζωῇ
410 μετ᾽ εὐθυμίας βιώσεις, ταῖς μακαρίαις ἐλπίσιν εὐφραινομένη· ἐν δὲ
τῇ ἐξόδῳ μετὰ παρρησίας μεταστήσῃ τῶν ὧδε καὶ εἰς τοὺς τόπους
τῆς ἀναπαύσεως, οὓς ἡτοιμάσατό σοι κύριος ἀπελεύσῃ, μισθοὺς τῶν
ἐνταῦθα πόνων ἀντιδιδούς σοι συμβασιλεύειν αὐτῷ· ᾧ πρέπει πᾶσα
δόξα, τιμὴ καὶ προσκύνησις, ἅμα τῷ ἀνάρχῳ αὐτοῦ πατρὶ καὶ τῷ
415 παναγίῳ καὶ ἀγαθῷ καὶ ζωοποιῷ αὐτοῦ πνεύματι νῦν καὶ ἀεὶ καὶ εἰς
τοὺς αἰῶνας τῶν αἰώνων. Ἀμήν.

prayer, they slink away in shame. When the ascetic tries to cut off by prayer the thoughts that trouble him, he cuts them off for a little while but rouses mental distractions associated with them, for he is contending with old foes; he is not entirely free, because he is attached to the causes of the thoughts that are disturbing him, namely, the relaxation of the flesh and the attraction of worldly honours, on which account he does not take the step towards confession. And so he enjoys no peace because the claims of his enemies hold sway. Who is there who holds the properties of others who will not be asked for them by the owners? And who will be set free by his accusers if he refuses, when asked, to give up what he wrongly holds?

33.   But when the ascetic who has been fortified by the remembrance of God prefers denial and mortification of the flesh and unabashedly confesses his thoughts, his enemies retreat straightaway and the discursive intellect, now being free, maintains continuity of prayer and meditation on divine things without interruption. Spurn completely any suspicion that arises in your heart against anyone, as breaking the bond of charity and peace. Accept with a good spirit every misfortune that comes your way from without, as offering a saving opportunity for patient endurance, a patient endurance that bestows an abode of rest in heaven. Passing your days in this way, you will live this present life with a cheerful heart, gladdened by blessed hopes, and in death you will confidently leave the things of this life and depart to the place of rest that the Lord has prepared for you, and as a reward for your labours here below he will grant you to reign with him.[49] To him be all glory, honour and worship together with his eternal Father and his all-holy, good and life-giving Spirit, now and always and unto the ages of ages. Amen.

[49] 2 Tim 2:12.

Λόγος περὶ νήψεως καὶ προσευχῆς, τῆς ἱερᾶς δυάδος καὶ μητρὸς τῶν
ἀρετῶν, ἀποτρεπόμενος τοὺς ἐξ ἀμαθείας γλῶσσαν κινοῦντας κατὰ
τῶν ἐπιμελουμένων αὐτῆς καὶ προτρεπόμενος παντὶ χριστιανῷ μετα-
μανθάνειν αὐτήν, ὡς δίκην πτερύγων, κουφίζουσαν τὸν αἰρόμενον ὑπ᾽
5 αὐτῆς καὶ πρὸς τὸν ἔρωτα τῆς μακαρίας τριάδος ἀναβιβάζουσαν

1. Τοῖς τὰς ἑαυτῶν ὄψεις ἀσθενεῖς κεκτημένοις, οἱ ἀνὰ χεῖρας
τὸ φῶς ἔχοντες καὶ προπορευόμενοι ἐνώπιον αὐτῶν ἐπαχθεῖς φαί-
νονται, οὐ διὰ τὸ εἶναι τὸ φῶς βλαβερόν, οὐδὲ διὰ τὸ πρὸς αὐτοὺς
κακῶς διακεῖσθαι τοὺς βαστάζοντας τὸ φῶς, ἀλλὰ διὰ τὴν ἐν τῷ βάθει
10 τῶν βλεφάρων αὐτῶν οἰκουροῦσαν ἀσθένειαν· ἥτις ὑπὸ τοῦ φωτὸς
ἐλεγχομένη καὶ εἰς τὸ ἔξω προσκαλουμένη, ταράττει σφόδρα τοὺς
ὀφθαλμούς. καὶ εἰ μὴ διὰ δακρύων ἐκφορηθείη ἡ ἐμφωλεύουσα
τούτοις δριμύτης, ἡμερωθῆναι καὶ πρὸς τὸ φῶς ἀτενίσαι οὐ δύνανται.
τὸ αὐτὸ τοῦτο συμβαίνει καὶ ἐν τοῖς καταπεπονημένοις ὑπὸ τῆς
15 ἐνοικούσης ἐν τῇ ψυχῇ ἁμαρτίας καὶ τῇ τῶν παθῶν ἀρρωστίᾳ
παραλελυμένα κεκτημένοις τὰ τοῦ ἔσω ἀνθρώπου αἰσθητήρια.
2. Οὗτοι καὶ γὰρ τοὺς τῆς ψυχῆς λογισμοὺς ἐσκοτισμένους
ἔχοντες ὑπὸ τῆς τῶν παρόντων ἐπιθυμίας πρὸς τὸ τῆς θεότητος φῶς
τὸ ἐν ταῖς καθαραῖς διανοίαις ἐλλάμπον οὐκ ἰσχύουσιν ἀναβλέψαι.
20 πῶς γὰρ ἂν τοῦ θείου φωτὸς ἀξιωθήσονται, οἱ τὴν ἐναντίαν αὐτῷ
διάθεσιν ἀσπαζόμενοι; διὸ καὶ οὓς ἂν τῶν ἀνθρώπων θεάσωνται τὰς
ἐν τῷ κρυπτῷ τῆς ψυχῆς τελουμένας ἐνεργείας τῆς ἁγίας γνώσεως
διὰ τοῦ λόγου φανεροῦντας πρὸς τὴν τῶν ἄλλων ὠφέλειαν, δυοῖν
θατέρω κρημνῷ περιπίπτουσιν, ὡς περὶ τὴν ἀληθῆ διάκρισιν σκοτεινοὶ
25 χρηματίζοντες· ἢ ἀδύνατα λέγειν αὐτοὺς ἰσχυρίζονται, ὡς πλάσματα
μᾶλλον λογικὰ ἢ πράγματα μυστικὰ φρονοῦντες τὰ ὑπ᾽ αὐτῶν
καταγγελλόμενα σωτήρια ῥήματα, ἢ φθόνῳ τηκόμενοι τὴν πνευματικὴν ἐργασίαν ὡς πλάνην διασύρουσι καὶ τοὺς ἔργῳ καὶ λόγῳ
ταύτην κηρύττοντας πεπλανημένους ἀποκαλοῦσιν.
30 **3.** Εἰς τὴν αὐτὴν τοῖς Ἰουδαίοις βλασφημίαν καταφερόμενοι· ὡς
γὰρ Ἰουδαῖοι τὸν κύριον ὁρῶντες ἐν ἐξουσίᾳ πολλῇ τὰς θεοσημίας
ποιοῦντα καὶ ἐν πνεύματι θεοῦ τὰ δαιμόνια ἐκβάλλοντα, πλάνον
ἀπεκάλουν καὶ δαιμονῶντα, καὶ ἐν τῷ Βεελζεβοὺλ ἐκβάλλειν αὐτὸν

---

6 ἀναχεῖρας OA   12 ἐμφωλεύουσα corr.: ἐμφολεύουσα OA   24 σκοτεινοὶ
corr.: σκοτινοὶ OA

DISCOURSE ON VIGILANCE AND PRAYER, THE HOLY DYAD AND MOTHER OF VIRTUES, TO DISSUADE THOSE WHO OUT OF IGNORANCE WAG THE TONGUE AGAINST THOSE WHO CULTIVATE THIS, AND TO PERSUADE EVERY CHRISTIAN TO LEARN THIS DYAD, WHICH RAISES UP, AS WITH A PAIR OF WINGS, THE ONE BORNE ALOFT BY IT AND GUIDES HIM UPWARDS TO THE LOVE OF THE BLESSED TRINITY

1. For those with weak eyesight those who precede them with a torch in their hands seem distressing, not because the light is harmful, nor because those who bear the light are maliciously disposed towards them, but because of the weakness that lurks in the depths of their own eyes. This weakness, which is exposed by the light and called out into the open, disturbs the eyes terribly. Unless the stinging lurking in them is expelled through tears, they cannot be soothed and cannot gaze at the Light. The same thing happens in the case of those who have been labouring under the burden of sin dwelling in the soul and have had the senses of the inner man paralyzed by the sickness of the passions.

2. Those who have the thoughts of their soul darkened by desire for the things of this present life are unable to look upon the Light of divinity which shines in pure minds. For how could they be considered worthy of the divine Light, who welcome a disposition opposed to it? And so, whenever they behold those whose words reveal for the benefit of others the workings of holy knowledge in the hidden place of the soul, blinded, as it were, in their capacity for true discernment, they fall over one or the other of two precipices: either they insist that these spiritual people are making impossible claims, regarding the saving words proclaimed by them more as verbal figments than as mystical realities; or, consumed by jealousy, they disparage spiritual activity as delusion and call them deceived who preach this in word and deed.

3. These people fall into the same sort of blasphemy as the Jews. For when the Jews saw the Lord working miracles with great authority and casting out demons by the Spirit of God, they called him deranged and possessed, and in the excess of their folly they claimed he was

τὰ δαιμόνια ἐξ ὑπερβαλλούσης ἀνοίας ἔλεγον, οὕτω καὶ αὐτοὶ τοῦ
35 παναγίου πνεύματος τὴν ἐνέργειαν τὴν ἀποκαλυπτομένην ἐν ταῖς
πισταῖς καρδίαις εἰς ἐνέργειαν πλάνης διαβάλλουσι· καὶ φιλοτιμίαν
ἐκ τῆς βλασφημίας ταύτης πορίζονται, τὸ μὴ ἀφεθῆναι αὐτοῖς μήτε
ἐν τῷ νῦν αἰῶνι μήτε ἐν τῷ μέλλοντι, τῆς τοιαύτης καταδίκης τῇ
σειρᾷ δικαιότατα ἑαυτοὺς ἐνδεσμοῦντες.
40 　**4.**　Ἐπειδὴ γὰρ διὰ τοῦ ἁγίου πνεύματος ἡ τῶν ἁμαρτημάτων
ἄφεσις τοῖς πιστεύουσι δωρεῖται – μετὰ γὰρ τὸ δοῦναι τὸν κύριον
τοῖς μαθηταῖς τὴν τοῦ πνεύματος χάριν καὶ εἰπεῖν, *λάβετε πνεῦμα ἅγιον,*
ἐπήγαγεν, ἄν τινων ἀφῆτε τὰς ἁμαρτίας ἀφίενται αὐτοῖς. οὗτοι δὲ τὸ
νοερὸν τῆς ψυχῆς μύσαντες τοῦ ἁγίου πνεύματος τὴν χάριν ἑαυτοῖς
45 ἀπέκλεισαν, δι' ἧς τῆς ἀφέσεως καταξιοῦται ὁ ἐν ἐπιγνώσει τὸν θεὸν
ἔχειν βουλόμενος – εἰκότως τῆς ἐλευθερίας ἀλλοτριοῦνται καὶ νῦν
καὶ τότε οἱ εἰς τὸ ἅγιον πνεῦμα βλασφημοῦντες.

　5.　*Ὁ γὰρ νόμος τοῦ πνεύματος τῆς ζωῆς ἠλευθέρωσέ με,* φησίν, *ἀπὸ*
τοῦ νόμου τῆς ἁμαρτίας καὶ τοῦ θανάτου· ὃν δὴ νόμον πνευματικὸν
50 πλαξὶ καρδίας διὰ προσευχῆς ἀναγινωσκόμενον μὴ φέροντες, πῶς
τὸ δόγμα τῆς ἐλευθερίας εἰσδέξονται καὶ εἰς τὴν ζωὴν εἰσελεύσονται,
τῇ τῶν παθῶν δουλείᾳ κεκρατημένοι καὶ τῷ τῆς ἀγνωσίας σκότει
κεκαλυμμένοι; οἳ καὶ ὡς τὸν ἀφεγγῆ χῶρον τῆς διανοίας οἰκοῦντες
καὶ ταῖς ἁλύσεσι τῆς ῥαθυμίας συνεχόμενοι οὐ δύνανται πρὸς τὸ φῶς
55 τῆς νήψεως βαδίσαι καὶ τὴν ἀνατολὴν τοῦ ἡλίου τῆς δικαιοσύνης
καταθρῆσαι, τὴν ἀπαρενόχλητον διάθεσιν τῆς ψυχῆς καὶ τὴν ἡμερότητα τῆς καρδίας, ὡς ἡμέραν, δημιουργοῦντος, καθ' ἣν τὰ μὲν
ὁρμήματα τῶν παθῶν, ὡς θηρία, φυγαδεύονται τῇ θέρμῃ τοῦ πνεύματος, ἐλαυνόμενα· ὁ δὲ νοῦς ἐπὶ τὸ ἔργον τῶν πνευματικῶν ἀρετῶν
60 ἐκπορεύεται, τῷ φωτὶ τῆς ὀρθῆς κρίσεως ὁδηγούμενος.

　6.　Τούτου δὲ τοῦ ἀγαθοῦ τὴν πεῖραν μὴ δοκιμάσαντες ἔχειν ἐν
ἑαυτοῖς, δι' ἧς εἰς τὸ ὄρος τῆς θείας ἐπιγνώσεως ἀναβαίνει καὶ
θεοφανείας καταξιοῦται καὶ θείας φωνῆς ἀκούει καὶ νόμον τὸν τοῦ
πνεύματος δέχεται ὁ τὸν ἐν Μωϋσεῖ τύπον εἰς τὴν ἐν τῇ ψυχῇ

---

34 ἐξυπερβαλλούσης OA

casting out demons by Beelzebul.[1] Similarly, these people, too, slander the working of the all-holy Spirit which is manifest in faithful hearts as a working of delusion. And from this blasphemy they procure for themselves their ambition, namely, to have forgiveness denied them both in this age and in the next:[2] with the cords of such a condemnation they most justly bind themselves.

4.   The forgiveness of sins is bestowed on believers through the Holy Spirit, for after the Lord granted to his disciples the grace of the Holy Spirit and said, "Receive the Holy Spirit," he added, "If you forgive the sins of any they are forgiven them."[3] But these people have closed the spiritual faculty of the soul, thereby excluding themselves from the grace of the Holy Spirit whereby the person who is willing to acknowledge God[4] is deemed worthy of forgiveness. On this account, those who blaspheme against the Holy Spirit are rightly alienated from freedom both now and in the future.

5.   As scripture says, "For the law of the Spirit of life has set me free from the law of sin and death."[5] If they do not bear this spiritual law, which can be read on the tablets of the heart[6] by prayer, how can they receive the teaching of freedom and enter into life when they are ruled by slavery to the passions and covered with the darkness of ignorance? Those who inhabit the lightless region of the discursive intellect and are held by the chains of sloth are unable to proceed towards the light of vigilance and to gaze upon the rising of the sun of righteousness[7] which creates an untroubled disposition in the soul and gentleness in the heart, as the sun creates the day. Thereby the impulses of the passions are put to flight by the warmth of the Spirit, like wild beasts being driven away, and the mind goes forth to the work of the spiritual virtues under the guidance of the light of right judgement.[8]

6.   But these critics have had no experience of this good, whereby the person who has chosen to advance towards the truth manifest in the soul, following the example of Moses, ascends the mountain of divine knowledge, is deemed worthy of the divine theophany, hears

---

[1] Mt 12:22-30, Mk 3:20-30, Lk 11:14-23.
[2] Mt 12:31-32.
[3] Jn 20:22-23.
[4] Cf. Rom 1:28.
[5] Rom 8:2.
[6] Cf. 2 Cor 3:3.
[7] Cf. Mal 3:20.
[8] Cf. Ps 103:22-23.

65 φανερουμένην ἀλήθειαν προβιβάζειν αἱρούμενος, παρεδόθησαν εἰς
ἀδόκιμον νοῦν φρονεῖν καὶ λαλεῖν τὰ μὴ καθήκοντα, ἵνα διὰ μὲν
τοῦ μάταια φρονεῖν αὐτοὺς καὶ περιττὰ σοφίζεσθαι, τῆς πνευματικῆς
τέχνης ἀμαθεῖς διατελῶσι· διὰ δὲ τῆς ἐκ τῶν ῥημάτων διαβολῆς τῆς
καθεζομένης ἐν ταῖς γλώσσαις αὐτῶν καὶ τοὺς γλιχομένους μετα-
70 μαθεῖν τὴν τοιαύτην φωτοβόλον τέχνην διακωλύωσιν, οὔτε αὐτοὶ
εἰσερχόμενοι καὶ τοῖς βουλομένοις εἰσέρχεσθαι ὁδὸν οὐ παρέχοντες.
καὶ εἰκότως, ἕκαστον γὰρ τὴν οἰκείαν θέλει συγγένειαν καὶ πρὸς
τὴν ἰδίαν γνώμην φιλεῖ ἐπισπᾶσθαι τὸ ἑτερόγνωμον· καὶ οὐκ ἂν
ἡσυχάσῃ ποτέ, μέχρις ἂν θατέρα διάθεσις ἐπικρατεστέρα γενομένη
75 τῆς ἐναντίας περιγένηται. καὶ ὅπερ ἐστὶν ἐπὶ τῶν ἐναντίων πραγμάτων,
τοῦτο καὶ ἐπὶ τῶν μαχομένων γνωμῶν ἐστιν ἰδεῖν. ὡς γὰρ ἐκεῖ τὸ
θερμὸν τοῦ ψυχροῦ καὶ τοῦτο πάλιν τοῦ θερμοῦ ἀναλωτικὸν γίνεται,
ὅταν ὑπερβάλλει τὸ ἓν τοῦ ἑτέρου, οὕτω καὶ ἐνταῦθα αἱ μὲν διαθέσεις
ὡς ἀντιδιαθέτως ἔχουσαι πόλεμον ἐγείρουσι καὶ μία τῆς ἄλλης
80 κατακρατῆσαι φιλονεικεῖ· ἡ δὲ ἀντίστασις, ὁρᾶται, ἕως οὗ θατέρα
ἴσην τὴν αἵρεσιν ἔχουσα, ἐφ᾽ ἑαυτῆς ποθεῖ μένειν.

7. Ἡ δὲ ὑποταγὴ τελεῖται, ὅταν τῆς μιᾶς ἡ ἧττα ἐξ ἀσθενείας
φανῇ, ᾧ γάρ τις ἥττηται, τούτῳ καὶ δεδούλωται. οὗτοι μὲν οὖν ἔξω
ἑαυτῶν φερόμενοι, τὴν τῆς διανοίας ὁδὸν περιπατεῖν οὐ βούλονται·
85 πνεύματι γὰρ περιπατεῖν κατὰ Παῦλον μὴ θέλοντες, τὴν μὲν πνευματικὴν ἐπιστήμην ἀπαιδευσίαν καὶ πλάνην, τοὺς δὲ ταύτης μαθητάς
τε καὶ κήρυκας ἀπαιδεύτους καὶ πλάνους κατονομάζουσιν· ὅθεν αὐτοὶ
μὲν τὴν τῆς ἐπιθυμίας αὐτῶν ὁδὸν πορευέσθωσαν.

8. Ἡμεῖς δὲ τῆς ἀπορρήτως ἀνατελλούσης φωτοτόκου ταύτης
90 ἐργασίας τὸ κάλλος πειρασόμεθα κατὰ δύναμιν ὑποδεῖξαι τοῖς
ἐρωτικῶς διακειμένοις τυπωθῆναι τὴν διάνοιαν πρὸς τὰ ἴχνη τῆς
σωτηρίου ταύτης ὁδοῦ. ἡ πνευματικὴ ἐργασία, ἤγουν ὁ πνευματικὸς
νόμος, κόσμος χρηματίζει ἐξαίρετος, τὴν θέσιν καὶ τὴν σύστασιν
εἰληφὼς ἐν τοῖς ἀδύτοις χωρίοις τῆς ψυχῆς, ἐν ᾧ ὁ ἐπουράνιος
95 δημιουργεῖται ἄνθρωπος, ἐκ προσοχῆς ἀκριβοῦς καὶ ἀδιαλείπτου
προσευχῆς συνιστάμενος, καθάπερ ἐκ ψυχῆς καὶ σώματος ὁ ὁρώμενος
ἄνθρωπος· οὗ τὸν τρόπον τῆς ἁπλουστάτης διαθέσεως καὶ ἀτυπώτου
διαπλάσεως ἐκ τῆς κατὰ τὸν αἰσθητὸν ἄνθρωπον δημιουργίας μάν-
θανε.

88 τὴν bis O

the divine voice and receives the law of the Spirit.[9] Accordingly, they were handed over to a base mind to think and speak improper things.[10] And so, on the one hand, they continue in their ignorance of the art of the Spirit, because they hold vain thoughts and contrive trivia. On the other hand, by the slanderous statements that sit ready on their tongues they hinder also those who strive to learn this light-bestowing art, neither entering in themselves, nor giving way for those who wish to enter.[11] And naturally so, for each wants its side to predominate and desires the other side to be drawn over to its own opinion, and it will not rest for a moment until one position gets the upper hand and prevails over its opposite. What occurs in the case of opposites found in nature can also be observed in the case of hostile opinions. In the former, heat can dissipate cold and cold in turn can dissipate heat, whenever one is in excess of the other. Similarly, in the latter, positions that are diametrically opposed incite hostility and one contends to overcome the other. But the opposition, it can be seen, desires to maintain its own quarter as long as one faction is equal to the other.

7. Submission comes about whenever the defeat of one party occurs as a result of weakness, for one becomes the slave of the man by whom one is defeated. Therefore, when these critics get carried away, they refuse to walk the way of the discursive intellect, for, since they are unwilling to walk in the Spirit, as Paul says,[12] they call spiritual knowledge ignorance and delusion and the disciples and heralds of this way ignorant and deluded. So let them proceed along the way of their desire.

8. But we, as best as we are able, shall try to show the beauty of this ineffably dawning, light-begetting activity to those who are disposed in love to have their discursive intellect formed with the imprints of this way of salvation. Spiritual activity, or the spiritual law, is an extraordinary world which finds its location and constitution in the inaccessible reaches of the soul where the heavenly man is formed and sustained by true attention and unceasing prayer, just as the visible man is made up of soul and body. From the creation of the sensible man, you can learn the manner of the heavenly man's utterly simple disposition and fashioning which is free from external impressions.

---

[9] Cf. Ex 19:1-25, 24:12-18, 33:17-23, 34:29-35.
[10] Cf. Rom 1:28.
[11] Cf. Lk 11:52.
[12] Cf. Rom 8:4.

100   **9.** Ἐν τῷ φαινομένῳ τούτῳ κόσμῳ κατὰ τὴν ἕκτην ἡμέραν ὁ
ἄνθρωπος ὑπο θεοῦ διεπλάσθη, καὶ ἐν τῷ νοουμένῳ τῆς διανοίας
κόσμῳ κατὰ τὴν πρὸς τὰ νοητὰ διάθεσιν ὁ οὐρανόφρων διαπλάττεται
παρὰ θεοῦ ἄνθρωπος. ὅταν γὰρ ἡ ἐπιθυμία τῆς ψυχῆς, τὴν τοῖς
αἰσθητοῖς προσκειμένην πενταδικὴν αἴσθησιν διαφυγοῦσα, πρὸς τὴν
105   τῶν νοητῶν διατεθῇ γνῶσιν, τότε ὁ θεὸς ἀπὸ τῆς κατὰ τὴν αἴσθησιν
ἐνεργείας, τὸν νοῦν, ὡς ἀπὸ γῆς χοῦν λαμβάνων, καὶ τὴν ἑαυτοῦ
θεωρίαν αὐτῷ ἐμπνέων, καὶ τὴν ἐπίκλησιν τοῦ ἐνδόξου ὀνόματος
αὐτοῦ παρέχων αὐτῷ, ποιεῖ τὸν ἔσω ἄνθρωπον εἰς ψυχὴν ζῶσαν καὶ
διάνοιαν πεφωτισμένην, ἀγγελικῶς αὐτῷ λειτουργοῦντα καὶ τὴν
110   λογικὴν λατρείαν ἀποπληροῦντα· διώκτην τῶν προσβολῶν ὁρώμενον,
διάκονον τῶν θείων ἐννοιῶν, ἀναιρέτην τῶν παθῶν, γεωργὸν τῶν
ἀρετῶν, πρὸς τὰς ἐπιθυμίας ἀνταγωνιστήν, ἐραστὴν τῆς τοῦ θεοῦ
ἀγαπήσεως, τῆς φαντασίας ἀφανιστήν, τῆς σοφίας φανερωτήν, βασιλέα τῶν τῆς φύσεως λογισμῶν ὑπὸ πνευματικοῦ λόγου βασιλευ-
115   όμενον, τῶν φροντίδων φιμωτήν, ἀμεριμνίας φροντιστήν, ξένον τῶν
αἰσθήσεων τοῦ αἰῶνος τούτου, φίλον τῶν γνώσεων τοῦ μέλλοντος
αἰῶνος, ἀπόδημον τοῦ φθειρομένου βίου, οἰκήτορα τοῦ μὴ παρερ-
χομένου κόσμου, τῆς πολεμουμένης πατρίδος φυγάδα, τῆς
ἀπολιορκήτου πόλεως πολίτην, τῶν προσκαίρων καταφρονητήν, τῶν
120   ἀθανάτων πραγματευτήν, ἀμαθῆ τῶν ἀνθρωπίνων πραγμάτων, μύστην
τῶν τοῦ θεοῦ θελημάτων.

    10.   Πρὸς τοὺς ἐπιγείους φρονίμους ἀλλόγλωσσον, πρὸς τοὺς ἐν
οὐρανοῖς τὸ πολίτευμα ποιουμένους ἑρμηνέα τῶν ἄνω, τὰ φαινόμενα
τερπνὰ ὡς ἀνύπαρκτα φεύγοντα, τὰ μὴ φαινόμενα ἀγαθὰ ὡς διαμένοντα
125   ποθοῦντα, νεκρὸν ταῖς ὑλικαῖς ἐπιθυμίαις, ζῶντα τὴν ἐν Χριστῷ
κεκρυμμένην ζωήν, οὐδενὸς τῶν ἐπιγείων ὀρεγόμενον – οὐ πλούτου
τὸν ἄσυλον πλοῦτον ἀφαιρουμένου, οὐ τρυφῆς τὴν ἀδάπανον τρυφὴν
δαπανώσης καὶ λιμὸν ἀπαράκλητον ἐργαζομένης, οὐ δόξης ἀδοξίας
προξένου, οὐ τιμῆς ἀτίμου τὸν πολύτιμον μαργαρίτην ἄτιμον ποιου-
130   μένης τῇ τῶν ἀτίμων τιμῇ, οὐκ ἀρχῆς καταδουλούσης τὸ τῆς ψυχῆς
ἀδούλωτον ταῖς ἀρχαῖς καὶ ταῖς ἐξουσίαις τῶν πονηρῶν πνευμάτων,

---

116 φίλον corr.: φίλων OA

9.   On the sixth day man was formed by God in this visible world;[13] in the thought world of the discursive intellect the heavenly-minded man is formed by God with a disposition towards spiritual realities. For when the desire of the soul has fled the fivefold sense faculty which is directed towards sensible things and has become disposed to the knowledge of spiritual realities, then, God takes the mind away from the activities of the senses, as he took dust from the earth,[14] and, breathing into it contemplation of himself and equipping it with the *Invocation of his Glorious Name*,[15] he creates the inner man as a living soul and an illumined discursive intellect to offer him angelic service and to perform spiritual worship.[16] The inner man is then seen to be a persecutor of temptations, a servant of divine thoughts, a destroyer of the passions, a cultivator of the virtues, an antagonist of the desires, a devotee of love for God, an obliterator of illusion, a revealer of wisdom, a king over the thoughts of nature who is ruled by the spiritual word, a muzzler of cares, a curator of tranquillity, a foreigner to the senses of this age, a friend of the knowledge of the age to come,[17] an emigrant from this corruptible life, an inhabitant of the world that does not pass away, a fugitive from a homeland at war, a citizen of the impregnable city, a despiser of transient things, a dealer in things immortal, an ignoramus in human affairs, an initiate in the will of God.

10.   The inner man is a speaker of a foreign language to the wise men of this world, an interpreter of the things above for those who make their home in heaven,[18] a fugitive from visible pleasures as things of no substance, a lover of invisible goods as realities that perdure, one dead to desire for material things, one alive to the life hidden in Christ,[19] a person with no longing for any earthly thing — not for wealth which deprives of inviolate wealth, not for a joy which exhausts the inexhaustible joy and causes a famine without hope for relief, not for honour which brings dishonour, not for worthless values which render the pearl of great price[20] worthless by placing value on worthless things, not for power that enslaves the unenslaved power of the soul

---

[13] Gen 1:31.
[14] Gen 2:7.
[15] I.e., the Jesus Prayer.
[16] Cf. Rom 12:1.
[17] Cf. Eph 1:21.
[18] Cf. Phil 3:20.
[19] Cf. Col 3:3.
[20] Mt 13:46.

οὐκ ἐπαίνων ἐκλυόντων τὴν πρὸς τὰς λειτουργίας τοῦ θεοῦ τῶν
λογισμῶν παράστασιν.

11.   Καὶ συνελὼν λέγω, οὐδὲν τῶν ὅσα τοὺς ἀνθρώπους ἢ θέλγει
135 ἢ θλίβει καταβιβάζει αὐτὸν τοῦ ὕψους τῆς θείας διακονίας· ἐν γὰρ
τῷ διακριτικῷ τῆς ψυχῆς ὡς ἐν παραδείσῳ ὁ λογισμὸς αὐτοῦ τέθειται,
ἐργαζόμενος τὴν εἰς θεὸν μνήμην διὰ τῆς εὐχῆς καὶ φυλάσσων τὸν
νοῦν διὰ τῆς προσοχῆς· ἐν ᾧ καὶ παραμένων ἐντολὴν μυστικῶς
δέχεται, διακρίνουσαν αὐτῷ τὰ καλὰ ἀπὸ τῶν κακῶν καὶ πᾶν νόημα
140 τοῦ θείου φωτὸς ἐξημμένον προτρεπομένην αὐτῷ ἐσθίειν, τὸν δὲ
λογισμὸν τῆς ἐπιθυμίας, ὡς γνῶσιν καλοῦ καὶ κακοῦ, εἴτουν ἡδονῆς
καὶ ὀδύνης ἔχοντα, φεύγειν πάσῃ σπουδῇ, ὡς θάνατον αἰώνιον
προξενοῦντα διὰ τῆς τοῦ θεοῦ ἀμνηστίας.

12.   Ταύτης τῆς διακρίσεως ὁ φωτισμὸς ἀνατέλλει ἐν τῇ ψυχῇ,
145 νήφοντος τοῦ νοῦ καὶ πρὸς τὴν ἑαυτοῦ καρδίαν ὁρῶντος καὶ τὸν
θεὸν προσκαλουμένου εἰς ἀναίρεσιν τῆς δαιμονικῆς ἀχλύος. καὶ
ὥσπερ ὁ ἐν τῷ οἴκῳ αὐτοῦ καθήμενος καὶ πάντων τῶν ἰδίων
πραγμάτων ἐπιμελούμενος, ἐπὰν ἴδῃ τινὰ θέλοντά τι ἁρπάσαι ἀπὸ
τῶν προσόντων αὐτῷ, λαμβάνει ἐκ τοῦ θησαυροῦ αὐτοῦ καὶ ἀπέρχεται
150 πρὸς ἐξουσίαν καὶ ἐκκαλεῖται αὐτὴν πρὸς τὴν ἑαυτοῦ βοήθειαν, οὕτω
καὶ ὁ νοῦς ἐν τῷ οἴκῳ τῆς γνώσεως μένων καὶ τῶν ἑαυτοῦ λογισμῶν
φροντίζων, ὅταν ἴδῃ τὴν σατανικὴν προσβολὴν πειρωμένην ἀδικῆσαι
αὐτόν, ἐπαίρει τὰ ἑαυτοῦ νοήματα ἀπὸ τοῦ κόσμου τούτου καὶ
ἀποτρέχει πρὸς τὸν θεόν, τὴν ἑαυτοῦ ταλαιπωρίαν ἐμφανίζων αὐτῷ.

155 **13.**   Ὁ δὲ τὸν στεναγμὸν τῶν πενήτων καὶ τὴν ταλαιπωρίαν τῶν
πτωχῶν μὴ παρορῶν κύριος δέχεται τὰ αὐτοῦ ξένια καὶ οἰκειοῦται
πᾶσαν αὐτοῦ τὴν διάθεσιν, καὶ εὐθέως ἡ ψυχὴ θρόνος γίνεται τοῦ
θεοῦ καὶ ὁ οἶκος τοῦ πένητος νοῦ οἶκος τοῦ βασιλέως ὁρᾶται καὶ
ἡ στρατιὰ τῶν ἀγγέλων κατὰ τῆς δαιμονικῆς φάλαγγος πέμπεται, τὴν
160 ἐκδίκησιν ἐργαζομένη τῆς ψυχῆς. εἰ μὲν οὖν γρηγοροῦσιν αἱ ἔννοιαι
τῆς ψυχῆς, ὁ φωτισμὸς τοῦ πνεύματος πληροῖ αὐτὴν πάσης δόξης·
εἰ δὲ ἀμελήσει ὁ νοῦς περὶ τὴν ἑαυτοῦ ἔρευναν καὶ ἀργὸς διατεθῇ
περὶ τὴν θείαν μελέτην, οἱ λογισμοὶ τῆς κακίας ἀναβαίνουσιν ἐν τῇ
καρδίᾳ κάλυμμα σκότους εἰς τὸν νοῦν φέροντες.

165 **14.**   Ὁ δὲ τὴν ἀπροσεξίαν νοσῶν τῷ μέρει τῆς ἀλογίας ὑποκλίνεται
καί, τὸν γνόφον ὑπερχόμενος τοῦ τῶν αἰσθήσεων ἔρωτος, τὸν ἔρωτα
τοῦ θείου φωτὸς ἀποτίθεται καὶ τοῦ λόγου διακρίνεται καὶ τῆς
γνώσεως ἐκβάλλεται καὶ εἰς τὴν χώραν τῶν παθῶν γίνεται. τότε τὰ

to the rulers and powers of the evil spirits,[21] not for praise which releases the attendance of the thoughts to the service of God.

11. In summary, none of the things that charm or afflict men can bring the inner man down from the height of divine service, for his thought has found its place in the soul's faculty of discernment, as in a paradise, where it labours at remembrance of God through prayer and guards the mind through attention. Abiding there, it receives mystically a commandment which discerns for it good from evil and encourages it to eat of every thought associated with the divine Light, but to flee with all haste the thought associated with desire, as involving the knowledge of good and evil or of pleasure and pain, because this is a harbinger of eternal death through forgetfulness of God.[22]

12. The illumination of this discernment dawns in the soul when the mind maintains vigilance and looks towards its own heart and beseeches God to dispel the demonic haze from it. In the case of a man abiding in his home and looking after all his property, whenever he sees someone who wants to make off with some of his belongings, he takes them out of his storeroom and goes off to the authorities to call them to his assistance. Similarly, in the case of the mind which abides in the household of knowledge and attends to its own thoughts, whenever it sees the approach of Satan attempting to put it in the wrong, it removes its thoughts from this world and runs off to God to show him its misery.

13. The Lord, who does not overlook the groaning of the poor and the misery of the indigent,[23] accepts the gift-offerings of the mind and conforms its entire disposition to himself. Immediately the soul becomes the throne of God, the house of the poor mind is seen to be the house of a king and the army of angels is sent against the demonic phalanx to avenge the soul. If, then, the thoughts of the soul remain vigilant, the illumination of the Spirit fills it with every glory. But if the mind is negligent in its self-examination and is disposed to be lazy about divine meditation, thoughts of wickedness arise in the heart bringing a veil of darkness upon the mind.

14. The man who suffers from the disease of inattention submits to the lot of irrationality and, slipping into the darkness of love for the senses, he abandons love for the divine Light, is separated from reason, exiled from knowledge and enters the land of the passions.

[21] Cf. Eph 6:12.
[22] Cf. Gen 2:15-17.
[23] Cf. Ps 11:6.

φρονήματα αὐτοῦ πονεῖν ἀπάρχονται περὶ τὴν τῶν κακῶν γεωργίαν
170 καὶ οἱ λογισμοὶ αὐτοῦ, καθάπερ μύρμηκες τὰς αἰσθήσεις διατρέχοντες,
νοήματα συλλέγουσιν ἐπιθυμίας φθειρομένης. τὴν ἀλόγιστον ταύτην
φορὰν τῆς ψυχῆς ἡ μετ' εὐχῆς ἵστησι νῆψις.

15. Νῆψίς ἐστι ῥεμβασμῶν κατάπαυσις, ἐπιστασία λογισμῶν,
στάσις τοῦ νοῦ, κίνησις λόγου. νῆψίς ἐστι νοῦ καθαρότης, ἠθῶν
175 κατάστασις, ψυχῆς ἐγρήγορσις, ἰσχὺς πρακτικῆς, σαρκικῆς πυρώσεως
ἀκινησία. νῆψις τοὺς πρὸς τὴν γῆν μετεωρισμοὺς καταργεῖ τῆς
ψυχῆς, ἡ δὲ εὐχὴ μετέωρον ποιεῖται τὴν ψυχὴν πρὸς τὰ οὐράνια.
νῆψις τόπος θεοῦ ἐν εἰρήνῃ ὁρώμενος, σκοπευτήριον ψυχῆς ἐν ᾧ
θεὸς κατοικεῖ, εἰς ὃ καὶ πᾶν μέλος ἐπιθυμίας κοσμικῆς συντριβόμενον
180 οἴχεται· *ἐγενήθη, γάρ φησιν ὁ προφήτης, ἐν εἰρήνῃ ὁ τόπος αὐτοῦ καὶ
τὸ κατοικητήριον αὐτοῦ ἐν Σιών· ἐκεῖ συνέτριψε τὰ κράτη τῶν τόξων,
ὅπλον καὶ ῥομφαίαν καὶ πόλεμον.* ἐκεῖ ποῦ; ὅπου ἡ νῆψις ὁρᾶται, ἐκεῖ
ἡ τοῦ θεοῦ μνήμη συντρίβει τὴν λήθην ὡς ὅπλον, τὴν ἄγνοιαν ὡς
ῥομφαίαν τὴν ῥαθυμίαν ὡς πόλεμον· αἵτινές εἰσι τὰ κράτη τῶν παθῶν,
185 ὡς ἐξ αὐτῶν ὁρμωμένων καὶ πρὸς αὐτὰς ὑπονοστούντων.

16. Νῆψις παραστάτην τοῦ θεοῦ τὸν νοῦν ἀπεργάζεται καὶ τοῦ
νοὸς τὸν θεὸν πάλιν ἐπόπτην δεικνύει· *τὸ πρωΐ, γάρ φησι, παραστήσομαί σοι καὶ ἐπόψει με.* τὸ πρωῒ τῆς πρωτονοίας μου παραστήσομαί
σοι διὰ προσευχῆς καὶ τῇ ἐπισκοπικῇ τῶν χαρισμάτων σου δυνάμει
190 ἐπόψει με, διδούς μοι εὐχὴν ἀμετεώριστον, εὐφροσύνην πνευματικήν,
ἀφάνταστον διάνοιαν, ἀληθινὴν ἀγάπην, πραότητα ψυχῆς καὶ καρδίας
εἰρήνην. νῆψις τὸν νοῦν ποιεῖται θεωρὸν τοῦ θεοῦ. *ἰδοὺ τόπος παρ'
ἐμοί, φησιν ὁ θεὸς πρὸς τὸν Μωϋσῆν,* ἐμφανίζων αὐτῷ ἑαυτόν, *καὶ
στήσῃ ἐπὶ τῆς πέτρας καὶ θήσω σε εἰς ὀπὴν τῆς πέτρας καὶ ὄψει τὰ
195 ὀπίσθιά μου.* τόπος δὲ πλησιάζων θεῷ ἡ νῆψίς ἐστι, δι' ἧς τῆς κατὰ
τὴν πέτραν τῆς πίστεως στάσεως ὁ νοῦς ἀξιούμενος, εἰς τὴν
ἀκαταίσχυντον ἐλπίδα τίθεται, ἐξ ἧς εἰς τὴν ἱερὰν ἀναβαίνων ἀγάπην
ὁρᾶται ὀπίσω τοῦ θεοῦ πορευόμενος, ἅτε δὴ τῆς θεοποιοῦ ἀγαπήσεως
τὴν τῆς ψυχῆς ἔννοιαν πηγνυούσης ἐν τῇ ὁσίᾳ μνήμῃ τοῦ θεοῦ.

200 **17.** Νῆψις τῶν ἀποκαλυπτομένων ἐν τῇ ψυχῇ κρυπτῶν θεαμάτων
σκοπεύει τὴν ἐμφάνειαν καὶ τῶν λαλουμένων μυστηρίων εἰς τὸ οὖς
τῆς διανοίας τὴν γνῶσιν δέχεται. ὁ μέγας Γρηγόριος τὴν τοῦ

183 συντρίβει corr.: συντρίβῃ ΟΑ

Then, his thinking begins to labour over the cultivation of evil and his thoughts, like ants, crawl over the senses and collect notions of corrupting desire. Vigilance coupled with prayer puts a stop to this irrational tendency of the soul.

15. Vigilance means the cessation of distractions, control of thoughts, stability of the mind, activation of reason. Vigilance means purity of mind, an orderly moral life, watchfulness of soul, fortitude in the practical life, steadfast resistance to the burning of the flesh. Vigilance renders impotent the earthbound distractions of the soul, but prayer raises the soul to heavenly things. Vigilance appears as a place of God in peace, a watchtower of the soul in which God dwells and where every bit of worldly desire is crushed and vanishes. For the prophet says, "His place has been established in peace and his dwelling place in Sion. There he smashed the strength of the bows, the shield, the sword and war."[24] Where is this? Where vigilance is apparent, there the remembrance of God crushes forgetfulness like a shield, ignorance like a sword, sloth like war. These are the powers of the passions since they originate in them and return to them.

16. Vigilance makes the mind attendant upon God and in turn shows God to be a watchman over the mind. For scripture says, "In the morning I shall attend upon you and you will watch over me."[25] With my first thought of the morning I shall attend upon you through prayer and with the directive power of your gifts you will watch over me, granting me undistracted prayer, spiritual joy, a discursive intellect untroubled by the imagination, true love, gentleness of soul and peace of heart. Vigilance brings the mind to the contemplation of God. "Behold, there is a place by me," God said to Moses when he manifested himself to him, "and you shall stand by the rock and I will put you in a cleft of the rock and you shall see my back."[26] Vigilance is a place near to God through which the mind is deemed worthy to stay by the rock of faith and sets itself to confident hope, from which it ascends to holy love and is seen to walk behind God, inasmuch as divinizing love keeps the thoughts of the soul fixed on the sacred remembrance of God.

17. Vigilance looks for the manifestation of hidden wonders revealed in the soul and receives the knowledge of mysteries spoken in the ear of the discursive intellect. Gregory the Great borrows the

[24] Ps 75:3-4.
[25] Ps 5:4.
[26] Ex 33:21-23.

Ἀββακοὺμ δανειζόμενος ῥῆσιν, τοῦτο παρίστησι λέγων· *ἐπὶ τῆς*
φυλακῆς μου στήσομαι, καὶ ἀποσκοπεύσω καὶ γνώσομαι τί ὀφθήσεται
205 *καὶ τί λαληθήσεταί μοι·* φυλακὴν λέγοντος τοῦ προφήτου τὴν τοῦ νοῦ
νῆψιν καὶ τὴν τῆς διανοίας ἡσυχίαν, ἐν ᾗ διὰ τὸ ἁπλούστατόν τε
καὶ ἄπλαστον ἡ γνῶσις τῶν ἀπορρήτων τικτομένη φανερὰ γίνεται
τῇ ψυχῇ. φυλακὴ δὲ λέγεται ἡ τοῦ νοῦ νῆψις, ὡς κήδεσθαι καὶ
φροντίζειν καταπείθουσα τὴν ψυχὴν περὶ τὰ ἑαυτῆς φύλλα, εἴτουν
210 μέρη, τῶν λογισμῶν γὰρ τῆς ψυχῆς συναγομένων πρὸς τὸν αὐτῆς
νοῦν, καὶ τοῦ νοῦ πάλιν τῆς ἑαυτοῦ καρδίας μὴ ἀφισταμένου, ἀλλὰ
πρὸς αὐτὴν ἐπιστρεφομένου καὶ τῆς τοῦ θεοῦ βασιλείας καὶ δικαιοσύνης μέριμνάν τε καὶ ζήτησιν ποιουμένου, ἡ τοιαύτη σπουδὴ καὶ
ἀκριβεστάτη φροντὶς φυλακὴ τῶν τῆς ψυχῆς μερῶν γίνεται, τῶν
215 γενικωτάτων ἀρετῶν τὴν τιμιότητα δι᾽ ἑαυτῆς συντηροῦσα.

18. Νῆψις συλλαμβάνει φόβον θεοῦ· ἀνάπαυσιν ἀπὸ θλίψεως
τίκτει· ἀνάβασίν τε μαιεύει καὶ ἔκστασιν. *ἐφυλαξάμην,* γάρ φησιν ὁ
αὐτὸς προφήτης, *καὶ ἐπτοήθη ἡ καρδία μου ἀπὸ φωνῆς προσευχῆς*
χειλέων μου, καὶ εἰσῆλθε τρόμος εἰς τὰ ὀστᾶ μου, καὶ ἐν ἐμοὶ ἐταράχθη
220 *ἡ ἰσχύς μου. ἀναπαύσομαι ἐν ἡμέρᾳ θλίψεώς μου τοῦ ἀναβῆναί με εἰς*
λαὸν παροικίας μου. καὶ πάλιν· *εἰσακήκοα, κύριε, τὴν ἀκοήν σου καὶ*
ἐφοβήθην, κατενόησα τὰ ἔργα σου καὶ ἐξέστην. εἰς ἑαυτόν, φησί,
συστραφεὶς καὶ ἐν ἐμαυτῷ γενόμενος καὶ τῶν περὶ ἐμὲ πάντων ἀφ᾽
ἑαυτοῦ τὴν ἔννοιαν ἀποστήσας, εἶδον τὴν συμβολὴν τοῦ ἐμφυλίου
225 πολέμου τῆς ψυχῆς· ἑώρακα τὴν κατὰ τοῦ λόγου τῶν ἀλόγων παθῶν
ἐπιβουλήν τε καὶ ἐνέδραν· ἔγνων τὸν κατὰ τοῦ θεοῦ ἀγῶνα τοῦ
διαβόλου καὶ τῶν δαιμόνων, τὴν κατὰ τῶν θείων ἀρετῶν ἐπανάστασιν
τῶν παθῶν, τὰ ἐπαιρόμενα ὑψώματα κατὰ τῆς γνώσεως τοῦ θεοῦ, τὴν
τῆς ἔχθρας ἀντίστασιν κατὰ τῆς εἰρήνης, τῆς κακίας τὴν πεφιλημένην
230 μανίαν καὶ κατὰ τῆς ψυχῆς μαινομένην, τὴν πεφαντασμένην καὶ
νενοθευμένην τῆς ἁμαρτίας ἐν ταῖς ἀρεταῖς συνεργίαν. ἀφόρατον δὲ
ἀφανισμὸν καὶ δολερὸν σκορπισμὸν τῆς οὐσίας τοῦ νοῦ καὶ πᾶσαν
ἄλλην τῶν πονηρῶν πνευμάτων πολυειδῆ κίνησιν φανερῶς τε καὶ
ἀφανῶς ὑφαινομένην καὶ ἐξαπλουμένην κατὰ τῆς διακρίσεως τοῦ

207 τικτομένη corr.: τυκτομένη OA   216 συλλαμβάνει corr.: συλαμβάνει OA
218 ἐπτοήθη corr.: ἐπτωήθη OA

saying of Habakkuk and presents this statement: "'I shall stand on my guard and watch,' and I shall know what will appear and what will be said to me."[27] By 'guard' the prophet means the vigilance of the mind and the quiet of the discursive faculty in which, by reason of its uttermost simplicity and absence of form, the knowledge of ineffable things is born and becomes manifest to the soul. Vigilance of the mind is called a guard because it persuades the soul to care and take thought for its leaves,[28] that is, its parts, for the thoughts of the soul are gathered towards its mind and the mind, in turn, does not shy away from its own heart but rather turns toward it, anxiously seeking the kingdom of God and his righteousness.[29] Such zeal and genuine way of thought constitute a guard over the parts of the soul, which through itself preserves the value of the cardinal virtues.[30]

18. Vigilance conceives the fear of God; it gives birth to rest from affliction; as a midwife it serves in the birthing of spiritual ascent and ecstasy. For the same prophet says, "I kept guard and my heart was terrified at the sound of the prayer of my lips. Trembling penetrated my bones and my strength was troubled within me. I shall rest on the day of my affliction so that I may go up to the people of my sojourning."[31] And again, "I have heard, O Lord, the report of you and I grew afraid. I considered your works and I fell into ecstasy."[32] Turning in upon myself, he says, and entering within while rejecting thought for anything around me, I beheld the encounter of the civil war in the soul. I saw the treacherous ambush of the irrational passions against the rational faculty of the soul. I perceived the struggle of the devil and the demons against God, the rebellion of the passions against the divine virtues, the high obstacles raised against the knowledge of God, the opposition of hostility to peace, the madness besotted with evil and raving against the soul, the deluded and corrupted conspiracy of sin against the virtues. And when I learned of the undetected destruction and treacherous scattering of the substance of the mind and every other sort of manifold movement of the evil spirits, contrived and disseminated openly and in secret against the discernment of the

---

[27] Gregory Nazianzen, Or. 45.1 — *In sanctam pascham* (PG 36:624A); cf. Hab 2:1.
[28] Theoleptos derives his curious etymology from the vocal similarity of the two words, φύλλα and φυλακή.
[29] Mt 6:33.
[30] In this context the cardinal virtues are presumably faith, hope and love, which Theoleptos mentioned at the end of the preceding paragraph.
[31] Hab 3:16.
[32] Ibid. 3:2. I have translated the verb ἐξέστην to accord with Theoleptos' exegesis.

235 λόγου καταμαθών, *ἐπτοήθη ἡ καρδία μου καὶ εἰσῆλθε τρόμος εἰς τὰ ὀστᾶ μου*.

   19. Ὅτι ὁ ἄνθρωπος, προσευχόμενος χείλεσι καὶ γλώσσῃ ψάλλων, εὑρίσκεται, ἐν καρδίᾳ συνδιάζων κακίᾳ, τοῖς χείλεσιν ἐγγίζει θεῷ, τῇ δὲ καρδίᾳ πόρρω ἀπέχει αὐτοῦ. διὸ καὶ φοβηθεὶς τὴν μετὰ τοῦ
240 ἐχθροῦ κρυπτὴν κοινωνίαν, ὁ κοινωνὸς τῆς θεότητος εἶναι ταχθείς, *ἐν ἐμοὶ ἐταράχθη ἡ ἰσχύς μου*. πάλιν δὲ διὰ τῆς τοῦ νοὸς φυλακῆς διδαχθείς, ὅτι ἡ τοῦ θεοῦ λόγου κατάβασις πρὸς τὸν ἄνθρωπον διὰ τοῦτο γίνεται, ἵνα τὸ λογικὸν τῆς ψυχῆς ἐλευθερώσῃ ἀλόγου δουλείας τῶν παθῶν καὶ τὴν ἀφαιρεθεῖσαν ὑπὸ τοῦ ἐχθροῦ ἐξουσίαν πάλιν
245 τῷ ἀνθρώπῳ χαρίσηται εἰς τὸ ἵστασθαι αὐτὸν γενναίως κατὰ τῆς ἁμαρτίας καὶ καθαρῶς λατρεύειν τῷ ζῶντι θεῷ, ἀναπαύσεως ἔτυχον καὶ ἐκουφίσθην ἀπὸ τῶν πολλῶν θλίψεων. διότι ἀναβαίνω διὰ τῆς ἐνανθρωπήσεως τοῦ υἱοῦ τοῦ θεοῦ εἰς ἄρνησιν σαρκικῆς ἡδονῆς καὶ τοῦ δεσμοῦ τῆς ἡδυπαθείας λύομαι.

250   **20.**   Εἰ γὰρ καὶ ἐκ τοῦ ἀκοῦσαί με μυστικῶς τὴν ἀκοὴν τῆς θείας ἐνανθρωπήσεως πεφόβημαι διὰ τὴν ἄστεκτον δύναμιν τῆς θεότητος, ἀλλ᾽ ἐκ τοῦ κατανοήσασθαι πάλιν τὰ ἔργα τῆς σωτηρίου ταύτης οἰκονομίας, ἐξέστην διὰ τὸν ἄπειρον πλοῦτον τῆς θείας χρηστότητος. νῆψις ὁδὸς τοῦ θεοῦ καὶ πορεία πρὸς τὴν ἀλήθειαν.
255 Δαβὶδ καὶ Ἡσαΐας διδάσκουσι τοῦτο· ὁ μὲν εὐχόμενος ὁδηγηθῆναι πρὸς αὐτήν, ὁ δὲ προτρεπόμενος τῷ λαῷ ἑτοιμάζειν αὐτήν· *κύριε, ὁδήγησόν με ἐν τῇ ὁδῷ σου καὶ πορεύσομαι ἐν τῇ ἀληθείᾳ σου*. *φωνὴ βοῶντος ἐν τῇ ἐρήμῳ, ἑτοιμάσατε τὴν ὁδὸν κυρίου, εὐθείας ποιεῖτε τὰς τρίβους αὐτοῦ*. ἐὰν γὰρ ἡ φυλακὴ τῆς καρδίας ἑτοιμασθῇ ἐν τῷ νῷ,
260 αἱ δυνάμεις τῆς ψυχῆς εὐθεῖαι ὁρώμεναι τρίβοι κυρίου γίνονται. *εὐθὺς κύριος ὁ θεὸς ἡμῶν καὶ εὐθύτητας εἶδε τὸ πρόσωπον αὐτοῦ*.

   21.   Νῆψις οἶκος θεοῦ καὶ σύζυγος προσευχῆς. *εἰσελεύσομαι εἰς τὸν οἶκον σου ἐν ὁλοκαυτώμασιν, ἀποδώσω σοι τὰς εὐχάς μου, ἃς διέστειλε τὰ χείλη μου καὶ ἐλάλησε τὸ στόμα μου ἐν τῇ θλίψει μου*, Δαβὶδ
265 ἐστιν ὁ λέγων. εἰσέρχεται ἡ ψυχὴ εἰς φυλακὴν τοῦ νοῦ, ὅτε πάντες οἱ λογισμοὶ αὐτῆς ὁλοκλήρως τῷ πυρὶ τῆς θείας ἀγάπης καίονται, ὧν καὶ ὁλοκαυτουμένων ὑπὸ τοῦ θείου ἔρωτος ἐν τῷ κατὰ τὴν νῆψιν θυσιαστηρίῳ οἱ ἀτμοὶ τῶν εὐχῶν πρὸς θεὸν πυκνοὶ ἀναφέρονται. διὸ

---

235 ἐπτοήθη corr.: ἐπτωήθη ΟΑ   251 πεφόβημαι corr.: πεφόβημε ΟΑ

rational faculty, "my heart was terrified and trembling penetrated my bones."

19. It can happen that the man who prays with his lips and sings psalms with his tongue, inasmuch as he associates with evil in his heart, draws near to God with his lips, but in his heart is far from him.[33] Wherefore, struck with fear at this secret association with the enemy, while I was ordained to be a partaker of divinity, my strength was troubled within me. And, in turn, I found rest and relief from my many afflictions when I was instructed through guarding my mind that the descent of God the Word to man has this purpose, namely, to free the rational faculty of the soul from irrational servitude to the passions and to bestow upon man once again the power taken from him by the enemy so that he may stand valiantly against sin and serve the living God in purity. And so I make my ascent through the incarnation of the Son of God to the denial of carnal pleasures and I am released from the bonds of pleasure.

20. If, when I heard mystically a voice telling me of the divine incarnation, I was struck with fear because of the unbearable power of the Godhead, I, in turn, fell into ecstasy over the boundless riches of the divine goodness, when I considered the works of this saving economy. Vigilance is the way of God and a path to the truth. David and Isaiah teach this, the one praying to be led to it and the other exhorting the people to prepare for it. "Lord, guide me in your way and I shall walk in your truth."[34] "A voice of one crying in the wilderness, 'Prepare the way of the Lord, make his paths straight.'"[35] For if the preparations have been made for the guarding of the heart in the mind, the powers of the soul are seen to be the straight paths of the Lord. The Lord our God is upright and "his face beheld righteousness."[36]

21. Vigilance is the house of God and the spouse of prayer. "I will come into your house with whole burnt offerings; I will pay you my vows, which my lips uttered and my tongue spoke in my affliction," as David says.[37] The soul enters upon the guarding of the mind when all its thoughts are utterly consumed by the fire of divine love, and when these are burned whole on the altar of vigilance by divine love

---

[33] Cf. Is 29:13, Mt 15:8, Mk 7:6.
[34] Ps 85:11.
[35] Is 40:3.
[36] Ps 10:7.
[37] Ps 65:13-14.

καὶ ὁ προφήτης κατευθυνθῆναι τὴν προσευχὴν αὐτοῦ ὡς θυμίαμα
270 παρακαλεῖ· *κατευθυνθήτω ἡ προσευχή μου ὡς θυμίαμα ἐνώπιόν σου.* ὡς
γὰρ τὸ θυμίαμα ἐκ πολλῶν εἰδῶν μυριστικῶν σκευαζόμενον μίαν
σύγκρατον ἐκπέμπει εὔπνοιαν, οὕτω καὶ ἡ ψυχὴ τὰς διαφόρους ἀρετὰς
ἀναματτομένη πρὸς ἑαυτὴν εἰς μονολόγιστον ἔννοιαν τῆς ἀγάπης
συνάγεται.
275   **22.** Ὡς γὰρ ἡ τῶν παθῶν ἕξις τὰς τῆς ψυχῆς δυνάμεις πρὸς τὰς
ἐπιθυμίας τοῦ κόσμου τούτου διασκορπίζει, οὕτως ἡ φύσις τῶν ἀρετῶν
συνάγει ταύτας πρὸς τὴν θείαν ἀγάπην, ὡς μήτηρ τὰ ἑαυτῆς τέκνα.
τὸ θυμίαμα ἔξω τοῦ πυρὸς μένων ὀλίγην ἔχει τὴν εὐωδίαν, ἐμβληθὲν
δὲ τοῖς ἄνθραξι δαψιλῶς ἡδύνει τῶν παρεστώτων τὴν αἴσθησιν, ὡς
280 τῆς ὀσμῆς διὰ τοῦ καπνοῦ ἐμπιπτούσης ταῖς τούτων ὀσφρήσεσι. καὶ
ἡ ψυχὴ ἔξω τῆς θείας ἀγάπης διατρίβουσα οὐκ εὐαρεστεῖ τῷ θεῷ.
ἡνίκα δὲ οἱ φωτοειδεῖς αὐτῆς λογισμοὶ τῷ θυμιατηρίῳ τῆς καρδιακῆς
ἡσυχίας προσχωρήσωσιν αὐτίκα τῷ πυρὶ τῆς ἀγάπης ἐκκαίεται καὶ
ὅλη ἀνωφερὴς καὶ μετάρσιος γίνεται, ἐνδημοῦσα γὰρ διὰ τῆς
285 γνώσεως τῷ θεῷ, ἐκδημεῖ τῶν τερπνῶν τοῦ παρόντος βίου διὰ τὸ
μηδεμίαν προσπάθειαν ἔχειν πρὸς τὰς τῶν αἰσθήσεων σχέσεις.
   23. Νῆψις καὶ γρηγοροῦντος τοῦ σώματος καὶ καθεύδοντος τὴν
καρδίαν ἐξυπνίζει καὶ φωτίζει κατὰ τὸν λέγοντα· *ἐγὼ καθεύδω καὶ
ἡ καρδία μου ἀγρυπνεῖ.* μαρτυρεῖ τοῦτο καὶ Ἰακὼβ μετανάστης γινό-
290 μενος καὶ ἐπὶ τοῦ ἐδάφους ἀνακλινόμενος καὶ κλίμακα ὀπτευόμενος,
ἀγγέλους ἔχουσαν ἀναβαίνοντας καὶ καταβαίνοντας. ἡνίκα γὰρ ἡ
ψυχὴ ξενιτεύσῃ ἀπὸ τῆς τῶν αἰσθητηρίων σχετικῆς οἰκειότητος καὶ
ἐν τῇ εὐνοίᾳ τῆς ταπεινοφροσύνης, ὡς ἀσκητικῇ εὐνῇ, ἁπλωθῇ καὶ
τὸ ἡγεμονικὸν αὐτῆς θήσῃ ἐν τῇ τοῦ Χριστοῦ πίστει, ὡς κεφαλὴν
295 ἐν λίθῳ, αἱ μὲν αἰσθήσεις τοῦ σώματος καθεύδουσι πρὸς τὴν τῶν
παρόντων ἀργοῦσαι διακονίαν, ἡ δὲ καρδία νήφουσα ἄγρυπνον
ποιεῖται τὸ ὄμμα τῆς ψυχῆς.
   24. Τότε ἡ φυλακὴ τῆς διανοίας ὡς κλίμαξ μετάρσιος ὁρᾶται,
ἐν ᾗ οἱ λογισμοὶ ὡς μὲν πονοῦντες τὰς ἀρετὰς καὶ πρὸς γνῶσιν τῶν
300 ἄνω ἐπεκτεινόμενοι ἀναβαίνουσι, καταβαίνουσι δὲ πάλιν ὡς ταπει-
νούμενοι διὰ τὴν τῆς φύσεως ἀσθένειαν. *νήψις προφητῶν παραγγελία·*
ἑτοιμάζου Ἰσραὴλ τοῦ ἐπικαλεῖσθαι τὸ ὄνομα κυρίου τοῦ θεοῦ σου.

---

278 εὐωδίαν corr.: εὐωδμίαν ΟΑ   290 ὀπτευόμενος corr.: ὀπταυόμενος Ο,
ὀπτανόμενος Α

thick clouds of prayers are borne upward to God. And so the prophet asks that his prayer be directed as incense: "May my prayer be directed as incense before you."[38] For as incense prepared from many kinds of fragrant substances gives off a single odour from the mixture, so too, when the soul takes upon itself the impressions of the different virtues, it is gathered together into the single thought of love.

22. As the habit of the passions disperses the powers of the soul among the desires of this world, so the nature of the virtues gathers these together unto divine love, as a mother does her children. Incense that remains outside the fire has little fragrance, but thrown upon the coals it gives abundant delight to the senses of those standing nearby, when the odour by means of the smoke falls upon their sense of smell. The soul that abides outside of divine love is not pleasing to God. But when the luminous thoughts of the soul approach the altar of the heart's tranquillity, the soul is immediately consumed by the fire of love and in its entirety soars upwards to the heights, for when it abides in God through knowledge, it departs from the pleasures of the present life because it has no attraction for the habits of the senses.

23. Both while the body is awake and while it is asleep, vigilance keeps the heart awake and illumines it, as scripture says, "I sleep and my heart wakes."[39] Jacob too bears witness to this; he left his country and lay down on the ground and saw a vision of a ladder with angels ascending and descending.[40] For when the soul exiles itself from its intimate relationship with the sense faculties and lies down on the goodwill of humility, as on the bed of asceticism, and lays its governing faculty on the faith of Christ, as Jacob lay his head on a rock,[41] the senses of the body sleep because they are not occupied with serving present needs, but the heart is vigilant and keeps the eye of the soul awake.

24. Then, the guarding of the discursive intellect appears like a ladder stretching upwards, on which the thoughts ascend by labouring at the virtues and reaching out toward knowledge of the things above, and descend again because they are humbled by the weakness of nature.[42] Vigilance is a precept of the prophets: "Be ready, Israel, to

---

[38] Ps 140:2.
[39] Cant 5:2.
[40] Gen 28:10-22.
[41] Gen 28:11.
[42] Gen 28:12. Cf. Hesychius, *On Vigilance and Virtue* 51, *Philokalia* 1:149 — "Vigilance is like Jacob's ladder."

Χριστοῦ ἐντολή· *γρηγορεῖτε καὶ προσεύχεσθε.* νῆψις ἐπήκοον ποιεῖται
τὸν θεὸν τοῦ ἀνθρώπου· *τῇ ἑτοιμασίᾳ τῆς καρδίας αὐτῶν, προσέσχε τὸ*
305 *οὖς σου·* Δαβὶδ ὁ μακάριος τοῦτο λέγει. τοὺς ταύτην ἀσπαζομένους
μακαρίζει Χριστός· *μακάριοι οἱ καθαροὶ τῇ καρδίᾳ, ἤγουν οἱ νήφοντες*
καὶ φυλάττοντες τὸν νοῦν· ἡ δὲ αἰτία, *ὅτι αὐτοὶ τὸν θεὸν ὄψονται.*
αὕτη ποθούμενον καὶ ζητούμενον ἀδιαλείπτως δῶρον, οὗ καὶ διψῶντες
τυχεῖν οἱ ἐφιέμενοι καθεκάστην εὔχονται οὕτως· *δώρησαι ἡμῖν ὁ θεὸς*
310 *γρήγορον νοῦν, σώφρονα λογισμόν, καρδίαν νήφουσαν, ὕπνον ἐλαφρόν καὶ*
πάσης σατανικῆς φαντασίας ἀπηλλαγμένον.

25. Ἡ καλοποιὸς αὕτη νῆψις τοὺς ταύτην φιλοῦντας ἀγαπᾷ· οἱ
δὲ ζητοῦντες αὐτὴν καὶ λέγοντες, *πότε ἥξεις πρὸς ἡμᾶς;*, εὑρήσουσιν
αὐτήν. ἐπιφαινομένη δὲ τοιαῦτα τοῖς ἐντυγχάνουσιν ὑποφωνεῖ· ἐγὼ
315 κρύπτομαι τοῖς νέφεσι τῆς ἀμελείας. ἐχθραίνει με ἡ ἀχλυοποιὸς λήθη.
ἀμαυροῖ με ἡ σκοτεινὴ ἄγνοια. διώκει με ἡ νεκροποιὸς ῥαθυμία.
ὀρθρίζω ἐν ἀπροσπαθεῖ νοΐ. ἀνατέλλω ἐν ἀφαντάστῳ διανοίᾳ.
ἐμφανίζομαι τερπνοτάτη ἐν πραείᾳ ψυχῇ. διαπορεύομαι ἐν ἀκακίᾳ
καρδίας. οὐ προτίθημι πρὸ ὀφθαλμῶν μου πονηρίαν· *προορῶ γὰρ τὸν*
320 *κύριον ἐνώπιόν μου διὰ παντός.* οἱ δὲ ἐμοῦ ἀλλότριοι ἐπανίστανται ἐπ᾽
ἐμὲ καὶ οὐ προτίθενται τὸν θεὸν ἐνώπιον αὐτῶν. οὐ προσκολλᾶταί μοι
καρδία σκαμβή. τὴν καταλαλιὰν ἐκδιώκω. ἑσπέρας καὶ πρωῒ καὶ
μεσημβρίας καὶ ἐν παντὶ καιρῷ σκοπεύω τὰς ὁδοὺς τῶν νοητῶν
ἐχθρῶν. καὶ διηγοῦμαι τῇ ψυχῇ τὰ ἐγκρύματα τῶν παθῶν καὶ
325 ἀπαγγέλλω τῷ νῷ τὴν κατ᾽ αὐτῶν νίκην· ἐγχειρίζω γὰρ τοῖς λογισμοῖς
τὸ ὅπλον τῆς εὐχῆς καὶ φωναῖς σιγηραῖς ὑπαγορεύω ψάλλειν αὐτοὺς
μετὰ Δαβίδ. *ὁ θεὸς ἡμῶν καταφυγὴ καὶ δύναμις, βοηθὸς ἐμπαθῶν*
ἐπαναστάσεσι ταῖς κινουμέναις καθ᾽ ἡμῶν σφόδρα. διὰ τοῦτο οὐ

---

311 ἀπηλλαγμένον corr.: ἀπηλαγμένον OA

call upon the name of the Lord your God."[43] It is a commandment of Christ: "Stay awake and pray."[44] Vigilance persuades God to listen to man: "Your ear attends to the readiness of their hearts," as blessed David says.[45] Christ blesses those who welcome it: "Blessed are the pure of heart," that is, those who are vigilant and guard the mind — and the reason, "because they shall see God."[46] This is the gift continuously longed for and sought after. Those who thirst after and long to attain it offer this prayer daily: "May God grant us a wakeful mind, chaste thoughts, a vigilant heart and a light sleep free of all satanic phantasy."[47]

25.   This beneficent vigilance loves those who befriend it, and those who seek after it, saying, "When will you come to us?,"[48] will find it. When it appears it will respond to those who encounter it with such answers as this: I am concealed by the clouds of indifference. Alienating forgetfulness sets me at enmity. Darkling ignorance obscures me. Death-purveying sloth hunts me down. I rise early in the mind free of passions. I dawn in the discursive intellect that is not governed by the imagination. In the gentle soul my manifestation brings the greatest delight. I make my paths in the heart that is free of evil. Wickedness I set not before my eyes.[49] "I keep the Lord always in my sight."[50] "My enemies rise up against me and they have not God before them."[51] "A crooked heart does not cling to me."[52] I drive away slander. Evening, morning, noonday and at all times I search out the paths of my spiritual enemies.[53] I tell the soul of the ambushes set by the passions and I announce to the mind the way of victory against them. I set the shield of prayer in the hands of the thoughts and I command them with silent voices to sing psalms with David. "God is our refuge and strength,"[54] a help against the fierce rebellion of the

---

[43] Am 4:12.

[44] Mt 26:41, Mk 14:38.

[45] Ps 9:38.

[46] Mt 5:8.

[47] From the prayer, καὶ δὸς ἡμῖν, δέσποτα, πρὸς ὕπνον ἀπιοῦσιν, which is said before retiring in the evening. It is found in the office of the Μικρὸν Ἀπόδειπνον and is sometimes attributed to the monk Antiochos. It can be found in the prayer book known as the *Horologion*.

[48] Ps 100:2.

[49] Cf. Ps 100:2-3.

[50] Ps 15:8.

[51] Ps 53:5.

[52] Ps 100:4.

[53] Cf. Ps 54:18.

[54] Ps 45:2.

φοβηθησώμεθα ἐν τῷ προσβάλλειν τὴν κακίαν καὶ πειρᾶν ἀποστῆσαι
330 ἡμᾶς τῆς Ἰησοῦ γλυκύτητος καὶ μεταθεῖναι εἰς ὀρέξεις σαρκικὰς καὶ
ἔρωτας κοσμικούς· *ἡμῖν γὰρ τὸ προσκολλᾶσθαι τῷ θεῷ ἀγαθόν ἐστι,*
τίθεσθαι ἐν κυρίῳ τὴν ἐλπίδα σωτήριον ἡμῖν ἐστιν.

26. Ἐπειδὴ ᾗ ὥρᾳ χωρισθῶμεν τῆς μνήμης τοῦ κυρίου ὑπακού-
σαντες τοῖς ἐχθροῖς δαίμοσι, τηνικαῦτα θανατούμεθα, ὅτι *οἱ μακρύν-*
335 *οντες ἑαυτοὺς ἀπ᾽ αὐτοῦ ἀπολοῦνται,* ταῦτα τοῖς εὑρίσκουσί με ὑπᾴδειν
εἰσηγοῦμαι καὶ πράττειν. τοιγαροῦν οἱ βουλόμενοι ἔλθετε πρός με
καὶ φάγετε πόνους τῶν ἐμῶν ἀρετῶν, πίετε οἶνον κατανύξεως καὶ
πένθους, ἀπολίπετε κτήσεις πραγμάτων καὶ ἡδονὰς σαρκὸς καὶ
κόπους ματαίους καὶ φροντίδας ἀνωφελεῖς. ζητήσατε πτωχείαν καὶ
340 κακοπάθειαν καὶ θλίψεις διὰ Χριστόν. κτήσασθε πραότητα καὶ πεῖναν
δικαιοσύνης, ἵνα ἐπιλάμψῃ ὑμῖν τῶν λογισμῶν ἡ εἰρήνη. ἀπαλείψατε
ἀπὸ τῶν καρδίων ὑμῶν τὰ τῶν παθῶν μορφώματα καὶ σχήματα καὶ
ἐγγράψατε εἰς τὰς διανοίας ὑμῶν τὸ τοῦ Χριστοῦ ὄνομα, ὅπως ἂν
μορφωθῇ Χριστὸς ἐν ὑμῖν, κληρονόμους θεοῦ καὶ συγκληρονόμους
345 αὐτοῦ ἐργαζόμενος ὑμᾶς.

27. Ἐπάρατε τοὺς λογισμοὺς ὑμῶν ἀπὸ τῆς μερίμνης τῶν σωματικῶν καὶ βλέψατε πρὸς τὴν μελέτην τῶν πνευματικῶν· τοῦ περιω-
νύμου Δανιὴλ ἀκούετε, *ἦρα τοὺς ὀφθαλμούς μου, λέγοντος, καὶ εἶδον.*
τὴν σωφροσύνην ἀγαπήσατε καὶ τὴν ἁγνείαν· οἱ γὰρ ὀφθαλμοί μου
350 ἐπὶ τοὺς ἠσφαλισμένους τῇ πίστει τοῦ μὴ ἀκολάστως ἀτενίζειν τοῖς
προσώποις τῶν γυναικῶν. ὁ ἐν τῇ ὁδῷ τῆς τῶν ἐντολῶν ἐργασίας
πορευόμενος οὗτός μοι λειτουργεῖ. ὁ ψευδόμενος καὶ ὑβρίζων καὶ
ὁ μνύων οὐ διακονεῖ μοι· ἐπὶ δὲ ἀργολογίαις οὐ συνήδομαι. εἰς τὰς
ἀναδιδομένας πρωτονοίας τῆς πονηρᾶς ἐπιθυμίας ἀποκτέννω πάντα
355 τὰ αἰσχρὰ πάθη· τὰς προσβολὰς γὰρ ὁρῶσα καὶ διακωλύουσα, οὐ
συγχωρῶ κινηθῆναι τοὺς λογισμούς. ἡνίκα γὰρ αἱ εἰκόνες τῶν
λογισμῶν τυπωθῶσι, τῆς διανοίας ἡ συγκατάθεσις γέγονε καὶ ἡ ψυχὴ
ὡς δούλη τοῖς ἐχθροῖς ἠχμαλώτευται καὶ ἐγὼ τῆς ἐμῆς ἀπελήλαμαι

---

329 προσβάλλειν conieci: προσβάλλ[...] textus mutilus in O; προσβάλλεται Α
338 ἀπολίπετε corr.: ἀπολίπεται ΟΑ   350 ἠσφαλισμένους corr.: ἠσφαλιμένους
ΟΑ

passions against us. On account of this, let us not fear when evil attacks and tries to distance us from the sweetness of Jesus and convert us to the desires of the flesh and love for the things of this world, for "it is good for us to cleave to God and it is our lot to place our hope of salvation in the Lord."[55]

26. The moment we have separated ourselves from the remembrance of the Lord and given ear to the hostile demons, we straightaway bring death upon ourselves, because "those who distance themselves from him shall perish."[56] I propose to sing accompaniment and do these things for those who find me. Therefore, you who are willing, come to me and partake[57] of the labours of my virtues, drink the wine of compunction and mourning, abandon the acquisition of things, the pleasures of the flesh, vain toils and worthless thoughts. Seek after poverty, mortification and afflictions for the sake of Christ. Acquire gentleness and thirst for righteousness in order that peace may shine upon you in your thoughts.[58] Wipe your hearts clean of the impressions and forms left by the passions, and engrave upon your discursive intellect the *Name of Christ* that Christ may leave his impress upon you[59] and make you "heirs of God and co-heirs with him."[60]

27. Raise your thoughts from anxiety over bodily matters and look to the study of spiritual things. Listen to the famous Daniel, "I lifted my eyes and I saw."[61] Love chastity and purity, for my eyes are upon those who are secure in their faith so that they will not gaze lustfully upon women's faces.[62] The person who serves me is the one who walks in the path of working at the commandments.[63] He who deals falsely, commits insults and swears oaths does me no service; I take no pleasure over idle chatter. At the first promptings of evil desire I slay all the shameful passions, for in noting and preventing temptations, I do not permit the thoughts to be moved. When the images of thoughts leave their impress, there has been an assent of the discursive intellect; the soul is taken captive as a slave to its enemies and I am banished from

---

[55] Ps 72:28.
[56] Ps 72:27.
[57] Cf. Prov 9:5-6.
[58] Cf. Mt 5:6.
[59] Cf. Gal 4:19.
[60] Rom 8:17.
[61] Dan 10:5.
[62] Cf. Sir 9:8.
[63] Cf. Ps 118:1.

χώρας. τοῦτο οὖν εἰδυῖα ἵσταμαι κατὰ τῆς φαντασίας τὸν συνδυασμὸν
360 αὐτῆς ἀποστρεφομένη.

28. ῾Ορῶσα δὲ πονοῦσαν οὕτως ἐμὲ ἡ ἐμὴ σύζυγος εὐχὴ συνάπ-
τεταί μοι αὐτίκα, πάνυ γάρ με φιλεῖ, ὡς τῶν κλεπτῶν καθυλακτοῦσαν
καὶ τὸν οἰκοδεσπότην νοῦν ἐξυπνίζουσαν, ἧς τῇ ἀκαταμάχῳ δυνάμει
ἐξολοθρεύονται ἐκ τῆς πιστῆς ψυχῆς οἱ ἐργαζόμενοι τὴν ἀνομίαν
365 πάντες λογισμοὶ μετὰ τῆς φαντασίας αὐτῶν. ἰδοὺ τὰς μυστικὰς ἐμὰς
ὁδοὺς ἐφανέρωσα. βαδίσατε ἐν αὐταῖς, πνεῦμα γὰρ θεοῦ ἡγεῖται
αὐτῶν, καὶ ὁ βαίνων ἐν αὐταῖς πνεύματι θεοῦ ἄγεται· ὁ δὲ ἀγόμενος
πνεύματι υἱὸς θεοῦ γίνεται· *ὅσοι γάρ, φησί, πνεύματι θεοῦ ἄγονται, οὗτοί
εἰσιν υἱοὶ θεοῦ.*

370 **29.** Ἀλλὰ προκυψάτω ἀφ᾽ ὑψηλοῦ τῆς καθαρότητός που καὶ αὕτη
ἡ βασιλὶς τῶν ἀρετῶν εὐχὴ καὶ πρὸς τοὺς ἑαυτῆς ὑποφόρους τὰ
ἑαυτῶν ἀποδυσαμένους καὶ αὐτὴν ἐνδυσαμένους δημηγορείτω τὰ
ἑαυτῆς. ἐγὼ διαναπαύω τοὺς ἀσκητὰς ἀπὸ τῶν τοῦ σώματος κόπων·
τοῖς γὰρ ἐμοὶ δασμοφοροῦσι τοὺς τῆς ψυχῆς καὶ τοῦ σώματος πόνους
375 τοὺς τοῦ πνεύματος καρποὺς ἀντιμισθοῦ παρέχω· δι᾽ ὧν ἀνώτεροι
δαιμόνων ἐπηρείας γίνονται, οἱ τούτων καταξιούμενοι. ἐγώ εἰμι ὁ
ἀγρὸς ὁ κεκρυμμένος, ὃν κτῶνται οἱ ἀποκτώμενοι πάντα τὰ τοῦ
κόσμου προθύμως· ἐγὼ νοῦν ἐξιστῶσα τῆς τῶν παρόντων αἰσθήσεως,
διακόπτων κεφαλὰς δυναστῶν, εἴτουν παθῶν φαντασίας, δυναστευ-
380 όντων τῇ ψυχῇ πρὸς συγκατάθεσιν τῆς ἁμαρτίας.

30. Ἐγώ εἰμι τὸ πῦρ ὃ ἦλθε βαλεῖν ὁ κύριος, ἀναπτομένη ἐν τοῖς
ἀΰλοις ἐνύλοις. ἐγὼ κατ᾽ ἐχθρῶν ἀμυντήριον· *πάντα τὰ ἔθνη ἐκύκλωσάν
με καὶ τῷ ὀνόματι κυρίου ἠμυνάμην αὐτούς.* ἐγὼ διδάσκαλος τῆς τοῦ
Χριστοῦ γνώσεως· *ἐν ᾗ ἂν ἡμέρᾳ ἐπικαλέσωμαί σε, ἰδοὺ ἔγνων ὅτι θεός
385 μου εἶ σύ.* ἐγὼ παραμυθία τῶν ἀθυμούντων· *εὐθυμεῖ τις; ψαλλέτω. ἀθυμεῖ
τις; προσευχέσθω.* ὁ ἡσυχάζων ἀπὸ παντὸς λογισμοῦ συλλαλεῖ μοι.
ὁ σιωπῶν ἀκούει μου. ὁ μὴ ῥεμβόμενος τοὺς ὀφθαλμοὺς φυλάσσει
με· ὁ γὰρ ἔρως τῶν σωματικῶν ὄψεων συλᾷ τοῦ ἐμοὶ προσομιλοῦντος

my country. Therefore, with this knowledge I take my stand against the imagination to divert collusion with it.

28. When prayer, my spouse, sees me labouring so, she joins herself to me immediately, for she loves me very much, because I bark at thieves and awaken the mind, who is the master of the household; by her invincible power all thoughts that work their wickedness, together with their imaginings, are completely eliminated from the faithful soul. Behold, I have revealed my mystic paths. Walk in them, for the Spirit of God governs them, and he who travels them is led by the Spirit of God, and he who is led by the Spirit becomes a son of God. For scripture says, "All who are led by the Spirit of God are sons of God."[64]

29. But let prayer, this queen of the virtues, stoop down from the heights of purity and speak publicly to her subjects who have stripped off their own garments and have clothed themselves in hers. I allow ascetics to rest awhile from the toils of the body, for to those who pay me the tribute of the labours of their soul and body I provide the fruits of the Spirit as a reward,[65] whereby those deemed worthy of these transcend the capricious treatment of demons. I am the hidden field acquired by those who eagerly divest themselves of all the goods of the world.[66] I am the one who diverts the mind from the perception of present realities, cutting off the heads of the mighty,[67] that is, phantasies associated with the passions that prevail upon the soul to consent to sin.

30. I am the fire which the Lord came to cast upon the earth,[68] now enkindled in material beings who have freed themselves from matter. I am a bulwark against enemies: "All the nations have surrounded me and in the Lord's name I warded them off."[69] I am the teacher of the knowledge of Christ: "On the day when I call upon you, behold I know that you are my God."[70] I am the consolation of the disheartened: "Is anyone cheerful? Let him sing psalms. Is any disheartened? Let him pray."[71] He who seeks tranquillity from all

---

[64] Rom 8:14.
[65] Cf. Gal 5:23.
[66] Theoleptos is presumably referring to the parable of the treasure hidden in the field (Mt 13:44).
[67] Hab 3:14.
[68] Lk 12:49.
[69] Ps 117:10.
[70] Ps 55:10.
[71] Cf. Jas 5:13.

τὸν ἔρωτα. ὁ διὰ θεωρίας ἀπλανοῦς ὁδεύων ἐν ἐμοὶ μένει, κἀγὼ ἐν
390 αὐτῷ. οὗτος φέρει καρπὸν ἀγαθωσύνης, πραότητος, ἐπιεικείας, ταπεινοφροσύνης, πίστεως, ἐγκρατείας καὶ τῶν ἄλλων χαρισμάτων. ὁ
δὲ μὴ συνὼν μετ' ἐμοῦ ἐβλήθη ἔξω τῆς θείας γνώσεως καὶ διεβλήθη
ὡς ὑπερήφανος καὶ ἐσκοτίσθη ὡς ἀκάθαρτος· ὃν λαμβάνουσιν οἱ
λογισμοὶ τοῦ κόσμου καὶ εἰς τὸ πῦρ τῶν σαρκικῶν ἡδονῶν βάλλουσι
395 καὶ καίεται. φλογίνη γάρ εἰμι καὶ στρεφομένη ρομφαία ἐν τῷ συνεχῶς
στρέφεσθαί με καὶ ἐκχέεσθαι ἐν τῇ καρδίᾳ ἐνθυμήσεσιν ἀλαλήτοις
καὶ ὑψοῦσθαι κατὰ τῶν πολεμουσῶν ἐννοιῶν, τὰς μὲν γνωστικὰς
δυνάμεις τῆς ψυχῆς διαφυλάττουσα, τὰς δὲ ἐπιθυμίας τῶν παρερχομένων καλῶν φλογίζουσα· καὶ τὸν μὲν ἐκκακοῦντα πρός με καὶ τοὺς
400 ἐμοὺς κόπους δι' ἐλπίδος καὶ ὑπομονῆς μὴ καταδεχόμενον ἔξω
ποιουμένη τῆς μακαρίας ζωῆς· τὸν δὲ ἐπιγινώσκοντά με καὶ προσ-
πίπτοντα καὶ ποθοῦντα ἀδιαλείπτως συνεῖναι μετ' ἐμοῦ διὰ τῆς
διηνεκοῦς μετανοίας καὶ καταδοχῆς τῶν θλιβερῶν καὶ τῶν πολλῶν
πειρασμῶν ἓν πνεῦμα τιθεμένη μετὰ τοῦ κυρίου.

405　**31.**　Εἰ γὰρ καὶ νέκρωσιν ποιοῦμαι τῶν σαρκικῶν κινημάτων, ἀλλὰ
καὶ ζώωσιν ἐργάζομαι τῶν τῆς ψυχῆς νοημάτων. πτῶσίς εἰμι τῶν
θελόντων ἐμοῦ ἐκπίπτειν καὶ ἀνάστασις τῶν ἱσταμένων ἐν ἐμοὶ καὶ
τὸν θεὸν δυσωπούντων καὶ ρῆμα ἀντιλεγόμενον πρὸς τὰ πνεύματα
τῆς κακίας. τὸ γὰρ *Κύριε Ἰησοῦ* ἀνενδότως φθεγγομένη ἐν τῷ βάθει
410 τῆς ψυχῆς, οἰκειοῦμαι τὸν νοῦν ὅλον καὶ τοὺς λογισμοὺς τῆς ψυχῆς
εἰς τὴν ἐμὴν θεωρίαν καὶ ὑπαγορείαν, καὶ εὑρίσκομαι ἀντιλέγουσα
τοῖς ἀλόγοις πάθεσι καὶ ταῖς κοιναῖς φροντίσιν.

　　32.　Ἡμέρα εἰμὶ κυρίου πεποιημένη ὑπ' αὐτοῦ, ὡς τὴν ἐπίκλησιν
ἐνεργοῦσα τοῦ πολυποθήτου ὀνόματος αὐτοῦ, εὐφραίνουσα πάντας
415 τοὺς εἰς ἐμὲ ὁρῶντας πάντοτε· ὃν καὶ ὁ προφήτης ὑποδεικνύει τοῖς
λαοῖς λέγων, *αὕτη ἡμέρα ἣν ἐποίησεν ὁ κύριος· ἀγαλλιασώμεθα καὶ*
εὐφρανθῶμεν ἐν αὐτῇ· καὶ πάλιν, ἐν ἐκείνῃ τῇ ἡμέρᾳ ἀπολοῦνται πάντες

thoughts holds converse with me. He who keeps silence hears me. He who does not allow his eyes to roam preserves me, for the love of bodily sights despoils the love of the one who converses with me. He who travels the way of unwavering contemplation abides in me and I in him. He bears the fruit of goodness, gentleness, forbearance, humility, faith, continence and the other gifts.[72] But he who is not in my company has fallen from divine knowledge: he has been discredited in his arrogance and has entered the darkness of impurity. The thoughts of the world seize him and cast him into the fire of the pleasures of the flesh and he is consumed.[73] For I am a fiery and turning sword as I turn constantly and pour myself out into the heart by means of ineffable ideas and am exalted against hostile thoughts.[74] I preserve the soul's powers of knowing but consume with fire the desires for passing goods. He who wearies of me and does not accept my labours in hope and patient endurance, I exclude from the blessed life; but he who comes to know me and falls down in supplication and continuously desires to be with me through unceasing repentance and acceptance of many oppressive trials, I make one spirit with the Lord.[75]

31.   For if I bring about the mortification of the movements of the flesh, I also effect the vivification of the thoughts of the soul. I am the downfall of those who would fall away from me, and the resurrection of those who stand by me entreating God, and a word that opposes the spirits of evil. Ceaselessly uttering the *Jesus Prayer* in the depths of the soul, I conform the entire mind and the thoughts of the soul to contemplation of me and my recitation of the prayer and I find myself able to oppose the irrational passions and vulgar notions.

32.   I am the day that the Lord has made, since I work at the *Invocation of his much loved Name*, gladdening all who have their gaze always fixed on me. This is what the prophet points out to the people when he says, "This is the day which the Lord has made. Let us rejoice and be glad in it."[76] And again, "On that day all their plans

---

[72] Cf. Jn 15:5, Gal 5:23.

[73] Cf. Jn 15:5-6.

[74] Cf. Gen 3:24. Cf. Hesychius, *On Vigilance and Prayer* 176, *Philokalia* 1:169 — "Let us hold fast, therefore, to prayer and humility, for together with vigilance they act like a fiery sword against the demons."

[75] Cf. 1 Cor 6:17.

[76] Ps 117:24.

οἱ διαλογισμοὶ αὐτῶν. καὶ γὰρ ἀληθῶς ἐμοῦ φωτοβολούσης ἐν ταῖς ψυχαῖς τῶν πιστῶν, οἱ διαλογισμοὶ τοῦ κοσμικοῦ φρονήματος ἐξ
420 αὐτῶν ἀφανίζονται, εἰς ἀθάνατον γὰρ κόσμον μεθίστημι αὐτούς, τυποῦσα ἐν αὐτοῖς τὴν εὐφροσύνην τῶν ἀπορρήτων ἀγαθῶν.

33. Ἐμὲ ἰδὼν Ἀβραὰμ ἐχάρη. ὃ γὰρ ἐκεῖνος ἐν τύπῳ θεασάμενος ἠγαλλιάσατο τῇ ψυχῇ, τοῦτο ἐγὼ ἐν ἀληθείᾳ δείκνυμι τοῖς ἐμὲ ἀνολιγώρως ἀσπαζομένοις. Ἀβραὰμ γὰρ εἰς ὄρος ἀνελθὼν ἐπὶ τὸ
425 θυσιάσαι τὸν Ἰσαάκ, ἐπεὶ συμποδίσας αὐτὸν σφαγιάζειν ἔμελλεν, ὑπὸ ἀγγέλου διεκωλύθη· καὶ τὸν μὲν Ἰσαὰκ ζῶντα ἀπροσδοκήτως ἀπέλαβεν, ἀντ᾽ αὐτοῦ δὲ κριὸν ἐθυσίασε· καὶ τῷ τύπῳ τῶν πραγμάτων τούτων τὴν ἡμέραν τῆς τοῦ Χριστοῦ ἀναστάσεως ἐμυήθη, ὅθεν καὶ ἐχάρη τοσούτου μυστηρίου ἀποκάλυψιν εἰληφώς.

430 34. Κράτησον ἐμὲ ἀσφαλῶς, ἄνθρωπε, ἐν μυχοῖς σῆς καρδίας καὶ ὄψει ἐναργῶς τοῦ μυστηρίου φανέρωσιν. ἄνελθε προθύμως εἰς τὸν ἐμὸν σταυρὸν καὶ φθέγγου νοερῶς καὶ νηφαλέως ἐν τῇ σῇ διανοίᾳ τὸ ὄνομα κυρίου τοῦ θεοῦ σου· καὶ ἴδοις τότε τῆς μὲν ὀρθῆς κρίσεως τὸν λογισμὸν ὑπὸ τοῦ ταπεινόφρονος καὶ πιστοῦ νοὸς συμποδιζόμενον
435 καὶ ὑπακούοντα πρὸς ὑπηρεσίαν τῶν τοῦ θεοῦ θελημάτων, οὐ μὴν ἀναιρούμενον. οὐ γὰρ πέφυκεν ἡ τοῦ πνεύματος μάχαιρα τὸν καθαρὸν τῆς φύσεως λογισμὸν τῆς καρδίας ἐκτέμνειν, διασώζειν δὲ μᾶλλον καὶ συντηρεῖν· αὐτοῦ γὰρ ἀναιρουμένου, ὁ νοῦς τίνι συνεργῷ πρὸς τὰ κάλλιστα χρήσεται; τῆς δὲ ἀλόγου αἰσθήσεως καὶ φαντασίας τὴν
440 σφαλερὰν καὶ ὑπερήφανον κρίσιν ἀναιρουμένην τῇ διακρίσει τῆς ἀληθείας.

35. Ταύτης γὰρ νεκρωθείσης τῇ τομῇ τοῦ λόγου, ἡ μὲν αἴσθησις ὄργανον ἀρετῶν τῶν ἐν τοῖς σωματικοῖς μέλεσιν ἐνεργουμένων γίνεται· ἡ δὲ σφραγιζομένη φαντασία ἐν τῇ διανοίᾳ τύπους φέρει
445 τῶν ἐν τοῖς σχήμασι κεκρυμμένων λόγων καὶ διὰ θεωρίας φανερουμένων ἐν τῇ ψυχῇ. λύσις εἰμὶ τῶν πεπεδημένων τῇ ῥαθυμίᾳ, φῶς τῶν ὑπὸ ἀγνοίας τυφλουμένων, ἀνόρθωσις τῶν καταπιπτόντων, φύλαξ τῶν προσερχομένων ἐμοί, ἀγάπησις τῶν ἀπαρνουμένων τὰ τοῦ κόσμου, κραταίωσις τῶν ἀγαθῶν λογισμῶν.

424 ἀνολιγώρως corr.: ἀνολιγόρως ΟΑ

come to naught."[77] For when my light truly shines in the souls of the faithful, the plans of their worldly attitude vanish from them, for I transport them to a world of immortality, impressing upon them the joy of ineffable goods.

33. When Abraham saw me he rejoiced.[78] What Abraham saw as a type which gladdened his soul I show in truth to those who welcome me without neglect. For Abraham went up the mountain to sacrifice Isaac and when, after binding his feet, he was about to offer sacrifice, he was prevented by an angel. Unexpectedly, he got Isaac back alive and sacrificed a ram in his stead.[79] And by the type of these events he was initiated into the day of Christ's resurrection, wherefore he rejoiced at having received a revelation of this mystery.

34. Hold fast to me, friend, in the innermost reaches of your heart and you will see clearly the disclosure of the mystery. Mount eagerly upon my cross and utter spiritually and soberly in your discursive intellect the *Name of the Lord your God*. Then, may you see the thought of right judgement bound by a humble and faithful mind and obedient to the service of God's will, but this living sacrifice like that of Isaac is not taken from you. The sword of the Spirit does not exist to cut away from the heart the pure thought of nature;[80] rather, to preserve and keep it; for if this is removed, what helper will the mind have for the best pursuits? Rather, it is the perilous and arrogant judgement of irrational sense perception and imagination that is removed by the discernment of the truth.

35. For when wrong judgement has been put to death by the sword-cut of reason, sense perception becomes an instrument of the virtues which are at work in the members of the body.[81] And when the imagination has been slain in sacrifice, it bears in the discursive intellect the likenesses of the reasons hidden in the outward forms and made manifest in the soul by contemplation.[82] I am the loosing of those bound with the bonds of sloth, a light to those blinded by ignorance, the righting of those who fall, a guardian of those who approach me, the love of those who renounce the things of the world, the confirmation of good thoughts.

---

[77] Ps 145:4.
[78] Jn 8:56.
[79] Gen 22:1-19.
[80] Cf. Eph 6:17.
[81] I.e., ascetic praxis.
[82] Here Theoleptos seems to be referring to what Evagrius called θεωρία φυσική. See *Praktikos* 1 (sc 171:498-499 and n. 1).

450   **36.** Ὀρφανὸν νοῦν ξενιτεύοντα κόσμου καὶ ψυχὴν χηρεύουσαν
ἀπὸ σχέσεως σαρκικῆς ἀναλαμβάνω. ὁδὸν παθῶν καὶ λογισμοὺς
ὑπερηφανίας ἀφανίζω καὶ βασιλεύω ἐν καρδίαις ταπεινῶν. οἱ ἐμοῦ
ἄγευστοι χαρᾶς ἀλλότριοι, λύπης μέτοχοι, δισταγμοῦ, μικροψυχίας,
ἀμφιβολίας καὶ δειλίας πλήρεις τῆς ἀπὸ δαιμόνων καὶ θηρίων καὶ
455 ἀνθρώπων καὶ ἀλλοιώσεως στοιχείων καὶ διαφόρων νοσημάτων·
πολλάκις δὲ καὶ ἀπὸ σκιῶν ἀνθρωπίνων τὸ ἀσθενέστατον.

     37. Τινὲς εἰς τελείωσιν ἀρετῆς ὑπολαβόντες ἀρκεῖν τὰ τοῦ
σώματος ἔργα, εἰς κόπους ἑαυτοὺς ἐκδεδώκασιν, ἐμοῦ δὲ ἐπιθυμίαν
οὐκ ἐκτήσαντο. οὐκ ἴσασι γὰρ ὅτι ἡ νηστεία καὶ ἡ ἐγκράτεια καὶ
460 ἡ πτωχεία καὶ ἡ ξηροκοιτία καὶ ἡ ἀγρυπνία καὶ ἡ γονυκλισία καὶ
πάντα τἆλλα τὰ διὰ τοῦ σώματος ἐπιτελούμενα διὰ τοῦτο γίνονται,
ἵνα ἐμὲ κτήσονται τὴν βασιλίδα τῶν ἀρετῶν καὶ πύλην τῶν τοῦ
πνεύματος καρπῶν· ὅθεν καὶ ἐν τῇ ἐργασίᾳ αὐτῶν θαρρήσαντες καὶ
φροντίδα τῆς ἀγάπης καὶ τῆς μελέτης μηδ’ ὅλως ἐμοῦ θέμενοι, ἀλλ’
465 ὡς Ἰουδαῖοι τῷ γράμματι, καὶ αὐτοὶ τῇ αἰσθήσει ἐναπομείναντες, ἐμοῦ
καὶ τῶν δι’ ἐμοῦ χορηγουμένων κρυπτῶν ἀρετῶν τυχεῖν οὐκ
ἐσπούδασαν. ἐνόμισαν γὰρ ὅτι τὴν τελειότητα ἤδη κατέλαβον καὶ
ἀμέριμνοι γεγόνασιν, ὅθεν καὶ ὡς ἀμελέτητοι περὶ τὰς μείζους τῶν
ἀρετῶν διακείμενοι, ὑπὸ τῶν κρυπτῶν παθῶν τῆς κακίας ἐσυλήθησαν.

470   **38.** Ὁ γεωργὸς διὰ τὴν ἐλπίδα τοῦ θερισμοῦ χειμῶνος ἐν τῇ γῇ
καταβάλλει τὰ σπέρματα· καὶ ὁ ἀσκητὴς διὰ τὴν ἐπιπόθησιν τῆς ἐμῆς
μελέτης ποιεῖται τοὺς κόπους ἐν τῷ σώματι αὐτοῦ. ὁ μὲν σπείρων
καὶ μὴ θερίζων λιμῷ ἀπόλλυται· ὁ δὲ κοπιῶν τῷ σώματι καὶ μὴ
εὐχόμενος τῇ καρδίᾳ, οἱ κόποι αὐτοῦ ἀνωφελεῖς εὑρίσκονται· ἐκ τοῦ
475 συναμφοτέρου γὰρ ἑκατέροις ἡ ἡδονὴ ἀκολουθεῖ. ὡρίμασαν οἱ
καρποί, καὶ ἐπελθοῦσα χάλαζα ἢ πνευμάτων ἐναντίων σφοδρότης
τούτους διέφθειρε καὶ ὁ γεωργὸς πάντων πενέστατος φαίνεται.
πλεονάζουσι καὶ οἱ τοῦ σώματος κόποι, καὶ μὴ ἐπιτελουμένης εὐχῆς
ἐν τῇ ψυχῇ τῆς ἐνδυναμούσης τὸν ἀγωνιστὴν εἰς τὰ ἔργα καὶ
480 συντηρούσης αὐτὰ καὶ τὴν ψυχὴν ἐξυπνιζούσης εἰς μελέτην ἐννοιῶν
ἀγαθῶν, πνέουσιν οἱ ἄνεμοι τῆς ὑπερηφανίας καὶ τοῦ θυμοῦ καὶ τῆς
ὀργῆς καὶ τῶν ἄλλων παθῶν τῶν κινουμένων ἀφανῶς, καὶ διασπεί-
ρουσι τὴν ψυχὴν εἰς τόπους ἐννοίας καὶ φαύλας ἐνθυμήσεις· καὶ τότε
ὁ ἄνθρωπος ὁρᾶται πάντων ἐλεεινότερος.
485   **39.** Ἐὰν γὰρ μὴ ἐγὼ παραγένωμαι, οὐκ ἀναιροῦνται οἱ πονηροὶ
λογισμοί, οὐ κραταιοῦται ἡ καρδία, οὐ κτᾶται ἡ ψυχὴ τὴν εἰρήνην
καὶ τὴν χαρὰν τοῦ πνεύματος, οὐ καταπίνεται ὁ νοῦς ἐν τῇ γνώσει

36. I adopt the orphan mind that is an exile from the world and the soul that is widowed from attachment to the flesh. I destroy the way of the passions and arrogant thoughts and I rule over the hearts of the humble. Those who have not tasted of me are strangers to joy and partakers of grief, full of doubt, faint-heartedness, uncertainty and cowardice before demons, wild beasts, men, changes of the elements and various diseases, and they are often at their weakest before human shadows.

37. Some, having undertaken to ward off the works of the body to reach the perfection of virtue, have given themselves over to toils but did not acquire desire for me. They did not know that fasting, continence, poverty, sleeping on the ground, vigils, genuflections and all other acts performed through the body are done for this purpose, namely, in order to acquire me, the queen of the virtues and the gate of the fruits of the Spirit. Thus, since they placed their confidence in their own labours and failed to set their thought of their love and meditation entirely on me but remained on the level of sense perception, as the Jews remained on the level of the letter of the Law, they did not make haste to attain me and the hidden virtues to which I would lead them. They thought they had already acquired perfection and became careless, and so they showed no diligence in disposing themselves towards the greater virtues and were carried off by the hidden passions of wickedness.

38. In the hope of a winter harvest, the farmer casts seed upon the earth: with a desire to practise my ways the ascetic undertakes the labours of the body. He who sows but does not reap perishes of famine. As for the man who labours in body and does not pray in his heart, his labours are found to be worthless. For in each case pleasure follows from both the elements put together. The fruits ripened but the coming of a hailstorm or the violence of contrary winds destroyed them and the farmer appears as the poorest of all men. Bodily labours are multiplied, but when prayer is not offered in the soul to strengthen the contestant in his works and preserve them and keep the soul awake for meditation on good thoughts, then blow the winds of arrogance, irascibility, anger and the other passions which have hidden movements, and they scatter the soul to places of bad thoughts and bad notions. Then, the individual is seen to be the most pitiable of all men.

39. If I am not present, evil thoughts are not destroyed, the heart receives no strength, the soul does not acquire the peace and joy of the Spirit, the mind does not drink of the knowledge of God, it is

τοῦ θεοῦ, οὐκ ἐξηλοῦται ἀπὸ τῶν σχημάτων τοῦ κόσμου, οὐκ ἐνδύεται
τὴν ἀγάπην, οὐ κινεῖται ἐν τῇ σοφίᾳ, οὐκ εἰσέρχεται εἰς τὸ φρούριον
490 τῆς ταπεινοφροσύνης, οὐ λάμπει τῶν θαυμασίων θεωριῶν ἡ ἀνατολή,
οὐκ ἄλλο οὐδὲν τῶν ὑπὸ τοῦ θεοῦ δωρουμένων τελεῖται.

40. Τούτων γὰρ καὶ ἄλλων ἀπείρων καὶ ἀπορρήτων ἀγαθῶν τῶν
ἄνωθεν καταπεμπομένων ἐγὼ μεσίτης πέφυκα· κινοῦμαι γὰρ ἐν τῷ
τῆς γνώσεως λογισμῷ καὶ λαμβάνω τὰς τῆς φύσεως δυνάμεις εἰς
495 ἑαυτὴν καὶ ἐπιρρίπτω ταύτας εἰς τὴν δύναμιν τοῦ θεοῦ καὶ προσε-
δρεύειν αὐτῷ ἀναπείθω δι᾿ ἐλπίδος καὶ κάμπτω τὰ σπλάγχνα τοῦ
ἀγαθοῦ, καὶ ἡ τῆς ψυχῆς μετὰ τοῦ θεοῦ καταλλαγὴ γίνεται. καὶ αὐτίκα
αἱ φωτειναὶ νεφέλαι συνάγονται καὶ ὑετοὶ τῶν χαρισμάτων καταχέ-
ονται ἐν τῇ διανοίᾳ καὶ πληροῦται ἡ γῆ τῆς καρδίας γνώσεως
500 πνευματικῆς. τότε οἱ θεῖοι λόγοι πηγάζουσι δαψιλῶς, συντηροῦντες
τὰ μέλη τοῦ σώματος ἐν τοῖς κόλποις τῆς πρακτικῆς, τὰς δὲ αἰσθήσεις
τῆς ψυχῆς ἐν ταῖς γνώσεσι τῶν θείων θεωρημάτων.

41. Ἐμὲ ὑπεδήλου Ἰακὼβ ἡνίκα ὠδύρετο, προδοθέντος τοῦ παγ-
κάλου Ἰωσὴφ ὑπὸ τῶν ἀδελφῶν εἰς δουλείαν. ὁ γὰρ ἐμὲ κτησάμενος
505 καὶ τῆς ἐξ ἐμοῦ ἡδονῆς ἀπολαύσας, ἀπαράκλητα ὀδυνηθήσεται τὴν
καρδίαν, ὅταν ἴδῃ προδιδομένην με ὑπὸ τῶν αἰσθήσεων καὶ τῆς
μερίμνης τῶν ἀνθρωπίνων πραγμάτων καὶ ἐκλείπουσαν ἀπὸ τῶν
ὀφθαλμῶν τῆς ψυχῆς καὶ ἁρπαζομένην ἀπὸ τῶν ἀγκαλῶν τῆς
ἀγαπητικῆς δυνάμεως αὐτῆς. ἥλιος δύνει καὶ τίς ἡμέρα ἀνατελεῖ;
510 κἀγὼ ὑποχωρῶ τοῦ χωρήματος τῆς διανοίας καὶ τίς παρακαλέσει τὴν
ψυχήν; ἥλιος ἀνατέλλει καὶ φεύγει τὸ σκότος ἀπὸ προσώπου αὐτοῦ·
κἀγὼ ὑποφωνοῦμαι ἐν τῇ καρδίᾳ καὶ ὡσεὶ καπνὸς ἐκλείπουσιν οἱ
ἐπίβουλοι τῆς ψυχῆς. δύνοντος ἡλίου, τὸ στερέωμα μένει· ἐμοῦ δὲ
μὴ ἀνατελλούσης ἐν τῇ ψυχῇ καὶ ἡ στερρότης τῆς καρδίας παρέρ-
515 χεται· ἐγὼ γὰρ δωροῦμαι δύναμιν καὶ κραταίωσιν τοῖς λογισμοῖς καὶ
ἐγὼ πέφυκα τὸ τῆς ψυχῆς στερέωμα. οἱ τὴν σοφίαν τὴν κοσμικὴν
ἀγαπήσαντες ἐμὲ οὐκ ἔγνωσαν, οὐδὲ ἠγάπησαν, οὐδὲ ἐζήτησαν,
ἠρκέσθησαν γὰρ ἐν τοῖς λογισμοῖς τῆς γνώσεως αὐτῶν τῆς
ἀναδιδομένης ἐκ τῆς πολλῆς μαθήσεως, ὡς οἱ ἐν νυκτὶ περιπατοῦντες
520 ἐν τῷ τῆς σελήνης φωτὶ τῆς ἐνδεοῦς οὔσης καὶ ἐκλειπούσης.

42. Ἀλλ᾿ οἱ μέν, εἰ καὶ παραμυθοῦνται ὑπὸ τοῦ σεληνιακοῦ
φωτός, ἀλλ᾿ ὡς τὸ φῶς τῆς ἡμέρας ἐπεγνωκότες, ποθοῦσι τὴν
ἀνατολὴν τοῦ ἡλίου πρὸς τὸ ἐπιτελέσαι τὰ χρειώδη αὐτῶν, οὐ γὰρ
δύνανται τὰ τῆς ἡμέρας ἔργα νυκτὸς ἐκπληροῦν. οἱ δὲ ὑπὸ τῆς
525 γνώσεως ἐπαιρόμενοι τῆς βρυούσης τὴν φυσίωσιν καὶ ὑπὸ τῆς

---

493 πέφυκα corr.: πέφηκα OA   509 ἡμέρα corr.: ἡμέραν OA

not pried loose from the forms of this world, it is not clothed with love, it is not moved in wisdom, it does not enter the fortress of humility, the dawn of wondrous contemplations does not shine, nor is there granted any other gift of God.

40. I am the mediatrix of these and other infinite and ineffable goods sent down from above, for I am active in the thought that bestows knowledge; I take the powers of nature to myself and I commit them to the power of God; I persuade them to attend to him in hope and I bend the heart of goodness, and the soul is reconciled with God. Immediately, the radiant clouds gather, a shower of gifts pours down on the discursive intellect and the earth of the heart is filled with spiritual knowledge. Then the divine words gush forth abundantly to preserve the body's members in the bosom of the ascetic life and the senses of the soul in the knowledge of divine contemplations.

41. Jacob secretly referred to me when he lamented over the ever good Joseph, who had just been handed over to slavery by his brothers.[83] He who has acquired me and has enjoyed the pleasure that comes from me will experience inconsolable grief in his heart when he sees that I am being handed over by the senses and the worries of human affairs and eclipsed from the eyes of the soul and snatched away from the embraces of the faculty of love. The sun sets and what day will dawn? So too I withdraw from the place of the discursive intellect and who will comfort the soul? The sun rises and the darkness flees before its face. I call quietly in the heart and like smoke the soul's attackers depart. When the sun sets the firmament remains, but if I do not dawn in the soul steadfastness of heart passes away, for I bestow power and strength on thoughts and I am the firmament of the soul. Those who have loved the world's wisdom have not known me, nor have they loved or sought me, for they contented themselves with the thoughts of their own knowledge, which is bestowed by much learning, like those who walk about at nighttime in the moonlight, which is meagre and faint.

42. But, even though some are comforted by the moonlight, nevertheless, since they have known the light of day, they are eager for the rising of the sun so they can do their necessary business, for they cannot complete the works of the day during the night. But those who are buoyed by the knowledge that is puffed up with pride[84] and

---

[83] Gen 37:34-36.
[84] Cf. 1 Cor 8:1.

κενοδοξίας παρακαλούμενοι τὸ ἐμὸν οὐκ ἐπόθησαν, οὐδὲ ἐπενόησαν
θεάσασθαι φῶς· ὅθεν καὶ εἰς χεῖρας τῆς ὑπερηφανίας καὶ τῆς ὀργῆς
καὶ τῆς ζηλοτυπίας καὶ τῆς ἔριδος καὶ τῆς πολυλογίας παρεδόθησαν.
καὶ ὥσπερ οὐκ ἐκλείπει ἡ σελήνη τοῦ πληροῦσθαι καὶ λήγειν ἀλλ᾽
530 ὅτε πληρωθῇ ἄρχεται κενοῦσθαι, οὕτω καὶ οἱ τῇ θύραθεν σοφίᾳ
ἐπερειδόμενοι, τῆς οἰήσεως ὄντες ἀνδράποδα, πλοῦτον ἔχειν φαν-
τάζονται γνώσεως· οἱ δὲ ταῖς ἀληθείαις πένητες ὄντες διὰ τὸ μὴ ἔχειν
ἴχνος ταπεινώσεως τῆς ὑπ᾽ ἐμοῦ χορηγουμένης καὶ ἀψευδὲς φρόνημα
βασταζούσης.
535   **43.**   Ὅταν δόξωσι πεπληρῶσθαι γνώσεως, τότε μακρὰν εὑρίσκονται γνώσεως τῆς τὴν ἀγάπην φερούσης καὶ τὴν πραότητα τῆς
καρδίας· γνῶσις γὰρ ἡ τῇ τῆς δόξης ἐπιθυμίᾳ δουλουμένη καὶ τῇ
οἰήσει δουλεύουσα καὶ τῷ τύφῳ τῆς ὑπερηφανίας συνεζευγμένη, ὄφις
ἐστὶ φρονιμώτατος τοῦ κατὰ τὴν θείαν γνῶσιν φωτὸς ἠλλοτριωμένη
540 ὡς ἐκεῖνος τῶν λογικῶν, καὶ θάνατον ψυχῆς ἐργαζομένη, ὅπερ ἐστὶ
μακρυσμὸς ἐμῆς ἀνατολῆς καὶ δύσις γνώσεως θεοῦ.

44.   Καὶ ἵνα μάθῃς τί ἐστι ζωὴ ψυχῆς λογικῆς, ἄκουε τοῦ λόγου
τῆς ζωῆς· *αὕτη δέ ἐστιν ἡ αἰώνιος ζωή, ἵνα γινώσκωσί σε τὸν μόνον*
ἀληθινὸν θεὸν καὶ ὃν ἀπέστειλας Ἰησοῦν Χριστόν. ὁ λόγος τῆς σοφίας
545 τοῦ αἰῶνος τούτου τὴν καταργουμένην γνῶσιν φέρει τοῦ κόσμου,
τὴν γεννῶσαν τὰς ἀλόγους ἐπιθυμίας καὶ συγκρινομένην τῇ ὁμοιότητι
τῆς νυκτός. ὁ δὲ λόγος ὁ ὑπ᾽ ἐμοῦ δυσωπούμενος καὶ ὃν ἐγὼ δείκνυμι
τοῖς ἐμοὶ προσκαρτεροῦσι θεοῦ λόγος ἐστὶ καὶ θεός, τὴν τοῦ παναγίου
πνεύματος αὐτοῦ γνῶσιν δωρούμενος, τὴν πηγάζουσαν τὴν ἀνώλεθρον
550 ζωήν, τοὺς ποταμοὺς τῆς ἀγάπης καὶ τὸ ὕδωρ τῆς ἀναψύξεως, τὴν
βρύουσαν ἡμέραν ταπεινώσεως καὶ υἱοὺς ἡμέρας ποιουμένην τοὺς
διψῶντας αὐτήν.
45.   Ὥσπερ οὖν ὁ ἐν τῷ σκότει τῆς νυκτὸς περιπατῶν προσκόμματα ποδῶν ἔχει καὶ πλάνην ὁδοῦ πεφόβηται καὶ κλεπτῶν ἐπιθέσεις
555 καὶ θηρίων ὁρμὰς τῶν διερχομένων ἐν νυκτί, οὕτω καὶ ὁ τῇ ἀφροσύνῃ
τῆς γνώσεως ταύτης ἐπινηχόμενος τοῖς δικτύοις τῆς παμπτώτου
οἰήσεως καὶ τῆς τῶν παθῶν πτοήσεως, ὡς ἀφώτιστον λογισμὸν
κεκτημένος, συνέχεται. καὶ ὥσπερ ὁ ἐν τῷ φωτὶ τῆς ἡμέρας περιπατῶν
πάντων τῶν συμπτωμάτων ἐκείνων ἀπήλλακται, οὕτω καὶ ὁ ἐμὲ
560 συνεχῶς ὑπάδων ἐκ τῆς ἀπαντήσεως τῶν παθῶν οὐ πτοεῖται, ἀλλὰ

531 ἐπερειδόμενοι corr.: ἐπαιρειδόμενοι OA

are encouraged by vainglory do not desire nor even think of gazing upon my light. And so, they have been given over to the hands of arrogance, anger, jealousy, rivalry and garrulity. Just as the moon does not leave off growing full and then stop, but when it is full it begins to wane, so too those who devote all their attention to profane wisdom, being captives of conceit, imagine that they have a wealth of knowledge, but in reality they are impoverished of truth because they have not a trace of the humility which is bestowed by me and which brings with it a way of thought free of deceit.

43.   When they think they have acquired the fullness of knowledge, then they are far from the knowledge which is a bearer of love and gentleness of heart, for knowledge that is enslaved to desire for honour, that serves conceit and that is yoked to the smoke of arrogance is the serpent of great cunning who was exiled from the light of divine knowledge just as he was from rational beings;[85] this knowledge brings about the death of the soul, which means separation from my rising, and the setting of the knowledge of God.

44.   And that you may learn what is the life of the rational soul, listen to the Word of life: "And this is eternal life, that they know you the only true God, and Jesus Christ whom you have sent."[86] The word of wisdom that belongs to this age bears this world's knowledge, which passes away, which begets irrational desires and which is compared with the night. But the word which is won over by me and which I show to those who attend to me is the Word of God, yea, even God himself, who bestows the knowledge of his all-holy Spirit, which is a spring of indestructible life, rivers of love and the water of refreshment, and which issues forth the day of humility making those who thirst for it sons of the day.[87]

45.   Therefore, just as the person who walks in the darkness of night encounters obstacles at his feet and fears wandering from the path and being set upon by thieves or being attacked by wild animals that go about at night, so too the man who swims in the folly of this knowledge is caught in the nets of all-destroying conceit and the excitement of the passions, because he has got for himself a way of reasoning without light. And just as the man who walks about in the light of day is spared all those falls, the one who attends to me continuously is not distraught at the encounter with the passions, but

---

[85] I.e., Satan exiled from his place among the angelic beings.
[86] Jn 17:3.
[87] Cf. 1 Thes 5:5.

τῇ συνεχεῖ ἐπικλήσει τοῦ κυρίου Ἰησοῦ τῇ κρουομένῃ ὡς ἐν κιθάρᾳ
τῇ καθαρᾷ καρδίᾳ φυγαδεύει τὸν σάλον τῆς ἁμαρτίας ἐκ τῆς αὐτοῦ
ψυχῆς, ὡς ὁ Δαβὶδ διὰ τοῦ ψαλμοῦ ἐκ τοῦ Σαοὺλ τὸ δαιμόνιον καὶ
τῆς τοῦ πνεύματος γαλήνης ἐν ἀπολαύσει γίνεται.

565   **46.**   Μωσαϊκὴ ῥάβδος εἰμί, εὐθείᾳ καὶ πλαγίᾳ πληγῇ τοὺς μὲν ἐμὲ
φιλοῦντας διασώζουσα, τοὺς δὲ μισοῦντας διαφθείρουσα, κατεχομένη
γὰρ ἀσφαλῶς ὑπὸ τοῦ εὐσεβοῦς νοός. διὰ μὲν τῆς νήψεως τῆς τὴν
εὐθύτητα τῆς καρδίας ὑπαγορευούσης διάκρισιν ἐν τῇ ψυχῇ ποιοῦμαι,
τὸ χαῦνον τῆς θηλυδριώδους ἐπιθυμίας ῥηγνύουσα, τὸ δὲ στάσιμον
570   τοῦ ἀνδρώδους φρονήματος ἀνακαλύπτουσα καὶ ἄμικτον σχέσεως
σαρκικῆς διατηροῦσα· ἐν ᾧ οἱ λόγοι τῶν ἀρετῶν διερχόμενοι
ἄψαυστοι διαφυλάττονται καὶ τῶν ἀριστερῶν καὶ τῶν δεξιῶν τῆς
κακίας ὁρμημάτων. διὰ δὲ τῆς ταπεινώσεως τῆς πλαγίῳ καὶ ὑπο-
πεπτωκότι φρονήματι τυπούσης τὴν διάνοιαν, τοὺς ὑπερηφάνους
575   λογισμοὺς τοὺς μετὰ τὴν διόρθωσιν τῶν ἀρετῶν ὀπίσω διώκοντας
τῆς ψυχῆς καὶ αὐτὴν ἐπειγομένους χειρώσασθαι ὀλοθρεύω καὶ
ἀφανίζω. ἡ λογικὴ φύσις διὰ τὴν παράβασιν ἀπεβάλετο τὴν διάκρισιν
καὶ λογισμῷ ἑνὶ τῆς ἀλόγου ἐπιθυμίας ὁδηγουμένη διετέλει τὰ ἔργα
αὐτῆς.

580   **47.**   Ἀλλ' ὁ τοῦ θεοῦ λόγος, τὴν ἀποβληθεῖσαν διάκρισιν βουληθεὶς πάλιν τῇ ἡμετέρᾳ φύσει δωρήσασθαι ἐν τῇ ἐνανθρωπήσει
αὐτοῦ, διὰ Μωσέως εἰκόνισε τὴν μετὰ πολλὰ ἔτη δοθησομένην τῇ
τῶν ἀνθρώπων φύσει χάριν τῆς διακρίσεως καὶ προσέταξε τῷ Μωϋσεῖ
ἐξαγαγεῖν τὸν Ἰσραὴλ ἀπὸ τῶν Αἰγυπτίων καὶ διαχωρίσαι τὸν λαὸν
585   τὸν εἰδότα τὸν θεὸν ἀπὸ τῶν μὴ εἰδότων τὸν θεόν. ὁ γοῦν Μωϋσῆς
ἐξαγαγὼν ἀπὸ τῆς Αἰγύπτου τοὺς Ἰσραηλίτας καὶ τῇ διττῇ πληξει
τῆς ῥάβδου διαιρήσας καὶ ἑνώσας τὴν θάλασσαν, προδιετύπου τὴν
ἐς ὕστερον γενησομένην τῆς φύσεως κατάστασιν εὐδιάκριτον καὶ
πρὸς ἑαυτὴν πάλιν ἐπάνοδόν τε καὶ ἕνωσιν.

590   **48.**   Διὰ μὲν γὰρ τῆς διαιρέσεως τὴν ὑγρὰν ξηρὰν ἀπεργασάμενος,
δίοδον τοῖς Ἰσραηλίταις ἐχαρίσατο καὶ τῆς κατὰ φύσιν τῶν τῆς
ψυχῆς λογισμῶν κινήσεως τὴν εἰκόνα ἐν τούτῳ ἐνεχάραξε. διὰ δὲ
τῆς ἑνώσεως τὸ ὕδωρ ἐπαναστρέψας ἐπὶ τοὺς Φαραωνίτας ἐκάλυψεν
αὐτοὺς καὶ ἐσήμανε διὰ τούτου, ὅτι ἡ διὰ τῆς φύσεως ἔχθρα διὰ τῆς
595   κατὰ τὴν ἀγάπην ἑνώσεως ἀναιρεῖται. ταῦτα δὲ ὄψει ἐναργῶς
τελούμενα, ἐὰν μετὰ νήψεως προσαρμοσθῇς ἐμοὶ διόλου· τῆς γὰρ

by the continuous *Invocation of the Lord Jesus*, which is plucked by the pure heart like a harp, he chases from his soul the agitation of sin, as David chased the demon from Saul by a psalm, and enjoys calm of spirit.[88]

46. I am the rod of Moses, saving those who love me and destroying those who despise me with a straight and a sideways blow, for I am held securely by a pious mind.[89] First by the vigilance which dictates uprightness of heart I work discernment in the soul, shattering the frivolity of effeminate desire, while revealing the stability of a manly attitude and preserving it free of association with the flesh. The words of the virtues which pass through here are kept untouched by the attacks of wickedness from the left and from the right. Then by a humility which impresses the mind with a dependent and submissive attitude, I destroy and annihilate the arrogant thoughts that pursue the soul after the virtues have set it right and that press hard to capture it. Because of the transgression rational nature rejected discernment and goes about its works led by the one thought of irrational desire.

47. But when the Word of God by his incarnation decided to restore to our nature the discernment that we cast aside, he used Moses as an image of the grace of discernment that would be given to man's nature many years later: he ordered Moses to bring Israel out of Egypt and to separate the people who know God from those who do not know God. Thus, when Moses brought the Israelites out from Egypt and separated and united the sea with a twofold striking of his rod, he foreshadowed the state of nature endowed with good discernment that would appear later, as well as its return to and reunion with itself.[90]

48. By parting the sea he made what was wet into dry land and gave the Israelites a way through, thereby inscribing on this event the image of the natural movement of the soul's thoughts.[91] By uniting the sea he turned back the water upon the Pharaoh's men and covered them, thereby signifying that the enmity present through our nature is destroyed by the union of love.[92] You will clearly see these things come about, if you conform yourself entirely to me with vigilance,

[88] 1 Kingdoms 16:14-23.
[89] Cf. Ex 4:2-5.17, 14:16; Num 20:7-13.
[90] Ex 14:15-31.
[91] Ex 14:21-22.
[92] Ex 14:27-28.

ἐξ ἐμοῦ ἀναδιδομένης γνώσεως ἐκχεομένης ἐν τῇ ψυχῇ, οἱ τῆς φύσεως λογισμοὶ διακρινόμενοι ἀπὸ τῆς ὀρέξεως τῆς ἀλόγου τοῦ σκοτασμοῦ τῆς ἀγνωσίας ἐκλυτροῦνται. ἡ δὲ ψυχὴ εἰς ἀγάπην ἐρχομένη τοῦ
600 θεοῦ συνάπτεται καὶ πρὸς τὰς ἑαυτῆς δυνάμεις καὶ πρὸς τὰς ὑποστάσεις τῶν ἀνθρώπων καὶ γίνεται φιλόθεος καὶ φιλάνθρωπος ἡ ψυχή· ὅθεν λοιπὸν ἡ ἀναιρετικὴ τῆς φύσεως ἔχθρα, μὴ ἔχουσα ποῦ ποτε κινηθῆναι, ἐξαφανίζεται.

49. Μωϋσῆς προσευχόμενος ἐδυνάμωσεν Ἰησοῦν καὶ Ἀμαλὴκ
605 ἐτροπώσατο. καὶ νοῦς εὐχόμενος κραταιοῖ λογισμὸν καὶ καταβάλλει ἐπιθυμίαν. ἐμὲ ὡς ἄμαχον ὅπλον κατὰ παθῶν καὶ ὀχυρὸν φρούριον τῶν ἀρετῶν συνεχῶς ἀνελίσσει τῷ στόματι Δαβὶδ ὁ μακάριος λέγων· *ἐμνήσθην τοῦ θεοῦ καὶ ηὐφράνθην· ἐμνήσθην ἐν νυκτὶ τοῦ ὀνόματός σου, κύριε, καὶ ἐφύλαξα τὸν νόμον σου· μνησθήσομαι τοῦ ὀνόματός σου ἐν*
610 *πάσῃ γενεᾷ καὶ γενεᾷ· μνησθήσονται καὶ ἐπιστραφήσονται πρὸς κύριον πάντα τὰ πέρατα τῆς γῆς· τὰς εὐχάς μου ἀποδώσω ἐνώπιον τῶν φοβουμένων αὐτόν· ἐν ἐμοί, ὁ θεός, εὐχαὶ ἃς ἀποδώσω αἰνέσεώς σου.* καὶ ἵνα μὴ πλῆθος ἀναλέγωμαι στίχων, δίελθε τοὺς ψαλμοὺς καὶ μαθήσῃ περὶ ἐμοῦ.

615 **50.** Ὁ κύριος ἡμῶν Ἰησοῦς Χριστὸς τὰς μὲν ἡμέρας ἐν ταῖς συναγωγαῖς ἐδίδασκε τὸν λαόν, τὰς δὲ νύκτας ἀναχωρῶν ἐν τῇ ἐρήμῳ προσηύχετο. διὰ τοῦ κατὰ τὴν χήραν καὶ τὸν ἄδικον κριτὴν παραδείγματος προσκαρτερεῖν ἡμᾶς τῇ εὐχῇ νενομοθέτηκεν. ἐρχόμενος πρὸς τὸ ὑπὲρ ἡμῶν σωτήριον πάθος, συνεχῶς προσηύχετο.
620 οἱ ἀπόστολοι, *ἡμεῖς δὲ τῇ προσευχῇ καὶ τῇ διακονίᾳ τοῦ λόγου προσκαρτερήσωμεν,* ἔλεγον. ὁ θεῖος Παῦλος, *παρακαλῶ, προσκαρτερεῖτε τῇ εὐχῇ γρηγοροῦντες,* γράφει. ἡ ἐκκλησία ὑπὲρ τοῦ Πέτρου ἐν τῷ δεσμωτηρίῳ ὄντος προσηύχετο· *προσευχὴ γὰρ ἦν, φησίν, ἐκτενὴς ὑπὲρ αὐτοῦ γινομένη ἐν τῇ ἐκκλησίᾳ.* διὸ καὶ ὁ δέσμιος τοὺς αὐτὸν δεσμεύ-
625 σαντας δυνάμει κρείττονι καταδεσμεύσας, τοῦ δεσμωτηρίου λέλυται.

---

621 προσκαρτερεῖτε corr.: προσκαρτερεῖται OA   623 ὄντος corr.: ὄντως OA

for when the knowledge I grant is poured forth in the soul the thoughts of nature are distinguished from irrational desire and are redeemed from the darkness of ignorance. When the soul approaches love of God it is joined both to its own powers and to other human persons and the soul comes to love God and men. So then, because the destructive enmity of nature no longer has anywhere to move, it is annihilated.

49. By his prayer Moses strengthened Joshua and overturned Amalek[93] and by its prayer the mind fortifies thought and suppresses desire. Blessed David spoke constantly of me as an invincible shield against the passions and a strong fortress of the virtues, declaring, "I remembered God and I rejoiced";[94] "I remembered your name in the nighttime, O Lord, and I kept your law";[95] "I will remember your name in every generation";[96] "All the ends of the earth will remember and return to the Lord";[97] "My vows I will pay before those who fear him";[98] "In me are the vows which I will render in praise of you, O God."[99] And so that I need not collect a multitude of verses, go through the psalms yourself and learn of me.

50. During the day our Lord Jesus Christ instructed the people in the synagogues, while at night he retreated to the desert to pray.[100] Through the example of the widow and the unjust judge he has counseled us to persevere in prayer.[101] As he came to his saving passion on our behalf he prayed continuously.[102] The apostles used to say, "But let us devote ourselves to prayer and the ministry of the word."[103] The divine Paul writes, "I exhort you, continue steadfastly in prayer and watchfulness."[104] The church prayed for Peter when he was in prison, for scripture says, "Earnest prayer was made in the church on his behalf."[105] And so, the prisoner was delivered from prison, having by a greater power imprisoned those who had imprisoned him. The

[93] Ex 17:8-16.
[94] Ps 76:4.
[95] Ps 118:55.
[96] Ps 44:18.
[97] Ps 21:28.
[98] Ps 21:26.
[99] Ps 55:13.
[100] Mk 1:35, Lk 6:12.
[101] Lk 18:1-8.
[102] Lk 22:44.
[103] Acts 6:4.
[104] Col 4:2.
[105] Acts 12:4.

ἱεραρχῶν, διδασκάλων, ὁσίων, δικαίων, μαρτύρων καὶ πάντων τῶν
ἁγίων οἱ χοροὶ δι᾽ ἐμοῦ τετελείωνται.

51. Τινὲς δὲ ἀβλεψίᾳ ψυχῆς κρατηθέντες καὶ τῆς ἐμοῦ μὴ
γευσάμενοι χάριτος, μηδὲ γνόντες οἷα ἐν τῇ ψυχῇ χαρίζομαι ἀγαθὰ
630 ἀδιαλείπτως ἐνεργουμένῃ, ἐνυβρίζουσιν εἰς ἐμὲ καὶ τοὺς διὰ πτωχείας
κτήτορας τοῦ ἐμοῦ πλούτου γινομένους ἐξουθενοῦσιν. ἀλλ᾽ εἰ μὲν
ὀψέ ποτε τῆς τοιαύτης ἀπονοίας παύσονται καὶ πρὸς ἐμὲ καὶ οὗτοι
ἐπιστραφῆναι θελήσουσιν, ἐπιστραφήσομαι κἀγὼ πρὸς αὐτοὺς καὶ
φωτίσω αὐτοὺς φῶς γνώσεως καὶ γνώσονται τὰ ἐπιτηδεύματα τῆς
635 πολεμούσης αὐτοὺς κρυπτῆς κακίας, ὡς ὁ προφήτης ὁ λέγων· *κύριε,*
γνώρισόν με καὶ γνώσομαι· τότε εἶδον τὰ ἐπιτηδεύματα αὐτῶν.

52. Εἰ δὲ μεῖναι βουληθεῖεν ἐν τῷ σκότει τοῦ φρονήματος αὐτῶν,
τοὺς τῇ τῶν ὀφθαλμῶν ἀποβολῇ τὸν αἰσθητὸν ἥλιον μὴ θεωμένους
ἐρωτησάτωσαν οἷα πείσονται. τοσαῦτα καὶ τοιαῦτα ῥήματα ζωῆς
640 αἰωνίου γέμοντα παρὰ τῆς βασιλίδος ταύτης ἀναμαθόντες δράμωμεν,
προσέλθωμεν πρὸς αὐτήν, ὅπως φωτισθῇ τὰ πρόσωπα ἡμῶν·
ἐρωτήσωμεν αὐτήν, οὐ γὰρ φθονήσει διδάξαι τὴν ἑαυτῆς πολιτείαν.
εὐηγγελισάμην δικαιοσύνην, φησί, ἐν ἐκκλησίᾳ μεγάλῃ· τὴν ἀλήθειάν σου
καὶ τὸ σωτήριόν σου εἶπα. ποῦ ποιμαίνεις, ἡ πανθέωρος ἡ ἀρετή; ποῦ
645 κοιτάζεις, τὸ ἀγαλλίαμα τῆς ψυχῆς; τίς ἀναβήσεται εἰς τὴν μελέτην
σου; τίς στήσεται ἐν τῇ ἀγάπῃ σου;

53. Ποιμαίνω ἐν νήψει, κοιτάζω ἐν ταπεινώσει· ἀναβαίνει πρός
με ὁ ἐν ὕψει κατορθωμάτων καταβαίνων τῷ φρονήματι· ἵσταται ἐν
τῇ ἐμῇ ἀγάπῃ ὁ προσεκτικὸς καὶ ὑπὸ τῶν ὀρέξεων μὴ ρεμβόμενος.
650 ταῦτα τὰ βραχέα ῥήματα κρατήσωμεν γνησίως καὶ κρατήσει ἡμῶν
αὕτη καὶ κατακράτος νικήσει τὰ φρονήματα ἡμῶν καὶ ἑτοιμάσει
μονὴν αὐτοῖς τὴν μακαρίαν καὶ ἐροῦμεν τὰ τοῦ Δαβίδ· *ἡ καρδία μου*
καὶ ἡ σάρξ μου ἠγαλλιάσαντο ἐπὶ θεὸν ζῶντα· καὶ γὰρ στρουθίον εὗρεν
ἑαυτῷ οἰκίαν καὶ τρυγὼν νοσσιὰν ἑαυτῇ, οὗ θήσει τὰ νοσσία ἑαυτῆς. ἐὰν
655 γὰρ νηφόντως καὶ διηνεκῶς εὐχόμεθα, ἐν ἀγαλλιάσει ἔσται ἡ καρδία
ἡμῶν, ἐπικαλουμένη τὸ ὄνομα τοῦ ζῶντος θεοῦ· εὑρήσει γὰρ ὁ νοῦς
ἡμῶν τότε οἰκίαν θεωρίας καὶ ἡ ψυχὴ ἡμῶν νοσσιὰν ἀγάπης, ἐν ᾗ
τοὺς λογισμοὺς αὐτῆς θήσει καὶ οὐ φοβηθήσεται ἀπὸ παθῶν καὶ

648 τῷ corr.: τὸ OA

companies of bishops, teachers, holy men, righteous men, martyrs and all the saints have attained perfection through me.

51. Seized by a blindness of soul, not having tasted my grace and unaware of what goods I bestow in the soul where I am unceasingly active, some people mock at me and treat with contempt those who come to possess my riches through poverty. But if sometime later they cease from such madness and wish to return to me, I shall return to them and illumine them with the light of knowledge and they will know the ways of the hidden evil that makes war against them, as the prophet says, "Lord, make it known to me and I will know. Then they knew their ways."[106]

52. But if they should want to remain in the darkness of their way of thinking, let them ask those who through the loss of their eyes cannot see the sensible sun what sufferings will befall them. Now, newly instructed by this queen in such words filled with eternal life, let us run, let us proceed to her, that our faces may receive light. Let us ask her, for she will not refuse to teach us her way of life. Scripture says, "I have told the good news of righteousness in the great assembly. I have spoken of your truth and your salvation."[107] Where do you pasture your flock, all-seeing virtue? Where do you lie down to sleep, the joy of my soul?[108] Who shall ascend to meditate on you? Who shall find a place in your love?

53. I pasture my flock in vigilance. I lie down to sleep in humility. He shall ascend to me who abases his thoughts even when he attains the height of virtuous conduct. He shall find a place in my love who is attentive and is not distracted by desires. Let us truly lay hold of these short words and prayer will lay hold of us; in strength she will conquer our thoughts and prepare a blessed abode for them and we shall speak the words of David, "My heart and my flesh have rejoiced in the living God, for even the sparrow has found a home for itself and the turtledove a nest where it can lay its young."[109] If we pray soberly and continuously our heart will know gladness, as it calls upon the *Name of the Living God*. Then our mind will find the abode of contemplation and our soul the nest of love where it can lay its thoughts and have no fear of the passions and demons. For scripture says, "You

[106] Jer 11:18.
[107] Ps 39:10-11.
[108] Cant 1:7.
[109] Ps 83:3-4.

δαιμόνων. τὸν ὕψιστον, γάρ φησιν, ἔθου καταφυγήν σου· οὐ προσελεύσεται
660 πρός σε κακά, καὶ μάστιξ οὐκ ἐγγιεῖ ἐν τῷ σκηνώματί σου.

54. Ὁ μετὰ ἀκριβείας εὐχόμενος θεὸν ἔχει ἀμέσως φωτίζοντα τὴν
διάνοιαν αὐτοῦ. δεῖ οὖν ἀεί ποτε τῇ εὐχῇ συνάπτειν νῆψιν, μήπως
εὑρισκώμεθα λογισμῷ εὐχόμενοι καὶ ἐννοίᾳ μετεωριζόμενοι. ὁ γὰρ
μὴ οὕτω ποιῶν οὐ δύναται τὸν ἑαυτοῦ νοῦν ἐξειλῆσαι τοῦ τῆς
665 προσπαθείας δεσμοῦ. διότι οὐκ ἐκ συμφωνίας τῶν ψυχικῶν δυνάμεων
ἡ εὐχὴ πρὸς θεὸν ἀνατείνεται. ὡς γὰρ τὸν Πέτρον ἡ τῆς ἐκκλησίας
σύμφωνος εὐχὴ τοῦ δεσμωτηρίου ἐλυτρώσατο, οὕτω καὶ ἡ ἐν ψυχῇ
ἀνυομένη ἐκτενὴς προσευχὴ ἐξ ὅλης τῆς διανοίας τὸν πιστὸν καὶ
πρακτικὸν νοῦν τοῦ δεσμωτηρίου τῶν αἰσθήσεων ἐξάγειν πέφυκε καὶ
670 ὅλον αὐτὸν εἰσάγειν εἰς γνῶσιν τοῦ θεοῦ.

55. Ὁ ἱερεὺς ἐὰν μὴ καταλείψῃ τὰ ἔξω τοῦ ναοῦ καὶ εἰσέλθῃ
εἰς τὰ ἄδυτα καὶ σταθῇ ἐπὶ τῆς ἱερᾶς τραπέζης, οὐ δύναται τὴν
ἀναίμακτον θυσίαν προσαγαγεῖν τῷ κυρίῳ. καὶ ὁ νοῦς ἐὰν μὴ τὴν
τῶν αἰσθήσεων ἐνέργειαν ἀφήσῃ, ἔτι δὲ καὶ τὴν τῶν λογισμῶν
675 κίνησιν, καὶ μείνῃ ἐν τῇ γνώσει, οὐ δύναται τὴν πνευματικὴν θυσίαν
τὴν ἐν τῇ καθαρᾷ εὐχῇ ἀνυομένην ἐπιτελέσαι. πρότερον ἵσταται ὁ
νοῦς καὶ τότε καθαρῶς κινεῖται καὶ ἡ καθαρὰ κίνησις αὐτοῦ εὐχὴ
εὑρίσκεται. καὶ ὥσπερ ὁ διαβήτης ἵσταται ἐν τῷ κέντρῳ καὶ ἀπαρτίζει
τὸν κύκλον, οὕτω καὶ ὁ νοῦς, ὡς ἐν κέντρῳ τῷ νοήματι τοῦ θεοῦ
680 ἐπερείδων ἑαυτόν, τὴν ἀνακύκλησιν ποιεῖται τῆς εὐχῆς αὐτοῦ. καὶ
ὥσπερ πάλιν τὸ κέντρον μέσον ὁρᾶται τοῦ κύκλου καὶ ὅλον τὸν γῦρον
τοῦ κύκλου ἔσωθεν αὐτοῦ ἔχει, οὕτω καὶ ὁ θεός, ἐν μέσῳ τῆς καρδίας
ὁρώμενος, πᾶσαν τὴν ψυχὴν εἴσω τῆς θεωρίας αὐτοῦ ποιεῖται. ὁ
κύκλος τῇ μὲν θέσει ἔξωθεν τοῦ κέντρου φαίνεται, τῇ δὲ περιγραφῇ
685 ἔσωθεν αὐτοῦ καὶ ὅλος ἐν αὐτῷ πέφυκε. καὶ πάντα τὰ ὄντα τῇ μὲν
φύσει διέστηκε τοῦ θεοῦ, τῇ δὲ δημιουργίᾳ καὶ τῇ προνοίᾳ καὶ τῇ
διαμονῇ τοῦ θεοῦ τὰ πάντα ἐστίν· ἐξ αὐτοῦ γὰρ καὶ δι᾽ αὐτοῦ καὶ εἰς
αὐτὸν τὰ πάντα.

56. Καὶ ἵνα μάθῃς ὅτι ἐὰν μὴ στῇ ὁ νοῦς, οὐ δύναται ἐλθεῖν εἰς
690 μελέτην καὶ εἰς σύνεσιν τῆς εὐχῆς, ἄκουσον τοῦ ὀφθέντος ἀγγέλου
τῷ Δανιήλ· τοῦ γὰρ προφήτου τῆς ἀγγελικῆς μορφῆς τὴν ἰδέαν μὴ
ἐνεγκόντος, εἴρηκεν αὐτῷ ὁ ἄγγελος· Δανιήλ, ἄνερ ἐπιθυμιῶν, στῆθι
ἐν τῇ στάσει σου καὶ σύνες ἐν τοῖς λόγοις τούτοις, ὅτι ἀφ᾽ ἧς ἡμέρας

---

660 ἐγγιεῖ corr.: ἐγκιεῖ ΟΑ   678 διαβήτης corr.: διαβίτης ΟΑ   681 γῦρον
corr.: γύρον ΟΑ

have made the Most High your refuge. No evil shall approach you and no scourge come near your tent."[110]

54. He who prays with exacting care experiences unmediated illumination of his discursive intellect by God. Therefore, it is always necessary to join vigilance to prayer lest ever we imagine we are praying while in fact our thoughts have wandered off. For without doing so he cannot free his mind of the bond of passionate attachments, because his prayer is not directed towards God from the concerted blending of the soul's powers. As the concerted prayer of the church ransomed Peter from prison,[111] so too the steadfast prayer in the soul effected by one's entire discursive intellect brings forth the faithful and practical mind from the prison of the senses and leads it to enter entirely into the knowledge of God.

55. Unless the priest leaves behind the outer parts of the temple and enters the sanctuary and stands before the sacred table, he cannot offer to the Lord the bloodless sacrifice. So too unless the mind abandons the activity of the senses and even the movement of thoughts and abides in knowledge, it is unable to perform the spiritual sacrifice which is effected in pure prayer. First, the mind stands still. And then, it moves purely and its pure motion is known as prayer. Just as the compass stands at the centre and describes the circle, so too when the mind fixes itself on the thought of God as its centre it makes a circle of its prayer. And further, just as the centre appears in the middle of the circle and holds the entire ring of the circle from within itself, so too God appears in the middle of the heart and places the entire soul within contemplation of him. By its position the circle appears outside the centre, but in reference to its circumference it is also entirely within it. So too all beings are by nature distant from God, but by their creation, providence and conservation all things belong to God, for "all things are from him and through him and unto him."[112]

56. And that you may learn that unless the mind stand still, it is unable to enter upon meditation and understanding in prayer, listen to the angel that appeared to Daniel. Because the prophet could not bear the sight of the angelic form, the angel said to him, "Daniel, man of desires, stand in your place and set your understanding on

---

[110] Ps 90:9-10.
[111] Acts 12:5.
[112] Rom 11:36.

ἔδωκας τὴν καρδίαν σου κακωθῆναι ἐναντίον τοῦ θεοῦ, ἠκούσθησαν οἱ
695 λόγοι σου.

57.   Ἀπόθου λοιπὸν σὺ τὸν σάλον τῶν παθῶν σου καὶ νήστευσον
ἀπὸ τῶν τῆς ἐπιθυμίας λογισμῶν καὶ στῆθι ἐν τῇ νήψει τῆς καρδίας
σου καὶ σύνες ἐν τῇ στενῇ μελέτῃ τῆς εὐχῆς τῇ παντοίων λόγων
ὑπερβαινούσῃ πλάτος· καὶ ἀπλανῶς ἐπιγνώσῃ, ὅτι ἀφ᾽ ἧς ὥρας
700 ἠγάπησας εὔχεσθαι ἐν ταπεινώσει, ἐκαθαρίσθη ἡ καρδία σου καὶ
εἰσηκούσθη ἡ δέησίς σου. ἡνίκα σταυρώσῃ ἑαυτὴν ἡ ψυχή, ὑψοῦται
ἐκ τῶν γηΐνων· ὑψουμένη δὲ εἰς μνήμην τῶν ἑαυτῆς παραπτωμάτων
ἔρχεται καὶ τῶν ἐπερχομένων θλιβερῶν τὴν δικαιοσύνην ἐπιγινώσκει
καὶ τοῦ θεοῦ λόγου τὴν οἰκονομίαν κατανοεῖ καὶ θαυμάζει. καὶ τοῖς
705 πειρωμένοις δυσφημεῖν καὶ διαβάλλειν τὴν πρόνοιαν ἐπιτιμᾷ καὶ
ἀντιλέγει. καὶ εἰς αὐτομεμψίαν κινεῖται καὶ τῷ θεῷ προσπίπτουσα,
αἰτεῖ τὴν συγχώρησιν.

58.   Κύριε, λέγουσα, ἐξάλειψον τὴν μνήμην τοῦ ματαίου κόσμου
ἀπ᾽ ἐμοῦ καὶ δός μοι τὴν ἐπιπόθησιν τῶν σῶν ἀκηράτων ἀγαθῶν.
710 θοῦ φυλακὴν τῇ καρδίᾳ μου καὶ θεωρίαν προσευχῆς περὶ τοὺς
λογισμούς μου. διέγειρόν με πρὸς τοὺς σοὺς ὕμνους τὴν δουλεύουσαν
τῇ ῥαθυμίᾳ. ἄναψον τὸν νοῦν μου τῷ φωτὶ τῶν προσταγμάτων σου
καὶ παῦσον τὸν οἶστρον τῶν παθῶν μου. οἶκτόν μοι παράσχου τὴν
σπλάγχνα συμπαθείας ἀποκλείσασαν βροτοῖς. τῶν ἁμαρτιῶν μου τὴν
715 ἄβυσσον ξήρανον ἀβύσσῳ τοῦ ἐλέους σου. οἰκείωσόν με τῷ χορῷ
τῶν ἁγίων, τὴν μετὰ δαιμόνων τοῖς πάθεσιν ἑορτὰς ἐπιτελοῦσαν.
κατάταξόν με ὅπου ἦχος καθαρὸς ἑορταζόντων καὶ φωνὴ ἀφράστου
ἀγαλλιάσεως, ἔνθα τῶν δικαίων οἱ δῆμοι, ὅπου τῶν ἀγγέλων αἱ τάξεις·
ὅπως τὸ κάλλος ἐνοπτριζομένη τῆς ἀγαθότητός σου, ἀμνήμων
720 γένωμαι τοῦ αἴσχους τῶν κακῶν μου. σὺ γὰρ εἶ ἡ ἀΐδιος εὐφροσύνη,
ἡ ἀκατάλυτος ἑορτή, ἡ αἰώνιος χαρὰ καὶ μακαρία ἀνάπαυσις, καὶ
σοὶ πρέπει πᾶσα δόξα, τιμὴ καὶ προσκύνησις σὺν τῷ ἀνάρχῳ σου
πατρὶ καὶ τῷ παναγίῳ καὶ ἀγαθῷ καὶ ζωοποιῷ σου πνεύματι, νῦν καὶ
ἀεὶ καὶ εἰς τοὺς αἰῶνας τῶν αἰώνων· Ἀμήν.

these words: 'From the day on which you gave your heart to be chastened before God, your words found a hearing.' "[113]

57. Put aside, then, the agitation of your passions, abstain from thoughts of desire, take a stand in the vigilance of your heart and set your understanding on the confined meditation of prayer which overcomes the broad expanse of words of all sorts, and unerringly you will realize that from the time you made humble prayer your preference, your heart was purified and your supplication gained a hearing. When your soul crucifies itself, it is lifted up from earthly things and, lifted up, it comes to the remembrance of its own transgressions and recognizes the justice of the afflictions that come upon it, and it understands and marvels at the Economy of God the Word. It rebukes and disputes those who try to slander and calumniate providence. It is moved to self-reproach and, falling down before God, it asks for forgiveness, saying this prayer.

58. "Lord, wipe away from me the memory of this vain world and grant me longing for your unfading goods. Place a guard over my heart[114] and contemplative prayer around my thoughts. Rouse me to sing your praises, I who am enslaved to sloth. Kindle my mind by the light of your commandments and stop the goading of the my passions. Grant me compassion, I who closed my heart of my compassion to mortal men. Dry up the abyss of my sins with the abyss of your mercy. Claim me for the company of the saints, I who by my passions celebrated feasts with demons. Place me in the ranks where there is the pure sound of those who celebrate and the voices of unutterable joy; the tribes of the just are where the ranks of the angels are — so that in gazing upon the beauty of your goodness I may forget the shame of my evil deeds. For you are eternal gladness, the perpetual feast, eternal joy and blessed rest, and to you belong all glory, honour and worship together with your Father without beginning and your all-holy, good and life-giving Spirit, now and forever and unto the ages of ages, Amen."

[113] Dan 10:11-12.
[114] Ps 140:3.

Ὅτι τὰ κατὰ τὴν Αἴγυπτον καὶ τὴν Ἐρυθρὰν Θάλασσαν γεγενημένα παραδόξως διὰ Μωσέως ἐνεργοῦνται πνευματικῶς ἐν τοῖς ἀγωνιζομένοις κατὰ Χριστόν

1. Εὐσύνοπτόν σοι παραίνεσιν ἐκθέμενος τῇ ἐκ τῆς περὶ τὰ καλὰ
5 προθυμίας ἐπερωτησάσῃ μοναχῇ ἐγχειρίζω πρὸς εὐχερῆ διάληψιν
τῆς κατὰ τὴν ἄσκησιν ὅλης πραγματείας. ὀφείλεις, ἡ φίλη τοῦ
Χριστοῦ, τὰ συμβάλλοντα τῇ σῇ σωτηρίᾳ καὶ τῇ ἐπαγγελίᾳ τῶν σῶν
χειλέων διανοεῖσθαι καὶ τῶν τοιούτων ἐξέχεσθαι διόλου, ἵνα τῇ σῇ
ἀγαθῇ προθέσει καὶ τῆς διὰ τῶν ἔργων ἐκβάσεως συναντησάσης τοῦ
10 σωτηρίου σκοποῦ μὴ διαμάρτῃς.

2. Τὰ δεσμοῦντα τὴν τοῦ ἀνθρώπου ψυχὴν ἐν τῷ κόσμῳ καὶ
στροβοῦντα τὴν διάνοιαν ταῦτά ἐστιν· ὕλη πραγμάτων καὶ ἔντευξις
γονέων, συγγενῶν, φίλων, συνήθων καὶ τῶν λοιπῶν ἀνθρώπων,
σαρκὸς ἄνεσις καὶ εὐπάθεια, καὶ ψυχῆς κενόδοξον φρόνημα. ταῦτά
15 ἐστιν ὁ ἀγρός, τὰ πέντε ζεύγη τῶν βοῶν καὶ ἡ γυνή, ὧν τὴν ἀπόλαυσιν
οἱ κληθέντες προτιμησάμενοι τὴν τοῦ δεσποτικοῦ δείπνου παρητή-
σαντο γεῦσιν. ταῦτα ὁ Ἀβραὰμ ἀποβαλόμενος διὰ τοῦ καταλιπεῖν
γῆν καὶ συγγένειαν καὶ οἶκον πατρικὸν, ξένος ὑπῆρξε τοῦ κόσμου·
καὶ ὁ τῶν ἰδίων ἀποξενωθεὶς κόλπος ἐγεγόνει τῶν ἀλλοτρίων καὶ
20 πατὴρ ἐθνῶν ἀνεδείχθη.

3. Τοίνυν καὶ σὺ βουληθεῖσα τοὺς τοιούτους δεσμοὺς διαρρῆξαι
κατὰ τὸν Ἀβραὰμ καὶ Χριστῷ ἀκολουθῆσαι κατὰ τοὺς ὁσίους
πατέρας· καὶ λέγειν μετὰ παρρησίας πρὸς τὸν καθηγητήν· *σὺ διέρρηξας*

The events which occurred miraculously through Moses in Egypt and at the Red Sea are wrought spiritually within those who struggle in Christ[1]

1. At your request, which you made as a nun zealous for the good, I have set forth and now entrust to you a readily grasped exhortation in the form of an easy, systematic treatment of the entire subject of the ascetic life. Friend of Christ, you ought to consider what contributes to your salvation and to the profession made with your lips and cling to such things wholeheartedly, lest you fall far short of the goal of salvation, even when the outcome of your works happens according to your good purpose.[2]

2. These are the chains that bind the soul of man to the world and the distractions that afflict his discursive intellect: material things; encounters with parents, relations, friends, acquaintances and other people; the indulgent and passionate disposition of the flesh; and an attitude of vainglory in the soul. These constitute the field, the five yokes of oxen and the wife which the invited guests preferred to enjoy, and so they declined to taste the banquet of the Lord.[3] These are the things Abraham rejected in leaving his land, relations and his father's house, becoming a stranger in the world. And the one who became estranged from his own people became a bosom for other peoples and was made known as a father of nations.[4]

3. Therefore, you too, like Abraham, decided to break these bonds and to follow Christ as the holy Fathers did and to say with boldness before your teacher: "You have broken my bonds and I will offer you

---

[1] Cf. Ex 14:15-29.

[2] Since the discourse is addressed to an individual in the second person, the individual must surely be Eulogia even though she is not named explicitly. The reference to her monastic profession may be an indication that her tonsure was still an event in the recent past. Further, this discourse represents a reply to a request that appears to be identical with that mentioned in MD 1.1.

[3] Lk 14:15-24.

[4] Gen 12:1-3. The symbolism of Abraham's migration had been used earlier in the patristic tradition. See Gregory of Nyssa, *Contra Eunomium* 2:84-95 (ed. Jaeger 1:251-254; PG 45:940-941).

τοὺς δεσμούς μου· σοὶ θύσω θυσίαν αἰνέσεως. κόσμον ἀπολιποῦσα καὶ
25 πᾶσαν τὴν ἐν αὐτῷ ματαιότητα καὶ ψευδῆ μανίαν ὡς ἄλλην Αἴγυπτον
ἀποφυγοῦσα, ἐπὶ φροντιστήριον φέρουσα ἑαυτὴν ἀνεχώρησας, καὶ
τὸν σύντονον τῆς ἀρετῆς δρόμον περιπατεῖν προείλου. γίνωσκε οὖν
ὡς εἰς ἀγῶνας ἐνέβαλες σεαυτὴν καὶ ἀγῶνας μεγάλους καὶ διηνεκεῖς,
ἐπειδὴ ὅσῳ χαυνουμένη πρότερον ἠρεμεῖν ἐποίεις τοὺς ἐχθρούς,
30 τοσούτῳ τούτους διηρέθισας κατὰ σεαυτῆς, τὴν ῥαθυμίαν ἀπεκδυ-
σαμένης καὶ τὰ τοῦ πνεύματος ὅπλα ἐπενδυσαμένης.

    4. Πρώην ὀπίσω τῶν ἐπιθυμιῶν ἐπορεύου τοῦ κόσμου· νῦν ὀπίσω
τοῦ ἐσταυρωμένου Χριστοῦ ἀκολουθοῦσα συνετάξω. οὐχ ἡσυχάζουσιν
οἱ κοσμοκράτορες τῶν ἐν τῷ αἰῶνι τούτῳ προσηλωμένων· ὀπίσω σου
35 δὲ καταδιώκουσι κραταιῶς, μηχανώμενοι ἢ τὸ σῶμα πάλιν ἐπιρρίψαι
εἰς τὸν περισπασμὸν ὧν ἀποφυγοῦσα πραγμάτων ἢ τὴν διάνοιαν
ταῖς μνήμαις τῆς ἀλόγου ἀναστροφῆς ἐγχρονίζουσαν καταρρυπαίνειν,
καὶ οὕτω τῆς πρὸς τὰ κρείττονα προκοπῆς ἀφιστᾶν τὴν ψυχήν. ὃ
δὴ καὶ πεπόνθασιν οἱ Ἰσραηλῖται, ὧν τὰ κῶλα κατεστρώθη ἐν τῇ
40 ἐρήμῳ, σώματι γὰρ αὐλιζόμενοι ἐν τῇ ἐρήμῳ, τῇ διανοίᾳ, περιεπόλουν
τὴν Αἴγυπτον καὶ τὰς ἐν αὐτῇ ἀπολαύσεις περιεσκόπουν, ἔπαθλον
τῆς ματαίας ἐπιθυμίας κληρωσάμενοι τὴν ἔκπτωσιν τῆς ἐπηγγελμένης
γῆς.

    5. Ταῦτα διανοοῦσα, μαθήτρια τοῦ Χριστοῦ, ὥσπερ ἀπέφυγες τὰ
45 κατασπῶντά σε πράγματα, ἐπείγου συναποφυγοῦσα καὶ τὰ συγχέοντα
τὴν ψυχήν σου νοήματα τούτων, ἵνα τῶν ὄπισθεν δεσμῶν λυθεῖσα
παντελῶς τὴν πρὸς τὰ πρόσω πορείαν τῶν καλῶν ἀνεμποδίστως
τρέχῃς. τότε δυνήσῃ καὶ τὰ κυματώδη θελήματα τῆς σαρκὸς ὡς ὕδατα
Θαλάσσης Ἐρυθρᾶς διατεμεῖν καὶ τὴν τραχεῖαν ὁδὸν τῆς ἀρετῆς τὴν
50 ἀτριβῆ καὶ παγίαν καὶ φέρουσαν εἰς τὴν ἔρημον τῆς ἀπαθείας βαδίζειν
μετ᾽ εὐκολίας, μήτε τοῖς ἐξ ἀριστερῶν, μήτε τοῖς ἐκ δεξιῶν κύμασι
περιαντλουμένη· ὡς ὑπερβολὰς καὶ ἐλλείψεις ἐκφεύγουσα καὶ τὰ τῆς
ψυχῆς καὶ τὰ τοῦ σώματος πάθη διακόπτουσα τῇ δυνάμει τοῦ σταυροῦ
καὶ τὴν μέσην καὶ βασιλικὴν ὁδὸν τῶν ἐντολῶν τοῦ Χριστοῦ μετὰ
55 Χριστοῦ πορευομένη, ἀπαρνησαμένη γὰρ ἑαυτὴν καὶ τὸν σταυρὸν
αἴρουσα καὶ τοῖς ἴχνεσι τοῦ σταυρωθέντος ἑπομένη. ἐκεῖ καταλύεις
ὅπου *πρόδρομος ὑπὲρ ἡμῶν εἰσῆλθε Χριστός.*

---

40 περιεπόλουν corr.: περιεπώλουν ΟΑ

a sacrifice of praise."[5] Having left the world and fled all the vanity and deceitful folly in it, as another Egypt, you betook yourself to a monastic retreat and chose to walk the straight course of virtue. Know then that you have cast yourself into the midst of struggles, struggles both mighty and perpetual, because, now that you have put off sloth and clothed yourself in the armour of the Spirit,[6] you have provoked your enemies to the same extent that you previously in your laxity allowed them to rest.

4.   Formerly you went after the desires of the world; now you have set yourself to follow after Christ crucified. The world-rulers will not rest over those who have crucified themselves in this present age. They will pursue you vigorously, scheming either to throw your body back among the distractions of the things you fled or to defile your mind with dalliance over the memories of your way of life when it was not governed by reason, and in this way cause your soul to abandon progress towards the better. This is what the Israelites experienced, whose limbs were scattered in the desert,[7] for while they were encamped bodily in the desert, mentally[8] they wandered in Egypt and sought for their enjoyments there and were allotted the rewards of vain desire, namely, exclusion from the Promised Land.[9]

5.   In consideration of these matters, dear disciple of Christ, just as you fled the things that drag you down, rouse yourself to flee also thoughts about them which cause confusion in the soul, so that, completely loosed from the bonds of the past, you might run ahead towards the good unhindered. Then you can split in two the stormy cravings of the flesh like the waters of the Red Sea and, without being inundated either to the left or to the right, you can walk with ease the rugged road of virtue which is little travelled but sure, for it leads to the desert of impassibility. This is in your power because you have escaped the excesses and deficiencies and have cut off the passions of soul and body by the power of the Cross and proceed in the company of Christ along the middle and royal road of Christ's commandments, for you renounced yourself, took up the Cross and followed in the steps of the Crucified.[10] There you take up your abode, where Christ has entered as a forerunner on our behalf.[11]

[5] Ps 115:7-8.
[6] Cf. Eph 6:10-13.
[7] Heb 3:17; cf. Num 14:23,28-35.
[8] I.e., "with their discursive intellect."
[9] Cf. Ex 16:3; Num 11:5.
[10] Cf. Mt 16:24, Mk 8:34, Lk 9:23.
[11] Heb 6:20.

6. Τότε καὶ τὰ προφητικὰ λόγια ἐναργῶς βλέπεις πληρούμενα·
πεσοῦνται ἐκ τοῦ κλίτου σου χιλιὰς καὶ μυριὰς ἐκ δεξιῶν σου, πρὸς σὲ
60 *δὲ οὐκ ἐγγιεῖ·* ἵστανται γὰρ αἱ ὁρμαὶ τῶν παθῶν ὡς νεκρουμένων τῷ
κέρατι τοῦ σταυροῦ. καὶ τοῦτο δηλῶν ὁ ἀπόστολος λέγει· *οἱ δὲ τοῦ*
Χριστοῦ τὴν σάρκα ἐσταύρωσαν σὺν τοῖς παθήμασι καὶ ταῖς ἐπιθυμίαις,
μήτε τοῖς ἐπαίνοις ἐκλυόμενοι, μήτε τοῖς ψόγοις τραχυνόμενοι. μηδὲ
τοῦτό σε λανθανέτω τὴν ἱερὰν ἀγωνίστριαν, ἐκ δὲ τοῦ κατὰ τὸν
65 Μωσέα τύπου χειραγωγουμένη, θέασαι τὴν ἐνέργειαν τοῦ Χριστοῦ,
δι' ὃν καὶ οἱ τύποι καὶ αἱ σκιαὶ παρελήφθησαν εἰς πίστωσιν τοῦ κατ'
αὐτὸν μυστηρίου. ὅταν ἀμεταστρεπτὶ τὸν δρόμον τῶν ἀρετῶν βαδί-
ζουσα, διὰ τῶν ἀρετῶν τὰ πάθη περάσασα καὶ πρὸς ἀπάθειαν φθάσῃς
ἰσχύϊ τοῦ τὸν κόσμον νικήσαντος Χριστοῦ, μὴ δημοσιεύσῃς τὴν ὁδὸν
70 τῶν κατορθωμάτων. εἰ τοῦτο ποιεῖς, σεαυτῇ τὴν νίκην ἐπιγράφεις·
καὶ ἰδοὺ τὰ τῆς ὑπερηφανίας πνεύματα ὀπίσω σου καταδιώκοντα διὰ
τὴν ἐκπόμπευσιν τῶν ἀρετῶν ματαιοῦσι τὸν κόπον σου καὶ τὸν μισθόν
σου ὑφαρπάζουσι.

7. Τῇ ταπεινοφροσύνῃ δὲ σεαυτὴν ἐξουδενοῦσα, συγκρύπτεις τὰς
75 ἀρετάς σου καὶ ἀφανίζεις τοὺς διὰ τῆς κενοδοξίας ἐπιβουλεύοντάς
σοι δαίμονας. ὡς γὰρ ὁ Μωϋσῆς μετὰ τὸ περάσαι τὸν Ἰσραὴλ τὴν
θάλασσαν πλαγίως πλήξας αὐτὴν τῇ ῥάβδῳ, τὰ διαιρεθέντα ταύτης
ὕδατα ἥνωσε· καὶ οὕτως ἣν διώδευσε τρίβον ξένην ὁ Ἰσραὴλ
ἠφάνισεν, ὁμοῦ δὲ συνηφάνισε καὶ τοὺς καταδιώκοντας Αἰγυπτίους
80 τὴν αὐτὴν ὁδὸν βαίνειν ἐπιχειρήσαντας καὶ κατεπόντισεν ἐν μέσῳ
τῆς θαλάσσης· οὕτω καὶ ὁ κατ' ἴχνος τοῦ Χριστοῦ περιπατῶν, διὰ
μὲν τῆς κατὰ τὰς ἀρετὰς δικαιοσύνης νεκροῖ τὸ σαρκικὸν θέλημα,
διὰ δὲ τῆς ταπεινοφροσύνης τὸ ὑπερήφανον φρόνημα καταργεῖ καὶ
εἰρήνης τῶν λογισμῶν ἀπολαύει καὶ τοὺς ἐπινικίους ὕμνους τῷ νικητῇ
85 θεῷ ἀναπέμπει. οὕτως οἰκονομῶν τὰ καθ' ἑαυτήν, μᾶλλον δὲ
οἰκοδομοῦσα, ἀπαρτίζεις τὸ σχῆμα τοῦ σταυροῦ, τὴν δύναμιν αὐτοῦ
ἐνεργουμένην συντηρεῖς ἐν ἑαυτῇ. συσταυροῦσαι Χριστῷ καὶ
συνθάπτῃ καὶ συνανίστασαι καὶ συνδοξάζῃ· κοινωνὸς γὰρ
ἀνυποκρίτως γεγονυῖα τῶν αὐτοῦ παθημάτων, κοινωνὸς γίνῃ καὶ τῆς
90 αὐτοῦ δόξης.
8. Οὐκ ἀπηλλάγη ὁ Ἰσραὴλ καὶ φόβου καὶ θορύβου, ἕως ἑώρα
τὴν καινισθεῖσαν ὁδὸν ἐν μέσῳ τῆς θαλάσσης τρέχοντας τοὺς

6. Then you will see the prophetic words clearly fulfilled: "A thousand will fall at your side, ten thousand at your right, but it will not come near you."[12] For the onslaughts of the passions will cease when they are put to death by the beam of the Cross. The Apostle points to this when he says, "Those who belong to Christ have crucified the flesh with its passions and desires,"[13] neither growing lax when they are praised nor growing angry when they are censured. Do not let this escape your notice, holy athlete, but guided by the example of Moses behold the activity of Christ, for whose sake both the types and the shadows were received as a confirmation of the mystery regarding him. Whenever you walk the way of the virtues and through the virtues put an end to the passions and attain impassibility by the strength of Christ, who conquered the world,[14] do not publish the way of achieving your successes. If you do this, you ascribe the victory to yourself, and behold, the spirits of pride will pursue you because you display your virtues publicly, and they will render your labour in vain and will snatch away your reward.

7. In humility treat yourself with contempt and hide your virtues and you will destroy the demons who attack you by means of vainglory. After Israel crossed the sea Moses struck it with a crosswise blow of his staff and brought together the divided waters, and in so doing he destroyed the extraordinary path by which Israel passed through, while at the same time he also destroyed the pursuing Egyptians who attempted to use the same road, and drowned them in the midst of the sea.[15] Similarly, too, one who walks in the footsteps of Christ puts to death the will of the flesh by the righteousness of the virtues and destroys the attitude of pride by humility; he enjoys peace of thoughts and sends up hymns of victory to God the victor. Arranging, or rather, building up your life in this way, you complete the form of the Cross, you keep its power at work in you. Crucify yourself, bury yourself, raise yourself, glorify yourself with Christ, for as you have shared sincerely in his sufferings, you share also in his glory.[16]

8. Israel was not delivered from its fear and trembling until it saw the Egyptians racing after them along the newly opened road in the

---

12 Ps 90:7.
13 Gal 5:24.
14 Cf. Jn 16:33.
15 Ex 14:26-29.
16 Cf. Gal 2:19, Rom 6:4-8, 8:17, Col 2:12-13.

Αἰγυπτίους ὀπίσω αὐτῶν. ὅτε δὲ τῇ μάστιγι τῆς ῥάβδου τὰ διηρημένα
ὕδατα τῆς θαλάσσης συνελθόντα ἐπὶ τὸ αὐτὸ καὶ τὴν γεωθεῖσαν
95 ἄβυσσον ἄβυσσον ὑγρὰν ἀναδείξαντα πάλιν καὶ τοὺς διώκοντας
συνελάβετο καὶ κατεπόντισε, τότε καὶ ὁ ἐπτοημένος λαὸς καὶ
τεταραγμένος καὶ διωκόμενος ἠγαλλιάσατο καὶ τὸν θεὸν ἐμεγάλυνε.
τὸ διὰ τῆς παραδοξοποιΐας ταύτης σημαινόμενον μυστικῶς διανοοῦ
καὶ πειρῶ συγκαλύπτουσα ἀεὶ τὰς ὑπὸ σοῦ τελουμένας θαυμασίας
100 ἀρετὰς διὰ τῆς ἐν ταπεινοφροσύνῃ προσευχῆς· οὕτω γὰρ καὶ τοὺς
διὰ τῆς κενοδοξίας βάλλοντας ἐχθροὺς ἀναιρεῖς προφανῶς καὶ
σεαυτὴν διασώζουσα ὡς τὸ ἀρέσκειν ἀνθρώποις παντάπασιν
ἀποπεμπομένη· ἐπειδὴ κατὰ μὲν τὰς ἄλλας ἀρετὰς συνεργεῖν ὑπο-
κρίνονται οἱ δόλιοι τοῖς ἀγωνισταῖς, καὶ τοῦτο δὲ μηχανῶνται οἱ
105 πονηροὶ πρὸς ἀπάτην καὶ ἀδόκητον ὄλεθρον τῶν φιλαρέτων, ταπείνωσιν δὲ σχηματίσασθαι οὐδόλως ἀνέχονται, ὡς ὑπερηφανίας γεννή-
τορες. διὸ καὶ ὁ προφήτης λέγει, *ἴδε τὴν ταπείνωσίν μου καὶ τὸν κόπον*
μου καὶ ἄφες πάσας τὰς ἁμαρτίας μου.
9. Φησὶ δὲ καὶ ὁ διὰ τῆς κλίμακος ἀπὸ γῆς ἀνυψῶν τοὺς
110 βουλομένους, *οὐ νενήστευκα, οὐκ ἠγρύπνησα, οὐκ ἐχαμεύνησα, ἀλλ᾽*
ἐταπεινώθην καὶ ἔσωσέ με συντόμως ὁ κύριος. οὔτε γὰρ τὸ ὄρθιον ξύλον
ἄνευ τοῦ πλαγίου σώζει τὸ σχῆμα τοῦ σταυροῦ, οὔτε αἱ ἀρεταὶ
ταπεινώσεως δίχα σώζουσι τὸν ἀσκητήν. ὑψουμένη οὖν τῶν γηΐνων
καὶ τῆς πρὸς αὐτὰ φιλίας διὰ τῶν ἀρετῶν, τοῦτο γὰρ τὸ ὄρθιον ξύλον,
115 χρήζεις πάντως αὐτῆς πλαγίας ταπεινοφροσύνης εἰς συμπλήρωσιν
τοῦ φωτίζοντός σε σταυροῦ, ὃν καὶ ᾑρετίσω βαστάζειν.

10. Τότε δὴ τότε καὶ ὑψηλὴ οὖσα καὶ ταπεινή, ὑψηλὴ διὰ τὴν
τῶν αἰσθητῶν περιφρόνησιν, ταπεινὴ διὰ τὸ ὑποκάτω πάντων φρονεῖν
ἑαυτὴν ἐκ τοῦ λογίζεσθαι μὴ εἶναι σὸν τὸ κατόρθωμα, ἀλλὰ τοῦ
120 εἰπόντος· *οὐ δύνασθε χωρὶς ἐμοῦ ποιεῖν οὐδέν.* μέγα μὲν τὸ νεκρῶσαι
τὸ θέλημα τῆς σαρκός, ἤτοι τὰς ἡδονάς, διὰ τῶν ἀρετῶν· μεῖζον δὲ
τὸ ἐν ὕψει ἀρετῶν ταπεινοῦν τὸ φρόνημα τῆς ψυχῆς. ὁ φεύγων τὰ
πάθη φεύγει ἀπὸ προσώπου τῶν ἐχθρῶν· ὁ δὲ ἐν κατορθώμασι
ταπεινούμενος ἀπαντᾷ κατὰ πρόσωπον τοῖς ἐχθροῖς· *κύριος γὰρ*

midst of the sea. And when the divided waters of the sea came together in the same place at the stroke of the staff, revealing the deep that had become land as once again a watery deep, and took and drowned those in pursuit, then the terrified, frightened and persecuted people rejoiced and magnified God.[17] Consider what is meant by this extraordinary event on a mystical level and try to keep always hidden the marvels of your virtuous accomplishments by means of prayer grounded in humility, for in this way you will clearly destroy the enemies who attack you through vainglory and you will keep yourself safe by rejecting outright the goal of pleasing people. In the case of the other virtues the treacherous demons are able to feign cooperation with ascetics, and the evil ones scheme at this to deceive and bring unexpected destruction upon those who love virtue, but they are absolutely incapable of simulating humility since they are progenitors of pride. Wherefore the prophet says, "Behold my humility and my toil and take all my sins away."[18]

9.   St. John, who raises those who are willing from the earth to the heights by means of his ladder, says, "I have not fasted, I have not kept vigils, I have not slept on the ground, but 'I humbled myself, and the Lord hastened to rescue me.' "[19] For neither does the vertical beam of wood maintain the form of the cross without the crossbeam, nor do the virtues preserve the ascetic without humility. Thus, exalted above earthly things and above affection for them by the virtues (for this constitutes the upright beam), you stand very much in need of the crossbeam of humility to complete the cross which illumines you and which you have chosen to bear.

10.   Then indeed you will be at one and the same time both exalted and humble, exalted because of your disdain for sensible things and humble because you consider yourself beneath all, in that you do not think of this accomplishment as your own but as that of the one who says, "Without me you can do nothing."[20] It is a great achievement to mortify the will of the flesh, that is the pleasures, by means of the virtues, but it is a greater one to keep the attitude of the soul humble when it is at the height of virtue. He who flees the passions flees from the face of his enemies, but he who maintains humility in the midst of his accomplishments confronts his enemies face to face,

---

[17] Ex 14:26-29.
[18] Ps 24:18.
[19] Ioannes Climacus, *Scala paradisi* 25.14 (PG 88:992D); Ps 114:6.
[20] Jn 15:5.

125 ὑπερηφάνοις ἀντιτάσσεται. ἡ ἀρετὴ τέμνει τὸ φιλήδονον θέλημα, ἡ δὲ
ταπείνωσις καταργεῖ τὸ φιλόδοξον φρόνημα.

11. Τὸ κατ᾽ ἀρετὴν ὀδυνηρὸν καὶ ἐπίπονον ἐλευθεροῖ τὸν
ἀγωνιστὴν τῆς καθ᾽ ἡδονὴν λειότητος καὶ σχέσεως. ἡ δὲ αὐτομέμψια
καὶ ἐξουδένωσις ποιεῖ τὸν ταπεινὸν ἀναιρέτην τῆς ὑπερηφανίας·
130 ὀδύνη δὲ καὶ ἀτιμία διὰ θεὸν τοῦ σωτηρίου σταυροῦ τὰ ὡραΐσματα.
εἰ κενοδοξεῖς ἐν ταῖς ἀρεταῖς ἐπιγινώσκει τῆς δεξιᾶς τὸ ἔργον ἡ
ἀριστερά· καὶ τρέχουσιν ὀπίσω σου οἱ Αἰγύπτιοι, ὡς ἐπιστάμενοι
τὴν ὁδόν σου. εἰ δὲ ἀκενοδόξως ἐκτελεῖς τὰ ἔργα σου, λανθάνει τὴν
ἀριστερὰν ἡ δεξιά, καὶ ὁρᾷς ἐναργῶς βυθιζομένους τοὺς ὑπερηφάνους
135 λογισμούς, ὡς ἄλλους Αἰγυπτίους ἐν τῇ θαλάσσῃ. τόπος τῆς ὑπερηφανίας τὸ φρόνημα. τόπος τῶν ἀλόγων παθῶν τῶν ἐν τῇ ψυχῇ
κινουμένων τὸ θέλημα. τόπος τῆς ἐν τῷ σώματι τελουμένης καθ᾽
ἡδονὴν ἁμαρτίας ἡ αἴσθησις. δεῖ οὖν τοὺς τρεῖς τούτους πολέμους
νικῆσαι τὸν ἀγωνιστήν. νικᾷ δὲ ὁ γνησίως ἑπόμενος τῷ διὰ θανάτου
140 νικητῇ τοῦ θανάτου Χριστῷ.

12. Εἰ μὴ ἐμαστιγώθη ἡ Αἴγυπτος, οὐκ ἀπελύθη ὁ Ἰσραήλ. εἰ
μὴ ἐπλήγη ἡ θάλασσα κατ᾽ εὐθεῖαν, οὐ διέβη ὁ διωκόμενος λαὸς
τὴν ὑγρὰν διὰ ξηρᾶς. εἰ μὴ πλαγίως ἐμαστίχθη πάλιν ἡ θάλασσα,
οὐκ ἠφανίζετο ὁ διώκων ἐχθρός. πλῆξον τὴν σάρκα τῇ δεκαλόγῳ
145 ἐργασίᾳ τῶν ἐντολῶν τοῦ Χριστοῦ, τῇ ἀκτημοσύνῃ, λέγω, τῇ φυγῇ
τῶν ἀνθρώπων, τῇ ἐγκρατείᾳ τῶν ἑκουσίων ἡδονῶν, τῇ ὑπομονῇ τῶν
ἀκουσίων θλιβερῶν, τῇ εὐρύθμῳ ψαλμῳδίᾳ, τῇ μετ᾽ ἐπιστασίας
ἀναγνώσει, τῇ μετὰ προσοχῆς προσευχῇ, τῇ συμμέτρῳ ἀγρυπνίᾳ, τῇ
εὐκατανύκτῳ γονυκλισίᾳ καὶ τῇ εὐλόγῳ σιωπῇ. εἰ ταῦτα κατέχεις
150 ἀνολιγώρως, φεύγεις τὴν ἁμαρτίαν τὴν δεκαχῶς τραυματίζουσάν σε
διὰ τῆς δουλείας τῶν κακῶν. ἡ γὰρ καθήδονος τῆς σαρκὸς ἀπόλαυσις
διὰ τῆς πενταδικῆς αἰσθήσεως καὶ τοῦ προφορικοῦ λόγου τὴν ψυχὴν
παραπείθουσα, τῇ ὕλῃ τῶν αἰσθητῶν προσηλοῖ, ὧν ἡ γένεσις ἡ
τετράστοιχος κτίσις ἐστί. συντιθεμένης οὖν τῆς τετρακτύος τῶν
155 αἰσθητῶν τῇ κατὰ τὰς αἰσθήσεις ἑξαδικῇ ἐνεργείᾳ, ὁ δέκατος ἀριθμὸς
συμπληροῦται, δι᾽ οὗ καὶ ὁ λόγῳ διοικούμενος ἄνθρωπος διδάσκεται
ἀπλανῶς τὴν ὁλοκλήρως κακουχοῦσαν ἁμαρτίαν τὸν καθ᾽ ἕκαστον
ἄνθρωπον.

---

for "the Lord opposes the proud."[21] Virtue cuts off the will's attraction
to pleasure, but humility destroys the mind's attraction to honours.

11.   The suffering and hardship involved in the acquisition of virtue
sets the ascetic free from the slippery road of attachment to pleasure.
Self-reproach and abnegation enable the humble person to destroy
pride. Suffering and dishonour for the sake of God are the adornments
of the saving Cross. If you take false pride in the practice of the virtues,
the left hand will know the work of the right,[22] and the Egyptians
will race after you, for they will know your route. But if you perform
your works with no attention to honours, the right hand will escape
the notice of the left, and you will see clearly your prideful thoughts
drowned in the deep, like another band of Egyptians. The mental
attitude is the place of pride. The will is the place of the irrational
passions that move in the soul. Sense perception is the place of sin
effected in the body by pleasure. The ascetic, then, must win these
three battles. He is victorious, who truly follows Christ who by his
death was victor over death.[23]

12.   If Egypt had not been struck with scourges, Israel would not
have been released. If the sea had not been struck straight across, the
people being pursued would not have passed through the water on
dry land. If the sea had not been struck again crosswise, the enemy
in pursuit would not have been annihilated. Strike the flesh by putting
into practice the decalogue of the commandments of Christ: namely,
freedom from possessions, flight from people, abstinence from willed
pleasures, patient endurance of unwilled afflictions, regular psalmody,
reading with concentration, attentive prayer, moderated denial of sleep,
genuflections performed with compunction, and eloquent silence. If you
hold diligently to these things, you will escape sin, which wounds you
in ten ways by enslaving you to evils. The pleasureful enjoyment of
the flesh wins over the soul through the five senses and the spoken
word and affixes it to the matter of sensible things, the generation
of which involved the creation of the four elements. So if the fourfold
nature of sensibles is added to the sixfold activity of the senses, the
number ten is complete. Through it the one who manages his life
according to reason is unerringly taught about the sin which deeply
afflicts each man.

[21] Prov 3:34; Jas 4:6.

[22] Cf. Mt 6:3.

[23] Cf. Heb 2:14. Note also the great Easter troparion: "Christ is risen from the
dead; in dying he slew death and brought life to those who lay in tombs."

13. Ἐπειδὴ τοῦτό σοι εὑρήσεις ὑποσημαίνοντα, οἶμαι, καὶ τὸν
160 χρόνον τῆς εἰς τὴν Αἴγυπτον παροικίας καὶ δουλείας τοῦ Ἰσραήλ·
τετρακόσια γὰρ ἔτη διετέλεσαν οἱ Ἑβραῖοι ταλαιπωρούμενοι ἐν τῇ
Αἰγύπτῳ. ὡς οὖν ἐκεῖ ἡ ἑκατοντὰς συμπλήρωσις οὖσα τῶν δεκάδων
τὴν τελειότητα ἔχει, τετραπλασιαζομένη δὲ ἀπαρτίζει τὸν τετρακόσια,
οὕτω καὶ ἡ τετρὰς ἐνταῦθα τῶν αἰσθητῶν προστεθεῖσα ταῖς πέντε
165 αἰσθήσεσι καὶ τῷ κατὰ προφορὰν λόγῳ, ἕκτῳ ἀριθμῷ ὄντι καὶ τελείῳ,
τὴν δεκάδα κεφαλαιοῖ.

14. Σὺ τοίνυν τὴν εἰρημένην δεκάδα τῶν σωτηρίων τρόπων
ἀντικατάστησον πρὸς τὴν πολεμίαν δεκάδα τῶν αἰσθητῶν καὶ τῶν
αἰσθήσεων τὴν ἀνενδότως καὶ ἀπατηλῶς προσβάλλουσαν καὶ συν-
170 θλίβουσαν τὴν ψυχήν σου. καὶ καταπολέμησον αὐτὴν καὶ ὄψει τὸν
νοῦν ἀπολυόμενον τῆς πολυειδοῦς καὶ δυσαπαλλάκτου δουλείας τῶν
ἀλόγων ἡδονῶν. ταύτης δὲ τῆς ἐλευθερίας ἀξιωθεῖσα, αὐτίκα καὶ
διάκρισιν ὀρθὴν προσλαμβάνεις, δι᾽ ἧς καὶ τὰ ἐμπαθῆ θελήματα
διαιροῦσα καὶ τὴν ταραχώδη τῶν παθῶν σύγχυσιν διαπερῶσα διὰ
175 τῆς πρὸς τὰς ἀρετὰς διαθέσεως καὶ τῆς τῶν θείων λογίων μελέτης·
ἐντεῦθεν καὶ τῇ μνήμῃ τῆς τοῦ κυρίου Ἰησοῦ ταπεινώσεως καθάπερ
ῥάβδῳ χρωμένη καὶ ὀχυρουμένη, τὴν ἐπ᾽ ἀρεταῖς ἔπαρσιν τοῦ
φρονήματος πλήττουσα καὶ καταστέλλουσα.

15. Ἵνα δὲ τρανοτέραν ἐπίδειξιν παρέξω σοι τοῦ κατὰ τὴν χάριν
180 μυστηρίου καὶ τὰ τῆς σκιᾶς παραβάλλω ταῖς τῆς χάριτος ἐνεργείαις,
ὅπως κατανοοῦσα τὰ πνευματικῶς σοι τελούμενα τὸ πρόθυμον τῆς
ψυχῆς διαναστήσῃς. ἐκεῖ Μωϋσῆς, ἐνθάδε Χριστός· ἐκεῖ δοῦλος,
ἐνταῦθα δεσπότης· ἐκεῖ ῥάβδος, ὧδε σταυρός· ἐκεῖ ἀπειλαὶ καὶ
πληγαί, ἐνταῦθα ἐντολαὶ καὶ ἐπαγγελίαι· ἐκεῖ ὁ παλαιὸς Ἰσραήλ, ὧδε
185 ὁ κατὰ Χριστὸν κτιζόμενος λαὸς καὶ ὁ νοῦς ἑκάστου πιστοῦ· ἐκεῖ
ἐξέλευσις ἀπ᾽ Αἰγύπτου καὶ λύτρωσις κακουχουμένου λαοῦ, ὧδε φυγὴ
κόσμου καὶ ἀποχὴ ἁμαρτίας καὶ ὑπακοὴ πρὸς Χριστόν· ἐκεῖ Φαραὼ
καὶ Αἰγύπτιοι καταβιαζόμενοι σώματα, ἐνταῦθα Σατᾶν καὶ δαίμονες
οἱ ψυχὰς ἀπολέσαι σπουδάζοντες· ἐκεῖ Θάλασσα Ἐρυθρὰ τὴν πρὸς
190 ἔρημον ἀπαγωγὴν κωλύουσα, ἐνθάδε θέλησις σαρκικὴ καὶ σχέσις
ῥεούσης ἐπιθυμίας εἴργουσα τὴν πρὸς τὴν θείαν ἀγάπην ὁδόν.

16. Ἐκεῖ παράδοξος διαίρεσις καὶ ἀποκατάστασις πάλιν τοῦ
ὕδατος, ἡ μὲν γέφυραν πρὸς σωτηρίαν τοῖς διωκομένοις, ἡ δὲ τάφον
πρὸς ἀπώλειαν τοῖς διώκουσι σχεδιάσασα, ἐνταῦθα ἑκούσιος ἐκκοπὴ
195 θελήματος καὶ ταπείνωσις, ἡ μὲν ἀπὸ τῶν καλῶν τὰ φαῦλα διακρί-
νουσα, ἡ δὲ ἐξουδένωσιν ἔμφρονα τῷ κατορθοῦντι προβαλλομένη

13. You will find significant, I think, also the length of time of Israel's sojourn and slavery in Egypt, for the Hebrews spent four hundred years of misery in Egypt. Since, in that case, the number one hundred represents perfection in that it completes the decads, and when it is multiplied by four makes up four hundred, so too in this instance the number four applied to sensible things, when it is added to the five senses and the spoken word, which fully make up the number six, tops off the decad.

14. You must therefore set the aforementioned decad of saving means over against the enemy's decad of sensible things and the senses, which inexorably and deceptively attacks and afflicts your soul. Fight against it and you will see your mind delivered from its manifold servitude to irrational pleasures, which is so difficult to overcome. When you have been deemed worthy of this freedom, straightaway you will receive also true discernment, whereby you can distinguish what movements of your will are bound to passion and pass through the troublesome confusion of the passions by means of your virtuous dispositions and your meditation on the divine scriptures. Then, using the remembrance of the humility of the Lord Jesus as a staff to lean on, you can strike and put down the arrogance of your mental attitude in your practice of the virtues.

15. In order to set out for you a clearer exposition of the mystery of grace, I will compare the types of the shadowy dispensation of the Old Law with the workings of grace, so that, by reflecting on what is wrought for you spiritually, you may rouse the zeal of your soul. There stands Moses, here Christ; there a servant, here a master; there a staff, here a cross; there threats and plagues, here commandments and promises; there the old Israel, here the people created in Christ and the mind of each faithful person; there the exodus from Egypt and the redemption of an afflicted people, here flight from the world, rejection of sin and obedience to Christ; there Pharaoh and the Egyptians oppressing bodies, here Satan and the demons eager to destroy souls; there the Red Sea blocking the route into the desert, here the will of the flesh and attachment to uncontrolled desire barring the way to divine love.

16. There an extraordinary parting and restoring of the water occurred, forming on the one hand a bridge to salvation for those pursued and on the other hand a grave of destruction for their pursuers, here a voluntary excision of the will accompanied by humility, the one discerning good from evil and the other putting forth a mental contempt as a shield for the one who does the right thing, while hiding

καὶ διὰ τῆς αὐτομεμψίας καὶ τὰ κατορθώματα καλύπτουσα, ὁμοῦ δὲ
καὶ τὴν ἀνθρωπαρέσκειαν ἀφανίζουσα. ἐκεῖ ἔρημος τὸν φυγάδα λαὸν
ἀναπαύουσα, ὧδε ἀπάθεια τῆς ταπεινώσεως ἡ διάδοχος, τὴν ὄχλησιν
200 τῶν παθῶν καταπαύουσα. ὅπου γὰρ ταπείνωσις, ἐκεῖ χάριτος
ἐνοίκησις· ὅπου δὲ χάριτος παρουσία, ἐκεῖ παθῶν ἀλλοτρίωσις· ὅπου
δὲ παθῶν μακρυσμός, κοιτασμὸς εἰρήνης· ὅπου δὲ εἰρήνη, πνεύματος
ἁγίου ἐπισκίασις, ὅλην παρακαλοῦσα τὴν ψυχὴν ὑπὲρ νοῦν.

17. Ταῦτα διαλογιζομένη ἀκενοδόξως καὶ ἀναβάσεις διανοίας
205 ποιοῦσα καὶ ἀπο δυνάμεως εἰς δύναμιν προβιβάζουσα, τριπλῆν
ἐρημίαν καὶ μόνωσιν μοναχῇ τὸ ὄνομά σου παρεγγυᾶταί σοι, ἐπειδὴ
καὶ τὸν προφήτην εὑρίσκεις συμμαρτυρούμενον καὶ διὰ τριῶν πα-
ραδειγμάτων τὴν τριττὴν σοι ταύτην τάξιν ὑπαινιττόμενον· ἡνίκα καὶ
γὰρ τῆς ὕλης μακρυνθῇς καὶ τῶν ἀνθρώπων, ὁμοιοῦσαι πελεκᾶνι ἐν
210 ἐρήμῳ αὐλιζομένῳ· ὅταν δὲ τὴν σάρκα διὰ τῶν κατὰ τὰς ἀρετὰς πόνων
καθυποτάξας, τῶν πρὸς αὐτὴν ἐπιθυμιῶν καὶ τῶν διαλογισμῶν τὴν
ψυχὴν ἀπορρήξῃς, νυκτικόρακι παραβάλλῃ παραμένοντι ἐν οἰκοπέδῳ·
ὅταν δὲ πάλιν τῶν ἐννοιῶν τοῦ κόσμου καὶ τῶν ἐνθυμήσεων
ἀποδιαστήσῃς τὸν νοῦν, στρουθίον εἰκονίζεις μονάζον ἐπὶ δώματος
215 – συνῳδὰ τῷ προφήτῃ καὶ αὐτὴ φθεγγομένη, *ὡμοιώθην πελεκᾶνι
ἐρημικῷ, ἐγενήθην ὡσεὶ νυκτικόραξ ἐν οἰκοπέδῳ, ἠγρύπνησα καὶ ἐγενόμην
ὡς στρουθίον μονάζον ἐπὶ δώματος.*

18. Οὕτως ἡ τρίβολος κακία συντρίβεται· οὕτως ὅλος ὁ πόθος
τῆς τριμεροῦς ψυχῆς πρὸς τὸν ἐν τριάδι θεὸν ἕνα συνάγεται·
220 φιλαργυρίας γὰρ ἀφανιζομένης ὑπὸ τῆς ἀκτησίας καὶ φιληδονίας
μαραινομένης διὰ τῆς κατὰ τὴν σάρκα κακοπαθείας καὶ κενοδοξίας
καταστρεφομένης ὑπὸ τῆς ταπεινοφροσύνης, πᾶσα ἡ διάθεσις τῆς
ψυχῆς τῷ θεῷ προσκολλᾶται καὶ τοῦ κατ᾽ εἰκόνα καὶ καθ᾽ ὁμοίωσιν
τὸ κάλλος ἀναζωγραφεῖται, καὶ τῆς παραγαγούσης καὶ ἐπισκοπούσης
225 καὶ συντηρούσης τὸ πᾶν ἁγίας τριάδος, ἡ ἐπίγνωσις φανεροῦται,
ἡδονῆς ἀρρήτου καταξιοῦσα τὸν ἑνούμενον αὐτῇ καθαρῶς καὶ ὁλικῶς
δοξάζοντα ταύτην ὡς μονάδα καὶ τριάδα· ὅτι τῷ ἐν τῇ μακαρίᾳ τριάδι
ἑνὶ θεῷ πρέπει πᾶσα δόξα, τιμὴ καὶ προσκύνησις καὶ μεγαλοπρέπεια,
νῦν καὶ ἀεὶ καὶ εἰς τοὺς αἰῶνας τῶν αἰώνων. Ἀμήν.

his accomplishments through self-reproach and at the same time destroying the desire for human applause. There the desert provides rest for the fugitive people, here impassibility, humility's successor, puts to rest the turmoil of the passions. For where there is humility there is the indwelling of grace; where grace is present there is alienation from the passions; where there is a distancing from the passions there is the establishment of peace; where there is peace there is the overshadowing of the Holy Spirit, which brings consolation to the entire soul in a manner beyond understanding.[24]

17.   When you have thought these matters through without vainglory, making ascents of the discursive intellect and progressing from strength to strength,[25] your name will entrust to you, sister, a threefold solitude and aloneness, since you will find the Prophet also bearing witness and alluding to your threefold station in life by means of three examples. For when you have distanced yourself from matter and from people, you become like a pelican dwelling in the wilderness; when you have brought your flesh into subjection by virtuous labours and have torn your soul away from the desires and thoughts of the flesh, you resemble an owl that stays on a house; when in turn you have removed your mind from thoughts and desires of the world, you are like a sparrow alone on a housetop — in accord with the prophet who made the utterance, "I was like a pelican in the wilderness; I became like an owl on a house; I kept watch and became like a sparrow on a housetop."[26]

18.   Thus the threefold attack of wickedness is crushed; thus all the yearning of the tripartite soul is gathered to the one God in Trinity. When greed is destroyed by divestment of property, when attachment to pleasure is extinguished by the mortification of the flesh, when vainglory is driven out by humility, the entire disposition of the soul cleaves to God and the beauty of the Image and Likeness is restored. When the Holy Trinity guides, watches over and preserves the whole, understanding manifests itself, deeming worthy of ineffable pleasure the person who is granted a pure and intimate union with it and who glorifies God with all its powers as Unity and Trinity, because all glory, honour, worship and majesty are due the one God in blessed Trinity, now and always and forever and ever. Amen.

---

[24] Cf. Phil 4:7.
[25] Cf. Ps 83:8.
[26] Ps 101:7-8.

Ἀναγωγὴ τοῦ εἰς τὴν συγκύπτουσαν θαύματος
διαγωγὴν ἀρίστην μυσταγωγοῦσα

1. Τῆς συγκυπτούσης γυναικὸς τὴν ἀσθένειαν καὶ τὴν παρὰ
Χριστοῦ θεραπείαν εἰς τὴν ἑκάστου ψυχὴν ἀνενεγκεῖν βουλόμενος,
5 τῆς τοῦ θεοῦ λόγου χρήζω ἐπιδημίας, ὅπως ἐπιστάς μου τῇ καρδίᾳ
καὶ τὸν ἐμὸν νοῦν ἀπὸ τὰ κάτω περισπασμοῦ ἀνανεῦσαι παρασκευάσῃ
τῇ θεϊκῇ ἐλλάμψει καὶ δυνάμει αὐτοῦ· τὸ μὲν εἰς τὸ ἀναβλέπειν τὴν
ἐν τοῖς οὐρανοῖς ἑτοιμασθεῖσαν ἀλήθειαν, τὸ δὲ εἰς τὸ ἀναγγέλλειν
τοῖς ἐπὶ γῆς τὸ θεῖον αὐτοῦ ἔλεος. οὕτω γὰρ καὶ οἱ διηγούμενοι τὰ
10 τοῦ θεοῦ καὶ οἱ ἀκούοντες ἐν συναισθήσει ψυχῆς εἴποιεν, *πλήρης*
ὁ οὐρανὸς καὶ ἡ γῆ τῆς δόξης σου, κύριε.

2. Τὴν τοίνυν πρόθεσιν εἰς ἔκβασιν ἀγαγεῖν πειρασώμεθα καὶ
πέρας τῷ σκοπῷ ἐπιθήσωμεν, χειραγωγὸν ἔχοντες Χριστόν, οὗ χωρὶς
οὐδεὶς δύναται ποιεῖν οὐδέν. τουτὶ τὸ γύναιον ταῖς ἐπιθυμίαις προσ-
15 κείμενον τῆς σαρκὸς καὶ ταῖς γηΐναις ἡδοναῖς προστετηκός, προ-
κεκυφυῖαν εἶχε τὴν διάνοιαν καὶ μηδόλως περί τι καλὸν ἀνανεύουσαν·
ὅθεν καὶ συγχωρήσει θεία παρεδόθη τὸ σῶμα εἰς τιμωρίαν. αἴτια γὰρ
τῶν ἀκουσίων κακῶν τὰ ἐκ προαιρέσεως ἁμαρτήματα· *μηκέτι, γάρ*
φησιν, ἁμάρτανε, ἵνα μὴ χεῖρόν τί σοι γένηται. διὰ τοῦτο καὶ συγκύπ-
20 τουσαν καλεῖ ὁ εὐαγγελιστὴς τὴν γυναῖκα, ὡς τῇ πρὸς τὰς ἡδονὰς
τῆς σαρκὸς κύψει τῆς ψυχῆς καὶ τὸ σῶμα παρὰ τὸ ὄρθιον σχῆμα
συγκεκυφὸς πρὸς τὴν γῆν. ἐκεῖνο γὰρ πέπονθε τὸ σῶμα, ὅπερ
προπέπονθεν ἡ ψυχή, ἵνα ἐκ τοῦ φαινομένου τῷ σώματι ἀσθενήματος
αἴσθησιν ἡ ψυχὴ λαμβάνῃ τοῦ ἀφανῶς νοσήματος.

25 **3.** Ἡ ψυχὴ διετέθη πρὸς τὴν σάρκα καὶ τὸ σῶμα νένευκε πρὸς
γῆν. ἡ πρὸς τὸ σῶμα σχέσις τῆς ψυχῆς ἔτεκεν ἡδονήν· ἡ πρὸς τὴν
γῆν τοῦ σώματος κύψις ἀνέδωκεν ὀδύνην. ἀμφότερα ἡδύνετο,
ἀμφότερα καὶ ὀδυνᾶται. ἁρμόζει τὰ τοῦ Ἡσαΐου λαλῆσαι· *ἔκυψεν*

---

7 ἐλλάμψει corr.: ἐλλάμψη OA

MD 4

INTERPRETATION OF THE MIRACLE GRANTED TO THE CRIPPLED WOMAN AS AN INITIATION INTO THE HIGHEST WAY OF LIFE[1]

1. If I am to apply the infirmity of the crippled woman and her healing by Christ to the individual soul, I stand in need of the visitation of God's Word to approach my heart and to prepare to raise my mind from distractions here below by his divine illumination and power, so that I can look upon "the truth prepared in his heavenly places"[2] and proclaim his mercy to those on earth. Thus those who explain the works of God and those who listen with the conscious perception of their souls could say, "Heaven and earth are full of your glory, O Lord."[3]

2. Let us therefore try to bring this intention into effect and attain our goal, having Christ to guide us by the hand, for without him no one can do anything.[4] This poor woman, attached to the desires of the flesh and engrossed in earthly pleasures, had her discursive intellect stooped over and completely incapable of looking up to anything good, and so by divine warrant her body was handed over for punishment. Sins committed by free will are the cause of unwanted ills, for scripture says, "Never commit sin, lest something worse happen to you."[5] Therefore, the evangelist calls the woman crippled because the upright form of her body had been bent towards the ground by the stooping of the soul to the pleasures of the flesh. The body suffered what the soul had already suffered so that by the visible infirmity of the body the soul might grasp an awareness of its invisible sickness.

3. The soul became disposed towards the flesh and the body became bowed to the ground. The soul's attachment to the body gave birth to pleasure; the body's stooping to the ground yielded torment. Both partook of pleasure; both partake also of torment. The words of Isaiah

---

[1] Lk 13:10-17. This is the Gospel text for the Tenth Sunday of Luke (beginning of December). Ἀναγωγή for Origen and Gregory of Nyssa refers to the movement of thought from the literal to the allegorical sense (e.g., Gregory of Nyssa, *Vita Moysi* 2.217 [SC 1 3rd ed.; PG 44:397C]).

[2] Ps 88:3.

[3] Is 6:3. Theoleptos confuses the verse with its liturgical form in the Sanctus.

[4] Jn 15:5.

[5] Jn 5:14.

ἄνθρωπος, καὶ ἐταπεινώθη ἀνήρ. ἔκυψεν ὁ ἐκ τῶν ἄνω καὶ τὰ ἄνω
30 βλέπειν γεγενημένος νοῦς καὶ συνυψοῦν καὶ τὸ κάτω βρῖθον τεταγμένος σῶμα, καὶ ἐταπεινώθη τὸ σῶμα κυρτωθὲν καὶ εἰς γῆν νενευκός.
εἰ γὰρ τὸ φῶς σκότος, τὸ σκότος πόσον.

4. Συμμαρτυρεῖ τοῖς λεγομένοις καὶ ὁ ἀριθμὸς τοῦ κατὰ τὴν
τιμωρίαν χρόνου· δέκα γὰρ ἔτη καὶ ὀκτὼ ἐδεσμεῖτο ὑπὸ τοῦ Σατανᾶ
35 ἡ γυνή, μήτε περὶ τὴν πρᾶξιν τῶν ἐντολῶν διὰ τοῦ δέκα δηλουμένων
διαπονουμένη, μήτε τοῦ μέλλοντος αἰῶνος διὰ τοῦ ὀκτὼ αἰνιττομένου
τὴν φροντίδα ποιουμένη. εὐφυῶς ἁρμόσειεν ἄν τις καὶ τὸ παρὰ τοῦ
προφήτου Δαβὶδ εἰρημένον· *κύψει καὶ πεσεῖται ἐν τῷ αὐτὸν κατακυριεῦσαι τῶν πενήτων.* κύψει τῇ διανοίᾳ διὰ τῆς φιλίας τῆς ἐν τῷ
40 παρόντι αἰῶνι καὶ συγκύψει τὸ σῶμα διὰ τῆς ἀπραξίας τῶν καλῶν.
ἡ δὲ αἰτία διὰ τὸ κατακυριεῦσαι καὶ ἐπαναστῆναι τὸν συγκύπτοντα
νοῦν τῷ ἔρωτι τῆς σαρκὸς κατὰ τῶν ἐνταλμάτων τοῦ πτωχεύσαντος
τὴν προσληφθεῖσαν ἐξ ἡμῶν σάρκα, ἵνα πλουτήσωμεν τοῦ προλαβόντος Χριστοῦ τὴν θεότητα.

45 **5.** Οὕτως οὖν ἔχουσαν τὴν συγκύπτουσαν καὶ ἐπὶ τοσούτοις
τιμωρουμένην ἔτεσιν ἰδὼν ὁ φιλάνθρωπος κύριος, καὶ ὡς τὰ μακρὰ
βλέπων ἐγγὺς οὖσαν τοῦ πιστεύειν αὐτὴν ἐπιστάμενος, ἐφώνησεν·
ἀπολέλυσαι τῆς ἀσθενείας σου. καὶ λόγῳ μὲν τὴν λογικὴν ψυχὴν
ἰάσατο. τῇ τῆς χειρὸς δὲ ἁφῇ τὸ σῶμα ἠνώρθωσε καὶ διπλῆν τῇ
50 γυναικὶ τὴν θεραπείαν ἐχαρίσατο. δείξας ἐναργῶς ὡς ὁ καταρχὰς
ἐμφυσήματι θείῳ τὸν πλασθέντα χειρὶ ἄνθρωπον εἰς ψυχὴν ζῶσαν
ἀπεργασάμενος, αὐτὸς καὶ νῦν διὰ σαρκὸς ἐπιστὰς τὸν τοῦ Σατανᾶ
πολυετῆ δεσμὸν λόγῳ καὶ χειρὶ παραχρῆμα διαλύσας τὴν διπλῆν
ἀνόρθωσιν τῇ γυναικὶ ἐδωρήσατο, ὡς διπλοῦς τῇ φύσει θεάνθρωπος.

---

are appropriate here: "Man bowed low and a man was humbled."[6] The mind with its origin from above and born to look upon the things above bowed low, even though it was ordained to raise the body from its downward penchant; and the body was humbled and became hunched and stooped towards the ground. "For if the light is darkness, how great will that darkness be!"[7]

4. The period of time set for the punishment also confirms what we have said, for the woman was bound by Satan for eighteen years. Neither did she labour at the practice of the commandments indicated by the number ten, nor did she give thought to the future age alluded to by the number eight.[8] Here one could fittingly apply the text of the prophet David: "He shall bend low and fall when he exercises dominion over the poor."[9] He shall bend low with his discursive intellect because of his affection for what belongs to this present age and his body shall stoop because of his failure to practise the good. The reason lies in the fact that the crippled mind exercises dominion and by means of its love for the flesh rebels against the precepts of the one who accepted the poverty of our flesh, which he assumed that we might be rich in the divinity of Christ, which he possessed from his pre-existence.[10]

5. So then, when the Lord who loves mankind saw that the woman who had been crippled and tormented for so many years was of this sort and, looking into the future, recognized that she was near the point of believing, he called to her, "You are freed from your infirmity."[11] By his word he healed her rational soul and with the touch of his hand he raised her body upright, granting the woman a twofold healing.[12] Having clearly shown that the one who in the beginning made man, formed by the hand of God, into a living soul by means of a divine insufflation is the same one who, now standing nearby in the flesh, instantly broke Satan's bond of many years asunder by his word and his hand,[13] he bestowed upon the woman a twofold restoration of health, for as the God-Man he is twofold in nature. The woman herself represents those among the Jews who came to

---

[6] Is 2:9.
[7] Mt 6:23. Cf. Euthymios Zigabenos, *Commentarius in Lucam* 13 (PG 129:1001CD).
[8] Cf. Theophylaktos of Bulgaria, *Enarratio in Evangelium Lucae* 13 (PG 123:917C).
[9] Ps 9:31.
[10] Cf. 2 Cor 8:9.
[11] Lk 13:12.
[12] Cf. Euthymios Zigabenos, *Commentarius in Lucam* 13 (PG 129:1001C).
[13] Lk 13:13.

55 αὕτη καὶ τοὺς ἐξ Ἰουδαίων πιστεύοντας τῷ Χριστῷ εἰκονίζει, οἱ
πεπιστευκότες γὰρ ἐξ αὐτῶν πρὸ τῆς τοῦ Χριστοῦ ἐπιδημίας συγκε-
κυφότες ὑπῆρχον τῇ διανοίᾳ καὶ τοῖς κατὰ τὸν νόμον ἀνυομένοις
ἔργοις, τῷ γράμματι προσκείμενοι καὶ τὸν σωματικὸν νόμον μετα-
διώκοντες καὶ μηδαμῶς ἀνανεῦσαι πρὸς τὸ πνεῦμα δυνάμενοι.

60 **6.** Ἐπεὶ δὲ ὁ ἄνω κάτω γέγονεν, ἵνα τὰ κάτω τοῖς ἄνω συνάψῃ,
καὶ τὸ ἀληθινὸν φῶς ἀνέτειλε τοῖς ἐν γῇ, τοὺς τύπους καὶ τὰς σκιὰς
περιαῖρον καὶ τοῦ πνεύματος ἀποκαλύπτον τὴν ὡραιότητα, ὅσοι μὴ
τῷ φθόνῳ πεπέδηντο, μηδὲ τῇ τοῦ γράμματος ἀχλύϊ τὸ τῆς ψυχῆς
ὀπτικὸν ἤμβλυναν, προσέδραμον τῷ Χριστῷ· λέλυνται γὰρ τῇ
65 ἐπιστασίᾳ τοῦ Χριστοῦ, ὡς ἡ συγκύπτουσα, ἀπὸ τοῦ κατὰ νόμον
ἀσθενήματος τοῦ δεσμοῦντος τὸν Ἰσραήλ, δέκα καὶ ὀκτὼ ἔτη ἅπερ
ἀλληγορικῶς λαμβανόμενα τὴν ὀκταήμερον τῆς σαρκὸς περιτομὴν
δηλοῖ καὶ τὴν ζωοθυσίαν· ἐπειδὴ τῇ δεκάτῃ τοῦ μηνὸς τὸ πρόβατον
λαμβανόμενον εἰς τὴν ἑορτὴν ἐτηρεῖτο τοῦ πάσχα. ἀμέλει καὶ
70 προσεδέθησαν τῷ Χριστῷ τῷ διὰ τοῦ βαπτίσματος πᾶσαν ἁμαρτίαν
περιτέμνοντι καὶ διὰ σταυροῦ θυσίαν ἑαυτὸν ἀνενεγκόντι ὑπὲρ ἡμῶν
καὶ τὴν ἁμαρτίαν ἀραμένῳ τοῦ κόσμου.

7. Ἐπεγνωκότες γὰρ ἀπὸ τοῦ κατὰ τὴν οἰκονομίαν τοῦ σωτῆρος
μυστηρίου καὶ τῶν τελουμένων ὑπ᾽ αὐτοῦ παραδόξως τὰ τοῦ νόμου
75 σύμβολα καὶ τῶν προφητῶν τὰ κηρύγματα ἐκβαίνειν εἰς Χριστὸν
καὶ ὅτι ὁ τοῦ γράμματος νόμος ἀσθενεῖ πρὸς τελείωσιν, ἡ δὲ τελείωσις
καὶ τὸ πλήρωμα τοῦ νόμου αὐτός ἐστιν ὁ Χριστός – *οὐκ ἦλθον, γάρ
φησι, καταλῦσαι τὸν νόμον ἀλλὰ πληρῶσαι* – τὸν σωματικὸν καταλε-
λειπότες ὡς παιδαγωγόν, τὸν τοῦ γράμματος καὶ τοῦ πνεύματος
80 νομοθέτην πεφθάκασι καὶ τοῦ πνευματικοῦ νόμου γεγόνασι μέτοχοι.
σοφῶς δὲ καὶ ἡ τοῦ σαββάτου ἡμέρα τῇ θεραπείᾳ τῆς συγκυπτούσης
συνέδραμε, τοῦ ποιητοῦ καὶ νομοθέτου καὶ θεραπευτοῦ δεικνῦντος
ὡς ἡ ἑκάστου διόρθωσις καὶ ἡ πρὸς τὸ κρεῖττον ἐπίδοσις ἐν τῷ
ἑβδοματικῷ τούτῳ αἰῶνι τελεῖ· καὶ ὁ μὴ ἐν τῇ παρούσῃ ζωῇ ἀπὸ
85 κακίας μεταβληθείς, μηδὲ τὰς ἑαυτοῦ κηλῖδας διὰ τῆς μετανοίας
ἀπονιψάμενος, ἀλλ᾽ ἐν ταῖς ἐπιθυμίαις τῆς σαρκὸς τὴν ζωὴν
ἐκμετρήσας, τὰς περιμενούσας τιμωρίας ἐν τῷ μέλλοντι αἰῶνι ἑαυτῷ
ταμιεύει.

8. Ἀλλ᾽ ὁ μὲν φορήσας ἡμᾶς θεὸς λόγος διὰ φιλανθρωπίαν, τὰ
90 τῆς φιλανθρωπίας ἔργα θεοπρεπῶς ἐπιτελῶν, καὶ σώματα ἐθεράπευε

---

62 ἀποκαλύπτον corr.: ἀποκαλύπτων OA

believe in Christ. For those among them who believed prior to the coming of Christ were crippled in their discursive intellect and in the works that they did according to the Law, and since they were attached to its letter and followed the corporeal law they were unable in any way to look up towards its spirit.

6. When the Most High came down to join the depths to the heights, and when the true Light dawned for those on earth removing the types and shadows and revealing the beauty of the spirit,[14] all those who had not been shackled by envy and had not dulled the soul's faculty of vision with the mists of the letter of the Law ran to Christ. For like the crippled woman, they had been set free by the authority of Christ from the infirmity of the Law which bound Israel. The eighteen years, taken allegorically, indicate the circumcision of the flesh on the eighth day and the practice of animal sacrifice, for on the tenth day of the month the lamb was taken and kept for the feast of the Passover.[15] They had in fact been bound over to Christ, who through baptism circumcises all sin and who through the Cross offers himself as a sacrifice on our behalf and takes away the sin of the world.[16]

7. From the mystery of the Saviour's Economy and the extraordinary things he did, these Jews realized that the symbols of the Law and the proclamations of the Prophets are fulfilled in Christ, that the letter of the Law is too weak to provide perfection and that Christ is himself both the perfection and the fulfilment of the Law. For he says, "I did not come to destroy the Law but to fulfil it."[17] Then, after they had abandoned the corporeal Law as their guide, they attained the giver of the Law of the letter and the spirit and have become partakers of the spiritual Law. The day of the Sabbath wisely coincided with the healing of the crippled woman,[18] for the creator, lawgiver and healer was indicating that each person's amendment and progress towards the better takes place in this age, symbolized by the week of seven days. Anyone who has not been converted from evil in the present life and has not washed away his defilements through repentance but has wasted his life in the desires of the flesh stores up for himself enduring punishments in the age to come.

8. But God the Word, who bore with us out of his love for mankind, performing his benevolent works in divinely fitting manner,

---

[14] I.e., the spirit of the Law.
[15] Ex 12:3.
[16] Cf. Heb 7:27, 10:10,14.
[17] Mt 5:17.
[18] Lk 13:10.

καὶ ψυχὰς διέσωζε καὶ διὰ τούτων ἐνῆγε τοὺς ἀνθρώπους εἰς
θεογνωσίαν καὶ φιλοθεΐαν. τερατουργῶν δὲ καὶ ἐν σαββάτῳ, παρε-
γύμνου ἑαυτὸν εἶναι τὸ νοητὸν καὶ ἀληθινὸν σάββατον· αὐτὸς γάρ
ἐστιν ὁ καταλύων τὴν ἁμαρτίαν καὶ αὐτός ἐστιν ἡ νέκρωσις τῶν
95   παθῶν καὶ ἡ πηγὴ τῶν ἀρετῶν καὶ τῶν ἀγωνιστῶν ἡ ἀνάπαυσις. δεῦτε,
γάρ φησι, πάντες οἱ κοπιῶντες καὶ πεφορτισμένοι, κἀγὼ ἀναπαύσω ὑμᾶς·
καὶ πάλιν, μάθετε ἀπ’ ἐμοῦ, ὅτι πρᾶός εἰμι καὶ ταπεινὸς τῇ καρδίᾳ, καὶ
εὑρήσετε ἀνάπαυσιν ταῖς ψυχαῖς ὑμῶν. ἄρατε τὸν ζυγόν μου ἐφ’ ὑμᾶς.
εἰ δὲ καὶ ζυγός ἐστι τὰ τοῦ Χριστοῦ ἐντάλματα, ἀλλὰ χρηστός ἐστι·
100 καὶ εἰ φορτίον ἐστὶν ἡ κατὰ τὸ εὐαγγέλιον ὑποταγή, ἀλλ’ ἐλαφρόν
ἐστιν· αἱ γὰρ ἐντολαὶ αὐτοῦ βαρεῖαι οὐκ εἰσί.

9.   Τί δὲ πρὸς ταῦτά φασιν οἱ τῆς συναγωγῆς ἄρχοντες, γραμματεῖς
καὶ φαρισαῖοι καὶ τοῦ ἰουδαϊκοῦ λαοῦ διδάσκαλοι; *ἓξ ἡμέραι εἰσὶν*
ἐν αἷς δεῖ ἐργάζεσθαι· ἐν ταύταις ἐρχόμενοι θεραπεύεσθε καὶ μὴ τῇ ἡμέρᾳ
105 *τοῦ σαββάτου.* ὑπὸ τοῦ φθόνου κεντούμενοι καὶ ὑπὸ τῆς βασκανίας
σκοτούμενοι τῆς κατὰ τὸ σάββατον νομοθεσίας ἀγνοοῦσι τὴν δύναμιν,
μᾶλλον δὲ κακουργοῦντες καὶ νόμον ἀθετοῦσι καὶ θεὸν ἐξουδενοῦσι
καὶ τὴν ἡμέραν τοῦ σαββάτου ἀσυντελῆ ἀποφαίνονται καὶ δοκοῦντες
τιμᾶν ἀτιμάζουσι.

110 **10.**   Ὁ νόμος ἐμέρισε τὰς ἡμέρας τῆς ἑβδομάδος, καὶ τὰς μὲν ἓξ
εἰς τὴν σωματικὴν ἐργασίαν, τὴν δὲ ἑβδόμην εἰς τὴν ψυχικὴν
ἐργασίαν ἀφώρισε. ἐπειδὴ γὰρ ὁ ἄνθρωπος τῶν πνευματικῶν χαρισμάτων ἅπαξ ἀποδιαστὰς καὶ τὴν τῶν θείων μελέτην καταλιπών, εἰς
τὴν τῶν γεηρῶν ἐπιθυμίαν κατωλίσθησε καὶ περὶ τὴν τοῦ σώματος
115 ἀπόλαυσιν ἀδολεσχῶν ὑπῆρχεν. ἵνα μὴ ἐκ τῆς παντελοῦς ἀργίας εἰς
ἀτόπους ἐπιθυμίας ἐμπίπτει καὶ περὶ τὴν τῶν παθῶν φροντίδα διόλου
σχολάζῃ, περιέκλεισεν ὁ νόμος τὴν διάνοιαν τοῦ ἀνθρώπου τὰς ἓξ
ἡμέρας εἰς τὰ διὰ τῶν τεχνῶν ἔργα, ἵνα ἐν τούτοις διαπονούμενος
ὁ ἄνθρωπος καὶ τὰ πρὸς διατροφὴν καὶ σκέπην τοῦ σώματος
120 πορίζηται καὶ τῶν κακῶν παντελῶς ἀπέχηται.

11.   Ἐπεὶ δὲ διπλοῦς ὁ ἄνθρωπος τελῶν ψυχὴν ἔχει καὶ σῶμα,
ἀπεκλήρωσε τὴν τοῦ σαββάτου ἡμέραν εἰς θεραπείαν τῆς ψυχῆς,
ὅπως τῆς ἑβδόμης ἡμέρας ἀναλισκομένης εἰς τὰς ἐν τῷ ἱερῷ συνάξεις
καὶ τοὺς θείους ὕμνους καὶ τὰ ἱερὰ ἄσματα καὶ εἰς τὰς ἀναγνώσεις
125 καὶ πᾶσαν ἄλλην τὴν πρὸς ἀλλήλους εὐποιΐαν, πιαίνηται ἡ ψυχὴ
καὶ ἐπιγινώσκει τὸν εὐεργέτην τοῦ παντὸς καὶ τὴν μνήμην τῶν διὰ
τοῦ νόμου διηγορευμένων περισώζει καὶ ἐν ταῖς ἐργασίμοις ἡμέραις.
εἰ γὰρ οὐκ ἔξεστιν ἀγαθοποιεῖν ἐν σαββάτῳ καὶ ἑαυτὸν καὶ τὸν

has granted healing to bodies and salvation to souls, and through these works has led men to the knowledge and love of God. By working a miracle on the Sabbath he revealed himself as the true spiritual Sabbath. For he is the destroyer of sin and he is death to the passions, the well-spring of the virtues and rest for ascetics. "Come, he says, all you who labour and are heavily burdened and I will give you rest";[19] and again, "Learn from me, for I am meek and humble of heart, and you will find rest for your souls. Take my yoke upon you."[20] If the precepts of Christ constitute a yoke, it is nevertheless a goodly one; and if submission to the Gospel is a burden, it is nevertheless a light one, for his commandments are not too heavy to bear.[21]

9. What did the presidents of the synagogue, the scribes, Pharisees, and teachers of the Jewish people say to this? "There are six days on which work ought to be done. Come on those days and be healed and not on the Sabbath day."[22] Pricked by envy and blinded by jealousy, they were unaware of the meaning of the Sabbath law; rather, in their malice they both rejected the Law and treated God with contempt. They emptied the Sabbath day of any meaning; in thinking they were honouring it, they deprived it of honour.

10. The Law divided up the days of the week and set aside six days for bodily labour and the seventh day for the labour of the soul. Once man had removed himself from the spiritual gifts and abandoned meditation on divine things, he sank to desire for earthly things and spent his time in idle chatter about the delights of the body. Lest out of total laziness man should fall prey to unnatural desires and devote his attention entirely to the passions, the Law restricted man's discursive intellect during the six days of the week to working with his skills, in order that by labouring with these he might provide sustenance and shelter for the body and abstain completely from evil works.

11. Since man is twofold in nature, possessing soul and body, God allotted the Sabbath day for the healing of the soul. In this way, if the seventh day is spent in liturgical assemblies, in divine hymns, sacred songs and readings and in any other good work done for one another, the soul will grow strong and recognize the Benefactor of the universe and preserve even on workdays the memory of the prescriptions of the Law. If it is not permissible for the Jew to do good on the Sabbath

[19] Mt 11:28.
[20] Mt 11:29.
[21] Mt 11:30.
[22] Lk 13:14.

πλησίον δι᾽ ἔργων πνευματικῶν, οὐδὲ ὑμνήσει λοιπὸν τὸν θεὸν ὁ
130 Ἰουδαῖος ἐν τῇ ἡμέρᾳ ταύτῃ, οὐδὲ εὔξεται, οὐδὲ ἀναγνώσει σχολάσει,
ἀλλ᾽ οὐδὲ φάγει οὐδὲ πίει, οὐδὲ ὑπνώσει, οὐδὲ στήσεται, οὐδὲ
κινηθήσεται, οὐδὲ καθίσει· ἔσται δὲ μόνον ἀναπεπτωκὼς ἐπὶ κλίνης.
    12. Τούτων γὰρ τὰ μὲν τῆς πίστεως, τὰ δὲ τῆς φύσεως ἔργα.
τούτων μὴ τελουμένων, εἰς τί χρήσιμον ἡ τοῦ σαββάτου ἡμέρα
135 δαπανηθήσεται; καίτοι γε ὁ νόμος μέχρι καὶ τῶν κτηνῶν ἐν τῷ
σαββάτῳ τὸν ἔλεον ἐκτείνει καὶ τοῦτο πάλιν διὰ τὴν ἀνάπαυσιν τοῦ
ἀνθρώπου, δι᾽ ὃν ὥσπερ τὰ ἄλλα πάντα, οὕτω δὴ καὶ τὸ σάββατον
γέγονε. καὶ γὰρ κινδυνεύοντι τῷ ζῴῳ κατὰ τὸ σάββατον βοηθεῖν ὁ
νόμος ἐπιτρέπει καὶ ὑγιαίνοντι τὰ πρὸς ζωὴν ὑπηρετεῖν διατάττεται·
140 καὶ ὁ μὲν ποιῶν ταῦτα φυλάττει τὸν νόμον, τὴν συμπάθειαν κηρύττει
τοῦ νόμου, τὸν νομοθέτην δοξάζει.
    13. Ὁ δὲ τὴν θεραπείαν καὶ τὴν σωτηρίαν ἐκτελῶν τοῦ ἀνθρώπου
ἐν τῷ σαββάτῳ καὶ διερμηνεύων τοῦ νόμου τὴν δύναμιν καὶ τῆς τοῦ
σαββάτου προσηγορίας ἀνακαλύπτων διὰ τῶν ἔργων τὸ μυστήριον
145 καὶ τὸν νοῦν ἐντεῦθεν διανοίγων εἰς τὴν τοῦ πνεύματος κατανόησιν,
παραλύει τὸν νόμον καὶ βεβηλοῖ τὸ σάββατον καὶ ἀντινομοθετεῖ; ὁρᾷς
πῶς οἱ τὸν νόμον περιέπειν ὑποκρινόμενοι τὰ ἐναντία τοῦ νόμου καὶ
φρονοῦσι καὶ λέγουσι; βλέπεις πῶς ἡ τοῦ φθόνου κακία ἐμποδὼν
τοῖς Ἰουδαίοις προσίσταται τοῦ μὴ ἐπιγνῶναι τὴν ἀλήθειαν; ἕκαστος
150 καὶ γὰρ αὐτῶν ἔδει συνιδεῖν τὴν τοῦ νόμου διάθεσιν ἀφ᾽ ἑαυτοῦ·
ἐθαυμαστώθη, γάρ φησιν, ἡ γνῶσίς σου ἐξ ἐμοῦ.

    14. Ἕκαστος γὰρ σῶμα τελεῖ καὶ ψυχὴ καὶ ὥσπερ ὁ μετά τινος
ὁμιλῶν καὶ τὴν ἔξωθεν αὐτοῦ ὄψιν ὁρᾷ καὶ τὴν ἔσωθεν τοῦ σώματος
ψυχὴν διὰ τοῦ λόγου νοεῖ, καὶ τὸ μὲν δυσειδὲς τῆς ὄψεως παρατρέχει,
155 τὴν δὲ κεκρυμμένην λαμπρότητα τῆς ψυχῆς φανερουμένην διὰ τοῦ
λόγου κατανοῶν θαυμάζει καὶ ἀποδέχεται, οὕτως εἰκάσαι δεῖ καὶ περὶ
τοῦ παλαιοῦ νόμου· πρόσωπον γάρ ἐστι καὶ οὗ τὸ σῶμα αὐτοῦ τὰ
ῥήματα, ψυχὴ δὲ ἡ θεωρία τοῦ πνεύματος. ὁ γοῦν τὰ ῥήματα
διερχόμενος ὀφείλει καὶ τὴν ψυχὴν ἀνιχνεύειν, ἤτοι τὸν πνευματικὸν
160 νοῦν. καὶ ὥσπερ ἡ ἱστορία τοῦ γράμματος εἰς τὴν θεωρίαν εἰσάγει
τοῦ πνεύματος, οὕτως ἡ θεωρία πάλιν ἀναπτύσσει τὴν ἱστορίαν, καὶ
οὕτω τῆς ἀληθείας ἡ ἐπίγνωσις διαυγάζει. ὁ δὲ τῇ παχύτητι τοῦ
γράμματος ἐναπομένων, ὡς σαρκικὰ φρονῶν, τῇ σαρκὶ τοῦ νόμου
προσφύεται καὶ ταῖς ψιλαῖς ἀφαῖς τῶν ῥημάτων καθηδυνόμενος,
165 πνευματικὸν καὶ οὐράνιον οὐδὲν ἐννοεῖ· ὅθεν καὶ τὸ σκότος ἀγαπῶν,

132 ἀναπεπτωκὼς corr.: ἀναπεπτωκὸς OA

either for himself or for his neighbour by means of spiritual works, for the rest neither will he praise God on this day, nor pray, nor devote time to reading; he does not eat or drink, nor will he sleep, stand, move about or sit down. He will only take to his bed.

12. Some of these are the works of faith, others are the works of nature. If these works are not done, what useful occupation is left for the Sabbath day? And yet the Law extends compassion even to cattle on the Sabbath. As in other matters, the purpose of the Sabbath is that man may find some rest. The Law allows one to assist an animal in danger on the Sabbath and commands one to provide the necessities of life for a healthy animal. The man who does this keeps the Law, proclaims the compassion of the Law, and glorifies the Lawgiver.

13. But if someone effects the healing and salvation of man on the Sabbath, explains the meaning of the Law, reveals in his works the mystery behind the name of the Sabbath, thus opening the mind to an understanding of the spirit of the Law, does he put an end to the Law and profane the Sabbath and introduce a rival law? Do you see how those who pretend to treat the Law with respect both think and say things contrary to the Law? Do you see how the evil of jealousy stands as a hindrance to the Jews so that they refuse to recognize the truth? Each of them on their own ought to have understood the intention of the Law. For scripture says, "Knowledge of you is too wonderful for me."[23]

14. Each person consists of body and soul. Someone conversing with another sees that person's outer appearance and conceives of the soul inside the body through what he says; he passes over the ugliness in the other's appearance while marveling at and receiving the hidden radiance of his soul, which he perceives and which is made manifest through speech. In just such a way should one portray the Old Law: it is like a person whose body is the words of the Law and whose soul is the contemplation of the spirit of the Law. Thus anyone perusing the words ought also to search out the soul, that is, the spiritual meaning. Just as the account of the letter leads to contemplation of the spirit, so contemplation in turn unfolds the literal sense; in this way, recognition of the truth bestows its radiance. But anyone who stays on the obtuse level of the literal sense, just as he thinks carnal thoughts, he clings to the flesh of the Law. Finding his delight in a mere grasp of the words, he understands nothing of their spiritual and heavenly meaning and so, in loving the darkness, he falls away from

[23] Ps 138:6.

τοῦ φωτὸς ἀποπίπτει· ὁ Ἰσραήλ, γάρ φησι, διώκων τὸν σωματικὸν
νόμον, εἰς τὸν πνευματικὸν νόμον οὐκ ἔφθασε.

    15. Καὶ τοῦτο κατάμαθε ἀπὸ τῶν τοῦ ἀρχισυναγώγου ῥημάτων·
ἓξ ἡμέραι εἰσὶν ἐν αἷς δεῖ ἐργάζεσθαι. ἓξ βίβλοι εἰσίν, ἡ πεντάτευχος
170 τοῦ Μωσέως καὶ ἡ τῶν προφητῶν. ταύτας δεῖ ἀναγινώσκειν ψιλῶς,
ταύτας φυλάττειν κατὰ τὸ γράμμα· ταύτας διερχόμενοι διὰ τῶν λέξεων
καὶ σωματικῶς ἐκλαμβάνοντες, θεραπεύετε τὰ σώματα καθ' ἡδονὴν
καὶ μὴ τῇ ἡμέρᾳ τοῦ σαββάτου θεραπεύεσθε κατὰ ψυχήν, μηδὲν πλέον
τῆς ἱστορίας κατὰ διάνοιαν προβαίνοντες.

175   **16.** Τὸ σάββατον κατάπαυσιν σημαίνει, καὶ ὁ συνιεὶς τὸ μυστήριον
τοῦ σαββάτου καταπαύει καὶ ἀργεῖ τὸν νόμον. ὁ τὰ τῆς χάριτος
ἐνεργῶν ἀργεῖ τὰ τοῦ νόμου. ὁ τὴν καινὴν διαθήκην στέργων τὴν
παλαιὰν οὐ τελεῖ. ἐν ταῖς ἓξ ἡμέραις ἐρχόμενοι θεραπεύεσθε καὶ μὴ τῇ
ἡμέρᾳ τοῦ σαββάτου. ὃ δὲ λέγει τοιοῦτόν ἐστιν· τῷ τύπῳ παραμένετε
180 καὶ μὴ τῇ ἀληθείᾳ προσδράμητε· τῇ σκιᾷ καλύπτεσθε καὶ μὴ πρὸς
τὸ φῶς ἀτενίζητε· τῆς σαρκὸς ποιεῖτε πρόνοιαν καὶ τῆς ψυχῆς τὴν
μέριμναν ἀπόθεσθε· τὸ γράμμα διέρχεσθε καὶ τὸ πνεῦμα μὴ διερευνᾶτε.
αὕτη τῶν τοῦ ἀρχισυναγώγου ῥημάτων ἡ διάνοια.

    17. Ἡ τοῦ σαββάτου ἡμέρα συμπλήρωσίς ἐστι τῆς ἑβδομάδος,
185 προστιθεμένη γὰρ ταῖς πρὸ αὐτῆς ἓξ ἡμέραις, ἑβδόμη εὑρίσκεται,
προσηγορεύθη δὲ σάββατον κατάπαυσιν σημαίνουσα, ἐπειδὴ ἐν ταῖς
ἓξ ἡμέραις τὰ πάντα δημιουργήσας ὁ θεός, ἐν τῇ ἑβδόμῃ κατέπαυσεν
ἀπὸ πάντων τῶν ἔργων. τὸ σάββατον τὸν μέλλοντα αἰῶνα ὑπαινίττεται,
ἐν ᾧ ἡ ἀποχήρωσις κατὰ τὰ βεβιωμένα ἑκάστῳ γίνεται· ὡς γὰρ ἡ
190 τοῦ σαββάτου ἡμέρα ἐπιστᾶσα τοὺς κατὰ τὰς πρὸ αὐτῆς ἡμέρας
κοπιῶντας διαναπαύει μὲν ἀπὸ τῶν σωματικῶν μόχθων, εἰς ὕμνους
δὲ θείους καὶ διηγήματα διεγείρει, οὕτω καὶ ὁ μέλλων αἰὼν τοὺς ὧδε
ὑπὲρ ἀρετῆς ἀγωνισαμένους καὶ μετὰ ἐφοδίων πνευματικῶν τοῦ τῇδε
βίου ἐκδεδημηκότας ἀνακλίνει καὶ τῶν βραβείων ἀξιοῖ.

195   **18.** Ἡ ἑβδόμη ἡμέρα ὡς μονὰς καὶ τὴν παρθενίαν ὑπεμφαίνει καὶ
τὴν ἀγγελικὴν ζωὴν ὑπογράφει, τὴν ἑτοιμασίαν τοῦ μὴ λυομένου

---

189 ἀποχήρωσις conieci: ἀποκήρωσις OA

the light. For scripture says, "In pursuing the Law of the body Israel failed to attain the Law of the spirit."[24]

15. And this is what you should learn from the words of the president of the synagogue: "There are six days on which work ought to be done."[25] There are six books, namely, the Pentateuch of Moses and the Book of the Prophets. You should read these in straightforward fashion; you should keep to their literal meaning. As you go through them according to what the words actually say with the corporeal sense in mind, heal your bodies as you please, but seek no healing for your soul on the Sabbath day, going no further in your discursive intellect than the literal sense.

16. The word 'Sabbath' means rest, and one who understands the mystery of the Sabbath puts an end to the Law and leaves it as no longer effectual. He who works by the activities of grace considers the teachings of the Law ineffectual. He who loves the New Covenant does not abide by the old one. "On the six weekdays come and be healed, but not on the Sabbath."[26] What the synagogue president is saying is this: "Stay with the type and do not run to the truth; hide yourself in the shadow and do not look towards the light. Make provision for the flesh and disregard the cares of the soul. Peruse the letter and do not search after the spirit." This is the meaning of the words spoken by the president of the synagogue.

17. The Sabbath day is the completion of the week, for when it is added to the preceding six days it makes up the seventh; and it was called 'Sabbath' meaning rest, since God created all things in six days and rested from all his works on the seventh.[27] The Sabbath alludes to the future age when for each man there will be a separation from his past life. Just as the Sabbath day, when it comes, grants to those who laboured on the preceding days rest from bodily toils and rouses them to divine hymns and readings, so too the future age grants repose[28] and reward to those who have struggled for virtue here below and who have departed from this life with spiritual provisions.

18. Since the seventh day stands alone, it alludes to virginity and represents the angelic life,[29] in that it announces beforehand readiness

---

[24] Cf. Rom 9:31.

[25] Lk 13:14.

[26] Lk 13:14.

[27] Gen 2:2.

[28] Literally, "causes to recline." The reference is to the Messianic banquet (cf. Mt 8:11, Lk 13:29).

[29] I.e., the monastic life.

αἰῶνος προκηρύττουσα, ἐν γὰρ τῇ ἀναστάσει πάντες ὡς ἄγγελοι διαμένουσιν. ἡ τοῦ σαββάτου ἡμέρα ὡς ἑβδόμη καὶ τὴν ἑπταδικὴν ἐνέργειαν τῶν τοῦ πνεύματος χαρισμάτων ὑποδηλοῖ· ὡς γὰρ αὕτη
200 καὶ τοὺς σωματικοὺς μόχθους κοιμίζει καὶ πρὸς τοὺς πνευματικοὺς τρόπους καὶ ὕμνους τοὺς ἀληθεῖς φύλακας τοῦ νόμου ἐξυπνίζει, οὕτω καὶ ὁ τοῦ εὐαγγελίου νόμος διπλῶς φιλοτιμεῖται τοὺς τῆς εὐσεβείας ἀγωνιστάς· καὶ τὴν τῶν παθῶν χαρίζεται κατάπαυσιν, τὴν σάρκα νεκρῶν καὶ δουλαγωγῶν· καὶ τὴν ψυχὴν ἐνισχύων πρὸς τὴν τῶν
205 ἀρετῶν κατόρθωσιν, τὸν νοῦν κραταιῶν τῶν τῆς σαρκὸς κρατεῖν θελημάτων.

19. Διὰ τοῦτο καὶ ὁ Χριστὸς τὰ πλεῖστα τῶν θαυμάτων καὶ μείζονα ἐν τῷ σαββάτῳ ἐτέλει, γνῶσιν ἐνιεὶς τοῖς Ἰουδαίοις καὶ διὰ τῆς ἡμέρας, τοῦ μὲν παχυτέρου φρονήματος ἀπάγειν τὸν νοῦν, πρὸς
210 δὲ τὰ τοῦ πνεύματος μεταβιβάζειν αὐτόν. ἀλλὰ προσεκτέον μήποτε ἅπερ ἐγκαλοῦμεν τοῖς ἀλλοτρίοις, ταῦτα καὶ ἡμῖν πρόσεστι τοῖς οἰκειουμένοις τῷ Χριστῷ διὰ τῆς πίστεως. φησὶ γὰρ ὁ ἀπόστολος, *οἱ δὲ τοῦ Χριστοῦ τὴν σάρκα ἐσταύρωσαν σὺν τοῖς παθήμασι καὶ ταῖς ἐπιθυμίαις·* τουτέστι τὰς τοῦ σώματος ἐμπαθεῖς πράξεις ἐνέκρωσαν
215 σὺν ταῖς κατὰ διάνοιαν ἀνατυπώσεσι τῶν ἀτόπων λογισμῶν καὶ ταῖς βλαβεραῖς ἐπιθυμίαις. ἤκουσαν γὰρ Ἱερεμίου τοῦ προφήτου λέγοντος, *θάνατος ἀνέβη διὰ τῶν θυρίδων.* ἤκουσαν τοῦ προφήτου Δαβίδ, *θοῦ, κύριε, φυλακὴν τῷ στόματί μου καὶ θύραν περιοχῆς περὶ τὰ χείλη μου,* φάσκοντος. ἤκουσαν τοῦ ἀποστόλου, *πνεύματι περιπατεῖτε καὶ ἐπιθυμίαν*
220 *σαρκὸς οὐ μὴ τελέσητε,* φθεγγομένου.

20. Καὶ ἐπειδὴ ὁ τῆς σαρκὸς νόμος κατὰ τὴν πενταδικὴν τοῦ σώματος αἴσθησιν καὶ τὴν τῆς γλώσσης κίνησιν ἐνεργούμενος ἔχει καὶ τὴν διάνοιαν φαντασίων ἀπρεπῶν καὶ ῥυπαρῶν λογισμῶν ἀναπεπλησμένην, ἔσπευσαν ὡς τοῦ πνεύματος ἐρασταὶ τὰς τοῦ
225 σώματος αἰσθήσεις καὶ τὸν κατὰ προφορὰν λόγον τοῖς τρόποις τῶν ἀρετῶν χαλινῶσαι καὶ ἀσφαλίσασθαι. εἶτα ὡς ἐν ἑβδόμῃ ἡμέρᾳ τῇ διανοίᾳ ἐπιστάντες, ἐν ᾗ τῶν λογισμῶν ἡ συναγωγὴ καὶ τὸ φρόνημα τῆς ψυχῆς τελεῖται, ἠγωνίσαντο διὰ προσευχῆς συντόνου καὶ τῆς τῶν γραφῶν μελέτης καὶ τῆς τῶν ἐν τῷ μέλλοντι αἰῶνι διηνεκοῦς
230 φροντίδος, καὶ κατέπαυσαν ἀπὸ τῶν παθῶν καὶ κατήργησαν τοὺς πονηροὺς λογισμούς.

for the age that knows no end, for in the resurrection all will live as angels.[30] The Sabbath, as the seventh day, points to the sevenfold operation of the gifts of the Spirit. Just as this day puts bodily toils to sleep and awakens the true guardians of the Law to spiritual ways and hymns, so too the Law of the Gospel bestows a twofold gift upon those who labour for piety: it grants relief from the passions by mortifying the flesh and bringing it into subjection[31] and it empowers the soul to attain the virtues while strengthening the mind to master the will of the flesh.

19. For this reason Christ worked most of his miracles, and the greater of these, on the Sabbath imparting knowledge to the Jews through this day so as to lead their minds out of their obtuse way of thinking and win them over to the ways of the Spirit. But we must take care lest we, who have assimilated our lives to Christ by faith, should ever be guilty of the same accusations we make against others. For the Apostle says, "Those who belong to Christ have crucified the flesh with its passions and desires":[32] that is, they have put to death the body's deeds of passion together with harmful desires and the impressions left on the discursive intellect by wicked thoughts. For they have given ear to the prophet Jeremiah, who says, "Death has come up through the windows."[33] They have heard the prophet David saying, "Set a guard over my mouth, O Lord, a door to encompass my lips."[34] They have listened to the voice of the Apostle, "Walk in the Spirit, and do not gratify the desires of the flesh."[35]

20. Because the law of the flesh, which operates according to the fivefold senses of the body and the movement of the tongue, leaves the discursive intellect filled with indecent phantasies and sordid thoughts, as devotees of the Spirit, they strove eagerly to rein in the senses of the body and the spoken word and keep them securely in check by the practice of the virtues. Then, when on the seventh day they came to a standstill in the discursive intellect, in which the thoughts are gathered and the soul's attitude is formed, they entered into the struggle with intense prayer and meditation on the scriptures and continual attention to the things of the future age; they found rest from the passions and rendered evil thoughts impotent.

[30] Cf. Mt 22:30.
[31] Cf. 1 Cor 9:27.
[32] Gal 5:24.
[33] Jer 9:20.
[34] Ps 140:3.
[35] Gal 5:16.

21. Ἀμέλει καὶ τὸν ἀληθῆ σαββατισμὸν αὐτῶν ὁρῶν ὁ διὰ προσευχῆς δυσωπούμενος κύριος, παραγίνεται ἐν ταῖς ψυχαῖς αὐτῶν καὶ τὸν συγκύπτοντα νοῦν εἰς τὰς ἐπιθυμίας τῶν αἰσθητῶν τὰ ἄνω
235 φρονεῖν ἐκπαιδεύει· καὶ λύων αὐτὸν τοῦ διπλοῦ δεσμοῦ, τοῦ τε κατὰ τὴν αἴσθησιν καὶ τὴν διάνοιαν, τὴν ἔφεσιν αὐτοῦ δεσμεῖ τῷ ἔρωτι αὐτοῦ καὶ δίδωσιν αὐτῷ μετὰ παρρησίας λέγειν. *διέρρηξας τοὺς δεσμούς μου, σοὶ θύσω θυσίαν αἰνέσεως.* θυσία δὲ αἰνέσεως ἡ κατὰ σῶμα πρᾶξις τῶν ἀρετῶν καὶ ἡ κατὰ διάνοιαν ἀπερίσπαστος προσ-
240 ευχή.
22. Κατὰ μὲν γὰρ τὸ παλαιὸν θυσίαν ἡ τοῦ νεκροῦ ζῴου προσ-ένεξις ἐτέλει, κατὰ δὲ τὴν χάριν τὸ νεκροῦν τὰ τοῦ σώματος μέλη πρὸς τὰς ἐμπαθεῖς πράξεις καὶ τὰς τῆς ψυχῆς δυνάμεις ἀκινήτους τηρεῖν πρὸς τὰς φαύλους ὁρμάς, τὸ σπουδαῖον εἶναι διὰ παντὸς πρὸς
245 τὴν τῶν θείων θελημάτων ἐκπλήρωσιν, τὸ ἐπὶ στόματος τοὺς θείους ὕμνους συνετῶς φέρειν καὶ τὸ ἐν τῇ διανοίᾳ διανύειν τὴν προσευχὴν νηφόντως. ταῦτά ἐστι θυσία ζῶσα καὶ εὐάρεστος καὶ λογικὴ λατρεία· θυσία διὰ τὸ ἀναισθήτως ἔχειν πρὸς τὴν ἁμαρτίαν, ζῶσα διὰ τὴν ἔφεσιν καὶ τὴν πρὸς τὰ καλὰ κίνησιν, εὐάρεστος διὰ τὸ ἀρέσκεσθαι
250 τὸν θεὸν ἐν τοῖς κατὰ πνεῦμα τελουμένοις, λογικὴ δὲ ὡς τοῦ λόγου τὴν φύσιν ἰθύνοντος τὰ κατ᾽ ἐντολὴν πράττειν. οὕτω μὲν οὖν οἱ κατὰ Χριστὸν ζῆν αἱρούμενοι τὸν ἑαυτὸν ἰθύνοντες βίον, εἰς τοὺς οὐρανίους καταπαύουσι κόλπους.

23. Οἱ δὲ τὰς αἰσθήσεις μόνας κοσμοῦντες καὶ τὴν διὰ τῶν λόγων
255 ὁμιλίαν περιποιούμενοι, τῆς διανοίας δὲ καταμελοῦντες καὶ τῆς τῶν κρυπτῶν παθῶν ἀποβολῆς οὐδόλως φροντίζοντες, οὗτοι καὶ καθηδυ-παθοῦσι καὶ κενοδοξοῦσιν. ὡς ἄλλῳ γὰρ ἀρχισυναγώγῳ, τῷ δαίμονι τῆς ὑποκρίσεως πειθαρχούμενοι, συνήδονται τοῖς λογισμοῖς καὶ τὴν πρὸς ἀνθρώπους ἐπίδειξιν ἀσπάζονται, ἀπωθούμενοι τὸν σαββατισμὸν
260 καὶ τὴν ἀπὸ τῶν παθῶν ἀναχώρησιν, ὡς τὸν ἔπαινον θηρώμενοι τὸν ἀνθρώπινον. ἀγνοοῦσι καὶ γὰρ ὅτι ὥσπερ *ἐξένευσεν ὁ Ἰησοῦς ὄχλου ὄντος ἐν τῷ τόπῳ,* οὕτω καὶ ἡμῶν ὑπὸ παθῶν ἐνοχλουμένων καὶ ὑπὸ λογισμῶν συγχεομένων ἀποχωρεῖ. ἐὰν δὲ ἴδῃ ἡμᾶς ῥίπτοντας ἑαυτοὺς εἰς ἀποφυγὴν τῶν ἀφανῶν παθῶν, ἐπιφαίνεται ἡμῖν καὶ πᾶσαν

21. And indeed, when the Lord is importuned through their prayer and sees their true Sabbath observance, he visits their souls and teaches the mind bowed down among desires for sensible things to think of the things above.[36] Loosing the mind from its twofold bondage, namely, in sense perception and in the discursive intellect, he binds its yearning to love for him and grants it the freedom to say, "You have loosed my bonds; I will sacrifice to you a sacrifice of praise."[37] A sacrifice of praise consists in the body's practice of the virtues and the undistracted prayer of the discursive intellect.

22. In the old dispensation the offering of a dead animal constituted a sacrifice, but in the dispensation of grace sacrifice involves mortifying the members of the body with respect to deeds of passion[38] and keeping the faculties of the soul from being moved by evil impulses; being always eager for the fulfilment of the divine will; singing the divine hymns intelligently with one's lips; and practising vigilant prayer in the discursive intellect. That is "a living and pleasing sacrifice, rational worship."[39] It is a sacrifice because it is insensible to sin; it is living because of its longing for and movement towards the good; it is pleasing because God is pleased with what is done according to the Spirit; it is rational in that reason guides nature in practising what is in accord with the commandments. In this way, then, those who choose to live according to Christ give direction to their lives and find rest in heavenly harbours.

23. People who adorn only their senses and busy themselves with the converse of speech, while neglecting their discursive intellect and paying no attention at all to repudiating their hidden passions, squander their lives in pleasure and vainglory. Offering their obedience to the demon of hypocrisy, as to another synagogue president, they find pleasure in their thoughts and welcome ostentation before men,[40] while rejecting the observance of the Sabbath and withdrawal from the passions, for they chase after human praise. They are unaware that just as "Jesus avoided the mob that was in that place,"[41] so, too, he withdraws from us when we are mobbed by the passions and thrown into confusion by our thoughts. But if he sees us throwing ourselves into flight from our hidden passions, he manifests himself to us and

---

[36] Cf. Col 3:2.
[37] Ps 115:7-8.
[38] Cf. Col 3:5.
[39] Rom 12:1.
[40] Cf. Mt 6:1, 23:5.
[41] Jn 5:13.

265 ταραχὴν διασκεδάζει, αὐτὸς γάρ ἐστιν καὶ ἡ νέκρωσις τῶν ἁμαρτημάτων καὶ ἡ ζώωσις τῶν κατορθωμάτων· *κύριος, γάρ φησι, θανατοῖ
καὶ ζωογονεῖ.*

24. Ἑτοιμάσωμεν οὖν ἑαυτοὺς ἀπομαθεῖν τὰ κακά, ἵνα κραταίωσιν
λάβωμεν εἰς τὸ ποιεῖν τὰ καλά. *ὁ κύριος, γάρ φησι, δώσει χρηστότητα,*
270 *γνῶσιν ἀληθείας καὶ δύναμιν.* καὶ ἡ φύσις ἡμῶν τελεσφορήσει τοὺς
καρποὺς τῶν καλῶν, δοξάζουσα Χριστὸν τὸν χορηγὸν καὶ συνεργὸν
καὶ τελειωτὴν τῶν ἀγαθῶν· ὅτι αὐτῷ πρέπει πᾶσα δόξα εἰς τοὺς
αἰῶνας. Ἀμήν.

scatters every disturbance, for he is death to sins and life to virtuous accomplishments. For scripture says, "The Lord bestows death and grants life."[42]

24.   Let us prepare ourselves, then, to unlearn our evil ways in order that we may receive the fortitude to do good. For scripture says, "The Lord will bestow kindness,"[43] knowledge of the truth and power. And our nature shall bring to perfection the fruits of good deeds, as it glorifies Christ, the provider, co-worker and perfecter of good things. To him be all glory forever. Amen.

[42] 1 Kingdoms 2:6.
[43] Ps 84:13.

Κατήχησις εἰς τὴν ἑορτὴν τῆς Μεταμορφώσεως τοῦ κυρίου καὶ θεοῦ καὶ σωτῆρος ἡμῶν Ἰησοῦ Χριστοῦ

1. Ἡ παροῦσα λαμπρὰ ἡμέρα τῆς Μεταμορφώσεως κατὰ τὴν δοθεῖσαν ἡμῖν χάριν παρὰ τοῦ μεταμορφωθέντος Χριστοῦ ἀπαιτεῖ
5 παραστῆσαι τῇ ὑμῶν ἀγάπῃ τῆς ἑορτῆς τὸ μυστήριον, ἵνα τὴν δύναμιν τοῦ μυστηρίου μαθόντες οὐ μόνον τοῖς ἱεροῖς ὕμνοις, ἀλλὰ καὶ τοῖς ἀγαθοῖς τρόποις τὴν τοῦ Χριστοῦ Μεταμόρφωσιν ἑορτάζωμεν· ἐπεὶ καὶ τοῦτό ἐστιν τὸ ἐπιγνῶναι ἡμᾶς τὴν δωρεὰν ἧς ἠξιώθημεν καὶ τὸν ταύτης θησαυρὸν ἀνακαλύπτειν διὰ τῆς τῶν ἀγαθῶν ἔργων
10 προκοπῆς, βίῳ καὶ λόγῳ τὴν ἑορτὴν σεβαζόμενοι.

2. Ὁ ἐν πεδιάδι βαδίζων γῇ μετ' ἀναπαύσεως περιπατεῖ διὰ τὴν ὁμαλότητα τοῦ τόπου καὶ τὴν εὐκολίαν τῆς ὁδοιπορίας· ὁ δὲ ἀναβαίνων ἐν ὄρει κοπιᾷ καὶ ἱδρῶτι περιχεῖται διὰ τὸ ἄναντες τοῦ τόπου καὶ τὴν ἐντεῦθεν τοῦ σώματος ἀγανάκτησιν. τὴν οὖν ὁμαλὴν
15 γῆν καὶ ὑπτίαν καὶ πρὸς τὸν δρόμον ῥᾳδίαν, εἰκόνα λάμβανε τοῦ καθ' ἡδονὴν βίου καὶ τῆς τρυφῆς καὶ τοῦ πλατυσμοῦ τῆς κατὰ σάρκα ζωῆς διὰ τὴν ἄνεσιν καὶ τὴν λειότητα τῶν ματαίων ἡδονῶν· τὸ δὲ ὄρος εἰκόνα λογίζου πάλιν τῆς ἐναρέτου διαγωγῆς διὰ τὴν ἐν πᾶσιν ἐγκράτειαν καὶ τὸ τραχὺ τῆς ἀσκήσεως καὶ τὸ ἐπώδυνον τῆς
20 ὑπομονῆς τῶν συναντώντων θλιβερῶν.

3. Ὁ τοίνυν ἐγκρατείᾳ συζῶν καὶ κατὰ τὰς ἐντολὰς τοῦ Χριστοῦ πορευόμενος καὶ τὰς ἡδονὰς τοῦ σώματος καταμαραίνων, πιστὸς καὶ θερμὸς μαθητὴς τοῦ κυρίου κατὰ τὸν Πέτρον ὁρᾶται. ὁ δέ γε καὶ τὸ φρόνημα τοῦ κόσμου θανατῶν καὶ λογισμοὺς σαρκικοὺς καταργῶν
25 καὶ πρὸς τὰς ὑπὲρ τοῦ εὐαγγελίου θλίψεις ἑτοιμαζόμενος καὶ τοὺς κακῶς βιοῦντας ἐλέγχων καὶ τὰς ἐξ αὐτῶν ὑπὲρ ἀληθείας κακώσεις

Catechesis on the feast of the Transfiguration of our Lord, God and Saviour, Jesus Christ[1]

1. The present, radiant day of the Transfiguration, according to the grace granted us by the transfigured Christ, invites us to present to your charity the mystery of this feast. For once we have learned the meaning of the mystery, we may celebrate the Transfiguration of Christ not only with sacred hymns but also with virtuous conduct. This indeed is the meaning of the feast, namely, that we recognize the gift of which we have been deemed worthy and that we reveal its treasure through our progress in good works, revering the feast both in our lives and in our words.

2. The person who travels on level ground walks about refreshed because of the evenness of the terrain and the ease of the journeying, but he who travels up a mountain grows weary with the effort and is drenched with sweat because of the steepness of the terrain and the strain that it places on the body.[2] Think of the even ground, the flat terrain and the facility of the march as an image of the life lived in pleasure and of the luxury and dissipation of the life of the flesh owing to the indulgence and lubricity of vain pleasures. Consider in turn the mountain as an image of the life lived in virtue through self-discipline in all things, the ruggedness of asceticism and the painfulness of enduring chance afflictions.

3. Therefore, the person who spends his life in the company of self-discipline and proceeds according to the commandments of Christ, disdaining the pleasures of the body, is seen to be, like Peter, a faithful and fervent disciple of the Lord. And someone who puts worldliness to death, abolishes carnal thoughts and prepares himself for afflictions on behalf of the Gospel, who reproves those living evil lives and yet

---

[1] Previously edited by H.-V. Beyer, "Die Katechese des Theoleptos von Philadelpheia auf die Verklärung Christi," jöb 34 (1984) 171-198. The feast of the Transfiguration is celebrated on 6 August. The Gospel used at Matins is Lk 9:28-36 and that for the Liturgy Mt 17:1-9.

[2] This imagery for the difficulty of virtue comes ultimately from a frequently quoted or paraphrased passage of Hesiod, *Opera et dies* 287-291. Cf. Basil, *Ad adolescentes* 5 (ed. Boulenger 46.8-47.13).

βαστάζων, τὸν τοῦ Ἰακώβου ζῆλον ἐνδείκνυται. ὁ δὲ πάλιν τὴν
διάνοιαν λογίων ἱερῶν πεποιηκὼς ἐνδιαίτημα καὶ τῇ τῶν θείων
ἐκκαιόμενος μελέτῃ καὶ περὶ τοὺς λόγους τῆς φύσεως ἀδολεσχῶν
30 εἰς τὴν τῆς ἀληθείας κατανόησιν, τὸν Ἰωάννου τρόπον μιμεῖται.
οὗτος σώματι καὶ ψυχῇ καὶ διανοίᾳ κατακολουθῶν τῷ κυρίῳ καὶ τὸν
θλιβερὸν τῆς ἀρετῆς δρόμον ἀεὶ τρέχων, ἀνέρχεται καὶ εἰς τὸ κατὰ
νοῦν ὄρος εἰς τὸ προσεύχεσθαι ἀπερισπάστως· ἐκεῖ γὰρ ἡ καθαρὰ
προσευχὴ   ἐκτελεῖται,   πᾶσαν   ἔννοιαν   τοῦ   αἰῶνος   τούτου
35 ἀπορραπίζουσα καὶ τὸν νοῦν ὅλον φωτεινὸν ἀπεργαζομένη, ἅτε τῷ
τῆς θείας ἀγάπης ἐλαίῳ πιαινόμενον καὶ ταῖς θείαις φωτοχυσίαις
ἐκλάμποντα.

4.   Τοῦ νοῦ δὲ φωτιζομένου τῇ τοῦ θεοῦ μνήμῃ καὶ διὰ προσευχῆς
ἀπερισπάστου τῇ τοῦ θεοῦ γνώσει ἐλλαμπομένου, καὶ τὰ τοῦ σώματος
40 κινήματα λευκὰ διατελεῖ, ῥήματα συνέσεως ἀπὸ τοῦ στόματος
προέρχονται, τὰ αἰσθητήρια σεμνότητος περιβάλλονται κόσμον, τὰ
μέλη τοῦ σώματος περὶ τὴν διακονίαν τῶν ἀγαθῶν πράξεων πονεῖ,
καὶ ὅλος ὁ ἄνθρωπος φῶς χρηματίζει, ἐπειδὴ λυχνία γίνεται ἡ ψυχὴ
αὐτοῦ φέρουσα *τὸ φῶς τὸ ἀληθινόν, ὃ φωτίζει πάντα ἄνθρωπον ἐρχόμενον*
45 *εἰς τὸν κόσμον* τῶν ἀρετῶν.
5.   Ὁ οὕτω πολιτευόμενος καὶ οὕτως ἀναγόμενος *οὐ συσχηματίζεται*
τῷ αἰῶνι τούτῳ τῷ ἀλλοιουμένῳ καὶ λυομένῳ· ἀκούων γὰρ τοῦ τὰ
ἀθέατα κατοπτεύσαντος Παύλου λέγοντος, *ὁ θεὸς παράγει τὸ σχῆμα*
τοῦ κόσμου τούτου, οὐκ ἐπιστρέφεται τῶν ἐπιγείων. παρατρέχει τὰ
50 παρατρέχοντα, ὡς σχῆμα μόνον ἀλλ' οὐχ ὕπαρξιν κεκτημένα· ὡς γὰρ
τὸ σχῆμα ἐν βραχεῖ φαινόμενον ἀφανίζεται, οὕτω καὶ τὰ παρόντα
οὐδὲν ἔχει βέβαιον οὐδὲ στάσιμον. ὅθεν καὶ τὸ φρόνημα ἑαυτοῦ
ἐπαίρων ἀπὸ τῆς τῶν φθειρομένων ἐπιθυμίας καὶ τὰ ἡδέα τοῦ βίου
ὡς ἀνυπόστατον σχῆμα διαπτύων, τὰ ἀθάνατα πράγματα τοῦ μέλλον-
55 τος αἰῶνος κατασπάζεται, μεταμορφούμενος ἀεὶ ἐν τῷ καθ' ἑκάστην
ἐπανάγεσθαι πρὸς ἑαυτὸν καὶ ἀνακαινίζεσθαι καθ' ὥραν τὴν διάνοιαν,
τοῦτο μὲν ταῖς τῶν κακῶν ἀποχωρήσεσι, τοῦτο δὲ καὶ ταῖς πρὸς τὰ
καλὰ προσχωρήσεσι καὶ ταῖς τῶν ἀρετῶν ἐπιδόσεσι.

bears with their evil deeds for the sake of the truth, such a man manifests the zeal of James. And in turn he who has made his discursive intellect a dwelling place of the sacred scriptures, is consumed with meditating on divine realities and ponders over the reasons of nature in order to comprehend the truth, such a person imitates the way of John. John, in following the Lord in body, soul and discursive intellect, and ever running the laborious race of virtue, ascends even to the mountain of the spiritual realm, where he attains undistracted prayer. In that realm pure prayer is brought to fulfilment in casting off all concern for this age and rendering the mind entirely luminous, as at the same time it is fed with the oil of divine love and illumined by the divine outpourings of Light.[3]

4. When the mind is illumined by the remembrance of God and through undistracted prayer is enlightened by the knowledge of God, the movements of the body become perpetually white and words of understanding come forth from the mouth; the organs of sense clothe themselves with the adornment of sanctity and the members of the body labour in the service of good deeds; the whole man is coloured with light, since his soul becomes a lamp bearing the true Light which "illumines every man who comes into the world" of the virtues.[4]

5. The person who lives and progresses in this manner "is not conformed to this age" of change and dissolution.[5] He gives no attention to earthly things, for he hearkens to Paul, who saw the unseeable and said, "God is making the form of this world to pass away."[6] He passes by passing things since they possess only form but not real existence. As form appears for a brief while and then disappears, so too, present realities possess nothing secure or stable. Thus, while he raises his mind above desire for things which decay and spurns the pleasant things of life as form without substance, he embraces the immortal realities of the age to come, ever being transformed because he is restored daily unto himself and is renewed hourly in his discursive intellect. The one he accomplishes by a retreat from evil, the other by an advance towards the good and by progress in the virtues.

---

[3] Both John Chrysostom and John Damascene attribute a specific reason or role in the choice of each of the three apostles: John Chrysostom, *In Matthaeum Homilia* 56.1 (PG 58:550); John Damascene, *Homilia in Transfigurationem* 9 (PG 96:560CD). Theoleptos, however, adopts a different interpretation from his predecessors.

[4] Jn 1:9.

[5] Cf. Rom 12:2, Gal 1:4.

[6] 1 Cor 7:31.

6. Τοιαύτας ἀναβάσεις ὁ τῆς εὐσεβείας ἀγωνιστὴς ἑαυτῷ προσ-
60 τιθεὶς καὶ προκόπτων, ὡς κατὰ θεὸν κτιζόμενος καὶ δίκην φωστῆρος
ἐκλάμπων καὶ πρὸς μίμησιν καλῶν παροξύνων καὶ ἄλλους, ὅλῳ
πνεύματι καὶ ὅλῳ σώματι τιμᾷ τὴν Χριστοῦ Μεταμόρφωσιν,
ἐπιγινώσκων τῆς ἑορτῆς τὸ μυστήριον καὶ τοῖς ὁρῶσιν ἐμπράκτως
διερμηνεύων· Χριστὸς γὰρ μεταμορφωθεὶς καὶ τὴν ἄρρητον δόξαν
65 μεθ᾽ ἧς ἐλεύσεται κρῖναι τὰ σύμπαντα προεμήνυσε καὶ τὴν λαμπρότητα ἧς μεθέξουσιν οἱ αὐτῷ εὐαρεστοῦντες παρεγύμνωσε καὶ πάντα
πιστὸν ἐδίδαξε παρασκευάζειν ἑαυτὸν ἐνταῦθα ἐπιτήδειον πρὸς
μετουσίαν τῆς ἀποκειμένης μακαριότητος, κηροῦ δίκην ἐνέργειαν
περισῴζοντα πρὸς τὸ παρὰ τοῦ θείου φωτὸς προσλαμβάνεσθαι.
70 **7.** Ὡς γὰρ ὁ κηρὸς τῇ τοῦ πυρὸς θέρμῃ λυόμενος ὑπέκκαυμα
τοῦ πυρὸς γίνεται διὰ τὴν προσοῦσαν αὐτῷ φυσικὴν λιπαρότητα –
ἐντεῦθεν καὶ τὸ φῶς τρεφόμενον καταλάμπει τοὺς πλησιάζοντας –,
οὕτω καὶ ὁ πιστὸς διὰ τῶν κατὰ τὰς ἀρετὰς ἀνθέων τὰ κηρία τῆς
θείας γνώσεως ἑαυτῷ συμπήξας καὶ τῇ τοῦ θείου ἔρωτος θέρμῃ ἀπὸ
75 πάσης ἐπιθυμίας γηΐνης λυθείς, ἡτοίμασεν ἑαυτὸν λύχνον ἐνταῦθα,
διὰ τοῦ νόμου τῆς θείας ἀγάπης ἐκδεχόμενος ἐν τῇ ἀποκαλύψει τοῦ
ἐλπιζομένου αἰῶνος τὸ θεῖον καὶ ἄρρητον ἐκεῖνο φῶς ὑποδέξασθαι
καὶ τῆς ἐκεῖθεν ἀποπαλλομένης ἀϊδίου λαμπρότητος ἐπαπολαῦσαι.
8. Ἡ φυλακὴ γὰρ τῶν τοῦ Χριστοῦ ἐντολῶν καὶ ὁ πόνος τῶν
80 ἀρετῶν, ὃν εἰς τὸν αἰῶνα τοῦτον κατεβάλλετο, τροφὴ τῆς θείας δόξης
ὑπάρχει· *ἀγαπήσω, γάρ φησι, τὸν φύλακα τῶν ἐμῶν ἐντολῶν καὶ
ἐμφανίσω αὐτῷ ἐμαυτόν.* καὶ ὥσπερ τὸ αἰσθητὸν φῶς δαπάνην ἑαυτοῦ
τὸ κηρίον ἔχει, οὕτω καὶ τοῦ θείου φωτὸς ἡ δόξα διαυγάζει ἐν τοῖς
οἰκειουμένοις αὐτῷ δι᾽ ἀρετῆς· *ἐμὸν γὰρ βρῶμά ἐστι, φησὶν ὁ Χριστός,*
85 *τὸ ποιεῖν τὸ θέλημα τοῦ πατρός μου τοῦ ἐν τοῖς οὐρανοῖς. ἐν δὲ τῷ θελήματι*
αὐτοῦ, φησὶν ὁ προφήτης, ζωὴ αἰώνιος.

9. Ὅθεν καὶ ζήσεται ὁ τῶν καλῶν ἐργάτης, θερίζων τοὺς πόνους
αὐτοῦ χάριτι τοῦ καθηγητοῦ τῆς σωτηρίας ἡμῶν Ἰησοῦ Χριστοῦ τοῦ
δοξάζοντος τοὺς δοξάζοντας αὐτόν· ᾧ πρέπει πᾶσα δόξα, τιμὴ καὶ
90 προσκύνησις, ἅμα τῷ ἀνάρχῳ αὐτοῦ πατρὶ καὶ τῷ παναγίῳ καὶ ἀγαθῷ
καὶ ζωοποιῷ αὐτοῦ πνεύματι, νῦν καὶ ἀεὶ καὶ εἰς τοὺς αἰῶνας τῶν
αἰώνων. Ἀμήν.

---

65 προεμήνυσε (cum Beyer) corr.: προεμύνησε OA

6. Such spiritual 'ascents' the champion of piety accrues to himself as he advances,[7] since he is a God-like creation,[8] shining forth like a heavenly light and spurring others on to the imitation of the good.[9] In so doing, he reveres the Transfiguration of Christ with his whole spirit and his whole body, recognizing the mystery of the feast and interpreting it effectively to those with sight. For when Christ was transfigured, he announced the ineffable glory with which he will come to judge the universe, revealed the radiance in which those who please him will share, and he taught every faithful man to share here below for participation in the blessedness stored up for him, by preserving his activity, like wax, to be received by the divine Light.

7. For wax dissolves in the heat of fire becoming fuel for the fire because of its natural oiliness, and the light is fed from this source and shines upon those who are near. In the same way, when the faithful man has fixed to himself the waxes of divine knowledge through the flowers of the virtues and has been released from all earthly desire by the warmth of divine love, he has prepared himself as a lamp here below; through the law of divine love he waits to receive that divine and ineffable Light in the revelation of the age we hope for and to enjoy the eternal radiance emanating therefrom.

8. The observance of Christ's commandments and the labour of the virtues which he laid down for this age constitute the food that nourishes us in our growth towards divine glory. For scripture says, "I shall love the man who keeps my commandments and I will manifest myself to him."[10] Just as the sensible light has wax for its fuel, so too the glory of the divine Light shines in those who have assimilated themselves to it through virtue. For Christ says, "My food is to do the will of my Father in heaven."[11] And the prophet says, "In his will is eternal life."[12]

9. Thus, the person who does good works shall live, for he reaps the harvest of his labours by the grace of the teacher of our salvation, Jesus Christ who glorifies those who glorify him.[13] To him is due all glory, honour and worship together with his Father without beginning and his all-holy, good and life-giving Spirit, now and always and unto the ages of ages. Amen.

[7] Cf. Ps 83:6.
[8] Cf. Eph 4:24.
[9] Cf. Mt 5:14,16.
[10] Jn 14:21.
[11] Jn 4:34.
[12] Ps 29:6.
[13] Cf. Jn 17:10,22.

Περὶ ἡσυχίας καὶ προσευχῆς

1. Ὁ χειροτέχνης, καθήσας εἰς τὸ ἔργον αὐτοῦ, πάσης ἄλλης φροντίδος ἐξίσταται, ὅλην δὲ τὴν μέριμναν αὐτοῦ καὶ τὴν σπουδὴν εἰς τὴν ἐργασίαν αὐτοῦ τίθησι· διὰ μὲν τῆς σπουδῆς τὴν ὀκνηρίαν, 5 διὰ δὲ τῆς φροντίδος τὴν ἀτεχνίαν διακρουόμενος. ἐπειδὴ τὸν ἐκ τοῦ ἔργου μισθὸν ἐπ᾽ ὄψεσι τῆς διανοίας ἔχει, ὅθεν καὶ φανταζομένη ἡ καρδία αὐτοῦ τὸ κέρδος, καὶ κόπου καὶ τροφῆς ὑπερορᾷ. καὶ ὁ μοναχὸς βουλόμενος τὴν ἑαυτοῦ ψυχὴν διατρέφειν ἔχεται διὰ παντὸς τοῦ ἔργου αὐτοῦ, δέδοικε γὰρ τὴν ἀργίαν καὶ τὴν ἐντεῦθεν ἀτροφίαν 10 κατὰ τὴν ἀποστολικὴν ἐντολήν, *ὁ ἀργὸς μὴ ἐσθιέτω*, λέγουσαν.

2. Ὡς γὰρ ὁ ἀργῶν ταῖς χερσὶν ἐπιθυμεῖ μὲν βρωμάτων – *ἐν ἐπιθυμίαις, γάρ φησι, πᾶς ἀεργός* –, οὐ μετέχει δὲ ἀλλὰ λιμώττει διὰ τὴν τῶν ἀναγκαίων στέρησιν, οὕτω καὶ ὁ τῆς κατὰ διάνοιαν ἐργασίας ἀμελῶν λογισμοῖς πολυειδέσιν εἴσοδον ἀνοίγει· καὶ τούτοις 15 συνδυάζων ἐκ ῥαθυμίας καὶ χρονίζων ἐν αὐτοῖς ὁμοιοῦται τῷ εἰς χώραν μακρὰν ἀποικισθέντι καὶ τὴν χοιρώδη τροφὴν δαπανῶντι καὶ μὴ χορταζομένῳ. καὶ ἰδοὺ ὡς μὴ ῥήματα θεῖα μελετῶν, ἀργὸς διατελεῖ· ὡς ἀργὸς οὐ διατρέφεται· ὡς μὴ τρεφόμενος ἄρτῳ θείων λόγων, θνήσκει ἄγνοιαν θεοῦ νοσῶν. ὡς γὰρ ὁ γνῶσιν ἔχων θεοῦ ζωῆς μετέχει 20 – *αὕτη δέ ἐστιν ἡ αἰώνιος ζωή, ἵνα γινώσκωσί σε τὸν μόνον ἀληθινὸν θεὸν καὶ ὃν ἀπέστειλας Ἰησοῦν Χριστόν* –, οὕτω καὶ ὁ ἄγνοιαν θεοῦ πάσχων θάνατον ἔχει ποιμαίνοντα αὐτὸν καὶ τῆς ἀληθινῆς ζωῆς ἐστέρηται.

3. Ἔργον δὲ τοῦ μοναχοῦ ἡ τοῦ θεοῦ μνήμη ἐστίν, ἔθετο, γάρ 25 φησιν, *ὁ θεὸς τὸν ἄνθρωπον ἐν τῷ παραδείσῳ ἐργάζεσθαι αὐτὸν καὶ*

MD 6

HESYCHIA AND PRAYER

1. The artisan seated at his work refrains from all other concerns and sets his entire concentration and effort to what he is working on, evading laziness through effort and incompetence through attention. Since his discursive intellect keeps in sight the reward of his work, and thus his heart too imagines what it stands to gain, he takes no notice of the labour involved or of his own need for food. And also, the monk who wishes to nourish his own soul holds continually to his work, for he is afraid of idleness and the consequent deprivation of food according to the apostolic precept which states, "The idle man is not to eat."[1]

2. Just as the person who is idle with his hands desires food — for scripture says, "Every sluggard is caught up in his cravings"[2] — but does not partake of any, going hungry instead because of deprivation of necessities, so too the person who neglects to occupy his discursive intellect opens an entrance way for thoughts in their many forms. If in his laziness he engages with these thoughts and dallies over them, he becomes like the prodigal son who left home for a far away country and consumed the food of swine but was unable to eat his fill.[3] Behold, since he does not meditate on divine words, he becomes idle. Because he is idle, he is given no nourishment. Because he does not feed on the bread of divine words, he dies suffering from the disease of not knowing God. The person who possesses knowledge of God partakes of life: "And this is eternal life, that they know you the only true God, and Jesus Christ whom you have sent."[4] Similarly, the man who suffers from ignorance of God has death to be his shepherd and is deprived of true life.[5]

3. The work of the monk consists in the remembrance of God, for scripture says, "God put man in paradise to work in it and keep

---

[1] Cf. 2 Thes 3:10.
[2] Prov 13:4.
[3] Lk 15:13-16.
[4] Jn 17:3.
[5] Ps 48:15.

*φυλάσσειν, ὅπερ ἐστὶ μνημονεύειν θεοῦ καὶ νήφειν, ἵνα μὴ ῥαθυμήσας
ὁ ἄνθρωπος ἀπὸ τοῦ ἐνατενίζειν θεῷ λήθην πάθῃ τῆς ἐντολῆς καὶ
πρὸς τὴν τῶν παρόντων ἡδονὴν ἀποβλέψῃ. ὃ δὴ καὶ πέπονθε τοῦτο
καὶ ὁ Χριστὸς τοῖς οἰκείοις μαθηταῖς ἐντελλόμενος, γρηγορεῖτε καὶ*
30 *προσεύχεσθε λέγει. ὡς γὰρ ἡ καλλιεργία τῶν λαχάνων καὶ ἡ τῶν
καρπῶν ἀφθονία ῥᾳδίως ὑπὸ τῶν παριόντων συλῶνται, μὴ ἔχουσαι
φυλακὴν ἐπίμονον, οὕτω καὶ διάνοια προσευχῆς ῥήματα διερχομένη,
μὴ ἔχουσα δὲ τὸν νοῦν ἐπιστατοῦντα τοῖς λεγομένοις, ἀνωφελῶς
εὔχεται. ἐπειδὴ ἐν ἄλλαις ἐννοίαις κλεπτόμενος ὁ νοῦς καὶ κενεμ-*
35 *βατῶν, τῆς κατὰ προσευχὴν γνώσεως ἀποδημεῖ.*

4. Ἐκείνοις ὁ θεὸς λόγος ἐμφανίζεται τοῖς καθαρῶς εὐχομένοις
καὶ τοῖς διὰ παντὸς ἐν τῇ μελέτῃ τῶν θείων λόγων διακαρτεροῦσιν.
*ὁ τηρῶν, γάρ φησι, τὰς ἐντολάς μου, ἐκεῖνός ἐστιν ὁ ἀγαπῶν με, καὶ
ἐγὼ ἀγαπήσω αὐτὸν καὶ ἐμφανίσω αὐτῷ ἐμαυτόν.* ἡ μετὰ προσοχῆς
40 προσευχὴ τὴν γνῶσιν τοῦ θεοῦ ἀνατέλλει. ἡ θεία γνῶσις, τὴν ἀγάπην
τῆς ψυχῆς ἐπισπωμένη, συνάπτει τὴν ψυχὴν τῷ θεῷ. ἡ δὲ ἀγάπη
ὅλην τὴν καρδίαν τῷ θεῷ προσηλώσασα, ἀναπόσπαστον ποιεῖται τὴν
τοῦ νοῦ θεωρίαν ἀπὸ τῆς τοῦ θεοῦ γνώσεως, δεσμὸς γὰρ τοῦ νοῦ
πρὸς τὸν θεὸν καὶ τὰ θεῖα ἡ ἀγάπη ἐστίν· αὕτη φωτοβολοῦσα τὴν
45 ψυχὴν πᾶσαν ἔννοιαν καὶ πάντα λογισμὸν τοῦ αἰῶνος τούτου, ὡς
ἀχλύν τινα διασκεδάζει, *ἡ ἀγάπη, γάρ φησιν, οὐ λογίζεται τὸ κακόν.*
5. Ψυχὴ γὰρ ἡ τὸ βέλος τῆς ἀγάπης εἰσδεξαμένη οὐκ ἀφίησι
τὸν νοῦν τῆς ἀρρήτου καὶ θείας ἡδονῆς ἀποστῆναι. ὡς γὰρ ὁ νοῦς
προστεθεὶς τῇ αἰσθήσει τοῦ σώματος τῆς τῶν παρόντων ἡδονῆς
50 αἰσθάνεται, οὕτω καὶ τῇ ἀγάπῃ τοῦ θεοῦ ὁλικῶς ἑνωθεὶς τῆς
μακαριωτάτης εὐφροσύνης ἐν ἀπολαύσει γίνεται. ἡ καρδία τοῦ
σώματος ὑπό τινος πάθους τρωθεῖσα νεκροῦται· ἡ δὲ διάνοια τῷ
δόρατι τοῦ θείου νυγεῖσα ἔρωτος ζωῆς καὶ φωτὸς ἐκβλύζει νοήματα.
ἡ ἀγάπη ποτὲ μὲν βυθίζουσα τὸν νοῦν εἰς τὴν γνῶσιν τοῦ θεοῦ καὶ
55 τὴν πρὸς αὐτὸν ἕνωσιν ἀγνώστως μεσιτεύουσα, ἐξίστησι τὴν ψυχὴν
πάντων τῶν ὄντων καὶ ἀντὶ διαλογῆς ἡδείας τὴν βαθεῖαν σιγὴν
προβάλλεται, καὶ διακονεῖ τῷ θεῷ διὰ τῆς ἐκκεχυμένης πρὸς αὐτὸν
διαθέσεως. ποτὲ δὲ εἰς τὴν τῶν ὄντων θεωρίαν εἰσάγουσα, τῇ ποικίλῃ
διαυγείᾳ τῶν νοημάτων καταθέλγει τὴν διάνοιαν· καὶ ἄλλοτε τοὺς

it,"[6] that is, to remember God and to keep vigilance, lest by slothfully slackening his intent gaze upon God he suffer forgetfulness of the commandment and look away to the pleasure found in present realities. This is also what Christ suffered when he commanded his disciples, saying, "Watch and pray."[7] For just as the good vegetable garden and an abundant stand of fruit are pilfered by passers-by if a continual guard is not kept, so too if the discursive intellect goes through the words of prayer without having the mind attend to what is being said, its prayer is useless. When the mind is spirited away among thoughts of other things and wanders aimlessly, it is estranged from the knowledge found in prayer.

4. God the Word manifests himself to those who practise pure prayer and to those who persevere continually in meditation on the divine words. For scripture says, "He who keeps my commandments, he it is who loves me; and I will love him and manifest myself to him."[8] Attentive prayer allows the knowledge of God to dawn in the soul. Divine knowledge draws to itself the love of the soul and joins the soul to God. Love rivets the entire heart to God and renders the mind's contemplation inseparable from the knowledge of God, for love constitutes the mind's bond with God and divine things. When it casts its light upon the soul, it scatters, like a mist, every concept and every thought belonging to this age, for scripture says, "Love thinks no evil."[9]

5. The soul that has received the arrow of love does not allow the mind to withdraw from this ineffable and divine pleasure. Just as the mind, when it is associated with the body's sense perception, perceives the pleasure of present things, so too when it is united entirely to the love of God it enjoys the most blessed happiness. When the heart in the body is wounded by some accident, it dies. But when the discursive intellect is pierced with the lance of divine love, it pours forth thoughts of life and light. Sometimes when love immerses the mind in the knowledge of God and becomes the mediator of union with him at a level beyond knowledge, it removes soul from all beings, and in place of a dialogue of sweetness it casts a profound silence over the soul, and the mind serves God in a disposition poured out towards him. But sometimes, by introducing the mind to the contemplation of beings, love enchants the discursive intellect with the

---

6 Gen 2:15.
7 Mt 26:41, Mk 14:38.
8 Jn 14:21.
9 1 Cor 13:5.

60 πολυειδεῖς τρόπους τῶν ἀρετῶν ἀνερευνῶσα καὶ τὰς τῶν καλῶν
πράξεις, καθάπερ σιτία τοῖς μέλεσι τοῦ σώματος διανέμουσα· ἔτι δὲ
καὶ ταῖς μελέταις τῶν θείων λόγων καταγλυκαίνουσα τὸν νοῦν, τὴν
τῶν εἰρημένων πάντων ἐδωδὴν ἀφθόνως τρυγᾶν προτρέπεται, ὡς ἀπὸ
παντὸς ξύλου τοῦ ἐν τῷ παραδείσῳ τὴν μετάληψιν, καὶ τῆς τῶν
65 νοητῶν καὶ θείων ἀποκειμένης κληρουχίας κατασκοπεῖ τὴν μεγα-
λοπρέπειαν.

6. Ἑώρακα γεωργὸν διαπονούμενον περὶ τὸ λήϊον αὐτοῦ, καὶ τὰς
μὲν ἐρριζωμένας πέτρας σκάπτων ἔξω ἔρριπτε, τῶν δὲ εἰς ὄψιν τῆς
γῆς κειμένων λίθων τὴν ἀποβολὴν ταῖς χερσὶν ἐποιεῖτο. καὶ τὸ μὲν
70 πρῶτον ἦν κοπηρόν, τὸ δὲ δεύτερον ῥᾳδίως ἐτελεῖτο. καὶ ὁ σπουδαῖος
μοναχὸς ζητῶν καθαρὰν ποιῆσαι τὴν καρδίαν τῷ ἀρότρῳ τῆς
νηφαλίου προσευχῆς πειρᾶται διόλου τὰς κινουμένας ὑπὸ τοῦ ἐχθροῦ
ὑποβολὰς ἐκτέμνειν καὶ ἔξω τῶν ταμείων τῆς ψυχῆς ἀπορρίπτειν·
ἔχων εἰς τοῦτο χειραγωγὸν τὸν λέγοντα, *πάντα τὰ ἔθνη ἐκύκλωσάν*
75 *με καὶ τῷ ὀνόματι κυρίου ἠμυνάμην αὐτούς.*

7. Κρεῖσσον γὰρ τὰς τοῦ πονηροῦ προσβολὰς ἐκ πρώτης ἐννοίας
ἐμπιπρᾶν τῷ πυρὶ τῆς προσευχῆς καὶ ἀτάραχον τηρεῖν τὴν διάνοιαν
πρὸς τὸ ἀνεμπόδιστον τελεῖσθαι τὴν μετὰ τοῦ κυρίου διαλογήν, ἢ
τῇ κολακείᾳ τῶν προσβολῶν ὑπακοῦσαι καὶ συλλαλῆσαι τῷ δολίῳ
80 καὶ παραδέξασθαι τὸ ἀλλότριον ὡς οἰκεῖον καὶ τὸ ὀλέθριον ὡς
ὠφέλιμον ἀγαπῆσαι· ἔπειτα συνιδόντα τὴν ἀπάτην, κόπου δεῖσθαι καὶ
ἐξαγορείας καὶ δακρύων πρὸς ἔκπλυσιν τῶν ἐξ ἀμελείας ῥυπασμάτων.

8. Ἐνθυμήθι τὸν προπάτορα ἡνίκα ἑώρα πρὸς τὴν ἐκ πλευρᾶς
αὐτοῦ ἀνοικοδομηθεῖσαν γυναῖκα, τίνα ἦν ἃ ἐλάλει καὶ ὁποῖοι
85 ἐτέλουν ἀμφότεροι. *ὅτι γυμνοὶ ἦσαν καὶ οὐκ ᾐσχύνοντο·* γυμνοὶ τῆς
πρὸς τὴν σάρκα φιλίας, γυμνοὶ τῆς τοῦ κόσμου σχέσεως, γυμνοὶ τοῦ
αἴσχους τῶν παθῶν· ἀπερίσπαστοι, ἄβιοι, ξένοι τοῦ κόσμου, ὡς μηδὲν
ἐπιφερόμενοι τῶν ἐπιγείων· καὶ βασιλεῖς πάλιν τοῦ κόσμου, ὡς
οὐρανόφρονες, στολὴν θείαν περιβεβλημένοι, ἀγάπης τοῦ θεοῦ
90 διαδήματι κατεστεμμένοι. οὗτοι, ἡνίκα ὁ μὲν ἐπαύσατο τοῦ πρὸς τὴν

shimmering radiance of thoughts. At other times love searches out the multiform ways of the virtues and the practice of good works, as though dispensing food for the bodily members; and on still other occasions, by granting sweetness to the mind through meditations on the divine words, love urges it to eat in plenty the food of everything that has been said, as it would partake of every tree in paradise,[10] and it searches out the majesty of the inheritance of intelligible and divine things which are held in store for it.

6. I once saw a farmer labouring over his crop. As he dug up the rocks that were buried he would throw them away, but those stones that were lying in plain sight on the surface of the ground he would remove with his hands. The first task was a laborious one but the second was easily dealt with. So too the diligent monk who seeks to purify his heart with the plow of vigilant prayer is ever trying to cut off the suggestions contrived by the enemy and to cast them out of the storehouses of the soul. He has to guide him the one who says, "All the nations surrounded me and in the Lord's name I fended them off."[11]

7. It is better to sear the attacks of the evil one with the flame of prayer from their first conception and to preserve the discursive intellect untroubled so that the dialogue with the Lord may be accomplished unhindered, than to yield to the flattery of these attacks and converse with the treacherous one, accepting what is alien as one's own and loving what is destructive as something beneficial. By the time one realizes the deceit, toil, confession and tears are necessary to wash away the defilements that resulted from one's carelessness.

8. Consider our forefather when he saw the woman who had been formed from his rib. What were the things he said and what was the state they both enjoyed? "They were naked and were not ashamed":[12] naked of affection for the flesh, naked of attachment to the world, naked of the shame that comes from the passions, undistracted by the world, their lives unattached to the world, strangers to the world, bearing with them no earthly goods. Conversely, they were rulers of the world because they were heavenly-minded;[13] they were robed in divine garments, crowned with the diadem of love for God. But when Adam ceased gazing upon and speaking with his wife and she ceased

---

[10] Cf. Gen 2:16.
[11] Ps 117:10.
[12] Gen 2:25.
[13] Cf. Col 3:2.

σύνοικον ἀτενίζειν καὶ λαλεῖν, ἡ δὲ τοῦ συνεῖναι τῷ ἀνδρὶ καὶ ἀκούειν τῶν λόγων αὐτοῦ, πάροδον τῷ ὄφει δεδώκασι. καὶ ἡ διάστασις τῶν ὁμοφύλων ἕνωσιν τοῦ ἀλλοφύλου εἰργάσατο, καὶ ἡ ῥαθυμία τῶν λογικῶν προθυμία γέγονε τῷ ἀλόγῳ ὄφει, καὶ τὰ δεινότατα ἔπαθεν
95 ἐκ τῆς ἀμελείας καὶ τοῦ χωρισμοῦ.

9. Καὶ ὁ νοῦς τοίνυν τοῦ μοναχοῦ, ἕως οὗ παραμένων ἐν τῇ διανοίᾳ τοῖς θείοις λόγοις ἐμμελετᾷ καὶ τοὺς τῆς ἀσκήσεως τρόπους διανοεῖται καὶ ἐπιτελεῖ, καὶ πρὸ τούτων καὶ μετὰ τούτων τῇ ἐπιμόνῳ προσευχῇ περιτειχίζει τὴν καρδίαν, οὔτε τόπον τῷ πονηρῷ παρέχει
100 καὶ τὰς ὑποβαλλομένας παρ' αὐτοῦ ἐνθυμήσεις εὐτόνως διακρούεται. καὶ πάλιν τοῦ ἰδίου ἔργου κραταιῶς ἔχεται, λέγων καὶ αὐτὸς μετὰ τοῦ προφήτου, *τὰ ἔργα τῶν χειρῶν ἡμῶν κατεύθυνον ἐφ' ἡμᾶς καὶ τὸ ἔργον τῶν χειρῶν ἡμῶν κατεύθυνον,* διὰ μὲν τῶν ἔργων τοὺς ἐπιτελουμένους ἐν τῷ σώματι τρόπους τῆς ἀσκήσεως παριστῶντος,
105 διὰ δὲ τοῦ ἔργου τὴν ἐν τῇ διανοίᾳ προσευχὴν ὑποσημαίνοντος καὶ κατευθύνεσθαι ἀμφότερα εὐχομένου, τὰς μὲν ἀγαθὰς πράξεις ἀκενοδόξως, τὴν δὲ προσευχὴν ἀρεμβάστως ἀνύεσθαι. τοῦτο γὰρ αἰνίττεται τὸ κατεύθυνον, ἤγουν ἀνελλιπῶς καὶ εἰλικρινῶς τὴν λογικὴν ταύτην θυσίαν ἀναφέρειν σοι, κύριε, καταξίωσον.
110 **10.** Ὑπὸ τῶν εἰρημένων τούτων ἐργασιῶν ἐξυπνιζόμενος ὁ νοῦς καὶ πιαινόμενος, οὐκ ἐπιστρέφεται πρὸς τὰς εἰσηγήσεις τοῦ ἐχθροῦ, λογισμοὺς σαρκικοὺς ἀθετεῖ, μνήμας παλαιὰς ἐξαλείφει, ἐπιθυμίας προσφάτους συναντώσας ἐκ τῶν καθεκάστην πραγμάτων διαπτύει, ὑπονοίας καὶ ὀργὰς ἀναδιδομένας κατὰ τοῦ πέλας ἀπὸ ἔργων ἢ
115 ῥημάτων ἢ σχημάτων ἀποκρούεται. οὕτως ὁ ἀγωνιζόμενος καθαρεύει, οὕτως ὁ σπουδάζων εἰρηνεύει, προσπίπτων γὰρ ἀεὶ τῷ θεῷ διὰ ταπεινώσεως καὶ δεήσεως, ῥίπτει τὸν ὑπερήφανον καὶ πατεῖ ἐπὶ πᾶσαν τὴν παράταξιν αὐτοῦ τῇ δυνάμει τοῦ καθελόντος αὐτὸν διὰ σταυροῦ Ἰησοῦ Χριστοῦ· ᾧ πρέπει πᾶσα δόξα, τιμὴ καὶ προσκύνησις, ἅμα
120 τῷ ἀνάρχῳ αὐτοῦ πατρὶ καὶ τῷ παναγίῳ καὶ ἀγαθῷ καὶ ζωοποιῷ αὐτοῦ πνεύματι, νῦν καὶ ἀεὶ καὶ εἰς τοὺς αἰῶνας τῶν αἰώνων. Ἀμήν.

staying with her husband and listening to his words, they gave an inroad to the serpent. The separation of those of the same race brought union with one of an alien race. The sloth of rational beings became eagerness on the part of the irrational serpent, and they suffered the most terrible things as a result of their neglect and separation.

9. Therefore, so long as the mind of the monk abides in the discursive intellect, devotes its study to divine words, ponders and fulfils the practices of asceticism, and both before and after doing this encircles its heart with the wall of steadfast prayer, it gives no ground to the evil one and forcibly drives off the ideas suggested by him. The monk, in turn, adheres vigorously to his own work, saying together with the prophet, "Make straight the works of our hands for us and make straight the work of our hands."[14] By 'works' the prophet suggests the practices of asceticism performed by the body and by 'work' he indicates the prayer in the discursive intellect, beseeching that both be set on a straight path, the good works to be done without vainglory and prayer without distraction. The phrase 'make straight' is an indirect way of saying, "Deem us worthy, Lord, to offer you this rational sacrifice without ceasing and with all sincerity."[15]

10. When the mind is awakened and nourished by these practices just mentioned, it pays no regard to the insinuations of the enemy, it rejects thoughts of the flesh, it blots out old memories, it spits upon desires that spring afresh from daily affairs, it drives away suspicions and angry feelings that arise against one's neighbour out of deeds or words or outward appearances. Thus the one who struggles achieves purity. Thus the one who strives eagerly finds peace, for by always making prostration before God in humble entreaty, he casts out the proud one and tramples on all his pomp by the power of the one who conquered him through the Cross, Jesus Christ. To him be all glory, honour and worship together with his eternal Father and his all-holy, good and life-giving Spirit, now and forever and unto the ages of ages. Amen.

---

14 Ps 89:17.
15 Cf. Rom 12:1.

Ὁ παρὼν λόγος τὰς σκοτεινὰς τῶν παθῶν διαθέσεις τῷ φωτὶ τῆς διακρίσεως ἐξελέγχει

1. Ἀδελφαὶ καὶ μητέρες, σκότος ὢν ὁ πονηρὸς καὶ νοήματα σκοτεινὰ ὑποβάλλει τῇ ψυχῇ, δι᾽ ὧν συνέχων τὴν καρδίαν τῆς
5 ἀληθοῦς γνώσεως ἀποστερεῖ τὸν ἄνθρωπον. δεῖται οὖν φωτεινῆς διανοίας καὶ τῷ φόβῳ δεσμουμένης τοῦ θεοῦ πρὸς διάγνωσιν αὐτῶν ὁ θέλων κατάδηλα ταῦτα ποιεῖσθαι τῇ ψυχῇ. οὔτε γὰρ ὁ ἐν νυκτὶ περιπατῶν τὴν ὄψιν τοῦ συναντῶντος αὐτῷ ἀνθρώπου ὁρᾷ, οὔτε ὁ ὑπὸ ζόφου παθῶν συνεχόμενος τὰ ἕρποντα κινήματα ἐν τῇ ψυχῇ αὐτοῦ
10 διακρίνει. καὶ τοσοῦτον ὁ ὑπὸ δαιμόνων ἐνεργούμενος τυφλώττει καὶ ἀπατᾶται, ὥστε τὴν κακίαν βαστάζων καὶ περιθάλπων αὐτὴν ἐν τῇ καρδίᾳ πρὸς τοὺς ἐγκαλοῦντας αὐτῷ ἢ παραινοῦντας ἀποστῆναι τοῦ πάθους διϊσχυρίζεσθαι μακρὰν εἶναι αὐτοῦ καὶ ἀπαθῆ φέρειν τὴν ψυχήν.

15 **2.** Ὃ δῆτα καὶ πολλάκις μεταξὺ ὑμῶν συμβαῖνον ὁρῶ. καὶ γὰρ ἐπηρείᾳ τοῦ ἐχθροῦ μέσον δύο τινῶν προβαίνει σκάνδαλον καὶ ῥήματα κινοῦνται παρ᾽ ἀμφοτέρων πλήττοντα τὰς ἀλλήλων ψυχάς, ἃ καὶ μνημονευόμενα μῖσος φέρει ἐν τῇ ψυχῇ καὶ τὴν προτέραν ἕνωσιν καὶ ὁμιλίαν διακόπτει. ὅτε δὲ ὁ πνευματικὸς πατήρ, ἐπιγνοὺς
20 τὴν διάστασιν, μιᾷ τῶν ὀργιζομένων παραινεῖν ἄρξεται τὴν ἔχθραν ἀφεῖναι καὶ πρὸς εἰρήνην χωρῆσαι διὰ τῆς πρὸς τὴν ἀδελφὴν καταλλαγῆς, αὐτίκα ἐκείνη λέγει· κακίαν οὐκ ἔχω, τὴν ἀδελφὴν ἀγαπῶ· ποιῆσαι δὲ μετάνοιαν αὐτῇ ἢ λαλῆσαι βραχὺ οὐ βούλομαι, ἐπειδὴ μῖσος οὐκ ἔχω πρὸς αὐτήν. ὢ τῆς ἀναισθησίας. ἐκπέμπει διὰ
25 τοῦ στόματος τὴν δυσωδίαν τοῦ μίσους καὶ βόρβορον ἐν τῇ ψυχῇ ἔχειν οὐ λέγει. καπνὸν προφέρει καὶ πῦρ ἀπαρνεῖται. τὴν ἔχθραν τῆς ψυχῆς δημοσιεύει καὶ φιλικῶς ἐπαγγέλλεται διακεῖσθαι. αἰσχύνης λέγει ῥήματα καὶ οὐκ ἐντρέπεται. τὸν ὄφιν τρέφει καὶ τὴν κεφαλὴν αὐτοῦ συντρίβειν φρονεῖ.

30 **3.** Λαλῆσαι οὐ θέλεις τῇ ἀδελφῇ, καὶ μῖσος οὐ φέρεις πρὸς αὐτήν; καταλλαγῆναι μετ᾽ αὐτῆς ἢ καταλλάξαι αὐτὴν ἑαυτῇ οὐ βούλει, καὶ

THE PRESENT TREATISE EXPOSES THE DARK DISPOSITIONS
OF THE PASSIONS BY THE LIGHT OF DISCERNMENT

1. Sisters and Mothers, in his darkness the evil one suggests to the soul darkling thoughts through which he distresses the heart and deprives man of true knowledge. Therefore, the person who wishes to make these thoughts plain to the soul must have an illumined discursive intellect, which is also bound to the fear of God, in order to discern them. For neither does the man who walks about at night see the faces of the people he encounters, nor does the man distressed by the darkness of the passions discern the movements that slither within his soul. Someone under the influence of the demons is blinded and deceived to such an extent that, even though he carries evil about and cherishes it within his heart, he insists before those who reproach him or encourage him to abstain from passion that he is far removed from it and is keeping his soul free of passion.

2. This is precisely what I often see happening among you.[1] By an assault of the enemy a stumbling block arises between two nuns and words are uttered by both parties that batter each other's souls; the memory of these words brings hatred to the soul and disrupts the unity and communion that formerly prevailed. But when the spiritual father becomes aware of the disagreement and begins to exhort one of those provoked to anger to let go of her enmity and proceed toward peace by reconciliation with her sister, immediately she says to him, "I hold no malice. I love my sister. I will not prostrate myself to her or have a brief word with her, since I hold no hatred towards her." What insensitivity! She expels through her mouth the stench of hatred but says she has no filth in her soul. She gives off smoke but denies there is fire. She makes public knowledge of the enmity in her soul but professes a charitable disposition. She speaks shameful words but feels no shame. She feeds the serpent but thinks she crushes his head.

3. You refuse to speak to your sister; yet you do not bear hatred towards her? You do not want to be reconciled with her or to have

---

[1] Such direct, personal familiarity with the monastery can only be explained either by frequent correspondence or by the presence of Theoleptos in Constantinople.

ἀγαπᾶν λέγεις αὐτήν; πίπτει καὶ χεῖρα οὐ δίδως αὐτῇ, καὶ πονεῖν
ὑπολαμβάνεις ἐπὶ τῷ πτώματι ταύτης; μᾶλλον δὲ πτῶμα κεῖσαι καὶ
ἵστασθαι προσδοκᾷς; τὸ μικρὸν οὐ παρέχεις, καὶ τὸ μεῖζον ἐπαγγέλῃ;
35 ῥῆμα ψιλὸν οὐκ ἀνέχῃ πρὸς τὴν λυπηθεῖσαν ἢ λυπήσασαν εἰπεῖν
καὶ διὰ μικρᾶς ἀπολογίας οἰκειώσασθαι ταύτην, καὶ ὅλῃ ψυχῇ
φάσκεις προσηλοῦσθαι τῇ ἐκείνης ἀγάπῃ;

4. Βλέπεις τοῦ δολίου τὰ ἔνεδρα; ὁρᾷς τοῦ πονηροῦ τὰ γεώργια;
σκότος ἐστὶ καὶ φῶς σχηματίζεται. ἐχθρὸς τυγχάνει καὶ φίλος
40 ὑποκρίνεται. πολέμιός ἐστι καὶ τὰ τῶν συμμάχων προσποιεῖται.
ἐπίβουλος πέλει καὶ σύμβουλος φαίνεται. ὁ θησαυρὸς αὐτοῦ κακία
καὶ ἀρετὰς μηχανᾶται δανίζειν, καὶ τούτῳ τῷ τρόπῳ κλέπτει τὰς
ἀγωνιζομένας ψυχάς· ἡ γὰρ τὰ καλὰ πραγματεύεσθαι ποθοῦσα ψυχή,
τὸν δόλον ἀγνοοῦσα τοῦ πονηροῦ, προσέρχεται τῇ φαινομένῃ δῆθεν
45 ἀρετῇ, ἁλίσκεται δὲ τῇ κρυπτομένῃ κακίᾳ καὶ ἀγνώστως εἰς χεῖρας
πίπτει τοῦ ἐχθροῦ καὶ ὡς οὐ θέλει δουλεύει τῷ τυράννῳ. καὶ ὥσπερ
οἱ ψεκτὴν πραγματείαν ἔχοντες κρείττονα μὲν πρὸς ἀπάτην τῶν
ἐμπόρων προβάλλονται, ἔρημα δὲ παραμιγνύντες τοῖς ἀρεσκομένοις,
τὸ χρυσίον τῶν ἀγοραστῶν ἐπισπῶνται καὶ εἰς ζημίαν ἀντὶ κέρδους
50 αὐτοὺς περιϊστῶσιν, οὕτω καὶ οἱ δαίμονες, τὰ χρηστὰ δῆθεν ὑπα-
γορεύοντες, τὰ πονηρὰ ἐν τῷ ἀφανεῖ κατέχουσι καὶ τῇ δοκήσει τῶν
ὠφελίμων τὸν καθαρὸν νοῦν τῆς ψυχῆς ὑποκλέπτοντες, τὰ ὀλέθρια
προσφέρουσι· καὶ ματαίους μὲν δεικνύουσι τοὺς ἀγῶνας τῆς ψυχῆς,
αὐτοὶ δὲ κέρδος ἔχουσι τὴν ἐκείνης ἀπώλειαν.

55 **5.** Μὴ οὖν ἀπατῶ τὴν ἐλευθερίαν ἔχειν, ὑπὸ δαιμόνων αἰχμαλω-
τιζομένη, ἀλλ᾽ εἰ θέλεις ἐπιγνῶναι τὰς μαγγανείας τῶν ἐχθρῶν σου,
κύψον εἰς τὰ βάθη τῆς ψυχῆς καὶ σκόπησον, εἰ οὐ πάσχεις ἐφ᾽ οἷς
ἐλοιδορήθης. εἰ τῶν ὕβρεων ἡ μνήμη τόπον οὐκ ἔχει ἐν τῇ σῇ καρδίᾳ,
εἰ εὐχαριστεῖς τῷ θεῷ ἐφ᾽ οἷς ἤκουσας, εἰ πρὸς δοκιμασίαν σου
60 φρονεῖς τὰ λυπηρά σοι ἐπέρχεσθαι, εἰ προσέχεις ταῖς ἀδελφαῖς ὡς
ἰατρευούσαις σου τὰ πάθη διὰ τῶν ὀνειδισμῶν καὶ τῶν μέμψεων, εἰ
εὔχεταί σου ἡ καρδία ὑπὲρ αὐτῶν, εἰ οὐ λογίζῃ κακὰ περὶ αὐτῶν,
εἰ φροντίζεις αὐτῶν εἰς ἀγαθά, εἰ οὐ δυσχεραίνεις ἐπαινουμένων
αὐτῶν, εἰ οὐ χαίρεις πάλιν ψεγομένων αὐτῶν, εἰ οὐκ ἀνέχῃ κατηγοριῶν
65 ἀκοῦσαι – εἰ ταῦτά ἐστιν ὁ θησαυρός σου, καλῶς λέγεις ἀγαπᾶν τὴν
ἀδελφήν. εἰ δὲ τούτων οὐδὲν θεωρεῖς ἐν ἑαυτῇ, τἀναντία δὲ μᾶλλον

her reconciled with you, yet you say you love her? She falls and you do not give her your hand, yet you maintain that you are suffering over her fall? Or rather, you fall and you expect to be helped up? You do not make the least concession, yet you profess the greatest? You do not want to speak a simple word to your sister, who is in distress or who is causing you distress, and by a little apology to be reconciled to her, yet you claim with all your soul to be riveted to love for her?

4. Do you see the snares of the cunning one? Do you notice the plantings of the evil one? He is darkness but takes on the form of light. He is an enemy but acts the part of a friend. He is a foe but pretends to be an ally. He is a treacherous plotter but appears as a counselor. His treasury is wickedness, yet he contrives to lend virtues and in this way he steals the souls of ascetics. For the soul that desires to deal in good works, unaware of the treachery of the evil one, approaches the apparent virtue and is caught in the hidden wickedness; unknowingly it falls into the hands of the enemy and, without intending to do so, it serves the tyrant. The purveyors of faulty merchandise allege their wares are better so as to deceive the buyers and by mixing defective goods with those that have pleasing qualities they attract the money of the shoppers and thus involve them in a loss instead of a profit. Similarly, the demons, while making apparently good suggestions, keep their evil ones out of sight and defrauding the pure mind of the soul by the appearance of beneficial goods they introduce destructive influences. They show up the struggles of the soul as vain and have as their profit its perdition.

5. Do not be deceived into thinking that you possess freedom, when you are held captive by the demons, but if you wish to recognize the tricks of your enemies, stoop into the depths of your soul and consider whether you are not suffering any of the things for which you have been reproached. If the memory of insults has no place in your heart, if you give thanks to God for what you have heard, if you consider that the vexations have come upon you to test you, if you give heed to your sisters as to those who can heal your passions by their criticisms and reproaches, if your heart prays for them, if you hold no evil thoughts concerning them, if you think well of them, if you are not annoyed when they are praised, if you do not rejoice in turn when they are blamed, if you cannot bear to hear accusations against them — if your treasure lies in these things, rightly do you say you love your sister. But if you see none of these attitudes within yourself but rather the opposite attitudes occupy the land of your soul, alas for

κατέχουσι τὴν χώραν τῆς ψυχῆς σου, φεῦ τῆς πλάνης, οὐαί σοι τῆς
ἀναισθησίας, ὅτι τὴν φυλακὴν ἀντὶ ἑορτῆς ἔχεις. τὰ δεσμὰ ἐλευθερίαν
νομίζεις, καὶ θάνατον ἀντὶ ζωῆς θερίζεις.

70   **6.**   Ἀλλὰ σὺ μὲν ἴσως οὐκ ἔχεις λύπην κατὰ τῆς ἀδελφῆς, ἀκούεις
δὲ ὅτι ἐκείνη λυπεῖται σφόδρα ἐπὶ τῷ ῥήματι τοῦ ὀνειδισμοῦ, ὃ
εἴρηκας ἐνώπιον αὐτῆς. πῶς εὐθυμεῖς; πῶς ἠρεμεῖς; καὶ οὕτως ἔχουσα,
ἐσχάτως νοσεῖς· τὸ μὲν ὅτι οὐκ αἰσθάνῃ τῆς λοιδορίας δι᾽ ἧς τὴν
καρδίαν τοῦ πλησίον ἔπληξας, τὸ δὲ ὅτι καὶ τὴν ὀδύνην ἐκείνης
75   μανθάνουσα ἀνωδύνως διατελεῖς. οὐ νεκρότητος ἄντικρυς γνώρισμα
τοῦτο; οὐ φρενῶν ἔκστασις καὶ ἀγνωσίας ὁμίχλη βαθυτάτη; ἔβαλες
εἰς τὸν οἶκον τῆς ἀδελφῆς πῦρ. ὁ πονηρὸς ὡς ἄνεμος ἄγριος
δραξάμενος τῆς ὕβρεως ταύτης, ἀνῆψε τὴν κακίαν ἐν καρδίᾳ,
ἐμπυρίζεται σφόδρα ὁ οἶκος τῆς ψυχῆς. ὁ τῶν φωνῶν καὶ τῶν
80   στεναγμῶν καπνὸς εἰς τὰς ἀκοὰς διήκει τῆς ὅλης ἀδελφότητος. πᾶσα
ἡ ἀδελφότης συμπαθεῖ, κάμπτεται, ἐπείγεται τῇ δρόσῳ τῆς νουθεσίας
σβέσαι τὴν φλόγα τῆς λύπης καὶ παρακαλέσαι τὴν ψυχήν. καὶ σὺ
οὔτε ὡς αἰτία γενομένη τῆς ὀργῆς, οὔτε ὡς μέλος τοῦ κοινοβιακοῦ
σώματος ὀδυνᾶσαι, ἵνα καὶ δράμῃς διὰ μετανοίας καὶ προσπέσῃς τοῖς
85   ἐκείνης ποσὶ καὶ δι᾽ ἀπολογίας ἀγαθῆς ἡμερώσῃς τὴν θηριωθεῖσαν
καρδίαν καὶ θεραπεύσῃς καὶ σεαυτὴν κἀκείνην.

7.   Εἰ μὲν ἐξ ὑπονοίας ἔπαθεν ἡ ἀδελφή, σοῦ μὴ δούσης πρόφασιν
ὅλως μηδὲ συνειδυίας πρᾶγμα ἢ ῥῆμα μεσολαβοῦν πρὸς ταραχήν,
καὶ σιγᾷ ἐκείνη τῷ στόματι, πάσχει δὲ τῇ καρδίᾳ, ἀνέγκλητος σὺ
90   καὶ ἀνεύθυνος, ἐπειδὴ τὸ λυποῦν ἐκείνην οὐδὲν ἕτερόν ἐστιν, εἰ μὴ
μόνη ὑπόνοια καὶ λογισμὸς ἀνέκφραστος, φθόνῳ τοῦ ἐχθροῦ καὶ
ἀμελείᾳ τῆς προαιρέσεως συλληφθεὶς ἐν τῇ ψυχῇ.

8.   Εἰ δὲ σὺ τὴν γλῶσσαν ἐνέτεινας καθάπερ τόξον καὶ ὡς ἀπὸ
ξιφοθήκης τῆς σῆς πονηρᾶς διανοίας ῥῆμα πικρὸν ὡς βέλος ὀξὺ
95   πρὸς τὴν καρδίαν ἐπαφῆκας τῆς ἀδελφῆς, τὰ τοῦ φονέως προφανῶς
εἰργάσω καὶ τὸν ἀδελφοκτόνον ἐμιμήσω Κάϊν. ἐκεῖνος φθόνῳ βληθεὶς
ἐν τῷ πεδίῳ τὸν Ἄβελ ἀπέκτεινε, καὶ σὺ κακίᾳ τρωθεῖσα ἐν τῷ
κοινωβίῳ τὴν ἀδελφὴν δι᾽ ὕβρεως ἐθανάτωσας. τοῦ φονευθέντος τὸ

your error, woe to you for your insensitivity, because you have a prison instead of a festival! You think of your bonds as freedom but you reap a harvest of death instead of life.

6.   But perhaps you have no grievance against your sister, but you hear that she is seriously distressed over a word of reproach which you have spoken in front of her. How can you be cheerful? How can you remain unmoved? If you maintain such an attitude, you are terminally ill, because, on the one hand, you have no perception of the reproach with which you have struck the heart of your neighbour, and, on the other hand, because in learning of your sister's suffering you feel no pain. Is this not an outright indication of death? Is this not a taking leave of your senses and the deepest darkness of ignorance? You cast fire into your sister's house. Like a violent wind, the evil one seized hold of this outrage and enkindled wickedness in her heart. The house of her soul is set on fire in a great blaze. The smoke of her cries and the groans reach the hearing of the entire sisterhood. The entire sisterhood shows its compassion, is moved to pity and makes haste to quench the flames of grief with the dew of admonition and to console her soul. But neither as the cause of her anger, nor as a member of the community body do you feel any pain so that you would run with repentance and fall at your sister's feet and pacify her raging heart with a good apology and heal both yourself and your sister.[2]

7.   If your sister has suffered because of some supposed injury, without your having given any apparent cause at all and without your knowing of any deed or word intervening to distress her, and she is silent in speech but suffers in her heart, you are without blame and free of censure, because what troubles her is nothing other than mere suspicion and an unspoken thought conceived in her soul by the jealousy of the enemy and by carelessness in her exercise of free choice.

8.   But if you have bent your tongue like a bow[3] and loosed a bitter word at the heart of your sister like a sharp arrow from the quiver of your wicked mind, you have obviously committed murder in imitation of Cain, the fratricide.[4] Struck with jealousy he slew Abel in the plain, while, wounded with wickedness, you have by your insult mortally offended your sister in the common life. The blood of the

---

[2] Dorotheus of Gaza speaks in somewhat similar fashion in treating the vice of rancour. See *Instructions* 7.89-95, especially 90 (sc 92:306-319).
[3] Cf. Jer 9:2.
[4] Gen 4:1-16.

αἷμα ὡς φθέγμα πρὸς τὸν θεὸν ἐβόα καὶ τῆς ὑβρισθείσης τὸ στόμα
100 τῆς λοιδορίας τὸ ῥῆμα ὡς αἷμα προβαλλόμενον, τὸν ἀέρα μὲν φωνῶν,
τὴν καρδίαν δὲ πικρίας πληροῖ. ἐκεῖ τὸ ἐκκεχυμένον αἷμα τοῦ Ἄβελ
φωνὴν ἠφίει καὶ ὁ ἐκχέας αὐτὸ Κάϊν, ὡς μὴ δράσας φόνον, διέκειτο
καὶ ἐσίγα· ὧδε τὸ πνεῦμα τῆς μισουμένης τεταραγμένον καὶ συγκε-
χυμένον τυγχάνον διὰ τὴν ὕβριν στενάζει, καὶ ἡ διὰ τῆς κακολογίας
105 ταράξασα καὶ λυπήσασα οὐ στυγνάζει, οὐ συντρίβεται, οὐ βάλλει
μετάνοιαν, οὐκ ἀπολογεῖται, οὐκ ἐπιμέμφεται ἑαυτήν· φαίνεται δὲ καὶ
συναναστρέφεται ἐνώπιον αὐτῆς, ὡς μὴ κακόν τι ποιησαμένη· ὥστε
καὶ εἴ ποτέ τις εἰρηνοποιὸς ἄνθρωπος εἰσηγεῖται αὐτῇ ταπεινωθῆναι
ἔμπροσθεν τῆς ὀργιζομένης καὶ παῦσαι τὴν λύπην διὰ τῆς μετανοίας,
110 αὐτίκα τὰ τοῦ Κάϊν παραπλησίως λέγει καὶ αὐτή. ὡς γὰρ ὁ φονευτὴς
Κάϊν ἐρωτηθεὶς περὶ τοῦ φονευθέντος ἀδελφοῦ ἀπεκρίθη, *οὐ γινώσκω·
μὴ φύλαξ εἰμὶ τοῦ ἀδελφοῦ μου;* οὕτω καὶ αὕτη, ἐρωτωμένη καὶ
νουθετουμένη πρὸς τὸ καταλλάξαι τὴν λυπουμένην, τοιαῦτα λέγει·
οὐ σύνοιδα ἐν τῇ ψυχῇ μου πονηρίαν. οὐκ εἶπα κατὰ τῆς ἀδελφῆς.
115 μὴ ἐνέχομαι, ὁσάκις σκανδαλίζεται, τοσαυτάκις ὑποπίπτειν αὐτῇ;

9. Ὦ τοῦ σκοτασμοῦ τοῦ καλύπτοντος τὸν ὀφθαλμὸν τῆς ψυχῆς
καὶ ἐμποδίζοντος τὴν κατανόησιν τῆς ἁμαρτίας. τί λέγεις μοναχὴ
ἡ τὸν κόσμον σεαυτῇ καὶ σεαυτὴν τῷ κόσμῳ ἐπαγγειλαμένη νεκρῶσαι
καὶ τὴν μετάνοιαν δι᾽ ὅλου τοῦ βίου προτιμησαμένη καὶ τὴν ἀνάγκην
120 τῆς φοβερᾶς ἡμέρας φυγεῖν ἐπειγομένη; εἰ μὴ διὰ τὴν ὕβριν ἦν
ἀπεστομάτισας, εἰ μὴ διὰ τὴν πικρίαν ἣν ἐκέρασας τῇ ψυχῇ τῆς
ἀδελφῆς σου, κἂν διὰ τὰ ἔργα τῆς ἀσκήσεώς σου, πορεύθητι καὶ
διαλλάγηθι αὐτῇ, ἵνα μὴ ἄπρακτος ἡ κουρά σου εὑρεθῇ καὶ ἡ ἐκ
τοῦ κόσμου φυγὴ εἰς οὐδὲν συντελέσει σοι.

125 **10.** Εἰ κάμνεις τῷ σώματι, ἔχεις δὲ μῖσος, τελεῖς ναῦς γόμον ἐν
τῇ ξηρᾷ δεχομένη καὶ τοῦτον ἀποβαλλομένη ἐν τῇ θαλάσσῃ διὰ τὴν
ζάλην. εἰ κοπιᾷς ἐν ἔργοις σωματικοῖς, θησαυρίζεις δὲ κακίαν ἐν
λογισμοῖς, στόμαχος εἶ, βρώματα δεχόμενος καὶ πάλιν ἀποπτύων αὐτὰ
διὰ τὸν ἐνοικοῦντα ἐν αὐτῷ νοσοποιὸν χυμόν. οὐδὲν ἡ νηστεία, οὐδὲν
130 ἡ ἀγρυπνία, οὐδὲν ἡ ψαλμῳδία, μίσους ἐμφωλεύοντος ἐν τῇ ψυχῇ·

---

124 συντελέσει: συντελέσῃ rectius

murder victim cried out to God like a voice; the mouth of the outraged victim sends forth words of reproach like blood and fills the air with cries and the heart with bitterness. In the former case, the blood of Abel which was spilt emitted a voice and Cain, who spilt the blood, acted as though he had committed no murder and kept silent. In the latter case, because the spirit of the sister who is the object of hatred is distressed and troubled, it groans on account of the outrage, but the one who has caused the distress and grief by her evil words is not saddened, is not contrite, does not make a prostration, does not offer an apology, does not blame herself; rather, she appears and goes about her business in her sister's sight, as though she had done nothing wrong. As a result, if ever a peacemaker proposes to her that she should humble herself before her angered sister and put an end to her grief by repentance, she immediately replies in a manner like Cain. For when the murderer Cain was asked about his murdered brother, he replied, "I do not know; am I my brother's keeper?"[5] So too in the case of this woman, when she is asked and admonished to be reconciled with the sister she has grieved, she makes a reply such as this: "I am not aware of any evil in my soul. I did not speak against my sister. Am I supposed to fall down before her whenever she is offended?"

9. O what darkness covers the eye of the soul and hinders the apprehension of sin! As a nun who has promised to mortify the world to herself and herself to the world, who has chosen penance for all of her life and is eager to flee the punishment of the terrible day of judgement, what do you have to say? If not on account of the insult which you repeated by word of mouth, if not on account of the bitterness which you poured into the soul of your sister, even if it is just for the sake of the works of your ascetic practice, go and be reconciled with her, lest your tonsure be found unavailing and your flight from the world amount to nothing.

10. If you toil in body but hold on to hatred, you are like a ship that takes on its cargo on dry land but throws it away at sea because of a storm. If you labour at corporeal works but store up evil in your thoughts, you are like a stomach that accepts food which it then disgorges on account of a sickening humour lying inside it. Fasting means nothing, vigils mean nothing, psalmody means nothing, if hatred is lurking in the soul, for when contentiousness intervenes it places

---

5 Gen 4:9.

ἡ γὰρ μεσολαβοῦσα φιλονεικία δεσμὸς γίνεται τῆς ψυχῆς, ἀποκλείουσα τὸν νοῦν ἐν οἷς εἶπας καὶ οἷς ἤκουσας.

11.   Ἀδιάλλακτος μένουσα, ἠβουλήθης πράξεις ἀρετῶν προσαγα-γεῖν τῷ θεῷ; ὡς ἄδεκτα δῶρα ταύτας ἡγεῖται καὶ ὡς θυσίαν ψεκτὴν
135 ἀποστρέφεται. *ἐὰν προσφέρῃς τὸ δῶρόν σου ἐπὶ τὸ θυσιαστήριον καὶ μνησθῇς ὅτι ὁ ἀδελφός σου ἔχει τι κατὰ σοῦ, ἄφες τὸ δῶρον, καὶ ὕπαγε διαλλάγηθι τῷ ἀδελφῷ, καὶ τότε πρόσφερε τὸ δῶρόν σου.* λῦσον, φησί, πρότερον τὴν μικροψυχίαν δι᾽ ἧς συνεδέθης τῇ ψυχῇ καὶ παράστησόν μοι τὸν νοῦν καθαρὸν ἀπὸ μίσους, καὶ τότε τὸν ἐν τῷ σώματι βίον
140 σου ὡς καθαρὰν θυσίαν προσδέχομαι. τί μοι τὸ κέρδος τῆς ἔξωθέν σου πολιτείας, τὴν ἐκ τοῦ μίσους ἔσωθεν ζημίαν βλέποντι τῆς ψυχῆς σου; τί σοι τὸ ὄφελος, ἐὰν τὸ σῶμα ὅλον κοσμήσῃς τοῖς τρόποις τῶν ἀρετῶν, τὴν δὲ ψυχὴν ἀχρειώσῃς τῇ πικρίᾳ τοῦ μίσους; τί τὸ ὄφελος, ὅταν τὸ σῶμα διὰ τῆς παννύχου στάσεως παριστᾷς ὡς
145 λαμπάδα, τὸ δὲ ἀπὸ τῆς τοῦ πλησίον ἀγάπης φῶς τῆς ψυχῆς οὐκ ἔχῃς, διὰ τῆς ὑπομονῆς τῶν θλιβερῶν καὶ τῆς θερμοτάτης καταλλαγῆς ἀγοραζόμενον.

12.   Ταῦτ᾽ οὖν ἀκριβῶς ἐπιγνοῦσαι, μητέρες, τὴν μὲν κατ᾽ ἀλλήλων λύπην ὡς νοσερὰν δίαιταν καὶ ἀηδίαν φέρουσαν τῇ ψυχῇ
150 ἀποστράφητε, τὴν δὲ πρὸς ἀλλήλας ἀγάπην ὡς εὔχρηστον τροφὴν καὶ ἡδονὴν προξενοῦσαν θείαν ἀσπάσασθε· ὅπως τῇ δυνάμει τῆς ἀγάπης συντηρούμεναι εἰς μέτρον ἡλικίας φθάσητε τοῦ πληρώματος τοῦ ἀγαπήσαντος ἡμᾶς Χριστοῦ· ᾧ ἡ δόξα καὶ τὸ κράτος εἰς τοὺς αἰῶνας τῶν αἰώνων. Ἀμήν.

the soul in bondage, shutting up the mind in what you said and what you heard.

11.   Did you want to bring your virtuous practices before God while remaining irreconcilable? He considers them as unacceptable gifts and refuses them as a blameworthy sacrifice. "If you are offering your gift at the altar, and remember that your brother has something against you, leave the gift and go, be reconciled with your brother, and then offer your gift."[6] God is saying, "First, let go of the pettiness by which you have been bound in soul and present to me your mind purified of hatred, and then I will accept your bodily life as a pure sacrifice. What value to me is your exterior way of life when I look upon the interior damage done to your soul by hatred? What benefit is there for you, if you adorn all your body with the ways of the virtues but damage your soul with the bitterness of hatred? What benefit is there when you present your body as a lamp by means of night-long vigils, but in your soul you do not have the light of love for your neighbour which is purchased by patient endurance of sufferings and the most fervent reconciliation?"

12.   Now that you are well informed on these matters, mothers, avoid causing one another grief as that brings upon the soul a diseased and odious way of life; welcome love for one another as a harbinger of valuable nourishment and divine pleasure. And so, in preserving yourselves by the power of love, you may attain the measure of the full maturity of Christ, who has loved us.[7] To him be the glory and the power unto the ages of ages. Amen.

---

[6] Mt 5:23-24.
[7] Eph 4:13.

Περὶ ὑποταγῆς πρὸς τὴν προεστῶσαν

1. Ἀδελφαὶ καὶ μητέρες, ὁ θέλων οἶκον ἑαυτῷ κατασκευάσαι, οἰκοδόμον προσκαλεῖται καὶ τὴν ἰδίαν βούλησιν ἐμφανίζει καὶ τὴν ποσότητα τῶν κατὰ τὴν ἰσχὺν αὐτοῦ ἀναλωμάτων ἀνακαλύπτει. ὁ
5 δὲ τὴν μὲν παρασκευὴν τῆς ὕλης αὐτῷ ἐπιτρέπει, τὴν δὲ κατασκευὴν τοῦ οἴκου αὐτὸς ἀναδέχεται. ἴδωμεν οὖν τί ποιεῖ ὁ τεχνίτης ἀρχόμενος οἰκοδομεῖν. πάντως πρὸ πάσης ἄλλης ἐργασίας θεμέλιον καταβάλλει καὶ θεμέλιον ἰσχυρόν, ἵνα καὶ ἅπας ὁ ὄγκος τοῦ οἴκου ἐν ἀσφαλείᾳ γενόμενος, ἀκράδαντος διαφυλάττηται.
10 **2.** Τὸν τρόπον τοῦτον τύπον τοῦ καθ᾽ ἡμᾶς βίου ποιησώμεθα. οἴδατε ὅτι ἑκάστη ὑμῶν ἀπὸ τοῦ ἁγίου βαπτίσματος οἶκος Χριστοῦ γέγονε· *ὅσοι, γάρ φησιν, εἰς Χριστὸν ἐβαπτίσθητε, Χριστὸν ἐνεδύσασθε·* καὶ πάλιν, *οὐκ οἴδατε ὅτι ναὸς τοῦ θεοῦ ἐστε καὶ τὸ πνεῦμα τοῦ θεοῦ οἰκεῖ ἐν ὑμῖν;* ἑκάστη οὖν ὑμῶν, οἶκος τελοῦσα διὰ τῆς δωρεᾶς τοῦ
15 Χριστοῦ, οὐκ ἐφύλαξε τὰς ἐντολὰς τοῦ Χριστοῦ τὰς καινιζούσας καὶ συντηρούσας τὸν οἶκον, τὴν καθαρότητά φημι τοῦ σωτηρίου λουτροῦ· ἀλλὰ τὸν παλαιὸν ἄνθρωπον ἀγαπήσασα, τὸν φθειρόμενον κατὰ τὰς ἐπιθυμίας τῆς ἀπάτης ἐσάθρωσεν ἑαυτήν, πάθεσι τῆς σαρκὸς δου- λωθεῖσα καὶ τὴν ἄλογον τοῦ κόσμου συνήθειαν ἀσπασαμένη· ἅτινά
20 ἐστιν ἰδιορρυθμία, ἀνυποταξία, ἀνηκοΐα, ἀντιλογία, φιλονικεία, αὐταρέσκεια καὶ τὰ λοιπὰ τοῦ φιληδόνου θελήματος ἐκτρώματα. ὅπου γὰρ οὐ κατοικεῖ Χριστός, αἱ τοιαῦται διαθέσεις ἐκεῖ φιλοχωροῦσιν. ἔνθα δὲ Χριστοῦ ἐντολὴ ἐνεργεῖται, ἐκεῖ καὶ Χριστός. *ὁ τηρῶν, φησί,*

20 φιλονικεία ΟΑ [cf. 80 φιλονεικίας]

MD **8**

On submission to the superior

1. Sisters and Mothers, someone who wishes to construct a house for himself summons a builder, makes known his plan and reveals the extent of the expenditure that is within his means. He entrusts to him the procuring of the materials and the builder undertakes the construction of the house. Let us see then what the artisan does when he begins to build. Of course, before any other work he lays down a foundation, a strong foundation in order that the entire weight of the building is secure and can be kept from shaking.[1]

2. Let us take this method of proceeding as a type of our own life. You know that each of you, from the time of holy baptism, has become a house of Christ, for scripture says, "As many as were baptized into Christ have put on Christ";[2] and again, "Do you not know that you are God's temple and that God's Spirit dwells in you?"[3] Each of you, I say, though you are a house through the gift of Christ, did not keep the commandments of Christ which renew and preserve the house,[4] I mean, the purity of the salvific bath. Rather, each has preferred the 'old man,'[5] which is corrupted in deceitful desires, and has enfeebled herself by servitude to the passions of the flesh and by welcoming the irrational habits of the world, namely, idiorrhythmy,[6] insubordination, disobedience, contrariness, contentiousness, self-satisfaction and the remaining miscarriages of a will addicted to pleasure. Where Christ does not dwell, such dispositions are wont to lodge. But in the place where the commandment of Christ is practised,

---

[1] Cf. *Apophthegmata patrum*, Poimen 130 (704), PG 65:353D-356A. Throughout this instruction Theoleptos draws upon the Gospel story, Mt 7:24-27 and Lk 6:47-49.

[2] Gal 3:27.

[3] 1 Cor 3:16.

[4] Cf. S. Salaville, "Prière inédite de Nicolas Cabasilas à Jésus Christ," EO 35 (1936) 43-50.

[5] Cf. Rom 6:6, Eph 4:22, Col 3:9. While keeping the masculine gender references of the scriptural allusions, Theoleptos puts most of his participles and pronouns in the feminine, as he is speaking to the nuns.

[6] In this context idiorrhythmy probably refers to any sort of singularity adopted by an individual in the practice of the monastic life.

τὰς ἐντολάς μου ἐκεῖνός ἐστιν ὁ ἀγαπῶν με, καὶ ἀγαπηθήσεται ὑπὸ τοῦ
25 πατρός μου, καὶ ἐγὼ καὶ ὁ πατὴρ ἐλευσόμεθα καὶ μονὴν παρ' αὐτῷ
ποιήσομεν.

3. Ὁρᾷς πῶς ἡ ποίησις τῶν ἐντολῶν συντηρεῖ τὸν οἶκον τῆς
ψυχῆς καὶ τὸν Χριστὸν ἔνοικον ποιεῖται; ἐντολαὶ δὲ Χριστοῦ πάντως
ἡ ἀποταγὴ οὐ μόνον πάντων τῶν συγγενῶν καὶ τῶν πραγμάτων τοῦ
30 κόσμου, ἀλλὰ καὶ τοῦ φρονήματος τοῦ κοσμικοῦ καὶ τῆς κατὰ τὴν
γλῶσσαν προπετείας καὶ πάσης τῆς κατ' αἴσθησιν ἀλόγου συνηθείας.
*εἴ τις, γάρ φησιν, οὐκ ἀποτάξεται πᾶσι τοῖς ὑπάρχουσιν αὐτῷ, οὐ δύναται
εἶναί μου μαθητής.* ἐντολὴ Χριστοῦ ἡ πρὸς τὴν προεστῶσαν ὑποταγὴ
τῆς ψυχῆς ὁμοῦ καὶ τοῦ σώματος, ἡ ἐκκοπὴ τοῦ ἰδίου θελήματος
35 καὶ τῶν ἄλλων πάντων, ὅσα τοῦ παλαιοῦ ἀνθρώπου, ὅς ἐστιν ἡ
παράβασις τῶν τοῦ Χριστοῦ ἐντολῶν καὶ ἡ κατὰ τὴν παράβασιν
ἁμαρτία ἡ καὶ τὸν οἶκον τῆς ψυχῆς καταλύσασα.

4. Τοῦτο ἐπιγνοῦσαι καὶ βουληθεῖσαι μονὴν ἐν τοῖς οὐρανοῖς
ἑτοιμάσαι, κατελείψατε τὸν κόσμον καὶ τὴν ὑπερκόσμιον τῆς
40 ἀσκήσεως διαγωγὴν ἡρετίσασθε, ἐπειγόμεναι τὸ καθαρὸν τοῦ Χριστοῦ
ταμιεῖον ἀνοικοδομῆσαι. ἐν γὰρ τῇ καθαρότητι ὁ Χριστὸς καὶ οἰκεῖ
καὶ ὀπτάνεται· *μακάριοι, γάρ φησιν, οἱ καθαροὶ τῇ καρδίᾳ, ὅτι αὐτοὶ
τὸν θεὸν ὄψονται.* ἐπεὶ γοῦν ποθεῖτε οἶκος Χριστοῦ γενέσθαι, χρῄζετε
πάντως καὶ τοῦ ἀρίστου τεχνίτου πρὸς τὴν τῆς σωτηρίας ὑμῶν
45 οἰκοδομήν, οὗ χωρὶς οὐ δύνασθε ποιεῖν οὐδέν. ὁ Χριστὸς οὗτός ἐστιν
ὁ τὴν ἡμῶν οἰκονομῶν καὶ οἰκοδομῶν σωτηρίαν, ὁ καὶ κτίστης τῶν
πνευμάτων καὶ τῶν σωμάτων· *ἡ σοφία, γάρ φησιν, ᾠκοδόμησεν ἑαυτῇ
οἶκον.* ὁ δὲ αὐτὸς καὶ θεμέλιός ἐστιν· *οὐδείς, γάρ φησιν ὁ ἀπόστολος,
ἄλλον θεμέλιον δύναται θεῖναι παρὰ τὸν κείμενον, ὅς ἐστιν ὁ Χριστός.*
50 αὐτὸς γὰρ ὡς παντελὴς ἀρετὴ τὴν ὑπακοὴν καὶ τὴν ὑποταγὴν καὶ
ἐνεδείξατο καὶ ἐνετείλατο, *ὑπήκοος γενόμενος μέχρι θανάτου, θανάτου
δὲ σταυροῦ.*

5. Κατανοήσατε παρακαλῶ τῶν ῥημάτων τὴν δύναμιν. ἡ καθαρότης τῆς καρδίας καὶ ὁ ἁγιασμὸς τοῦ σώματος, ταῦτά ἐστιν ὁ οἶκος
55 τοῦ Χριστοῦ· θεμέλιον τοῦ τοιούτου οἴκου ἡ πρὸς τὴν προεστῶσαν

there also dwells Christ. He says, "He who keeps my commandments, he it is who loves me; and he will be loved by my Father, and I and my Father will come to him and make our abode with him."[7]

3. Do you see how the practice of the commandments preserves the house of the soul and makes Christ its tenant? The commandments of Christ certainly involve the renunciation not only of all family relations and of the affairs of the world, but also of worldly attitudes, rash speech and any other irrational habits of the senses. For scripture says, "If any man will not renounce all that he has, he cannot be my disciple."[8] Christ's commandment involves submission of both soul and body to the superior, the excision of one's personal will and everything else that belongs to the old man. The 'old man' refers to the transgression of the commandments of Christ and the sin involved in the transgression, which destroys the house of the soul.

4. Now that you realize this and have made your decision to prepare an abode in the heavenly places, you have abandoned the world and chosen for yourself the other-worldly, ascetic way of life, for you are eager to build a pure treasury for Christ. For in purity Christ makes his abode and vouchsafes a vision of himself, for scripture says, "Blessed are the pure of heart, for they shall see God."[9] Therefore, since you long to become a house for Christ, by all means employ the very best craftsman for the construction of your salvation, without whom you can do nothing,[10] namely, Christ, who is the dispenser and architect of our salvation. He is also the creator of spirits and bodies, for scripture says, "Wisdom has built for herself a house."[11] He is also himself the foundation, for the apostle says, "No other foundation can anyone lay than that which is laid, which is Christ."[12] He himself, as the example of perfect virtue, has both demonstrated and commanded obedience and submission, "for he became obedient unto death, even death on a cross."[13]

5. Please consider the meaning of these words. Purity of heart and sanctification of the body, these constitute the house of Christ; the foundation of such a house lies in submission and obedience to the

---

[7] Jn 14:21, 23.
[8] Lk 14:33.
[9] Mt 5:8.
[10] Cf. Jn 15:5; Heb 11:10.
[11] Prov 9:1.
[12] 1 Cor 3:11.
[13] Phil 2:8.

διὰ Χριστὸν ὑποταγὴ καὶ ὑπακοή· οἰκοδομὴ τῆς καθαρότητος ἡ πρὸς
Χριστὸν ἐξ ὅλης ψυχῆς ἀγάπη καὶ ἡ πρὸς τὰς ἀδελφὰς γνησία
διάθεσις· ἡ γνῶσις, γάρ φησι, φυσιοῖ, ἡ δὲ ἀγάπη οἰκοδομεῖ. ὡς γὰρ
ἡ φιλία τῆς σαρκὸς ἅπαν πάθος ἐργάζεται, οὕτως ἡ ἀγάπη τοῦ
60 Χριστοῦ ἅπαν εἶδος τῆς ἀρετῆς κατασπάζεται.
    6. Ὡς γοῦν τῆς οἰκίας ἡ οἰκοδομὴ τῇ πρὸς ἀλλήλας ἐπιθέσει
τῶν πετρῶν εἰς ὕψος ἐκτείνεται, οὕτω καὶ ἡ ἄσκησις ἐξ ἀρετῆς εἰς
ἀρετὴν προϊοῦσα, προκοπὴν τῇ ψυχῇ ἐμποιεῖ. ἐντεῦθεν ἄρχεται ἡ
ψυχὴ ὑψοῦσθαι καὶ ὑπερηφανεύεσθαι διὰ τὴν τῶν ἀρετῶν ὡς εἴρηται
65 προκοπήν. διὸ καὶ δεῖται, καθάπερ ὀρόφου τινός, τῆς ταπεινοφροσύνης. ὡς γὰρ ἡ ἐπικειμένη στέγη σκέπει τὴν τοῦ οἴκου οἰκοδομήν,
οὕτω καὶ ἡ ταπείνωσις τὴν διὰ τῶν ἀρετῶν καθαρότητα περιέπει καὶ
συντηρεῖ· ὡς γὰρ ἀκάθαρτος παρὰ κυρίῳ πᾶς ὑψηλοκάρδιος, καθαρὰ
παρὰ θεῷ πάντως ἡ ταπεινόφρων ψυχή· μάθετε, γάρ φησιν, ἀπ᾽ ἐμοῦ,
70 ὅτι πρᾶός εἰμι καὶ ταπεινὸς τῇ καρδίᾳ, καὶ εὑρήσετε ἀνάπαυσιν ταῖς ψυχαῖς
ὑμῶν. τίς δέ ἐστιν ἡ ἀνάπαυσις τῆς ψυχῆς; ἡ ἐνοίκησις τοῦ Χριστοῦ,
τῆς ταπεινοφροσύνης γὰρ τὴν ταραχὴν τῶν παθῶν κοιμιζούσης,
ἐπιφαίνεται ἡ χάρις τοῦ Χριστοῦ καὶ γαληνιᾷ ἡ καρδία καὶ μετ᾽
ἀγαλλιάσεως εὐχομένη λέγει· ἡδυνθείη αὐτῷ ἡ διαλογή μου, ἐγὼ δὲ
75 εὐφρανθήσομαι ἐπὶ τῷ κυρίῳ. ἐν πραείαις γὰρ ψυχαῖς ὁ θεὸς
ἀναπέπαυται καὶ τοῖς ταπεινοῖς δίδοται χάρις ταῖς ὑποτασσομέναις·
οὐ ταῖς ἀνυποτάκτοις, ταῖς τὴν ὑπακοὴν τιμώσαις διὰ τῶν ἔργων,
οὐ ταῖς παρακοὴν ἀσπαζομέναις, ταῖς καταδεχομέναις τὸ θέλημα τῆς
προεστώσης, οὐ ταῖς ἀντεχομέναις τῶν ἰδίων θελημάτων καὶ πρὸς
80 φιλονεικίας κινουμέναις.
    7. Ἡ τῇ καταστάσει τῶν πρώτων στηριζομένη ψυχὴ τεθεμελίωται
ἐπὶ τὴν πέτραν, τὴν φυλακὴν δηλονότι τῶν ἐντολῶν τοῦ Χριστοῦ.
ὅθεν καὶ ὑπὸ τῆς βροχῆς τῶν ἐμπαθῶν λογισμῶν οὐκ ἐμπνίγεται,
ὑπὸ τῶν πνευμάτων τῆς κενοδοξίας οὐκ ἐπαίρεται, οὐδ᾽ εἰς ἀντιλογίας
85 χωρεῖ. οὔτε μὴν ὑπὸ τῶν ἔξωθεν ἐπερχομένων αὐτῇ δίκην ποταμῶν
πειρασμῶν σαλευομένη καὶ ἡττωμένη ἀμύνεται τὰς λυπούσας
ἀδελφάς· κατέχουσα δὲ τὴν ὑπομονὴν τοῦ Χριστοῦ, φέρει τὰ πάντα
μακροθύμως.

80 φιλονεικίας ΟΑ [cf. 20 φιλονικεία]

superior for the sake of Christ. The edifice of purity is made up of love for Christ with all one's soul and a sincere disposition towards one's sisters. For scripture says, "Knowledge puffs up, but love builds up."[14] For as the affection of the flesh sets every passion to work, so the love of Christ embraces every form of virtue.

6. Thus, as the construction of the building is extended upwards by laying the stones on top of one another, so too the ascetic life proceeds from virtue to virtue[15] and brings progress to the soul. Then the soul begins to be exalted and overbearing through its aforementioned progress in the virtues. And so it also has need of humility as a kind of roof, for as the placement of a roof shelters the edifice of the house, so too humility tends and preserves the purity attained through the virtues. As "every haughty heart is impure before the Lord,"[16] the humble soul is truly pure before God. For scripture says, "Learn of me for I am meek and humble of heart, and you will find rest for your souls."[17] What is rest for the soul? The indwelling of Christ — for, when humility has put to sleep the disquietude of the passions, the grace of Christ appears and the heart grows calm and praying with joy it says, "May my conversation be pleasing to him, and I shall rejoice in the Lord."[18] For the Lord has taken his rest in gentle souls and his grace is given to the humble, to docile souls,[19] not to disobedient ones; to those that honour obedience by their works, not to those that welcome disobedience; to those who accept the will of the superior, not to those who hold to their own wills and are motivated by contentiousness.

7. The soul that is firmly fixed in the condition of the former is founded on rock, namely, the keeping of the commandments of Christ. On this account it is not drowned by the torrent of impassioned thoughts; it is not stirred by the spirits of vainglory; it is not moved to controversy. Unshaken and unconquered by the temptations that, like rivers, come over it from without, it guards itself from the sisters who grieve it; holding to patient endurance in Christ, it bears all things with long-suffering.[20]

---

[14] 1 Cor 8:1.
[15] Cf. Ps 84:8.
[16] Prov 16:5.
[17] Mt 11:29.
[18] Ps 103:34.
[19] Cf. Prov 3:34, Jas 4:6, 1 Pet 5:5.
[20] Cf. Mt 7:24-25; Lk 6:47-48.

8. Ἡ δὲ τῇ διαθέσει τῶν δευτέρων κατεχομένη ψυχὴ τὴν ἄμμον
90 τοῦ φιληδόνου θελήματος ἔχει θεμέλιον. ἀμέλει καὶ ὑπὸ λογισμῶν
ἀλλεπαλλήλων καὶ ὑπονοιῶν καὶ κενοδόξων ἐννοιῶν ταράσσεται καὶ
πρὸς οὐδεμίαν συμβαίνουσαν θλίψιν διὰ καρτερίας ἀντιστῆναι δύνα-
ται· πρὸς ἐπιθυμίας δὲ καὶ ὀργὰς καὶ κραυγὰς καὶ ἀκαταστασίας
τρόπον φερομένη, πτῶσιν ὑπομένει μεγάλην. ἐπειδὴ κόσμον ἔφυγε,
95 συνήθειαν δὲ κοσμικὴν οὐκ ἀπέλιπε· σχῆμα μοναδικὸν περιεβάλετο,
φρόνημα δὲ σαρκικὸν οὐκ ἀπεδύσατο· τῆς Αἰγύπτου ἐξῆλθεν, εἰς τὴν
ἐπηγγελμένην δὲ γῆν κατὰ τὴν φυλακὴν τῶν ἐντολῶν, οὐκ εἰσῆλθε·
διότι τὰ φρονήματα αὐτῆς καθάπερ κῶλα κατεστρωμένα ἔχει ἐν ταῖς
ματαίαις προλήψεσι τῆς κοσμικῆς ἀναστροφῆς καὶ ὁμοιοῦται μωρῷ
100 ἀνδρί, κόπον ὑπομένοντι καὶ κέρδος οὐκ ἔχοντι, ἐπαγγελλομένῳ
καμεῖν τὸν ἀμπελῶνα, οὐκ ἀπερχομένῳ δέ, διὰ τοῦτο καὶ μισθὸν οὐ
λαμβάνοντι. ῥῦσαι ἡμᾶς, κύριε, τοιαύτης διαθέσεως πρεσβείαις τῆς
παναχράντου σου μητρὸς καὶ τῶν ἠγαπηκότων σε ἁγίων. Ἀμήν.

8. But the soul that adheres to the disposition of the second group has a foundation based on the sandy ground of the will's attachment to pleasure. And so it is troubled by a constant parade of thoughts, suspicions and vainglorious notions. It cannot patiently withstand any affliction that comes upon it, but, borne along towards desires, anger, shouting, and all manner of instability, it suffers a great fall.[21] Because it has fled the world but not abandoned worldly customs, has put on the monastic habit but not shed the attitude of the flesh, has departed from Egypt but not entered into the promised land by keeping the commandments, it thus has its attitudes, like its members, spread out among the empty preoccupations of a worldly way of life[22] and resembles the foolish man who patiently endures toil but gets no benefit, who promises to labour in the vineyard but does not go and for this reason receives no pay.[23] Save us, Lord, from such a disposition by the intercessions of your most pure Mother and the saints who have loved you. Amen.

[21] Cf. Mt 7:26-27; Lk 6:49.
[22] Cf. Num 14:32-33.
[23] Cf. Mt 21:28-31.

Διδασκαλία διαλαμβάνουσα τὴν ὀφειλομένην διαγωγὴν τῶν ἐν τῷ κοινοβίῳ μοναχῶν

1. Δότε μοι μικρὸν τὴν διάνοιαν παρακαλῶ καὶ τὴν ἀκοὴν χαρίσασθε τοῖς ἐμοῖς λόγοις πρὸς τὸ συνιέναι τοῦ πονηροῦ τὴν
5 ἐνέργειαν, κλέπτοντος ἡμᾶς καὶ πείθοντος πράττειν τὰ αὐτοῦ θελήματα ὡς ἡμέτερα· ἐπιγνόντες γὰρ τὴν πονηρίαν αὐτοῦ, δυνήσεσθε σὺν θεῷ πρὸς τὴν κακουργίαν αὐτοῦ ἀντιστῆναι καὶ τὰ κέντρα αὐτοῦ συντρίψαι. ὁ γεωργὸς ἐρανιζόμενος διάφορα κλήματα εἰς ἕνα τόπον φυτεύει καὶ ἀμπελῶνα συνίστησι καὶ πολλὴν ἐπιμέλειαν ἐπιδείκνυται
10 πρὸς τὸν καρπὸν ἀφορῶν. καὶ ὁ γεωργὸς τῶν καλῶν Χριστὸς ἐκ διαφόρων τόπων ὑμᾶς εἰς μίαν μονὴν συνήγαγε καὶ κοινόβιον συνεστήσατο, ἵνα ὁμονοίας καὶ ἀγάπης πάντες τῷ δεσπότῃ καρπὸν προσφέρητε.

2. Κοινόβιον οὖν ἐστι Χριστοῦ ἐκλογή, χορὸς ἐκλεκτῶν, πληθὺς
15 ἀνατεθημένη θεῷ, συνοδία ἑπομένη Χριστῷ, σταυρὸν κρατοῦσα καὶ σταυρῷ κρατυνομένη. κοινόβιόν ἐστι θεία παρεμβολή, παράταξις ἱερά, στρατὸς τοῦ πνεύματος πρὸς τὰ πνεύματα τῆς πονηρίας ἀπομαχόμενος. τὸ κοινόβιον διὰ τοῦτο ὠνομάσθη κοινόβιον ἐκ τοῦ τοὺς μιγάδας μοναχοὺς εἰς μίαν καὶ τὴν αὐτὴν μονὴν συνελθόντας
20 κοινὴν ποιεῖσθαι καὶ τὴν κατοικίαν καὶ τὴν ζωὴν καὶ τὴν θέλησιν καὶ τὴν γνώμην καὶ μηδένα τῶν τοῦ κοινοβίου ἴδιον ἔχειν τι, ὡς ἀπορρήγνυσθαι τῆς κοινῆς συμφωνίας καὶ τοῦ κατὰ θεὸν συνθήματος καὶ ἐπαγγέλματος, οὗ ἐποιήσατο ἕκαστος καθυποσχόμενος ἐνώπιον τοῦ Χριστοῦ τὴν ὑπακοὴν ἀπονέμειν τῷ προεστῶτι καὶ πάσῃ τῇ
25 ἀδελφότητι.

3. Σχιζομένου γὰρ ἑνὸς κατὰ γνώμην τῆς κατὰ τὴν ὁμοφροσύνην συνοδίας τῶν ἀδελφῶν, ὁ ἐχθρὸς εὐθὺς τόπον εὑρίσκει καὶ διὰ τοῦ ἑνὸς ἐπείγεται κρατῆσαι καὶ τῶν λοιπῶν. ἐντεῦθεν οἱ μερισμοὶ γίνονται καὶ διχόνοιαι καὶ διχοστασίαι καὶ κατατομαὶ καὶ ταραχὴ
30 καὶ σύγχυσις. ὁ μὲν πρὸς τὸν δεῖνα διάκειται καὶ πρὸς τοὺς ἄλλους

---

6 ἡμέτερα corr.: ὑμέτερα OA   26 ὁμοφροσύνην corr.: ὁμοφροσύνης OA

INSTRUCTION DEFINING THE CONDUCT PROPER TO MONKS LIVING IN COMMUNITY[1]

1. Please give me your attention for a little while and grant a hearing to my words that you may understand the working of the evil one, who cheats us and persuades us to do his wishes as our own. Once you have recognized his wickedness, you will be able, with God's help, to resist his malevolence and shatter his darts. The farmer gathers together different sorts of vine shoots and plants them in one spot; he establishes his vineyard and exhibits great diligence as he watches for the fruit. Christ, the farmer of good things, has brought you together from different places into a single abode and established you as a monastery, that all of you may offer the master the fruit of concord and love.

2. The monastery then is the chosen portion of Christ, a band of elect, a multitude dedicated to God, a company of fellow travellers in the following of Christ, holding to the Cross and upheld by the Cross. The monastery constitutes a divine army, a sacred battle line, a battalion of the Spirit to fight off the spirits of wickedness. The monastery has been called an abode of the common life for this reason, namely, because a varied group of monks has come together into one and the same abode to form a common habitation, life, will and purpose, and to hold nothing in the monastery as a private possession that would be divisive of the common harmony, covenant and profession which each of you made in promising before Christ to render obedience to the superior and the entire brotherhood.

3. If one person intentionally separates himself from the harmonious fellowship of the brothers, the enemy immediately finds a foothold and through the one hastens to control the rest. Consequently, factions arise as well as disagreements, dissensions, divisions, trouble and confusion. One person is favourably disposed towards one individual but is hostile towards others. Another person agrees with an individual

---

[1] For a study and partial translation of this text see S. Salaville, "La vie monastique grecque au début du xive siècle d'après un discours inédit de Théolepte de Philadelphie," *Études Byzantines* 2 (1944) 119-125.

ἀπεχθῶς ἔχει. ἕτερος συμφωνεῖ μεθ᾽ οὗ βούλεται καὶ πρὸς τοὺς ἄλλους
ἀντιλέγει καὶ μάχεται. καὶ οὔτε σῶμα ὁρᾶται κοινόβιον καὶ κεφαλὴν
ἀποβάλλεται, ἐξουθενεῖται γὰρ ὁ προεστώς, μᾶλλον δὲ ὁ Χριστὸς
οὗ καὶ μέλη ἐσμὲν οἱ πάντες, καὶ αὐτός ἐστιν ἡ κεφαλὴ τῶν ἁπάντων.

35   **4.** Ὁ ἡσυχάζων ῥᾳδίως ἐπιβουλεύεται, ἐπειδὴ μεμονωμένος τρέχει
καὶ προσκόψας οὐκ ἔχει τὸν βοηθοῦντα. ὁ δὲ τεταγμένος ἐν τῇ
ἀδελφότητι μετὰ πληροφορίας ἀγωνίζεται. πολλῶν εὐμοιρεῖ τῶν
βοηθούντων, φέρει γὰρ ἐπὶ μνήμης, *οὐ καλὸν εἶναι μόνον τὸν ἄνθρωπον*
ἐπὶ τῆς γῆς· ποιήσωμεν αὐτῷ βοηθὸν κατ᾽ αὐτόν. οὐ καλὸν τῷ ἑνὶ ἡ
40 μόνωσις, ὡς οὐδὲ τῷ ἰδιογνώμῳ ἡ μονοτονία. *οὐαὶ γὰρ τῷ ἑνί.*
ἀσφαλὴς ἡ μετὰ πολλῶν διαγωγή· *ἰδοὺ δή,* γάρ φησι, *τί καλὸν ἢ τί*
τερπνὸν ἀλλ᾽ ἢ τὸ κατοικεῖν ἀδελφοὺς ἐπὶ τὸ αὐτό; καὶ *ἀδελφὸς ὑπὸ*
ἀδελφοῦ βοηθούμενος ὡς πόλις ὀχυρά· καὶ εἷς τὸν ἕνα οἰκοδομείτω.

    5. Αὕτη ἡ χάρις τοῦ κοινοβίου· τοιαύτη τῆς συνοδίας ἡ βοήθεια.
45 ἡ περιοχὴ τῶν μονῶν μία· ὁ οἶκος τῶν ἱερῶν ὕμνων ὁ αὐτός· τῆς
ἑστιάσεως ἡ τράπεζα ἡ αὐτή. τὰ πάντα κοινὰ καὶ τοῖς πᾶσι τὰ αὐτά,
ἵνα ὥσπερ τὰ ἔξω οὕτω καὶ τὰ ἔσω κοινὰ τυγχάνῃ, καὶ πλέον τὰ
ἔσω, ὥστε τὰ αὐτὰ φρονεῖν, τὰ αὐτὰ θέλειν, ἐν τοῖς αὐτοῖς συμφωνεῖν,
ὡς εἶναι τῶν πάντων τὴν γνώμην ἑκάστου κρίσιν, καὶ τοῦ ἑνὸς αὖθις
50 τὴν θέλησιν τῶν ὅλων διάθεσιν. τὴν τοιαύτην ὁμόνοιαν βλέπων ὁ
ἐχθρὸς καὶ σχίσμα μὴ εὑρίσκων, οὐκ ἔχει ποῦ τὴν προσβολὴν τῆς
διχονοίας, ὡς κεφαλήν, ἐμβαλεῖν, ἵνα καὶ τὸν λοιπὸν ὁλκὸν εἰσωθήσῃ
καὶ τῆς φιλονεικίας τοὺς τρόπους ἐνδείξηται. διὰ τοῦτο καὶ ὑποχωρεῖ
τῆς ἱερᾶς ὁμοφροσύνης τῶν ἀδελφῶν τὴν παρεμβολὴν δεδοικώς. καὶ
55 ὁ μὲν πολέμιος ἄπρακτος ἀποπέμπεται.

    6. Ἕκαστος δὲ ὁράτω τὰς χάριτας τῶν μιγάδων μοναχῶν. ὁ ἐν
συνοδίᾳ τυγχάνων ὕλην ἰδίαν οὐκ ἐπιφέρεται, οὐδὲ ἰδικὸν περισπασμὸν κέκτηται. εἰ δὲ καὶ ὕλην διοικεῖ καὶ περισπᾶται, διὰ τὴν
κοινότητα τοῦτο ποιεῖ καὶ τὴν κοινὴν ἀνάπαυσιν περιποιεῖται. καὶ

of his choosing but speaks against and fights with others. And so the monastery does not prove to be a body and it loses its head, for the superior is ignored, or rather, Christ whose members we all are, and he himself is the head of all.[2]

4. The solitary monk is an easy prey for treachery, since he runs the course alone, and if he stumbles he has no one to help him. But the monk who has joined the ranks of the brotherhood endures the struggle with full assurance. He is in happy possession of many helpers, for he bears in mind that "it is not good for man to be alone on earth; let us make for him a helper after his own kind."[3] Solitude is not good for the individual, just as obstinacy is not good for the self-willed person. "Woe to the solitary man."[4] A life lived among the many is safe, for scripture says, "Behold, what is good or what pleasant, except for brothers to live in unity?";[5] and "A brother helped by a brother is like a strong city";[6] and "let the one edify the other."[7]

5. This is the grace of the common life; such is the assistance provided by the fellowship: a single enclosure for the cells, the same chapel for the sacred hymns, the same table for meals. All things are held in common and the same things belong to all, so that interior goods as well as external goods are common property, and all the more so in the case of interior goods. And so all hold the same thoughts and the same wishes and all agree on the same things so that the opinion of all is the judgement of each, and in turn the will of the individual is the disposition of the whole. When the enemy sees such concord and finds no division he has nowhere to introduce the assault of discord, like his head, so as to force a way in for the rest of his serpent's body and display the ways of contention. For this reason he withdraws from the holy unanimity of the brethren in fear of their army, and the enemy is sent away unsuccessful.

6. Let each take a look at the graces received by monks living together. One who lives in community does not bring along private property, nor does he possess anything of his own to distract him. But even if he manages property and is distracted, he does this for the sake of the common good and concerns himself with the common

---

[2] Cf. 1 Cor 6:15, 12:27, Eph 4:15, Col 1:18.
[3] Gen 2:18.
[4] Eccl 4:10.
[5] Ps 132:1.
[6] Prov 18:19.
[7] 1 Thes 5:11.

60 τοῦτό ἐστιν αὐτῷ τὸ γέρας, τὸ κοπιᾶν καὶ διακονεῖν τῷ κατὰ τὸ
    κοινόβιον σώματι, ἐπειδὴ καὶ ἕκαστον μέλος τοῦ σώματος διὰ τῆς
    ἰδίας ἐνεργείας τὴν τοῦ ὅλου σώματος χρείαν ἀποπληροῖ.

7. Τροφῆς καὶ ἐνδύματος οὐ φροντίζει. ὅτε θέλει καὶ ὡς θέλει,
    οὐχ ὑπνοῖ, τὸ κροῦμα γὰρ τοῦ ξύλου καὶ τὸ ὄφλημα τῆς προσούσης
65 διακονίας οὐκ ἀφιᾶσιν αὐτὸν ἠρεμεῖν. ὁρᾷ τὸν ἀπαντῶντα ταχέως
    εἰς τὴν σύναξιν τῶν θείων ὕμνων καὶ ἢ προθυμούμενος ἢ αἰσχυνόμενος
    ταχύνει καὶ αὐτὸς πρὸς τὴν σύναξιν. ἐργαζόμενος ἀγαθόν, οὐκ
    ἐπιγράφεται ἑαυτῷ, τῇ δὲ βοηθείᾳ τῶν ἀδελφῶν τοῦτο ἐπιγράφεται·
    ὅθεν καὶ οὐκ ἐπαίρεται, ὡς ἄλλων καὶ οὐχ ἑαυτοῦ τὸ κατόρθωμα
70 λογιζόμενος. ἡττώμενος ἐν ἐλαττώματι, καταγινώσκει ἑαυτοῦ, ὡς τὴν
    γνωμικὴν ἀσθένειαν συνορῶν· ἐντεῦθεν καὶ λυπεῖται καὶ ταπεινοῦται.
    συναγόμενος ἐν τῷ ναῷ ἐπὶ τὸ ἐκτελέσαι τὴν ψαλμῳδίαν, εἰ μὲν
    γρηγορεῖ, διϋπνίζει καὶ τὸν ῥαθυμοῦντα· εἰ δὲ ῥαθυμεῖ, ἐξυπνίζεται
    ὑπὸ τοῦ πέλας. καὶ πόλις ὀχυρὰ γίνονται ὡς ὑπ᾽ ἀλλήλων βοηθού-
75 μενοι.

8. Ἀκούσας τι λυπηρὸν ἠὸ παθῶν ἀηδὲς παρὰ τοῦ πέλας, ἢ
    ὑπέμεινε καὶ τὴν λύπην ἀφῆκε καὶ τὸν λυπήσαντα ὠφέλησε καὶ
    ἑαυτὸν ὡς νικητὴν ἐστεφάνωσεν, ἢ ἐταράχθη καὶ οὐκ ἐλάλησε καὶ
    ἀγωνιστὴς ὁρᾶται, ὡς τὸ ἥμισυ τῆς κακίας τροπωσάμενος· ἢ μὴ
80 ἐνεγκὼν ὡς μικρόψυχος ἀντελύπησε, καὶ ἡ πτῶσις αὐτοῦ πολλάκις
    ἀνάστασις γέγονεν. εἰς αἴσθησιν οὖν ἐλθὼν τῆς κατὰ τὴν ἧτταν τοῦ
    πάθους δυσωδίας, ὠχύρωσεν ἑαυτὸν τοῦ μηκέτι τῇ μικροψυχίᾳ
    ὑποπεσεῖν, ἑαυτὸν δὲ καθοπλίζειν διὰ προσευχῆς καὶ ὑπομονῆς
    καὶ τοιουτοτρόπως τὸ πάθος καταγωνίσασθαι. καὶ τίς ἀναγγελεῖ
85 ὅσα καὶ οἷα κερδαίνει ὁ ἐν τῷ μέσῳ συναυλιζόμενος μετὰ συνέσεως,
    τὸν πρὸ τῆς παρακοῆς Ἀδὰμ μιμούμενος; ὡς *ἀπὸ παντὸς ξύλου τοῦ*
    ἐν τῷ παραδείσῳ ἐκεῖνος, οὕτω καὶ οὗτος πάντας τοὺς ἀδελφοὺς εἰς
    οἰκοδομὴν ἑαυτοῦ ἐν ἀγάπῃ κατανοῶν.

9. Τοῦ μὲν μιμεῖται τὸ πρὸς τὴν σύναξιν πρόθυμον, τοῦ δὲ τὴν
90 ἔμφοβον παράστασιν· καὶ τοῦ μὲν τὴν ἐν πᾶσιν ἐγκράτειαν, τοῦ δὲ
    τὴν σύμμετρον νηστείαν, καὶ ἄλλου μὲν τὸ ἐν προσευχαῖς ἐπίμονον,
    ἑτέρου δὲ τὴν εὔλογον σιωπήν, καὶ ἄλλου πάλιν τὴν ἐν πειρασμοῖς
    καρτερίαν. καὶ ἁπλῶς εἰπεῖν, τὰ προσόντα τοῖς πᾶσι δρεπόμενος

weal. This is his privilege — to labour and to serve the body of the community — since every member of the body fulfils the needs of the body as a whole through his own activity.

7. He gives no thought to food and clothing. He does not sleep when he wishes and as he wishes, for the sound of the simandron and the duty of the service at hand do not allow him to rest. He sees the monk going quickly to the assembly for the divine hymns and, either out of eagerness or shame, he hastens himself to the assembly. When he does a good deed, he does not attribute it to himself; he attributes it to the help of his brothers. Thus he does not exalt himself because he considers the accomplishment as belonging to others and not to himself. When he is overcome in a failing, he accuses himself because he realizes the weakness of his will. Consequently he is both grieved and humbled. When he gathers with the others in the church to perform the psalmody, if he stays awake, he rouses the one who is lazy, but if he is the lazy one, he is awakened by his neighbour. And they become a strong city, for they receive help from one another.[8]

8. If he heard something distressing or suffered something painful at the hands of his neighbour, either he endured it patiently, forgave the hurt, helped its perpetrator and crowned himself as victor, or he was troubled and did not speak and is considered a combatant for having furnished half the evil; or else he did not bear with it and was vexed in return because he was mean-spirited, and yet his fall often became a resurrection. Thus, when he came to realize the foulness of the passion involved in his defeat, he fortified himself so that he would fall into pettiness no more, but would arm himself with prayer and patient endurance and in this way struggle against the passion. Who will declare the number and kind of benefits he receives who lives wisely in the midst of a community, imitating the state of Adam before his disobedience? As Adam was given to eat of every tree in paradise,[9] so too this monk looks to all his brothers to build him up in love.

9. He imitates one monk's eager attendance at chapel, another's ardour of reverent fear; one monk's self-discipline in all things; another's measured fasting; still another's persistence in prayers, another's eloquent silence and yet another's perseverance in the face of temptations. In general terms, by culling everyone's particular

[8] Cf. Prov 18:19.
[9] Gen 2:16.

προτερήματα, τοῦ μέλιτος τῆς κατ' ἀρετὴν προκοπῆς γεύεται καὶ τοῦ
95 φωτισμοῦ τῆς θείας ἀγάπης μέτοχος γίνεται.

10. Οὗτος καὶ εἴ ποτε γένηται ἀπὸ συναρπαγῆς ἢ ἀγνοίας ἔν
τινι σφάλματι περιπεσεῖν, ὑπομνησθῆναι δὲ ὑπό τινος τῶν ἀδελφῶν,
αὐτίκα τὴν ὑπόμνησιν οὐχ ὡς τοῦ τυχόντος ἀδελφοῦ συμβουλὴν
λογιζόμενος παραιτεῖται, ἀλλ' ὡς τοῦ προεστῶτος παραίνεσιν· μᾶλλον
100 δὲ τοῦ Χριστοῦ ἐντολὴν δεχόμενος, διορθοῦται. καὶ πρῶτα μὲν
δοξάζει τὸν θεὸν τὸν κινήσαντα τὸν ἀδελφὸν ἐξ ἀγάπης εἰπεῖν αὐτῷ
τὸ προσῆκον. ἔπειτα χάριτας ὁμολογεῖ καὶ τῷ ἀδελφῷ, ὡς εἰς
διόρθωσιν αὐτὸν ἀγαγόντι. ἀμέλει καὶ τὴν παρ' αὐτοῦ εἰσήγησιν ὡς
ἐντολὴν καὶ τὸν ἔλεγχον ὡς θείαν κρίσιν λογιζόμενος, σοφὸν καὶ
105 δίκαιον ἐκ τῶν ἔργων ἑαυτὸν παρίστησιν· *ἔλεγχε, γάρ φησιν, σοφόν,*
καὶ ἀγαπήσει σε. δίδου σοφῷ ἀφορμήν, καὶ σοφώτερος ἔσται· γνώριζε
δικαίῳ, καὶ προσθήσει τοῦ δέχεσθαι.

11. Ταῦτα τῶν κατὰ θεὸν ἀγωνιζομένων τὰ ἐπιτηδεύματα καὶ τῶν
μετὰ γνώσεως συνασκουμένων τὰ μελετήματά τε καὶ τὰ γνωρίσματα.
110 ἐγὼ δὲ δίκαιον ἔκρινα καὶ ἅπερ ἔφθασα ἰδεῖν καὶ μαθεῖν, εἴπω δὲ
καὶ παθεῖν, κοινωνὸς γὰρ ἐγενόμην τῶν μακαρίων ἐκείνων καὶ ἁγίων
ἀνδρῶν, εἰς μέσον ὑφηγήσασθαι, ἵνα καὶ ζηλῶσαι θελήσητε καὶ μὴ
τῇ ἀλόγῳ συνηθείᾳ ἑπόμενοι πρὸς τῷ μακρύνεσθαι τοῦ καλοῦ καὶ
τοῖς κακοῖς περιπίπτητε.

115 **12.** Παρέβαλον πολλάκις εἰς διαφόρους συνάξεις ἀδελφῶν ὑπο-
ταγῆς κάλλει λαμπρυνομένων καὶ πειθομένων ἀνδράσι τοῦ πνεύματος·
γηραιοῖς μὲν τὰ σώματα, νεαροῖς δὲ τὰς ψυχὰς καὶ τῷ διαπύρῳ πόθῳ
τοῦ Χριστοῦ φλεγομένοις, πολυπειροτάτοις καὶ ὀνομαστοῖς καὶ τὸ
δοκίμιον τῆς ἀρετῆς ἐκ πίστεως εἰλικρινοῦς καὶ ἐκ πράξεως καὶ
120 θεωρίας κομισαμένοις. τῇ τοιαύτῃ ἱερᾷ ὁμηγύρει τῶν ἀδελφῶν
συνδιατρίβων, πράγματα εἶδον κατανύξεως καὶ ταπεινώσεως καὶ
ἀγάπης μεστά, μὴ μόνον ἐν ταῖς ἀγρυπνίαις τελούμενα, ἀλλὰ καὶ ἐν
τῇ συνάξει τῆς τραπέζης καὶ τῶν λοιπῶν διακονημάτων.

13. Καὶ γὰρ εἴ ποτέ τις τῶν ἱερῶν ὕμνων τελουμένων εἰς μνήμην
125 ἐλθὼν ἀστείου τινὸς παλαιοῦ ῥήματος ἢ πολλάκις τι προσφάτως

advantages, he tastes the honey of progress in virtue and comes to partake of the illumination of divine love.

10. Even if it should happen that this monk fall into some sin by accident or by ignorance and has it brought to his attention by one of the brothers, he does not immediately reject the reminder because he considers it as the counsel of just some ordinary brother; rather, by accepting it as he would the advice of the superior, or better, the commandment of Christ, he receives correction. First, he glorifies God, who moved the brother out of love to say to him what was needed. Then, he acknowledges his gratitude to the brother for having led him to correction. And indeed, by considering his brother's admonition as a commandment and his reproof as a divine judgement, he shows himself to be wise and just on the basis of works. For scripture says, "Reprove a wise man, and he will love you. Give occasion to a wise man, and he will be still wiser. Give knowledge to a righteous man and he will add to it so as to receive more."[10]

11. These are the pursuits of those who live their struggle according to God, the practices and marks that identify those who live the ascetic life in the company of knowledge. I have judged it best to describe publicly the things that I had the opportunity to see and to learn — and which, I may say, I also experienced, for I was a confrère among those blessed and holy men — so that you may wish to emulate them and not fall into evils by following irrational habits to the point of alienation from the good.

12. I often attended different assemblies of brethren who were illumined by the beauty of submissiveness and who were obedient to men of the Spirit, to men who were old in body but young in their souls, who burned with ardent desire for Christ, men of great experience and renown who acquired the steadfastness of virtue from their pure faith and from both the ascetic and contemplative life. While I lived in such a holy company of brothers, I saw deeds filled with compunction, humility and charity, performed not only during vigils but also in the assembly of the table and the remaining services.[11]

13. And if ever someone, while the sacred hymns were being performed, happened to remember some witty remark of the past or, perhaps thought of some brother's recent chance remark and permitted

---

[10] Prov 9:8-9.

[11] The autobiographical experiences recounted by Theoleptos in the following paragraphs are reminiscent of certain passages in Ioannes Climacus, *Scala paradisi* 4 — de oboedientia, PG 88:677-728 (especially 684D ff.).

εἰρημένου ὡς ἔτυχεν ἔκ τινος ἀδελφοῦ γνούς, γέλωτα ἐκίνησεν ἐν
τῇ καρδίᾳ ἢ τοῖς χείλεσιν ἢ λογισμὸν ἐμπαθῆ κατεδέξατο ἢ λόγους
οὐ σπουδαίους μετὰ τοῦ πέλας συνελάλησε, ταῦτα ἐσημειοῦτο καὶ
ἢ ἐν καιρῷ τοῦ ἀναγνώσματος ἢ μετὰ τὸ τέλος τῶν ἱερῶν ὕμνων,
130 καθεσθέντων τῶν ἀδελφῶν παρὰ τῷ γέροντι, ἐθριάμβευε τὴν ἰδίαν
ἀβουλίαν ἐνώπιον τῶν ἀδελφῶν καὶ ᾐτεῖτο συγχώρησιν· ἧς καὶ τυχὼν
καὶ διδαχθεὶς παρὰ τοῦ γέροντος διὰ τὴν ἧτταν καὶ ἐπαινεθεὶς διὰ
τὴν μετάνοιαν καὶ τὸ πεπαρρησιασμένον τῆς ἐξαγορεύσεως, ἀπελύετο
εἰς τὸν οἶκον αὐτοῦ.
135 **14.** Εἶτα ὁ γέρων, ἀφορμῆς λαβόμενος, ἐδίδασκε τοὺς ἀδελφούς,
δεικνύων αὐτοῖς τὴν ἀκριβῆ προσοχὴν τοῦ τὴν μετάνοιαν πεποιηκότος καὶ τὸ εὐθὲς τῆς γνώμης διὰ τὴν φανερὰν ἐξομολόγησιν τῆς
αἰσχύνης αὐτοῦ, ἔτι δὲ καὶ τὴν κατάνυξιν αὐτοῦ, ἀφ᾽ ἧς ὁρμώμενος
ἐξωμολογεῖτο πεπαρρησιασμένως. ταῦτα δὲ πάντα ἐνωτιζόμενοι οἱ
140 ἀδελφοὶ καὶ ἐπήνουν τὸν ἀδελφὸν καὶ ᾠκοδομοῦντο, βελτιούμενοι
καθ᾽ ἑαυτοὺς ἐν τῷ εἰς μίμησιν ἔρχεσθαι τῶν τοιούτων.
15. Καὶ τοῦτο μὲν ἐτελεῖτο ἐν τῇ συνάξει τῆς ψαλμῳδίας, ἐν
δὲ τῇ συνάξει τῆς τραπέζης τοιοῦτόν τι ἐπράττετο. σιγὴ ἦν πᾶσα
ἐν πᾶσι καὶ μετάληψις τῶν παρακειμένων καὶ ἀκρόασις τῶν
145 ἀναγινωσκομένων. εἰ δέ τινι συνέβη λαλεῖν μετὰ τοῦ πέλας ἡσύχως
ἢ εἰς ἐπήκοον πάντων εἰπεῖν τι, ἢ παρὰ τοῦ πέλας ὑπεμιμνήσκετο
ἢ παρὰ τοῦ ἐπιστημονάρχου· καὶ ὃς ἠγείρετο εὐθὺς καὶ μετάνοιαν
ἐποίει τῷ γέροντι, εἶτα καὶ τῷ ὑπομνηματίσαντι, καὶ οὕτω ποιῶν
ἐκαθέζετο εἰς τὸν τόπον αὐτοῦ καὶ ἤσθιε τοῦ λοιποῦ μετὰ σιγῆς
150 ἁπάσης.
16. Ὠφέλιμον καὶ τοῦτο διηγήσασθαι πρὸς τὴν ὑμῶν σύνεσιν.
εἷς ἀδελφὸς ἀπεστάλη παρὰ τοῦ γέροντος εἴς τινα δουλείαν, ὁ δὲ
βραδύνας παρεγένετο μετὰ τὴν ἑστίασιν τῶν ἀδελφῶν. ἐπεὶ δὲ ἀνάγκη
ἦν φαγεῖν καὶ αὐτὸν προετράπη παρὰ τοῦ διακονητοῦ τροφῆς
155 μεταλαβεῖν. καθεσθέντων οὖν ἀμφοτέρων, τοῦ μὲν εἰς τὸ διακονεῖν,
τοῦ δὲ εἰς τὸ διακονεῖσθαι, ὁ ἐσθίων ὑπὸ τῆς γαστριμαργίας πολε-
μούμενος καὶ θέλων λάβρως ἐσθίειν, κωλυόμενος δὲ ὑπὸ τῆς κενοδοξίας διὰ τὸ παρεῖναι τὸν διακονητὴν καὶ ὁρᾶσθαι ὑπ᾽ αὐτοῦ,
ἀφορμὰς ὑποθέσεων καὶ ἀργολογίας εἰς τὰς ἀκοὰς ἐποιεῖτο τοῦ
160 διακονητοῦ, ὅπως, τούτου ἀσχολουμένου εἰς τὰς ἀπολογίας τῶν
ἀργῶν λόγων, μετὰ πάσης ἀδείας ἐσθίει ὁ διακονούμενος, ὁμοῦ δὲ
καὶ τὴν παρὰ τοῦ διακονητοῦ κατάγνωσιν διαδιδράσκῃ ἐκ τοῦ μὴ
κατανοεῖσθαι τὸν γαστρίμαργον τρόπον αὐτοῦ.
17. Ταῦτα μὲν ὑπέβαλε τὸ πάθος καὶ κατὰ τὴν ὑποβολὴν καὶ
165 τετέλεσται. ἐπεὶ δὲ τὴν γαστέρα ἐπλήρωσε καὶ τοῦ μαστίζειν αὐτὸν
ἡ γαστριμαργία ἐπαύσατο ἡ ἀνηλεὴς κυρία, διαδέχεται τοῦτον ὁ τῆς

laughter in his heart or on his lips, or allowed himself an impassioned thought, or exchanged frivolous words with his neighbour, he took note of these things and either at the time of the reading or after the end of the sacred hymns, when the brothers took their seats before the elder, he made public his thoughtlessness in the presence of his brothers and asked for forgiveness. When he had got this and received instruction from the elder on his failure and been commended for his repentance and his frankness in confession, he was dismissed to his cell.

14.   Then, taking this opportunity, the elder instructed the brothers, showing them the scrupulous diligence of the monk who had made repentance, the rectitude of his resolve to make an open confession of his shame, and also his compunction by which he was moved to give free expression to his confession. When they heard all this, the brethren praised their brother and were edified and moved to better themselves by entering into the imitation of such virtues.

15.   This is what happened in the assembly for psalmody, but something similar took place in the assembly for the table. There was complete silence among all; they partook of what was laid out and listened to what was being read. If it happened that someone spoke quietly with his neighbour or said something in everybody's hearing, he was reminded either by his neighbour or by the disciplinarian. He would immediately get up and make a prostration to the elder and then to the one who had reminded him, and so doing he would sit down in his place and eat the rest of the meal in complete silence.

16.   It is worthwhile to relate this too for the benefit of your understanding. A brother was sent by the elder to perform a errand, but he was delayed and arrived after the brethren had eaten. Since he too had to eat, he was urged by the brother who was serving the meal to take some food. So when both had sat down, the one to serve and the other to be served, the monk who was eating was besieged by gluttony and wanted to eat greedily, but he was hindered by vainglory because the server was present and would see him. He made overtures for discussion and idle chatter in the hearing of the server so that while the latter was busy excusing himself from idle talk, the one being served could eat with complete abandon and still escape the server's condemnation because he would not notice his gluttonous manner.

17.   These were the suggestions proposed by the passion and the monk's conduct followed suit accordingly. When he had filled his belly, and gluttony, the merciless mistress, ceased to whip him, the reproof

συνειδήσεως ἔλεγχος, πλήσσων αὐτὸν καὶ ὑπ᾽ ὄψιν τιθεὶς τὰ πλημ-
μελήματα· ὅτι τε δοῦλος τῆς γαστριμαργίας γέγονε καὶ τῆς κενοδοξίας, τῆς μὲν διὰ τὴν ἡδονήν, τῆς δὲ διὰ τὸ μὴ καταγνωσθῆναι,
170 καὶ ὅτι διὰ ταῦτα δόλιος ἀνεφάνη τῷ διακονοῦντι, μισθοὺς αὐτῷ
ἀντιμετρῶν καὶ παρεχόμενος τὰς ἀφορμὰς τῆς ἀργολογίας.

18.   Τούτοις τοῖς λογισμοῖς τρωθεὶς τὴν ψυχήν, ἐγείρεται παρευθὺς
καὶ βαλὼν μετάνοιαν τῷ ἀδελφῷ, ἀνακαλύπτει πάντα καὶ συγχώρησιν
ἐξαιτεῖται. ὁ δὲ εἰς ἑαυτὸν ἀνετίθη τὸ τοῦ ἀδελφοῦ πλημμέλημα
175 καὶ θερμοτέραν ἀντεποίει μετάνοιαν καὶ συγχώρησιν ἐξῃτεῖτο.
συγχωρήσας οὖν καὶ συγχωρηθεὶς τοιαῦτα μετὰ πραότητος ἐφθέγξατο.

19.   Ἐγώ, ἀδελφέ, λέγων, ἐγεγόνειν αἴτιος τοῦ σοῦ πλημμελήματος
καὶ τοῦ ἐμοῦ· ἔδει γάρ με παραθέμενον τὰ χρειώδη ὑποχωρῆσαι καὶ
δοῦναί σοι ἄδειαν μεταλαβεῖν τροφῆς, ὡς ἐβούλου. εἰ δὲ καὶ
180 ὑπουργῆσαί σοι ᾑρετισάμην δι᾽ ἀνάπαυσίν σου πλείονα, προσῆκε
πάλιν παρόντα με σιγᾶν καὶ μετὰ προσευχῆς ἐξυπηρετεῖν σοι. ἡ
ἀμέλειά μου δὲ χώραν ἔδωκε τῷ διαβόλῳ πειράσαι τοὺς ἀμφοτέρους,
σὲ μὲν διὰ τῆς γαστριμαργίας, ἐμὲ δὲ διὰ τῆς ἀργολογίας. εἰ δὲ ἐγὼ
προσεῖχον καὶ προσηυχόμην, καί σε τῆς φαύλης ὁρμῆς ἀνέκοψα καὶ
185 ἐμαυτὸν διεφύλαξα. δῶμεν οὖν συγγνώμην ἀλλήλοις καὶ διαλύσωμεν
τὰ μηχανήματα τοῦ πειραστοῦ καὶ ἀσφαλισώμεθα τοῦ λοιποῦ, μὴ
ὑπείκειν ταῖς παρ᾽ αὐτοῦ ὑποβολαῖς, ἀλλ᾽ ἐκ πρωτονοίας καταβάλλειν
αὐτὰς τῷ δόρατι τῆς προσευχῆς.
20.   Τοιοῦτόν τι ἐτελεῖτο καὶ συναγομένων τῶν ἀδελφῶν εἴς τινα
190 διακονίαν. εἰ γάρ τινες ἀβουλίας προέφερον ῥήματα, ὁ σπουδαῖος
ἀνιστάμενος ἐποίει μετάνοιαν τοῖς λαλοῦσι τὰ μάταια, οἱ δὲ διαγιν-
ώσκοντες τὸν τῆς μετανοίας σκοπόν, ἐγειρόμενοι ἐποίουν μετάνοιαν
τῷ ὑπομνήσαντι, ἀποδεχόμενοι τὴν ὑπόμνησιν καὶ εὐχαριστοῦντες
τῷ ἀδελφῷ, καὶ τοῦ λοιποῦ μετὰ σιγῆς τὸ διακόνημα ἐκτελοῦντες.
195 οὕτω ποιοῦντες, ὁ μὲν ἐκήρυττε τὴν ἀγάπην, οἱ δὲ ἐδημοσίευον τὴν
ταπείνωσιν.

21.   Εἶδες ἅμιλλαν ἀγαθὴν καὶ οἰκοδομὴν ἀδελφότητος; ἀλλὰ νῦν
τὰ ἐναντία ἐν τοῖς κοινοβίοις διαπράττεται· συναγόμενοι γὰρ οἱ
μοναχοὶ ἐν τῷ ναῷ καὶ ἐν τῇ τραπέζῃ καὶ ἐν τοῖς διακονήμασι, καὶ
200 τῷ νῷ μετεωρίζονται καὶ τῇ γλώσσῃ ἀκαιρολογοῦσι, καὶ οὐδεὶς ὁ
ἀνακόπτων εὑρίσκεται. καὶ εἴ τις ἢ κατανυγεὶς θριαμβεύσει ἐνώπιον
τῶν μοναχῶν τὸ ἴδιον πταῖσμα πρὸς τὸ τυχεῖν συγχωρήσεως ἢ
ζηλωτὴς ὢν τοῦ καλοῦ τὸν πταίοντα ὑπομνηματίσει διὰ τῆς μετα-

of conscience took her place, beating him and bringing his failings to his view: namely, that he had become a slave of both gluttony and vainglory, the first for the sake of pleasure, the second so as to avoid condemnation, and that on this account he acted deceitfully towards the one serving him in meting out to him in return for his services the offer of an occasion for idle talk.

18. With his soul wounded by these thoughts, he got up straightaway and making a prostration to his brother he revealed everything and asked his forgiveness. But this second brother took his brother's fault upon himself and made in return an all the more fervent prostration and asked forgiveness. So, in forgiving and receiving forgiveness, he gently said something like this.

19. "Brother, I was responsible for your fault and my own, for having set out what was necessary I should have withdrawn and allowed you to partake of the food as you wanted. But if I chose to serve you so that you might relax more easily, it would have been more fitting for me to be there in silence and to serve you with prayer. My carelessness gave the devil a chance to tempt both of us, you through gluttony and me through idle talk. But if I had been paying attention and praying, I could have restrained you from your bad impulse and preserved myself. So let us forgive each other and undo the machinations of the tempter, and henceforth let us keep ourselves safe so as not to give in to his suggestions, but rather strike them down with the spear of prayer at their inception."

20. Something similar used to take place also when the brethren were gathered together to perform some service. If some of the monks were uttering thoughtless words, a zealous monk would rise and make a prostration to those engaged in vain speech. Acknowledging the intention of the prostration, they would get up, make a prostration to the one who had reminded them, accepting the reminder and thanking the brother, and for the rest of the time they would perform the service in silence. In so doing, the one proclaimed his love and the others exhibited their humility.

21. Have you noted the goodly rivalry and the edification of the brotherhood? But now the practice in the monasteries is the opposite, for when the monks assemble in the church or at the table or for services, their minds are distracted, their tongues wag with untimely chatter and no one can be found to put a stop to it. And if someone out of compunction exposes his own fault in front of the monks in order to obtain forgiveness, or if out of zeal for the good he offers a prostration as a reminder to one who commits a fault so that the

νοίας ἐπὶ τὸ διορθώσασθαι τὸν σφαλόμενον, αὐτίκα εἰρωνεύονται,
205 ἀποτρέπονται τοῦτον, γογγύζουσι, διασύρουσιν, ὀνειδίζουσιν· οἱ μὲν
βάλλοντες τοῖς σκώμμασιν, οἱ δὲ κακίζοντες ὑποχωροῦσι, μήτε τὴν
ταπείνωσιν τοῦ ἀδελφοῦ κατανοοῦντες, μήτε τὴν ἑαυτῶν διόρθωσιν
οἰκονομοῦντες. οὗτοί εἰσιν οἱ μήτε εἰσελθεῖν βουλόμενοι εἰς τὴν
βασιλείαν καὶ τοὺς εἰσερχομένους κωλύοντες.

210   **22.** Ὁρᾶτε καὶ μὴ διαφευγέτω ὑμᾶς ἡ ἔννοια τῆς πονηρᾶς
φάλαγγος, ἥτις μέλλει συναντᾶν ἡμῖν ἐν τῇ ἐξόδῳ τῶν ψυχῶν ἡμῶν,
κατέχουσα τὰς σειρὰς τῶν ἑκουσίων παθῶν καὶ τὴν ἄνοδον διακωλύουσα. τοῦτο πεισόμεθα, εἰ μεριζόμεθα τῷ φρονήματι, εἰ ταρασ-
σόμεθα, εἰ κτώμεθα κατ᾽ ἀλλήλων ὑπονοίας, εἰ μικροψυχοῦμεν ἐν
215 τοῖς συμβαίνουσι παρ᾽ ἀλλήλων ἀνιαροῖς. τότε γὰρ οὐκέτι στρατὸς
Χριστοῦ ἐσμεν, οὐδὲ τῷ θελήματι τοῦ στρατολογήσαντος ἀκο-
λουθοῦμεν, οὐδὲ ἀδελφοὶ καὶ συστρατιῶται συμμαχοῦντες ἀλλήλοις
κατὰ τοῦ κοινοῦ ἐχθροῦ, ἀλλ᾽ ἕκαστος ἰδίῳ θελήματι ἀγόμενος
ὑπερμαχεῖ τῆς ἰδίας γνώμης· καὶ κατὰ σάρκα ζῶμεν καὶ πάλιν
220 μέλλομεν ἀποθνήσκειν κατὰ τὸν ἀπόστολον.

23.   Πῶς οὖν οἱ ταῖς ἰδίαις ὀρέξεσι φερόμενοι καὶ κατ᾽ ἀλλήλων
κινούμενοι, δυνησόμεθα τροπώσασθαι τὴν μαινομένην καθ᾽ ἡμῶν
δαιμονικὴν παράταξιν; ὃ γὰρ ἐκεῖνοι καθ᾽ ἡμῶν βούλονται δρᾶν καὶ
ἀδυνατοῦσιν ἡμῶν σπουδαζόντων, τοῦτο ἡμεῖς ἐκ ῥαθυμίας κατ᾽
225 ἀλλήλων πράττομεν. καὶ ἡμεῖς μὲν ἐν σκοτομήνῃ μένοντες, κατα-
τοξεύομεν ἀλλήλους, οἱ δὲ ἐχθροὶ διαρπάζουσιν ἡμᾶς ὡς λάφυρα καὶ
εἰς τὸν ἡτοιμασμένον αὐτοῖς τόπον τῆς Γεέννης ὡς αἰχμαλώτους
ἀπάγουσι. τί τούτου ἀθλιώτερον; ὅτι δύναμιν εἰληφότες παρὰ Χριστοῦ
καὶ δυνατὰ ὅπλα ἔχοντες καταργεῖν τοὺς ἐχθροὺς ἡμῶν, αὐθαιρέτως
230 προδιδοῦμεν ἑαυτοὺς εἰς χεῖρας τῶν ἐχθρῶν.

24.   Θέλεις τὸν ἐχθρὸν πλῆξαι καιρίως καὶ εἰς βάθος ἐλάσαι τὸ
δόρυ καὶ διαρρῆξαι αὐτοῦ τὰ σπλάγχνα; ἐγώ σοι χαλκεύσω τὰ βέλη,
ἃ λαβὼν ἔχω παρὰ Χριστοῦ τοῦ τὰς χαλκᾶς πύλας τοῦ θανάτου
συντρίψαντος καὶ τοὺς σιδηροὺς μοχλοὺς τοῦ Ἅιδου συνθλάσαντος.
235 βούλει νικῆσαι τὰ πάθη καὶ τὴν χάριν ἣν ἔλαβες συντηρῆσαι καὶ

---

206 σκώμμασιν corr.: σκόμμασιν OᵖᶜA: κόμμασιν Oᵃᶜ

one who has fallen might be set right, the monks at once make sarcastic remarks and turn their backs on him; they grumble, ridicule and upbraid him. Some make fun of him, while others abuse him, and they withdraw without taking note of the brother's humility and without dealing with their own correction. These are the ones who refuse to enter the Kingdom and prevent others from doing so.[12]

22. Take note and do not let the designs of the evil phalanx escape you; it will gather to meet us when our souls go forth, grabbing the chains of our willful passions and preventing our ascent.[13] This is what we will experience if we are divided in our thoughts, if we are troubled, if we harbour suspicions against one another, if we are petty-minded about the annoyances we cause one another. Then we are no longer the army of Christ, nor are we following the will of the one who enlisted us in his army, nor are we brothers and fellow soldiers fighting together against the common enemy; rather, each man, acting according to his own will, fights for his own opinion. We live according to the flesh and consequently we will die, as the Apostle says.[14]

23. If then we get carried away by our desires and turn against one another, how will we be able to rout the demonic army that rages against us? For out of our slothfulness we do to one another what the demons would do to us but are unable to do when we are zealous. Abiding in the darkness of a moonless night, we shoot arrows at one another,[15] while our enemies seize us as spoils and lead us off as their captives to the place of Gehenna that is prepared for them.[16] What more miserable fate could there be than this? Though we have received strength from Christ and possess powerful weapons to annihilate our enemies, we voluntarily surrender ourselves into the hands of our adversaries.

24. Do you wish to smite the enemy in good time, drive your spear deep within him and rip apart his guts? I will forge the darts for you, which I have received from Christ who shattered the bronze gates of death and broke the iron bars of Hades.[17] Do you want to conquer the passions, preserve the grace which you received and in all your

---

[12] Lk 11:52.

[13] Theoleptos may well have in mind the graphic depictions of the heavenly ladder of St. John Climacus: see for example the 12th-century icon now at St. Catherine's in Sinai — K. Weitzmann, *The Icon* (New York, 1978), plate 25.

[14] Rom 8:12-13.

[15] Cf. Ps 10:2.

[16] Cf. Mt 25:41.

[17] Cf. Ps 106:16.

ἐν πᾶσί σου τοῖς μέλεσι δοξάσαι τὸν Χριστόν, οὗ καὶ κτίσμα διὰ
τὴν δημιουργίαν καὶ σῶμα διὰ τὴν οἰκονομίαν ἐσμέν; ἐγώ σοι καὶ
τὸν τρόπον ὑποδείξω τῆς νίκης, ὃν μεμάθηκα παρὰ Χριστοῦ τοῦ τὸν
κόσμον νενικηκότος.

240   **25.** Χρηστὸς ἔσο περὶ τὸν ἀδελφόν. ὑπόνοιαν μηδόλως κατὰ τοῦ
πλησίον παραδέχου, φθοροποιὸς γὰρ αὕτη τῆς ἀγάπης. τὴν παρὰ
τοῦ ἀδελφοῦ συναντῶσάν σοι μικροψυχίαν ὡς ἰδίαν καταδέχου, ὡς
σὸν μέλος ἀρρωστοῦν τὸν λυπήσαντα λογιζόμενος καὶ παντὶ τρόπῳ
τοῦτον εἰς τὴν ἀγάπην ἀνακαλούμενος. οὕτω διανοούμενος καὶ
245 διακείμενος, τὸν μὲν λελυπηκότα, τρωθέντα ἐξ ὑποβολῆς τοῦ ἀοράτου
ἐχθροῦ, ὠφέλησας καὶ ἐθεράπευσας διὰ τῆς ἀνεξικακίας· τὸν δὲ
ἀφανῶς πλήξαντα πολέμιον ἐτροπώσω περιφανῶς. ἐπειγομένου γὰρ
αὐτοῦ καὶ σὲ βλάψαι διὰ τῆς ἀντιλυπήσεως, σὺ καὶ τὸν πεσόντα
ἀδελφὸν ἐπανορθώσω διὰ τῆς ἀγάπης καὶ τῆς ὑπομονῆς καὶ τὸν
250 ἐχθρὸν ἀσθενῆ διήλεγξας καὶ ἀφῆκας ἐμπαιζόμενον μαίνεσθαι.

26. Σπουδάσωμεν τοιγαροῦν τὴν πανοπλίαν Χριστοῦ ἣν
ἐνεδύθημεν, ταύτην ἀναλαβέσθαι, ἵνα καὶ τὴν δοθεῖσαν δύναμιν
περισώζωμεν καὶ τὰ πεμπόμενα καθ' ἡμῶν ἀφανῶς βέλη τοῦ Βελίαρ
ἀποκρουώμεθα. πανοπλία δὲ Χριστοῦ ἡ τριὰς τῶν ἀρετῶν, ἡ πίστις
255 φημὶ καὶ ἡ ἐλπὶς καὶ ἡ ἀγάπη. πίστιν ἔχομεν, εἰ τὰ παρόντα φεύγομεν,
τοῖς δὲ μέλλουσι προσηλούμεθα. ἐλπίδα δὲ πάλιν, εἰ τὰ καλὰ
ἐργαζόμεθα καὶ τὰ μέλλοντα ἀγαθὰ ὡς συνόντα ἡμῖν καθορῶμεν.
ἀγάπην δὲ εἰ Χριστῷ καὶ ἀλλήλοις συνδεδέμεθα, εἰ διὰ Χριστὸν καλὰ
προνοούμεθα περὶ παντὸς ἀδελφοῦ καὶ τὰ συμπίπτοντα ἡμῖν λυπηρὰ
260 μακροθύμως φέρομεν.

27. Ἡ ἀγάπη, γάρ φησιν, *οὐ λογίζεται τὸ κακόν καὶ πάντα ὑπομένει*
διὰ τὴν στοργὴν τοῦ ἀγαπήσαντος ἡμᾶς Χριστοῦ καὶ ἕνωσιν ἡμῶν
συστησαμένου· αὐτῷ ἡ δόξα εἰς τοὺς αἰῶνας. Ἀμήν.

members glorify Christ, whose creatures we are by his creation and whose body we are by his Economy? I will show you also the way of victory, which I have learned from Christ, who has conquered the world.[18]

25.   Be kindly towards your brother. Entertain no suspicion whatsoever against your neighbour, for this is what destroys love. Accept the pettiness you may encounter from your brother as your own, considering the one who caused you hurt as one of your own limbs that is unwell, and restore him to love in any way you can. Being so minded and disposed, you benefitted and healed by your forbearance the one who had hurt you, for he was wounded by a suggestion of the unseen enemy. And you openly routed the foe who struck from hiding, for when he was eager to cause you harm by having you return the hurt, in charity and patient endurance you set right your brother who has fallen and exposed the enemy in his weakness and left him furious at being fooled.

26.   Let us therefore hasten to take up again the full armour of Christ with which we were clothed,[19] in order that we may safeguard the power given us and repel the darts of Beliar hurled at us in secret. The full armour of Christ is made up of the triad of the virtues, namely, faith, hope and love. We have faith, if we flee present realities and fix ourselves upon future realities. We in turn possess hope, if we perform good works and keep in sight the goods that will be ours as though we now partake them. And we have love, if we have bound ourselves to Christ and to one another, if for the sake of Christ we presume good of every brother and bear patiently the sufferings that befall us.

27.   For scripture says, "Love takes no account of evil and endures all things"[20] for the sake of the love of Christ, who has loved us and brought us together in unity. To him be glory forever. Amen.

---

[18] Cf. Jn 16:33.
[19] Cf. Eph 6:11, 13.
[20] 1 Cor 13:15.

Περὶ σιωπῆς

1. Πολλὴν ὀφείλομεν τὴν περὶ τὰς αἰσθήσεις τοῦ σώματος ἐπιδείκνυσθαι φυλακήν, ἀδελφοί, ἐπειδὴ τὸ κέντρον τῆς ἁμαρτίας δι᾿ αὐτῶν εἰσδῦνον ἐν τῇ ψυχῇ θανατοῖ αὐτὴν καὶ ἀκίνητον πρὸς
5 πᾶν ἔργον ἀγαθὸν ἐκτελεῖ· *θάνατος, γάρ φησιν, ἀνέβη διὰ τῶν θυρίδων.* πλείονα δὲ ποιεῖσθαι ὑμᾶς χρὴ τὴν περὶ τὴν γλῶσσαν ἀσφάλειαν, ὡς ὄργανον αὐτὴν γινομένην τῷ ἀπροσεκτοῦντι μυρίων κακῶν· τοσοῦτον γάρ ἐστι δεινὸν τὸ ἐκ τῆς γλώσσης ὀλίσθημα, ὡς κρεῖττον πεσεῖν ἀπὸ ὕψους εἰς γῆν ἢ ἀπὸ γλώσσης ὥσπερ ἀκούομεν. τῷ μὲν
10 γὰρ ἀπὸ ὕψους πεσόντι ἢ νόσος ἢ θάνατος σωματικὸς ἠκολούθησε, ψυχῆς δὲ ὄλεθρον ὁ τοιοῦτος οὐκ οἶδεν, ὡς διὰ τῆς αὐτομεμψίας καὶ τῆς εὐχαριστίας ἐλπίδα ἀνέσεως τὸν πικρὸν θάνατον εὑρηκώς· ὁ δὲ μὴ φυλάσσων τὸ ἑαυτοῦ στόμα καὶ ἑαυτοῦ τὴν ψυχὴν ἐλυμήνατο καὶ τὸν πλησίον τὰ μέγιστα ἔβλαψε. καὶ ὁ μὲν σωματικὴν βλάβην
15 ὑπέστη, ὁ δὲ ψυχῆς κίνδυνον ἔπαθε. κἀκεῖ μὲν εἰς ἕνα καὶ μόνον τὸ βλάβος περιΐσταται, ἐνταῦθα δὲ εἰς πολλούς· ὥστε καὶ πολλάκις ὁ ἀναιδῆ γλῶσσαν φέρων, τῆς ἑαυτοῦ καταγνοὺς προπετείας, ἑαυτὸν μὲν διὰ τῆς μεταμελείας τοῦ πτώματος ἀνεκαλέσατο· τῷ δὲ ὑβρισθέντι ἢ τοὺς βλαβεροὺς δεξαμένῳ λογισμοὺς μνήμην καὶ μάθησιν κακίας
20 ἐνέθηκε καὶ τὴν καρδίαν αὐτοῦ οἰκίαν τῷ διαβόλῳ κατεσκεύασεν. ὅθεν καὶ ὁ προφήτης εἰδὼς χαλεπώτατον εἶναι τὸ ἐκ τῆς γλώττης πτῶμα προσκαλούμενος τοὺς υἱοὺς τῆς ἐκκλησίας καὶ τὴν ὁδὸν τῆς σωτηρίας αὐτοῖς ὑποδεικνύων, πρῶτον τοῦ καλοῦ τρόπον αὐτοῖς ὑποτίθεται· τὸ χαλινὸν ἐπὶ τῇ γλώσσῃ φορεῖν καὶ δεσμὸν ἐπὶ τοῖς
25 χείλεσιν ἔχειν· *εἰ θέλεις, γάρ φησι, ζωὴν εὑρεῖν καὶ ἡμέρας ἰδεῖν ἀγαθάς, παῦσον τὴν γλῶσσάν σου ἀπὸ κακοῦ καὶ χείλη σου τοῦ μὴ λαλῆσαι δόλον·*

MD **10**

ON SILENCE

1. We ought to display great watchfulness regarding the senses of the body, brothers,[1] since through them the sting of sin finds its way into the soul and deadens it, rendering it immobile with regard to any good work. For scripture says, "Death has come up through our windows."[2] You should take special precautions in the case of the tongue, because for the careless man it can become an instrument of countless evils.[3] So terrible is a lapse of the tongue that, as we often hear it said, a fall to the ground from a height is preferable to a slip of the tongue.[4] The person who falls from a height suffers either infirmity or bodily death, but he does not experience the destruction of his soul, for in the bitterness of death he has found hope of forgiveness through self-reproach and an attitude of thanksgiving.[5] On the other hand, the person who neglects to keep watch over his mouth inflicts damage upon his soul and does the greatest harm to his neighbour. The former suffers bodily harm, but the latter endangers his soul. In the first case the harm involves one person only, but in the latter it affects many. Thus, the man with a shameless tongue often condemns his own rashness and recollects himself through repentance for his fall, but he has instilled the memory and experience of evil in the one who has been insulted or who has been the object of injurious thoughts, and has made that person's heart a dwelling for the devil. So, the prophet, recognizing the grievous danger in a lapse of the tongue, called upon the sons of the church and, showing them the path of salvation, he laid down for them the foremost way towards the good, namely, wearing a bit on the tongue and a rein on the lips. For the Psalmist says, "If you would find life and see good days, keep

---

[1] This is the only one of the *Monastic Discourses* with a direct indication that it was addressed to monks, presumably those of the adjacent monastery under the same name of Philanthropos Soter.

[2] Jer 9:20.

[3] Cf. Jas 3:6, 8.

[4] Unidentified proverb.

[5] Or perhaps this should be taken as a reference to the deathbed reception of holy viaticum: i.e., "through self-reproach and the reception of the Eucharist."

διὰ μὲν τοῦ κακοῦ πᾶσαν ὑβριστικὴν ἐκφορὰν καὶ κακολογίαν
ἀπαγορεύσας, διὰ δὲ τοῦ δόλου πονηρίαν καὶ τὰ ταύτης ἀκόλουθα
κωλύσας, εἰρωνείαν φημὶ καὶ κολακείαν, καὶ ψεῦδος καὶ λόγους
30 αἰνιγματώδεις ἀφανῶς πλήττοντας τὸν ἀδελφόν.

2.   Φεῦ μοι τῷ ταλαιπώρῳ, ὥσπερ τῶν ἄλλων μου μελῶν τὴν
χρῆσιν ἀντέστρεψα, οὕτω δὴ καὶ τῆς γλώσσης. ἔλαβον γὰρ τὸ
τοιοῦτον ὄργανον παρὰ θεοῦ, οὐχ ἵνα βλασφημίας κατὰ θεοῦ προφέρω,
οὐδὲ ἵνα ὑβρίζω τὸν ἀδελφὸν ἢ καταλαλῶ καὶ κατακρίνω αὐτὸν ἢ
35 κατηγορῶ καὶ ψεύδομαι ἢ ἄλλο τι κακίας εἶδος ὃ διὰ τοῦ τοιούτου
μέλους τὴν σύστασιν ἔχει ἐκπληρῶ, ἀλλ᾽ ἵνα δόγματα ὀρθὰ προφέρω
καὶ λόγους θεοῦ ἀπαγγέλω καὶ ἀνυμνῶ τὸν ποιητὴν καὶ ἐπαινῶ τὸν
πλησίον καὶ ὑπαγορεύω αὐτῷ τὰ χρήσιμα καὶ κατακρίνω ἐμαυτὸν
καὶ δικαιῶ τὸν ἀδελφὸν καὶ θριαμβεύω τὸν διάβολον ὡς τοῦ γένους
40 ἡμῶν κοινὸν πολέμιον.
3.   Τίς οὖν σοφὸς καὶ φυλάξει τὴν γλῶσσαν καὶ συνήσει τῆς ἐν
γνώσει σιωπῆς τὰς ἀρετάς; τῷ κλείοντι τὴν γλῶσσαν ἀνοίγεται ἡ
θύρα τῆς γνώσεως. ὁ φυλάσσων τὸ ἑαυτοῦ στόμα ἄσυλον τὸν ἑαυτοῦ
νοῦν διατηρεῖ. ὁ δεσμεύων τὰ ἑαυτοῦ χείλη ἐν περιοχῇ καθίσταται
45 τῶν οἰκείων λογισμῶν. ἀνὴρ σιωπηλὸς ἀναιχμαλώτιστον φυλάττει
τὴν ἑαυτοῦ καρδίαν. ἀνὴρ σιωπηλὸς κατασκοπεύει τῶν νοητῶν
θηρίων τὰ θήρατρα.
4.   Ἀνὴρ ἐγκρατὴς γλώσσης ἐπιστρέφει τὴν ἑαυτοῦ ψυχὴν πρὸς
τὸν θεὸν καὶ σκοπεύων ἑτοιμάζει ἑαυτὸν πρὸς ὑποδοχὴν τῶν θείων
50 χαρισμάτων. ψάλλει γὰρ μετὰ τοῦ προφήτου· *ἀκούσομαι τί λαλήσει*
ἐν ἐμοὶ κύριος, ὅτι λαλήσει εἰρήνην ἐπὶ τὸν λαὸν αὐτοῦ καὶ ἐπὶ τοὺς ὁσίους
αὐτοῦ καὶ ἐπὶ τοὺς ἐπιστρέφοντας καρδίαν ἐπ᾽ αὐτόν. ὁ γλώσσης κρατῶν
εὐχερῶς παθῶν κατεκράτησεν. ὁ γλώσσης κρατῶν τοὺς λόγους τῶν
θείων ἐντολῶν μελετᾷ, ὅπως ἂν μὴ λαλήσει τὸ στόμα αὐτοῦ τὰ ἔργα
55 τῶν ἀνθρώπων.

5.   Ὁ ἐν γνώσει σιωπῶν τὸν κατ᾽ αἴσθησιν ἐνέκρωσεν ἄνθρωπον,
τὸν δὲ κατὰ νοῦν ἀνεζώωσεν. *ἐγὼ γὰρ ἀποκτενῶ καὶ ζῆν ποιήσω.*

---

57 ἀνεζώωσεν corr.: ἀνεζώοσεν OA

your tongue from evil and your lips from speaking guile."[6] By the word 'evil' he forbade any insulting utterance and malicious talk, and by the word 'guile' he put a stop to wickedness and its attendant vices, namely, dissembling and flattery, as well as falsehood and enigmatic words[7] which strike secretly against one's brother.

2. Woe is me in my wretched state, for just as I reversed the proper use of my other members, so I did also with my tongue. I received this organ from God not that I might utter blasphemy against God, nor that I might insult my brother, or speak against him and condemn him, or accuse him and make false statements about him, or commit any other kind of evil which has its origin in this member. Rather, I received this member that I might utter orthodox doctrines, proclaim the words of God, laud the creator, praise my neighbour and make useful suggestions to him, condemn myself and vindicate my brother, and triumph over the devil as the common enemy of our race.[8]

3. Who then is the wise man who will keep guard over his tongue and understand the virtues of silence in his knowledge? The door of knowledge opens for the person who has bolted his tongue. The person who keeps watch over his own mouth preserves his mind unsullied. The person who fetters his lips stands in the fortification of his own thoughts.[9] The man of silence keeps his heart free of captivity.[10] The man of silence spies out the snares laid by the spiritual beasts.

4. A person with a disciplined tongue turns his soul towards God and by his watchfulness prepares himself for the reception of divine gifts. For he sings together with the prophet, "I shall hear what the Lord has to say to me, for he shall speak of peace with his people and with his holy ones and with those who turn their hearts to him."[11] The person who controls his tongue easily attains mastery over the passions. The person who controls his tongue meditates upon the words of the divine commandments, "lest his tongue speak of the works of men."[12]

5. The person who knows silence has put to death the sensible aspect of his person and restored the life of the mind. "For I shall kill and make alive."[13]

---

[6] Ps 33:13-14; 4 Kingdoms 19:28.
[7] Perhaps 'doubles entendres'?
[8] This passage is a commentary on Jas 3:9-10.
[9] Cf. Ps 140:3.
[10] Cf. Prov 13:3, 21:23.
[11] Ps 84:9.
[12] Ps 16:4.
[13] Deut 32:39; cf. 1 Kingdoms 2:6.

6. Ὁ ἐν γνώσει σιωπῶν τοὺς τοῦ σώματος ὀφθαλμοὺς ἔκλεισε, τοὺς δὲ τῆς ψυχῆς ἤνοιξε· καὶ τὸν νοητὸν ἑώρακεν ἥλιον καὶ τῶν
60 παρόντων ὑπερορᾷ καὶ τὰ μέλλοντα ἐνοπτρίζεται.

7. Ὁ ἐν γνώσει σιωπῶν φόβον θεοῦ συνέλαβε καὶ εἰς μνήμην τῶν ἑαυτοῦ πταισμάτων ἦλθε καὶ τῆς μελλούσης κρίσεως τὴν ἔννοιαν ἔλαβε καὶ ἔτεκε πνεῦμα κατανύξεως καὶ πένθος ἔπλεξε· καὶ ὡς ἐν μνημείῳ τῷ ἑαυτοῦ κελλίῳ παραμένων, τὸν ἴδιον νοῦν ταῖς ἐπιθυμίαις
65 νεκρωθέντα ἐθρήνησε καὶ συμπονούντων αὐτῷ καὶ παρακαλούντων αὐτῷ ἀγγέλων ἐπέτυχε. μακάριοι, γάρ φησιν, οἱ πενθοῦντες, ὅτι αὐτοὶ παρακληθήσονται.

8. Ὁ ἐν γνώσει σιωπῶν καὶ ὃν θησαυρὸν ἔχει φυλάττει καὶ ὃν οὐκ ἔχει πορίζεται. ὁ δὲ προπετὴς χείλεσι καὶ ὃν ἔχει σκορπίζει καὶ
70 τὸν ἐν ἄλλοις συλλέξασθαι οὐκ ἀνέχεται.

9. Ὁ ἐν γνώσει σιωπῶν ἐξενώθη τοῦ κόσμου καὶ ἐν τῷ μέλλοντι αἰῶνι τὸν ἑαυτοῦ παραπέμψας νοῦν κατέπαυσεν ἀπὸ πάντων ἐν οἷς οἱ τοῖς κύμασι τοῦ ταραχώδους τούτου βίου ἐνσκιρτῶντες ἐμπλέουσιν.

10. Ὁ ἐν γνώσει σιωπῶν τὰς ἑαυτοῦ ἐννοίας ἀπὸ τοῦ πρὸς τὰς
75 αἰσθήσεις μετεωρισμοῦ συνάγει καὶ τοῦ καπνοῦ καὶ τῶν ἰδίων παθῶν αἰσθάνεται καὶ τὴν καθήδονον τῆς σαρκὸς σχέσιν τῷ στεναγμῷ καὶ τῇ λύπῃ ἀπομαραίνει καὶ τὸ πῦρ ἐπείγεται τῆς θείας ἀγάπης ἀναφθῆναι.

11. Ὁ ἐν γνώσει σιωπῶν τὴν ἑαυτοῦ καρδίαν ὡς ἐν ἀρότρῳ τῷ
80 θείῳ φόβῳ ἐνέωσε καὶ λογισμὸν μετανοίας ἐφύτευσε καὶ τῇ τοῦ θανάτου ἐννοίᾳ κατήρδευσε καὶ ἀπροσπαθείας καρπὸν ἐγεώργησεν.

12. Ὁ ἐν γνώσει σιωπῶν πρὸ τῆς ἐξόδου τῶν τερπνῶν ἐκδημεῖ τοῦ βίου· καὶ ὢν ἐν τῷ κόσμῳ ὡς μὴ ὢν διατελεῖ· καὶ φαινόμενος οὐ γνωρίζεται, μετά τινος γὰρ μὴ ποιούμενος λόγον, τοῖς ὀφθαλμοῖς
85 τῶν ὁρώντων ἀνεπίγνωστος μένει. ὁ τοιοῦτος ἐπαινούμενος ταλανίζει ἑαυτόν, ὅτι τοὺς ὁρῶντας ἠπάτησε. κατηγορούμενος δὲ συγκατακρίνει ἑαυτόν, ὅτι ἀληθεύοντας ἐπιγινώσκει τοὺς κρίνοντας αὐτόν. διὸ καὶ οὐ φροντίζει ἀπολογίαν ἑαυτοῦ ποιήσασθαι, τὴν γὰρ μέριμναν αὐτοῦ πᾶσαν παρέστησε τῷ φοβερωτάτῳ βήματι τοῦ Χριστοῦ, μελετῶν
90 ἡμέρας καὶ νυκτὸς πῶς καταλλάξει ἑαυτῷ τὸν ἀδέκαστον κριτὴν ἐν τῇ τῆς κρίσεως ἡμέρᾳ.

6. The person who knows silence has closed the eyes of the body and opened those of the soul; having seen the spiritual sun, he disdains the present and beholds the future as in a mirror.

7. The man who knows silence has comprehended the fear of God, become mindful of his own failings, grasped the meaning of the judgement to come, given birth to a spirit of compunction and embraced suffering. Staying in his cell as in a tomb, he lamented for his mind which has been deadened by desires; he encountered angels who share his labours and comfort him. For scripture says, "Blessed are those who mourn, for they shall be comforted."[14]

8. The person who knows silence guards the treasure he has and the one he does not have he procures. But the person who is rash in speech scatters the one he has and does not allow the treasure in other people to be gathered in.

9. The person who knows silence is a stranger to the world and with his mind on the age to come he rests from all the cares in which sail those who dance upon the waves of this troubled life.

10. The person who knows silence gathers together his thoughts from the distractions of the senses; he perceives the smoke even of his own passions and with grieving and groaning he obliterates the orientation of the flesh towards pleasure and is eager to have the fire of divine love set alight.

11. The person who knows silence has harrowed his heart with divine fear as with a plough; he has planted the thought of repentance, watered it with the notion of death and cultivated the fruit of indifference to passion.

12. The man who knows silence takes leave of life before the emergence of pleasures and while he is in the world he goes on as if he were not.[15] He is seen but is not known, for by holding converse with no one he remains unrecognized in the eyes of his beholders. When such a man is praised he considers himself miserable because he has deceived his observers. But when he finds himself accused, he condemns himself because he recognizes that his judges are right. And so, he takes no thought for defending himself, for he has laid his every care before the most fearsome tribunal of Christ, pondering day and night on how he will reconcile himself with the impartial judge on the day of judgement.

---

[14] Mt 5:4.
[15] Cf. 1 Cor 7:31.

13.   Ταῦτ' οὖν καὶ ἡμεῖς διὰ παντὸς ἐννοοῦντες, βοήσωμεν πρὸς
τὸν θεόν· *θοῦ, κύριε, φυλακὴν τῷ στόματι ἡμῶν καὶ θύραν περιοχῆς περὶ
τὰ χείλη ἡμῶν*, καὶ γνῶσιν συνετίζουσαν τοὺς λογισμοὺς ἡμῶν, ὅπως
95 φυλάξωμεν τὰς ὁδοὺς ἡμῶν τοῦ μὴ ἁμαρτάνειν ἡμᾶς ἐν γλώσσῃ καὶ
ἐν γνώσει, θείῳ δὲ φόβῳ ἀνοίγειν καὶ κλείειν τὰ ἡμέτερα στόματα.
σὺ γὰρ μόνος δυνατὸς ὑπάρχεις φυλάξαι τὴν ἐν τῇ γνώσει εἴσοδον
τοῦ νοῦ ἡμῶν καὶ τὴν ἐν τῇ γλώσσῃ ἔξοδον αὐτοῦ. καὶ σοὶ πρέπει
δόξα, τιμὴ καὶ προσκύνησις, τῷ πατρὶ καὶ τῷ υἱῷ καὶ τῷ ἁγίῳ
100 πνεύματι, νῦν καὶ ἀεὶ καὶ εἰς τοὺς αἰῶνας τῶν αἰώνων. Ἀμήν.

95, 98 γλώσσῃ corr.: γλώσσει OA

13. Therefore, reflecting on these matters at all times, let us also cry out to God, "Set, O Lord, a guard at my mouth and a door to encompass my lips"[16] and knowledge to grant understanding to our thoughts, so that we may keep watch over our ways and not sin in speech and in knowledge, but rather, open and close our mouths in godly fear. For you alone are able to keep guard over the entrance of our mind in knowledge and over its going forth in speech. To you is due glory, honour and worship, the Father and the Son and the Holy Spirit, now and always and forever and ever. Amen.

[16] Ps 140:3.

Λόγος περὶ νηστείας
ἀναγινωσκόμενος κατὰ τὴν κυριακὴν τῆς τυροφάγου

1. Ἡ τοῦ χρόνου ἤδη περίοδος ἤγαγεν ἡμᾶς εἰς τὰς πανσέπτους ἡμέρας τῆς ἐγκρατείας, ὡς ἀπὸ ζάλης κυμάτων τῆς σαρκικῆς ἀνέσεως
5 εἰς τὸν εὐρύχωρον καὶ γαληνὸν λιμένα τῆς κατὰ τὴν νηστείαν στενότητος καταντήσασα· ἀπὸ γὰρ τῆς αὔριον ἀρχόμεθα βαδίζειν τὸν ταύτης δρόμον. ὡς οὖν τῆς ἀρχῆς ἐφαπτόμεθα, οὕτως ἐπιλαβόμεθα καὶ τοῦ τέλους, ὅπως ὅλην τὴν νηστείαν κρατήσαντες, ὅλην καὶ τὴν ἐκ ταύτης θεραπείαν δρεψώμεθα. ἀρχὴν δὲ λέγω τῆς ἐγκρατείας, οὐ
10 τὴν πρώτην ἡμέραν τῶν μετ' αὐτὴν συναριθμουμένων, καὶ τέλος πάλιν φημί, οὐ τὴν ἐσχάτην ἡμέραν τὴν καὶ συμπληροῦσαν τὴν τεσσα-ρακοστήν, τελευταίαν οὖσαν τῶν πρὸ αὐτῆς. ὁ γὰρ σκοπεύων τὸ μέτρον τῶν νηστίμων ἡμερῶν καὶ τὴν κατὰ μικρὸν παραδρομὴν αὐτῶν λογιζόμενος δημοσιεύει τὴν ἡδυπάθειαν τῆς ψυχῆς αὐτοῦ· ἣν καὶ
15 κωλυομένην ὑπὸ τῆς νηστείας δυσχεραίνων, φαντάζεται τὸ ὡρισμένον μῆκος αὐτῆς καὶ κουφίζει τὸ ἐκ τῆς ἡδυπαθείας αὐτοῦ βάρος, ὡς μετὰ τὴν παρέλευσιν τῶν τεσσαράκοντα ἡμερῶν μέλλων πάλιν ἐμφορεῖσθαι ἀδεῶς τῶν παχυτέρων καὶ ποικίλων βρωμάτων. οὐ ταῦτα γοῦν λέγω ἀρχὴν καὶ τέλος νηστείας, φιληδόνων γὰρ τὸ μετρεῖν τὰς
20 ἡμέρας καὶ τῶν σχῆμα νηστείας ἀλλ' οὐχ ὑπόστασιν κεκτημένων.

2. Ἀρχὴν δὲ λέγω νηστείας τὴν ἀποχὴν τῶν πολλῶν καὶ λιπαρῶν βρωμάτων, τέλος δὲ νηστείας ἐκκοπὴν τῶν παθῶν καὶ τῶν πταισμάτων, δι' ἣν καὶ ἡ σωματικὴ νηστεία νενομοθέτηται, ὄφελος ἐμποιοῦσα εἰ συνημμένην ἔχει καὶ τὴν πνευματικὴν νηστείαν, τὴν τῶν κακῶν
25 ἀποβολὴν τὴν καὶ τὸν ὅρον τῆς νηστείας συμπληροῦσαν. καὶ ἵνα μάθῃς ὅτι τοῦτό ἐστιν ἀληθὴς νηστεία, λάβε κατὰ νοῦν τὸν γραπτὸν νόμον, ὃς εἰς γράμμα καὶ πνεῦμα μεριζόμενος ἀπὸ τοῦ γράμματος ἐπὶ τὸ πνεῦμα καθοδηγεῖ τὸν τῆς διανοίας τοῦ νόμου ἐχόμενον. διὸ καί φησιν ὁ ἀπόστολος, *τὸ γράμμα ἀποκτένει, τὸ δὲ πνεῦμα ζωοποιεῖ.*
30 τοιοῦτόν τι καὶ ὁ τῆς νηστείας νόμος διασημαίνει, ἀποχὴν γὰρ βρωμάτων καὶ παθῶν ἀποβολὴν διαλαμβάνων διὰ τῆς ἐνδείας τῶν

TREATISE ON FASTING, READ ON CHEESEFARE SUNDAY[1]

1. The march of time has already brought us round to the most sacred days of abstinence; it has led us back from the storm waves of carnal licence to the spacious, calm harbour of the strict way of the fast, for tomorrow we begin to tread this course. Thus, as we touch the beginning, so we grasp hold also of the end that, in keeping to the fast in its entirety, we may gather all the fruits of the healing coming from it. I speak of the beginning of abstinence, not in the sense of the first day of those counted from it and, again, I speak of the end, not in the sense of the final day that completes the forty, namely, the last day of those preceding it. He who considers the number of days set for the fast and figures to get through them little by little makes public display of his soul's attachment to pleasure. Since he is annoyed at having his pleasures curbed by the fast, he imagines its duration to be limited and lightens the weight of his attachment to pleasure, because after the passage of the forty days he will again stuff himself with rich and varied foods without scruple. Therefore, this is not what I mean by a beginning and end of the fast, for to calculate the number of days is the way of pleasure-lovers and those who have adopted the outward form of the fast but not its inner substance.

2. By 'the beginning of the fast' I mean abstinence from the many kinds of rich foods; by 'the end of the fast' I mean the eradication of passions and failings. The bodily fast has been ordained for this purpose and is beneficial if it has joined to it the spiritual fast, namely, the rejection of evil, which completes the definition of the fast.[2] And that you may learn that this is the true fast, bear in mind the written Law, which is divided into letter and spirit and which guides the person who holds fast to the meaning of the Law from the letter to the spirit. And so the Apostle says, "The letter kills, but the spirit gives life."[3] The law of the fast has a somewhat similar significance, for it embraces

---

[1] Namely, the last Sunday preceding Great Lent. The Gospel for this Sunday is Mt 6:14-21.

[2] John Chrysostom, *Hom. 15 in Genesim*, PG 53:124.

[3] 2 Cor 3:6.

τοῦ σώματος τροφῶν εἰς τὴν τῆς ψυχῆς καθαρότητα κατευθύνει τὸν νηστεύοντα.

3. Ὅρα γοῦν μὴ νηστεύων ἀπὸ βρωμάτων ἀρκετόν σοι τοῦτο
35 μόνον νομίσῃς εἶναι καὶ τῆς κρείττονος νηστείας ὑπεριδὼν τοῖς τῷ γράμματι προσηλώσασιν ἑαυτοὺς Ἰουδαίοις, ὡς παχὺς τὴν διάνοιαν, ὁμοιωθῇς καὶ ἰουδαϊκὴν νηστείαν εὑρεθῇς ἐκτελῶν· οἳ τὸν σωματικὸν νόμον διώκοντες, εἰς τὸν πνευματικὸν νόμον οὐκ ἔφθασαν. ὁ γοῦν μέχρι τῆς τῶν βρωμάτων ἀποχῆς τὴν νηστείαν ὁρίζων ἀσιτίαν μὲν
40 αἰσθητὴν ἀσκεῖ, βρωματίζει δὲ τὴν ψυχὴν ἀπὸ παθῶν ἀλόγων καὶ λόγων καὶ φαύλων τρόπων, καὶ διπλῷ βάλλεται βέλει, διὰ μὲν τὴν πρὸς τὰ πάθη φιλίαν ἡδυπαθῶν, διὰ δὲ τὴν νενοθευμένην νηστείαν κενοδοξῶν. ἡδονὴ δὲ καὶ κενοδοξία τομώτατα βέλη τοῦ πονηροῦ. ἔπαρον τὴν ψυχὴν ἀπὸ τοῦ σώματος καὶ νεκρὸν ὁρᾶται τὸ σῶμα.
45 χώρισον τὴν νηστείαν ἀπὸ τῆς ψυχῆς καὶ νεκροῦται ὑπὸ τῶν παθῶν ἡ ψυχή. σύναψον τῷ σώματι τὴν ψυχὴν καὶ ἀνίσταται εἰς παλινζωΐαν. ἕνωσον τῇ ψυχῇ τὴν νηστείαν καὶ ζῶσαν ἔχεις ψυχὴν καὶ νήφουσαν εἰς ἀγαθὰς πράξεις.

4. Ἐγὼ δὲ καὶ δι' ὑποδείγματος παραστήσω σοι τὴν ἀληθινὴν
50 νηστείαν καὶ τὸ ταύτης κατόρθωμα. ὅπερ ἡ γέφυρά ἐστιν ἐν τόπῳ κρημνώδει καὶ χασματώδει ἢ ἐν ποταμῷ διείργοντι τὴν κατ' ὄψιν τῆς γῆς ἐπιφάνειαν, τοῦτο ποιεῖ καὶ ἡ νηστεία μεταξὺ σαρκὸς καὶ πνεύματος. ἐκεῖ γὰρ ἡ γέφυρα τοῖς δυσὶν ἄκροις τῶν διϊσταμένων δύο γαιῶν συνημμένη καὶ τοῖς ἰδίοις νώτοις τοὺς παριόντας ὑπο-
55 δεχομένη, τὸ ἄβατον χωρίον βάσιμον ποιεῖ καὶ ἀκινδύνως εἰς τὸ πέραν διαβιβάζει.

5. Ἐνταῦθα ἡ νηστεία τῶν ἰδίων ἐπιτηδευμάτων τὰ φάρμακα προσφέρουσα, θεραπεύει τὰ νενοσηκότα, καὶ τὸν μερισμὸν καὶ τὴν μάχην διαλύουσα, διαλάττει τὰ μαχόμενα καὶ συνάπτει. τῇ γὰρ λιτῇ
60 διαίτῃ καὶ τῇ βραχυφαγίᾳ τοῦ σώματος τὴν ζωὴν συντηροῦσα, τὸ μὲν σῶμα ἀπερίσπαστον καὶ κοῦφον καὶ εὔτονον πρὸς τοὺς ἀσκητικοὺς ἀγῶνας ποιεῖ, ὥστε δύνασθαι προθύμως καὶ ἀγρυπνεῖν καὶ ψάλλειν καὶ κλίσεις γονάτων ποιεῖν καὶ πρὸς τὰς ἐν τῷ ναῷ συνάξεις ἀπαντᾶν καὶ τὴν ἐγκεχειρισμένην διακονίαν ἐπιτελεῖν
65 εὐτόνως. τὸν νοῦν δὲ πάλιν νηφάλιον καὶ διεγηγερμένον οἰκονομεῖ, ὡς κάρου καὶ φαντασίας ἀπηλλαγμένον, διὰ τὴν σύμμετρον καὶ ἁπλὴν μετάληψιν τῶν ἀναγκαίων. τότε γὰρ ἀθόλωτος ὁ νοῦς μένων καὶ τὴν ἰδίαν ἐντρέχειαν διασώζων, διὰ τὸ μὴ βαρεῖσθαι, ὡς εἴρηται, ὑπὸ

---

36 παχὺς corr.: παχεῖς OA   43 βέλη corr.: βελει OA   51 κρημνώδει corr.:
κρυμνώδει OA

abstinence from foods and rejection of the passions and guides the one who fasts through privation of bodily nourishment to purity of soul.

3. Beware, then, lest in abstaining from food you think that this alone is sufficient for you and lest in disregarding the better fast you become thick-headed, like the Jews who fastened on the letter of the Law, and be found performing a Judaic fast. The Jews in their pursuit of the bodily law did not attain to the spiritual law. He then who limits his fast to abstention from food practises fasting in the sensible sphere, but feeds his soul with irrational passions and evil words and manners and is struck with a double-pointed dart: he enjoys himself through his attachment to the passions, yet takes false pride in his observance of the fast. Pleasure and vainglory are the sharpest darts of the evil one. Take the soul away from the body and the body appears dead. Separate the fast from the soul and the soul is deadened by the passions. Join the soul to the body and it rises up to renewed life. Unite the fast to the soul and you have a living soul that is vigilant in the practice of good deeds.

4. I will show you by way of example the true fast and what it accomplishes. The fast works between flesh and spirit in the same way as a bridge over a precipitous canyon or over a river that divides the visible surface of the earth, for in that case the bridge joins together the two extremities of the two separated points of land and, taking upon its back those who pass over, it makes the impassable region passable and provides a passage free of danger to the other side.

5. In our case the fast offers medicines through its own practice and heals what is diseased. In dissolving factions and quarrels, it reconciles and joins together contending parties. For by means of a frugal lifestyle and moderation in diet it preserves the life of the body and leaves it undistracted, light and vigorous for the struggles of asceticism, so that it can with eagerness perform vigils, psalmody and genuflections, frequent the church assemblies and carry out with enthusiasm the service at hand. And to the mind, in turn, it gives a vigilant and watchful disposition, freed from stupor and phantasy, because of a measured and simple partaking of necessities. Then the mind remains untroubled and preserves its readiness. Because it is not weighed down, as we said, by the mist of gluttony, it keeps its faculty

τῆς κατὰ τὴν ἀδδηφαγίαν ὀμίχλης, καθαρὸν ἔχει τὸ ὀπτικὸν ἑαυτοῦ·
70 ὅθεν καὶ κατανοεῖ τῆς ματαίας συνηθείας τοὺς τρόπους καὶ τὰ
προπετῶς καὶ ἀκρίτως ἐκπηδῶντα τοῦ στόματος ῥήματα.

6. Διορᾷ τοὺς ἕρποντας λογισμοὺς ἐν τῇ διανοίᾳ. κατασκοπεῖ τῶν
παθῶν τὴν ἀσχημοσύνην καὶ τὴν ἀηδίαν μὴ φέρων τῆς αἰσχύνης
ἀποστρέφεται τὰ κακά, ὡς τὴν ἐλπίδα τῆς σωτηρίας καὶ τὴν εἰς θεὸν
75 παρρησίαν ἀφαιρούμενα· διακρίνει γὰρ ἀπλανῶς τότε ὡς οὐδὲν
ὄφελος τῆς τῶν βρωμάτων ἀποχῆς, τῶν παθῶν δίκην σκυλάκων
καθυλακτούντων διὰ τῶν λογισμῶν καὶ τῶν φαύλων λόγων καὶ
δακνόντων τὴν ψυχὴν διὰ τῶν ἀτόπων τρόπων.

7. Τίς συγγένεια φωτὶ καὶ σκότει; τίς κοινωνία Χριστῷ καὶ
80 Βελίαρ; Χριστῷ δουλεύω διὰ τῆς ὁρωμένης νηστείας· Βελίαρ λατρεύω
διὰ τῶν παθῶν καὶ τῆς λοιπῆς κακῆς ἀναστροφῆς. οὐαί μοι τῷ πλάνῳ,
οὐαί μοι τῷ ὑποκριτῇ. Χριστοῦ μαθητὴς εἶναι σχηματίζομαι καὶ τοῦ
ἐχθροῦ δοῦλος καθίσταμαι διὰ τῆς ἁμαρτίας. καπηλεύω τὴν χάριν
τῆς νηστείας καθάπερ οἶνον ὕδατι μίγνυμι τὴν ἀσιτίαν τῇ ἀσωτείᾳ.
85 κρέας οὐκ ἐμβάλλω τῷ στόματι, ἀλλὰ τοῖς ὀδοῦσι τῆς καταλαλιᾶς,
τῆς κατακρίσεως, τῆς ὕβρεως καὶ τῆς εἰρωνείας κατεσθίω τὸν
ἀδελφόν. ἰχθύος ἀπέχομαι, ἀλλ᾽ ἐν τῇ ψυχῇ τὴν μνησικακίαν
ὑφέρπουσαν ἔχω καὶ διὰ τῶν ἀφώνων λογισμῶν πλήττω τὸν ἀδελφόν.
τυρὸν οὐκ ἐσθίω, ἀλλὰ τυρεύω κατὰ τοῦ πέλας καὶ ἐνεδρεύω τοῦ
90 καταβαλεῖν αὐτόν. ἔλαιον οὐ λιπαίνει τὸν ἐμὸν φάρυγγα, ἀλλ᾽ αἱ
ἡδοναὶ τῆς σαρκὸς λιπαίνουσι βδελυρῶς τὴν ψυχήν· καὶ ταῦτα
καθεκάστην τὸν στίχον τοῦ ψαλμοῦ ἐν τῷ στόματι φέρων καὶ λέγων,
παιδεύσει με δίκαιος ἐν ἐλέει καὶ ἐλέγξει με, ἔλαιον δὲ ἁμαρτωλοῦ μὴ
λιπανάτω τὴν κεφαλήν μου.

95 **8.** Παιδεύσει καὶ συνετίσει με διὰ τῆς συμμέτρου ἀτροφίας ἡ
δικαιοῦσά με νηστεία, ἡ πρεσβυτάτη καὶ σύνοικος ἀρετή. *παιδεύσει*
με δὲ ἐν ἐλέει, τουτέστιν, ἐν μικρᾷ θλίψει τῆς στενῆς διαίτης· *ἐν θλίψει,*
γάρ φησι, μικρᾷ ἡ παιδεία σου ἡμῖν. καὶ *ἐλέγξει με,* μὴ ἐξ ἡμισείας
ἐπιτελεῖν τὴν νηστείαν, ὥστε βρωμάτων ἀπέχεσθαι καὶ παθῶν μὴ
100 καθαρεύειν. *ἔλαιον δὲ ἁμαρτωλοῦ,* ἡ λεαίνουσα δηλαδὴ ἡδονὴ τῆς
ἁμαρτίας, *μὴ λιπανάτω* ἀπατηλῶς *τὴν κεφαλήν μου,* τὸν ἡγεμονεύοντα
νοῦν τῶν αἰσθήσεών μου.

9. Οἰνοποσίαν φεύγω καὶ μέθην ἀλόγου θυμοῦ στέργω. σιωπὴν
ἀσκῶ καὶ ὀργῆς κραυγὰς ἐκφέρω. γυναικὸς ἀποδιΐσταμαι καὶ τοὺς

---

69 ἀδδηφαγίαν sic in OA: cf. Nilus, Ep. 3.106 (PG 79:433C); Synesius, Ep. 132 (PG 66:1517B)   91 βδελυρῶς corr.: βδελυρῶς OA

of vision pure, and thus it perceives the ways of vain habits and the words that leap rashly and indiscreetly out of the mouth.

6. The mind sees clearly the thoughts that slink about in the discursive intellect; it searches out the shamefulness of the passions and, refusing to bear the odiousness of shame; it rejects evils as detrimental to its hope for salvation and its freedom in God. For it then unerringly discerns that there is no advantage in abstaining from foods when the passions are barking like dogs by their thoughts and evil words and are biting the soul by their wicked ways.

7. What kinship is there between light and darkness? What is there in common between Christ and Beliar?[4] I serve Christ by the visible fast; I am a servant of Beliar by the passions and the rest of my evil conduct. Woe upon me in my error! Woe upon me in my hypocrisy! I make an outward show of being a disciple of Christ, but I become a slave of the enemy by my sin. I peddle the grace of the fast. I mix profligacy with fasting, as water with wine. I put no meat in my mouth, but I devour my brother with the teeth of slander, condemnation, insolence and sarcasm. I abstain from fish, but I have rancour lurking in my soul and strike my brother with my unspoken thoughts. I eat no cheese, but I churn out mischief against my neighbour and set an ambush to strike him down. I do not season my food with oil,[5] but the pleasures of the flesh grease my soul with a loathsome oil. Yet every day I bear on my lips the verse of the Psalm, "The just man will discipline me in mercy and will reprove me, but let not the oil of the sinner anoint my head."[6]

8. The fast that justifies me, the most important virtue to have as one's companion, will grant me discipline and understanding through the measured deprivation of food. It will discipline me in mercy, that is, in the small trials of a strict way of life, for scripture says, "In small trials your discipline came to us."[7] It will reprove me lest I keep the fast half-heartedly to the point where I abstain from foods but am not free of passions. Do not let the oil of the sinner, namely, the lubricious pleasure of sin, deceitfully anoint my head (the mind that exercises dominion over my senses).

9. I avoid drinking wine, yet indulge in the intoxication of irrational anger. I practise silence, but let loose cries of wrath. I stay away from

---

[4] 2 Cor 6:14-15.
[5] Literally, " ... anoint my throat."
[6] Ps 140:5.
[7] Is 26:16.

105 ὀφθαλμοὺς ἐμπιπλῶ πορνικῆς ἐπιθυμίας. σωφρονῶ τῇ σαρκὶ καὶ τῇ
διανοίᾳ ζωγραφῶν τὰς εὐπρεπεῖς ὄψεις συνήδομαι τοῖς λογισμοῖς.
βραδυφαγῶ καὶ κατὰ τοῦ πέλας ταχὺ λαλῶ. κυπτάζω πρὸς τὰς
προσκυνήσεις καὶ οὐδαμῶς κάμπτω τὸ φρόνημα πρὸς ταπείνωσιν.
γονυκλιτῶ δεόμενος καὶ ταῖς πτέρυξι τῆς ὑπερηφανείας ἀεροβατῶ.
110 τοῖς λόγοις ἑαυτὸν καθαρὸν ἀποφαίνομαι, ὑψηλὰ δὲ φανταζόμενος
ἐν ἑαυτῷ ἀκάθαρτον ἑαυτὸν καθίστημι· *ἀκάθαρτος γὰρ παρὰ κυρίῳ*
πᾶς ὑψηλοκάρδιος. ἐλέγχειν ἄλλους ὡς δίκαιος οὐχ ὑποστέλλομαι,
παραίνεσιν δὲ ἢ τὴν τυχοῦσαν ὑπόμνησιν παρ᾽ ἄλλου δέξασθαι οὐκ
ἀνέχομαι. καταλέγειν τὰ ἀλλότρια πταίσματα καὶ διασύρειν τὸν
115 ἀδελφὸν οὐ κοπιῶ, τὰ ἐμαυτοῦ δὲ πλημμελήματα διαλογίζεσθαι καὶ
τὴν ἐπὶ τούτοις ὡς εἰκὸς συντριβὴν ἐπιδείκνυσθαι ὀκνῶ καὶ
ἀναβάλλομαι.

10. Τὴν ἔμπρακτον προκοπὴν τοῦ πλησίον, ἢ ὡς φθονερὸς
διαβάλλω, ἢ ὡς ὑπερήφανος ἐμαυτῷ ἐπιγράφομαι ὡς μυσταγωγῷ. τὴν
120 δὲ νομιζομένην πλημμέλειαν αὐτοῦ ὡς ἀληθινὴν προβαλλόμενος
θριαμβεύω. τὸν ὑποπίπτοντά μοι δουλικῶς ἀδελφὸν ὡς ὑπερήφανος
ἐπαινῶ, ἐπειδὴ κρίνει με ὑπερέχοντα, καὶ τὸν ἐπαινοῦντά με πάλιν
ὡς κενόδοξος μεγαλύνω κυροῦν τοὺς περὶ ἐμοῦ ἐπαίνους βουλόμενος
ὡς παρὰ μεγάλου λεγομένους. τὸν προσέρχεσθαί μοι καὶ προσλαλεῖν
125 βουλόμενον ὡς βδέλυγμα ἀποστρέφομαι, καὶ τούτου συστελλομένου
διὰ τὴν παραίτησιν μανίας πληροῦμαι.

11. Τὰς ἀφανεῖς καὶ πολυειδεῖς ταύτας σχέσεις καὶ ὁρμὰς καὶ
πράξεις ὁρᾶν ἡ νηστεία χαρίζεται τῷ νῷ. ὁ νοῦς δὲ ταῦτα πάντα
διορῶν, ὡς ἐναιθρία τελῶν, διὰ τὸ γαληνιᾶν ἐκ τῆς ἐγκρατείας, τῆς
130 τῶν παθῶν αἰσθάνεται βδελυρίας· κατανοεῖ τὴν ἀηδίαν τῶν κακῶν.
ὅθεν καὶ τῷ φωτὶ τῆς διακρίσεως περιλαμπόμενος, εἰς διαλογισμοὺς
ἀγαθοὺς κινεῖται, τοὺς τρόπους τῆς διορθώσεως ὑπαγορεύοντας.

12. Τὰ βρώματα θρασύνει τὸ σῶμα. τὰ φαῦλα σκληρύνει τὴν
ψυχήν. ἡ οἰνοποσία εἰς πύρωσιν ἐξάπτει τὴν σάρκα. τὰ ἀλόγιστα
135 πάθη πύρωσιν τῇ διανοίᾳ ἐργάζονται. ἤργησα τὰ πολυτελῆ καὶ
λιπαρὰ ἐδέσματα, ὀσπρίων δὲ καὶ λαχάνων καὶ ὕδατος συμμέτρως
μεταλαμβάνω, ἵνα καθαρὸν ποιήσω τὸ σῶμα. καταργήσω καὶ τὰ
αἴσχιστα πλημμελήματα, τοὺς δὲ τρόπους τῶν ἀρετῶν ἐνστερνίσομαι,
ἵνα καθαρίσω καρδίαν καὶ ναὸς θεοῦ γένωμαι. καὶ Χριστὸς ἐνοικήσει
140 διὰ προσευχῆς καὶ ἐμπεριπατήσει διὰ νηστείας, ἅπαν νόημα φαῦλον

---

130 βδελυρίας corr.: βδελλυρίας OA　　　135 πύρωσιν corr.: πήρωσιν OA

women, but fill my eyes with unchaste desires. I preserve chastity in the flesh, but paint pretty pictures in my discursive intellect and take pleasure in thoughts. I am slow in eating, but quick to speak against my neighbour. I stoop to make prostrations, but bow my attitude not at all to humility. I bend the knee to make petition, but I fly off on the wings of pride. I make a show of being clean in speech, but make myself unclean by imagining lofty things to be within my power, for "Everyone with an arrogant heart is unclean before the Lord."[8] As if I were a just man, I have no qualms about reproaching others, but I refuse to accept from another advice or a chance reminder. I do not weary of denouncing another's faults and disparaging my brother, but I hang back and delay calculating the number of my own failings and displaying a fitting contrition for them.

10. Either out of jealousy I slander the active progress of my neighbour, or out of pride I ascribe it to myself as his guide, but I am eager to denounce his reputed error as true. In my pride I praise the brother who fawns on me in servile fashion when he judges me to be his superior, and in my vainglory I in turn extol the man who praises me, but out of my desire to establish that the praises spoken of me come from somebody important. I reject as an abomination the man who wants to come and speak to me and, when he humbles himself to make his supplication, I am filled with rage.

11. The fast grants the mind to see these hidden and manifold attachments, impulses and deeds. Because of the state of calm that comes from abstinence the mind perceives all these things as though it were doing them out in the open; it realizes the loathsomeness of the passions and recognizes the odiousness of evil deeds. Thus, illumined by the light of discernment, it is prompted to good thoughts which suggest ways for amendment.

12. Food emboldens the body. Wicked deeds harden the soul. The imbibing of wine sets the flesh on fire. The irrational passions start a fire in the discursive intellect. I have set aside a varied diet of rich foods and partake of vegetables, greens and water in moderation in order to purify the body. I will also do away with shameful offences and cherish the ways of the virtues in order to purify my heart and become a temple of God.[9] Through prayer Christ will come to dwell within me and through fasting he will tarry within me,[10] driving from me every wicked thought, word and deed, just as he drove the buyers

---

[8] Prov 16:5.
[9] Cf. 1 Cor 3:16, 2 Cor 6:16.
[10] Cf. 2 Cor 6:16.

καὶ ῥῆμα καὶ ἔργον ἀπ᾽ ἐμοῦ ἐξελαύνων, καθάπερ, σαρκὶ διατρίβων
ἐπὶ τῆς γῆς, τοὺς πωλοῦντας καὶ ἀγοράζοντας ἐκ τοῦ ἱεροῦ.

13. Εἰ ταῦτα διανοοῦμαι καὶ τοὺς λόγους εἰς ἔργα ἐκβάλλω, τὴν
ἀληθῆ νηστείαν ἐπιδείκνυμι καὶ τιμῶ τὴν ἐγκράτειαν. καὶ τοῦτο
145 καταμάθοις ἂν ἐκ τοῦ πρὸ τῆς παρακοῆς Ἀδάμ, ἐκεῖνος γὰρ ἕως
τὴν νηστείαν εἶχε χειραγωγὸν καὶ σύμβουλον, τῶν ἐν παραδείσῳ
ξύλων κατετρύφα καὶ τοῦ κεκωλυμένου ξύλου ἀπείχετο. ἐπεὶ δὲ τὴν
σύντροφον νηστείαν ἀπεστράφη καὶ πρὸς τὴν σύζυγον Εὖαν ἐστράφη
καὶ τῆς ἀπηγορευμένης βρώσεως ἐνεφορήθη, αὐτίκα καὶ τῆς ἐδωδῆς
150 τῶν ἐν παραδείσῳ ξύλων ἐστέρηται καὶ τοῦ παραδείσου ἐκβέβληται.

14. Ἰδοὺ καὶ ἐνταῦθα ξύλα τοῦ παραδείσου, ἀφ᾽ ὧν ἐσθίειν
προσετάγημεν· ἡ πρᾶξις τῶν ἐντολῶν, ὁ ἐπὶ τοῦ στόματος ὕμνος καὶ
ἡ ψαλμῳδία, οἱ τρόποι τῶν ἀρετῶν, ἡ τῶν χειλέων ἀλήθεια, ἡ πρὸς
τὸν πέλας παραίνεσις, ἡ πρὸς θεὸν εὐχαριστία, ἡ διήγησις τῶν αὐτοῦ
155 θαυμασίων, ἡ τῶν θείων γραφῶν ἀνάγνωσις, ἡ ἔμμονος μελέτη τῶν
λογίων τοῦ θεοῦ, ἡ ἀδιάλειπτος προσευχὴ καὶ κατάνυξις τῆς ψυχῆς,
ἡ ἐξομολόγησις τῶν ἁμαρτημάτων καὶ τῶν ῥυπαρῶν λογισμῶν, ἡ
τῶν θλιβερῶν ὑπομονὴ καὶ ἡ πρὸς πάντας ἀνθρώπους εἰλικρινὴς
ἀγάπη καὶ ταπείνωσις.

160 **15.** Ταῦτα ἡ φυτεία τοῦ θεοῦ· τὰ ἀθάνατα ξύλα, οἱ ἄφθαρτοι
καρποί, ὧν καὶ τὴν ἀπόλαυσιν ἐλάβομεν. ὡσαύτως ὁρᾶται ἐν ἡμῖν
καὶ ξύλον ἀπώμοτον, ἀφ᾽ οὗ μὴ φαγεῖν ἐκελεύσθημεν· τὰ παρὰ φύσιν
πάθη, ἡ παράλογος χρῆσις τῶν ἐν ἡμῖν φυσικῶν δυνάμεων, αἱ
διαβεβλημέναι ἡδοναὶ τῆς σαρκός, ἡ ἐπιθυμία τῶν ὀφθαλμῶν, ἡ τῶν
165 ματαίων ἡδονή, τὰ ἀναιδῆ τῆς γλώσσης ῥήματα, ὁ ἄσεμνος τῶν
βρωμάτων κόρος, ἡ ἀσελγὴς μέθη, ὁ προπετὴς θυμός, ἡ δεινὴ καὶ
φλογώδης ὀργή, ἧς καπνὸς ἡ μνησικακία, ἡ κατὰ τοῦ πέλας ὑπόνοια
καὶ ὁ λοιπὸς ὁρμαθὸς τῶν ἐν τῇ διανοίᾳ κινουμένων παθῶν.

16. Ταῦτα τῆς παρακοῆς τὰ βλαστήματα, τὰ παραφυόμενα τοῦ
170 πονηροῦ ζιζάνια, τῇ δικέλλῃ τῆς προσευχῆς καὶ τῆς νηστείας
ἀπορριζούμενα. *τοῦτο, γάρ φησι, τὸ δαιμόνιον οὐκ ἐξέρχεται, εἰ μὴ ἐν
προσευχῇ καὶ νηστείᾳ.* τούτων οὕτως ἐχόντων, ἡ προαίρεσις ἔστηκε
μέση, ἐξουσίαν ἔχουσα ἑνὶ τούτων δοῦναι τὴν ῥοπὴν τοῦ θελήματος.
ἀλλ᾽ εἰ καὶ δύναμαι πράττειν ἐξουσιαστικῶς ὃ βούλομαι, ἀλλ᾽ οὐ

162 παραφύσιν OA

and sellers from the Temple, when he was living in the flesh upon earth.[11]

13. If I consider these things and turn my words into deeds, I am displaying the true fast and honouring self-discipline. This you could learn from Adam's state before his disobedience, for as long as he kept the fast as his guide and counsellor, he delighted in the trees of paradise and abstained from the forbidden tree. But when he abandoned the companionship of the fast and turned to Eve, his spouse, and took his fill of the forbidden food, he was straightaway deprived of the food of the trees in paradise and was expelled from paradise.[12]

14. Behold, in our case too there are trees of paradise from which we have been commanded to eat: the practice of the commandments, the singing of hymns and psalms, the ways of the virtues, truth upon our lips, counsel given to our neighbour, thanksgiving to God, the recounting of his wonderful deeds, the reading of the divine scriptures, steadfast meditation on the sayings of God, unceasing prayer and compunction of soul, the confession of sins and base thoughts, patient endurance of sufferings, and pure love and humility towards all men.

15. These constitute God's plantation, the immortal trees, the incorruptible fruits of which we have received the enjoyment. Similarly, there can also be seen within us the tree that is forsworn, from which we have been commanded not to eat,[13] namely, the passions contrary to nature, the irrational use of our natural powers, the discredited pleasures of the flesh, the lust of the eyes, pleasure in vanities, the shameless words of the tongue, the indecent surfeit of foods, wanton drunkenness, uncontrolled wrath, terrible and fiery anger from which comes the smoke of rancour, suspicion against one's neighbour and the remaining links in the chain of passions that move about in the discursive intellect.

16. These are the offshoots of disobedience, the weeds of the evil one[14] that grow up beside it and are uprooted by the two-pronged garden fork of prayer and fasting. For scripture says, "This sort of demon does not come out except by prayer and fasting."[15] This being the case, the choice hangs in the balance with the power to give the weight of the will to one or the other of these alternatives. But if I

---

[11] Mt 21:12, Mk 11:15, Lk 19:45, Jn 2:14-16.
[12] Gen 2:7-3:24.
[13] Cf. Gregorios Palamas, *Capita 150*, c. 55.
[14] Cf. Mt 13:25.
[15] Mt 17:21, Mk 9:29.

175 παραχρήσομαι τῇ ἐξουσίᾳ καὶ ἀπολέσω τὴν ταύτης τιμὴν ἐν τῷ
δουλῶσαι τὸ κρεῖττον τῷ χείρονι. εἰ γὰρ καὶ θέλησιν ἔσχον εἰς τὸ
ποιεῖν τὰ κατὰ γνώμην, ἀλλὰ καὶ διάκρισιν ἔλαβον. εἰς τὸ χωρίζειν
τὸ κακὸν ἀπὸ τοῦ καλοῦ καὶ τὴν θέλησιν συνάπτειν τῷ καλῷ μόνῳ,
ἵνα διὰ μὲν τῆς ἀπταίστου διακρίσεως γινώσκων τὸ καλόν, συντηρῶ
180 τὸ κατ' εἰκόνα, καθάπερ ὀφθαλμῷ τῇ γνώσει χειραγωγούμενος· διὰ
δὲ τῆς πρὸς τὸ καλὸν θελήσεως ἀγαπῶν τὸ καλὸν μόνον, τὸ καθ'
ὁμοίωσιν διαζωγραφῶ, ὡς πάντα τὰ κατὰ λόγον καὶ φρονῶν καὶ
λαλῶν καὶ ποιῶν.

17. Ἀπὸ γοῦν τῆς διακρίσεως καὶ τῆς ἐκ τῶν θείων γραφῶν
185 διδασκαλίας, εὑρίσκω τὴν νηστείαν, θύραν καὶ φυλακὴν τῶν καλῶν
πάντων. αὕτη τῶν καλῶν τὴν μετάληψιν δαψιλῶς χαριζομένη καὶ
χορτάζουσα τὸν ἐσθίοντα ἀπὸ τῶν τῆς ἀρετῆς καρπῶν, οὐ καλύπτε-
σθαι παρασκευάζει τῶν φθειρομένων τῇ ἀπολαύσει τὸν προτιμώμενον
τὴν εἰς τὰ πάντα ἐγκράτειαν. αὕτη τηρουμένη στολὴν κοσμιότητος
190 καὶ παρρησίας περιβάλλει τοὺς φύλακας· οἱ δὲ ἀθετοῦντες αὐτὴν
ἀκοσμίας καὶ αἰσχύνης καὶ ἀσχημοσύνης χιτῶνα ἐνδύονται.

18. Ἡ νηστεία τοὺς ταύτην φιλοῦντας τῶν χαμερπῶν καὶ γηΐνων
ἀπάγει καὶ εἰς ὄρος τῆς προσευχῆς ἀνάγει καὶ εἰς γνόφον τοῦ ὑπὲρ
γνῶσιν ὄντος εἰσάγει καὶ γνῶσιν ἀληθείας εἰσδέχεται· καὶ πλάκες
195 αὐτῷ γίνονται, ἡ διάνοια καὶ τὸ σῶμα, καὶ λόγοι σοφίας ἐγγράφονται
καὶ τρόποι ἀρετῶν ἐγχαράττονται καὶ τὸν Ἰσραηλίτην νοῦν
ἀκαταρρυθμίζουσιν. ἡ νηστεία τὸν ἐγκρατῆ ζηλωτὴν διάπυρον
ἀναδείκνυσι καὶ τῇ κτήσει τῶν γενικῶν ἀρετῶν τὸ τετράστοιχον σῶμα
ὑψοῦσα, ἁρπάζει τῶν ἐπιγείων καὶ εἰς πόθον τῶν οὐρανίων τὴν ψυχὴν
200 ἀναλαμβάνει.

177 καταγνώμην ΟΑ   194 ὄντος ... γνῶσιν om. Α

am able to do freely what I want, I will not misuse the power and destroy its value by subjecting the superior to the inferior. For if I possess the will to do purposeful acts, I also have received discernment to distinguish evil from good and to join my will to the good alone. Thus, by knowing the good through an unerring discernment, I may preserve the Image, being guided by knowledge as though by my eyes, and by loving the good alone through willing the good I may paint the Likeness in thinking, saying and doing all things according to reason.[16]

17. On the basis, therefore, of discernment and the teaching of the divine scriptures I find fasting to be the door and watchguard of all things good. In bestowing a plentiful partaking of what is good and feeding the diner on the fruits of virtue, it accustoms the man who prefers discipline in all things not to cover himself with the enjoyment of corruptible things. When it is observed, it clothes those who keep it with a garment of comeliness and boldness, but those who reject it wear a garment of ugliness, shame and guilt.[17]

18. Fasting leads those who love it away from things that are earthbound and earthly, guides them up the mountain of prayer,[18] leads them into the darkness[19] of the Being who is beyond knowing and grants them admission to knowledge of the truth. Mind and body become tablets,[20] and words of wisdom are inscribed on them and the ways of the virtues are engraved there, and they throw the Israelite mind into disorder. Fasting brings out the fervour of the disciplined zealot, and by exalting the body composed of the four elements through the acquisition of the cardinal virtues[21] it snatches the soul away from earthly realities and raises it up to yearn for heavenly things.

---

[16] Cf. Gen 1:26.

[17] Cf. Gen 3:7, 21. Cf. also the Sticheron for Vespers on Cheesefare Sunday (*The Lenten Triodion*, p. 168): "I have cast off the robe woven by God ... I am clothed now in fig leaves and garments of skin." There is a long tradition of patristic exegesis on the nature of these garments. See the examples given in Lampe, *Patristic Greek Lexicon*, pp. 1525-1526.

[18] Cf. the Ninth Ode for Matins on Tuesday of the first week of Great Lent (*The Lenten Triodion*, p. 215): "Through fasting let us draw near to the mountain of prayer; and with pure hearts like Moses let us also look on God, receiving inwardly the tablets of the commandments and shining with glory in the presence of God's love."

[19] Cf. Ex 20:21.

[20] Cf. Ex 31:18, 32:15, 34:1.

[21] For the body composed of four elements see Pseudo-Gregory of Nyssa, *Ad imaginem Dei et ad similitudinem* (PG 44:1328B). The cardinal virtues are mentioned in Nilus of Ancyra, *Epistula* 1.223 (PG 79:164D). The four virtues are φρόνησις, ἀνδρεία, σωφροσύνη, δικαιοσύνη.

19. Ἡ νηστεία θυμοῦ καὶ ὀργῆς καὶ κραυγῆς καὶ μήνιδος τὰς
κατὰ τοῦ πέλας ὁρμὰς χαλινοῦσα καὶ γλώσσης ἀκρατοῦς καὶ χειρῶν
προπετῶν κινήσεις καταστέλλουσα, ὑπήκοα καὶ τιθασσὰ τὰ ἔμφυτα
πάθη τῷ νηστεύοντι καθιστᾷ, καθάπερ πάλαι τοὺς λέοντας τῷ Δανιήλ.
205 ἡ νηστεία καὶ τῆς σαρκικῆς πυρώσεως ἀποτινάσσει τὴν φλόγα καὶ
τὸν διορατικὸν νοῦν ἐνισχύει πρὸς νῆψιν, ὃς καὶ ἐν μέσῃ τῇ καρδίᾳ
τὸν τῆς προσευχῆς ἦχον διασυρίζων, ἔχει μεθ' ἑαυτοῦ τὸν τῆς
μεγάλης βουλῆς ἄγγελον, Ἰησοῦν Χριστόν, τῷ φωτὶ τῆς θεότητος
αὐτοῦ τὴν διάνοιαν καταυγάζοντα καὶ τῇ δρόσῳ τῆς πρὸς αὐτὸν
210 ἀγάπης τὴν ψυχὴν ἀναψύχοντα, δι' ἧς πᾶσαν ἐπιθυμίαν τοῦ αἰῶνος
τούτου ἡ ψυχὴ ἀπομαραίνουσα, ἄλυπός τε αὐτὴ τελεῖ, ἐπειδὴ χαρᾷ
χαίρει διὰ τὴν γλυκυτάτην ὁμιλίαν τοῦ νυμφίου Χριστοῦ καὶ
ἀπαρενόχλητον τὴν καρδίαν καθιστᾷ· *πνεύματι γὰρ περιπατεῖ καὶ τόπον*
τῆς σαρκικῆς ἐπιθυμίας οὐκ ἔχει. ὅθεν καὶ τὴν εὐχαριστίαν τῶν τριῶν
215 παίδων μιμουμένη, ὑμνεῖ καὶ εὐλογεῖ καὶ δοξάζει τὸν κύριον.

20. Ἐξυμνεῖ διὰ τῶν ἐν τῇ διανοίᾳ λογισμῶν, εὐλογεῖ διὰ τῶν
ἐν τῇ γλώσσῃ ῥημάτων, δοξάζει διὰ τῶν ἐν τῷ σώματι τῆς δικαιοσύνης
ἔργων. *λαμψάτω, γάρ φησι, τὸ φῶς ὑμῶν ἔμπροσθεν τῶν ἀνθρώπων,*
ὅπως ἴδωσι τὰ καλὰ ὑμῶν ἔργα καὶ δοξάσωσι τὸν πατέρα ὑμῶν τὸν ἐν
220 *τοῖς οὐρανοῖς.* ἀφίημι τοὺς οἰκέτας καὶ τρέχω πρὸς τὸν δεσπότην, τὸν
καὶ νομοθετήσαντα τὴν νηστείαν ὡς θεὸν καὶ ὡς ἄνθρωπον πάλιν
τὸν αὐτὸν νηστεύσαντα ἐν τῇ ἐρήμῳ καὶ διὰ νηστείας τὸν πειραστὴν
καταβαλόντα.
21. Ἐπειδὴ γὰρ ὁ θεὸς λόγος ἐν ἀρχῇ τῶν αἰώνων ἐνετείλατο
225 τῷ Ἀδὰμ νηστεύειν ἀπὸ τοῦ τῆς βρώσεως ξύλου, ὁ δὲ τῆς κατὰ τὴν
νηστείαν ἐντολῆς ἐπιλαθόμενος, ἔφαγεν ἀπὸ τοῦ καρποῦ καὶ ἐπιτίμιον

---

206 ἐνισχύει corr.: ἐν ἰσχύει OA   210 ἀναψύχοντα corr.: ἀνὰ ψύχοντα OA
216 ἐξυμνεῖ corr.: ἐξ ὑμνεῖ OA

19. The fast bridles the impulses of wrath, anger, shouting and malice against one's neighbour and restrains the movements of an uncontrolled tongue and rash hands, thereby rendering the inborn passions obedient and tame for the one who fasts, as of old it disposed the lions towards Daniel.[22] Fasting extinguishes the flame of fleshly conflagration and gives to the clear-sighted mind the strength for vigilance. The mind, whistling the tune of prayer in the midst of the heart, has in its company the angel of great counsel,[23] Jesus Christ who illumines the discursive intellect with the Light of his divinity and refreshes the soul with the dew of love for him.[24] With this love the soul obliterates all desire for this age and is freed of grief since it rejoices in joy on account of its most sweet converse with Christ, its bridegroom, and sets the heart free of disturbance, for "it walks by the Spirit and has no place for desires of the flesh."[25] And so, in imitating the thanksgiving prayer of the three children,[26] it praises, blesses and glorifies the Lord.

20. The soul gives praise through the thoughts in the discursive mind; it offers blessing through words on the tongue; it gives glory through works of righteousness in the body. For scripture says, "Let your light shine before men that they may see your good works and give glory to your Father in heaven."[27] I release the servants and run to the master who ordained the fast as God and again as man kept the fast himself in the desert and through fasting cast down the tempter.[28]

21. When God the Word at the beginning of the ages commanded Adam to abstain from the tree of food, but the latter forgot the commandment of fasting and ate of the fruit, immediately he received

[22] Dan 6:16-24.

[23] Cf. Is 9:5.

[24] Dan 3:49-50. Note Ode Two of the Second Canon for Matins on Tuesday of the first week in Lent (*The Lenten Triodion*, p. 213): "What quenched the fire? What stopped the mouths of the wild beasts? It was fasting that delivered the Children from the furnace and Daniel the Prophet from the jaws of the lions. Brethren, let us also fast like them."

[25] Gal 5:16.

[26] Odes 8 (Dan 3:52-88).

[27] Mt 5:16.

[28] Mt 4:1-11, Mk 1:12-13, Lk 4:1-13. Christ's fast in the desert is mentioned several times in the liturgical office for the first week of Lent. See for example Ode Eight of Matins for Monday (*The Lenten Triodion*, p. 193): "Fasting for the space of forty days, the Lord consecrated and made holy this present Fast." Cf. Ode Nine of Compline on the same day (*The Lenten Triodion*, p. 208).

αὐτίκα τὸν θάνατον ἔσχε κατὰ τὴν πρόρρησιν, τούτου χάριν ἐν τῷ
τέλει τῶν αἰώνων τὴν ἀδαμιαίαν φύσιν ἐν ἑαυτῷ ἀναλαβόμενος, ἀπὸ
νηστείας ἤρξατο καὶ διὰ νηστείας τὸν ἐχθρὸν προσβαλόντα κατη-
230 γωνίσατο, ἵνα καὶ τοῖς ἀνθρώποις δείξῃ τίσιν ὅπλοις δύνανται τὸν
ἐχθρὸν καταργεῖν, ὁμοῦ δὲ καὶ διδάξῃ, ὅτι ὁ πάλαι τῷ πρώτῳ Ἀδὰμ
τὴν νηστείαν νομοθετήσας ὡς θεός, αὐτὸς καὶ νῦν ὡς δεύτερος ... .

the penalty of death in accordance with God's previous warning.[29] For this reason God the Word at the end of the ages, assuming to himself Adam's nature, began with a fast and by means of fasting struggled against the enemy's onslaught in order to show men the weapons with which they can destroy the enemy[30] and at the same time to teach that the one who of old ordained the fast for Adam as God, the same now as a second [Adam] ... .[31]

[29] Gen 2:15-17.

[30] See Ode Nine of Matins for Tuesday of the first week (*The Lenten Triodion*, p. 215): "As the Lord overcame the enemy by fasting, so by fasting let us also break in pieces his arrows and his snares."

[31] The text breaks off here in mid-sentence and is followed by one blank folio.

Περὶ νηστείας

1. Τὴν εὐσταλῆ καὶ σεμνοτάτην νηστείαν παραγενομένην ἀσπασίως ὑποδεξώμεθα οἱ διὰ τὴν ἄνεσιν ταύτης λήθην παθόντες. αὕτη καὶ γὰρ ἐπιστάσα εἰς μνήμην αὐτίκα ἡμᾶς ἄγει, ὧν τε κακῶν
5 ἐπειράθημεν διὰ τὴν ταύτης παράβασιν καὶ ὧν ἀγαθῶν αὖθις ἠξιώθημεν διὰ τὴν αὐτῆς τήρησιν. μάρτυρες τῶν λεγομένων ὁ πρῶτος Ἀδὰμ καὶ ὁ δεύτερος· ὁ μὲν τῆς φθορᾶς ἀρχηγὸς γεγονώς, ἐπειδὴ οὐκ ἐνήστευσεν· ὁ δὲ τῆς ἀφθαρσίας ἀπαρχὴ χρηματίσας, ἐπειδὴ τὴν ἡμῶν ἀναλαβόμενος φύσιν τὰς ἐλλείψεις ἡμῶν ἀνεπλήρωσε.
10 **2.** Χριστὸς γὰρ ἐν τῇ ἐρήμῳ νηστεύσας, τὸν πειραστὴν ἐτροπώσατο καὶ τὴν νίκην ἡμῖν περιεποιήσατο. δεῖ τοίνυν ἐπιδημήσασαν τὴν νηστείαν ἐκ τῶν αὐτῆς ἔργων διαγνωρίσαι, ὅπως ἐκ τῶν ἰδίων ταύτης κατορθωμάτων ἐπιγνόντες τὸν ἀληθῆ χαρακτῆρα τῆς ἐγκρατείας, ἐρασταὶ τοῦ κάλλους αὐτῆς γενώμεθα. χρεὼν δὲ τοὺς τῆς
15 νηστείας ἀγῶνας κεφαλαιῶσαι· οὕτω γὰρ τοῦ ταύτης εἴδους διαμορφωθέντος ἀναγνωρισμὸς γένηται τοῖς διὰ φιληδονίας τῶν ταύτης ἀγκαλῶν, ἁγνείας λέγω καὶ σεμνότητος, μακρυνομένοις.
3. α΄. Ἀγὼν τῆς νηστείας πρῶτος, τῶν πολυτελῶν καὶ λιπαρῶν βρωμάτων ἡ ἀποχή, ἡ τοῦ ἐκ τοῦ πλήθους τῶν σιτίων βάρους τὴν
20 κοιλίαν ἀποφορτίζουσα, καὶ τὸ μὲν σῶμα ἐλαφρύνουσα πρὸς τὴν τῶν καλῶν ὑπηρεσίαν, τὴν δὲ διάβλεψιν τοῦ νοῦ καθαρὰν διατηροῦσα, ὡς τὴν ἐκ τῶν ἀναθυμιάσεων ἀχλὺν τῶν ἐδεσμάτων τῇ λεπτῇ διαίτῃ διασκεδάζουσα καὶ καθάπερ τι σκότος διαχωρίζουσα τῷ ἑαυτῆς φωτί.
4. β΄. Δεύτερος ἀγών, ἡ διὰ τῶν λαχάνων καὶ ὀσπρίων καὶ τοῦ
25 ἄρτου καὶ τὸ ὕδατος σύμμετρος μετάληψις, στηρίζουσα τὸ σκληρὸν τῆς νηστείας καὶ δίκην στερεώματος τὴν ἐκ τοῦ κόρου πλημμύραν διαχωρίζουσα καὶ τὴν χάριν τῆς ἐγκρατείας μὴ ἀτιμάζουσα.
5. γ΄. Τρίτος ἀγών, τὸ πᾶσαν πονηρὰν πρᾶξιν ἀπονεκρῶσαι καὶ γλωσσαλγίας ῥύμην ἀναστεῖλαι. τῆς καθ᾽ ἡδονὴν γὰρ ἐνεργείας

9 ἐλλείψεις corr.: ἐλλείψις ΟΑ   cc. 3-8 Numeri marginales desunt in A
18 λιπαρῶν corr.: λυπαρῶν ΟΑ   26 πλημμύραν Α   29 γλωσσαλγίας corr.:
γλωσαλγείας ΟΑ

ON FASTING

1. Let us gladly welcome the arrival of the orderly and most venerable fast, because by neglecting it we have succumbed to forgetfulness. The nearness of the fast immediately reminds us of the evils we have experienced when we transgressed this command and, in turn, of the good things of which we have been deemed worthy when we kept it. The first and the second Adam are witnesses to our words: the first, in that he became the author of corruption because he did not keep the fast;[1] the second, in that he was called the first-fruit of incorruption[2] because by assuming our nature he made up for what we lacked.

2. By fasting in the desert Christ put the tempter to flight and secured for us the victory. We must therefore make known the advent of the fast through its works, so that from our own successful observance of it we may recognize the true character of self-discipline and come to love its beauty. It is necessary, then, to list the struggles associated with fasting, so that those who by the pursuit of pleasure have distanced themselves from its embrace, that is, from chastity and piety, may have way of recognizing its form.

3. (i) The first struggle associated with fasting is abstinence from costly, rich foods. This unburdens the stomach from the heaviness of a multitude of foods. It lightens the body for the service of the good, while keeping the clear vision of the mind pure, as if scattering the mist of food vapours by a simple regimen and separating it like some sort of darkness by its own light.

4. (ii) The second struggle involves a moderate consumption of food, consisting of greens, vegetables, bread and water. This supports the austerity of fasting and like a firmament[3] it separates the flood-waters of satiety without depreciating the grace of self-discipline.

5. (iii) The third struggle entails killing off every evil practice and restraining the impulse of talkativeness. For when an activity based

---

[1] Gen 3:6.
[2] Cf. 1 Cor 15:20.
[3] Cf. Gen 1:6.

30 καταργουμένης τῆς καὶ τὴν ψυχὴν καὶ τὸ σῶμα ἐκλυούσης καὶ
χαυνούσης, οἱ κατ' ἀρετὴν τρόποι βλαστάνουσι, καὶ οἱ καίριοι λόγοι
καὶ οἱ θεῖοι ὕμνοι τοῦ στόματος ἐξανθοῦσι.

6. δ'. Τέταρτος ἀγών, τὸ τὰς προσβαλλούσας μνήμας τῶν ὁρα-
θέντων καὶ πραχθέντων ἐμπαθῶς ἐκ πρώτης ἐννοίας ἀποκρούεσθαι
35 καὶ μὴ διὰ τῆς τῶν λογισμῶν πολυνοίας ἐᾶν συνήδεσθαι τὴν ψυχὴν
καὶ πρὸς τὸ τῆς συγκαταθέσεως φρέαρ κατασύρεσθαι ταύτην.

7. ε'. Πέμπτος ἀγών, τὸ τὴν ἐπιθυμίαν τῶν ὀφθαλμῶν καὶ τῶν
πονηρῶν ἀκουσμάτων ἀποδιαστῆσαι, ὅπως τῶν κατὰ τὴν ὄψιν καὶ
τὴν ἀκοὴν θυρίδων καλῶς ἀνοιγομένων καὶ κλειομένων, ἀνενόχλητος
40 ἡ διάνοια μένῃ καὶ τῷ φωτὶ τῆς γνώσεως ὁ νοῦς ἐνδιατρίβῃ.

8. ς'. Ἕκτος ἀγών, τὸ καὶ τὰς ἐν τῇ διανοίᾳ τυπουμένας ψιλὰς
φαντασίας ἐξαλείφειν τῇ νηφαλίῳ προσευχῇ καὶ τῇ μετὰ ταπεινοῦ
φρονήματος διηνεκεῖ μελέτῃ τῶν θείων λόγων.

9. Τοῖς τοσούτοις ἄθλοις τῆς νηστείας ὁ νοῦς ἐξεταζόμενος καὶ
45 τῆς τῶν παρόντων ἐπιθυμίας ἀπολυόμενος καὶ τῆς τῶν γηΐνων
φροντίδος ἀπαλλαττόμενος καὶ πάσης ἐννοίας τῶν ὄντων ἐξιστάμενος,
πρὸς τὸν θεὸν διαβαίνει· καὶ τὴν ἐπιθυμίαν δεσμεύων αὐτῷ καὶ δι'
ἀγάπης ἑνούμενος, τῆς ἐκεῖθεν ἐκβλυζούσης εὐφροσύνης καταπολαύει
καὶ τῆς ἀπορρήτου μακαριότητος καταξιοῦται. εἴθιστο καὶ γὰρ τῇ
50 νηστείᾳ τῷ τηροῦντι ταύτην συντηρεῖν τὰ ἐκ θεοῦ δεδομένα χαρίσματα. καὶ τοῦτο διδάχθητι ἀπὸ τοῦ προπάτορος. ἕως καὶ γὰρ ἐκεῖνος
τὴν νηστείαν εἶχε χειραγωγὸν καὶ τῆς ἐδωδῆς τοῦ ἀπηγορευμένου
ξύλου ἀπείχετο, καὶ ἡ πάντων τῶν ἐν τῷ παραδείσῳ ξύλων τράπεζα
παρὰ τῆς νηστείας αὐτῷ παρετίθετο· ἡνίκα δὲ τὴν νηστείαν ἀπώσατο,
55 τοῦ μὲν ἀπωμότου καρποῦ ἐγεύσατο, ἐκείνων δὲ πάντων ἀπώλεσε τὴν
ἀπόλαυσιν.

10. Οὕτως ἡ νηστεία τοὺς αἱρουμένους συζῆν αὐτῇ τῆς τῶν
φθειρομένων ἐπιθυμίας ἀπογυμνοῦσα τὴν τῆς θείας ἀγάπης περιβολὴν
ἐπενδύει καὶ χαρᾶς ἀϊδίου πληροῖ· ἐν Χριστῷ Ἰησοῦ τῷ κυρίῳ ἡμῶν,
60 αὐτῷ ἡ δόξα εἰς τοὺς αἰῶνας. Ἀμήν.

---

43 διηνεκεῖ corr.: διηνεκῇ OA   48 ἀγάπης corr.: ἀγάπην OA

on pleasure — one that leaves both soul and body in a lax and lazy condition — has been destroyed, the ways of virtue begin to grow and timely words and divine hymns blossom forth from the mouth.

6. (iv) The fourth struggle involves driving away, right from the first moment of their conception, the attacks brought on by memories of things seen and done in passion. It also involves not allowing the soul to share any pleasure from the distraction of thoughts and to be pulled down into the pit of consent.

7. (v) The fifth struggle involves putting aside the lust of the eyes as well as of all evil talk, so that the discursive intellect may remain undisturbed by the natural opening and closing of the doors of sight and hearing and that the mind may linger in the light of knowledge.

8. (vi) The sixth struggle entails the eradication even of the impressions of simple phantasies in the discursive intellect by means of vigilant prayer and constant, humble-minded meditation on divine words.

9. Through such contests of fasting, the mind is tested and set free from desire for present realities, delivered from thoughts of earthly things, and passing beyond every concept of beings it wins through to God. Binding its desire to him and uniting itself with him in love, it enjoys to the full the joy that issues forth from him, and is deemed worthy of ineffable blessedness. For by its nature fasting preserves in the one who observes it the gifts received from God. This is the lesson you should learn from our forefather Adam. As long as he kept the fast as his guide and avoided eating from the forbidden tree, the table of all the trees in paradise was set before him by the fast. But when he spurned the fast, he ate of the proscribed tree and lost the enjoyment of all those others.[4]

10. In this way, the fast strips those who choose to live by it of desire for the things that perish, clothes them with the garment of divine love and fills them with eternal joy in Christ Jesus our Lord, to him be glory forever. Amen.

---

[4] Gen 2:7–3:24.

Διδασκαλία πρὸς μοναζούσας εὐφυῶς τὸ μυστήριον
τῆς Χριστοῦ γεννήσεως προσαρμόζουσα τῇ μοναδικῇ πολιτείᾳ

1. Ἀδελφαὶ καὶ μητέρες, εἰ καὶ τῷ σώματι ἀπόδημός εἰμι ἐξ ὑμῶν,
ἀλλὰ τῷ πνεύματι ἐπιδημῶ ἐν ὑμῖν· πολυειδῆ γὰρ τὸν τῆς ἑνώσεως
5 τρόπον ὁ πλάσας ἐν οἰκτιρμοῖς θεὸς ἐποιήσατο, ἵνα μὴ διὰ τὴν τῶν
ἔργων πενίαν ὁ τῆς ἑνώσεως πλοῦτος ἡμᾶς φεύγει. καὶ γὰρ οὐ μόνον
δι' αὐτοπροσώπου παρουσίας ἡ ἕνωσις γίνεται, ἀλλὰ καὶ διὰ τῆς
ὁμογνωμοσύνης καὶ διὰ τῆς ὑπὲρ ἀλλήλων εὐχῆς καὶ διὰ τῆς πρὸς
ἀλλήλους ἀγάπης καὶ διὰ τῶν τῆς ἐπιστολῆς γραμμάτων καὶ διὰ τῆς
10 ἐκ τῶν ῥημάτων ὁμιλίας τὸ τῆς κατὰ θεὸν ἑνώσεως ἔργον συνίσταται·
ἃ δὴ πάντα κατὰ τὸν παρελθόντα καιρὸν ἐτελεῖτο.

2. Νῦν δὲ εἰ καὶ τοῦ σώματος ἡ παρουσία καὶ τοῦ στόματος ἡ
ζῶσα διδασκαλία οὐκέτι τελεῖται, ἀλλ' ἡ ὑπὲρ ὑμῶν εὐχὴ καὶ ἡ
ὀφειλομένη κατὰ θεὸν ἀγάπη διηνεκῶς ἐνεργοῦνται. διὰ γοῦν τοῦτο
15 καὶ σήμερον κέκριταί μοι ὁμιλῆσαι ὑμῖν καὶ διὰ τῆς παρούσης
κατηχήσεως, εἰς τοῦτο κινησάσης με τῆς κατὰ σάρκα τοῦ κυρίου
γεννήσεως, ἧς τὸ μυστήριον τὰς ὁδοὺς τῆς σωτηρίας ἡμῖν ὑπογράφει
καὶ τὴν οὐράνιον πολιτείαν σοφώτατα ἐκπαιδεύει τοὺς ἐπαγ-
γελλομένους ἡμᾶς ἀκολουθεῖν αὐτῷ.
20 **3.** Ὁ μονογενὴς υἱὸς τοῦ θεοῦ, δίχα μητρὸς ἐκ τοῦ πατρὸς
γεννώμενος, γεννᾶται καὶ δίχα πατρὸς ἐκ τῆς μητρός, ἵνα σύ, ἡ πατέρα
καὶ μητέρα καὶ συγγένειαν πᾶσαν καταλιποῦσα, τῷ δὲ κυρίῳ προσ-
κολληθεῖσα, ψάλλῃς διηνεκῶς· *ὁ πατήρ μου καὶ ἡ μήτηρ μου ἐγκατέλιπόν
με, ὁ δὲ κύριος προσελάβετό με.* Χριστὸς ἐκ παρθένου γεγένηται καὶ
25 τὴν παρθένον μητέρα πεποίηκε καὶ ἡ μήτηρ παρθένος μεμένηκεν·
ἀμφότερα παράδοξα καὶ νόμον ἀνθρώπινον ὑπερβαίνοντα, ἵνα σύ,
ἡ τὴν γαμικὴν συνάφειαν ἀποστραφεῖσα καὶ τῆς τοῦ κόσμου ὁμιλίας

---

6 φεύγει OA: φεύγῃ rectius   8 ὁμογνωμοσύνης corr.: ὁμογνομοσύνης OA

MD 13

AN INSTRUCTION ADDRESSED TO NUNS, CLEVERLY COMPARING
THE MYSTERY OF CHRIST'S BIRTH TO THE MONASTIC WAY OF LIFE[1]

1. Sisters and Mothers, though I am absent from you in body, still I am present among you in spirit, for God, who in his mercy fashioned us, has provided for many different kinds of unity, lest the riches found in unity escape us on account of the poverty of our works. Unity is brought about not only by personal presence, but also by like-mindedness, by prayer on one another's behalf, by the mutual practice of charity, by the exchange of letters and through instructive discourses is the work of godly unity realized. All these have been our practices in times past.

2. But now, even though my bodily presence and personal instruction by word of mouth are not now possible, still my prayer on your behalf and the charity I owe you in God are my constant concern. For this reason, then, I have decided to converse with you today by means of the present instruction, having been moved to do so by the Lord's birth in the flesh. This mystery delineates for us the ways of salvation and provides the wisest of teachings on the heavenly life to us who profess to follow him.

3. The only-begotten Son of God, begotten from the Father without a mother, is also born from his mother without a father,[2] that you, who have abandoned father and mother and all family relations and have joined yourself to the Lord, may continually sing the Psalm verse: "My father and my mother have forsaken me, but the Lord received me."[3] Christ was begotten of a virgin and has made the virgin a mother and the mother has remained a virgin — two wondrous realities that go beyond the laws of human nature — that you, who have renounced

---

[1] The text and translation of this discourse was published by S. Salaville, "Un directeur spirituel à Byzance au début du xivᵉ siècle: Théolepte de Philadelphie. Homélie inédite sur Noël et la vie religieuse" in *Mélanges Joseph de Ghellinck* (Museum lessianum. Section historique 14; Gembloux, 1951), pp. 877-887.

[2] This is a loose paraphrase of the kontakion of Romanos the Melodist sung at Matins on December 26, the Synaxis of the Most Holy Theotokos: ὁ πρὸ ἑωσφόρου ἐκ πατρὸς ἀμήτωρ γεννηθείς, ἐπὶ γῆς ἀπάτωρ ἐσαρκώθη σήμερον ἐκ σοῦ ... . See *The Festal Menaion*, translated by Mother Mary and Kallistos Ware, p. 292.

[3] Ps 26:10. Note that most of the references in the text are singular and thus are addressed in a particular way to the abbess Eulogia.

ἀποχωρήσασα ἑαυτήν, οὐ μόνον τῷ σώματι ἀλλὰ καὶ τῷ πνεύματι
παρθένος τελῇς· καὶ ὡς ἀπώσω τὰς κατὰ πρᾶξιν σαρκικὰς ἡδονάς,
30 ἀποκρούσῃς καὶ τὰς διὰ τῶν λογισμῶν ψυχικὰς ἐπιθυμίας, τὸν τοῦ
κόσμου συνδυασμὸν ἐν τῷ φρονήματι μὴ ποιουμένη, σώματι δὲ καὶ
ψυχῇ μοναχῇ θεωρουμένη, καὶ τὸν ὅρον τῆς μοναδικῆς ζωῆς καὶ
ἐν τῷ ἔξωθεν σχήματι καὶ ἐν τῷ ἔσωθεν φρονήματι ἀληθῶς διασώζουσα.
35 **4.** Σοῦ δὲ καθαρευούσης ἀπὸ σαρκικῶν πράξεων καὶ λογισμῶν
ἐμπαθῶν, ἡ τῆς παρθενίας φαιδρότης ἐν σοὶ ἀνατέλλει καὶ αὐτίκα
συλλαμβάνεις τὸν τοῦ θεοῦ λόγον, μηδὲν ἄλλο βαστάζουσα ἐν τῇ
καρδίᾳ ἢ τὴν μελέτην τῆς ἀποταγῆς καὶ τῆς ὑπακοῆς, τὴν φροντίδα
τῶν θεοποιῶν ἐντολῶν καὶ τὴν μνήμην τῶν ἐν ἀρχῇ συνθηκῶν· καὶ
40 οὕτω χρηματίζεις μήτηρ Χριστοῦ, πειθομένη καὶ ὑπείκουσα τῇ
προεστώσῃ σου διηνεκῶς. καὶ γὰρ ὅταν ἔργοις πρὸς αὐτὴν ὑποταγὴν
δεικνύῃς καὶ ὅταν πράγμασιν αὐτοῖς τὴν ὑπακοὴν ἐκπεραίνῃς, τότε
σωματοποιεῖς τὸν τῆς ἀρετῆς λόγον, γεννῶσα καὶ γεωργοῦσα αὐτὸν
διὰ τῶν τοῦ σώματος πράξεων καὶ φανεροποιοῦσα τοῖς ἔξω τὸν ἔσω
45 τῆς ψυχῆς σου διαλογισμὸν τῶν ἐντολῶν καὶ ὁρατὸν καθιστῶσα τοῖς
ἀνθρώποις διὰ τοῦ τρόπου ἀόρατον ὄντα τὸ πρότερον.

5. Χριστὸς ἐν τῷ σπηλαίῳ γεγένηται, ἵνα σὺ ἐν ᾧ εἰσῆλθες
μοναστηρίῳ προσμένουσα διὰ τῆς τῶν ἐντολῶν ἐργασίας πνευματικῶς
ἀναγεννηθῇς. ποθοῦσα γὰρ ἐν τοῖς οὐρανοῖς ἀπογραφῆναι, κατέλιπες
50 πάντα τὰ ἐπὶ τῆς γῆς καὶ αὐτὴν τὴν ὀνομασίαν ἤλλαξας, ἐκείνων
πάντων ἀλλοτριωθεῖσα, ὅσοι τὰ ὀνόματα αὐτῶν ἐπὶ τῶν γαιῶν
ἐκτήσαντο. διὸ καὶ τόπον μὴ ἔχουσα εἰς τὸ καταλῦσαι, παρεγένου
ἐν τῷ μοναστηρίῳ ὡς ἐν σπηλαίῳ τινὶ καὶ τίκτεις διὰ τῆς ἐμπράκτου
ἀποταγῆς τὸν τῆς ἐντολῆς λόγον, ὃν συνέλαβες ἐν τῇ ψυχῇ διὰ τῆς
55 παρθένου διανοίας καὶ καθαρᾶς ἀπὸ κοσμικῆς ἐπιθυμίας.

6. Χριστὸς σπαργάνοις περιεδέθη, διδάσκων καὶ σὲ τὰ εὐτελῆ
ῥάκη ἃ περιεβάλου ἀσπάζεσθαι καὶ ἀρκεῖσθαι τοῖς μοναδικοῖς καὶ

the marriage bond and retired from converse with the world, may make yourself a virgin not only in body but also in spirit. As you have eliminated from your conduct the pleasures of the flesh, may you oust also the wrongful desires of the soul from your thoughts. While you give no ground in your attitudes to worldly attachment, consider yourself a nun in body and soul, truly preserving the prescriptions of the monastic life both in outward form and in interior attitude.

4.   When you are purified of carnal practices and impassioned thoughts, the radiance of virginity will dawn within you and straight-away you will conceive the Word of God, bearing naught else in your heart but concern for renunciation and obedience, mindfulness for the divinizing commandments, and remembrance of the vows you made in the beginning. And so you are called mother of Christ, if you are ever obedient and submissive to your superior. Whenever you demonstrate your submission to her in deeds and whenever you achieve complete obedience in your very acts, then you give bodily existence to the word of virtue, begetting and cultivating it by the practices of the body, manifesting in your external actions the soul's interior understanding of the commandments and by your conduct making visible to men what was formerly invisible.[4]

5.   Christ was born in a cave,[5] that you remaining in the monastery you entered may be reborn spiritually through the practice of the commandments. Longing to have your name enrolled in heaven,[6] you abandoned everything on earth and even your name you changed because you had estranged yourself from all those who acquired their names in earthly ways. And so, with no place to lodge,[7] you came to the monastery as to a kind of cave and through your actual practices of renunciation you give birth to the word of the commandment, which you conceived in your soul through your virginal mind, pure of all worldly desire.

6.   Christ was wrapped in swaddling clothes to teach you to welcome the simple rags with which you are clothed,[8] to be satisfied with the

---

[4] Cf. Mt 5:16.

[5] Christ's birth in a cave is frequently mentioned throughout the liturgy for December 25: e.g., the Sticheron of Anatolios at the end of Great Compline (*Festal Menaion*, p. 266).

[6] Cf. Lk 2:2-3.

[7] Cf. Lk 2:7.

[8] This is undoubtedly a reference to the Sixth Ode of the First Canon sung at Matins on Christmas: ἐν φάτνῃ τῶν ἀλόγων ἀνακλίνεται· ῥάκει σπαργανοῦται (*Festal Menaion*, p. 276; cf. Lk 2:7). The term ῥακενδύτης, 'rag-wearer', was occasionally used of monks.

ἀναγκαίοις ἐνδύμασι καὶ μήτε περιττὰ περιβόλαια κτᾶσθαι, μήτε τὰ
τῶν χρωμάτων βαθύτερα ζητεῖν καὶ περὶ πολλοῦ ποιεῖσθαι. εἰ γὰρ
60 ἀνερευνᾷς τὰ τοιαῦτα καὶ χρῶμα βαθὺ σκοπεῖς καὶ κατάκορον καὶ
ἐρίου ἁπαλότητα καὶ νημάτων λεπτότητα καὶ ὑφασμάτων
ἐπιτηδειότητα, πολλάκις δὲ καὶ τὰ διὰ τῆς μετάξης ἱστουργούμενα
πολυπραγμονεῖς, ἐν ὑποκρίσει τὴν ἐπαγγελίαν ἐποίησω. οὐ γὰρ
ἔφυγες κόσμον, ἀλλ᾽ ὃν ἔδοξας κόσμον ἀρνεῖσθαι ἀμειβομένη τὸ
65 σχῆμα, μᾶλλον τούτῳ προσήρμοσαι καὶ τῶν ἑταιρίδων οὐδὲν δια-
φέρεις. δεῖ οὖν τοῖς σεμνοτάτοις ἀμφίοις στοιχεῖν καὶ περιδεσμεῖν
ἑαυτὴν τοῖς εὐτελέσι ῥάκεσι, ὅπως τῇ τούτων τραχυτάτῃ περιβολῇ
τῶν σαρκῶν ἡ ἁπαλότης περιστελλομένη τὴν ἐκ τῆς ἁφῆς λειότητα
ἀποπέμπηται, μήτε εἰς ὑπόμνησιν ἐρχομένη τῶν ἡδονῶν, καὶ τὸν
70 ὄγκον τῆς ματαίας δόξης ὑποχαλῶσα διὰ τῆς εὐτελείας τῶν ἐνδυμάτων
καὶ τοῦ ἀπεριέργως διακεῖσθαι πρὸς ταῦτα.

7. Χριστὸς ἐν τῇ φάτνῃ τῶν ἀλόγων ἀνεκλίθη, παιδεύων σε τὴν
γλωσσαλγίαν τῶν κατεσθιόντων σε ἀνθρώπων ταῖς λοιδορίαις καὶ
ταῖς συκοφαντίαις γενναίως φέρειν καὶ ἀνάπαυσιν ἡγεῖσθαι τοὺς ὑπὲρ
75 ἀρετῆς ἐπερχομένους πειρασμοὺς καὶ ὀνειδισμούς, καὶ μὴ
ἀντιμάχεσθαι τοῖς κακολογοῦσι, σιωπᾶν δὲ καὶ καταφρονεῖν τῆς ἰδίας
τιμῆς, ἵνα τῶν σῶν ὕβρεων τὴν ὑπομονὴν ὁρῶντες οἱ ἄνθρωποι δίκην
ἀστέρος λάμπουσαν, τὴν κοσμικὴν σύγχυσίν τε καὶ ταραχὴν ὡς
ἄλλην Περσίδα καταλιπόντες, πρὸς τὸν κατὰ θεὸν βίον ὁδοιπορήσ-
80 ωσι, τὴν μονὴν ὡς Βηθλεὲμ καταλαβόντες καὶ μιμηταὶ τοῦ σοῦ βίου
γενέσθαι ποθοῦντες.
8. Ἢ γὰρ τῶν κοσμικῶν πολλοί, τὴν ἐπαινετήν σου ἀναστροφὴν
καὶ τὸν ἀπέριττόν σου βίον ἐκπλαγέντες, πρὸς τὸν ἴσόν σοι τῆς
ἀποταγῆς δρόμον βαδίσουσι καὶ ὡς δῶρα τῷ θεῷ τὴν ἑαυτῶν
85 περιουσίαν προσοίσουσιν· ἢ πολλαὶ τῶν συνασκουμένων μοναχῶν,
ἰδοῦσαι τὴν ταπείνωσιν φρονήματός σου καὶ τὴν ἐν τοῖς λυπηροῖς
ὑπομονὴν καὶ καρτερίαν, ἀποστήσονται τῆς πονηρᾶς συνηθείας καὶ
ὑπακούσονται τῷ θελήματί σου, ἀλλὰ καὶ ὡς δῶρα προσκομίσουσί
σοι πληροφορίαν καὶ ἀγάπην καὶ εὐλάβειαν. καὶ οἱ ποιμαίνοντές σε

---

65 τούτῳ corr.: τοῦτο OA　　προσήρμοσαι corr.: προσήρμωσαι OA　　80 Βηθλεὲμ corr.: Βιθλεὲμ OA

essential monastic garments and not acquire extra clothing, nor seek with much to-do those with more richness of colour. For if you pursue such things and look for deep, rich colours, softness in wool, fine quality in linen and skilfully woven garments, and if you are too often concerned about clothing woven of silk, you have made an hypocrisy of your profession. You have not fled the world; rather, you have attached yourself to the world you thought you denied by exchanging your outer garment and you are no different from the courtesans. You must therefore be content with your most sacred robes and clothe yourself with simple rags so that the delicacy of the flesh wrapped in this very rough clothing that these provide will be deprived of the pleasantness that comes from touch; you will not suffer the remembrance of pleasures and you will lay down the burden of empty honours through the simplicity of your clothing and through your indifference to these things.

7.   Christ was laid in a manger for irrational animals[9] to teach you to suffer valiantly the prating of people who would prey upon you with abuses and slanders, and to consider as your rest the trials and reproaches occasioned by virtue, to refrain from fighting back against malicious talk, and to keep silence and despise your own honour. Then, when people see your patient endurance of insults shining like a star, they will abandon the confusion and disturbance of the world, like another Persia, and will make their way towards a life in God, arriving at the monastery, like Bethlehem, and desiring to become imitators of your way of life.[10]

8.   Either many of those in the world will be struck by your praiseworthy way of life and your frugal lifestyle and will walk the same route of renunciation as you did, bringing their riches to God as gifts; or many of your fellow nuns, seeing the humility of your attitude and your patient endurance and perseverance in sufferings, will refrain from their evil habits and submit to your will, and moreover they will bring you as gifts their confidence, charity and reverence.[11]

---

[9] Same liturgical reference as in the preceding note; cf. Lk 2:7.

[10] Cf. Mt 2:1-20 (the Gospel at the Liturgy on December 25, also read at the Great or Royal Hours on the previous evening). The liturgical texts refer frequently to the Magi travelling from the East, guided by the Star, to their encounter with Herod, to the gifts they presented to the Christ child and to the flight of the Holy Family into Egypt. At Great Compline a hymn by John the Monk refers to the Magi as 'Kings of the Persians' (*Festal Menaion*, p. 264).

[11] The gifts, here mentioned twice, are seen in association with the gifts brought by the Magi to the Christ child. The second half of the sentence appears to be a direct reference to Eirene-Eulogia.

90 δὲ πνευματικῶς ἐν πᾶσιν οἷς ὁρῶσιν ἐν σοὶ ἔργοις καὶ οἷς ἀκούουσι
παρὰ σοῦ λόγοις θαυμάσουσι καὶ δοξάσουσι τὸν θεόν, τὸν
οἰκονομοῦντα τὴν σωτηρίαν τῶν ἀνθρώπων· *λαμψάτω, γάρ φησι, τὸ*
φῶς ὑμῶν ἔμπροσθεν τῶν ἀνθρώπων, ὅπως ἴδωσι τὰ καλὰ ὑμῶν ἔργα
καὶ δοξάσωσι τὸν πατέρα ὑμῶν τὸν ἐν τοῖς οὐρανοῖς.
95 **9.** Χριστὸς γάλακτι ἐκτρέφεται, ἵνα καὶ σὺ τὰ ἁπλῶς ἐκτεθειμένα
τοῦ εὐαγγελίου μαθήματα μανθάνῃς καὶ τοὺς βίους τῶν ἐν ἁπλότητι
ζησάντων μακαρίων πατέρων ἀναγινώσκῃς, οἵ σε πρὸς τὴν γαλήνην
τοῦ ἐπουρανίου λιμένος προσορμίζουσι, τὴν τῶν δικαίων λαμπρότητα
διασκοπουμένην, ταῖς μὲν θεωρίαις ταῖς ἀνωτάτω πιαινομένην, πρὸς
100 δὲ τοὺς ἐκ τοῦ κόσμου λόγους καὶ τὴν καταργουμένην σοφίαν
ὑπνώττουσαν.
10. Ἡρώδην φεύγει Χριστός, νουθετῶν καὶ σὲ σαρκὸς
ἐπαναστάσεις φεύγειν. εἰς Αἴγυπτον ἔρχεται, ἐντελλόμενός σοι κόποις
ἀσκήσεως τὰ σκιρτήματα τῶν παθῶν καταβάλλειν καὶ μνήμῃ γεέννης
105 τὴν πύρωσιν τῆς σαρκὸς παύειν.
11. Ἐὰν οὖν τῇ κακώσει τῆς σκληραγωγίας ταπεινώσῃς τὴν
σάρκα καὶ ἐὰν τῷ φόβῳ τῶν κολάσεων τὸν παλαιὸν ἀποβάλῃς
ἄνθρωπον, τὸν κατὰ τὰς ἐπιθυμίας τῆς ἀπάτης φθειρόμενον, ἀκούσεις
καὶ σύ· *πορεύου εἰς γῆν Ἰσραήλ,* ἤτοι τοῦ νοῦ τοῦ ὁρῶντος τὸν θεόν.
110 ἀκούσεις δὲ καὶ τοῦτο, ἐπειδὴ τεθνήκασιν οἱ τῆς ἡδυπαθείας λογισμοὶ
οἱ ζητοῦντες ἀποκτεῖναι τὴν κατὰ Χριστὸν νηπιάζουσαν ψυχὴν καὶ
ζῶσαν ἐν τῷ Χριστῷ· *ἐὰν μὴ ἐπιστραφῆτε,* φησί, *καὶ γένησθε ὡς τὰ*
παιδία, οὐ μὴ εἰσέλθητε εἰς τὴν βασιλείαν τῶν οὐρανῶν· καὶ πάλιν, *ἄφετε*
τὰ παιδία· τῶν γὰρ τοιούτων ἐστὶν ἡ βασιλεία τῶν οὐρανῶν.

115 **12.** Καὶ γὰρ ἀληθῶς ἡ ἐπιτεταγμένη ἐγκράτεια καὶ ἡ ἐπίμονος
μνήμη τοῦ θανάτου καὶ τοῦ αἰωνίου πυρὸς καὶ τῶν λοιπῶν κολάσεων
μαστίζουσαι τὸ φρόνημα τῆς σαρκός, ἀπονεκροῦσιν αὐτὸ καὶ ζῆν
προξενοῦσι τῇ ψυχῇ τὴν ἐν Χριστῷ κεκρυμμένην ζωήν, εἰσάγουσαι
αὐτὴν εἰς τὴν πνευματικὴν γνῶσιν, γῆν τυγχάνουσαν τοῦ καθαρῶς
120 εὐχομένου νοός, ὥστε δύνασθαι καὶ σὲ τότε μετὰ τοῦ ἀποστόλου
λέγειν· *ζῶ δὲ ἐγὼ οὐκέτι, ζῇ δὲ ἐν ἐμοὶ Χριστός,* ὁ ὢν εὐλογητὸς εἰς
τοὺς αἰῶνας τῶν αἰώνων. Ἀμήν.

---

99 ἀνωτάτω corr.: ἀνοτάτω OA   115 ἐπιτεταγμένη corr.: ἐπιτεταμένη OA

Further, your spiritual shepherds will marvel at all the works they see in you and at all the words they hear from you and will give glory to God, who bestows salvation on men.[12] For scripture says, "Let your light shine before men that they may see your good works and give glory to your Father in heaven."[13]

9.   Christ is nourished with milk in order that you may learn the teachings set out simply in the Gospel and read the lives of the blessed Fathers who lived in simplicity; they will bring you to anchor in the calm of the heavenly harbour, you who look for the radiance of the just and are enriched with the highest contemplations but are asleep to the discourse of the world and the wisdom that passes away.[14]

10.   Christ flees from Herod to counsel you to flee from the rebellions of the flesh. He goes to Egypt to command you to subdue the unruliness of the passions by ascetic labours and to halt the burning of the flesh with the memory of Gehenna.[15]

11.   If then you humble the flesh by the infliction of austerities and if through the fear of punishments you cast off the 'old man' now corrupted with deceitful desires,[16] you too will hear the words, "Proceed into the land of Israel,"[17] that is, the land of the mind that sees God. And when you have put to death the thoughts of pleasureful satisfaction which seek to kill the soul that becomes like a little child and lives in Christ, you will hear this too: "Unless you turn and become like children," as scripture says, "you will never enter the kingdom of heaven";[18] and again, "Give leave to the little children, for to such belongs the kingdom of heaven."[19]

12.   For indeed the imposed discipline and the constant remembrance of death, the eternal fire and the other punishments scourge the carnal attitudes, deadening them, while procuring for the soul to live the life hidden in Christ.[20] They introduce the soul to spiritual knowledge, which is the land of the mind that practises pure prayer, so that you too can say with the apostle, "It is no longer I who live, but Christ who lives in me,"[21] who is blessed forever and ever. Amen.

[12] Cf. Lk 2:8-12 (Lk 2:1-20 is read on the evening of December 24).
[13] Mt 5:16.
[14] Cf. 1 Cor 1:20, 13:8.
[15] Mt 2:13-15
[16] Cf. Eph 4:22.
[17] Mt 2:20.
[18] Mt 18:3.
[19] Mt 19:14.
[20] Col 3:3
[21] Gal 2:20.

Περὶ ταπεινώσεως καὶ διαφορᾶς ἀρετῶν

1. Ὥσπερ ὁ πεινῶν καὶ ζητῶν ἄρτον ἄρτον φαντάζεται καὶ ἄρτον ἐπιποθεῖ, οὕτω καὶ ὁ τὴν τοῦ καλοῦ ζήτησιν ποιούμενος γνῶσιν ἔχει καλοῦ καὶ ἔφεσιν, ἐκ δὲ τῆς γνώσεως καὶ τῆς ἐφέσεως τοὺς
5 καθήκοντας ἐξευρίσκει τρόπους πρὸς τὴν τοῦ ἀγαθοῦ κτῆσίν τε καὶ ἀπόλαυσιν· *οἱ δὲ ἐκζητοῦντες, φησί, τὸν κύριον οὐκ ἐλαττωθήσονται παντὸς ἀγαθοῦ.* ἀγαθὸν οὖν κυρίως καὶ φύσει ἀγαθὸν καὶ πρῶτον ὁ θεός, παρ' οὗ καὶ ἅπαν καλὸν πρὸς ἡμᾶς καταπέμπεται. ὡς γὰρ ἀπὸ τοῦ ἡλιακοῦ δίσκου αἱ ἀκτῖνες ἐξικνούμεναι τὰ ἐπίγεια καταφωτί-
10 ζουσιν, οὕτω καὶ τὰ θεῖα χαρίσματα ἐκ τοῦ μεγάλου καὶ ἀπροσίτου φωτὸς προϊόντα τοὺς μετόχους ἀγαθοποιεῖ ἐξαλλάσσοντα αὐτοὺς διὰ τοῦ κατὰ τὰς ἀρετὰς πόνου καὶ τοῦ πρὸς τὸν θεὸν πόθου· *πᾶν, γάρ φησι, δώρημα τέλειον ἄνωθέν ἐστι καταβαῖνον.* αἱ τοίνυν κατὰ τὰς σωτηρίους ἐντολὰς ἀρεταί, καθάπερ σπέρματα τῇ καρδίᾳ καταβληθεῖ-
15 σαι, τὴν προαίρεσιν ὡς γεωργὸν ἐκκαλοῦνται πρὸς προκοπὴν τοῦ πληρώματος τοῦ Χριστοῦ.

2. Πᾶσαι μὲν οὖν αἱ ἀρεταὶ ὡς θλίψεις διὰ θεὸν κόσμου καὶ σαρκὸς τὴν ψυχὴν ἀποδιϊστῶσαι, τὸ τῆς ἡδονῆς καταλύουσι τεῖχος, τὸν δὲ οἶκον τῆς ἁγίας γνώσεως ἀνοικοδομοῦσι. μέσον δὲ τούτων
20 ὁρᾶται διαφορὰ τὸν ἐργάτην ἀπαιτοῦσα ἐπιστημόνως ταύτας μετέρ-χεσθαι πρὸς ἀπαρτισμὸν τῆς καλῶς ἡρμοσμένης ὁλοκληρίας. ἐγκράτεια γὰρ καὶ ὑπομονὴ τὸν θεμέλιον συνιστῶσι, τὸ τῆς ἡδονῆς ἀποξέουσαι λεῖον τῇ τῶν πόνων ἐπιμόνῳ τραχύτητι. ἐπειδὴ γὰρ ἡ ἡδονὴ τοῖς φθειρομένοις τὸν νοῦν προσηλοῖ, ἐπείγονται αὗται αἱ
25 ἀρεταὶ τὸν πρὸς τὴν σάρκα καὶ τὸν κόσμον δεσμὸν τῆς ψυχῆς λῦσαι διὰ τῆς ὑπομονῆς τῶν ἑκουσίων πόνων καὶ τῶν ἀκουσίως ἐπερχομένων θλιβερῶν. αὗται μὲν οὖν αἱ ῥηθεῖσαι δύο ἀρεταὶ τὸν θεμέλιον κατατίθενται τῆς ζητουμένης καθαρότητος.

3. Ἀγρυπνία δὲ καὶ προσευχὴ καὶ ψαλμῳδία καὶ ἀνάγνωσις καὶ
30 τῶν θείων λογίων ἡ ἔμμονος μελέτη καὶ ἡσυχία τὴν πρὸς τὰ καλὰ

---

11 ἐξαλλάσσοντα corr.: ἐξαλάσσοντα OA   21 ἡρμοσμένης corr.: εἱρμοσμένης
OA (cf. 180)

ON HUMILITY AND THE DIFFERENT VIRTUES

1. Just as a hungry person in search of bread phantasizes about bread and yearns for bread, so too someone in search of the good knows and desires the good, and out of knowledge and desire he searches for appropriate ways to acquire and enjoy the good. For scripture says, "Those who seek the Lord will lack for no good thing."[1] God, then, is truly the good and by nature the primary good, from which every good thing is sent down to us.[2] As the rays of the sun's disk reach the earthly regions and illumine them, so too the gifts of God proceed forth from the mighty, inaccessible Light and bestow goodness on those who partake of them, changing them completely by their labour in the virtues and their desire for God. For scripture says, "Every perfect gift comes down from above."[3] Thus, when the virtues associated with the saving power of the commandments have been cast like seeds upon the heart, they call forth the free will like a farmer to effect progress in the fullness of Christ.[4]

2. All the virtues, like hardships suffered for God, distance the soul from the world and the flesh, breaking down the wall of pleasure but rebuilding the house of holy knowledge. But among them there are notable differences, which require the labourer to engage in an intelligent search for those virtues that will complete a well-rounded whole. Self-discipline and patient endurance constitute the foundation, for they scrape off the smooth surface of pleasure with the permanent roughness of labours. Since pleasure fixes the mind upon things that pass away, these particular virtues quickly loose the soul's bondage to the flesh and the world by the patient endurance of willingly accepted labours as well as sufferings that occur against our will. Therefore, these two virtues just mentioned lay down the foundation for the purity we seek.

3. Vigils, prayer, psalmody, reading and constant meditation on the divine scriptures, and tranquillity bring to completion the edification

---

[1] Ps 33:11.
[2] Cf. Gregorios Palamas, *Capita 150*, cc. 34-35.
[3] Jas 1:17.
[4] Cf. Eph 4:13.

οἰκοδομὴν τῆς ψυχῆς διὰ τῆς κατὰ μικρὸν προσθήκης ἀπαρτίζουσαι,
τὴν μὲν τοῦ κόσμου σχέσιν ἐξορίζουσι, τὴν δὲ διάνοιαν ὑψοῦσι τοῦ
μηκέτι ἕρπειν ἐν τοῖς τῶν γηΐνων λογισμοῖς· τὸν δὲ νοῦν πάσης
ἐμπαθοῦς φαντασίας ἀπαλάττουσαι, τὸν καθαρὸν ἀέρα τῶν θείων
35 θεωριῶν ἐμφανίζουσι. τότε δὴ τότε καὶ ἡ κορυφαία ἀγάπη τὸν
καθαρὸν νοῦν διαδεχομένη συνάπτει τῷ θεῷ καὶ τὴν πρὸς αὐτὸν
ἕνωσιν ἀπεργάζεται, τῇ γλυκύτητι τοῦ θεοῦ τὴν θεωρίαν τοῦ νοῦ
κατευφραίνουσα καὶ τὴν μνήμην τῆς φωτοβολούσης αὐτὸν ὑπερβαλλούσης λαμπρότητος ἀναπόσπαστον ποιουμένη. αὕτη ἐστὶν ἡ τῆς
40 καθαρότητος στέγη, πᾶσαν ἡδονὴν καὶ λύπην σαρκὸς καὶ κόσμου
περιαιροῦσα καὶ τὰ ἐπίπονα ἡδέως καταδεχομένη καὶ παρακαλοῦσα
τὴν ψυχὴν διὰ τῆς πρὸς τὸν παρακαλοῦντα θεὸν ἐντεύξεως. ἡ ἀγάπη,
γάρ φησιν, οὐ λογίζεται τὸ κακόν· πάντα στέγει, πάντα ὑπομένει. ἀλλὰ
παρίτω καὶ ἡ σκυθρωπὸς καὶ φαιδρὰ ταπείνωσις, καθάπερ τι
45 ἀκατάλυτον δέμα, συνέχουσα τὴν τῶν ἀρετῶν οἰκοδομὴν καὶ τὴν
καθαρότητα περιέπουσα ἐν τῷ τὴν ῥυπῶσαν κενοδοξίαν ἐκτρίβειν
ἐκ τοῦ μὴ φρονεῖν ὑψηλὰ καὶ τὴν καρδίαν συντρίβειν καὶ τὴν σοφὴν
εὐτέλειαν κατασπάζεσθαι.

4. Ἀλλ᾽ ἐπεὶ τὸ τῶν ἀρετῶν σύστημα τὴν ὁσίαν ταπείνωσιν εἰς
50 μέσον παρήγαγον, καὶ ἡ ἱερὰ ταύτης ἀνέκυψε μνήμη, ἐσχάτως
παραβαλοῦσα ἡ τὰ πρῶτα φέρουσα, ὅπως κἀκ τούτου τὴν οἰκείαν
διάθεσιν ὑποδείξῃ καὶ διδάξῃ· ὁ θέλων, γάρ φησι, πρῶτος εἶναι ἔστω
πάντων ἔσχατος. φέρε, κατὰ τὸ μέτρον τῆς ἐν ἡμῖν διακρίσεως διὰ
βραχέων τὰ ταύτης παραστήσωμεν ἔργα, τοῖς μὲν ἀμελοῦσι χεῖρα
55 βοηθείας παρεχόμενοι πρὸς ἀνόρθωσιν, τοὺς δὲ ἀγωνιζομένους
στηρίζοντες εἰς τὸ μὴ πτῶσιν ἰδεῖν.

5. Ἡ ταπείνωσις δεσμός ἐστι τῶν κατορθωμάτων καὶ ἀφανισμὸς
τῶν ἁμαρτημάτων. ἡ ταπείνωσις συντηρεῖ τὰς ἀρετάς, μὴ ἐῶσα πρὸς
ἐπίδειξιν ποιεῖν τὰ τελούμενα. ἡ ταπείνωσις ἐξαλείφει ἁμαρτήματα,
60 πείθουσα τὸν ῥάθυμον ἐξαγγέλλειν ταῦτα πρὸς ἐξουδένωσιν. ἡ
ταπείνωσις σχῆμα ἑρπετοῦ περιτίθησι τῷ ταπεινόφρονι· ὡς περιστερὰ
δὲ χρυσαυγίζουσα, εἰς οὐρανοὺς αὐτὸν ἀναφέρει καὶ καταπαύει. ἡ
ταπείνωσις δύο πτερὰ περίκειται, τὸν ἐποχούμενον αὐτῇ ὡς ὄρνεον
ἐκ βρόχου καὶ παγίδος λυτρουμένη· ποιεῖ γὰρ αὐτὸν μήτε τὰ οἰκεῖα
65 βλέπειν κατορθώματα, μήτε τὰ ἀλλότρια σκοπεῖν ἁμαρτήματα· φεύγειν

---

38 κατευφραίνουσα conieci: κατευφραίνουσαν ΟΑ

of the soul in good things by gradual accretions. They root out the attachment to the world and raise high the discursive intellect so that it no longer slinks about among the thoughts of earthly things; and by delivering the mind from all impassioned imagining, they reveal the pure air of divine contemplations. Then, and only then, love, the chief of the virtues, takes possession of the pure mind, joins it to God and brings about union with him, gladdening the mind's contemplation with the sweetness of God and rendering inalienable the remembrance of the illuminating radiance that transcends the mind. Love constitutes the roof of purity, which removes all pleasure and grief that comes from the flesh and the world, gladly accepting toil and trouble and consoling the soul in the encounter with God, who consoles us. For scripture says, "Love takes no account of evil; it bears all things, endures all things."[5] Humility in both its sombre and more radiant moments must be your companion since it holds together the edifice of the virtues, like an indissoluble mortar, and takes diligent care of purity by wiping out defiling vainglory because it does not think arrogant thoughts but renders the heart contrite and welcomes wise lowliness.

4. When the assembly of the virtues welcomed holy humility into its midst, the sacred remembrance of this virtue emerged; even though it came along last of all, it passes to the first rank so as to show and teach thereby its proper position among the virtues. For scripture says, "Let the one who would be first take the last position of all."[6] Come, then, and according to the measure of discernment at our disposal, let us set out briefly the works belonging to humility, extending to the negligent a helping hand to set them straight and to strengthen the diligent so that they do not fall.

5. Humility is the bond of our accomplishments and the extermination of our sins. Humility preserves the virtues by not allowing us to do our deeds for show. Humility wipes away sins by persuading the lazy man to confess and so to reject them. Humility wraps the humble person in the guise of a reptile; but then, making him shine like a golden dove, it raises him to the heavens and grants him repose.[7] Humility is equipped with two wings, enabling the man who mounts upon it to escape like a bird from snares and traps,[8] for it prevents him from seeing his own achievements or looking for sins in others;

---

[5] 1 Cor 13:5, 7.
[6] Mk 9:35.
[7] Cf. Ps 54:7, 67:14.
[8] Cf. Ps 123:7.

δὲ τοὺς ἔξωθεν ἐπαίνους καὶ κατακρίνειν ἑαυτὸν τοῖς ἔσωθεν ἐλέγχοις. ἐκεῖνο τὴν κενοδοξίαν ἀναιρεῖ· τοῦτο τὴν ὑπερηφανίαν καταργεῖ. ἡ ταπείνωσις δυσὶν ἔργοις κοσμεῖ τὸν μετριόφρονα, τῇ σιωπῇ τῶν κατορθωμάτων καὶ τῇ προφορᾷ τῶν πλημμελημάτων. ἄλλους μεγαλ-
70 ύνει καὶ ἑαυτὸν σμικρύνει· ἄλλους ἐπαινεῖ καὶ ἑαυτὸν ἐξουθενεῖ· ἄλλους λογίζεται σωτηρίας ἀξιοῦσθαι, ἑαυτοῦ δὲ τὴν σωτηρίαν διστάζει.

    6. Ὁ μετριάζων κρύπτει τὰς ἀρετὰς καὶ ἡ μὲν καρδία αὐτοῦ βλέπει πρὸς τὸν τὰ κρυπτὰ εἰδότα, παρ᾽ οὗ καὶ τὰς ἀμοιβὰς προσδοκᾷ· τὰ
75 δὲ χείλη ἔχει καταμαρτυροῦντα ἑαυτοῦ καὶ ἀμφοτέρωθεν κέρδος ἑαυτῷ περιποιεῖται. οὐ πέφυκε θησαυρὸς ἐν ἀφυλάκτῳ τόπῳ κείμενος ἀσύλητος διαμένειν· οὐδὲ ἀρετὴ ἐκπομπευομένη ἐνταῦθα συναποδημοῖ τῷ ἀπιόντι πρὸς τὰ ἐκεῖθεν. εἶδόν τινας ἀποκρύπτοντας θησαυρὸν καὶ μηχανὴν συνεώρων βαθεῖαν καὶ ἀσφαλῆ· τὴν γὰρ κατάθεσιν τοῦ
80 χρυσίου ἐν τοῖς κόλποις τῆς γῆς ποιούμενοι, τὴν ὄψιν τῆς γῆς ἠχρειωμένῃ ἐπεκάλυπτον ὕλῃ, καὶ διὰ τῆς ἀτίμου κοπρίας τὸν πολύτιμον διέσωζον θησαυρόν.

    7. Τοιοῦτόν τι καὶ τῆς ταπεινοφροσύνης τὸ ἐπιτήδευμα· τὸ γὰρ ὁρώμενον αὕτη εὐτελίζουσα, τὴν ἀξίαν τοῦ νοουμένου φυλάττει καί,
85 τὴν παρατρέχουσαν δόξαν τῶν ἀνθρώπων παρατρέχουσα διὰ τῆς ἐξουδενώσεως, τὴν παρὰ τοῦ θεοῦ δόξαν κληρονομεῖ. τὸ χεῖρον ὑψοῖ σῶμα ταῖς ἀρεταῖς καὶ τὸ κρεῖττον, φημὶ τὸν νοῦν, κάμπτει διὰ τὴν συνεζευγμένην σάρκα. τὴν γῆν σάρκα κουφίζει διὰ τῶν ἐντολῶν, ἐπιτηδείαν παρασκευάζουσα πρὸς ἁρπαγὴν εἰς τὴν τοῦ κυρίου
90 συνάντησιν, καὶ ἵνα μὴ λατρεύσῃ τῇ κτίσει παρὰ τὸν κτίσαντα διὰ τῆς πρὸς τὰ κάτω φιλίας. τὸν δὲ οὐράνιον νοῦν κλίνει πρὸς τὸ ὁρᾶν τὴν εὐτέλειαν τοῦ σώματος, ἵνα μὴ ὁμοιωθῇ τῷ εἰπόντι· *θήσω τὸν θρόνον μου ἐπὶ τῶν νεφελῶν καὶ γενήσομαι ὅμοιος τῷ ὑψίστῳ.* οὕτως ἡ ταπείνωσις ἀντισοφιζομένη τὸν σοφιστὴν τῆς κακίας, θραύει τὰ
95 κέντρα αὐτοῦ, τὴν σκοτοποιὸν ἡδονὴν φημι καὶ τὴν καταργουμένην δόξαν, δι᾽ ὧν δάκνει καὶ φαρμακεύει καὶ θανατοῖ τοὺς πειθομένους αὐτῷ· διὰ μὲν τῆς ἡδονῆς εἰς πρόνοιαν τῶν τῆς σαρκὸς ἐπιθυμιῶν τὸν νοῦν κατασπῶν καὶ χωρίζων ἀπὸ τοῦ θεοῦ, διὰ δὲ τῆς δόξης τοὺς κατ᾽ ἀρετὴν πόνους ματαιῶν τοῦ ἀγωνιστοῦ – ἐκεῖνο πρὸς τὸ

---

89 ἐπιτηδείαν corr.: ἐπιτηδίαν OA

rather, it has him flee outward praises and condemn himself with inward reproofs. In the former instance it destroys vainglory; in the latter it abolishes pride. Humility adorns the modest person with two works, namely, with silence about his accomplishments and a forthright profession of his failings. He extols others and belittles himself; he praises others and disparages himself. He deems others worthy of salvation, but feels uncertain about his own salvation.

6. The modest person hides his virtues and his heart looks to the one who knows hidden things, from whom he awaits also his recompense, but he has his own lips to bear witness against him. He gains profit for himself on both accounts. A treasure lying in an unguarded place does not stay untouched: virtue which is publicly touted here below does not accompany a man when he passes on to the life above. I once saw some men hiding away a treasure and I was able to spot their crafty and sure ruse. They buried the treasure in the depths of the earth and covered the visible surface of the ground with useless junk, and by means of worthless garbage they preserved a treasure of great value.

7. The practice of humility is something of this sort, for in treating the visible as unimportant it guards the value of what is apprehended spiritually, and in bypassing the passing honour of men through disdain it inherits the honour that comes from God. By the virtues it exalts the inferior body and bows down the superior, namely, the mind, on account of the flesh to which it is yoked. It lightens the earthbound nature of the flesh by means of the commandments so as to make it ready to be snatched away to meet the Lord,[9] and so that it will not serve creation rather than the creator because of its attachment to inferior things.[10] But, it inclines the heavenly mind to look upon the body's lowly estate, lest it be likened to the one who said, "I will set my throne in the clouds and I shall become like unto the Most High."[11] In this way humility counters the devices of the sophist of wickedness and blunts his stings, namely, darkening pleasure and transitory honour, by which means the sophist stings, drugs and puts to death those who are swayed by him.[12] By means of pleasure he drags the mind down to a preoccupation with the desires of the flesh and separates it from God, while by means of honour he nullifies the

---

[9] 1 Thes 4:17.

[10] Rom 1:25.

[11] Is 14:13-14.

[12] I.e., by the devil.

100 κολάζειν τὴν ψυχὴν διὰ τῶν παθῶν, τοῦτο πρὸς τὸ ἀγέραστον
ἀποδεῖξαι τὸν ἀγωνιστὴν ἐν τῷ βλέπειν πρὸς ἀνθρώπους καὶ μὴ πρὸς
θεόν.

8. Ἐξαίρετον τῆς ταπεινοφροσύνης τὸ χρῆμα δείκνυται καὶ ἡ
ταύτης καλλονὴ ἀριδήλως πλεονεκτεῖ τὰς ἄλλας ἀρετάς. καὶ ὅρα τὴν
105 ταύτης δύναμιν. πᾶσαι μὲν αἱ ἀρεταὶ τὰς ἀντικειμένας αὐταῖς κακίας
ἀναιροῦσιν· ἡ δικαιοσύνη τὴν ἀδικίαν, ἡ σωφροσύνη τὴν ἀκολασίαν,
ἡ ἐγκράτεια τὴν ἀκρασίαν, ἡ ὑπομονὴ τὴν μικροψυχίαν, ἡ προσευχὴ
τὴν ἀνελπιστίαν, ἡ ἡσυχία τὴν πολυλογίαν. καὶ αἱ λοιπαὶ ὡσαύτως
τὰς παρεπομένας ἐναντιότητας καταργοῦσι. πάσαις δὲ ἀρεταῖς
110 ἐπιβουλεύει καὶ λυμαίνεται ἡ κενοδοξία· πᾶς γὰρ ὁ τὴν οἱανδήτινα
μετερχόμενος ἀρετὴν ἐνοχλεῖται ὑπὸ τῆς κενοδοξίας, ἐπαιρόμενος
ἐφ᾽ ᾗ ἐργάζεται ἀρετῇ, ἀφανίζει δὲ πάλιν τὴν ἐπίβουλον κενοδοξίαν.

9. Ἡ ταπείνωσις τὸν δίκαιον ἐκδικοῦσα καὶ κατευφραίνουσα·
εὐφρανθήσεται, γάρ φησι, *δίκαιος, ὅταν ἴδῃ ἐκδίκησιν·* ἡ δέ ἐστιν, ὁ
115 τῆς ἀθέου ὑπερηφανίας ἀφανισμός. καὶ τοῦτο δηλῶν ὁ προφήτης
ἐπάγει, *νίψεται τὰς χεῖρας αὐτοῦ ἐν τῷ αἵματι τοῦ ἁμαρτωλοῦ·* ἐν γὰρ
τῷ ἀφανισμῷ τῆς κενοδοξίας, τοῦτο γὰρ δηλοῖ τὸ *αἷμα τοῦ ἁμαρτωλοῦ·*
καθαρὰν ἔχει τὴν καρδίαν ὁ δίκαιος, τοῦτο γὰρ σημαίνει, τὸ *νίψεται*
τὰς χεῖρας· ἀφανὴς μένων ἐν τῷδε τῷ βίῳ διὰ τὸ ἀκενόδοξον, καὶ
120 ἀναμένων σὺν Χριστῷ φανερωθῆναι διὰ τὴν λανθάνουσαν τοὺς
ἀνθρώπους κρυπτὴν ἐργασίαν ἐκ ταπεινώσεως. εἰ γὰρ ἀκάθαρτος ὁ
ὑψηλοκάρδιος, καθαρὸς πάντως ὁ ταπεινόφρων. καὶ βλέπε τὴν καλὴν
τῆς ταπεινώσεως πλεονεξίαν, ὡς ἄνωθεν εἴρηται· οὐ γὰρ τὸν δίκαιον
μόνον ἐκδικεῖ καὶ χαροποιεῖ, τοὺς κλέπτοντας τὸν αὐτοῦ πλοῦτον
125 λογισμοὺς κενοδόξους ἐξορίζουσα καὶ καταργοῦσα, ἀλλὰ καὶ τὸν
ἁμαρτωλὸν δικαιοῖ καὶ παρακαλεῖ, αἴρουσα τὸ φορτίον τῶν ἁμαρτημάτων διὰ τῆς μετανοίας καὶ διὰ τῆς ἐξαγγελίας θριαμβεύουσα καὶ
σκορπίζουσα πρὸς τοὺς ὑποβάλλοντας τὰ κακὰ δαίμονας· *δίκαιος*, γάρ
φησιν, *ἐν πρωτολογίᾳ ἑαυτοῦ κατήγορος·* καὶ *λέγε σὺ πρῶτος τὰς*
130 *ἁμαρτίας σου, ἵνα δικαιωθῇς.*

ascetic's efforts at virtue. His purpose in the first instance is to punish the soul with the passions and in the second to show the ascetic deprived of his reward because he looked to men and not to God.

8. The practice of humility exhibits an extraordinary quality and its beauty clearly excels that of the other virtues. Mark then its force. All the virtues destroy their opposing vices: righteousness destroys iniquity, chastity licentiousness, discipline lack of self-control, patient endurance faintheartedness, prayer despair, quiet (hesychia) talkativeness, and in similar fashion the other virtues exterminate their corresponding opposites. But vainglory plots injury and harm against all the virtues, for anyone who attains any particular virtue is troubled by vainglory in that he is puffed up by pride in the virtue he is working at, but humility in its turn destroys the vainglory that preys upon him.

9. Humility vindicates the just man and brings him joy. For scripture says, "The just man will rejoice when he sees his vindication,"[13] that is, the destruction of ungodly pride. This is what the Prophet points to when he adds, "He will wash his hands in the blood of the sinner."[14] In the destruction of vainglory (indicated by 'the blood of the sinner') the just man possesses a pure heart (this is what is meant by 'washing his hands'); in this life he goes unnoticed because of his detachment from vainglory and awaits his appearance in the company of Christ because his hidden activity[15] escaped the notice of men on account of his humility. If the proud-hearted man is impure, the humble man is pure indeed. Observe the beautiful excellence of humility, as noted above. For humility vindicates and bestows its grace not only on the just man by rooting out and exterminating the vainglorious thoughts that steal his riches; it also justifies and consoles the sinner by removing the burden of his sins through repentance, by making them public through confession[16] and by scattering them among the demons who make evil suggestions. For scripture says, "The just man is the first to speak in self-accusation";[17] and again, "Be the first to tell your sins that you may receive justification."[18]

---

[13] Ps 57:11.

[14] Ibid.

[15] 'Hidden activity' or the 'hidden life in Christ' are key terms for Theoleptos; MD 1, as the title indicates, is devoted to an exposition of their meaning.

[16] The primary meaning here is confession of thoughts to one's spiritual father (usually the abbot) which may or may not involve sacramental confession. On this monastic practice see K. Ware, "Introduction," in *John Climacus, The Ladder of Divine Ascent*, pp. 37-43.

[17] Prov 18:17.

[18] Is 43:26.

10. Εἶδες ταπεινώσεως δύναμιν καὶ πλοῦτον ξένον καὶ βάθος σοφίας; κάτω κεῖται καὶ τοὺς κάτω κειμένους ἄνω τίθησι· τοὺς ἁμαρτωλοὺς διὰ τὴν ἐπίγνωσιν καὶ τὴν φανέρωσιν τῆς ἀσχημοσύνης καὶ τὴν αὐτομεμψίαν δικαιοῖ καὶ σῴζει· τοὺς δὲ δικαίους πάλιν, διὰ
135 τὴν ἐκ τοῦ μετρίου φρονήματος ἐξουδένωσιν καὶ τὴν σοφῶς περι-ποιουμένην εὐτέλειαν τὴν ἐπινοουμένην εἰς ἄμυναν τῶν χριστοφανῶς πολεμούντων αὐτοὺς ὑπερηφάνων λογισμῶν, δοξάζει καὶ μεγαλύνει· πύρινον γὰρ ὄχημα γενομένη τῶν ἀσπαζομένων αὐτὴν καὶ τὰ ἐπηρμένα πνεύματα καὶ πονηρὰ κατατεφροῦσα, ἀκώλυτον ποιεῖται
140 τὴν ἄνω πορείαν τῶν ἀπολιπόντων τὸν τῇδε βίον.

11. Ἐπείγου, ὁ τῆς εὐσεβείας ἀγωνιστής, διὰ τῆς κάτω κρυπτῆς ἐργασίας πρὸς τὰ ἄνω βραβεῖα, καὶ μὴ διὰ τὴν ἐψευσμένην ἐν τῷ παρόντι δόξαν τῶν καμάτων σου τοὺς ἱδρῶτας διακενῆς κενώσῃς· τοὺς μὲν μαραινομένους ἐπαίνους πιαίνων καὶ τρέφων τὰς ἀκοὰς δι'
145 ἀέρος καὶ ἀπέχων σου τὸν μισθὸν ἐνταῦθα· ἐκεῖ δὲ τῷ Ἅιδῃ παραπεμπόμενος καὶ λιμώττων καὶ κατάξηρος ὢν ἐν τῇ παντελεῖ ἐκπτώσει τῆς ἀπορρήτου δόξης, ἣν οἱ ταπεινοὶ περιβάλλονται.

12. Διανάστηθι, ὁ ἁμαρτάνων, διὰ μετανοίας καὶ θριάμβευσον τὰ ἁμαρτήματά σου, παραβλέπων τὴν ἀνθρωπίνην αἰσχύνην καὶ ἀφορῶν
150 πρὸς τὸν τελώνην καὶ ταπεινούμενος. ὁ φεύγων τὴν κενὴν τῶν ἀνθρώπων δόξαν καὶ τὴν πρόσκαιρον ἐξουδένωσιν ἀποδεχόμενος τῆς ταπεινοφροσύνης ἔχει τὰς πτέρυγας, δι' ὧν ὁ δίκαιος ἱστάμενος ἄπτωτος μένει καὶ ὁ κείμενος ἁμαρτωλὸς ἐγειρόμενος δικαιοῦται. ὁ ἀγαπῶν τὴν ἄνω δόξαν οὐ μισεῖ τὴν ἐξουδένωσιν, ὁ δὲ μὴ ἀθετῶν
155 τὴν ἐξουδένωσιν τὴν ἀνθρωπίνην ἀθετεῖ δόξαν. εἰ ὁ σῳζόμενος δίκαιος ἐξουδενεῖ ἑαυτόν – ὅταν, γάρ φησι, πάντα τὰ διατεταγμένα κατορθώσητε, λέγετε ὅτι ἀχρεῖοι δοῦλοί ἐσμεν – πόσῳ μᾶλλον ὁ ἀπὸ ἁμαρτίας ἐπιστρεφόμενος ἐξουδενεῖν ἑαυτὸν ὀφείλει καὶ κατακρίνειν;

13. Ἡ ταπείνωσις, τὰς ἑαυτῆς πτέρυγας διαπλοῦσα καθάπερ
160 ὄρνις, σκεπάζει καὶ τὸν μετριάζοντα δίκαιον καὶ τὸν ἐπιστρέφοντα ἁμαρτωλόν· ἐκεῖνον θέλγει κἀκεῖνον θάλπει. ἔχεις δικαιοσύνην ὁ κατορθῶν; ἔφυγες τὰς χεῖρας τῆς κακίας; ἔλυσας τὰ δεσμὰ τῆς αἰχμαλωσίας; εἶδε τοῦτο ὁ ἐχθρὸς καὶ μανικώτερον διανίσταται καὶ καταδιώκει ὀπίσω σου δι' ὑπερηφανίας. μίμησαι Μωσέα. βόησον

---

137 αὐτοὺς conieci: αὐτὸν ΟΑ

10. Do you realize the power of humility, its extraordinary riches and depth of wisdom? It assumes a lowly position, but those who keep themselves lowly it sets on high. It justifies and saves sinners because they acknowledge and make known their shame and abase themselves. As for the just, it raises them to honour and greatness because of their humble attitude and their modesty which, wisely acquired, is contrived as a defence against the prideful thoughts that war against them under the guise of Christian conduct. For when humility has become a fiery chariot[19] for those who welcome it, reducing the arrogant wicked spirits to ashes, it leaves unhampered the upward progress of those who have abandoned the life here below.

11. O contestant in piety, by your hidden activity here below press on towards the prizes on high and do not void the sweat of your labours to no purpose for the sake of false honour in this present age. By growing fat on passing flatteries and cherishing vaporous speeches, you receive in full your reward here below, but there, when you are sent off to hell, you will go hungry and thirsty because you fell away completely from the ineffable glory with which the humble surround themselves.

12. Sinner, raise yourself up again by repentance and divulge your sins, disregarding human shame and humbling yourself with your eyes directed at the example of the tax collector.[20] He who flees empty human honours and accepts a temporary self-abnegation possesses the wings of humility, by which the just man can stand firm without fear of falling and the sinner can raise himself up from his fallen state and receive justification. The person who loves the honour that is above is not averse to self-abnegation. He who does not reject self-abnegation rejects human honour. If the just man who is saved despises himself — for scripture says, "When you have done all that is commanded, say, 'We are unworthy servants.' "[21] — how much more ought the man who is converted from sin to despise and condemn himself?

13. As it unfolds its wings like a bird, humility gives shelter both to the just man in his lowliness and to the sinner in his repentance; the one it charms and the other it warms. Do you possess righteousness in your success? Have you fled the clutches of evil? Have you loosed the bonds of captivity? The enemy marks this and rising up ever more insanely follows close behind you by pride. Imitate Moses. Call to

[19] Cf. 4 Kingdoms 2:11.
[20] Lk 18:10-14.
[21] Lk 17:10.

165 πρὸς θεὸν διὰ καρδιακῆς προσευχῆς. προσλαβοῦ τὴν ταπείνωσιν τοῦ
διὰ σὲ σταυρωθέντος Χριστοῦ καὶ πλῆξον ἐν αὐτῇ καθάπερ ῥάβδῳ
τὸ σάρκινον καὶ φιλόδοξον φρόνημά σου, ὡς ἄλλην ἐρυθράν· καὶ
κρύψον τὰς ἀρετάς σου διὰ τῆς ἐξουδενώσεως καὶ τοῦ κατακρίνειν
ἑαυτόν, καὶ τοιουτοτρόπως ἀφανίζεις τοὺς ἐχθρούς σου.

170 **14.** Σύζευξον τοῖς σοῖς κατορθώμασι καὶ τὴν διὰ τῆς ἐξουδενώσεως ταπείνωσιν· καὶ δι' ὀδύνης καὶ ἀτιμίας σταυρὸν αἴρεις καὶ
ἀκολουθεῖς Χριστῷ· καὶ τῆς τῶν γηΐνων φιλίας καὶ συνηθείας
ὑψούμενος, ἅπαν ἀπονεκροῖς σαρκικὸν φρόνημα καὶ ἕλκεις Χριστὸν
διὰ τῆς ἀγάπης, καὶ ζῇ Χριστὸς ἐν σοὶ ἀγομένῳ ὑπὸ τοῦ πνεύματος
175 αὐτοῦ.

15. Ὁ μετανοῶν, σύζευξον τῷ πλήθει τῶν ἐξαγορευομένων ἁμαρτημάτων σου καὶ τὴν ταπείνωσιν, καὶ ὡς φάρμακον αὕτη δραστήριον
πάντα μολυσμὸν σαρκὸς καὶ πνεύματος ἀποτρίψει· ἐνέχυρον ἔχων
τὸν τελώνην δικαιωθέντα οὐκ ἀπὸ τῆς ἀληθείας, ἀλλ' ἀπὸ τῆς
180 ἡρμοσμένης αὐτῇ ταπεινώσεως. εἰ γὰρ ἀπὸ τῆς ἀληθείας διεσώζετο,
διεσώζετο ἂν καὶ ὁ Φαρισαῖος, ἀληθῆ κατορθώματα διηγούμενος.
κατὰ γὰρ τὴν ἀλήθειαν ἴσοι ἐτύγχανον, ὁ μὲν γὰρ ἀρετάς, ὁ δὲ
ἁμαρτίας ἐκέκτητο καὶ οὐδεὶς ἐψεύδετο. καὶ εἰ ἀπὸ τῆς ἀληθείας
ἐδικαιώθη ὁ τελώνης, μᾶλλον ἂν ὁ Φαρισαῖος ἐδικαιώθη ἀπὸ ταύτης
185 διὰ τὰ κατορθώματα.

16. Οὐ τοίνυν ἡ ἀλήθεια ἢ τὸν τελώνην ἐδικαίωσεν ἢ τὸν
Φαρισαῖον κατέκρινεν, ἀλλ' ἡ διάφορος γνώμη τοὺς ἡνωμένους διὰ
τὴν ἀλήθειαν δικαίως διέστησε· καὶ τὸν μὲν Φαρισαῖον κεράσαντα
τῇ ἀληθείᾳ τῶν κατορθωμάτων τὴν ὀλέθριον ἔπαρσιν ἀθλίως κατέ-
190 κρινε, τὸν δὲ τελώνην συνάψαντα τῇ ἀληθείᾳ τῶν παραπτωμάτων
τὴν ταπείνωσιν ἐδικαίωσε. καὶ ὅρα τῆς ταπεινοφροσύνης τὰ ἰδιώματα·
ἱστάμενος ἐν τῷ ἱερῷ καὶ προσευχόμενος, οὐκ ἔβλεπεν εἰς τὸν
οὐρανόν, ἐσκυθρώπαζεν, ἐστέναζεν, ἔτυπτε τὸ στῆθος, ἐφαύλιζεν
ἑαυτόν, τὸν ἐφάμαρτον ἑαυτοῦ βίον ἐδημοσίευεν, ἐξουδενούμενος ὑπὸ
195 τοῦ Φαρισαίου οὐδὲν ἀπεκρίνατο. εἶδες τὴν βοηθὸν ταπείνωσιν, ἣν
ἁρμοσάμενος ὁ τελώνης ἑαυτῷ δι' αἰσχύνης καὶ αὐτομεμψίας καὶ
κατακρίσεως δεδικαίωται;

17. Τῷ ταπεινόφρονι ἕπεται καὶ τὸ ἀληθεύειν, οὐ μὴν τῷ
ἀληθεύοντι ἀκολουθεῖ καὶ τὸ ταπεινοφρονεῖν· πολλοὺς γὰρ ὁρῶμεν

---

180 ἡρμοσμένης corr.: εἱρμοσμένης ΟΑ (cf. 21)   190 παραπτωμάτων conieci:
κατορθωμάτων ΟΑ   198 τῷ¹ corr.: τὸ ΟΑ

God in the prayer of the heart.[22] Grasp hold of the humility of Christ, who was crucified for you, and use it like a staff to strike your flesh-bound and honour-seeking attitudes like another Red Sea.[23] Hide your virtues in self-abnegation even to the point of condemning yourself, and in this way you will destroy your enemies.

14. Yoke to your successes also the humility found in self-abnegation, and through suffering and dishonour take up your cross and follow Christ.[24] Exalted above earthly attachments and affairs you can put to death any attitude of the flesh and draw Christ to you with your love; and Christ lives in you when you are led by his Spirit.[25]

15. O repentant sinner, yoke humility alongside the multitude of the sins you have to confess and like an effective tonic it will purge every defilement of flesh and spirit. You have as your guarantee the example of the tax collector, who was justified not because of his truthfulness but because of the humility joined to it. If he had been saved because of his truthfulness, the Pharisee would also have been saved in that he recounted his true achievements.[26] As far as truthfulness was concerned they were equals, for one had acquired virtues and the other sins and neither was lying. If the tax collector had been justified by his truthfulness, the Pharisee would have been justified by this to an even greater degree because of his achievements.

16. Truthfulness, therefore, neither justified the tax collector nor condemned the Pharisee, but a different judgement rightly separated those united in truthfulness. It condemned to wretchedness the Pharisee, who mingled ruinous pride together with the truth of his accomplishments, but it justified the tax collector, who joined humility to the truth of his transgressions. Note too the characteristics of his humility. Standing in the Temple and praying, he did not look up to heaven, but with gloomy countenance he moaned, struck his breast, disparaged himself and disclosed his sinful life, and when he was disparaged by the Pharisee, he gave no answer back. Do you see the helpfulness of humility? The tax collector was justified because he bound humility to himself by his shame, self-reproach and condemnation.

17. Truthfulness accompanies the humble man, but humility does not follow in the wake of the truthful man, for we see many truthful

---

[22] This should very likely be taken as a reference to the Jesus Prayer.

[23] Cf. Ex 14:15-21.

[24] Cf. Mt 10:38, 16:24, Mk 8:34, Lk 9:23.

[25] Cf. Rom 8:14, Gal 2:20.

[26] Dorotheus also notes the truthfulness of the Pharisee and how it was not for this reason that he was condemned: *Instructions* 6.70 (sc 92:270-272).

200 ἀληθεύοντας καὶ ἐπαιρομένους, οὔτε κερδαίνοντας διὰ τὴν ἀλήθειαν
καὶ ζημιουμένους μᾶλλον διὰ τὴν ἀπόνοιαν. καὶ τὰ παραδείγματα
ἐγγύθεν Φαρισαῖος καὶ τελώνης· ὁ μὲν ἐξ ἐπάρσεως δημοσιεύων ἅπερ
εἶχε κατορθώματα, ὁ δὲ ἐκ ταπεινώσεως θριαμβεύων ὅλον τὸν
ἐφάμαρτον αὐτοῦ βίον. ὁ πολέμιος τῶν ἡμετέρων ψυχῶν ὥσπερ ταῖς
205 ἄλλαις ἀρεταῖς ἀναλόγως ἀντίκειται, τὴν ἀναίρεσιν αὐτῶν ἐπισπεύδων
διὰ τῶν ἐναντίων, οὕτω καὶ τῇ ἀληθείᾳ μαχόμενος ἐπείγεται καταλύειν
αὐτὴν διὰ τοῦ ψεύδους· τοῦτο δὲ μὴ δυνηθείς, μίγνυσι τῇ ἀληθείᾳ
τὴν ὑπερηφανίαν, ἵν᾽ ὅπερ οὐχ εὑρίσκει φανερῶς μαχόμενος, τοῦτο
λάθρα δολερῶς κατορθώσει. τὸ ψεῦδος ὡς ἐχθρὸς εἰσηγεῖται καὶ ὡς
210 φίλος διὰ τῆς ὑπερηφανίας συντρέχει τῇ ἀληθείᾳ· ἐκεῖνο εἰς κατάλ-
υσιν τῆς ἀληθείας, τοῦτο εἰς κατηγορίαν καὶ κατάκρισιν τῆς συνειδήσεως, ὁμοῦ δὲ καὶ ἀντιλογίαν καὶ φιλονεικίαν. ἔμαθε τὰς
ἠπειλημένας τοῖς ἁμαρτωλοῖς κολάσεις· ἔγνω τὰς ἐπηγγελμένας τοῖς
δικαίοις ἀναπαύσεις. ὅθεν καὶ σπουδάζει τοὺς μὲν φιληδόνους διὰ
215 τῆς κατὰ τὴν ἁμαρτίαν ἡδονῆς μισῆσαι τὰς ἀρετάς, τοὺς δὲ φιλαρέτους
διὰ τῆς κενῆς δόξης τοῦ τῶν ἀρετῶν ἀποπεσεῖν μισθοῦ· τὸ μὲν ἵνα
εἰς κόλασιν ἐμβάλῃ, τὸ δὲ ὅπως τὰς ἀρετὰς ἀνωφελεῖς δείξῃ.
ἐπίβουλός ἐστι προφανὴς καὶ σύμβουλος τελεῖ· δολερὸς ἐπίβουλος,
ὅταν εἰσάγῃ τὰ ἀριστερά· σύμβουλος, ὅταν ὑποβάλῃ τὰ δεξιά. πρὸς
220 τοὺς ἀγαθοὺς ἐν ἀρχῇ φιλίαν ὑποκρινόμενος, ἐν τῷ τέλει τὴν ἔχθραν
ἐμφανίζει· πρὸς δὲ τοὺς φαύλους οἷός ἐστιν ἐκ προοιμίων φαίνεται.

18. Ὁ ἐρωτώμενος εἰπεῖν τὴν ἀλήθειαν καὶ ταύτην ἀποκρύπτων
καὶ ψεύδεται καὶ κενοδοξεῖ· ὁ δὲ ἐλεγχόμενος καὶ ὁμολογῶν μὲν τὴν
ἀλήθειαν, ἐπ᾽ ἄλλῳ δὲ τιθεὶς τὴν αἰτίαν, οὐκ ὠφελεῖται ἀληθεύων,
225 ἐπειδὴ ὑπερηφανεύεται καὶ κρίνει ἕτερον καὶ ἐν τῷ κρίνειν ἕτερον
ἑαυτὸν κατακρίνει. εἶδες πῶς πανταχοῦ παρεπομένη ἡ κενοδοξία
ζημιοῖ τοὺς ταύτην παραδεχομένους;

19. Ἡ Αἴγυπτος χώρα τοῦ Φαραὼ καὶ ἡ ἁμαρτία χώρα τοῦ
διαβόλου, πρὸς ἣν καὶ ὁ ἄσωτος ἀπεδήμησεν. ὁ Ἰσραὴλ φυγὼν τὴν
230 Αἴγυπτον, τὴν θάλασσαν χερσωθεῖσαν ἐβάδισε· καὶ ὁ τὴν ἁμαρτίαν
ἀφεὶς τῆς ἀρετῆς ἐπιλαμβάνεται. ἡ ξένη ὁδὸς τῆς ἐρυθρᾶς τὴν ἀρετὴν
ὑπογράφει σοι, καὶ ὡς ὀπίσω τοῦ ταύτην ὁδεύοντος Ἰσραὴλ ὁ Φαραὼ

people who are also arrogant. They gain no profit on truthfulness' account and come to greater ruin because of their desperate folly. The Pharisee and the tax collector are examples near at hand. The former out of pride proclaimed the accomplishments that he had attained; the latter out of humility disclosed the whole of his sinful life. The enemy of our souls, just as he opposes the other virtues to the same degree and hastens their destruction by means of their contrary vices, so too in fighting against the truth he rushes to destroy us by falsehood, but if he is unable to do this, he mixes arrogance in with the truth in order to accomplish deceitfully and in secret what he cannot find a way to fight in the open. As an enemy he introduces falsehood, but through pride he goes along with the truth as though he were a friend — in the former to destroy the truth and in the latter to accuse and condemn the conscience, as well as to introduce contrariness and contention. The enemy learned of the punishments threatened against sinners; he knew about the repose promised to the just. And so he urged the libertines to hate the virtues for the sake of sinful pleasure, and for the sake of empty honours he encouraged the virtuous to let the reward of the virtues slip away. In the first case his intention was to cast them into punishment and in the second case to show the virtues voided of profit. The enemy is a blatant trickster and counselor: a trickster full of deceit whenever he introduces sinister ideas and a counselor whenever he suggests clever notions. Among good people, though in the beginning he feigns friendship, in the end he makes plain his hostility, but among bad people he appears exactly as he really is right from the start.

18. If someone is asked to speak the truth and he conceals it, he is both deceitful and vainglorious, but if someone is upbraided and acknowledges the truth, but places the responsibility on somebody else, his truthfulness has no value because he is acting arrogantly and is judging another, and in judging another he condemns himself. Do you see how, in following you about everywhere, vainglory ruins those who give it admittance?

19. Egypt is the domain of Pharaoh and sin is the domain of the devil; it was there that the prodigal went off to on his journey.[27] When Israel fled from Egypt, it crossed the sea on dry land.[28] When someone puts sin aside, he lays hold of virtue. The strange passage through the Red Sea is for you an allusion to virtue. And as Pharaoh pursued

[27] Lk 15:13.
[28] Ex 14:22.

κατεδίωκεν, οὕτω καὶ σοὶ τὴν ἀρετὴν μετιόντι ἡ κενοδοξία παρέπεται, εἰς χεῖρας τῆς ὑπερηφανίας ζητοῦσα δουλῶσαί σε. ἔχεις ἀντὶ Μωσέως
235 τὸν τοῦ Μωσέως δεσπότην, ἀντὶ ῥάβδου τὸν σταυρὸν τοῦ διὰ σὲ σταυρωθέντος. ἡ ξηρὰ ὁδὸς τῆς θαλάσσης τὸ ὄρθιον σχῆμα τοῦ σταυροῦ ἐγχαράττει· ἡ δὲ πλαγία πλῆξις, ἡ τὴν διαιρεθεῖσαν θάλασσαν ἑνώσασα καὶ τὴν χερσωθεῖσαν γῆν καλύψασα, τὸ πλάγιον εἰκονίζει τοῦ σταυροῦ.
240 **20.** Σύναψον καὶ σὺ τῇ ἀρετῇ τὴν ταπείνωσιν καὶ ἀφανίζεις ἡδονὴν καὶ δόξαν, καὶ συσταυροῦσαι Χριστῷ καὶ τοῦ νοητοῦ Φαραὼ λυτροῦσαι· καὶ διὰ μὲν τῆς κατὰ τὴν ἀρετὴν ἐργασίας ὑψοῦσαι ἀπὸ τῆς γῆς, διὰ δὲ τοῦ ταπεινοῦ φρονήματος διαβαίνεις τὸν ἀέρα καὶ φθάνεις εἰς οὐρανόν. καὶ τοὺς πολεμίους ἐκφεύγεις καὶ τὰ πεμπόμενα
245 τῆς ὑπερηφανίας ὑπερβαίνεις βέλη. ἡ διαίρεσις τῆς θαλάσσης διήγαγε τὸν Ἰσραὴλ εἰς τὴν ἔρημον καὶ ἡ ἕνωσις ταύτης πάλιν τὸν διώκοντα κατεπόντισε. καὶ ὁ τὴν ἱερὰν δυάδα, ἀρετὴν λέγω καὶ ταπείνωσιν, οἰκειωσάμενος, διὰ μὲν τῆς ἀρετῆς εἰς ἀπάθειαν φθάνει, διὰ δὲ τῆς ταπεινώσεως τοὺς παρεδρεύοντας κλέπτας ἀφανίζει· καὶ
250 γαλήνην βαθεῖαν ἄγει, τῶν ἐνοχλούντων παθῶν ἀπαλλαττόμενος, ἐν Χριστῷ τῷ τοῖς σωτηρίοις αὐτοῦ παθήμασι τὴν ἀπάθειαν ἡμῖν δωρησαμένῳ.

21. Ἡ διαίρεσις τοῦ ὕδατος καὶ ἡ διάβασις τοῦ Ἰσραὴλ θαυμαστὴ καὶ διασῴζουσα τὸν Ἰσραὴλ παραδόξως· ἡ ἕνωσις πάλιν τοῦ ὕδατος
255 καὶ ὁ ὄλεθρος τῶν ὑπεναντίων θαυμαστά, ἐπειδὴ ἀμφότερα προτυπώματα τῶν ἐνεργημάτων τοῦ δεσποτικοῦ σταυροῦ. ὁ γὰρ ὑπὲρ ἡμῶν σταυρωθεὶς Χριστὸς διὰ τοῦ σταυροῦ καὶ ἡμᾶς ἔσωσε καὶ τοὺς δαίμονας κατήργησεν. εἰ τὴν μνήμην τοῦ κυρίου φέρεις ἐν ἑαυτῷ ἐστηριγμένην καὶ τὴν εἰς αὐτὸν τρέφεις ἀγάπην, δύνασαι ἀπορρίπτειν
260 ἀφ' ἑαυτοῦ τοῦ σαρκικοῦ ἤτοι τοῦ διαβολικοῦ φρονήματος τὰ ἐπαναστήματα· ἅτινά ἐστιν ἔπαρσις, ὑπερηφανία, ὑψηλοφροσύνη, οἴησις, τῦφος, κενοδοξία, ἀνθρωπαρέσκεια καὶ ὑπόκρισις· ταῦτα γὰρ ἐστιν εὑρήματα καὶ γεννήματα τοῦ πονηροῦ, οἷς καὶ καθάπερ ἅρμασιν ὁπλιζόμενος καθ' ἡμῶν ἐκστρατεύει.

265 **22.** Ὅταν οὖν κατέχεις ταῦτα καὶ ἐκπληροῖς, σὺ μὲν θανατοῦσαι, ζωογονεῖς δὲ τὸν ἐχθρόν· βρῶμα γὰρ αὐτῷ ἐστι τὰ παρ' ἡμῶν ἐνεργούμενα καὶ στεργόμενα πάθη. ὅταν δὲ πάλιν, δυναμούμενος ὑπὸ

---

249 παρεδρεύοντας corr.: παραδρεύοντας OA

Israel as it travelled on this road, so too does vainglory accompany you in your quest for virtue, seeking to make you a slave at the hands of pride. In Moses' place you have the Lord of Moses; instead of the staff you have the Cross of the one who was crucified for your sake. The dry passage through the sea is a representation of the vertical form of the Cross. The crosswise blow that brought together the divided sea and covered again the dried ground is an image of the transverse beam of the Cross.[29]

20. Join humility to your virtue and you too will do away with pleasure and false honour, crucifying yourself with Christ[30] and ransoming yourself from the spiritual Pharaoh. By means of virtuous acts you raise yourself up from the earth. By a humble attitude you pass through the air and attain to heaven; you escape from your enemies and pass beyond the darts of pride hurled against you. The parting of the sea allowed Israel to pass through to the desert and its re-uniting drowned their pursuers. Someone who has appropriated to himself the holy dyad, I mean virtue and humility, attains to impassibility by means of virtue and destroys its attendant thieves by means of humility. When freed from the disturbances of the passions he leads a life of deep calm in Christ who has granted us impassibility by his salvific sufferings.

21. The dividing of the water and the passage of Israel is a marvel that saved Israel in an extraordinary manner; in turn, the uniting of the water and the destruction of their adversaries are also marvels. This is because both sets of events are prefigurations of what would be wrought by the Lord's Cross, for Christ, crucified for us, by his Cross, both saved us and annihilated the demons. If you bear remembrance of the Lord firmly fixed within you and nurture your love for him,[31] you will be able to cast off from yourself the rebellious attitudes that arise from the flesh or indeed from the devil: namely, haughtiness, arrogance, proud-heartedness, presumption, conceit, vainglory, sycophancy and hypocrisy. These are inventions and products of the evil one with which he arms himself, as with war chariots, to make war against us.

22. Therefore, when you hold on to these vices and carry them out, you bring death upon yourself and give life to the enemy, for the passions that we show fondness for and give vent to are his

---

[29] Cf. Ex 14:26-28.

[30] Cf. Gal 2:19.

[31] Probably a reference to the Jesus Prayer. Note the association with love, which is developed in detail in MD 1.17-20.

κυρίου, ἐκτελεῖς τὰς ἐντολὰς καὶ κρύπτεις τὰς ἐργασίας διὰ τὸ
ἐξουδενεῖν ἑαυτόν, σὺ μὲν ζωοῦσαι, ὁ δὲ διάβολος θανατοῦται·
270 μυρμηκολέων, γάρ φησιν, ὤλετο παρὰ τὸ μὴ ἔχειν βοράν.

23. Διαιρεθείσης τῆς θαλάσσης τῇ εὐθείᾳ πληγῇ τῆς ῥάβδου, τὸ
μὲν μέσον τῆς ἀβύσσου πέδον ξηρὸν γέγονε, τὸ δὲ διαιρεθὲν ὕδωρ
εἰς δύο τείχη ἐπάγη – τὸ μὲν ἐκ δεξιῶν, τὸ δὲ ἐξ εὐωνύμων – καὶ
ὁ Ἰσραὴλ ἐπορεύθη διὰ ξηρᾶς ἐν μέσῳ τῆς θαλάσσης, ἵνα μάθωμεν
275 πραγματικῶς τὰς ἀρετὰς εἶναι μεσότητας, καὶ οἱ τὸν δρόμον τῆς
ἀρετῆς τρέχοντες καὶ πρὸς τὴν τῆς ἀπαθείας ἔρημον ἀποσκοποῦντες
ὀφείλουσιν ἐκκλίνειν τὰς ὑπερβολὰς καὶ τὰς ἐλλείψεις, ὡς τοῦ
διαβολικοῦ φρονήματος μηχανήματα καὶ τὸ σαρκικὸν θέλημα συν-
ιστῶντα· ἃ δὴ καὶ ἐπαφιέμενα ὡς ἀλλότρια τῶν ψυχῶν πρὸς τοὺς
280 εἰσηγουμένους ταῦτα δαίμονας καταργεῖ αὐτοὺς ὡς τοῖς οἰκείοις
βέλεσι πληττομένους. ὡς γὰρ ὁ γαιωθεὶς τόπος τῆς ἀβύσσου εἰς
σωτηρίαν ᾠκονόμηται τῷ Ἰσραήλ, ὃν καὶ φόβῳ πολλῷ καὶ σπουδῇ
συντόνῳ διέβαινον, ἐπειδὴ καὶ τὰ κύματα τῶν διαιρεθέντων ὑδάτων
ὑπὲρ κεφαλῆς αὐτῶν ἑώρων ἱστάμενα καὶ τοὺς Αἰγυπτίους αὖθις
285 ὀπίσω διώκοντας καὶ μανικὸν πνέοντας, οὕτω καὶ τὰ ἐπηρμένα ὡς
ὄρη τοῦ ὕδατος τμήματα καὶ πεπαγιωμένα ὡς τείχη ἑτερατουργήθη
πρὸς καταποντισμὸν τῶν καταδιωκόντων τὸν τοῦ θεοῦ λαὸν κατα-
δουλώσασθαι.
24. Τὸν φεύγοντα τὴν ἁμαρτίαν ἡ πρᾶξις διαδέχεται τοῦ καλοῦ
290 καὶ ἡ ποίησις τοῦ ἀγαθοῦ ἕξις ἐστὶ τῆς τοῦ κακοῦ φυγῆς. εἰ μὴ
ἐπέρασε τὴν ἐρυθρὰν ὁ Ἰσραήλ, οὐκ ἂν ἀπηλλάττετο τοῦ φόβου καὶ
τοῦ περισπασμοῦ τῶν Αἰγυπτίων. καὶ εἰ μὴ τὴν πρὸς τὴν σάρκα
σχέσιν τῆς ψυχῆς ἐκκόψῃς ἀπὸ σοῦ, οὐ φθάνεις εἰς τὴν τοῦ θεοῦ
ἀγάπην. καὶ εἰ μὴ κατασκηνώσῃς ἐν τῇ τοῦ θεοῦ ἀγάπῃ, οὐ σύνοικον
295 λαμβάνεις τὴν ταπείνωσιν. καὶ ὅταν αὐτὴν συνάψῃς ἑαυτῷ, ῥᾳδίως
τοὺς πολεμίους καταργεῖς. πρῶτον ἐμαστιγώθη ἡ Αἴγυπτος ταῖς δέκα
πληγαῖς· εἶτα τῆς δουλείας ὁ Ἰσραὴλ ἀπελύθη. καὶ ἡ κακοῦσα τὴν
ψυχὴν σάρξ, εἰ μὴ ἀντικακωθῇ τῇ δεκαλόγῳ ἐντολῇ, οὐ δύναται ὁ
νοῦς τῆς κατὰ τὴν ἐνεργουμένην ἡδονὴν δουλείας ἐλεύθερος γεγε-
300 νῆσθαι· καὶ αὐτὴ δὲ ἡ πρᾶξις ἀπρόσδεκτός ἐστι τῶν καλῶν, τῆς
διανοίας μὴ καθαρευούσης ἀπὸ παθῶν. καὶ μάρτυς ὁ νόμος· μὴ
προσιέμενος εἰς θυσίαν τὸ ἐπίμωμον πρόβατον.

---

298 ἀντικακωθῇ corr.: ἀντικακοθῇ ΟΑ

nourishment. But when in turn under the Lord's influence you fulfil the commandments and conceal your activities in order to disparage yourself, you find life but the devil finds death. For scripture says, "The ant-lion perished for want of food."[32]

23. When the sea was divided by the straight blow of the staff, the ground in the midst of the abyss became dry; the divided water formed two walls, one on the right and the other on the left; and Israel passed through the middle of the sea on dry land. This took place that we might learn in a practical way that the virtues constitute a middle ground and those who run the course of virtue searching for the desert of impassibility ought to avoid excesses and deficiencies as devices of the diabolic mind which preserve the will of the flesh. If these devices are turned back upon the demons who introduced them as alien to the soul, they will destroy the demons by hitting them with their own darts. For just as the place in the deep which was turned into solid ground was arranged for Israel's salvation and they crossed over it in great fear and mighty haste because they saw the swells of the parted waters standing over their heads and the Egyptians breathing madly in pursuit behind them, so too the sections of water raised as high as mountains and as solid as walls were wondrously wrought so as to drown those who were pursuing God's people in order to enslave them.

24. The practice of goodness overtakes the man who flees from sin; and doing good is a habit that derives from flight from evil. If Israel had not crossed the Red Sea, it would not have been delivered from the fear and the anxiety caused by the Egyptians. If you do not detach yourself from your soul's adherence to the flesh, you will not attain the love of God; and if you do not make your abode in the love of God, you will not have humility as your companion. When you join humility to yourself, you will easily eradicate your enemies. First, Egypt was scourged with the ten plagues;[33] then, Israel was released from slavery. As for the flesh that brings ruin upon the soul, unless it is ruined in return by the decalogue of the commandments, the mind cannot be freed from the slavery inflicted by the pleasure at work within it. And unless the discursive intellect is purified of the passions, its practice of the good will be ineffective. The Law bears witness to this: "Do not allow in sacrifice the sheep that is blemished."[34]

---

[32] Job 4:11.
[33] Ex 7:14-10:29, 12:29-30.
[34] Deut 17:1.

25. Ὀφείλει καὶ γὰρ ὁ πρακτικός, ὥσπερ τὴν ἐνήδονον πρᾶξιν τοῦ σώματος ἀποδιέστησε καὶ τοῦ πράγματος σωματικῶς ἠλ-
305 λοτρίωται, οὕτω συναποβαλέσθαι καὶ τὴν πρὸς τὸ πρᾶγμα τοῦ λογισμοῦ σχέσιν καὶ τὴν ψυχὴν ἀμιγῆ τοῦ πάθους διατηρεῖν τῇ τμητικῇ διακρίσει· ἡ ὀρθὴ γὰρ τῆς γνώσεως διάκρισις καὶ τὴν τῆς πράξεως προσένεξιν ὀρθὴν ἀποτελεῖ. ἡ τοίνυν διάκρισις δεικνύουσα τὸ καλὸν τόπος ἐστὶ τῆς ἀρετῆς, ἐν ᾗ ὁδεύουσα ἡ ψυχὴ ἀποπέμπεται
310 τὸ φαῦλον.

26. Ἡ ἀρετὴ τρόπος ἐστὶ μετ' εὐσεβοῦς διαθέσεως τελούμενος καὶ πρὸς τὴν τελείωσιν ἐπειγόμενος, ἐπειδὴ καὶ λόγον ἔχει θεμέλιον καὶ λόγου φέρει φανέρωσιν. ἡ τελείωσις τῆς ἀρετῆς στολὴν ἀγάπης ὑφαίνει, ἡ δὲ ἀγάπη συνέχει καὶ ἀγλαΐζει καὶ καθηδύνει τὴν ψυχὴν
315 τῇ ὡραιότητι τῆς πρὸς θεὸν ἑνώσεως· ὁρῶσα γὰρ ἡ ἀγάπη γυμνωθεῖ-σαν τὴν ψυχὴν διὰ τῶν ἀρετῶν πάσης ἐπιθυμίας κοσμικῆς, αὐτίκα δίκην περιβολῆς περιπλέκεται αὐτὴν καὶ συνάπτει Χριστῷ· ἥτις καὶ τῷ κάλλει τῆς θείας ἑνώσεως ὡραϊζομένη, πάσης μὲν γηΐνης ἐννοίας ἐπιλανθάνεται, χαρᾷ δὲ καὶ εἰρήνῃ ἐνανακλίνεται. καὶ τοῦτο δηλῶν
320 ὁ τοῖς τοῦ πνεύματος χαρίσμασιν ἐπεντρυφῶν πλουσίως Παῦλος λέγει, *ὁ καρπὸς τοῦ πνεύματός ἐστιν ἀγάπη, χαρά, εἰρήνη.* ἐκ γοῦν τῆς κατὰ τὴν ἀγάπην τοῦ θεοῦ συναφείας ἡ ψυχὴ φωτιζομένη εἰς ταπείνωσιν ἔρχεται· ἡ δὲ ταπείνωσις ἐπίγνωσίς ἐστι τῆς ἀνθρωπίνης πτωχείας καὶ τοῦ θείου πλούτου, πείθουσα τὸν προκόψαντα ἡγεῖσθαι
325 ἑαυτὸν μηδὲν εἶναί τι ταῖς ἀληθείαις, κἂν καὶ τὰ μεγάλα τύχῃ οὗτος κατωρθωκώς. καὶ τοῦτο καταμάθῃς ἂν καὶ ἀπὸ τῶν καθ' ἡμᾶς.

27. Τίς γὰρ ἐξ ἀπορίας πολλῆς προσελθὼν πλουσίῳ καὶ μετὰ πολλὰς δεήσεις χρυσίον εἰληφὼς εἰς ἐμπορίαν, ἡγεῖται τὸ ἀλλότριον ὡς ἴδιον καὶ ἐπαίρεται ἐπὶ τῷ δανείσματι; καὶ οὐχὶ μᾶλλον δέδοικε
330 τὸν δανειστὴν καὶ διόλου ὑποπίπτει αὐτῷ καὶ ταπεινοῦται καὶ εὐγνωμονεῖ διὰ παντὸς καὶ εὐχαριστεῖ; πτοούμενος γὰρ τὴν ἐπαίτησιν καὶ λογιζόμενος τὴν ἀπόδοσιν τοῦ καταβληθέντος χρυσίου καὶ τὴν ἐντεῦθεν καταλαμβάνουσαν αὐτῷ ἔνδειαν καὶ αἰσχύνην, ἐπείγεται πάσῃ δυνάμει τοῦ δανειστοῦ τὴν ψυχὴν ἀγαθύνειν, ἵνα, τοῦ χρέους
335 παρατεινομένου, τὰ πρὸς τροφὴν ὁ χρεώστης ἐκ τῆς ἐμπορίας πορίζηται. τοιαύτην λογίζου καὶ τοῦ ταπεινόφρονος τὴν διάθεσιν.

---

327 ἐξ ἀπορίας corr.: ἐξαπορίας ΟΑ   331 διαπαντὸς ΟΑ   332 ἀπόδοσιν corr.: ἀπόδωσιν ΟΑ

25. Just as the person engaged in the practice of virtue has separated from the body that conduct associated with pleasure and was delivered bodily from objective reality, so he ought also to cast off the attachment of his thoughts to such things and to preserve his soul free of any mingling with passion by means of an incisive discernment. An upright discernment derived from knowledge also renders the offering of one's activity upright. Thus, discernment which points out the good is the place of virtue, in which the soul makes its way and repels what is bad.

26. Virtue is a way of acting effected and brought to perfection in association with a pious disposition, since it both has reason as its foundation and brings about the manifestation of reason.[35] The perfection of virtue weaves a garment of love; love preserves the soul and bestows splendour and pleasure on it through the beauty of union with God. When love sees that the soul is stripped by the virtues of all worldly desire, it immediately enfolds the soul as with a garment and unites it to Christ. And when the soul takes on the beauty of divine union, it forgets all thoughts of earth and finds rest in joy and peace. Paul, who enjoyed an abundance of the charisms of the Spirit, indicates this in saying, "The fruit of the Spirit is love, joy, peace ... ."[36] So when the soul is illumined by its union with God in love, it attains to humility. Humility is a recognition of human poverty and divine wealth, which persuades the person who has made progress to consider himself as truly nothing at all, even though he has had the good fortune to accomplish great things. This you could learn also from ordinary experience.

27. After going to a rich man out of great need and after many petitions receiving money to make purchases, who considers this other man's property as his own and boasts about the loan? Rather, does he not fear the money-lender and act before him with complete subservience and humility, offering him perpetual goodwill and thanksgiving? Terrified in his begging, and thinking about the repayment of the money that was paid to him and the poverty and shame that befall him as a result, he makes haste with all his strength to benefit the soul of the money-lender so that by an extension of the loan the debtor can get the food he needs to live on out of the profit. Consider how this is also the disposition of the humble man. As the eye of the body,

---

[35] The mention of reason here and of discernment in the preceding paragraph should be understood in the light of what is said about them in MD 23.1-4.

[36] Gal 5:22.

ὡς γὰρ ὁ τοῦ σώματος ὀφθαλμὸς τοῦ ἔξωθεν φωτὸς ἀποστάς, οὐ
δύναται βλέπειν τὰ προκείμενα καὶ διακρίνειν, οὕτω καὶ ὁ κατορθῶν
ἀρετάς, ἡνίκα ἑαυτὸν λογίζεται ἑαυτὸν εἶναί τι καὶ περιβλέπων τὸ
340 κάλλος τῶν κατορθωμάτων ἡδύνηται, οὗτος τῷ τῆς οἰήσεως καὶ τῆς
ἐπάρσεως νέφει καλύπτεται καὶ τῇ ἰδίᾳ γνώμῃ τὰ χαρίσματα
ἐπιγράφει· ὅθεν καὶ ὡς φύλλον ἐν καιρῷ χειμῶνος τῆς χάριτος
ἀποπίπτων, ὡς ὑπερήφανος καὶ πίπτει καὶ κατακρίνεται.

28. Ὁ ἀποστὰς τοῦ κακοῦ καὶ ποιῶν τὸ ἀγαθὸν φεύγει τὰς χεῖρας
345 τοῦ ἐχθροῦ. χεῖρες δὲ τοῦ πονηροῦ ἡ πρᾶξις τοῦ κακοῦ καὶ ἡ ἀπραξία
τοῦ καλοῦ. ὁ ἐκκόπτων τὰ θελήματα αὐτοῦ καὶ ὑπείκων πατρὶ
πνευματικῷ εὐχερῶς ἀφανίζει τὸν ἐχθρόν. τὸ θέλημά ἐστιν ἡ θάλασσα·
ἔκοψας τὸ θέλημα; ἐξήρανας τὴν θάλασσαν. τὴν τραχεῖαν ὁδὸν τῆς
ἀρετῆς ἠγάπησας; παρῆλθες τὸν ἐκλελυμένον καὶ φιλήδονον βίον
350 καὶ τὴν ἔρημον κατέλαβες. ἔκρυψας τὴν ἀρετὴν καὶ ἐπεγράψω τὸ
κατορθούμενον τῷ βλέποντι τὰ κρυπτά; κατεπόντισας τὴν ὑπερηφανίαν καὶ ἰδοὺ ἐρεῖς μετὰ παρρησίας πρὸς τὰς δυνάμεις τῆς ψυχῆς
καὶ τὰ μέλη τοῦ σώματός σου. ἄσωμεν τῷ κυρίῳ, ἐνδόξως γὰρ
δεδόξασται ὁ τρισυπόστατος θεός, ὁ τοὺς πολεμοῦντας σῶμα ψυχὴν
355 καὶ πνεῦμα τριστάτας δαίμονας ἐξαφανίσας καὶ τὴν τριμερῆ ψυχὴν
διασώσας· ὅτι αὐτῷ πρέπει πᾶσα δόξα, τιμὴ καὶ προσκύνησις, τῷ
πατρὶ καὶ τῷ υἱῷ καὶ τῷ ἁγίῳ πνεύματι, νῦν καὶ ἀεὶ καὶ εἰς τοὺς
αἰῶνας τῶν αἰώνων. Ἀμήν.

337 ἔξωθεν corr.: ἔξοθεν ΟΑ

if it withdraws from the exterior light, cannot see and distinguish what is in front of it, so too the man who is successful in the practice of virtue, when he thinks something of himself and finds pleasure in looking at his fine accomplishments, he is covered with the cloud of presumption and haughtiness and ascribes the charisms to his own will-power. And so, like a leaf in winter time, he drops away from virtue and falls under the condemnation of pride.

28.   He who withdraws from evil and does good escapes the hands of the enemy. The doing of evil and the avoidance of doing good are the hands of the evil one. He who excises his own will and submits to a spiritual father easily does away with the enemy. The will is represented by the sea. Have you struck your will? Then you have dried up the sea. Have you preferred the rough road of virtue?[37] Then you have passed through the life of dissolution and pleasure and arrived at the desert. Have you concealed your virtue and ascribed what you accomplish to the one who sees hidden things?[38] Then you have drowned your pride and behold, you can speak with freedom to the powers of your soul and the members of your body. Let us sing to the Lord, for the tri-hypostatic God is gloriously glorified[39] — he who has utterly destroyed the threefold ranks of demons who make war against body, soul and spirit, he who has preserved the tripartite soul. To him belongs all glory, honour and worship, to the Father and to the Son and to the Holy Spirit, now and always and unto the ages of ages. Amen.

[37] Note the similar imagery in MD 5.2.
[38] Cf. Mt 6:4,6.
[39] Ex 15:1.

Περὶ ἀγάπης πνευματικῆς

1. Ἀδελφαὶ καὶ μητέρες, ὑμνῆσαι βούλομαι τὸ τῆς ἀγάπης χρῆμα, καὶ πάλιν οὐ δύναμαι λόγῳ παραστῆσαι τὴν ταύτης εὐπρέπειαν· αὕτη γὰρ ἡ καλλίστη τῶν ἀρετῶν, ὡς κεφαλὴ τῶν καλῶν, ἔργῳ καὶ πείρᾳ
5 καταλαμβάνεται. διὸ καὶ τὴν θαυμασίαν ταύτην ἀγάπην ἀκριβῶς ἴσασιν οἱ τὴν ὁδὸν αὐτῆς ἀξιωθέντες περιπατῆσαι. οἱ μὲν γὰρ στόματι τὴν ἀγάπην φέροντες διηγοῦνται περὶ αὐτῆς, οἱ δὲ ἐν καρδίᾳ ταύτην κτησάμενοι διὰ τῶν ἀρίστων ἔργων δημοσιεύουσιν· οὗτοι πολλῷ κρείττονες τῶν προτέρων τυγχάνουσιν. ἀλλ᾽ εἰ καὶ τὸ τῆς ἀγάπης
10 ἐξαίρετον ὑπερβαίνει τὸν ἡμέτερον λόγον, ἀλλ᾽ οὖν διὰ βραχέων ἐξυμνήσωμεν ταύτην πρὸς τὸ πολλοὺς ἐραστὰς αὐτῆς καταστῆναι.

2. Ἡ ἀγάπη, ἀγαπηταὶ ἀδελφαί μου, ἔργον ἐστὶν ἐν τῇ ψυχῇ τελούμενον, θερμαῖνον τὴν καρδίαν, φωτίζον τὸν νοῦν, ἐξυπνίζον τὴν διάνοιαν εἰς μελέτην τῶν λογίων τοῦ θεοῦ, ὅλον τὸ σῶμα διεγεῖρον
15 εἰς σκοποὺς τῶν θείων ἐντολῶν. τῆς ἀγάπης τὸ δῶρον ὁ θεὸς ἐξ ἀρχῆς ἐχαρίσατο τῷ ἀνθρώπῳ, ἣν καὶ λαβὼν ὁ ἄνθρωπος ὥσπερ τινὰ στολὴν κοσμιωτάτην ἐνεδύσατο ταύτην· ἀλλὰ διαρρήξας ταύτην ὁ τῶν ἡμετέρων ψυχῶν λῃστὴς γυμνὸν ἀπέδειξε τὸν ἄνθρωπον καὶ ἀσχημο-σύνης πάσης πεπληρωμένον. πῶς δὲ διαρρήσσεται ὁ τῆς ἀγάπης
20 χιτών; καὶ πῶς πάλιν περισῴζεται; ἀκούετε.

3. Ἡνίκα ὁ ἄνθρωπος ἀγαπᾷ ἐξ ὅλης καρδίας τὸν θεὸν καὶ τὰ ἀρεστὰ αὐτοῦ ποιῇ, τότε ἡ πᾶσα ἀγάπη τῆς ψυχῆς ἀδιαμέριστος ὑπάρχει, ὡς ὅλης τῆς ἀγαπητικῆς δυνάμεως προσκολλωμένης τῷ θεῷ. τότε ἡ ψυχὴ τὴν τῆς ἀγάπης καλλονὴν ὥσπερ τινὰ πορφύραν
25 ἐνδυομένη λαμπρύνεται καὶ καθάπερ τις χρυσαυγίζουσα περιστερὰ θεωρεῖται. ὅτε δὲ ἄρξηται ὁ ἄνθρωπος ἀγαπᾶν χρυσίον, ἀργύριον, λίθους τιμίους καὶ πᾶσαν ἄλλην ὕλην τῆς γῆς, ἔτι δὲ καὶ τὴν τρυφὴν καὶ πᾶσαν τὴν ποικιλίαν τῶν βρωμάτων καὶ τὴν θνήσκουσαν ζωὴν τῆς σαρκὸς καὶ τὴν πρὸς ὀλίγον φαινομένην παρὰ τῶν ἀνθρώπων
30 δόξαν – ὅτε εἰς ταῦτα πάντα τὰ πράγματα θήσει ὁ ἄνθρωπος τὴν ὄρεξιν τῆς ἑαυτοῦ ψυχῆς, τότε διαμερίζεται ὁ τῆς ἀγάπης χιτὼν καὶ κατακόπτεται· τῆς ἀγάπης δὲ λυθείσης καὶ διαδοθείσης εἰς τὸν

---

23 προσκολλωμένης corr.: προσκολωμένης OA

MD **15**

On spiritual love

1. Sisters and Mothers, I want to praise the subject of love and yet I am unable to represent its loveliness in words. It is the most beautiful of the virtues and as the crown of moral beauty it is acquired by works and through experience. And so they have a genuine knowledge of the wondrous nature of love who have been deemed worthy to walk upon its path. Those who carry on about love in their speech can describe it, but those who have acquired it in their hearts display it in the noblest works. The latter are better off by far than the former. Yet even though the extraordinary nature of love exceeds our rhetorical skills, let us nevertheless sing its praises briefly so as to strengthen its many devotees.

2. Love, my beloved sisters, is a work that is brought to perfection in the soul, that warms the heart, illumines the mind, wakes the discursive intellect to meditate on the words of God, rouses the entire body to observe the divine commandments. In the beginning God bestowed on man the gift of love, which man received and put on like a most splendid garment. But the robber of our souls has rent this asunder and left man naked and full of all manner of shamefulness.[1] How is the garment of love rent asunder? And, in turn, how is it rescued from ruin? Listen!

3. When man loves God with all his heart and does what is pleasing to him, then all love in the soul is indivisible, since its entire capacity for love cleaves to God. Then when the soul is clothed with the radiant beauty of love as with a garment of royal purple, it appears as a sort of golden dove.[2] But when man begins to love gold, silver, precious stones and any other material object from the earth, not to mention luxury, every variety of foods, the mortal life of the flesh and the transient honour bestowed by men — when man sets the desire of his soul to all these pursuits, then the robe of love is divided and cut in pieces.[3] When love has been let loose and given over to this

---

[1] An allegorical exegesis of the parable of the Good Samaritan (Lk 10:25-37) that goes back to Clement of Alexandria. See G.J.M. Bartelink, "Les démons comme brigands," in *Vigiliae christianae* 21 (1967) 12-24.

[2] Cf. Ps 67:14.

[3] Cf. Jn 19:23-24.

κόσμον τοῦτον, ἔρημος καὶ γυμνὸς καὶ ἐλεεινὸς ὁρᾶται ὁ ἄνθρωπος.
ὡς γὰρ ἐάν τις διαρρήξας τινὸς ἀνθρώπου ἱμάτιον τὴν ἀσχημοσύνην
35 τῆς σαρκὸς αὐτοῦ καταφανῆ ποιεῖ, ὡς ἀπογυμνώσας αὐτὸν τῆς ἰδίας
σκέπης, οὕτω καὶ ὁ διάβολος τῆς ψυχῆς τὴν καλὴν ἐπιθυμίαν ἣν
ἔλαβεν ἀπὸ θεοῦ ἁρπάσας καὶ κατατεμὼν καὶ εἰς τὰ πράγματα τοῦ
φθειρομένου κόσμου διασκορπίσας, ἐγύμνωσε τὴν ψυχὴν τῆς ἀγαθῆς
ἀγάπης καὶ συναπεγύμνωσεν αὐτὴν καὶ τῆς τοῦ θεοῦ βοηθείας.
40 **4.** Ὅταν γὰρ ἀποστῇ ἡ ψυχὴ τῆς θείας ἀγάπης, τότε μακρύνεται
καὶ τῆς τοῦ θεοῦ βοηθείας. καὶ ὅτι ὁ μὴ ἀγαπῶν τὸν θεὸν ἐστέρηται
καὶ τῆς αὐτοῦ βοηθείας, τὸ τροπάριν ὃ ψάλλομεν δηλώσει ἡμῖν. ἡ
γὰρ ψυχὴ ἡ οὖσα γυμνὴ τῶν ἀρετῶν καὶ τῆς ἀγάπης καὶ τὴν ἑαυτῆς
ἀκοσμίαν ὁρῶσα καὶ πενθοῦσα ἐπὶ τῇ ἑαυτῆς ἐλεεινότητι λέγει· *τὸν*
45 *νυμφῶνα σου βλέπω, σωτήρ μου, κεκοσμημένον, ἀλλ' ἔνδυμα οὐκ ἔχω*
ἵνα εἰσέλθω· λάμπρυνόν μου τὴν στολήν.
5. Τὸν νυμφῶνά φησι τῆς σῆς βοηθείας ὁρῶ, σωτήρ μου,
πεπληρωμένον πάσης ἀγαθότητος, ἀλλ' ἔνδυμα ἀγάπης οὐκ ἔχω ἵνα
καὶ εἰς τὸ φρούριον τῆς σῆς βοηθείας εἰσέλθω· διὸ λάμπρυνόν μου
50 τὴν διάνοιαν τῇ τῆς ἀγάπης στολῇ, φωτοδότα, καὶ σῶσόν με, ὅπως
κοσμηθεῖσα ὑπὸ τῆς ἀγάπης, καὶ σωτηρίας ἀξιωθήσωμαι. ταύτην τὴν
ἀγάπην πάλιν φυτεῦσαι θέλων ἐν ταῖς καρδίαις τῶν ἀνθρώπων ὁ τοῦ
θεοῦ υἱὸς ἦλθεν ἐπὶ τῆς γῆς, καὶ τὴν ψυχὴν ἣν κατεμέρισεν ὁ
διάβολος εἰς τὴν ἐπιθυμίαν τοῦ κόσμου, συρράψας καὶ συναγαγὼν
55 καὶ ὁλοκλήρως ἀναβιβάσας αὐτὴν εἰς τὴν ἀγάπην τοῦ θεοῦ, ἐνεδύσατο
τὴν ψυχὴν τὴν προτέραν αὐτῆς στολὴν καὶ ὡραιοτάτην εἰργάσατο.

6. Διὸ καὶ λέγει· *πῦρ ἦλθον βαλεῖν ἐπὶ τὴν γῆν, καὶ τί θέλω εἰ ἤδη*
ἀνήφθη. πῦρ οἶμαι τὴν ἀγάπην ἐνταῦθα καλῶν, ἥνπερ ἔσβεσε μὲν ὁ
διάβολος, ἀνῆψε δὲ πάλιν ὁ Χριστὸς διὰ τῆς ἁγίας αὐτοῦ πολιτείας
60 καὶ τῶν σεπτῶν ἐντολῶν. ἡ ἀγάπη σύσσημον καὶ γνώρισμα Χριστοῦ·
ἐν τούτῳ γνώσονται, φησί, πάντες ὅτι ἐμοὶ μαθηταί ἐστε, ἐὰν ἀγαπᾶτε
ἀλλήλους. ἡ πλησμονὴ τῶν ἁμαρτημάτων ἀφανίζει τὴν ἀγάπην· *διὰ*
γὰρ τὸ πληθυνθῆναι, φησί, τὴν ἀνομίαν, ψυγήσεται ἡ ἀγάπη τῶν πολλῶν.
ὡς γὰρ τὰ πλήθη τῶν ὑδάτων σήπτει τὰ σπέρματα, οὕτως καὶ τὰ
65 πλήθη τῶν ἀνομημάτων ἐξαλείφει ἐκ τῆς ψυχῆς τὰ τῆς ἀγάπης
κινήματα. ὑπὸ ταύτης τῆς ἀγάπης τρωθεὶς ὁ μέγας ἀπόστολος Παῦλός

---

42 αὐτοῦ conieci: αὐτῆς OA   58 ἥνπερ Oᵖᶜ: ἥπερ OᵃᶜA

world, man appears deserted, naked and miserable. If someone tears apart a man's garment, he reveals the shamefulness of his flesh, since he has stripped him of his covering. Similarly, when the devil robbed the soul of the noble desire which it received from God, cutting it up and scattering it among the affairs of this world which is perishing, he deprived the soul of the goodness of love and at the same time stripped it also of God's help.

4. Whenever the soul abandons divine love, it sets itself far from God's help. The troparion we sing will show us that the person who does not love God is deprived also of his help. For when the soul is stripped of the virtues and of love and beholds its own want of adornment, it mourns over its own piteous state, saying, "I see your bridal chamber adorned, O my Saviour, and I have no wedding garment that I may enter there. Make my robe to shine."[4]

5. "I see the bridal chamber of your help (the soul says), O my Saviour, filled with all goodness, but I have no wedding garment of love that I may enter the citadel of your help. Therefore, make my discursive intellect to shine with the robe of love, O Giver of Light, and save me, so that adorned by love I shall be deemed worthy of salvation too." Wanting to plant this love once again in the hearts of men, the Son of God came to earth, and the soul, which the devil had dispersed among the desires of this world, the Saviour stitched together, united it and lifted it up in its entirety into the love of God, clothing the soul with its former garment and making it an object of beauty.

6. And so he says, "I came to cast fire upon the earth; and would that it were already kindled."[5] I think fire here refers to the love of the good, which the devil extinguished but Christ kindled again through his holy way of life and sacred commandments. Love is a sign and token by which Christ is known. Scripture says, "By this all men will know that you are my disciples, if you love one another."[6] A surfeit of sins does away with love, for scripture says, "Because wickedness is multiplied, most men's love will grow cold."[7] As an abundance of water causes seeds to rot, so too an abundance of transgressions obliterates from the soul the movements of love. Wounded by this

---

[4] Exaposteilarion of Matins for the first three days in Holy Week. See *The Lenten Triodion*, p. 514. The citation of this text strongly suggests that the discourse was actually given at this time. Note the demotic form τροπάριν.

[5] Lk 12:49.

[6] Jn 13:35.

[7] Mt 24:12.

φησι· ἀνάθεμα εἶναί με ἀπὸ Χριστοῦ ὑπὲρ τῶν ἀδελφῶν μου τῶν συγγενῶν μου τῶν κατὰ σάρκα.

7. Τοιοῦτον γὰρ ἡ ἀγάπη· ὡς γὰρ ὁ τῆς λαμπάδος κηρὸς καίεται
70 μὲν ὑπὸ τοῦ πυρός, φῶς δὲ τὸ πῦρ γίνεται καὶ φωτίζει τὸν κατέχοντα, οὕτω καὶ ἡ τοῦ θεοῦ ἀγάπη κατοικοῦσα ἐν τῇ ψυχῇ ἐκκαίει τὴν καρδίαν καὶ διαθερμαίνει τὴν ψυχὴν προδοῦναι τὴν ἰδίαν σάρκα εἰς κόπους καὶ κινδύνους ὑπὲρ τῆς τῶν ἀνθρώπων σωτηρίας. ταύτης τῆς ἀγάπης τὸν σπινθῆρα ἑώρακα ἐν τῇ ἐμῇ ψυχῇ, ὑφ' οὗ πυρωθεὶς
75 παρέβλεψα τὴν ἐμαυτοῦ ζωήν, θαλάσσας καὶ ποταμοὺς διεπέρασα καὶ ὀρέων κρημνοὺς διῆλθον καὶ χειμῶνες δριμύτατοι κατεπίεσάν μου τὸ σῶμα, ἀλλ' ἐν τούτοις πᾶσιν ἡ ἀγάπη πιαίνουσα τὴν ψυχήν μου, ὑπομένειν με τὰ θλιβερὰ ἐνεποίει· τὸ γὰρ διάπυρον τῆς πρὸς ὑμᾶς διαθέσεως τὸν χειμῶνα τῶν ἐπερχομένων μοι πειρασμῶν διε-
80 σκέδασεν. ἵνα τί γένηται καὶ τί προξενήσω ὑμῖν; ἵνα τῶν πιεζουσῶν ὑμᾶς θλίψεων ἀπαλλάξω ὑμᾶς καὶ πληροφορίαν δωρήσωμαι ὑμῖν τοῦ ἀγαπᾶν ὑμᾶς καὶ τῆς ὑμῶν σωτηρίας ὀρέγεσθαί τε καὶ κήδεσθαι.

8. Ὁ καρπὸς οὖν ἑκάστου τῶν ἀνθρώπων ἀπὸ τῆς ἰδίας πολιτείας καὶ ἀναστροφῆς διαγινώσκεται· ἀπὸ γὰρ τῶν καρπῶν αὐτῶν, φησὶν
85 ὁ κύριος, ἐπιγνώσεσθε αὐτούς. ὡς γὰρ τοὺς καρποὺς τῶν δένδρων ὁρῶντες καὶ γευόμενοι, ἐξ αὐτῶν τὰ καλὰ δένδρα ἐπιγινώσκομεν, οὕτως καὶ τοὺς φιλοθέους καὶ τὰς φιλανθρώπους ψυχὰς ἐκ τῶν ἔργων καταλαμβάνομεν καὶ τοὺς λόγους αὐτῶν πιστοὺς καὶ βεβαίους ἡγούμεθα, ὡς ἐκ τῶν θείων γραφῶν καὶ τῆς πείρας αὐτῶν στηριζο-
90 μένας. διὸ μὴ παντὶ ἀνέμῳ ψευδοδιδασκάλῳ φερόμεναι, τὴν χάριν τοῦ ἁγίου πνεύματος ἀφ' ἑαυτὰς ἐκδιώκετε, τῆς ἐκκλησίας ἀπο-διϊστάμεναι καὶ εἰς ἀδιαφορίας ἀναστρεφόμεναι. καὶ ἐν τῇ πρὸς ἀλλήλας πληροφορίᾳ συνδεόμεναι, τὸν ἀγαπήσαντα ἡμᾶς κύριον καὶ τῷ τιμίῳ αὐτοῦ αἵματι κτησάμενον ἡμᾶς καὶ εἰς μίαν ἐκκλησίαν καὶ
95 ποίμνην συστησάμενον ὑμνεῖν μὴ ἀπολίποιτε· ὅτι αὐτῷ πρέπει πᾶσα δόξα, τιμὴ καὶ προσκύνησις, νῦν καὶ ἀεὶ καὶ εἰς τοὺς αἰῶνας τῶν αἰώνων. Ἀμήν.

79-80 διεσκέδασεν corr.: διεσκέδαζεν ΟΑ

love, the great apostle Paul says, "I am outcast from Christ for the sake of my brethren, my natural kinsfolk."[8]

7. Love operates in the following way. As the wax of a candle is burned by the fire and the fire produces light and illuminates the one holding the candle, so does God's love dwelling in the soul kindle the heart and warm the soul in order to deliver its flesh to labours and dangers for the salvation of others. In my own soul I have seen the spark of this love; set aflame by it, I disregarded my own life, crossed seas and rivers, passed between mountainous cliffs; the most bitter winters bore down upon my body. But in all these trials love enriched my soul and made me capable of enduring afflictions, for the fervour of my disposition towards you dispersed the winter of trials that had come upon me.[9] What is the reason for this and why do I do this for you? In order that I may deliver you from the afflictions that oppress you and assure you of my love for you and of my desire and concern for your salvation.

8. Thus, the fruit each man bears is recognized in his own life and conduct. For the Lord says, "By their fruits you shall know them."[10] By observing and tasting the fruits from trees we get to know the good trees thereby. Similarly, we recognize from their works the people who love God and those souls concerned with their neighbour and we consider their words to be trustworthy and secure, since they receive strength from the divine scriptures and from their own experience. Therefore, do not banish the grace of the Holy Spirit from yourselves by allowing yourselves to be borne about by every wind of false teaching, by separating yourselves from the church and turning to indifference.[11] Uniting yourselves to one another in full assurance, may you not cease praising the Lord, who loved us and bought us by his precious blood[12] and brought us together as one church and flock.[13] To him be all glory, honour and worship, now and forever and unto the ages of ages. Amen.

[8] Rom 9:3.

[9] This appears to be a reference to the hardships of travel between Philadelpheia and Constantinople, especially in winter. It also suggests that Theoleptos was actually in Constantinople sometime during the winter prior to this Lenten season. In all probability Theoleptos travelled between Constantinople and Phokaia by sea and then went overland to Philadelpheia. At some point he would have had to cross the Hermus River. In EP 1 (December 1321) Theoleptos spoke of the hardships of one such trip from the Capital to his see: EP 1, ed. Hero, pp. 6-9.

[10] Mt 7:16.

[11] Cf. Eph 4:14.

[12] Cf. 1 Pet 1:19.

[13] Cf. Jn 10:16.

1. Ἀδελφαὶ καὶ μητέρες, εἰώθασιν οἱ ἀπὸ πλούτου εἰς πενίαν καταβαίνοντες δανεισταῖς προσέρχεσθαι· οἳ καὶ ὅτε μὲν δανείζονται, ἡδύνονται ὡς ἐπιτυγχάνοντες τοῦ ζητουμένου δανείου· ὅτε δὲ ἀπαιτοῦνται παρὰ τῶν δανειστῶν τὰ χρέη, πικραίνονται σφόδρα. καὶ
5 εἰ μὲν εὐποροῦσι κἂν ἀποδοῦναι τὸ δάνειον, ἐλεεινοὶ πάλιν καὶ ἄποροι ἀπομένουσιν. εἰ δὲ οὐ δύνανται ἀποφλῆσαι τὸ χρέος, τὰς χεῖρας καὶ τὴν τυραννίδα τῶν ἀπαιτητῶν οὐ διαφεύγουσι. κατέστημεν καὶ ἡμεῖς ἀπὸ θεοῦ ἐν τῷ πλούτῳ τῶν ἀρετῶν, ἀλλὰ καταδαπανήσαντες τὴν δύναμιν τῆς ψυχῆς ἡμῶν ἐν τοῖς ματαίοις, ἐγενόμεθα πένητες
10 καὶ ἄποραι κατ' ἐκεῖνον τὸν ἄσωτον υἱὸν τὸν καταφαγόντα τὴν πατρικὴν οὐσίαν καὶ τοῦ πατρὸς ἀποδημήσαντα καὶ εἰς τὸ βόσκειν χοίρους καταντήσαντα.

2. Ἐπεὶ οὖν ἐξεπέσαμεν ἀπὸ τῶν καλῶν, προσήλθομεν ὡς δα-νειστῇ τῷ πονηρῷ καὶ ἐδανεισάμεθα παρ' αὐτοῦ ἐπιθυμίας αἰσχρὰς
15 καὶ πονηροὺς λογισμούς. ἀπωλέσαμεν τὴν ἀγάπην καὶ ἐκτησάμεθα τὸ μῖσος· ἀπελύσαμεν τὴν δικαιοσύνην καὶ ἐπιάσαμεν τὴν ἀδικίαν· ἀπεβαλόμεθα τὴν ἐγκράτειαν καὶ ἐκρατήσαμεν τὴν ἀκρασίαν· ἐδιώξαμεν τὴν εἰρήνην καὶ ἐπεσπασάμεθα τὴν μάχην· ἐμισήσαμεν τὴν ἡμερότητα καὶ ἠγαπήσαμεν τὴν ὀργὴν καὶ τὴν σκληρότητα.

20 3. Πάσας τοίνυν ταύτας τὰς πονηρὰς διαθέσεις δανειακῶς ἐλάβομεν ἐκ τοῦ διαβόλου· ξένα γὰρ τῆς ἡμετέρας φύσεως τὰ τοῦ πονηροῦ θελήματα. ὡς γὰρ ὁ δανειζόμενος ἀλλότρια λαμβάνει πράγματα, ἐπειδὴ ἀφ' ἑαυτοῦ οὐκ ἔχει, οὕτως καὶ ἡμεῖς τὰ ἴδια τῆς ψυχῆς ἡμῶν ἀπολέσαντες ἀγαθά, ἐλάβομεν τὰ πονηρὰ θελήματα τοῦ
25 ἀλλοτρίου δαίμονος. διὸ καὶ καθ' ἑκάστην ὥραν καὶ ἡμέραν ἀπαιτεῖ ἡμᾶς ὁ δαίμων ἐργάζεσθαι διὰ τοῦ σώματος ταῦτα. Ὡς γὰρ ὁ δανειστὴς ἀπαιτεῖ ἐκ τοῦ χρεωφειλέτου τὰ δανεισθέντα πράγματα, οὕτω καὶ ὁ διάβολος ἀναγκάζει ἡμᾶς τὰς κακὰς πράξεις ποιεῖν καὶ ὡς τόκους ἀπαιτεῖ τὰς αὐξήσεις τῶν κακῶν ἔργων.

11-12 ἀποδημήσαντα ... καταντήσαντα corr.: ἀποδημήσαντος ... καταντήσαντος ΟΑ
17 ἀπεβαλόμεθα corr.: ἀπεβαλλόμεθα ΟΑ

MD **16**

Untitled [The tyranny of sin]

1.   Sisters and Mothers, those who have fallen from wealth into penury customarily have recourse to money-lenders. And when they borrow money they are pleased when they get the loan they are seeking. But when the debts are collected by the money-lenders, they complain bitterly. Even if they have the means to pay back the loan, they are once again in a pitiable condition of poverty. But if they are unable to discharge their debt, they do not escape the tyrannous clutches of the loan collectors.[1] We too were established by God in the wealth of the virtues, but when we squandered the strength of our souls in empty pursuits we became poor and impoverished in the manner of the prodigal son who consumed the wealth he inherited, left his father to go abroad and was reduced to feeding swine.[2]

2.   Therefore, when we fell away from the good we had recourse to the evil one as to a money-lender and borrowed from him shameful desires and evil thoughts. We lost love and acquired hatred. We gave up righteousness and laid hold of iniquity. We discarded discipline and grabbed hold of licentiousness.[3] We drove away peace and welcomed strife. We hated gentleness and loved anger and obduracy.

3.   We have thus acquired all these evil dispositions on loan from the devil, for the will of the evil one is foreign to our nature. As the borrower accepts things that are not his own, since he does not possess them in his own right, so, in losing the proper goods of our soul, we accepted the evil will of the alien demon. And so at every day and hour the demon requires us to do his will through our body. As the money-lender demands from the debtor the money he owes, so too the devil requires us to do evil deeds and demands as interest increments in evil works.

---

[1] On this and related subjects see N. Oikonomidès, *Hommes d'affaires*, especially pp. 53-63.

[2] Lk 15:11-16.

[3] Note the alliteration in the Greek.

30 **4.** Ἰδὼν οὖν ἡμᾶς ὁ τοῦ θεοῦ υἱὸς καταπονουμένους ὑπὸ τῆς ἁμαρτίας καὶ τυραννουμένους ὑπὸ τῶν παθῶν καὶ βιαζομένους ὑπὸ τοῦ διαβόλου, γενόμενος ἄνθρωπος, ἔδωκεν ἑαυτὸν ἀντίλυτρον ὑπὲρ ἡμῶν. ὑπέμεινε σταυρὸν καὶ θάνατον, δι᾽ ὧν ὁ θάνατος τῶν ἡδονῶν καταργεῖται. ὀφείλομεν τοιγαροῦν ὁρᾶν πρὸς τὴν ἁγίαν πολιτείαν

35 τοῦ κυρίου καὶ μιμεῖσθαι τὴν σωτήριον ἀναστροφὴν αὐτοῦ, ἣν ἐν τῷ παρόντι κόσμῳ σωματικῶς ὁμιλῶν ἡμῖν καθυπέδειξε· τοὺς κόπους γὰρ τῶν ἔργων αὐτοῦ κρατοῦντες καὶ τοὺς λόγους τῶν ἐντολῶν αὐτοῦ τηροῦντες, ἐλεύθεραι γενώμεθα τῆς τοῦ διαβόλου τυραννίδος. ὀργὴν ἐξορίζωμεν καὶ πραότητα κτώμεθα, μῖσος ἀπελαύνωμεν καὶ ἀγάπην

40 ἀγκαλιζώμεθα, ἀδικίαν διώκωμεν καὶ δικαιοσύνην ἀσπαζώμεθα· καὶ πᾶσαν ἄλλην παθῶν ἐνέργειαν ἀποτρέπουσαι, τὰς ἀρετὰς ἐργαζώμεθα καὶ διὰ τῆς τῶν ἀρετῶν ἐργασίας καὶ μελέτης λυτροῦται ἡ ψυχὴ ἡμῶν τῶν πονηρῶν λογισμῶν καὶ τῶν ἔργων τῆς ἁμαρτίας καὶ ὁ διάβολος φεύγει ἐξ ἡμῶν.

45 **5.** Μὴ γοῦν θελήσωμεν τυραννεῖσθαι ὑπὸ τοῦ πονηροῦ αἱ τοσαύτης ἐλευθερίας τυχοῦσαι. τίς γὰρ καλούμενος λαβεῖν δωρεὰν πράγματα καὶ τὸ ἴδιον χρέος ἀποφλῆσαι καὶ παραιτεῖται τὴν κλῆσιν καὶ ἀποστρέφεται τοῦ ἐλεοῦντος τὴν χάριν; οἱ δὲ τοῦτο οἱ ἄνθρωποι οὐ ποιοῦσιν· ὁ δὲ ποιῶν ὑπὸ ἀφροσύνης συνέχεται καὶ καταδίκῃ

50 καθυποβάλλεται. πῶς ἡμεῖς τὰς σωτηριώδεις πράξεις καὶ τὰ ὑπὲρ ἡμῶν τοῦ σωτῆρος παθήματα οὐ ζηλοῦμεν οὐδὲ μιμούμεθα; διὸ σπουδάσωμεν βαστάσαι ταῦτα ἐν τοῖς ἡμετέροις σώμασιν, δίκην ἐμπλάστρων ἁπλοῦντές τε καὶ τιθέμεναι ἐν τοῖς τοῦ σώματος αἰσθητηρίοις καὶ μέλεσι. καὶ εἰ τοῦτο ποιοῦμεν, θεραπεύονται τὰ

55 διανοήματα τῶν ψυχῶν ἡμῶν καὶ ὑπὸ τῆς μελέτης καὶ τῆς γνώσεως τῶν δεσποτικῶν παθῶν διαβαστάζεται ἡ ψυχὴ καὶ οὐ πίπτει εἰς τὰ πονηρὰ τῆς σαρκὸς θελήματα· δουλεύουσα γὰρ τῷ κυρίῳ διὰ τῶν ἀρίστων ἔργων, τῆς δουλείας τῶν παθῶν ἀπαλλάττεται. ἐν αὐτῷ Χριστῷ τῷ κυρίῳ ἡμῶν ᾧ ἡ δόξα εἰς τοὺς αἰῶνας τῶν αἰώνων. Ἀμήν.

39-41 ἐξορίζωμεν ... ἀπελαύνωμεν ... ἀγκαλιζώμεθα ... διώκωμεν ... ἐργαζώμεθα conieci: modus indicativus OA

4.   Therefore, when the Son of God saw us labouring under the burden of sin, tyrannized by the passions and overpowered by the devil, he became man and gave himself as a ransom for us.[4] He endured the Cross and death, whereby the death brought on by sinful pleasures is destroyed. We ought then to look upon the Lord's holy way of life and imitate his saving conduct which he showed us while he lived among us bodily in the present world. Enduring the labours of his works and keeping the words of his commandments, let us free ourselves of the devil's tyranny. Let us banish anger and acquire gentleness. Let us eschew hatred and embrace love. Let us chase away iniquity and welcome righteousness. And rejecting every other activity of the passions, let us labour at the virtues, and through our studious efforts to practise them our soul will be ransomed from evil thoughts and sinful works and the devil will flee from us.

5.   Once we have attained so great a freedom, let us not then wilfully place ourselves under the tyranny of the evil one. When invited to accept money as a gift so as to discharge one's debt, who would decline the invitation and repudiate the favour of him who shows us pity? People do not act this way. But someone who does act this way is held fast by stupidity and is subjecting himself to condemnation. How can we not strive after and imitate the saving deeds and the sufferings of the Saviour on our behalf? And so, let us hasten to bear these sufferings in our bodies, applying and setting them like poultices on the senses and members of the body. If we do this, the thoughts of our souls receive healing, the soul is borne up by meditation and knowledge of the Lord's passions and does not fall prey to the evil inclinations of the flesh, for when the soul serves the Lord through the noblest works it is delivered from servitude to the passions. In Christ our Lord to whom be glory forever and ever. Amen.

[4] 1 Tim 2:6.

Τῇ λαμπρᾷ κυριακῇ
καὶ περὶ τοῦ θανάτου τοῦ ἀδελφοῦ Λέοντος

1. Ἀδελφαὶ καὶ μητέρες, ἡ μὲν παροῦσα ἡμέρα τὴν ἀνάστασιν φέρουσα τοῦ Χριστοῦ προτρέπεται λέγειν περὶ αὐτῆς, ἡ δὲ ἐκδημία
5 καὶ ἀπὸ τοῦ βίου τούτου αἰφνίδιος καὶ ἀνέτοιμος μετάστασις τοῦ ἀδελφοῦ ἡμῶν Λέοντος, οὗ τὸ ἐπίκλην ὁ Μονομάχος, ἀναγκάζει με λαλῆσαι πρὸς τὴν ὑμετέραν ἀγάπην περὶ ἐξόδου τῆς ψυχῆς, ἵν᾽ ἐκ τοῦ συμβεβηκότος αἰφνιδίου θανάτου τῷ ἀδελφῷ ἡμῶν καὶ ἐκ τῆς παρούσης κατηχήσεως τυπωθῇ ἐν ταῖς καρδίαις ὑμῶν ἡ τοῦ θανάτου
10 μνήμη πρὸς τὸ ἐξυπνίζειν ὑμᾶς ἀπὸ τῆς συνεχούσης ὑμᾶς ῥαθυμίας καὶ διεγείρειν εἰς ἀγαθά, προσδοκωμένας ἀεί ποτε αὐτὸν καὶ φοβου- μένας τὴν αἰφνίδιον ἔφοδον αὐτοῦ.

2. Οἴδατε, ἀδελφαί μου, ὅτι ὀφθαλμοῖς ἰδίοις ἑωράκατε αὐτὸν καὶ συνεστιάτορα καὶ συνοδοιπόρον εἴχετε αὐτόν, καὶ ἅμα διεπλέετε τὴν
15 θάλασσαν τοῦ βίου τούτου· ἀλλ᾽ αἰφνιδίως ἔπνευσεν ὁ τοῦ θανάτου κλύδων καὶ διαχωρίσας τὴν ψυχὴν αὐτοῦ ἀπὸ τοῦ σώματος παρέδωκε τὸ σῶμα αὐτοῦ εἰς τὸν τῆς γῆς βυθὸν καὶ τῆς παρούσης ζωῆς ἀπεστέρησε, τὴν δὲ ψυχὴν αὐτοῦ παρεσκεύασεν ἀνέτοιμον εὑρεθῆναι, ὃ δὴ καὶ λυπεῖ με τὰ μέγιστα.
20 3. Τὸ μὲν γὰρ θνήσκειν τὸν ἄνθρωπον, τοῦτο φύσεως νόμος καὶ τοῦ δεσπότου ἀπόφασις, δικαιοῦσα τὸν μεθιστάμενον ἀπὸ ἁμαρτίας καὶ εἰς τὸν ἀεὶ διαμένοντα παραπέμπουσα κόσμον· τοὺς δὲ ἔτι ζῶντας σωφρονίζουσα καὶ πρὸς τὰ μέλλοντα μεθαρμόζουσα. τὸ δὲ ἀνέτοιμον εἶναι τὸν τελευτῶντα καὶ ἀπαρασκεύαστον εὑρίσκεσθαι εἰς τὰ τῆς
25 σωτηρίας αὐτοῦ ἔργα, τοῦτο τῆς προαιρέσεως καὶ τῆς γνώμης ἀμέλεια· ὅπερ οὐκ ἔδει ποιεῖν ἐκεῖνον. οὐ γὰρ ἐνδέχεται τὸν χρι- στιανικῶς ζῶντα ἄνθρωπον ἀμελεῖν ἐν τῷ τῆς ὑγιείας καὶ τῆς ζωῆς αὐτοῦ καιρῷ, ἀλλὰ γρηγορεῖν εἰς τὰς καλὰς πράξεις καὶ τρέχειν πρὸς

11 προσδοκωμένας cum Sal. corr.: προσδοκωμέναις O, προδοκωμέναις A   11-
12 φοβουμένας cum Sal. corr.: φοβουμέναις OA

THE RADIANT DAY OF EASTER AND THE DEATH OF BROTHER LEO[1]

1. Sisters and Mothers, the present day, which brings us the Resurrection of Christ, presses me to speak of it, but the sudden untimely departure from this life and passing away of our brother Leo, surnamed Monomachos, compels me to speak to you concerning the soul's departure. Thus, by the sudden death that befell our brother and by the present instruction the memory of death may leave its impression on your hearts so as to waken you from the sloth holding you in its grip and to rouse you to good works, while your attitude towards death is always and ever one of ready expectation and fear of its sudden onslaught.

2. You know, my sisters, you saw him with your own eyes and had him as a guest at table and as a fellow traveller on the way; together you plied the sea of this life. But suddenly the sea-storm of death blew forth and separating his soul from the body, it committed his body into the depths of the earth, deprived him of the present life and let his soul be caught unprepared: this is what grieves me most.[2]

3. For man to die is a law of nature and a sentence imposed by the Lord, one which vindicates the person who repents of sin and guides him to the world of eternity and which chastens those still living and prepares them properly for the life to come. But for a man to be caught unready for death and ill-prepared in the works of his salvation is a matter of freely chosen and intentional negligence; this he ought not to have allowed. The person who lives a Christian life

---

[1] An edition, translation and commentary on this text was published by S. Salaville, "Une lettre et un discours inédits de Théolepte de Philadelphie," REB 5 (1947) 108-115.

[2] The suggestion here is that Leo Monomachos was the hieromonk who served the community of nuns both liturgically and perhaps also in matters of spiritual direction while Theoleptos was absent. Since he is spoken of as a fellow traveller, he was probably from the adjacent men's monastery of the Philanthropos Soter. Theoleptos' grief over his soul's unreadiness is a little puzzling. Perhaps, it means no more than that Leo had no opportunity to make specific preparation for death by confession of sins. That would certainly serve as an example to the nuns to maintain holiness of life and not depend on the opportunity of a deathbed confession.

τὴν ἐξομολόγησιν καὶ ἀπέχεσθαι ἀπὸ τῶν πονηρῶν τρόπων. ὡς γὰρ
30 ὁ πλέων ἐν τῇ θαλάσσῃ, ἡνίκα γαλήνην ἄγει, κωπηλατεῖ σπουδαίως
καὶ σπεύδει πρὸς τοὺς τόπους ἐγγίζειν τοῦ λιμένος, μήπως αἰφνιδίως
ἐπαναστῇ ἄγριος ἄνεμος καὶ εὑρήσῃ αὐτὸν εἰς τὸ πέλαγος καὶ
βυθισθῇ ὑπὸ τῶν μεγάλων καὶ ἀπείρων κυμάτων. τὸ αὐτὸ τοῦτο
ἑκάστη ὑμῶν ὀφείλει ποιεῖν, ζῶσα ἐν τῷ κόσμῳ τούτῳ καὶ συνα-
35 ναστρεφομένη.

4. Ὑγιαίνων γὰρ ὁ ἄνθρωπος καὶ καλῶς ἔχων τῷ σώματι διὰ
τὴν τῶν στοιχείων εὐκρασίαν, γαλήνης ἀπολαύει διὰ τὴν τῶν
ἀρρωστημάτων ἀπουσίαν καὶ τὴν κατὰ φύσιν τῆς δυνάμεως αὐτοῦ
κίνησιν. δεῖ οὖν αὐτὸν ὑγιαίνοντα καὶ περιπατοῦντα ἐν τῷ κόσμῳ
40 κωπηλατεῖν, ἤγουν εἰς κόπους παραμένειν τῶν τοῦ κυρίου ἐντολῶν
καὶ τρόπους ἀρίστους ἐπιζητεῖν. καὶ ὥσπερ οἱ πλέοντες ἐν ταῖς χερσὶ
τὰς κώπας κατέχοντες τέμνουσι τὸ τῆς θαλάσσης ὕδωρ καὶ διαπερῶσι
τὸ πλοῖον, οὕτω καὶ ὁ ἄνθρωπος ὀφείλει πράττειν διηνεκῶς τὰ καλὰ
ἔργα καὶ διαπερᾶν τὸν χρόνον τῆς ζωῆς αὐτοῦ μετὰ δικαιοσύνης καὶ
45 σπουδάζειν τὰς ἐν ὑγείᾳ ἡμέρας αὐτοῦ ἀναλίσκειν ἐν τῇ μετανοίᾳ
καὶ τῇ ἐξομολογήσει, ἵνα ἐὰν ἀσθένημά τι ἐπέλθῃ αὐτῷ ἢ αἰφνίδιος
θάνατος, εὑρεθῇ εἰς τοὺς λιμένας τῆς σωτηρίας. πᾶς γὰρ μετανοῶν
καὶ ἐξομολογούμενος, ἐν ὅσῳ ὑγιαίνει καὶ ζῇ, εἰς τοὺς κόλπους τοῦ
λιμένος εἰσάγεται καὶ οὐ φοβεῖται ἀσθένειαν ἢ θάνατον· διαλογίζεται
50 γὰρ ὅτι ἐὰν ἔλθῃ αὐτῷ ἀσθένεια, ὠφελήσει πλέον τὴν ψυχὴν αὐτοῦ
ταπεινώσασα αὐτήν. εἰ γὰρ ὅτε ἠδύνατο τὸ σῶμα αὐτοῦ ἐνεργεῖν τὴν
ἁμαρτίαν, οὐκ ἐκίνει τὰ μέλη αὐτοῦ πρὸς τὰς πράξεις τῶν κακῶν,
ἀλλὰ διεκώλυεν ἑαυτὸν ἀπὸ παντὸς πονηροῦ πράγματος καὶ ταπεινόφρων ἐφαίνετο, πολλῷ μᾶλλον ταπεινωθήσεται ἐν τῇ ἀσθενείᾳ τοῦ
55 σώματος καὶ γνησίως εὐχαριστήσει τῷ θεῷ ὡς εὐεργετούμενος διὰ
τῆς ἀρρωστίας. εἰ δὲ θάνατος συμβῇ αὐτῷ, ἰδοὺ μετακομίζει αὐτὸν
εἰς τὴν ἐκεῖθεν ἀνάπαυσιν, πρὸς ἣν ἠπείγετο φθάσαι διὰ τῆς καλῆς
πολιτείας αὐτοῦ. διὸ καὶ χαρὰ ἐν οὐρανῷ γίνεται ἐπὶ τῇ μετανοίᾳ
τοῦ ἀνθρώπου καὶ τῇ μεταστάσει τοῦ ἐν ἑτοιμασίᾳ ψυχῆς μεταστάντος
60 ἀπὸ τοῦ βίου. καὶ ὥσπερ οἱ συγγενείας νόμῳ δεσμούμενοι, ὁρῶντες
τὸν ἑαυτῶν συγγενῆ ἐν ἀξιώματι προκόπτοντα καὶ ἐν τιμῇ
ἀναβαίνοντα, χαίρουσι διὰ τὸ διαβαίνειν τὴν αὐτοῦ τιμὴν καὶ πρὸς
αὐτούς, οὕτω καὶ οἱ ἄγγελοι χαίρουσιν ἐπὶ τῇ μετανοίᾳ καὶ τῇ
προκοπῇ τῶν ἡμετέρων ψυχῶν ὡς συγγενεῖς ἡμῶν.

32 εὑρήσῃ cum Sal. corr.: εὑρήσει ΟΑ   46 ἀσθένημά τι cum Sal. conieci:
ἀσθενήματος ΟΑ

cannot be negligent during the times when he enjoys health and life; rather, he must be vigilant in performing good works, in hastening to confess his sins and in avoiding evil ways. The situation is comparable to that of a sailor travelling on the sea: when the sea is calm he rows vigorously and is anxious to be near a place of harbour, lest a fierce squall arise, find him in the open sea and leave him swamped by innumerable mighty waves.[3] Each of you should do the same while you live and conduct your lives in this world.

4. For while a man is in good health and is sound in body because of the harmonious mixing of the elements, he enjoys a calm owing to the absence of sickness and also to the natural functioning of his faculties. Therefore, while he enjoys health in his traversal through this world, he must keep rowing, that is, he must persevere in labouring at the Lord's commandments and seek after the noblest ways of virtue. As sailors hold the oars in their hands and cut through the water of the sea, sending the boat forward, so too man ought continuously to practise good works and pass through his lifetime in righteousness, earnestly spending his healthy days in repentance and confession of his sins, so that, if an illness or sudden death should overtake him, he may be found within the harbours of salvation. Any man who while he is alive and healthy repents and confesses his sins, enters the inner reaches of the harbour and has no fear of sickness or death, for he figures that if sickness befalls him it will bring greater benefit to his soul by humbling it. For if, when his body was capable of committing sin, he did not allow his members to engage in evil deeds but restrained himself from any evil deed and adopted a humble attitude, all the more, then, will he be humbled when his body is sick and he will give sincere thanks to God for being granted the benefit of illness. And if death does come upon him, behold, it transports him to that rest which he had been hastening to attain through his good conduct. And so there is joy in heaven over a man's repentance and over his passing from this life with his soul prepared.[4] As those bound by the law of kinship look upon their kinsman advancing in social position and rising in honour and rejoice that his honour redounds even to them, so too do the angels rejoice over the repentance and progress of our souls, as they are kindred to us.[5]

---

[3] A similar image and application can be found in Pseudo-Macarius, *Homilia* 43.4 in *Die 50 geistlichen Homilien des Makarios*, ed. H. Dörries, E. Klostermann and M. Kroeger (Patristische Texte und Studien 4; Berlin, 1964), p. 287.

[4] Cf. Lk 15:7.

[5] Cf. Lk 15:10.

65   **5.** Καὶ οὕτω μὲν εἰς τὴν ἄφεσιν τῶν ἑαυτοῦ ἁμαρτιῶν φθάνει
καὶ τῆς βασιλείας τῶν οὐρανῶν ἀξιοῦται ὁ μετανοῶν καὶ διηνεκῶς
ἑτοιμαζόμενος εἰς τὴν ὥραν τῆς ἐξόδου αὐτοῦ. εἰ δὲ ὅτε ζῇ καὶ
ὑγιαίνει ὁ ἄνθρωπος ἐν ἁμαρτίαις διάγει καὶ εἰς μερίμνας βιωτικὰς
σχολάζει, ἰδοὺ ματαίας καὶ ἀργὰς διαβιβάζει τὰς ἡμέρας αὐτοῦ καὶ
70 καθεύδει ὁ τοιοῦτος καὶ ὑπνοῖ· ὃν καταλαμβάνει ἢ δεινὴ ἀσθένεια
ἢ αἰφνίδιος θάνατος καὶ ἀνέτοιμον εὑρίσκει τὴν αὐτοῦ ψυχὴν καὶ
ἐλεεινὸν ἀποδεικνύει καὶ μεμακρυσμένον ἀπὸ τοῦ θεοῦ. ὡς γὰρ ὁ
κυβερνήτης ὑπνώττων ὑπὸ σπιλάδος αἰφνιδίως ἐπιπεσούσης τῷ πλοίῳ
βυθίζεται καὶ ἐμπνίγεται, οὕτω καὶ ὁ ἐν τῇ ὑγείᾳ αὐτοῦ διατελῶν
75 ἀμετανόητος καὶ ἀνεξομολόγητος ὑπὸ αἰφνιδίου θανάτου ἁρπάζεται
καὶ εἰς θάνατον αἰώνιον παραπέμπεται. καὶ ὥσπερ πικρότατόν ἐστι
τὸ ἀπὸ φυλακῆς εἰς φυλακὴν ἐμβάλλεσθαι τὸν κατακεκριμένον
ἄνθρωπον, οὕτως ἀφόρητος ἡ κόλασις ὑπάρχει καὶ τῷ ἀνετοίμως
ἐξερχομένῳ ἐκ τοῦ βίου τούτου.

80   **6.** Διὸ φοβηθεῖσαι τὸν αἰφνίδιον θάνατον τοῦ ἀδελφοῦ ἡμῶν,
γρηγορήσωμεν ἡμεῖς ἐν ὅσῳ ζῶμεν, καὶ διὰ μετανοίας καὶ ἐξομολογήσεως καὶ ἐλεημοσύνης καὶ τῆς πρὸς τοὺς θείους ναοὺς
συνάξεως θεραπεύσωμεν τὸν θεόν, ἵνα ταῖς φρονίμοις παρθένοις
ὁμοιωθέντες ἕτοιμαι εὑρεθῶμεν ἀκολουθῆσαι τῷ κυρίῳ. εἰ δὲ ἐν
85 παιγνίοις καὶ ματαίοις ἔργοις καὶ βιωτικαῖς μερίμναις ἀναστρεφόμεθα,
ὡς τὰς λαμπάδας ἡμῶν, ἤτοι τὰς ψυχὰς ἡμῶν, ἐσβεσμένας καὶ
σκοτεινὰς φέρουσαι, ἀπομένομεν ἔξω τοῦ νυμφῶνος Χριστοῦ ὡς
ἀνέτοιμαι. ὡς γὰρ ἐπὶ τῶν παρθένων μέσον νυκτὸς ἡ κραυγὴ γέγονε,
καὶ αἱ μὲν ἕτοιμαι εἰς τὸν νυμφῶνα εἰσῆλθον, αἱ δὲ ἀνέτοιμαι
90 ἐκλείσθησαν ἔξω, οὕτως καὶ ἡμῖν τοῖς ἀνθρώποις ἀδήλως καὶ
αἰφνιδίως ὁ θάνατος ἐπέρχεται, καὶ αἱ μὲν ἔλαιον ἐξομολογήσεως
καὶ μετανοίας φέρουσαι ἐν ταῖς ψυχαῖς αὐτῶν συγκληρονόμαι γίνονται
τοῦ Χριστοῦ καὶ εἰς τὴν βασιλείαν αὐτοῦ εἰσέρχονται, αἱ δὲ ἀμελῶς
καὶ ῥαθύμως περιπατοῦσαι μακρὰν τῆς σωτηρίας εὑρίσκονται καὶ
95 ἀκούουσι παρὰ τοῦ σωτῆρος· οὐκ οἶδα ὑμᾶς.

       7. Ἀλλὰ μὴ γένοιτο, ἀγαπηταί μου ἀδελφαί, τινὰ ἐξ ὑμῶν
δέξασθαι τὴν ἀπόκρισιν ταύτην· ἀξιωθείημεν δὲ πᾶσαι συγκοινωνῆσαι
Χριστῷ διὰ τῆς καλῆς ἀναστροφῆς καὶ τοῦ περιπατεῖν ἡμᾶς πρὸς
δόξαν θεοῦ· ὅτι αὐτῷ πρέπει πᾶσα δόξα εἰς τοὺς αἰῶνας. Ἀμήν.

---

73 ἐπιπεσούσης cum Sal. corr.: ἐπισπεσούσης ΟΑ   91 ἔλαιον cum Sal. corr.:
ἔλεον ΟΑ   98 ἡμᾶς corr.: ὑμᾶς ΟΑ

5. Thus, the penitent who is continually preparing himself for the hour of his death attains the forgiveness of his sins and is deemed worthy of the Kingdom of Heaven. But if a person when he is alive and well spends his time in sin and occupies himself with the concerns of this life, behold, he passes his days in empty idleness; he sleeps and slumbers. Either a terrible disease or sudden death seizes him, finds his soul unprepared and reveals him to be in a wretched state, alienated from God. As a helmsman who falls asleep is swamped by a squall that falls suddenly upon his boat and is drowned, so too the healthy man who goes unrepentant and unconfessed is snatched off by sudden death and conveyed to a death that is eternal.[6] Just as it is the most bitter fate for a condemned man to be incarcerated first in one prison and then in another, so is the punishment unbearable also for the man who departs from this life unprepared.

6. So then, prompted by fear at the sudden death of our brother, let us be watchful while we have life and let us serve God by repentance, confession of sins, almsgiving and by assembling for prayer in the divine churches, so that, like the wise virgins, we may be found ready to follow the Lord. But if we pass our time occupied with games, empty pursuits and worldly cares, with our lamps (that is, our souls) extinguished and dark, we shall be left outside the bridal chamber, because we are unprepared. For just as in the middle of the night the cry went up among the virgins and those who were ready entered the bridal chamber, while those who were not prepared were shut outside,[7] similarly does death come suddenly and secretly upon us. Those who bear in their souls the oil of confession of sins and of repentance become co-heirs with Christ and enter into his Kingdom, while those who in their indifference and sloth are found wandering far from salvation shall hear from the Saviour, "I know you not."[8]

7. But may it not happen, my dear sisters, that any of you should receive this reply. Rather, may we all be found worthy to enjoy communion with Christ through our good conduct and our journey towards the glory of God, for to him belongs all glory forever. Amen.

---

[6] A similar image but rather different application is given in Hesychius, *On Vigilance and Virtue* 169, *Philokalia* 1:167.

[7] Mt 25:1-13.

[8] Mt 25:12.

1. Ἀδελφαὶ καὶ μητέρες, ἐνδέχεται ἡμᾶς τοῦ μακαρίου Ἰωσὴφ
τοῦ ἀπὸ Ἀριμαθαίας τὴν ἐπαινετὴν τόλμαν καὶ τὸ θαυμάσιον ἔργον
5 ἐνθυμεῖσθαι διηνεκῶς καὶ μιμεῖσθαι αὐτοῦ τὴν ἀγαθὴν προαίρεσιν
καὶ πρᾶξιν. ἐὰν γὰρ τὸ ἀγαθὸν ἔργον ὃ ἐποίησεν εἰς τὸν κύριον ἡμῶν
Ἰησοῦν Χριστὸν μελετῶμεν ἐν τῇ ψυχῇ, ἰδοὺ καὶ ἡμεῖς, καθάπερ
σινδόνι, τῇ ἡμετέρᾳ καρδίᾳ ἐντυλίσομεν τὸ σῶμα τοῦ κυρίου,
συστρέφουσαι ἐν τῇ διανοίᾳ τὴν ἁγίαν ταφὴν αὐτοῦ καὶ ἐν τῇ μνήμῃ
10 τῆς ψυχῆς κατατιθέμεναι, ὡς μηδέποτε ἐπιλανθάνεσθαι τοῦ μυστηρίου
τούτου.

2. Τίς οὖν οὐ θαυμάσειε τὸν εὐσχήμονα Ἰωσήφ, ὃς τὴν εἰς
Χριστὸν τὸν θεὸν εὐσέβειαν καὶ ἀγάπην προτιμησάμενος, πάντα τὰ
τοῖς ἀνθρώποις ἐπίφοβα ὑπερεῖδε καὶ πρὸς τὸν Πιλᾶτον ἀπῆλθε καὶ
15 τὸ σῶμα ᾐτήσατο τοῦ κυρίου. οὐκ ἔσβεσεν αὐτοῦ τὴν πίστιν τὸ
βουλευτικὸν ἀξίωμα. οὐκ ἐνεπόδισεν αὐτῷ ὁ πλοῦτος αὐτοῦ. οὐκ
ἐκώλυσεν αὐτὸν ὁ τῆς σωματικῆς κακώσεως φόβος. ἀλλὰ καὶ τὸ
ἀξίωμα, βουλευτὴς γὰρ ἦν, ἤγουν ἔφορος τῶν τῆς ἀγορᾶς πραγμάτων,
καὶ τὸν πλοῦτον καὶ τὸ σῶμα αὐτοῦ προδούς, ἔσπευσε λαβεῖν ἀντὶ
20 πάντων τὸν Χριστόν. οὐκ ἐφόβησεν αὐτὸν ἡ κατὰ Χριστοῦ μάχη
τῶν Ἰουδαίων, ἀλλὰ τολμήσας ἐζήτησε καὶ ἔλαβε καὶ ἠξίωσε ταφῆς
τὸν κύριον.

---

2 Ἀριμαθαίας corr.: Ἀριμαθαία OA   17 ἐκώλυσεν corr.: ἐκώλησεν OA

THE SUNDAY OF THE MYRRH-BEARING WOMEN; AND ON JOSEPH OF ARIMATHAEA[1]

1. Sisters and Mothers, it behooves us to ponder continuously the praiseworthy courage and wondrous work of Joseph of Arimathaea and to imitate his good resolve and conduct. For if we meditate in our souls upon the good deed which he performed for our Lord Jesus Christ, behold we too shall wrap the Lord's body in our heart as in a shroud, gathering his holy burial into our discursive intellect and depositing it in the remembrance of our soul so as never to forget this mystery.[2]

2. Who then would not marvel at the noble Joseph?[3] Preferring piety and love for Christ God and disdaining anything to be feared from the hands of men, he went off to Pilate and asked for the Lord's body. His position as a member of the council did not extinguish his faith.[4] His wealth did not deter him. The fear of bodily harm did not stop him. Rather, forsaking his wealth and his personal safety, in addition to his rank, for he was a member of the council (that is, an official in charge of public affairs), he hastened to receive Christ in preference to all else. The Jews' hostility towards Christ did not intimidate him; rather, taking courage, he sought out the Lord, received him and considered him worthy of his tomb.

[1] The Gospel for this the Third Sunday after Easter is Mk 15:43-16:8 (the burial in Joseph of Arimathaea's tomb and the visitation of the tomb by the myrrh-bearing women, Mary Magdalene, Mary the mother of James, and Salome). Cf. the note in the Pentekostarion's Synaxarion for this Sunday: τῇ αὐτῇ ἡμέρᾳ, κυριακῇ τρίτῃ ἀπὸ τοῦ Πάσχα, τὴν τῶν ἁγίων μυροφόρων ἑορτὴν ἑορτάζομεν· ἔτι δὲ μνείαν ποιούμεθα καὶ τοῦ ἐξ Ἀριμαθαίας Ἰωσήφ, ὃς ἦν μαθητὴς κεκρυμμένος· πρὸς δὲ καὶ τοῦ νυκτερινοῦ μαθητοῦ Νικοδήμου.

[2] Mk 15:43-46, Lk 23:53, Mt 27:59. Note the word-play on μνήμη (remembrance), which suggests μνῆμα or μνημεῖον (tomb).

[3] The epithet 'noble' is taken from Mk 15:43 and is found also in the hymn Ὁ εὐσχήμων Ἰωσήφ, sung at Vespers on Good Friday, at Matins on Holy Saturday and on the Sunday of the Myrrh-bearing Women. See *The Lenten Triodion*, pp. 616, 622.

[4] Cf. Mk 15:43. Note also the verse from one of the troparia for Matins on the Third Sunday of Easter: Ἰωσὴφ τὸν εὐσχήμονα, ζηλωτὴν εὐσεβείας, βουλευτὴν καὶ μαθητήν, σὺν Μυροφόροις τιμήσωμεν καὶ ἀποστόλοις, κράζοντες σὺν αὐτοῖς καὶ πιστῶς ἀνυμνοῦντες τοῦ σωτῆρος τὴν ἀνάστασιν φαιδρῶς.

3. Ἐπαινῶ σου τὴν πίστιν Ἰωσήφ, μακαρίζω σου τὴν προαίρεσιν, σεβάζομαί σου τὸ ἔργον. ταλανίζω τοὺς ἀνθρώπους τοὺς ἐν καιρῷ
25 μὲν εὐπραγίας ἀγαπῶντας τοὺς φίλους καὶ πλησιάζοντας αὐτοῖς, ἐν δὲ καιρῷ πειρασμῶν ἀποστρεφομένους καὶ φεύγοντας αὐτούς. ἐπεὶ οὖν τὸ τοῦ Ἰωσὴφ ἔργον μακάριόν ἐστι, μιμησώμεθα αὐτό. πῶς δὲ μιμησώμεθα; ἀκούετε, ἀδελφαί μου. ἔστι τις ἐν φυλακῇ κεκλεισμένος, κατακεκριμένος, παρεωραμένος, μεμισημένος ὑπὸ συγγενῶν καὶ φίλων
30 καὶ γειτόνων; ἀπέλθωμεν εἰς φυλακὴν καὶ ἐπισκεψώμεθα αὐτόν, ἐλευθερώσωμεν αὐτὸν ἀπὸ τῆς φυλακῆς, ἐγγυησώμεθα αὐτόν, συνδοσίαν ποιήσωμεν· καὶ τῇ σινδόνι τῆς συγκροτήσεως καὶ τοῦ ἀναβασταγμοῦ περικαλύψαντες αὐτοῦ τὰ χρέη, θάψωμεν αὐτά.

4. Κατάκειται ἄλλος ἐν ἀσθενείᾳ; δουλεύσωμεν αὐτῷ, παραμείν-
35 ωμεν αὐτῷ, τὰ παρηγοροῦντα τὴν ἀσθένειαν αὐτοῦ χορηγήσωμεν αὐτῷ, συνδήσωμεν τὰ τραύματα αὐτοῦ καὶ τῇ θεραπείᾳ τῆς ὑγείας ἐνθάψωμεν αὐτοῦ τὰς ὀδύνας. ἕτερος τυγχάνει αἰχμάλωτος; ἐκπριώμεθα αὐτόν, ἐκβάλλωμεν αὐτὸν ἀπὸ τῶν χειρῶν τῶν κατεχόντων αὐτόν, ἀνασώσωμεν αὐτὸν καὶ εἰς τὴν πατρίδα αὐτοῦ
40 ἀναγάγωμεν, ἵνα καὶ εἰς τὴν εὐσέβειαν συντηρήσωμεν αὐτόν.

5. Ἄλλος ἀναστρέφεται ἐν τῇ τοῦ βίου τρυφῇ καὶ διάγει διόλου ἐν τοῖς τοῦ κόσμου πράγμασι; παραινέσωμεν αὐτὸν καὶ διὰ τῆς ἀγαθῆς συμβουλῆς συλληψώμεθα αὐτὸν καὶ πρὸς τὴν ἐκκλησίαν συνεισφέρωμεν καὶ διὰ τῆς ἐν αὐτῇ παραστάσεως ἐξηλώσωμεν αὐτοῦ
45 τὰς ματαίας ὁδούς. εἰ ταῦτα ποιοῦμεν, τὸ σῶμα τοῦ Ἰησοῦ ὁσίως ἐνταφιάζομεν καὶ εἰς μίμησιν τοῦ Ἰωσὴφ ἐρχόμεθα. ἀλλὰ μάθετε, ἀδελφαί μου, πῶς ἐν ἑαυτῇ ἑκάστη ὑμῶν δύναται πληρῶσαι τοῦ Ἰωσὴφ τὸν τρόπον. ἡ κακὴ συνήθεια καὶ ἡ πονηρὰ ἕξις τῆς ἁμαρτίας Πιλάτος ἐστί. ἑκάστης ὑμῶν σῶμα καὶ μέλος Χριστοῦ ἐστι, πάντες
50 γὰρ οἱ χριστιανοὶ σῶμα καὶ μέλη Χριστοῦ ἐσμεν.

6. Ὁ θεοφιλὴς λογισμὸς καὶ τὴν ἐργασίαν τῶν ἐντολῶν τοῦ Χριστοῦ ἀγαπῶν μαθητὴς τοῦ Χριστοῦ ἐστι καὶ Ἰωσὴφ ὀνομάζεται. ὅστις οὖν τὰ μέλη τῆς σαρκὸς καὶ τὰ αἰσθητήρια τοῦ ἰδίου σώματος ἐλευθερώσει ἐκ τῆς πονηρᾶς συνηθείας καὶ ἀποστήσει αὐτὰ ἐκ τῆς
55 κακῆς πολιτείας καὶ διαγωγῆς, δεόμενος πρὸς τὸν θεὸν νυκτὸς καὶ ἡμέρας τοῦ λυτρωθῆναι ἀπὸ τοῦ ἐργάζεσθαι τὴν ἁμαρτίαν, οὗτος αἰτεῖ καὶ λαμβάνει τὸ σῶμα τοῦ Ἰησοῦ· πᾶς γὰρ ὁ αἰτῶν λαμβάνει καὶ ὁ ζητῶν εὑρίσκει. ὁ Ἰωσὴφ αἰτήσας ἔλαβε τὸ σῶμα τοῦ κυρίου· καὶ

3. I praise your faith, Joseph; I bless your free decision; I revere your deed. I denounce those men who love their friends and stand by them in times of prosperity, but who in times of trial turn away and flee from them.[5] Since, then, Joseph's deed is a blessed one, let us imitate it. But how are we to imitate it? Listen, my sisters. Is there someone shut up in prison, condemned, neglected, hated by relatives, friends and parents? Let us go to the prison and visit him. Let us free him from prison, pledge surety for him, make a contribution. Wrapping his debts in the shroud of our support and assistance, let us bury them.

4. Does another lie sick in bed? Let us take care of him; let us stay by his side. Let us furnish him with things to comfort him in his illness. Let us bind up his wounds and bury his sufferings in the healing of health. Is another held in captivity? Let us pay his ransom; let us wrest him from the hands of his captors. Let us rescue him and bring him back to his homeland so that we can preserve him for piety.[6]

5. Is there another wandering around in the midst of life's delights and living entirely in the affairs of the world? Let us exhort him and assist him by our good counsel and bringing him to church, by his presence there detach him from his empty ways. If we do these things, we bury the body of Jesus with reverence and come to imitate Joseph. Learn, then, my sisters, how each of you in her own life can practise the way of Joseph to the full. Pilate represents the established practice of evil and the wicked habit of sin. The body of each of you is a member of Christ, for as Christians we all constitute the body and members of Christ.[7]

6. A godly way of thought is a disciple who loves to practise Christ's commandments and is given the name Joseph. Whosoever will free the members of his flesh and the sense faculties of his own body from evil practices and will keep them from a wicked way of life and conduct, beseeching God night and day to deliver him from committing sin, this person asks for and receives the body of Christ, for "everyone who asks receives and he who seeks finds."[8] When Joseph asked, he received the body of the Lord,[9] and when you ask God to keep you

---

[5] Cf. Sir 6:8-12, 12:8.

[6] This may well be a reference to the Christians captured by the Turks. They were under considerable pressure to convert to Islam.

[7] Cf. 1 Cor 6:15, 12:27, Eph 5:30.

[8] Mt 7:8, Lk 11:10.

[9] Mk 15:43-45, Lk 23:52.

σὺ αἰτῶν τὸν θεὸν τῆς ἁμαρτίας ἀποστῆσαι, λαμβάνεις τὸ αἴτημά
60 σου καὶ τὸ σῶμά σου ἐκβάλεις τῆς δουλείας τῶν κακῶν.

7. Ὁ Ἰωσὴφ καθελὼν τὸ σῶμα τοῦ κυρίου καὶ ἀγοράσας σινδόνα
καὶ ἐντυλίξας αὐτό, κατέθετο ἐν τῷ καινῷ αὐτοῦ μνημείῳ. καὶ πᾶς
ἄνθρωπος καταλείψας τὴν ἁμαρτίαν καὶ ἐν σωφροσύνῃ διάγων καὶ
ἐν ἐκκλησίᾳ σχολάζων καὶ δικαιοσύνην ἀγαπῶν καὶ ἐλεημοσύνην
65 μετερχόμενος καὶ ἀκτημοσύνην ἀσπαζόμενος καὶ νηστείᾳ προσασ-
χολούμενος, εἰς ὑψηλοφροσύνην καὶ κενοδοξίαν ἐπαίρεται ἡ καρδία
αὐτοῦ, ἀναλογιζόμενος τὰς ἀρετὰς αὐτοῦ. ὅταν δὲ ἐπικαλεῖται τὸν
κύριον καὶ εἰς μνήμην τῶν ἑαυτοῦ ἁμαρτημάτων ἔρχεται, καθέλκει
τὸ φρόνημα αὐτοῦ καὶ παρακαλῶν τὸν κύριον ἀποκαθηλωθῆναι ἐξ
70 αὐτῶν οὐχ ὑπερηφανεύεται καὶ ὑψηλοφρονεῖ. ὁ γοῦν διὰ τῆς μνήμης
τῶν ὧν ἔπραξε κακῶν καθελὼν τὸ φρόνημα αὐτοῦ ἀπὸ τῆς ὑψηλο-
φροσύνης τῶν ἰδίων κατορθωμάτων καὶ εἰς ταπεινοφροσύνην ἐλθών,
οὗτος καὶ τὴν ἑαυτοῦ ψυχὴν ἐκ τῶν παθῶν ἐξαγοράζει καθάπερ
σινδόνα.

75 **8.** Ὁ γὰρ ταπεινούμενος τῷ φρονήματι καὶ κοπιῶν τῷ σώματι
ἐν τοῖς ἀγαθοῖς ἔργοις ἄφεσιν εὑρίσκει τῶν ἰδίων πλημμελημάτων.
ὁ δὲ ἀφεθεὶς τὰ ἁμαρτήματα καὶ ἐλευθερωθεὶς ἐξ αὐτῶν ἐξαγοράζει
πάντως τὴν ἰδίαν ψυχήν· πᾶσα γὰρ ψυχὴ ἐργαζομένη τὴν ἁμαρτίαν
πεπραγμένη ἐστὶν ὑπὸ τῆς ἰδίας προαιρέσεως καί, ἕως κατέχεται ἐν
80 τοῖς ἁμαρτήμασιν, δούλη ἐστὶ καὶ πεπαλαιωμένην καὶ ῥερυπωμένην
συνείδησιν φέρει. ὅτε δὲ διὰ ταπεινώσεως καὶ κόπου σωματικοῦ
ἐλευθερωθῇ τῶν κακῶν, καθαρὰ θεωρεῖται, ἄφεσιν γὰρ ἁμαρτιῶν
λαμβάνουσα τὸν ἐκ τῶν παθῶν ἀποβάλλει ῥῦπον. ἴδε, γάρ φησι, *τὴν*
ταπείνωσίν μου καὶ τὸν κόπον μου καὶ ἄφες πάσας τὰς ἁμαρτίας μου.
85 ὅτε οὖν ἄφεσιν τῶν ἰδίων ἁμαρτημάτων εὑρήσει ἡ ψυχή, τότε σινδὼν
λευκὴ χρηματίζει, ἅτε καθαρὰν καρδίαν κεκτημένη καὶ ῥύπου παντὸς
κεχωρισμένην. καταλειψάτω τοιγαροῦν τὴν ἣν ἐργάζεται ἁμαρτίαν
ἑκάστη, καὶ εὑρεθήσεται ἐξαγοράζουσα τὴν ἰδίαν ψυχὴν καὶ καθαρὰν
αὐτὴν ποιοῦσα.

90 **9.** Τότε καὶ ὁ λογισμὸς αὐτῆς εἰς μελέτας ἀγαθὰς κινεῖσθαι
διεγείρεται· καὶ τὸ σῶμα ὑπὸ τῆς ἐναρέτου καὶ καθαρᾶς ψυχῆς
καθάπερ ὑπὸ λευκῆς ὀθόνης συστρεφόμενον καὶ συνδεσμούμενον
οὐκέτι δύναται κινεῖσθαι πρὸς ἐνέργειαν τῆς ἁμαρτίας. ὅπερ γὰρ
ἐργάζεται ἡ ψυχὴ διὰ τοῦ σώματος, τοῦτο μελετᾷ καὶ συστρέφει διὰ
95 τῶν λογισμῶν· καὶ ὅπερ λογίζεται ἐν τῇ διανοίᾳ, τοῦτο καὶ πράττει
διὰ τῶν μελῶν τοῦ σώματος. καλὰ οὖν λογιζομένη καὶ διαπράττουσα,

---

60 ἐκβάλεις corr.: ἐκβάλῃς ΟΑ　　85 σινδὼν corr.: σινδὸν ΟΑ

from sin, you receive what you asked for and release your body from slavery to evil deeds.

7.   After Joseph took down the Lord's body and bought a shroud and wrapped him in it, he placed him in a newly wrought tomb.[10] Every person who has abandoned sin, who lives a chaste life and attends church assiduously, who loves righteousness and practises almsgiving, who welcomes poverty and engages in fasting — if he keeps an account of his virtues, his heart swells in arrogance and vainglory. But whenever he calls upon the Lord and comes to remember his sins, he drags his attitude down; he is not proud or haughty in appealing to the Lord to release him from his sins. Thus, the person who by remembrance of the evils he has done abases his attitude from arrogance over his virtuous accomplishments and arrives at humility buys back his own soul from the passions like a shroud.

8.   The humble-minded person, who labours at good works in his body, finds forgiveness for his failings. When he is forgiven for his sins and is freed from them, he does indeed buy back his soul, for every soul involved in sinful works is belaboured by its own free choice and, as long as it is caught in its sins, it is enslaved and bears a wizened and befouled conscience. But when the soul has been freed of evils by humility and bodily labour, it appears pure, for in receiving forgiveness for its sins it casts off the filth of the passions. For scripture says, "Behold my humility and my labour and forgive all my sins."[11] So when the soul finds forgiveness for its sins, it is then like a white shroud inasmuch as it has acquired a pure heart free of attachment to any defilement. Thus, let each one of you abandon her works of sin and she will be found to be ransoming her soul and rendering it pure.

9.   Then, her thoughts will be stirred towards meditation on the good; and since her body is wrapped and bound by a virtuous and pure soul as by a white linen cloth,[12] it is no longer capable of being moved towards sinful actions. The soul studies and mulls over in its thoughts what it works through the body; through the members of the body it puts into practice what it thinks of in the discursive intellect. Thus when the soul thinks about and practises good deeds, it is

---

[10] Lk 23:53, Mt 27:59-60.
[11] Ps 24:18.
[12] Cf. Jn 19:40.

συστέλλεται ἀπὸ τῶν κακῶν, δεσμεῖται γὰρ τὸ σῶμα ὑπὸ τῆς καθαρᾶς καρδίας καὶ οὐ πράττει τὰ κακά.

10. Οὕτως οὖν πορευόμενος ὁ ἄνθρωπος καὶ διὰ τῶν ἔργων τῆς
100 μετανοίας καὶ τῆς μνήμης τῶν ἰδίων ἁμαρτημάτων ταπεινούμενος τὴν σωτήριον πολιτείαν τοῦ Χριστοῦ ἐν τῷ μνημονευτικῷ τῆς ψυχῆς κατατίθησι. καὶ ὥσπερ ὁ Ἰωσήφ, θάψας τὸ σῶμα τοῦ κυρίου, προσεκύλισε λίθον μέγαν τῇ θύρᾳ τοῦ μνημείου, οὕτω καὶ ὁ τὰ καλὰ ἐργαζόμενος ἄνθρωπος, καθάπερ τι μνημεῖον καινὸν τὴν ἑαυτοῦ
105 καρδίαν ποιῶν, θάπτει καὶ θησαυρίζει ἐν αὐτῇ τὴν ἐπὶ γῆς ἀναστροφὴν τοῦ κυρίου, καὶ ἐν ταῖς θύραις τῆς ψυχῆς, αἵτινές εἰσιν αἱ αἰσθήσεις τοῦ σώματος, ἀσφάλειαν ἐπιτίθεται, ἵνα μὴ κλαπῇ ὁ ἀγαθὸς θησαυρός.

11. Γένοιτο δὲ ἡμᾶς, ἀγαπηταὶ ἀδελφαί, τὸν πλουτίζοντα ἡμᾶς θησαυρὸν μὴ ἀπολέσαι, ἀλλὰ τοῦτον φέρουσαι ἐν τῇ καρδίᾳ ἄσυλον
110 ζωῆς ἐν ἀπολαύσει τυγχάνειν. εἰ γὰρ ὁ τοῦ χρυσοῦ θησαυρὸς ἐννοούμενος εὐφραίνει τὰς καρδίας τῶν κεκτημένων αὐτόν, πολλῷ μᾶλλον ὁ θησαυρὸς τῆς ζωῆς ἡμῶν, Ἰησοῦς Χριστός, ἐν ταῖς ψυχαῖς ἡμῶν ταμιευόμενος, χαροποιήσει ἡμᾶς καὶ διατηρήσει ἡμᾶς ἐν τοῖς ἀγαθοῖς· ὅτι αὐτός ἐστιν ἡ πηγὴ τῶν ἀγαθῶν καὶ αὐτῷ πρέπει πᾶσα
115 δόξα, τιμὴ καὶ προσκύνησις σὺν τῷ ἀνάρχῳ αὐτοῦ πατρὶ καὶ τῷ παναγίῳ καὶ ἀγαθῷ καὶ ζωοποιῷ πνεύματι, νῦν καὶ ἀεὶ καὶ εἰς τοὺς αἰῶνας τῶν αἰώνων. Ἀμήν.

108 ἡμᾶς¹ Oᵖᶜ: ὑμᾶς OᵃᶜΑ

restrained from evil works, for the body is bound by the pure heart and does not practise evil.

10. Thus, the man who proceeds in this fashion and humbles himself by works of repentance and by the remembrance of his sins deposits Christ's salvific way of life in his soul's memory faculty. Just as Joseph buried the Lord's body and rolled a great stone against the door of the tomb, so too the man who performs good works makes his heart like a new tomb and buries and stores up within it the treasure of the Lord's way of life on earth; at the doors of his heart, which are the senses of the body, he sets a guard, lest the good treasure be stolen.

11. My beloved sisters, let it not happen that we lose the treasure that enriches us; rather, bearing it in our hearts safe from harm, may we come into the enjoyment of life. If thinking about a treasure of gold gladdens the hearts of those who have acquired it, how much more will the treasure of our life, Jesus Christ, stored up in our souls bring us joy and preserve us in good works. For Christ himself is the source of good works and to him belongs all glory, honour and worship together with his eternal Father and all-holy, good and life-giving Spirit, now and always and unto the ages of ages. Amen.

Τῇ δ΄ κυριακῇ
Ἐξήγησις εἰς τὸ θαῦμα τοῦ παραλύτου

1. Ἀδελφαὶ καὶ μητέρες, κατὰ τὴν παρελθοῦσαν κυριακὴν τῶν ἐνταῦθα τόπων ἀποδημῶν, οὐκ ἔφθασα παραθεῖναι ταῖς ὑμετέραις
5 ψυχαῖς τὴν συνήθη τῆς διδασκαλίας βρῶσιν. διὸ καὶ τοῦ εἰς τὸν παράλυτον θαύματος ἡ ἐξήγησις τὰς ὑμετέρας διαφυγοῦσα καρδίας ἀδιήγητος κατελείφθη· καὶ ὡσεὶ παράλυτος ἐτελεῖτε καὶ ὑμεῖς, ἐν τῇ κλίνῃ τῆς ἀδιδάκτου γνώσεως κατακείμεναι, οὐ γὰρ εἴχετε ἄνθρωπον, ἤγουν ἐμέ, τὸν διδάσκαλον ὑμῶν τὸν πονοῦντα ὑπὲρ τῆς
10 σωτηρίας ὑμῶν ἐμβαλεῖν ὑμᾶς ὡς κολυμβήθραν εἰς τὴν διάνοιαν τοῦ γενομένου θαύματος ὑπὸ τοῦ κυρίου. ὅθεν καὶ κατὰ τὴν ἐνεστῶσαν κυριακὴν μεθ' ὑμῶν ἀναστρεφόμενος, παρατίθημι ταῖς ὑμετέραις ψυχαῖς τὴν κατήχησιν. τοιγαροῦν καὶ μετὰ προσοχῆς ἀκούετε, ὅπως τῇ γνώσει τῆς διδασκαλίας τὰ παραλελυμένα νοήματα τῶν ὑμετέρων
15 ψυχῶν στερεωθέντα διεγερθήσονται εἰς τὸ βαστάζειν τὴν φροντίδα τῆς ὑμῶν σωτηρίας καὶ περιπατεῖν ἐν τοῖς ἀγαθοῖς ἔργοις.

2. Ἑορτὴ ἦν τῶν Ἰουδαίων, ἡ λεγομένη πεντηκοστή, καὶ ὁ Ἰησοῦς ἀνέβη εἰς Ἱεροσόλυμα. ἵνα μὴ καταλύτης δόξῃ τοῦ νόμου ὁ τοῦ νόμου δοτήρ, παρεγένετο μετὰ τῶν ἄλλων καὶ αὐτὸς εἰς τὴν ἑορτὴν καὶ
20 οὐ διὰ τοῦτο μόνον ἦλθεν εἰς τὴν ἑορτήν, ἀλλ' ἵνα καὶ τὸ συνδραμὸν πλῆθος εἰς πίστιν ἀγάγῃ διὰ τῶν θαυμάτων καὶ τῆς διδαχῆς. ἀκουέτωσαν οἱ πρὸς τὰς πανηγύρεις ἀποτρέχοντες καὶ οἱ τὰς ἑορτὰς τῶν ἁγίων ἐπιτελοῦντες διὰ συμποσίων καὶ χορευμάτων καὶ ᾀσμάτων δαιμονικῶν καὶ παιγνίων διαφόρων. παρεγένετο ὁ κύριος εἰς τὴν
25 ἑορτήν, οὐχ ἵνα φάγῃ καὶ πίῃ, οὐδ' ἵνα ἐργάσηται κοσμικὰ καὶ νεωτερικὰ πράγματα, ἀλλ' ἵνα ἀγαθοποιήσῃ καὶ φωτίσῃ πάντας διὰ τῶν σημείων καὶ τῆς διδασκαλίας.

3. Δεῖ οὖν καὶ ἡμᾶς ἐν ταῖς ἑορταῖς τῶν ἁγίων ἀπερχομένους εἰς τοὺς θείους ναοὺς πανηγυρίζειν πνευματικῶς καὶ ἀγρυπνοῦντας ἐν
30 ταῖς ψαλμῳδίαις προσκαρτερεῖν, θεραπεύειν τε τοὺς ἁγίους διὰ τῆς παννύχου στάσεως καὶ τῆς ἐμπόνου παρακλήσεως καὶ τιμᾶν τὰς ἡμέρας τῶν ἑορτῶν διὰ τοῦ λαλεῖν ἀγαθὰ καὶ ἀκούειν καὶ ἀλλήλους

20 συνδραμὸν O^{pc}: συνδραμῶν O^{ac}A

FOURTH SUNDAY [AFTER EASTER]:
INTERPRETATION OF THE MIRACLE OF THE PARALYTIC[1]

1. Sisters and Mothers, as I was away from these parts last Sunday, I did not manage to present to your souls the usual food of instruction and so the interpretation of the miracle of the paralytic escaped your hearts and was left untold. And you too became like the paralytic, lying on the bed of uninformed knowledge,[2] for you did not have someone, namely, myself, as your teacher to labour on behalf of your salvation, to plunge you into the meaning of the miracle worked by the Lord, as into a pool.[3] Therefore, since I am with you this Sunday, I present my instruction to your souls.[4] Listen, then, with attention so that by the knowledge you gain from my teaching the paralyzed thoughts of your souls shall rise up strengthened to carry the thought of your salvation and walk in good works.

2. "There was a feast among the Jews," called Pentecost, "and Jesus went up to Jerusalem."[5] That the giver of the Law would not seem to undo the Law, he too attended the feast together with the others. But it was not for this reason alone that he went to the feast, but to lead the assembled multitude to faith by means of his miracles and teaching. Those who go off to the festivals and celebrate the feasts of the saints with drinking parties and dancing and demonic songs and other sorts of merrymaking should give ear. The Lord attended the feast not to eat and drink, not to perform worldly novelties, but to bestow goodness and light upon all by his signs and his teaching.

3. Therefore, on the feasts of the saints we too must make our celebrations spiritual by going off to the churches of God and faithfully keeping the vigils of psalmody; we must perform the services for the

[1] Jn 5:1-15 is the Gospel read on this Sunday.
[2] Cf. Mt 9:2.
[3] Jn 5:7.
[4] Theoleptos was apparently away from Constantinople on the Sunday of the Paralytic and decided to deliver his sermon on that subject on the following Sunday, which would have been the Fifth Sunday after Easter, the Sunday of the Samaritan Woman.
[5] Jn 5:1.

παρακινεῖν εἰς μίμησιν τῶν καλῶν. *ἀνέβη ὁ Ἰησοῦς εἰς Ἱεροσόλυμα.*
βλέπετε τὸ *ἀνέβη. ἀνέβη ὁ Ἰησοῦς,* τὴν ἡμετέραν προκοπὴν καὶ
35 ἀνάβασιν οἰκονομῶν· ἡμῶν γὰρ καταβάντων εἰς τὰ πάθη καὶ εἰς τὴν
ἁμαρτίαν πεσόντων, ἀναβαίνει ὁ Ἰησοῦς εἰς Ἱεροσόλυμα τὴν ἀπὸ
τῶν παθῶν καὶ τῆς ἁμαρτίας πρὸς ἀπάθειαν καὶ ἀρετὴν ἀνάβασιν
ἡμῶν πραγματευόμενος. ἡνίκα γὰρ μεριμνῶμεν τὰ καλὰ καὶ
ἐργαζώμεθα δικαιοσύνην, ἑορτὴν ἄγωμεν ἐν ταῖς ψυχαῖς καὶ οἱ
40 ἄγγελοι πανήγυριν μίαν μεθ' ἡμῶν συγκροτοῦσι καὶ ἀναβαίνομεν εἰς
Ἱεροσόλυμα, ἤγουν καταντῶμεν εἰς τὸ καταγώγιον τῆς εἰρήνης καὶ
τῆς σωτηρίας.

4. *Ἦν ἐν τοῖς Ἱεροσολύμοις προβατικὴ κολυμβήθρα, πέντε στοὰς*
ἔχουσα. ἐν ταύταις κατέκειτο πλῆθος πολὺ τῶν ἀσθενούντων, ἄγγελος γὰρ
45 *κατὰ καιρὸν διετάρασσεν αὐτήν· καὶ ὁ πρῶτος ἐμβὰς ὑγιὴς ἐγένετο ᾧ*
δήποτε κατείχετο νοσήματι. κολυμβήθρα ἐστὶν ἡ μετάνοια, ἥτις καὶ
προβατικὴ λέγεται διὰ τὸ πραεῖς καὶ ἀκάκους ἀποτελεῖν τοὺς ταύτην
ἀσπαζομένους. ὡς γὰρ ἡ ἐν Ἱεροσολύμοις κολυμβήθρα προβατικὴ
ἐλέγετο διὰ τὸ ἐκπλύνειν τὰ ἐντόσθια καὶ τὰ ἔγκατα τῶν θυσιαζομένων
50 προβάτων, οὕτω καὶ ἡ μετάνοια, διὰ τῶν δακρύων ἐκπλύνουσα τὰ
ἐντόσθια μέλη τῆς ψυχῆς καὶ τοὺς ἔνδον λογισμοὺς καθαίρουσα,
ἡμέρους καὶ προσηνεῖς ποιεῖται τοὺς ἀνθρώπους. καὶ διὰ τοῦτο καὶ
ἡ τῆς μετανοίας κολυμβήθρα, προβατικὴ λέγεται· ὡς γὰρ ἔγκατα τὰ
ἔσχατα ἀποβαλλομένη ἁμαρτήματα, τὰ πρῶτα γεννήματα τῆς ψυχῆς
55 ἀσπάζεται, προβιβάζοντα αὐτὴν εἰς ἀοργησίαν καὶ θείαν ἀγάπην.

5. Πρῶτα δὲ γεννήματα τῆς ψυχῆς εἰσιν αἱ ἀρεταὶ αἱ πρότερον
ἐν τῇ φύσει σπαρεῖσαι ὑπὸ τοῦ θεοῦ· αἳ καὶ ὑπὸ τῶν προβάτων
εἰκονίζονται. ἔγκατα δὲ τὰ δυσώδη πάθη τὰ καὶ ἐσχάτως ἐπιγενόμενα
τῷ τῶν ἀνθρώπων γένει, ἅπερ καὶ ἡ ἀληθινὴ μετάνοια ἀποστρεφομένη
60 εἰς τὴν πρώτην κατάστασιν ποιεῖ τὴν ψυχὴν ἐπανέρχεσθαι. *πέντε*
στοὰς ἔχουσα· πέντε γὰρ εἰσιν οἱ τρόποι τῆς μετανοίας· ἀποχὴ κακῶν,
ἐργασία τῶν καλῶν, μνήμη τῶν ἁμαρτημάτων, ἐξομολόγησις καὶ τὸ
διηνεκὲς πένθος.

6. Ἐν τούτοις τοῖς πέντε τρόποις τῆς μετανοίας οἱ ἀσθενοῦντες
65 τοῖς ἁμαρτήμασι προσερχόμενοι διαναπαύονται· ὁ γὰρ πρώτως
ἐμβαλλόμενος τῷ ὕδατι τῆς μετανοίας εἰς ὑγείαν ψυχικὴν ἐπανέρχεται
καὶ οἷον ἀρά ἐστι τὸ νοσοποιὸν πάθος ἀποβάλλεται, κἂν πορνείαν
εἴπῃς, κἂν μοιχείαν, κἂν μέθην, κἂν ἀδικίαν, κἂν μνησικακίαν.
πάντα γὰρ τὰ ἐνεργήματα τῶν ἁμαρτημάτων τῷ ὕδατι τῆς μετανοίας
70 ῥιπτόμενα ἐμπνίγονται καὶ νεκροῦνται· ἀλλὰ καὶ τὰ μετὰ τὴν ἐνέργειαν

saints with night-long stations and patient entreaties and honour their feast-days by speaking and listening to good things and encouraging others to imitate what is good. "Jesus went up to Jerusalem."[6] Note the phrase 'went up': 'Jesus went up' to provide for our progress and ascent. Because we went down to the passions and fell into sin, Jesus goes up to Jerusalem to bring about our ascent from the passions and sin to impassibility and virtue. For whenever we are anxious for the good and work at righteousness, we hold a feast in our souls and the angels gather together in a single festival with us and we go up to Jerusalem, that is, we arrive at the abode of peace and salvation.

4. "There was in Jerusalem a sheep pool with five porticoes. In these lay a great number of invalids, for an angel from time to time stirred up the pool and the first to step in was cured of whatever disease he had."[7] The pool represents repentance, which is referred to as a pool for sheep because it renders those who give it welcome gentle and free of wickedness. Just as the pool in Jerusalem was called a sheep pool because they washed there the entrails and viscera of the sheep for sacrifice, so too repentance, by washing with tears the inner members of the soul and purifying the interior thoughts, makes men mild and gentle. This is why the pool of repentance is called a sheep pool, because when it carries away the worst sins, like the viscera, it gives welcome to the first fruits of the soul which lead it on to divine love and freedom from anger.

5. The first fruits of the soul are the virtues which were previously sown in its nature by God; they are represented by the sheep. The entrails are the foul passions inflicted latterly on the race of men; in abandoning these, true repentance allows the soul to return to its original state. The sheep pool 'has five porticoes,' for the means of repentance are fivefold: abstention from evil deeds, practice of good works, remembrance of one's sins, confession and perpetual sorrow.

6. When those who are infirm with their sins come to these five ways of repentance, they find rest, for the first to plunge himself in the water of repentance returns to health of soul; the disease-bearing passion, whatever it is, is cast away, whether you speak of fornication or adultery or drunkenness or wrong-doing or rancour. When all the workings of sin are cast into the water of repentance they are drowned and put to death. Even the thoughts left imprinted on the soul after

---

[6] Jn 5:1.
[7] Jn 5:2-4.

τῆς ἁμαρτίας τυπούμενα ἐνθυμήματα ἐν τῇ ψυχῇ καὶ αὐτὰ ὑπὸ τῶν
δακρύων τῆς μετανοίας καὶ τῆς ἐξομολογήσεως ἐξαλείφονται.

7. Συντριβομένη γὰρ ἡ ψυχὴ καὶ κλαίουσα καὶ μεταμελομένη
ἐφ᾽ οἷς ἔπραξε κακοῖς, τὸν ῥύπον τῶν αἰσχρῶν πράξεων αὐτῆς μισεῖ
75 καὶ ἀποστρέφεται παντελῶς. καὶ ὥσπερ ἱμάτιον ῥερυπωμένον ὕδατι
ἐμβαλλόμενον καὶ χερσὶ προστριβόμενον λευκὸν ἀποτελεῖται, οὕτω
καὶ ψυχὴ λογισμὸν ἀκάθαρτον φέρουσα διὰ τῆς ἐξομολογήσεως καὶ
τῆς συντριβῆς τοῦ ἰδίου συνειδότος κεκαθαρμένη γίνεται. ἀλλ᾽
ἀκούετε προσεκτικῶς, πεποθημένα μου τεκνία. ἡ τοῦ ἀνθρώπου ψυχή,
80 ὑπὸ τῶν ἡδονῶν ἐκλυθεῖσα καὶ ἐν τῇ ἐπιθυμίᾳ τοῦ κόσμου τούτου
καταπεσοῦσα, πάρετος ἐγεγόνει καὶ ὅλοι οἱ λογισμοὶ αὐτῆς παρα-
λελυμένοι εἰσὶ καὶ πάντα τὰ μέλη τοῦ σώματος αὐτῆς ἀκίνητα πρὸς
ἐργασίαν τοῦ ἀγαθοῦ τυγχάνει. οὔτε γὰρ τὰς τρεῖς δυνάμεις αὐτῆς
ὑγιεῖς ἔχει, ἤγουν τὸν λογισμόν, τὸν θυμὸν καὶ τὴν ἐπιθυμίαν, οὔτε
85 ἀπὸ τῶν ὀκτὼ γενικῶν παθῶν ἐκτὸς διατρίβει. ὅθεν καὶ ἑκάστης ὑμῶν
ἡ ψυχὴ τριάκοντα καὶ ὀκτὼ ἔτη ἔχει ἐν τῇ ἀσθενείᾳ ὡς ὁ παράλυτος.

8. Ἀδύνατον γὰρ ἡ κατὰ λογισμὸν καὶ θυμὸν καὶ ἐπιθυμίαν
νοσοῦσα μὴ καὶ τὰ ὀκτὼ πάθη ἐπισύρεσθαι καὶ εἰς τὴν δουλείαν
αὐτῶν ὑποκλίνεσθαι. πῶς γὰρ ἀρρωστοῦσιν αἱ τρεῖς δυνάμεις τῆς
90 ψυχῆς καὶ τίνα εἰσὶ τὰ ὀκτὼ πάθη ἅπερ ἡ ψυχὴ ἐπιφέρεται; ἐμοῦ
λέγοντος, προσέχετε. ὅταν ὁ λογισμὸς φροντίζῃ περὶ ἀδικίας καὶ
μελετᾷ περὶ πονηρίας καὶ μελετᾷ πῶς ψεύσεται, πῶς ἐπιορκίσει, πῶς
ἐπιτελέσει τὸ ἔργον τῆς πορνείας ἢ τῆς μοιχείας ἢ τοῦ φόνου ἢ τῆς
μαγείας ἢ ἄλλου τινὸς κακοῦ, τότε ἀρρωστῇ ὁ λογισμός.

95 9. Ὅτε δὲ ὀργίζεται κατὰ τοῦ πλησίον ὁ ἄνθρωπος καὶ μαίνεται
κατὰ τοῦ γείτονος αὐτοῦ καὶ κινεῖται κακῶσαι αὐτὸν καὶ παροξύνεται
κατὰ τοῦ ἀδελφοῦ αὐτοῦ, τότε ἀρρωστῇ ὁ θυμὸς τῆς ψυχῆς. ὅτε δὲ
πάλιν ἐπιθυμεῖ τοῦ κόσμου καὶ τῶν ἐν τῷ κόσμῳ πραγμάτων καὶ δόξης
κοσμικῆς ἐρᾷ καὶ τοῦ παρὰ τῶν ἀνθρώπων ἐπαίνου, τότε ἀρρωστῇ
100 ἡ ἐπιθυμία τῆς ψυχῆς. οὕτως οὖν διακειμένων τῶν τριῶν μερῶν τῆς
ψυχῆς, τὰ ὀκτὼ πάθη νομὴν καὶ χώραν ἐν τῇ καρδίᾳ τοῦ ἀνθρώπου
καὶ ἐν τοῖς μέλεσι τοῦ σώματος ἔχουσι καὶ εὑρίσκεται ἡ ψυχὴ
τριάκοντα καὶ ὀκτὼ ἔτη ἔχουσα ἐν τῇ ἀσθενείᾳ.

10. Τίνα δέ εἰσι τὰ ὀκτὼ πάθη; ἡ γαστριμαργία, ἡ πορνεία, ἡ
105 φιλαργυρία, ἡ ἀκηδία, ἤγουν ἡ ἀφροντισία, ἡ ὀργή, ἡ λύπη, ἡ

---

75 ῥερυπωμένον corr.: ῥερυπομένον OA   85 διατρίβει corr.: διατρίβη OA

the sinful act are themselves wiped away by the tears of repentance
and confession.

7.   If the soul shows contrition, weeps and is repentant for the evil
deeds it committed, it despises the sordidness of its shameful actions
and avoids them completely. Just as a soiled garment is made white
by being plunged into water and being hand-scrubbed, so too the soul
that carries impure thoughts attains purity by confession and contrition
of its conscience. But listen attentively, my beloved children. Once a
person's soul has become dissipated by pleasures and has fallen among
the desires of this world, it is palsied, all its thoughts are paralyzed
and all the members of its body are incapable of good works. For
its three faculties, namely, the rational, the irascible and the concupiscible, are not healthy, nor does it live free of the eight principal
passions. Thus, the soul of each of you has spent thirty-eight years
in its infirmity, like the paralytic.[8]

8.   The soul that is diseased in its rational, irascible and concupiscible
faculties cannot help but be impeded by the eight passions and be
subjected to their enslavement. How can the three faculties of the soul
get sick and what are the eight passions that the soul brings upon
itself? Pay attention while I speak. When the rational faculty gives
thought to wrongdoing and meditates on wickedness and on how it
will lie, how it will swear falsely, how it will commit an act of
fornication, adultery, murder, sorcery or some other evil deed, then
the rational faculty is sick.

9.   When a man gets angry with a friend, annoyed at his neighbour
and starts maltreating him, or when he is irritated with his brother,
then the irascible faculty of his soul is sick. And in turn when he desires
the world and the things in the world and loves worldly honour and
the praise that comes from men, then the concupiscible faculty of the
soul is sick. Thus, when the three parts of the soul are so disposed,
the eight passions possess a portion and place in the heart of man
and in the members of his body, and the soul finds itself with an
infirmity that lasts for thirty-eight years.

10.   What are the eight passions? Gluttony, lust, avarice, acedia (or
indifference), anger, dejection, vainglory and pride.[9] What man is there

---

[8] Jn 5:5.

[9] See the useful discussion of the eight passions and their relationship to the three
faculties by K. Ware in his introduction to *John Climacus, The Ladder of Divine
Ascent*, translated by C. Luibheid and N. Russell (New York, 1982), pp. 62-66. Further
references and bibliography are given there.

κενοδοξία καὶ ἡ ὑπερηφανία. τίς οὖν τῶν ἀνθρώπων οὐ πονηρεύεται
καὶ δολιοῦται καὶ οὐκ ὀργίζεται καὶ οὐκ ἐπιθυμεῖ πλούτου καὶ δόξης;
καὶ τίς πάλιν οὕτως ἔχων καὶ εἰς τὰ ἠριθμημένα ὀκτὼ πάθη οὐκ
ἐμπίπτει;

110   **11.** Ἠκούσατε τὴν ἀρρωστίαν τῆς ψυχῆς; ἔγνωτε πῶς ἑκάστη
ἀσθενεῖ τριάκοντα καὶ ὀκτὼ ἔτη καθάπερ ὁ παράλυτος; λοιπὸν μάθετε
καὶ τὸν τρόπον τῆς θεραπείας. καὶ σπεύσατε ἄνθρωπον εὑρεῖν, ἤγουν
φρόνιμον λογισμὸν κτήσασθαι, δυνάμενον ποιῆσαι τὴν ἴασιν τῶν
ψυχῶν ὑμῶν· καὶ γὰρ ἔστι καὶ ἐν ἡμῖν κολυμβήθρα, ἡ ἐπαινετὴ καὶ
115 ἰαματικὴ μετάνοια, πέντε τρόπους καθάπερ στοὰς ἔχουσα, καθὼς
ἄνωθεν εἰρήκαμεν· τὴν ἀποχὴν τῶν κακῶν, τὴν ἐργασίαν τῶν καλῶν,
τὴν ἐξομολόγησιν, τὴν μνήμην τῶν ἰδίων ἁμαρτημάτων καὶ τὸν
κλαυθμόν. ἐν τῇ κολυμβήθρᾳ τῶν Ἱεροσολύμων ἄγγελος διαταράσ-
σων τὸ ὕδωρ, ἰαματικὴν ἐδίδου δύναμιν.

120   **12.** Ἐνταῦθα δὲ ἑκάστη ὑμῶν κακῶς πολιτευομένη διαταράττει
τὸ συνειδὸς καὶ ἐκφοβεῖ καὶ θορυβεῖ τὴν ψυχήν· παριστᾷ γὰρ ἐν
τῇ μνήμῃ τῆς καρδίας τὰ ἁμαρτήματα καὶ τὴν μέλλουσαν κρίσιν
καὶ τὰ φοβερὰ κολαστήρια καὶ ὑπὸ τὴν ὄψιν τῆς ψυχῆς τίθησιν,
ὑφ᾽ ὧν ἐλεγχομένη καὶ θορυβουμένη καὶ φοβουμένη τὴν ἑαυτῆς
125 καταδίκην, βαπτίζεται εἰς τὴν μετάνοιαν καὶ κλαίει πικρῶς, καὶ οὕτως
ἐλευθεροῦται ἀπὸ τῆς ἁμαρτίας. ὁ ἀπεχόμενος ἀπὸ τῶν κακῶν καὶ
μετανοῶν καὶ ἐξομολογούμενος εὑρίσκει ἔμφρονα λογισμόν, ὑφ᾽ οὗ
καὶ εἰς μετάνοιαν εἰσαγόμενος ὑγιὴς γίνεται. εἰ δὲ πρῶτον μὲν ἄρξεται
μετανοεῖν, ὕστερον δὲ ἀναβάλλεται καὶ ὑπερτίθεται καὶ τὴν σήμερον
130 ἡμέραν καταφρονεῖ, πρὸς δὲ τὴν αὔριον ἀεὶ ἑτοιμάζεται, ἄνθρωπον
οὐκ ἔχει, ἤγουν ἀνθρώπινον φρόνημα, κτηνώδη δὲ καὶ ἄλογον γνῶσιν
φέρει. ἐν ὅσῳ γὰρ τὸ δοκεῖν πορεύεται πρὸς μετάνοιαν διὰ τοῦ
ἐλέγχου καὶ τῆς μεταμελείας, ὁ τῆς ὑπερθέσεως καὶ τῆς ἀναμονῆς
λογισμὸς προλαμβάνων ἀφαιρεῖται τὴν ἴασιν ἐκ τῆς ψυχῆς. καὶ πάλιν
135 ὁ ἄνθρωπος ἐν ἁμαρτίαις διάγει καὶ ἀρρωστῶν κατὰ ψυχὴν πορεύεται,
μὴ λυτρούμενος ἐκ τῶν παθῶν.

   13. Ἀλλ᾽ ἵνα φανερώτερον τὸν λόγον ποιήσομαι, ἀκούετε. ὁ
ἄνθρωπος ὁ μὴ εἰσερχόμενος εἰς τὴν ἐκκλησίαν ἀλλὰ διόλου
ἀναστρεφόμενος εἰς ματαιότητας καὶ μανίας ψευδεῖς παράλυτός ἐστι·
140 ὃς καὶ ἐλεγχόμενος ὑπὸ τῆς ἰδίας συνειδήσεως, ὅτι κακῶς ποιεῖ
διάγων ἔξω τῆς ἐκκλησίας, μεταμέλεται καὶ λυπεῖται καὶ ἄρχεται
πορεύεσθαι πρὸς τὴν ἐκκλησίαν. ἐὰν οὖν εἰσέλθῃ εἰς τὴν ἐκκλησίαν
καὶ παραστῇ μετὰ φόβου καὶ τὴν ψαλμῳδίαν ἀκούσει, θεραπεύεται

---

118 κλαυθμόν corr.: κλαθμόν OA

then who does not act wickedly and treacherously, who does not get angry and who does not desire wealth and honour? And who in turn, by acting thus, does not fall into the eight passions just enumerated?

11.   Have you heard of sickness of soul? Did you realize that each soul endures an infirmity of thirty-eight years like the paralytic? Then, learn also the way of healing. Make haste to find someone, that is, acquire a sensible way of thinking that is capable of effecting the healing of your souls. For within you too there exists a pool, namely, praise-worthy repentance, endowed with healing power and possessed of five ways like porticoes, as we mentioned above:[10] abstention from evil deeds, practice of good works, confession, remembrance of one's sins, and weeping. In the pool in Jerusalem, when an angel troubled the water, he gave it a healing power.[11]

12.   In your case, when each of you conducts herself here below in an evil manner, she troubles her conscience and brings fear and confusion upon her soul. For sin puts both the future judgement and its fearsome punishments in the remembrance of the heart and places them within the sight of the soul. Made by these thoughts to feel reproach, confusion and fear for its own condemnation, it is immersed in repentance and weeps bitterly and in this way is freed from sin. He who refrains from evil deeds, who repents and confesses, discovers a sensible way of thinking whereby he is guided towards repentance and recovers his health. But if one starts to repent at first and later delays, temporizes, spurns the present day and is always putting it off till the morrow, he has no one to help him, that is, no truly human attitude; rather, he carries about a knowledge that is brutish and irrational. For while he apparently is proceeding towards repentance through reproach and regret, the thought of delay and tarrying get there first and take away the healing from his soul. And the fellow again passes his life in his sins and continues to be sick in soul without finding deliverance from the passions.

13.   But give ear that I may make the matter more clear. A person who does not go to church but spends all his time in empty pursuits and misdirected inanities is a paralytic. When he is reproached by his conscience for doing wrong in spending his time outside the church, he repents, feels remorse and starts going to church. If then he enters the church and assists there with fear and listens to the psalmody, his soul finds healing and salvation, for he has an upright way of

[10] MD 19.5.
[11] Jn 5:4.

ἡ ψυχὴ αὐτοῦ καὶ σώζεται· καθάπερ γὰρ ἄνθρωπον ἔχει λογισμὸν
145 ὀρθόν, ἐλέγχοντος τοῦ συνειδότος, ἐμβάντα αὐτὸν εἰς τὴν ἐκκλησίαν
ὡς εἰς κολυμβήθραν. εἰ δὲ ἐλεγχθῇ μὲν ὑπὸ τῆς ἰδίας συνειδήσεως
καὶ τὸ δοκεῖν μεταμεληθῇ μὲν ὡς μὴ σχολάζων ἐν τῇ ἐκκλησίᾳ, οὐκ
ἀπέλθῃ δέ, ἀλλ᾽ εἴπῃ ἐν ἑαυτῷ – ποιήσω καὶ ταύτην τὴν δουλείαν,
ἀποκαταστήσω καὶ ταύτην μου τὴν πραγματείαν καὶ μετὰ ταῦτα
150 φθάσω εἰς τὴν ἀπόλυσιν τοῦ ἑσπερινοῦ. εἰ δὲ καὶ οὐ φθάσω, αὔριον
εἰς τὸν ὄρθρον ἢ εἰς τὴν λειτουργίαν ἀπελεύσομαι –, ἀθεράπευτος
μένει καὶ τῆς ἰδίας σωτηρίας στερεῖται. ἐν ὅσῳ γὰρ τὸ δοκεῖν
ἐλογίζετο ἀπελθεῖν εἰς τὴν ἐκκλησίαν, ἡ τοῦ βίου μέριμνα καὶ ἡ
φιλία τοῦ κόσμου, προλαβοῦσα αὐτόν, ἀπεστέρησε τῆς εἰς τὴν
155 ἐκκλησίαν εἰσόδου καὶ τῆς τῶν θείων λογίων ἀκροάσεως καὶ τὴν
ἴασιν τῆς ψυχῆς αὐτοῦ ἀφείλετο. καὶ πληροῦται τὸ *ἐν ᾧ πορεύομαι,*
ἄλλος προλαμβάνει με καὶ λαμβάνει τὴν ἴασιν, ἐγὼ δὲ ἀσθενῶν πορεύομαι.
ἐν ᾧ μεριμνῶ εἰς τὴν ἐκκλησίαν ἀπελθεῖν, ἡ φιλία τοῦ κόσμου καὶ
τῶν πραγμάτων προλαμβάνει καὶ προκατέχει με καὶ οὐκ ἀφίησί με
160 δραμεῖν αὐτίκα εἰς τὴν ἐκκλησίαν, ἀλλὰ λαμβάνει καὶ ἐπαίρει τὴν
ἀγαθὴν μέριμναν ἐκ τῆς ψυχῆς μου, ἐγὼ δὲ πάλιν ἔξω τῆς ἐκκλησίας
εὑρίσκομαι.

14. Πάλιν πορνεύει τις καὶ κατάκειται ἐν τῇ ἐνεργείᾳ τῆς
μοιχείας, ἐλέγχεται δὲ ὑπὸ τοῦ συνειδότος, ὅτι κακῶς περιπατεῖ. ἐὰν
165 οὖν ἐλεγχόμενος ἀποστῇ τῆς πορνείας καὶ εἰσέλθῃ εἰς τὴν κολυμβήθραν τῆς σωφροσύνης, θεραπεύεται ἡ ψυχὴ αὐτοῦ καὶ σώζεται. εἰ
δὲ μεριμνήσει μὲν δῆθεν ἀποστῆναι τῆς πορνείας, οὐκ ἀγαπήσῃ δὲ
τὴν σωφροσύνην, ἐγείρεται πάλιν ὁ τῆς πορνείας λογισμὸς καὶ διὰ
τῆς προλήψεως προφθάνει τὴν ψυχὴν αὐτοῦ καὶ λαμβάνει τὴν ἔννοιαν
170 τῆς σωφροσύνης ἐκ τῆς καρδίας αὐτοῦ, καὶ πάλιν πίπτει ὁ ἄνθρωπος
εἰς τὴν πρᾶξιν τῆς πορνείας. καὶ πληροῦται τὸ *ἐν ᾧ δὲ πορεύομαι,*
ἄλλος προλαμβάνει με καὶ λαμβάνει τὴν ἴασιν, ἐγὼ δὲ ἀσθενῶν πορεύομαι.

15. Ἐν ᾧ λογίζομαι, φησίν, εἰς σωφροσύνην ἐλθεῖν, ὁ τῆς
πορνείας λογισμὸς προλαμβάνων με ἁρπάζει τὴν γνῶσιν τῆς σωφρο-
175 σύνης ἐξ ἐμοῦ, ἐγὼ δὲ πάλιν πορνεύων εὑρίσκομαι. πάλιν ἀδικεῖ τις
τὸν πλησίον αὐτοῦ καὶ κατάκειται ὡς ὁ παράλυτος ἐν τῇ κλίνῃ τῆς
πλεονεξίας, ἀλλ᾽ ἐλέγχεται ὑπὸ τοῦ συνειδότος, ὅτι κακῶς ποιεῖ. ἐὰν
οὖν ἐλεγχόμενος καταλείψῃ τὴν ἀδικίαν καὶ εἰσέλθῃ εἰς τὴν κο-

thinking, which like a man plunges him into the church as into a pool when his conscience reproves him. But if he is reproached by his conscience and apparently regrets his irregular attendance at church, yet does not go but says to himself, "I am going to do this errand and settle this business as well and after that I will go to the concluding part of the Vespers service. But if I do not get there, tomorrow I will attend Matins or the Liturgy" —, he remains unhealed and is deprived of his salvation. For while he apparently considered going to church, the cares of life and attachment to the world got the better of him and deprived him of the occasion of entering the church and hearing the divine scriptures and dispossessed him of healing for his soul.[12] This fulfils the statement of the paralytic, "When I approach, someone else gets there ahead of me and receives healing, while I continue in my sickness."[13] When I make up my mind to go to church, my attachment to the world and my affairs gets ahead of me, holds me back and does not allow me to run off straightaway to church. Instead it snatches away and removes the good intentions from my soul, and consequently I find myself outside the church.

14. In another case someone committed fornication and continued in his licentious activity, but he was reproached by his conscience for walking an evil path. If then because of the reproach he abstains from fornication and enters the pool of chastity, his soul receives healing and salvation. If he then makes up his mind to abstain from fornication but has no love for chastity, the thought of fornication arises again, overtakes his soul by means of his predisposition and snatches the idea of chastity from his heart, and once again the man falls into the practice of fornication. And the saying is fulfilled: "When I approach, someone else gets there ahead of me and receives healing, while I continue in my sickness."

15. In other words, "When I think of entering the path of chastity, the thought of fornication gets ahead of me and robs me of the knowledge of chastity, and I find myself once again caught in fornication." In another case someone wronged his neighbour and remained, like the paralytic, on the bed of his covetousness, but was reproached by his conscience for doing evil. If then because of the

---

[12] Cf. Mt 13:22, Mk 4:19.

[13] This quotation from the liturgical office is repeated as a refrain in the following paragraphs (14-17). It is taken from Vespers of the Sunday of the Paralytic (in the Pentekostarion) and the hymn is attributed to Koumalas: ἐν ᾧ δὲ πορεύομαι, ἄλλος προλαμβάνει με καὶ λαμβάνει τὴν ἴασιν, ἐγὼ δὲ ἀσθενῶν κατάκειμαι. Cf. Jn 5:7.

λυμβήθραν τῆς δικαιοσύνης, θεραπεύεται ἡ ψυχὴ αὐτοῦ καὶ σώζεται.
180 εἰ δὲ μεριμνήσει μὲν δῆθεν ἀποστῆναι τῆς ἀδικίας, οὐκ ἀγαπήσει
δὲ τὴν δικαιοσύνην, προλαμβάνει πάλιν αὐτὸν ὁ τῆς πλεονεξίας
λογισμὸς καὶ ἀφαιρεῖται ἐξ αὐτοῦ τὴν ἔννοιαν τῆς δικαιοσύνης, καὶ
πάλιν πίπτει ὁ ἄνθρωπος εἰς ἐνέργειαν τῆς ἀδικίας καὶ ἁρπάζει τὰ
πράγματα τοῦ ἀδελφοῦ αὐτοῦ. *καὶ πληροῦται τὸ ἐν ᾧ δὲ πορεύομαι,*
185 *ἄλλος προλαμβάνει με καὶ λαμβάνει τὴν ἴασιν, ἐγὼ δὲ ἀσθενῶν πορεύομαι.*

16. Ἐν ᾧ *λογίζομαι,* φησί, *δικαιοσύνην ποιῆσαι,* ὁ τῆς ἀδικίας
λογισμὸς προλαμβάνων με ἁρπάζει τὴν γνῶσιν τῆς δικαιοσύνης ἐξ
ἐμοῦ, ἐγὼ δὲ πάλιν ἀδικῶ τὸν ἐμὸν ἀδελφόν καὶ ὡς παράλυτος εἰς
τὸν κράββατον τῆς πλεονεξίας καταπίπτω.
190 **17.** Πάλιν δανίζει τίς τινι ἀνθρώπῳ χρήματα καὶ λαμβάνει τόκους
ἐξ αὐτοῦ καὶ κατάκειται ἐν τῇ κλίνῃ τῆς φιλοχρηματίας ὡς παράλυτος,
ἀλλ᾽ ἐλέγχεται ὑπὸ τοῦ συνειδότος καὶ ὑπὸ τῆς θείας γραφῆς, ὅτι
κακῶς ποιεῖ καὶ διπλασιάζει τὸ κεφάλαιον. ἐὰν οὖν ἐλεγχόμενος
ἀφήσει τὸ λαμβάνειν τόκους καὶ εἰσέλθῃ εἰς τὴν κολυμβήθραν τῆς
195 ἐλεημοσύνης καὶ τοῦ δανίζειν τοῖς πτωχοῖς κατὰ θεόν, θεραπεύεται
ἡ ψυχὴ αὐτοῦ καὶ σώζεται. εἰ δὲ ἄρξεται λογίζεσθαι ἐν ἑαυτῷ –
ἐξόδους ἔχω καὶ χρήζω πολλῶν καὶ δέομαι οἰκονομίας μεγάλης, καὶ
δέον ἐπαρεῖν τόκους, ἵνα καὶ τὸν λαόν μου διαθρέψω καὶ ἐλεημοσύνην
ποιήσω –, προλαμβάνει αὐτὸν ὁ τῆς φιλοχρηματίας λογισμὸς καὶ
200 ἐπαίρει ἐξ αὐτοῦ τὴν ἔννοιαν τῆς ἐλεημοσύνης, καὶ πάλιν πίπτει ὁ
ἄνθρωπος εἰς φειδωλίαν καὶ ἀσπλαγχνίαν, καὶ ἀμετάδοτος γίνεται.
καὶ πληροῦται τὸ ἐν ᾧ δὲ πορεύομαι, ἄλλος προλαμβάνει με καὶ λαμβάνει
τὴν ἴασιν, ἐγὼ δὲ ἀσθενῶν πορεύομαι.

18. Ἐν ᾧ, φησί, *λογίζομαι λαβεῖν τόκον* πρὸς τὸ δοῦναι
205 ἐλεημοσύνην, ἡ φειδωλία προλαμβάνει με καὶ μετὰ τὸ λαβεῖν τοὺς
τόκους οὐδὲ ὀβολὸν μεταδίδωμι· ἁρπάζει γὰρ ἐξ ἐμοῦ τὴν μνήμην
τῆς συμπαθείας, ἐγὼ δὲ πάλιν εἰς ἀσπλαγχνίαν κατασύρομαι καὶ πρὸς
μετάδοσιν οὐκ ἐκτείνω τὴν χεῖρά μου. ἀλλὰ γένοιτο, ἀδελφαί μου
ἠγαπημέναι, τὸν τοῦ εὐαγγελίου λόγον ἐν ταῖς καρδίαις δεξάμεναι,
210 ὑπακοῦσαι αὐτῷ, ὅπως ταῖς ἐντολαῖς τοῦ Χριστοῦ πειθαρχήσασαι
διαναστῶμεν ἀπὸ τοῦ κοσμικοῦ φρονήματος καὶ εἰς πνευματικὰ
φρονήματα περιπατήσωμεν.

---

209 δεξαμέναι corr.: δεξαμέναις ΟΑ

reproach he abandons his wrongdoing and enters the pool of righteousness, his soul finds healing and salvation. If he then makes up his mind to abstain from wrongdoing but has no love for righteousness, the thought of covetousness again gets the better of him and takes from him the idea of righteousness, and once again the man falls into the activity of covetousness and makes off with his brother's goods. And the saying is fulfilled: "When I approach, someone else gets there ahead of me and receives healing, while I continue in my sickness."

16. In other words, "When I consider acting justly, the thought of wrongdoing gets the advantage of me and robs me of the knowledge of justice. Once again I find myself wronging my brother and like the paralytic I fall back upon the pallet of my covetousness."

17. In another case someone loaned money to a man and received interest from him and he continued to lie on the bed of his miserliness like the paralytic, but he was reproached by his conscience and by divine scripture[14] for doing evil and doubling his capital. If then because of the reproach he gives up taking interest and enters the pool of almsgiving and of lending to God's poor, his soul finds healing and salvation. But if he starts thinking to himself, "I have payments to make and need a lot of money and require a large administration; it is necessary to raise interest in order both to feed my people and to give alms" —, the thought of miserliness gets the better of him and lifts from him the idea of almsgiving, and once again the fellow falls into niggardliness and heartlessness and becomes unwilling to share his goods.[15] And the saying is fulfilled: "When I approach, someone else gets there ahead of me and receives healing, while I continue in my sickness."

18. So he is saying to himself, "When I think of taking interest in order to give alms, niggardliness gets the better of me and after taking interest I share not a penny of it; for miserliness snatches away from me the remembrance of compassion, and once again I slip into heartlessness and fail to hold out my hand to share." But, my beloved sisters, after you have received the word of the Gospel in your hearts, you must give heed to it so that, obedient to the commandments of Christ, we may stay aloof from the world's way of thinking and walk according to spiritual attitudes.

---

[14] E.g., Ex 22:24, Lev 25:37, Deut 23:20-21.
[15] Cf. Nilus of Ancyra, *De monastica exercitatione* 73 (PG 79:805D): ἀσπλαγχνία ἣν γεννᾷ φιλοχρηματία.

19. ῾Ως γὰρ ὁ παράλυτος ἐπιστάντι τῷ ᾿Ιησοῦ καὶ κελεύσαντι ἆραι τὴν κλίνην καὶ περιπατεῖν ὑπήκουσεν ἀδιακρίτως καὶ ἠγέρθη, οὕτω
215 καὶ ἡμεῖς ἐὰν ταῖς εὐαγγελικαῖς ἐντολαῖς ὑπακούσωμεν κελευούσαις ἡμῖν κουφίσαι τὴν ἐπιθυμίαν ἡμῶν ἀπὸ τῆς ὕλης τοῦ κόσμου τούτου καὶ ὑψῶσαι τὸν λογισμὸν ἡμῶν, καθάπερ κράββατον, καὶ θεῖναι ἐν τοῖς ὤμοις τῶν ἀρετῶν, ἀξιωθείημεν περιπατῆσαι τὴν ὁδὸν τῆς σωτηρίας ἡμῶν καὶ καταντῆσαι εἰς τὴν ὁδὸν τῆς βασιλείας τῶν
220 οὐρανῶν χάριτι καὶ φιλανθρωπίᾳ τοῦ κυρίου ἡμῶν ᾿Ιησοῦ Χριστοῦ· ᾧ πρέπει πᾶσα δόξα, τιμὴ καὶ προσκύνησις εἰς τοὺς αἰῶνας τῶν αἰώνων. ᾿Αμήν.

19.   As the paralytic obeyed Jesus and got up without reserve when Jesus stood there and ordered him to take up his bed and walk,[16] so too if we are obedient to the Gospel commandments which order us to lighten our desires of the matter of the world and lift our thoughts up like a pallet and place them on the shoulders of the virtues, we might be deemed worthy to walk in the path of our salvation and reach the path of the kingdom of heaven by the grace and clemency of our Lord Jesus Christ. To him be all glory, honour and worship unto the ages of ages. Amen.

---

[16] Jn 5:8.

Τῇ πέμπτη κυριακῇ
τῆς Σαμαρείτιδος

1. Ἀδελφαὶ καὶ μητέρες, ἡνίκα θελήσῃ ὁ ἁλιεὺς ἀγρεῦσαι ἰχθύας, ἀπέρχεται εἰς τὴν θάλασσαν καὶ βάλλει τὸ ἄγγιστρον αὐτοῦ εἰς τὸν
5 βυθὸν καὶ ἀνάγει τοὺς ἐκεῖ νηχομένους ἰχθύας. τοῦτο καὶ ὁ τὴν ἡμετέραν οἰκονομῶν σωτηρίαν πραγματεύομενος Ἰησοῦς ὁ Χριστὸς καθέζεται πρὸς τῇ πηγῇ· καὶ τὴν ἐν τῷ φρέατι παραγενομένην Σαμαρεῖτιν ἐπὶ τὸ ἀντλῆσαι ὕδωρ ζωγρήσας διὰ τῆς πίστεως, πέμπει κηρῦξαι τοῖς Σαμαρείταις τῆς θεότητος αὐτοῦ τὴν δύναμιν. ὁρᾶτε
10 σοφωτάτην ἁλίαν; βλέπετε ἄγραν ἐπαινετήν; πηγῇ προστρέχει ἡ Σαμαρεῖτις δίψαν ἰωμένη πρὸς βραχὺ καὶ πηγῇ ἐντυγχάνει ἀληθινῇ πινομένη καὶ μηδέποτε παραχωρῆσαι διψῆσαι τὸν πίνοντα· *ὁ γὰρ πίνων, φησίν, ἐκ τοῦ ὕδατος τούτου διψήσει πάλιν· ὁ δὲ πίνων ἐκ τοῦ ὕδατος οὗ ἐγὼ δώσω, οὐ μὴ διψήσει εἰς τὸν αἰῶνα.* ἀντλῆσαι ὕδωρ
15 παραγίνεται καὶ τὸ ζῶν ὕδωρ ἐμπορεύεται. ζητεῖ λαβεῖν ὕδωρ ὁ κύριος καὶ ζητῶν οἰκονομεῖ τὴν ζητουμένην. ὁ ζητῶν ζητεῖται καὶ ὁ ζητῶν λαβεῖν δίδωσιν.

2. Ὦ βάθος γνώσεως, ὦ δωρεᾶς ἀνυπερβλήτου. ὡς σοφὸς ἁλιεὺς καθάπερ δέλεαρ τὴν τοῦ ὕδατος ζήτησιν προβάλλεται καὶ τὴν γνῶσιν
20 τοῦ ζωηροῦ καὶ πνευματικοῦ ὕδατος καθάπερ ἄγγιστρον ἐμβαλὼν τῇ ψυχῇ τῆς Σαμαρείτιδος καὶ εἰς τὸν πόθον αὐτοῦ κρεμάσας αὐτήν, ἕλκει πρὸς τὴν ἑαυτοῦ πίστιν διὰ τῆς ἐπιγνώσεως. *δός μοι, λέγει, καὶ δός μοι, ἀκούει.* τὸ ῥεῦμα γὰρ τοῦ ζητηθέντος αἰσθητοῦ ὕδατος ἐφανέρωσε τῇ γυναικὶ τῆς νοητῆς πηγῆς τοὺς ποταμούς· ὅθεν καὶ
25 εἰς δίψαν ἐλθοῦσα ζητεῖ καὶ λαμβάνει καὶ πίνει καὶ τῆς πόσεως τὴν ἡδονὴν ἀπαγγέλλει καὶ τὴν μυστικὴν πηγὴν ἀνακαλύπτει. καὶ ὡς

---

4 ἄγγιστρον OA [cf. 20]: rectius ἄγκιστρον   10 ἁλίαν OA: rectius ἁλείαν vel ἁλιείαν

MD **20**

THE FIFTH SUNDAY [AFTER EASTER]: THE SAMARITAN WOMAN[1]

1. Sisters and Mothers, when a fisherman wants to catch fish, he goes to the sea and throws his fishing line out into the deep water and he brings back the fish that swim there. Providing for our salvation, Jesus Christ was doing just this when he sat down at the well.[2] After he had caught in the net of faith the Samaritan woman who had come to the well to draw water, he sent her to the Samaritans to proclaim the power of his divinity.[3] Do you see the great wisdom in this fishing? Do you appreciate this praiseworthy catch? The Samaritan woman ran to the well to cure her thirst for a little while and she encountered the true well-spring which, once drunk, nevermore allows the one who drinks of it to thirst. For scripture says, "The one who drinks of this water will thirst again, but the one who drinks of the water that I shall give will never thirst."[4] She came to draw water and procured living water. The Lord sought to receive water and in seeking he provided for her who was seeking for herself. The one who was seeking was sought after; the one who was seeking to receive gave.

2. O the depth of the knowledge![5] O what an unsurpassable gift! Like a wise fisherman he put forward his request for water as bait and sinking the knowledge of the living and spiritual water, like a hook, into the soul of the Samaritan woman, he caught her on her desire for the water and drew her to faith in himself by means of understanding. "Give me," he says and "Give me," she hears.[6] For the stream of the sensible water which he requested revealed to the woman the rivers of the spiritual spring. Thus, coming to thirst for it, she seeks and takes and drinks, and she announces the delight of the drinking and reveals the mystical well-spring. And as the deer runs

---

[1] Jn 4:5-42 is the Gospel read at the Liturgy on this Sunday.
[2] Jn 4:6.
[3] Jn 4:7, 29-30, 39.
[4] Jn 4:13-14.
[5] Cf. Rom 11:33.
[6] Jn 4:7.

ἡ ἔλαφος ἐπὶ τὰς πηγὰς τῶν ὑδάτων ἀποτρέχει, ἐξέρχονται τῆς πόλεως
καὶ οἱ Σαμαρεῖται καὶ πρὸς τὸν Ἰησοῦν ἔρχονται. ὦ πλοῦτος σοφίας,
ὦ ὕδατος γλυκεροῦ. ὄντως ὕδωρ ζῶν καὶ ἀλλόμενον οἱ λόγοι τοῦ
30 κυρίου· ὕδωρ μὲν ὡς δροσίζοντες καὶ ἀναψύχοντες τοὺς ὑπὸ καύσωνος
τῆς πονηρᾶς ἐπιθυμίας φλογιζομένους· ζῶν δὲ ὡς τοὺς νενεκρωμένους
ὑπὸ ῥαθυμίας διανιστῶντες καὶ εἰς προθυμίαν διεγείροντες, ἀλλόμενον
δὲ ὡς μὴ συστελλόμενοι καὶ κρυπτόμενοι ἐν καρδίᾳ ἀλλ' ἐκπηδῶντες
διὰ τοῦ στόματος διὰ τὴν ἐκβλύζουσαν ἐν τῇ ψυχῇ ἀγάπην καὶ τῷ
35 ἤχῳ τοῦ κηρύγματος κατευφραίνοντες τὰς τῶν ἀνθρώπων καρδίας
διὰ τὴν προσοῦσαν ἐν αὐτοῖς χάριν.
    3.   Τὸ μὲν αἰσθητὸν ὕδωρ πινόμενον οὐ μόνον οὐκ αὐξάνει, ἀλλὰ
καὶ διαφορούμενον ἐκλείπει· διὸ καὶ πάλιν ὑπὸ δίψης συνέχεται ὁ
πίνων τοῦτο τὸ ὕδωρ. τὸ δὲ ὑπὸ τοῦ κυρίου διδόμενον ὕδωρ οὐ μόνον
40 διαμένει ἀεί, ἀλλὰ καὶ πληθυνόμενον ὑπερεκβλύζει καὶ τοὺς δεχο-
μένους ἀρδεύει τῇ δαψιλείᾳ καὶ τοὺς δωρουμένους πιαίνει τῇ διαμονῇ
καθάπερ πηγῇ καὶ ὁλοκλήρους ποταμοὺς πεμπούσῃ καὶ τοῦ
ἐκβλύζοντος ὕδατος μὴ ἐξισταμένῃ.

    4.   Περὶ ὥραν ἕκτην οἱ ἄνθρωποι βρωμάτων μεταλαμβάνουσι καὶ
45 ὁ Ἰησοῦς περὶ ὥραν ἕκτην βρῶμα ποιεῖται τὴν σωτηρίαν τῆς
Σαμαρείτιδος. ἐν τῇ ἕκτῃ ὥρᾳ ἡ Εὔα θηρεύεται ὑπὸ τῆς ὁμιλίας τοῦ
ὄφεως καὶ ἐν ἕκτῃ ὥρᾳ ἡ Σαμαρεῖτις ζωγρεῖται ὑπὸ τῆς σοφίας τοῦ
ζῶντος λόγου. ἐν πέντε ἡμέραις ἡ κτίσις πᾶσα δημιουργηθεῖσα, τῇ
ἕκτῃ ἡμέρᾳ διεπλάσθη ὁ ἄνθρωπος ὑπὸ θεοῦ. καὶ τοῖς πέντε βιβλίοις
50 τοῦ Μωσέως ἡ Σαμαρεῖτις ὁδηγηθεῖσα πρὸς γνῶσιν τοῦ Χριστοῦ,
ἐν τῇ ἕκτῃ ὥρᾳ ἀναπλάττεται ὑπὸ κυρίου.
    5.   Εἰποῦσα γὰρ ὅτι *οἶδα ὅτι ἔρχεται ὁ Μεσίας Χριστός*, ὑπὸ τοῦ
Ἰησοῦ διδάσκεται αὐτὸν εἶναι τὸν Μεσίαν τὸν λαλοῦντα μετ' αὐτῆς.
ἐκεῖ χοῦν λαβὼν ὁ θεὸς ἀπὸ τῆς γῆς, ἔπλασε τὸν ἄνθρωπον· ἐνταῦθα

29 ἀλλόμενον hic et alibi scriptum cum spiritu leni OA   35 καρδίας corr.:
καρδίαν OA   38 ὑπὸ δίψης: ὑποδίψης OA   52 Μεσίας OA [cf. 53]: rectius
Μεσσίας

to the springs of water,[7] the Samaritans too go forth from the city
and come to Jesus.[8] O the riches of wisdom![9] O what sweet water!
Truly the words of the Lord are a living and flowing water: water,
in that his words refresh and cool those being consumed by the burning
heat of evil desire; living, in that they raise up those deadened by
indolence and stir them to enthusiasm; flowing, in that they are not
gathered up and hidden in the heart, but gush forth through the mouth
because of the love that issues forth in the soul, and by the sound
of their proclamation they gladden the hearts of men because of the
grace present within them.

3.   When ordinary water is drunk, not only does it fail to increase
in quantity, but it also gives out as it is dispersed, and so the one
who drinks this water is once again caught by thirst. The water given
by the Lord not only lasts forever, but it also gushes forth in
superabundance. It waters with plenty those who receive it and enriches
those who offer it freely to others as by an abiding spring which sends
forth entire rivers, yet is not deprived of the water that issues forth
from it.

4.   About the sixth hour people partake of food and about the
sixth hour Jesus prepared food, namely, the salvation of the Samaritan
woman.[10] At the sixth hour Eve fell prey to the serpent's conversation[11] and at the sixth hour the Samaritan woman was ensnared by
the wisdom of the living Word.[12] After all creation had been made
in five days, on the sixth day man was formed by God.[13] And after
the Samaritan woman was led to the knowledge of Christ by the five
books of Moses, she was formed anew by the Lord at the sixth hour.

5.   For when she said, "I know Christ the Messiah is coming," she
was taught by Jesus that the one speaking to her was the Messiah.[14]
In the first case, God took earth from the ground and formed man;[15]

---

[7] Ps 41:2.
[8] Jn 4:39-40.
[9] Rom 11:33.
[10] Jn 4:6.
[11] Gen 3:1-7.
[12] Cf. Pseudo-Chrysostom, *In Samaritanam* (PG 59:537). The reference can also
be found in one of the opening stichera for Vespers on the Sunday of the Samaritan
Woman: ἐπὶ τὴν πηγὴν ἐπέστη ἡ πηγὴ τῶν θαυμάτων ἐν τῇ ἕκτῃ ὥρᾳ τῆς Εὔας
ζωγρῆσαι καρπόν· ἡ γὰρ Εὔα ἐν ταύτῃ ἐξελήλυθεν ἐκ τοῦ παραδείσου ἀπάτῃ τοῦ
ὄφεως.
[13] Gen 1:1-31.
[14] Jn 4:25-26.
[15] Gen 2:7.

55 ὁ κύριος ὕδωρ ζητήσας λαβεῖν ἀπὸ γυναικός, διήγειρεν αὐτὴν εἰς
ἔφεσιν καὶ ζήτησιν τοῦ ἰδίου ὕδατος· ὅθεν καὶ δοὺς αὐτῇ τὸ ζῶν
ὕδωρ, ἐνέπλησεν αὐτῆς τὴν ψυχὴν χάριτος πνευματικῆς. οἱ ἀπόστολοι
ἀπῆλθον εἰς τὴν πόλιν ἵνα τροφὰς ἀγοράσωσι, καὶ ὁ κύριος τὴν
Σαμαρεῖτιν χειροτονεῖ ἀπόστολον καὶ εἰς τὴν πόλιν πέμπει, ἵνα ψυχὰς
60 ἐπιστρέψει πρὸς αὐτόν. ἡ Σαμαρεῖτις καταλιποῦσα τὴν πόλιν, εἰς τὴν
πηγὴν ἦλθε καὶ τῇ πηγῇ τῶν ἰαμάτων ἐνέτυχε καὶ τοῦ ἁλλομένου
ὕδατος εἰς ζωὴν αἰώνιον ἠξίωται.

   6. Τὴν ὑδρίαν ἐν τῷ φρέατι ἀφῆκε καὶ τὴν καρδίαν ὑδρίαν διὰ
τῆς πίστεως πεποίηκε καὶ ἤντλησε τὸ ζῶν ὕδωρ ἐκ τῆς πηγῆς τοῦ
65 κυρίου καὶ λαβοῦσα ἀπῆλθεν εἰς τὴν ἰδίαν πόλιν καὶ ἐπότισε νάμα
ἐπιγνώσεως τοὺς ὑπὸ αὐχμοῦ ἀγνωσίας κρατουμένους. ταύτης τὴν
πίστιν καὶ τὸν τρόπον ζηλώσωμεν πᾶσαι καὶ ὡς ἐκείνη τῆς πόλεως
ἐξελθοῦσα πρὸς τὴν πηγὴν ἔδραμε καὶ τῷ κυρίῳ ἐνέτυχεν, καταλείψ-
ωμεν καὶ ἡμεῖς τῆς κακῆς ἡμῶν πολιτείας τὴν συνήθειαν καὶ πρὸς
70 τὴν πηγὴν τῆς μετανοίας καὶ τῶν δακρύων δράμωμεν καὶ τὸν Ἰησοῦν
ὀψώμεθα δωρούμενον τὴν ἄφεσιν. ἡ ὀργιζομένη ἀποστήτω τῆς
μνησικακίας καὶ προσελθέτω τῇ πηγῇ τῆς μετανοίας καὶ εἰπάτω ἐν
ἑαυτῇ, δός μοι, κύριε, τὸ ὕδωρ τῆς μετὰ τῆς ἀδελφῆς μου καταλλαγῆς,
παράσχου μοι τὸ νάμα τῆς πρὸς αὐτὴν ἀγάπης. καὶ εὐθὺς ἡ πηγὴ
75 τῆς ἀφέσεως καὶ τῆς ἀγάπης ἀναδοθήσεται ἐν τῇ σῇ καρδίᾳ καὶ
ἴδῃς ἐν τῇ τοιαύτῃ καταστάσει καθάπερ πηγῇ καθεζόμενον καὶ
ἀρεσκόμενον τὸν Ἰησοῦν καὶ σωτηρίαν παρέχοντα τῇ σῇ ψυχῇ.

   7. Ἐπαναπαυόμενος γὰρ ὁ κύριος ἐν τῇ ἀγαθῇ διαθέσει τῆς ψυχῆς
σου, ἀναπαύει σε ἀπὸ τοῦ φορτίου τῆς ὀργῆς καὶ τῆς μνησικακίας,
80 αἴρων καὶ ἀφανίζων αὐτὴν ἀπὸ σοῦ· κουφίζει γὰρ τὴν ψυχήν σου
τοῖς τῆς ἀγάπης καὶ τῆς καταλλαγῆς πτεροῖς. ὕδωρ ἐζήτησε παρὰ
γυναικὸς λαβεῖν καὶ ὕδωρ ἔδωκεν αὐτῇ. οὕτω ζητεῖ καὶ παρὰ σοῦ
ὕδωρ ἐξομολογήσεως καὶ μετανοίας καὶ δωρεῖταί σοι ὕδωρ τῆς
ἀφέσεως· ζητεῖ παρὰ σοῦ ὕδωρ αὐτομεμψίας καὶ καταλλαγῆς καὶ
85 παρέχει σοι ὕδωρ τῆς ἀγάπης. ἀναπαύεις αὐτὸν διὰ τῆς ἀγαθῆς σου
προθέσεως καὶ ἀναπαύει σε διὰ τῶν χαρισμάτων τοῦ ἁγίου αὐτοῦ
πνεύματος. *δεῦτε, γάρ φησι, πάντες οἱ κοπιῶντες καὶ πεφορτισμένοι,
κἀγὼ ἀναπαύσω ὑμᾶς.*

in this case the Lord sought to take water from a woman and roused her to long and seek for the water he offered. Thus, in giving to her the living water,[16] he filled her soul with spiritual grace. The apostles went to the city to buy food and the Lord ordained the Samaritan woman as an apostle and sent her into the city to convert souls for him.[17] When the Samaritan woman left the city and came to the well-spring, she encountered the well-spring of healing and was deemed worthy of the water welling up to eternal life.[18]

6. She left her water-jar at the well and by faith has made her heart into a water-jar.[19] She drew the living water from the well-spring of the Lord and when she received it she went into her city and watered with the flowing water of understanding those who were gripped by the drought of ignorance.[20] Let us all emulate the faith and manner of this woman. As she left the city and ran to the well and met the Lord, let us too abandon the habits of our evil way of life and run to the well of repentance and tears and look upon the Lord, who grants us forgiveness. Let she who is angered refrain from rancour and come to the well of repentance and let her say within herself, "Lord, give me the water of reconciliation with my sister. Provide for me the flowing water of love for her." Immediately the well-spring of forgiveness and love will issue forth in your heart and in these circumstances you will see Jesus seated as he was at the well and he will reconcile you and grant salvation to your soul.

7. When the Lord rests content in the good disposition of your soul, he will grant you rest from the burden of anger and rancour, lifting it up and removing it from you, for he will lighten your soul with the wings of love and reconciliation. He sought to receive water from the woman and he gave water to her. Thus does he seek also from you the water of confession and repentance and he grants you the water of forgiveness. He seeks from you the water of self-reproach and reconciliation and he grants you the water of love. You give him rest by means of your good intentions and he grants you rest by means of the gifts of his Holy Spirit. For scripture says, "Come all you who labour and are heavily burdened and I will give you rest."[21]

---

[16] Jn 4:10.
[17] Jn 4:28-30, 39-42.
[18] Jn 4:14.
[19] Jn 4:28.
[20] Jn 4:29-30.
[21] Mt 11:28.

8. Καταλειψάτω ἑκάστη ὑμῶν, καθάπερ Σαμάρειαν, τὴν φροντίδα
90 τοῦ ματαίου βίου καὶ πορευέσθω πρὸς τὴν πηγήν, τὴν ἐκκλησίαν
φημί, καὶ ἀξιωθήσεται τῆς ὁμιλίας τοῦ κυρίου. ὡς γὰρ ὁ πρὸς τὰ
βασίλεια ἀπερχόμενος τὸν βασιλέα ὁρᾷ καὶ ἐντυγχάνει αὐτῷ, οὕτω
καὶ ἡ πρὸς τὸν οἶκον τοῦ θεοῦ ἀποτρέχουσα τῷ θεῷ ὁμιλεῖ καὶ τοῦ
ὕδατος τῆς σωτηρίας μεταλαμβάνει· ἱσταμένη γὰρ ἐν τῇ ἐκκλησίᾳ
95 καὶ τῶν τοῦ θεοῦ λόγων ἀκρωμένη, καταλιμπάνει καθάπερ ὑδρίαν
τὴν γηΐνην καὶ κοσμικὴν ἀναστροφὴν καὶ ἐπανέρχεται πρὸς τὴν
πρώτην πολιτείαν, ἤγουν τὴν πρὸ τῆς παραβάσεως. καὶ οὔτε
αἰσχύνεται ἀνακαλύπτουσα τὰ ἑαυτῆς ἁμαρτήματα, καὶ μεγαλύνει τὸν
κύριον τὸν λυτρωσάμενον αὐτὴν ἐκ τῆς δουλείας τῶν κακῶν. τὰ
100 ῥεύματα τῆς πηγῆς ἀντλοῦσα ἡ ὑδρία λαμβάνει. τὰ δὲ ῥήματα τοῦ
θεοῦ λόγου ἡ διάνοια εἰσδέχεται.

9. Ἐὰν οὖν σχολάζομεν ἐν ταῖς ἐκκλησίαις καὶ μετὰ συνέσεως
τῶν θείων ᾀσμάτων ἀκρωμένα, δυνησόμεθα καὶ μετὰ τὸ ἐξελθεῖν
ἐκεῖθεν τὴν μνήμην τῆς ἀκροάσεως ἐν ἑαυταῖς φέρειν καθάπερ ὑδρίαν,
105 τὴν ἡμετέραν ψυχὴν τῇ γνώσει τῶν ἐν ἐκκλησίᾳ τελουμένων
ἐναποτιθέμεναι καὶ ὅπουπερ ἂν διάγωμεν τὰ τοῦ θεοῦ λόγια
ἀπαγγέλουσαι. κοπιάσωμεν, ἀδελφαί, ἐν τῷ παρόντι αἰῶνι, ἵνα
εὕρωμεν ἀνάπαυσιν ἐν τῷ μέλλοντι, ὅτι δὲ ἐὰν κοπιάσωμεν ὀλίγον,
εἰς αἰῶνας ἀναπαυόμεθα. ὁ ὁδηγῶν ἡμᾶς εἰς τὴν οὐράνιον ὁδὸν
110 Ἰησοῦς, δι' ὧν ἔργων ἐποίησε, τοῦτο παρέστησε.

10. Φησὶ γὰρ ὁ εὐαγγελιστής, *Ὁ δὲ Ἰησοῦς κεκοπιακὼς ἐκ τῆς
ὁδοιπορίας, ἐκαθέζετο.* ὃς καὶ πᾶσαν τὴν ὑπὲρ ἡμῶν τελέσας οἰκονομίαν
καὶ κεκοπιακὼς εἰς τὴν ἀνάβασιν τοῦ σταυροῦ καὶ καταβὰς εἰς Ἅιδην
καὶ ἀναστὰς καὶ ἀναβὰς εἰς τοὺς οὐρανούς, ἐκάθισεν ἐκ δεξιῶν τοῦ
115 θεοῦ καὶ πατρός. ἀλλὰ καὶ οἱ ἀπόστολοι, κοπιάσαντες ἐν τῷ παρόντι
αἰῶνι καὶ τὸ κήρυγμα τοῦ εὐαγγελίου σπείραντες ἐν ταῖς καρδίαις
τῶν ἀνθρώπων καὶ πεζῇ τὴν οἰκουμένην διελθόντες, καθεσθήσονται
ἐπὶ θρόνων τοῦ κρῖναι πᾶσαν τὴν οἰκουμένην. κακοπαθήσωμεν
λοιπὸν ἐν ἔργοις τῆς δικαιοσύνης, ὅπως ἐν ταῖς ἐπ' οὐρανίοις μοναῖς
120 ἀνακλιθεῖσαι τὴν αἰώνιον ἀνάπαυσιν λάβωμεν ἐν Χριστῷ Ἰησοῦ τῷ
κυρίῳ ἡμῶν, ᾧ ἡ δόξα καὶ τὸ κράτος εἰς τοὺς αἰῶνας τῶν αἰώνων.
Ἀμήν.

120 ἀνακλιθεῖσαι corr.: ἀνακλιθῆσαι OA

8. Let each of you leave behind the attitudes of her empty way of life, like Samaria, and proceed to the well, I mean the church, and she will be deemed worthy of converse with the Lord. As someone who goes to the palace to see and meet the emperor, so too the sister who runs to the house of God converses with God and partakes of the water of salvation. Standing in the church and listening to the words of God, she abandons her earthly and worldly conduct like a water-jar and returns to the original way of life, namely, that before the transgression. She is not ashamed to reveal her sins and she glorifies the Lord who redeemed her from slavery to evil. The jar for drawing water receives flowing streams from the well and the discursive intellect accepts the sayings of God the Word.

9. Therefore, if we are regular in our church attendance and listen intelligently to the divine chants, we shall be able even after we leave there to carry within ourselves the remembrance of what we heard like a water-jar, storing it up in our soul by means of the knowledge of the mysteries celebrated in church and announcing the words of God wherever we pass our lives. Sisters, let us labour in the present age that we may find rest in the age to come, because if we labour a little while we shall find eternal rest.[22] Jesus, who leads us on the heavenly path, proved this through the works he did.

10. The evangelist says, "Jesus, wearied from the journey, sat down."[23] Having accomplished the entire salvific dispensation for our sake and wearied in the ascent to the cross, he descended to Hades, rose again and ascended into heaven; then he sat down at the right hand of God the Father. But the apostles also laboured in this present age and sowed the seed of the Gospel proclamation in the hearts of men. After traversing the world on foot, they shall be seated on thrones to judge the whole world.[24] In the time that remains let us mortify ourselves in the works of righteousness so that we may recline in heavenly abodes and receive eternal rest in Christ Jesus our Lord, to whom be glory and might unto the ages of ages. Amen.

---

[22] Cf. 2 Cor 4:17.
[23] Jn 4:6.
[24] Mt 19:28.

Τῇ ἕκτῃ κυριακῇ·
εἰς τὸ θαῦμα τοῦ ἐκ γενετῆς τυφλοῦ

1. Ἀδελφαὶ καὶ μητέρες, *τίς λαλήσει τὰς δυναστείας τοῦ κυρίου, ἀκουστὰς ποιήσει πάσας τὰς ἐργασίας αὐτοῦ;* ἰδοὺ καὶ πάλιν ὁ σωτήρ,
5 τοῦ γεγεννημένου τυφλοῦ τοὺς ὀφθαλμοὺς ἀνοίξας, διανοίγει καὶ τὰ ὄμματα τῶν ψυχῶν ἡμῶν εἰς ἐπίγνωσιν τῆς ἀρρήτου δυνάμεως αὐτοῦ. ὡς γὰρ τὸν ἐκ γενετῆς τυφλὸν ὀμματώσας πεποίηκε καὶ τὴν ψυχὴν αὐτοῦ ἀναβλέψαι καὶ ἐπιγνῶναι αὐτὸν δημιουργὸν τῶν κτισμάτων καὶ υἱὸν θεοῦ καὶ θεὸν πιστεῦσαι καὶ προσκυνῆσαι αὐτῷ, οὕτω καὶ
10 ἡμᾶς διὰ τοῦ πρὸς τὸν τυφλὸν σημείου ἀνάγει εἰς ἔκπληξιν καὶ ἀγάπην τῆς ἀγαθότητος αὐτοῦ. ἡ τῶν σωματικῶν ὀφθαλμῶν ἀνάβλεψις γέγονε καὶ τῶν ψυχικῶν ὀφθαλμῶν ἀνάβλεψις. ὁ τυφλὸς διπλῆν ἐκέκτητο πήρωσιν. ἡ σωματικὴ τύφλωσις ἀορασίαν ἔχει τοῦ αἰσθητοῦ φωτός· ἡ ψυχικὴ πήρωσις ἀγνωσίαν ἔχει τοῦ θεϊκοῦ φωτός. ὁ γοῦν
15 τυφλὸς καὶ τὸν αἰσθητὸν ἥλιον οὐχ ἑώρα διὰ τὸ πεπηρωμένους ἔχειν τοὺς τοῦ σώματος ὀφθαλμοὺς καὶ τὸν ἥλιον τῆς δικαιοσύνης Ἰησοῦν τὸν Χριστὸν τὸν υἱὸν τοῦ θεοῦ ἀγνοῶν οὐκ ἐπίστευεν. ἀλλ᾽ ὁ σωτὴρ ἡμῶν καὶ τοὺς τοῦ σώματος ὀφθαλμοὺς αὐτοῦ ἀνέῳξε καὶ ἐχαρίσατο αὐτῷ ὁρᾶν τὸ τῆς παρούσης ἡμέρας φῶς καὶ τοὺς τῆς ψυχῆς
20 ὀφθαλμοὺς αὐτοῦ ἐφώτισε καὶ ἠξίωσεν αὐτὸν ἐπιγνῶναι τοῦ θερα- πευτοῦ τὴν θεότητα ὡς τῶν ψυχῶν καὶ σωμάτων ποιητὴς καὶ δεσπότης. ὅθεν καὶ πάντες οἱ ὁρῶντες τὸν τυφλὸν ὀμματωθέντα φωτίζονται, καὶ αὐτοὶ καὶ καθοδηγοῦνται πρὸς τὸ ἰδεῖν τὴν ἑαυτῶν τύφλωσιν καὶ ἐπιγνῶναι τὴν εὐεργεσίαν ἧς ἠξιώθη ἡ ἡμετέρα φύσις.
25 καὶ γὰρ καὶ ἡ ψυχὴ ἡμῶν, τοῖς γεννητοῖς καὶ φθαρτοῖς προστεθεῖσα καὶ ὅλην τὴν ἑαυτῆς διάθεσιν τοῖς πράγμασι τοῦ αἰῶνος τούτου προσηλώσασα, τυφλὴ διατελεῖ, μηδόλως ὁρῶσα πρὸς τὴν τῶν ἀρετῶν ἐπίκτησιν, ἣν καὶ ὁ κύριος ἡμῶν Ἰησοῦς Χριστὸς καθεκάστην ἐπισκέπτεται διὰ τῆς σωτηριώδους αὐτοῦ οἰκονομίας καὶ τῆς σαρ-
30 κικῆς αὐτοῦ διατριβῆς.

---

2 γενετῆς corr.: γεννετῆς ΟΑ   7 γενετῆς corr.: γεννητῆς ΟΑ   25 γεννητοῖς ΟᵃᶜΑ   27 διατελεῖ corr.: διατελῇ ΟΑ

MD 21

THE SIXTH SUNDAY OF EASTER:
THE MIRACLE OF THE MAN BLIND FROM BIRTH[1]

1. Sisters and Mothers, "Who will tell the mighty deeds of the Lord, make heard all his doings?"[2] Behold once again, when the Saviour opened the eyes of the man who had been born blind, he opened also the eyes of our souls to the recognition of his ineffable power. As the Saviour, after giving sight to the man blind from birth, also granted his soul to see again, to recognize him as creator of created things and Son of God and to believe in God and worship him, so too by the sign granted to the blind man he leads us to admiration and love for his goodness. The restoration of sight to the bodily eyes has become also a restoration of sight to the eyes of the soul. The blind man had contracted a twofold defect. His bodily blindness involved the incapacity of seeing the sensible light. The defect in his soul involved an ignorance of the divine Light. Thus the blind man both failed to see the sensible sun because the eyes of his body were defective and he failed to believe the Sun of Righteousness[3] because he did not know that Jesus Christ was the Son of God. But our Saviour opened the eyes of his body and granted him to see the light of the present day; he also illumined the eyes of his soul and deemed him worthy to recognize the divinity of his healer, the creator and master of souls and bodies. And so all those who see the blind man with his sight restored are also illumined and they too make their way towards seeing their own blindness and recognizing the beneficence of which our nature has been deemed worthy. For truly our souls as well are blind because of their attachment to things that are subject to generation and corruption and because they fix their entire disposition on the affairs of this world, failing completely to look towards the acquisition of the virtues. This was the daily concern of our Lord Jesus Christ in his saving Economy and his life in the flesh.

---

[1] Jn 9:1-38 is the Gospel read on this Sunday.
[2] Ps 105:2.
[3] Cf. Mal 3:20.

2. Βουλόμενος γὰρ ὁ κύριος ὁδὸν ἡμῖν ὑποδεῖξαι σωτηρίας, ἄνθρωπος γέγονε καὶ θαυμάτων ἐπιδείξεσι καὶ διδασκαλίαις τὰ τῆς ἁμαρτίας περιεῖλε προσκόμματα. καὶ δεῖ τοὺς πιστεύοντας ἡμᾶς εἰς αὐτὸν τοῖς ἔργοις καὶ τοῖς λόγοις αὐτοῦ ἐνατενίζειν διηνεκῶς, ὅπως
35 ἐκ τοῦ μελετᾶν ἡμᾶς τὰ ποιήματα τῶν χειρῶν αὐτοῦ καὶ τὰ ῥήματα τοῦ σεβασμίου στόματος αὐτοῦ φωτιζώμεθα τὰς ψυχάς. φῶς γάρ ἐστι τὰ προστάγματα αὐτοῦ· *ἐκ νυκτός, γάρ φησιν ὁ προφήτης, ὀρθρίζει τὸ πνεῦμά μου πρὸς σέ, ὁ θεός, διότι φῶς τὰ προστάγματά σου ἐπὶ τῆς γῆς.*

40 **3.** Ὡς γὰρ ὁ ἥλιος, τὸν αἰσθητὸν τοῦτον φωτίζων κόσμον, ὁρᾶν παρέχει τοῖς τοῦ σώματος ὀφθαλμοῖς καὶ πρὸς τὴν τῶν θαυμάτων ὁδηγεῖ γνῶσιν, οὕτω καὶ ἡ μελέτη τῶν τοῦ Χριστοῦ ἔργων καὶ λόγων τοὺς τῆς ψυχῆς ὀφθαλμοὺς διανοίγει καὶ πρὸς τὴν ἀληθινὴν γνῶσιν χειραγωγεῖ τὸν ἄνθρωπον. ἀλλ᾽ ἵνα γνῶτε ὃ λέγω, προσεκτικῶς
45 ἀκούετε. ὁ σωτὴρ ἡμῶν πτύσας χαμαὶ καὶ πηλὸν ποιήσας ἐκ τοῦ πτύσματος, ἐπέχρισε τὸν πηλὸν ἐπὶ τοὺς ὀφθαλμοὺς τοῦ τυφλοῦ καὶ εἶπεν αὐτῷ· *ὕπαγε νίψαι εἰς τὴν κολυμβήθραν τοῦ Σιλωάμ. ἀπῆλθεν οὖν καὶ ἐνίψατο καὶ ἦλθε βλέπων.* τοῦτο κηρύττει μὲν τὸν σωτῆρα τρανότατα δημιουργὸν τοῦ ἀνθρώπου. τίς γὰρ τῶν ἀνθρώπων δυνή-
50 σεται πηλῷ διανοῖξαι τυφλοῦ ὀφθαλμούς, εἰ μὴ ὁ ἀπὸ γῆς πλάσας τὸν ἄνθρωπον οὗτος καὶ τὸν πηλὸν λαμβάνει καὶ πλάττει τοὺς τοῦ σώματος ὀφθαλμούς;

4. Διδάσκει δὲ τοὺς προσέχοντας καὶ τρόπον μυστικῆς ἀρετῆς, δι᾽ οὗ ἡ ψυχὴ χριομένη καὶ νιπτομένη τοὺς ἐκ τῆς τῶν παθῶν
55 πηρώσεως τύπους ἀποβάλλεται καὶ βλέπειν ἀξιοῦται τὸν ἑαυτῆς εὐεργέτην. τὸ πτύσμα τὸ τῆς ταπεινώσεως φρόνημα ἡμῖν εἰκονίζει. ἡ δὲ γῆ τῆς ὀργίλου καὶ σκληρᾶς ἡμῶν προαιρέσεως τύπον φέρει. ὁ δὲ πηλὸς τὴν ἐκ ταπεινοφροσύνης καὶ ἀγαθοεργίας ἐγγινομένην τῇ ψυχῇ πραότητα ὑποσημαίνει. ὡς γὰρ ὁ πηλὸς μαλασσόμενος
60 ὑπείκει ταῖς χερσὶ καὶ διαπλάττεται κατὰ βούλησιν τοῦ μαλάσσοντος, οὕτω καὶ ὁ ἄνθρωπος ὁ τὴν μελέτην τῆς ταπεινώσεως φέρων μαλάσσεται τὴν ψυχὴν καὶ ἀπαλύνεται ἡ καρδία αὐτοῦ καὶ πειθήνιος καὶ πρᾶος γίνεται· καὶ οὔτε κακὸν ἀντὶ κακοῦ ἀποδοῦναι θέλει, οὔτε μὴν φιλονεικεῖν ἔν τινι πράγματι ἢ ἐκδικεῖν ἑαυτόν. ἑτοιμάζει δὲ
65 ὅλον ἑαυτὸν εἰς τὴν τῶν ἀδελφῶν ἀνάπαυσίν τε καὶ ἀγαθὴν θέλησιν. καὶ καθάπερ τὸ πτύσμα ἐκ τοῦ στόματος ἐξερχόμενον ἐκ τοῦ ἄνω πίπτει πρὸς τὰ κάτω καὶ μίγνυται τῷ τῆς γῆς χώματι καὶ ἀπαλύνει τὴν σκληρὰν φύσιν τῆς γῆς, τοιούτους καὶ ἡμᾶς δεῖ καταφαίνεσθαι,

2. Because the Lord wanted to show us the way of salvation, he became man and by the evidence of his miracles and by his teachings he removed the obstacles caused by sin. We who believe in him must unceasingly devote our attention to his deeds and words so that by studying the works of his hands and the words of his sacred mouth we may find illumination for our souls. His commands are light, for the prophet says, "In the nighttime, O God, my spirit keeps watch for you, because your commands are light upon the earth."[4]

3. As the sun, when it illumines this sensible world, provides sight to the eyes of the body and guidance in the knowledge of the world's wonders, so too meditation on the deeds and words of Christ opens the eyes of the soul and leads man to true knowledge. Listen attentively, that you may know what I am talking about. After our Saviour spat on the ground and made clay with the spittle, he anointed the eyes of the blind man with clay and said to him, " 'Go and wash in the pool of Siloam.' So he went and washed and came back seeing."[5] This deed proclaims the Saviour to be very clearly the creator of man. For who is there among men who could open the eyes of a blind man with clay, unless the one who formed man from the earth is also the very same who took clay and formed the eyes of the body?[6]

4. To those who are attentive it teaches also the way of mystical virtue whereby the soul, when it is anointed and washed, casts off the marks left by the disabling effects of the passions and is deemed worthy to look upon its benefactor. The spittle represents for us the attitude of humility. The earth bears the type of our irascible and hardened free will. The clay indicates the gentleness that arises in the soul as a result of humility and good works. As the clay, worked into suppleness, yields to the hands and is fashioned according to the intention of the one who works it, so too the man who is studied in humility works his soul into suppleness and his heart is softened and becomes docile and gentle. He wants neither to return evil for evil[7] nor indeed to act contentiously in any matter or to avenge himself. He devotes himself entirely to the relief of his brothers and goodwill towards them. As spittle coming from the mouth falls down from above and mixes with the soil of the earth and softens the earth's hard nature,

---

[4] Is 26:9.
[5] Jn 9:6-7.
[6] Cf. Gen 2:7.
[7] Cf. Rom 12:17, 1 Thes 5:15, 1 Pet 3:9.

ἵνα, ὅταν ἐπαιρώμεθα κατὰ ψυχὴν ὡς ἄνωθεν γεγενημένην, ἀπο-
70 βλέποντες πάλιν πρὸς τὴν ἀσθένειαν τῆς συνεζευγμένης αὐτῇ σαρκός,
συστελλώμεθα διὰ τὴν θνητότητα τῆς φύσεως ἡμῶν.

5. Ἡ φύσις ἡμῶν ἁμαρτωλὸς γενομένη διὰ τὴν παράβασιν τῆς
θείας ἐντολῆς ἀνυπότακτος καὶ σκληρὰ διετέλει. καὶ καθάπερ τρα-
χυτάτη σάρξ καὶ νευρώδης οὐχ ὑπείκει τοῖς ὀδοῦσιν, οὕτω καὶ ὁ
75 ἄνθρωπος οὐδόλως καταπειθὴς γενέσθαι τῶν τοῦ θεοῦ προσταγμάτων
ἠβούλετο. ἀλλ᾽ ὁ τοῦ θεοῦ υἱός, κλίνας οὐρανοὺς καὶ καταβὰς δίκην
πτύσματος καὶ σκηνώσας ἐν τῇ μήτρᾳ τῆς ἁγίας παρθένου καὶ
θεοτόκου, ἐκ τῶν παναγνῶν αὐτῆς αἱμάτων, καθάπερ γῆν, ἐν ἑαυτῷ
τὴν ἀνθρωπίνην προσλαβόμενος φύσιν καὶ πληρώσας αὐτὴν τῶν
80 ἰδίων ἀγαθῶν καὶ χρίσας αὐτὴν τῷ ἐλαίῳ τῆς θεότητος αὐτοῦ καὶ
νιψάμενος ὑπὲρ ἡμῶν διὰ τοῦ βαπτίσματος οὗ ἔδωκεν, ἐθεοποίησεν
ἡμᾶς καὶ πάντα πρὸς δόξαν τοῦ θεοῦ θεωρεῖν ἡμᾶς παρεσκεύασεν.
6. Εἴ τις οὖν θέλει τὴν ἐκ τῆς κενοδοξίας καὶ τῆς ἀλαζονείας
τύφλωσιν τῆς ἑαυτοῦ ψυχῆς ἀποβαλέσθαι καὶ φωτισθῆναι τοὺς
85 λογισμούς, ἐνθυμείσθω τὴν τοῦ κυρίου πρὸς ἡμᾶς διὰ σαρκὸς
κατάβασιν καὶ τὴν θαυμαστὴν ταπείνωσιν καὶ τὴν ὑπερβάλλουσαν
πτωχείαν, καὶ πάντως τὸ ὑπερήφανον καὶ ὑψηλὸν φρόνημα κατα-
βληθήσεται τῆς ἑαυτοῦ καρδίας καὶ χρισθήσονται οἱ ὀφθαλμοὶ ἡμῶν
τῷ τῆς ταπεινοφροσύνης πηλῷ, γῆν καὶ σποδὸν ἑαυτοὺς φρονοῦντες
90 καὶ μετὰ τοῦ προφήτου λέγοντες· ἐγὼ δέ εἰμι σκώληξ καὶ οὐκ ἄνθρωπος,
ὄνειδος ἀνθρώπου καὶ ἐξουθένημα λαοῦ.
7. Οὕτω δὲ πραϋνθέντες καὶ ταπεινοφροσύνης ἐννοίαις χρισθέντες,
ἐν τῇ πολιτείᾳ βαδίσωμεν τοῦ Χριστοῦ, ἐν αὐτῇ καθάπερ ἐν τῇ τοῦ
Σιλωὰμ κολυμβήθρᾳ νιψάμενοι τοὺς πόδας εἰς ἑτοιμασίαν τοῦ
95 εὐαγγελίου καὶ ἀποστολὴν τοῦ τῆς σωτηρίας κηρύγματος· μάθετε,
γάρ φησιν, ἀπ᾽ ἐμοῦ ὅτι πρᾶός εἰμι καὶ ταπεινὸς τῇ καρδίᾳ· καὶ ὅτι
ἐγώ εἰμι τὸ φῶς τοῦ κόσμου, καὶ εὑρήσουσιν οἱ λογισμοὶ ὑμῶν
ἀνάβλεψιν καὶ αἱ ψυχαὶ ὑμῶν ἀνάπαυσιν. ἐὰν γρηγορῶμεν, ἀγαπηταί
μου, μιμηταὶ γενησόμεθα τοῦ Χριστοῦ καὶ ὀμματώσομεν καὶ ἡμεῖς
100 τυφλούς, καθάπερ ἐκεῖνος τὸν ἐκ γενετῆς τυφλόν.

89 σποδὸν corr.: σπονδὸν ΟΑ   100 γενετῆς corr.: γεννετῆς ΟΑ

so we too should conduct ourselves: whenever we feel elated because of our soul's high origins, we should look back at the weakness of the flesh which is yoked to it and humble ourselves on account of the mortality of our nature.

5. When our nature was rendered sinful through the transgression of the divine commandment, it became unruly and hardened. As very tough and gristly flesh does not yield to the teeth, so too man was totally unwilling to be obedient to God's commands. But the Son of God bent the heavens and came down[8] like spittle; he made his dwelling in the womb of the holy virgin and Theotokos, taking human nature, like earth, to himself from her all-holy blood, filling it with his goodness and anointing it with the oil of his divinity; after his own washing in the Jordan he divinized us through the baptism which he instituted and he prepared us to behold all things for the glory of God.

6. If then someone wants to cast off the blindness of his soul that results from vainglory and arrogance and to receive illumination in his thoughts, let him ponder on the Lord's descent among us in the flesh, his wondrous humility, his exceeding poverty. The arrogant and haughty attitude of his heart will certainly be cast to the ground; his eyes will be anointed with the clay of humility; and he will consider himself earth and dust, saying together with the prophet, "I am a worm and no man, the reproach of men and the scorn of people."[9]

7. After we have attained gentleness and received the anointing of humility in our thoughts, let us walk in Christ's way of life, for in this conduct, as in the pool of Siloam,[10] we wash our feet in preparation for the Gospel[11] and for the mission of proclaiming salvation. For scripture says, "Learn from me for I am gentle and humble in heart";[12] and because "I am the Light of the world," your thoughts will find their sight restored and your souls will find rest.[13] If we are watchful, my dear sisters, we shall become imitators of Christ and we too will restore sight to the blind, as he did for the man blind from birth.

---

[8] Cf. Ps 17:10, 143:5.
[9] Ps 21:7. Note that in the Greek text Theoleptos switches somewhat awkwardly from the third person singular to the first person plural.
[10] Jn 9:7.
[11] Cf. Eph 6:15.
[12] Mt 11:29.
[13] Jn 8:12. Cf. Mt 11:29.

8. Οἷον, ἔστι τις ἄνθρωπος μὴ σχολάζων ἐν τῇ τοῦ θεοῦ ἐκκλησίᾳ, ἀλλὰ βιωτικοῖς περισπασμοῖς ἑαυτὸν ἐκδεδωκώς; οὗτος τυφλός ἐστι μὴ βλέπων τὴν ἀλήθειαν. ὁ οὖν ἀναπτύξας τὴν καρδίαν αὐτοῦ διὰ διδασκαλίας καὶ ῥῆμα ἀγαθὸν καθάπερ πτύσμα βαλὼν εἰς τὴν ψυχὴν
105 αὐτοῦ καὶ ὑπαλείψας αὐτὸν πρὸς τὸ ἀπελθεῖν εἰς τὴν τοῦ Χριστοῦ ἐκκλησίαν, οὗτος ἤνοιξεν ὀφθαλμοὺς τυφλοῦ. ὁ ὑπὸ πτωχείας πιε- ζόμενος καὶ τῆς ἀναγκαίας τροφῆς ἀπορῶν καὶ βλασφημῶν τυφλός ἐστι, μὴ βλέπων τὴν ὑπομονὴν καὶ τὴν ἐν Χριστῷ καρτερίαν. ὁ οὖν κλάσμα ἄρτου ἢ ἔνδυμα ἢ ἀργύριον δεδωκὼς αὐτῷ, οὗτος πτύει
110 χαμαί, βλέπει γὰρ τὸν χαμαὶ κείμενον ἀδελφὸν καὶ διατρέφει πεινῶντα τοῦτον καὶ ἀγαθύνει τὴν καρδίαν αὐτοῦ καὶ τῷ χρίσματι τῆς ἐλεημοσύνης κινεῖ τὴν ψυχὴν αὐτοῦ εἰς χαρὰν καὶ διανοίγει τὸ στόμα αὐτοῦ εἰς δοξολογίαν καὶ εὐχαριστίαν θεοῦ, ὁ τοῦτο ποιῶν ἀνοίγει τυφλοῦ ὀφθαλμούς, ὁ γὰρ δοξάζων τὸν θεὸν καὶ εὐχαριστῶν αὐτὸν
115 ἀνεῳγμένους ἔχει τοὺς ὀφθαλμοὺς τῆς ψυχῆς.

9. Ὁ σκανδαλισθεὶς καὶ ὀργιζόμενος τῷ ἀδελφῷ αὐτοῦ τυφλός ἐστιν, οὐ βλέπει γὰρ τὴν ἐντολὴν τοῦ Χριστοῦ. ἐὰν οὖν σὺ μὴ ἀναμείνῃς τὸν σκανδαλιζόμενον ἐλθεῖν πρός σε, ἀπέλθῃς δὲ σὺ μᾶλλον πρὸς αὐτὸν καὶ πέσῃς εἰς τοὺς πόδας αὐτοῦ, ἰδοὺ ἔπτυσας
120 χαμαί. καὶ ἐὰν διὰ ῥημάτων ταπεινῶν μαλάξῃς τὴν ψυχὴν αὐτοῦ, ἐποίησας πηλόν. καὶ ἐὰν θήσεις τὸ πταῖσμα ἐπάνω σου καὶ ἐκεῖνον ἀθωώσῃς ὡς ἀναίτιον καὶ εἰς τὴν κολυμβήθραν τῆς εἰρήνης εἰσαγάγῃς αὐτόν, ἤνοιξας τοὺς ὀφθαλμοὺς αὐτοῦ καὶ εἰς τὴν σὴν ἀγάπην ἐπεσπάσω αὐτόν· ὅθεν καὶ περιπατῶν ἐπαινεῖ καὶ εὐχαριστεῖ σοι καὶ
125 ἐνώπιον τῶν λοιδορούντων σε μεγαλύνει σε, καθάπερ ὁ τυφλὸς τὸν Χριστὸν ἐν μέσῳ τῶν Ἰουδαίων· καὶ ὅταν συναντήσῃ σοι χαιρετίζει σε ἐνδόξως καὶ προσκυνεῖ σοι μετὰ τιμῆς πολλῆς.

10. Σπουδάσωμεν τοιγαροῦν ἐν ἐκκλησίαις πορεύεσθαι, ὅπως ἐν τῷ βαδίζειν ἐν αὐτῇ νιπτόμεναι καὶ καθαιρόμεναι ἀπὸ τῶν κηλίδων
130 τῆς ἁμαρτίας, φωτισθῶσιν οἱ ὀφθαλμοὶ τῶν ψυχῶν ἡμῶν καὶ οὐ μὴ ὑπνώσομεν εἰς θάνατον, ἀλλὰ τῆς αἰωνίου ζωῆς ἀξιωθείημεν ἐν Χριστῷ Ἰησοῦ τῷ κυρίῳ, ᾧ πρέπει πᾶσα δόξα, τιμὴ καὶ προσκύνησις σὺν τῷ ἀνάρχῳ αὐτοῦ πατρὶ καὶ τῷ παναγίῳ καὶ ζωοποιῷ πνεύματι, νῦν καὶ ἀεὶ καὶ εἰς τοὺς αἰῶνας τῶν αἰώνων. Ἀμήν.

8. For example, is there a man who does not attend the church of God regularly, but devotes himself to the distractions of life? This man is blind because he does not see the truth. If then someone opens up this fellow's heart through instruction, lets good words fall, like spittle, into his soul and encourages him to soften his attitude so he will go to the church of God, that person has opened the eyes of a blind man. The man who blasphemes because he is oppressed by poverty and is lacking the food he needs is blind in that he does not see the patient endurance and perseverance to be found in Christ. Thus the person who has given him a piece of bread or a garment or money spits on the ground as Christ did, for seeing his brother lying on the ground he feeds this hungry man and cheers his heart; with the chrism of almsgiving he moves the man's soul to joy and opens his mouth to offer praise and thanksgiving to God. The person who does this opens the eyes of a blind man, for he who glorifies God and offers him thanksgiving has the eyes of his soul opened.

9. He who takes offence and is angry at his brother is blind, for he does not see the commandment of Christ. If then you do not wait for the one who is offended to come to you, but rather you go to him and fall at his feet, behold you have spit upon the ground. And if by your humble words you have softened his soul, you have made clay; if you take his fault upon yourself and exonerate him of all blame and lead him to the pool of peace, you have opened his eyes and drawn him to your love. And so he goes away praising and thanking you; before your detractors he extols you as the blind man extolled Christ in the midst of the Jews; whenever he meets you he greets you with esteem and bows to you with much respect.

10. Therefore, let us be earnest in attending church so that in entering the church we may be washed and purified from all the stains of sin and the eyes of our souls may be illumined and we may never fall asleep in death,[14] but be deemed worthy of eternal life in Christ Jesus the Lord. To him belongs all glory, honour and worship together with his eternal Father and the all-holy and life-giving Spirit, now and always and unto the ages of ages. Amen.

---

[14] Cf. Ps 12:4.

Τῇ πεντηκοστῇ·
εἰς τὴν ἐπιφοίτησιν τοῦ παναγίου πνεύματος

1. Ἀδελφαὶ καὶ μητέρες, πολλὴ τοῖς χριστιανοῖς ἡμῖν ἡ εὐφροσύνη ἐκ τῶν πνευματικῶν ἑορτῶν ἀνατέλλει· ἀεί ποτε γὰρ
5 ἀνακαινίζονται αἱ ψυχαὶ ἡμῶν ἐκ τῶν ἐν τῇ ἐκκλησίᾳ τελουμένων καὶ λαλουμένων. καὶ ὥσπερ ὁ εἰς κλίμακα ἀναβαίνων ἀπὸ βαθμίδος εἰς βαθμίδα προβαίνει καὶ διόλου ὁ δρόμος αὐτοῦ εἰς τὴν ἄνω φορὰν γίνεται, οὕτω καὶ τῶν χριστιανῶν τὸ πλήρωμα ἐν οὐρανοῖς τὸ πολίτευμα ἔχειν ἐπαγγειλάμενοι ἀπὸ ἑορτῆς εἰς ἑορτὴν μεταβαίνουσι
10 καὶ ἐκ δυνάμεως εἰς δύναμιν πορεύονται καὶ ἀναβάσεις ἐν τῇ καρδίᾳ διατίθενται· καὶ αἱ ψυχαὶ αὐτῶν ἐκ τῶν γηίνων ἀνυψοῦνται φροντίδων καὶ οἱ λογισμοὶ αὐτῶν διηνεκῶς εἰς τὸν οὐρανὸν ἀτενίζουσιν. ὡς γὰρ ὁ ἀπὸ τῶν ἄνω πρὸς τὰ κάτω ἐρχόμενος ὅλως πρὸς τὰ κατώτερα καὶ βαδίζει καὶ βλέπει, οὕτω καὶ ὁ πρὸς οὐρανὸν βλέπων διηνεκῶς
15 τὸ φρόνημα αὐτοῦ ἐν τοῖς πνευματικοῖς ἔργοις τε καὶ νοήμασιν ἐπαίρει. καὶ δὴ προσέχετε, παρακαλῶ.
2. Χθὲς ἑωρτάσαμεν τὴν ἀνάληψιν τοῦ κυρίου· σήμερον πανηγυρίζομεν τὴν ἐπιδημίαν τοῦ πνεύματος. χθὲς ἀπὸ τῆς γῆς ἤρθημεν τῷ φρονήματι καὶ εἰς οὐρανοὺς ἀνήλθομεν ὅπου *πρόδρομος ὑπὲρ ἡμῶν*
20 *εἰσῆλθε* Χριστός· σήμερον ἡ γῆ οὐρανὸς γίνεται καὶ τὸ πῦρ τοῦ παρακλήτου τοὺς ἀποστόλους ὡς λύχνους ἀνάπτει καὶ φωτίζει τῆς οἰκουμένης τὰ πέρατα. χθὲς οἱ ἀπόστολοι εἰς τὸν οὐρανὸν ἦσαν ἀτενίζοντες· σήμερον ἐν τῷ οἴκῳ καθήμενοι τὸ πνεῦμα καθήμενον ἐφ᾽ ἕνα ἕκαστον αὐτῶν ὑποδέχονται. χθὲς ἡ φύσις ἡμῶν εἰς οὐρανοὺς
25 ἀνερχομένη καὶ τῷ θεῷ καὶ πατρὶ προσαγομένη, ἡ ἔχθρα ἐλύετο καὶ ἡ καταλλαγὴ ἐπραγματεύετο· σήμερον τὸ πνεῦμα τοῖς ἀποστόλοις καταπτὰν τὰ οὐράνια δῶρα τοῖς ἐπὶ γῆς χαρίζεται καὶ ἡ ἡμῶν πρὸς τὸν θεὸν εἰρήνη καὶ καταλλαγὴ πιστοῦται.

17 ἑορτάσαμεν OA

MD **22**

PENTECOST:
THE VISITATION OF THE ALL-HOLY SPIRIT

1. Sisters and Mothers, for us Christians great joy arises from spiritual feasts, for our souls are ever being renewed by the rites that are celebrated and the words that are spoken in church. Just as a man climbing a ladder proceeds from one rung to another with his entire course directed upward, so too the commonwealth of Christians, proclaiming their citizenship in heaven,[1] pass from feast to feast and "proceed from strength to strength, making spiritual ascent their heart's resolve."[2] Their souls are lifted up from earthbound ponderings and their thoughts are focused continuously on heaven.[3] For as a person going from high ground to low ground walks with his attention focused entirely downwards, so too the person who gazes continuously towards heaven raises his thoughts to spiritual works and considerations. So now please pay heed.

2. Yesterday we celebrated the feast of the Lord's Ascension; today we celebrate the coming of the Spirit. Yesterday our thoughts were lifted up from the earth and we ascended into heaven where Christ "entered as a forerunner on our behalf";[4] today earth is become heaven and the fire of the Counsellor lights up the apostles like lamps and illumines the ends of the earth. Yesterday the apostles "were gazing heavenward";[5] today, seated in the house, they receive the Spirit alighting on each one of them.[6] Yesterday when our nature ascended to heaven and was brought before our God and Father, the enmity was ended and reconciliation was wrought; today the descent of the Spirit upon the apostles bestows heavenly gifts upon those on earth, and our peace and reconciliation with God are assured.

---

[1] Phil 3:20.
[2] Ps 83:6, 8.
[3] Cf. Col 3:2.
[4] Heb 6:20.
[5] Acts 1:10.
[6] Cf. Acts 2:3.

3. Χθὲς ἡ τῆς ἐπιδημίας τοῦ παρακλήτου ὑπόσχεσις ἐτελεῖτο –
30 ἐὰν γὰρ μὴ ἐγώ, φησίν, ἀπέλθω, ὁ παράκλητος οὐκ ἐλεύσεται πρὸς ὑμᾶς·
σήμερον τὰ τῆς ἐπαγγελίας πέρας λαμβάνει – ἐν γὰρ τῷ συμπληροῦσθαι
τὴν πεντηκοστὴν ἦσαν ὁμοθυμαδὸν οἱ ἀπόστολοι πάντες. καὶ ἐγένετο ἄφνω
ἦχος ἐκ τοῦ οὐρανοῦ καὶ ὤφθησαν αὐτοῖς διαμεριζόμεναι γλῶσσαι ὡσεὶ
πυρός, καὶ ἐκάθισεν ἐφ' ἕνα ἕκαστον αὐτῶν. καὶ προεφήτευον ξέναις
35 γλώσσαις τὰ μεγαλεῖα τοῦ θεοῦ. ὢ μυστηρίων φρικτῶν. ὢ παραδόξων
ἔργων. μεσίτης ὁ Χριστὸς θεοῦ καὶ ἀνθρώπων γίνεται· ἀναιρεῖ τὴν
ἔχθραν· βραβεύει τὴν εἰρήνην· ἑνοποιεῖ τὰ διεστῶτα· ἔλαβε σάρκα
καὶ ἔδωκε πνεῦμα· ἀνήνεγκε τὴν ἡμετέραν φύσιν καὶ κατήνεγκε τὸ
πνεῦμα αὐτοῦ.
40 **4.** Ἐπὶ τῆς γῆς βαδίζων, καθάπερ ἀρότρῳ, τῷ σταυρῷ τῷ τιμίῳ
τὰς ὑλομανούσας καρδίας τῶν ἀνθρώπων ὑπὸ τῆς ἀπιστίας καὶ τῆς
ἁμαρτίας νεώσας καὶ καινοποιήσας, σπέρματα θεογνωσίας καὶ ἀρετῆς
κατεβάλλετο ἐν ταῖς ψυχαῖς αὐτῶν· εἰς οὐρανοὺς ἀνελθών, τοῖς
μαθηταῖς αὐτοῦ ἐργάταις οὖσι τοῦ εὐαγγελίου αὐτοῦ ἔδωκε τὸ πνεῦμα
45 αὐτοῦ ὡς δρέπανον καὶ ἀπέστειλεν εἰς πᾶσαν τὴν οἰκουμένην θερίζειν
τῶν ἀνθρώπων τὴν σωτηρίαν, συνάγειν τε τοὺς μετεωριζομένους εἰς
διαφόρους δόξας καὶ ἀποκλείειν αὐτοὺς εἰς τὰς ἀποθήκας τῆς μιᾶς
πίστεως καὶ τῆς μιᾶς ἐκκλησίας. καὶ καθάπερ τὸ δρέπανον τοῦ
στάχυος ὅσον μέν ἐστιν ἄνω καὶ πρὸς τὸν ἀέρα τεινόμενον τέμνει
50 καὶ εἰς τὰς χεῖρας εἰσάγει τοῦ θερίζοντος· ὅσον δέ ἐστι κάτω καὶ
τῇ γῇ πλησιάζον ἀφίησιν ὡς ἀσυντελῆ καὶ ἀχρήσιμον, ὃ καὶ τοῦ
πυρὸς δαπάνη εὑρίσκεται· οὕτω καὶ τὸ πνεῦμα τὸ ἅγιον τὸ ἐν τοῖς
ἀποστόλοις λαλῆσαν διαιροῦν ὑπῆρχε τὸν πιστὸν ἐκ τοῦ ἀπίστου
καὶ τὸν πονηρὸν ἐκ τοῦ ἀγαθοῦ.
55 **5.** Ὅσοι μὲν γὰρ καρπὸν πίστεως ἐλάμβανον ἐκ τοῦ κηρύγματος,
οὗτοι τῷ πνεύματι τῷ ἁγίῳ τεμνόμενοι ἐκ τῆς ἀπιστίας καὶ τῆς
συγγενείας τῶν γεννητόρων, τῇ τοῦ Χριστοῦ πίστει προσήρχοντο
καὶ ἐβαπτίζοντο εἰς τὸ ὄνομα τοῦ πατρὸς καὶ τοῦ υἱοῦ καὶ τοῦ ἁγίου
πνεύματος. ὅσοι δὲ τῇ γῇ τῆς ἀπιστίας ἦσαν προσπεφυκότες καὶ τῇ
60 τοῦ κόσμου ἐπιθυμίᾳ προσηλωμένοι, οὗτοι ἐναπέμειναν ἐν τῷ τοῦ
κόσμου φρονήματι καὶ τῇ πλάνῃ τοῦ βίου ὕλην τοῦ αἰωνίου πυρὸς
ἑαυτοὺς ἑτοιμάσαντες.

---

38 ἡμετέραν A: ἡμέτερα O

3.   Yesterday the promise of the Counsellor's coming was made —
scripture says, "For if I do not go away, the Counsellor will not come
to you";[7] today the substance of that promise finds its fulfilment —
"When Pentecost had come, all the apostles were together. And
suddenly a sound came from heaven, and there appeared to them
tongues as of fire, distributed and resting on each one of them. And
in strange tongues they prophesied the mighty deeds of God."[8] O
fearsome mysteries! O extraordinary works! Christ is become an
intermediary between God and men;[9] he destroys the enmity, awards
peace, unites the separated.[10] He took flesh and gave Spirit; he bore
our nature up to heaven and brought his Spirit down upon us.

4.   When he walked upon the earth, by his venerable Cross, as
with a plough, he harrowed and renewed the hearts of men that had
run wild with the weeds of unbelief and sin, and sowed the seeds of
divine knowledge and virtue in their souls. When he ascended to heaven
he gave his Spirit, like a sickle, to his disciples, who were labourers
in the service of his Gospel, and sent them into all the world to reap
mankind's salvation,[11] to gather in those distracted by various opinions
and to shut them up in the granaries of the one faith and the one
church. The sickle cuts off the upper part of the corn stalk, which
extends into the air, and directs it into the harvester's hands; the lower
part of the stalk, which is near the ground, it leaves as worthless and
of no use except as fuel for the fire. Similarly, the Holy Spirit, who
spoke in the apostles, distinguished the believer from the unbeliever
and the evil man from the good man.

5.   As many as received the fruit of faith from the preaching of
the Gospel were cut off by the Holy Spirit from unbelief and from
family ties; they came to faith in Christ and were baptized in the name
of the Father and of the Son and of the Holy Spirit. But as many
as took to growing in the ground of unbelief and became bound to
worldly desires were content with the thoughts of this world and, by
the error of their way of life, prepared themselves as fuel for the eternal
fire.[12]

---

[7] Jn 16:7.
[8] Acts 2:1-4.
[9] Cf. 1 Tim 2:5.
[10] Cf. Eph 2:14.
[11] Cf. Mt 28:19.
[12] Cf. Mt 13:30.

6.   Τὸ πνεῦμα τὸ ἅγιον καὶ δρέπανον καὶ πῦρ γίνεται· δρέπανον,
ὡς τέμνον καὶ διακρίνον τὰ καλὰ ἐκ τῶν κακῶν· πῦρ, ὡς ἀναλωτικὸν
65 πάσης ἁμαρτίας. διὰ τοῦτο γὰρ *ὤφθησαν ἐν τοῖς ἀποστόλοις διαμεριζόμεναι γλῶσσαι ὡσεὶ πυρός*, ἵνα καὶ τὸ κοῦφον καὶ ἀνωφερὲς τῆς
ἐνεργείας τοῦ πνεύματος μάθῃς καὶ τὸ δαπανητικὸν πάσης κακίας
καὶ τὸ φωτιστικὸν τῶν προαιρουμένων ψυχῶν. *καὶ ἐκάθισεν ἐφ᾽ ἕνα
ἕκαστον αὐτῶν.* διατί ἐκάθισεν; ἵνα μονὴν ἐν ἡμῖν ποιήσῃ ἣν σχόντες
70 ἐξ ἀρχῆς ἀπωλέσαμεν.

66 γλῶσσαι corr.: γλῶσαι OA

6.   The Holy Spirit is both sickle and fire: sickle, as one who discerns and cuts off good from evil; fire, as one who destroys all sin. For this reason "there appeared to the apostles distinct tongues as of fire,"[13] that you might learn both the buoyant and upward-bearing character of the Spirit's activity and its ability to consume all evil and illumine chosen souls. "And he rested on each one of them."[14] Why did he rest? In order that he make in us his abode which we originally possessed but lost.[15]

---

[13] Acts 2:3.
[14] Acts 2:3.
[15] The homily appears to break off incomplete.

Μερικὴ διατράνωσις πρὸς ὑπόμνησιν ἄγουσα τῶν παρὰ τοῦ ταπεινοῦ Φιλαδελφείας Θεολήπτου διαφόρως λαληθέντων τῇ σεβασμιωτάτῃ βασιλίσσῃ Εὐλογίᾳ μοναχῇ καὶ τῇ μετ᾽ αὐτῆς καὶ ὑπ᾽ αὐτὴν Ἀγαθονίκῃ μοναχῇ

5   **1.** Ὁ νοῦς λογιστικὴν ἔχων δύναμιν καὶ ἐρωτικήν, διὰ μὲν τῆς λογικῆς δυνάμεως ἐργάζεται τοὺς τρόπους τῶν ἀρετῶν, θείοις λόγοις καὶ διανοήμασιν ἐμμελετᾷ, διασκέπτεται τὰ ὄντα ἀπταίστως, διαλαμβάνει τὴν ἐν τοῖς οὖσιν ἀλήθειαν ἀπλανῶς, καὶ διὰ τῆς ἀληθείας εἰς θεογνωσίαν ἔρχεται.

10   **2.** Διὰ μὲν οὖν τῆς λογικῆς δυνάμεως διακρίνων τὰ κακὰ ἀπὸ τῶν καλῶν καὶ ποιῶν τὰ καλά, καὶ ζητῶν καὶ εὑρίσκων τὸν θεόν, ὡς εἴρηται, ἑνοῦται αὐτῷ διὰ τῆς ἐρωτικῆς δυνάμεως, διὰ τῆς ἀγάπης αὐτῷ συναπτόμενος καὶ τῷ κάλλει τῆς θεωρίας αὐτοῦ μόνης ἐνευφραινόμενος, ὡς τὸ ἑστὼς καὶ ἀκρότατον καὶ κατὰ φύσιν ὀρεκτὸν 15 πεφθακώς· καὶ διὰ τοῦτο μηδὲν τῶν ὄντων ἢ λογιζόμενος ἢ ἐννοῶν, σχολάζουσαν γὰρ ἔχων τὴν λογικὴν ἑαυτοῦ δύναμιν διὰ τὴν ἕνωσιν τοῦ ὑπερουσίου καὶ ὑπὲρ πᾶσαν γνῶσιν ὄντος θεοῦ. καὶ μόνῃ τῇ ἀκαταλήπτῳ θεωρίᾳ καὶ τῇ διαπύρῳ ἀγάπῃ αὐτοῦ καθηδυνόμενος, ὑπὸ τοῦ ἐκεῖθεν πηγάζοντος γλυκυτάτου καὶ ἀρρήτου φωτὸς κατα-20 λαμπόμενος, διαναπαύεται· *χορτασθήσομαι, γάρ φησιν, ἐν τῷ ὀφθῆναί μοι τὴν δόξαν σου.* οὕτω μὲν οὖν ἐνεργεῖ ὁ νοῦς τῇ τοῦ λόγου δυνάμει παρέχων τὸ κράτος καὶ οὕτως ἐνεργεῖται τῷ πρὸς θεὸν θερμοτάτῳ ἔρωτι συνδεόμενος.

  3. Ὅταν δὲ τοῖς αἰσθητηρίοις ἐπιβάλλων τοῦ σώματος εἰς αἴσθη-25 σιν ἔρχηται διὰ τῆς τῶν αἰσθητῶν ἀντιλήψεως. εἰ μὲν τὸν λόγον ἐπιστάτην ποιήσεται τῆς αἰσθήσεως, συνάπτων ὁ λόγος τὴν ἐπιθυμίαν ἑαυτῷ, κατορθοῖ τὰ προειρημένα καὶ εἰς προκοπὴν ὁ νοῦς ἀναβαίνει, καθὼς δεδηλώκαμεν. εἰ δὲ πρὸς τὴν τῶν αἰσθητῶν ἐπιθυμίαν κλίνει

MD 23

A PARTIAL REMINDER CLARIFYING THE STATEMENTS MADE ON VARIOUS OCCASIONS BY THE HUMBLE THEOLEPTOS OF PHILADELPHEIA TO THE MOST AUGUST PRINCESS AND NUN, EULOGIA, AND TO HER COMPANION AND SUBORDINATE, THE NUN AGATHONIKE[1]

1. The mind is endowed with the powers of reason and love, and through its rational power the mind devotes its labour to the ways of the virtues, meditates on divine words and thoughts, conducts precise examination of beings, inerrantly distinguishes the truth in them and through the truth attains to knowledge of God.

2. Thus, when the mind uses its rational power to discriminate between good and evil, to do the good, and to seek and find God, as scripture says,[2] the mind enters into union with him through its power of love, joining itself to him by means of love and finding its sole joy in the beauty of contemplating God, since it has attained what is permanent, supreme and desirable by nature. Therefore, it neither ponders nor considers any created beings, for its power of reason is at rest in its union with God, who is transcendent and beyond all knowledge. Finding its delight solely in incomprehensible contemplation and fervent love for him and receiving illumination from the most sweet, ineffable light that springs forth from there, the mind takes its rest, for scripture says, "I shall be satisfied when I behold your glory."[3] In this way then the mind is active when it provides strength to the power of reason and it becomes passive when it finds itself bound by a most fervent love for God.

3. But whenever the mind gives attention to the body's faculties of sensation, it becomes involved in sense perception through the apprehension of sensible things. On the one hand, if the mind places reason in control of sense perception, reason joins desire to itself and brings the aforementioned to their true fulfilment and the mind makes

---

[1] There is a reference to this work and the circumstances of its composition in Hero, *Letter* 2.231-239. Note the phrase τετραδόπουλα τρία ἔστειλά σοι μερικὴν ὑπόμνησιν διαλαμβάνοντα τῶν λαληθέντων πρὸς ὑμᾶς.

[2] Mt 7:7-8.

[3] Ps 16:15.

ὁ νοῦς διὰ τῆς ἀλόγου αἰσθήσεως, ἡ ἐπιθυμία τῇ ἀλόγῳ αἰσθήσει
30 προστεθεῖσα διὰ τῆς αὐτεξουσίου προαιρέσεως κραταιὰν ποιεῖται
τὴν ἐπανάστασιν τῆς σαρκὸς κατὰ τῆς ψυχῆς· καὶ ὁ νόμος τῆς
σαρκὸς κυριεύων, ὑπερήφανον καὶ κενόδοξον καὶ ὑποκριτὴν καὶ
ἀνθρωπάρεσκον ποιεῖ τὸν νοῦν, τὸν δὲ λογισμὸν πονηρὸν καὶ
περίεργον· πάσῃ δυνάμει ἐπινοούμενον καὶ διαπονούμενον, πρὸς τὴν
35 εὕρεσιν τῶν καθ᾽ ἡδονὴν τρόπων καὶ τὴν τῆς ἐπιθυμίας ἐκπλήρωσιν,
σαρκὸς οὖσαν ἀπόλαυσιν· ἀπόλαυσις γὰρ σαρκικὴ ἐπιθυμία ἐστὶν
ἐνεργουμένη ἐν τοῖς τοῦ σώματος μέλεσι καὶ ἡδονὴ προσαγορευο-
μένη.

4. Ὁ νοῦς τοίνυν ἐνδυόμενος τὴν αἴσθησιν καὶ δι᾽ αὐτῆς τῇ τῶν
40 αἰσθητῶν ἐπιθυμίᾳ θελγόμενος ἀλογίστως, τὴν ἡδονὴν μετὰ τοῦ
σώματος καὶ τῶν αἰσθητῶν ἐκτελεῖ· πράγματα δὲ μὴ ἔχων εἰς
ἐκπλήρωσιν τῆς σαρκικῆς ἡδονῆς, ἡδύνεται κατὰ διάνοιαν διὰ τῆς
ἀλόγου φαντασίας καὶ τῶν λογισμῶν. ἡ γὰρ ἐπιθυμία τῆς ψυχῆς ἡ
τὴν διάκρισιν ἀποβαλοῦσα τοῦ λόγου διὰ τοῦ συναφθῆναι τῇ ἀλόγῳ
45 αἰσθήσει, εἰς ἡδονὴν μεταπεσοῦσα διὰ τῆς ἐνεργείας τοῦ σώματος,
τοὺς ἐνηδόνους τρόπους τῆς σαρκὸς διατυποῦσα ἐν τῇ διανοίᾳ, καὶ
διὰ τῆς φαντασίας τῶν αἰσθητῶς πεπραγμένων συνέχουσα καὶ
συγκλείουσα τὸν νοῦν, ἀνακινεῖ τοὺς λογισμοὺς εἰδοποιοῦντας τὰς
πράξεις τῆς διαβεβλημένης ἡδονῆς.

50 **5.** Καὶ ἐν τῷ χρονίζειν ἐν τῇ διανοίᾳ τὴν φαντασίαν τὴν γεννῶσαν
τοὺς λογισμοὺς τῶν καθύγρων τρόπων τῆς ἡδονῆς, εἰς διάθεσιν
αἰσχρὰν ἐρχόμενος ὁ νοῦς, καθηδυπαθεῖ καὶ ἀνενεργήτως ἡδύνεται.
ὃ γὰρ ἐτέλει διὰ τῆς αἰσθήσεως καὶ τῶν αἰσθητῶν πραγμάτων, τοῦτο
ποιεῖ διὰ τῆς φαντασίας καὶ τῶν λογισμῶν· καὶ πραγμάτων μὲν
55 εὐπορῶν καὶ εὐκολίαν εὑρίσκων, τὴν κατ᾽ ἐπιθυμίαν ἡδονὴν
ἐκπεραίνει· πράγματα δὲ μὴ ἔχων, ἐκτελεῖ λογιστικῶς ἅπερ ἐποίει
σωματικῶς.

6. Ὁ τοίνυν βουλόμενος καταμαραίνειν τὰς ἡδονὰς τῆς σαρκὸς
καὶ σεμνότητι τὸ σῶμα κατακοσμεῖν καὶ καθαρὸν ἔχειν, σπουδαζέτω
60 φεύγειν ἀεὶ τὰ τοῦ σώματος αἰσθητήρια, δι᾽ ὧν ἡ κατ᾽ αἴσθησιν ἡδονὴ
ἐν τοῖς μέλεσιν ἐνεργουμένη τὸν νοῦν προσηλοῖ τοῖς αἰσθητοῖς.

7. Φεύγων γὰρ ὁ νοῦς τὰ ἔξω καὶ συναγόμενος ἐπὶ τὰ ἔνδον, πρὸς
ἑαυτὸν ἐπανάγεται· εἴτουν τῷ φυσικῶς κατὰ διάνοιαν κρυπτομένῳ

progress, as we have shown. On the other hand, if the mind inclines towards desire for sensible things through a sense perception not governed by reason, desire by means of our free choice comes in alongside a sense perception not governed by reason and adds strength to the rebellion of the flesh against the soul. And when the law of the flesh is in command, it renders the mind full of pride, vainglory, hypocrisy and sycophancy, and it makes our way of thinking evil and idly curious, plotting and labouring with all its might to discover the ways of pleasure and the fulfilment of its desire, which is the enjoyment of the flesh. Fleshly enjoyment consists of desire at work in the members of the body and is called pleasure.

4. Therefore, when the mind puts on the garment of sense perception and is thereby irrationally bewitched by it with a desire for sensible things, it takes pleasure in the body and in sensible things. And when it lacks the means for fulfiling fleshly pleasure, it finds pleasure in the discursive mind through irrational phantasies and thoughts. Desire present in the soul expels the discernment of reason through its close association with irrational sense perception, and it changes to pleasure through the activity of the body, imprinting within the discursive intellect the pleasureful ways of the flesh; it constrains and encloses the mind through the imagining of sensible activities of the past and it gives impetus to the thoughts that fashion the deeds of discredited pleasure.

5. When phantasies that produce thoughts about the pleasure of sexual gratification[4] become the habitual pastime of the discursive faculty, the mind becomes involved in a shameful disposition and revels in dissipation and loses its effectiveness through self-gratification. What it used to do through sense perception and sensible things, it does through imagination and thoughts. When it has an abundance of sensible objects, it is content and attains the pleasure it desires, but when these are lacking to it, it achieves in thought what it used to do in body.

6. Therefore, anyone who wants to eradicate the pleasures of the flesh and adorn the body with chastity and keep it pure should always make haste to flee the sense faculties of the body through which sensible pleasure, by its activity in our members, rivets the mind to sensible things.

7. When the mind flees externals and is drawn inwards, it returns to itself: then it holds converse with its own word, which is naturally

---

[4] Literally, "thoughts of the moist ways of pleasure."

ἑαυτοῦ λόγῳ συγγίνεται, καὶ διὰ τοῦ συνόντος αὐτῷ οὐσιωδῶς λόγου
65 συνάπτεται τῇ εὐχῇ, καὶ διὰ τῆς εὐχῆς εἰς γνῶσιν τοῦ θεοῦ ἀναβαίνει
μεθ᾽ ὅλης τῆς ἀγαπητικῆς δυνάμεώς τε καὶ διαθέσεως.

8.   Τότε σαρκὸς μὲν ἐπιθυμία οἴχεται, πᾶσα δὲ ἡ καθήδονος ἀργεῖ
αἴσθησις καὶ τὰ ὡραῖα τῆς γῆς ἀηδῆ καταφαίνεται· ὀπίσω γὰρ ἑαυτῆς
ἡ ψυχὴ πάντα τὰ τοῦ σώματος καὶ τὰ περὶ τὸ σῶμα θεμένη, ὀπίσω
70 τῆς ὡραιότητος τοῦ Χριστοῦ γίνεται, αὐτῷ κατακολουθοῦσα μετὰ
τῶν ἔργων τῆς σεμνότητος καὶ τῆς κατὰ διάνοιαν ἁγνείας· καὶ
ψάλλουσα, *ἀπενεχθήσονται τῷ βασιλεῖ παρθένοι ὀπίσω αὐτοῦ·* Χριστὸν
φανταζομένη καὶ προορῶσα καὶ λέγουσα, *προωρώμην τὸν κύριον
ἐνώπιόν μου διὰ παντός·* Χριστῷ προσκολλωμένη διὰ τῆς ἀγάπης καὶ
75 κράζουσα, *κύριε, ἐναντίον σου πᾶσα ἡ ἐπιθυμία μου·* Χριστῷ διὰ παντὸς
ἐνατενίζουσα καὶ βοῶσα, *οἱ ὀφθαλμοί μου διὰ παντὸς πρὸς τὸν κύριον·*
Χριστῷ διαλεγομένη διὰ τῆς καθαρᾶς προσευχῆς καὶ ἡδύνουσα καὶ
εὐφραινομένη, *ἡδυνθείη αὐτῷ ἡ διαλογή μου, ἐγὼ δὲ εὐφρανθήσομαι ἐπὶ
τῷ κυρίῳ.*
80 **9.**   Ἀποδεχόμενος γὰρ ὁ θεὸς τὴν ἐκ τῆς εὐχῆς διαλογὴν καὶ ὡς
ἀγαπώμενος καὶ ὡς ὀνομαζόμενος καὶ ὡς ἐπιζητούμενος εἰς βοήθειαν,
τὴν ἄρρητον τῇ δεομένῃ ψυχῇ χαρὰν χαρίζεται· μνημονεύουσα γὰρ
θεοῦ διὰ τῆς κατὰ τὴν προσευχὴν διαλογῆς, κατευφραίνεται ὑπὸ
κυρίου· *ἐμνήσθην, γάρ φησι, τοῦ θεοῦ καὶ εὐφράνθην.*
85 **10.**   Οὔτε ἀλλόγλωσσοι διὰ λόγων ὁμιλῆσαι δύνανται δίχα ἑρ-
μηνέως διὰ τὸ μὴ ἐπίστασθαι τὴν ἀλλήλων διάλεκτον, οὔτε νοῦς τὴν
ἐν τοῖς αἰσθητοῖς ἡδονὴν ἰσχύει τελέσαι, δίχα τῶν αἰσθήσεων τοῦ
σώματος· οὔτε πάλιν ἐν τῇ διανοίᾳ κατ᾽ ἐπιθυμίαν ψυχικὴν ἡδυπαθῆ-
σαι ἐν τοῖς λογισμοῖς δίχα τῆς τῶν ἡδέων φαντασίας.

90 **11.**   Φεῦγε γοῦν τὰς αἰσθήσεις καὶ ἤργησας τὴν ἡδονὴν τῶν
αἰσθητῶν. φεῦγε καὶ τὰς κατὰ διάνοιαν φαντασίας τῶν ἡδέων καὶ
ἤργησας τὴν ἡδυπάθειαν τῶν λογισμῶν. ἀφάνταστος δὲ μένων ὁ νοῦς
ὡς μὴ καταδεχόμενος μήτε ὑπὸ τῶν καθ᾽ ἡδονὴν τρόπων, μήτε ὑπὸ
τῶν κατ᾽ ἐπιθυμίαν λογισμῶν τυποῦσθαί τε καὶ σφραγίζεσθαι, ἐν

hidden within the discursive intellect; through the word essentially associated with it the mind joins itself to prayer; and through prayer it ascends to knowledge of God with all its power and disposition of love.

8. Then, desires of the flesh pass away and all sense perception associated with pleasure comes to an end and the beauties of the earth appear to hold no delight. When the soul has placed behind itself all the things of the body and all bodily concerns, it goes after the beauty of Christ, following him with the works of chastity and the purity of its discursive intellect, while singing with the Psalmist, "The virgins are borne away to the king behind him."[5] The soul holds Christ before its eyes and in its imagination, saying, "I held the Lord always before my eyes."[6] It cleaves to Christ in love and cries out, "All my desire lies before you, O Lord."[7] With its gaze set always on Christ, it shouts, "My eyes are always on the Lord."[8] It finds its pleasure and joy in speaking with Christ in pure prayer: "May my speech be pleasing to him, and I shall rejoice in the Lord."[9]

9. When God accepts the dialogue of prayer as one who is beloved, called by name, and sought out for help, he grants ineffable joy to the soul that has made the request. The soul that remembers God in the dialogue of prayer receives joy from the Lord, for scripture says, "I remembered the Lord and I rejoiced."[10]

10. People who speak foreign tongues are unable to converse with one another in words without an interpreter, because they do not understand one another's language. So too the mind is incapable of taking pleasure in sensible things without the senses of the body; nor, in turn, is it able to find emotional pleasure in thoughts without the imagining of pleasant things in the discursive intellect.

11. Flee, then, the senses and you have rendered the pleasure of sensible things ineffectual. Flee also the imagining of pleasant things in the discursive intellect and you have rendered the self-gratification found in thoughts ineffectual. When the mind remains free from the imagination by not allowing itself to be imprinted or impressed either by the ways of pleasure or by thoughts encumbered by desire, it finds

[5] Ps 44:15.
[6] Ps 15:8.
[7] Ps 37:10.
[8] Ps 24:15.
[9] Ps 103:34.
[10] Ps 76:4.

95 ἁπλότητι εὑρίσκεται· καὶ ὑπεράνω πάντων τῶν αἰσθητῶν καὶ τῶν
νοητῶν γενόμενος, εἰς θεὸν τὴν ἔννοιαν ἀναβιβάζει, μηδὲν ἕτερον
ὅτι μὴ τὸ ὄνομα κυρίου διὰ τῆς συνεχοῦς μνήμης βαθέως ὑποφωνῶν,
ὡς βρέφος τὸν πατέρα αὐτοῦ· καλέσω, γάρ φησι, τῷ ὀνόματί μου κύριον
ἐναντίον σου.
100   12.   Καὶ ὥσπερ ὁ Ἀδὰμ χειρὶ θεοῦ πλασθεὶς ἀπὸ χοὸς γέγονεν
εἰς ψυχὴν ζῶσαν ἐμφυσήματι θείῳ, οὕτω καὶ ὁ νοῦς ταῖς ἀρεταῖς
διαπλασθείς, πυκνῇ ἐπικλήσει κυρίου ἐκ καθαρᾶς διανοίας καὶ
θερμῆς διαθέσεως ὑπᾳδομένη, τὴν θείαν ἀλλοιοῦται ἀλλοίωσιν,
ζωογονούμενος καὶ θεοποιούμενος ἐκ τοῦ γινώσκειν καὶ ἀγαπᾶν τὸν
105 θεόν.
     13.   Ὁ θεὸς λόγος τὸν ἀνθρώπινον νοῦν λογικὸν διαπλάσας,
συνέζευξεν αὐτῷ καὶ τὴν τοῦ ἔρωτος δύναμιν, ὅπως ὁ τῆς φύσεως
λόγος τῷ πόθῳ τῆς ψυχῆς συνεργῷ χρώμενος ἐπιτελεῖ τὰς ἀγαθὰς
πράξεις, ἵνα αἱ ἀρεταὶ ἐπιτιθέμεναι τῇ ψυχῇ, καθάπερ χρώματα τῇ
110 εἰκόνι, τὴν ἀκριβῆ μίμησιν τῆς θείας ὁμοιώσεως διασώζωσι, καὶ οὕτω
τὸ κατ᾽ εἰκόνα καὶ καθ᾽ ὁμοίωσιν διαφυλάττηται.
     14.   Τὸ μὲν γὰρ κατ᾽ εἰκόνα ἐν τῇ ἀξίᾳ τοῦ λόγου διαδείκνυται,
τὴν δὲ θείαν ὁμοίωσιν ἡ ἀγάπη περιποιεῖ. καὶ ὁ μὲν λόγος τὴν
ἀλήθειαν γνωρίζει, ἀρχή, γάρ φησι, τῶν λόγων σου ἀλήθεια· ἡ δὲ ἀγάπη
115 τὰς ἀρετὰς οἰκοδομεῖ· καὶ πᾶσα μὲν γνῶσις ἀπλανὴς εἰς τὴν ἀλήθειαν
ἀναφέρεται, ἅπαν δὲ ἀγαθὸν τελούμενον εἰς τὴν ἀγάπην ἀνάγεται.
     15.   Ὁ μὲν λόγος διὰ τῆς γνώσεως τῶν ὄντων πρὸς τὸν τῶν ὄντων
αἴτιον, τὸν ἀληθῆ θεόν, χειραγωγεῖ τὸν νοῦν· ἡ δὲ ἀγάπη τὴν πρὸς
θεὸν ἕνωσιν ἐργαζομένη οὐκ ἐᾷ τὸν νοῦν ἔξω τῆς τοῦ θεοῦ μνήμης
120 φέρεσθαι. ἀλλ᾽ ὥσπερ αὕτη κεκόλληται πρὸς θεόν, οὕτω καὶ τὸν νοῦν
προσηλοῦσθαι τῇ τοῦ θεοῦ θεωρίᾳ παρασκευάζει· ἐμοί, γάρ φησι,
τὸ προσκολλᾶσθαι τῷ θεῷ ἀγαθόν ἐστι, τίθεσθαι ἐν τῷ κυρίῳ τὴν ἐλπίδα
μου.
     16.   Ἡ πρὸς τὴν σάρκα καὶ τὰ αἰσθητὰ διάθεσις καὶ φιλία ἀθετεῖ
125 τὴν τοῦ θεοῦ ἀγάπην. ἡ τῆς θείας ἀγάπης ἀθέτησις τὴν σκοτοποιὸν
τίκτει λήθην. ἡ λήθη τὴν ἄγνοιαν τοῦ θεοῦ φέρει, ἄγνοια δὲ θεοῦ
ψυχῆς θάνατος· ἀγνοούμενος γὰρ ὁ θεὸς θανατοῖ, γινωσκόμενος δὲ

---

95 ὑπεράνω corr.: ὑπὲρ ἄνω OAM   101 ἐμφυσήματι corr. (M): ἐν φυσήματι
OA   126 ἄγνοιαν corr. (M): ἄγνειαν OA   ἄγνοια corr. (M): ἄγνεια OA

itself in simplicity. Passing beyond all sensible and intelligible things, it raises its thoughts to God, giving voice to nothing but the *Name of the Lord* in the depth of continuous remembrance, as a child calls upon its father. For scripture says, "By my name I shall call upon the Lord before you."[11]

12. As Adam was fashioned from the earth by the hand of God and became a living soul by the divine insufflation,[12] so, too, the mind, formed by the virtues, undergoes a divine transformation by means of the frequent *Invocation of the Lord* which is sung by a pure discursive intellect and a warm disposition. Thus does the mind receive life and divinization from knowing and loving God.

13. When God the Word fashioned the human mind with a faculty of reason, he joined to it also the power of love so that the natural word may use the soul's desire as an aid in performing good deeds, in order that the virtues applied to the soul, like colours to an icon,[13] may assure the exact imitation of the divine likeness, and thus the Image and Likeness may be preserved.

14. The Image is clearly manifest in the dignity of the word, but love secures the divine Likeness. The word makes known the truth, for scripture says, "Truth is the source of your words,"[14] but love builds up the virtues."[15] All knowledge that is free of error has reference to the truth, but every good you do leads to love.

15. Through knowledge of beings the word guides the mind towards the cause of beings, the true God, but, when love brings about union with God, it does not allow the mind to be distracted from the remembrance of God. Just as love clings to God, so too it prepares the mind for attachment to the contemplation of God. For scripture says, "For me it is good to cling to God, to place my hope in the Lord."[16]

16. A disposition and attraction to the flesh and sensible things involves rejection of God's love. Rejection of divine love engenders a forgetfulness that brings darkness upon us. Forgetfulness brings ignorance of God and ignorance of God means death for the soul. When God is ignored he bestows death, but when he is known he

---

[11] Cf. Is 45:4.
[12] Gen 2:7.
[13] Cf. Gregory of Nyssa, *De perfectione christiana* (PG 46:272AB).
[14] Ps 118:160.
[15] Cf. 1 Cor 8:1.
[16] Ps 72:28.

ζωογονεῖ· αὕτη, γάρ, ἐστιν ἡ αἰώνιος ζωή, ἵνα γινώσκωσί σε τὸν μόνον ἀληθινὸν θεὸν καὶ ὃν ἀπέστειλας Ἰησοῦν Χριστόν.

130   **17.** Διὰ γοῦν ταῦτα ἐπείγεται ὁ λόγος διὰ τῶν ἀρετῶν τὴν ἐπιθυμίαν ἀποστῆσαι τῆς σαρκὸς καὶ τοῦ κόσμου καὶ προσαρμόσαι τῷ θεῷ λόγῳ· συνδεθείσης γὰρ τῆς ψυχῆς τῷ θεῷ διὰ τῆς ἀγάπης, καὶ ἡ μνήμη τοῦ νοῦ τῆς τοῦ θεοῦ θεωρίας οὐκ ἐξίσταται· ᾧ γὰρ δέδεται ἡ ψυχὴ διὰ τῆς ἀγάπης, τούτῳ καὶ ὁ νοῦς διὰ τῆς γνώσεως
135 ἐνατενίζει διὰ παντός. ἐπειδὴ τὰς οἰκείας δυνάμεις ἀποδίδωσιν ἡ ψυχὴ τῷ δεδωκότι θεῷ, καὶ ταύτας ἀφοσιοῖ πρὸς τὴν αὐτοῦ διακονίαν καθὼς καὶ προσετάγη, ὅθεν καὶ ἀντιλαμβάνει παρὰ τοῦ πεποιηκότος θεοῦ τῆς πρὸς αὐτὸν εὐνοίας καὶ εὐγνωμοσύνης τὰς ἀμοιβάς.

18. Ὁ ἐν ἡμῖν λογικὸς νοῦς τὸν ἔξωθεν αἰσθητὸν κόσμον
140 ἀπολιπών, ἔτι δὲ καὶ τὰ κατὰ διάνοιαν σχήματα τοῦ κόσμου καὶ πάντα τὰ μετὰ θεὸν αἰσθητά τε καὶ νοητά, θεὸν αὐτίκα ὁρᾷ καὶ καλεῖ ὅσον ἐφικτὸν καθαρῷ νοΐ. ὁ γὰρ ἔσωθεν ἐξ αὐτοῦ φυσικῶς ἀναδιδόμενος νοερὸς λόγος, τὸν θεὸν λόγον εἰκονίζων, ὡς εἰκὼν ἐπὶ τὸ πρωτότυπον εἰς τὸν θεὸν ἀναφέρει τὸν νοῦν, ὡς ἐξιστάμενον πάντων τῶν ὄντων
145 καὶ πρὸς τὸν ὑπὲρ τὰ ὄντα γενόμενον.

19. Ἔκστηθι πάντων τῶν κατ᾽ αἴσθησιν καὶ κατάλιπε τὸν τῆς σαρκὸς νόμον, καὶ ὁ τοῦ πνεύματος νόμος ἐγγραφήσεται τῇ σῇ διανοίᾳ. ὡς γὰρ ὁ πνεύματι περιπατῶν ἐπιθυμίαν σαρκὸς οὐ τελεῖ κατὰ τὸν ἀπόστολον, οὕτω καὶ ὁ ἐξιστάμενος αἰσθήσεων καὶ
150 αἰσηθτῶν, σαρκὸς δηλονότι καὶ κόσμου, εἰς τὸ πνεύματι περιπατεῖν καὶ τὰ τοῦ πνεύματος φρονεῖν ἔρχεται. καὶ τοῦτο διδάχθητι, ἐξ ὧν ὁ θεὸς εἰς τὸν Ἀδὰμ πρὸ τῆς παρακοῆς κατειργάσατο.

20. Ὁ Ἀδὰμ φυλάττων τὴν ἐντολὴν ἐν τῷ παραδείσῳ ηὐλίζετο· καὶ βουληθεὶς ὁ θεὸς τὴν Εὔαν δημιουργῆσαι, *ὑπέβαλεν ἔκστασιν ἐπὶ*
155 *τὸν Ἀδὰμ καὶ ὕπνωσεν.* ἤργησεν ὁ Ἀδὰμ ἀπὸ πάσης τῆς κατ᾽ αἴσθησιν ἐνεργείας διὰ τοῦ ὕπνου, καὶ παρήγαγεν ὁ θεὸς τὴν γυναῖκα *καὶ ἤγαγεν αὐτὴν πρὸς τὸν Ἀδάμ.* καὶ ὁ ἐκστήσας θεὸς τὸν Ἀδὰμ διὰ τοῦ ὕπνου, διεφώτισεν αὐτὸν διὰ τῆς γυναικός. διὸ καὶ πρὸς αὐτὴν ἀτενίζων, ἅπερ οὐχ ἑώρακε τοῖς ὀφθαλμοῖς καὶ τοῖς λογισμοῖς οὐκ ἔγνω,
160 διελάλει τρανῶς.

146 κατ᾽ αἴσθησιν corr. (M): καταίσθησιν O, κατταίσθησιν A

bestows life, for "This is eternal life, that they know you, the only true God, and Jesus Christ, whom you have sent."[17]

17. For these reasons, then, by the practice of the virtues the word hastens to put aside the desire of the flesh and of the world and to attach itself to God the Word. When the soul is bound to God by love, even the remembrance of the mind is not distracted from the contemplation of God, for through knowledge the gaze of the mind is ever fixed on the one to whom the soul is bound by love. When the soul delivers up its faculties to the God who granted them, it sanctifies these for his service, as it was commanded. Then the soul receives from God, its creator, the rewards of its good will and affection towards him.

18. When the rational mind within us has left behind the external world of the senses and even the forms of the world in the discursive intellect as well as all sensible and intelligible things posterior to God, it beholds God forthwith and calls to him as much as possible with a pure mind. The spiritual word within, which issues forth naturally from the mind, is an image of God the Word and, like an image to its prototype, it brings the mind back to God, when the mind has transcended all beings and belongs to the one who is beyond all beings.

19. Shun all the things of the senses, abandon the law of the flesh, and the law of the spirit[18] shall be engraved upon your mind. For as the person who walks in the Spirit does not gratify the desires of the flesh, according to the Apostle,[19] so too the person who shuns the senses and sensible things, that is, the flesh and the world, comes to walk in the Spirit and to think thoughts inspired by the Spirit. You can learn this from what God wrought for Adam before his disobedience.

20. While Adam kept the commandment he dwelt in paradise, and when God wanted to create Eve, "he put Adam under a trance and he slept."[20] Because of the sleep, Adam lost awareness of all sensible activity, and God brought forth the woman "and led her to Adam."[21] God, who had put Adam to sleep in a trance, illumined him through the woman. And so, gazing upon her, he spoke clearly of what he had not seen with his eyes nor known in his thoughts.

[17] Jn 17:3.

[18] Cf. Rom 8:2.

[19] Gal 5:16.

[20] Gen 2:21. Note that Theoleptos is commenting in this passage on the Greek word ἔκστασις. The 'ecstasy' mentioned here refers to the sleep of the senses.

[21] Gen 2:22.

21. Καὶ σὲ τοίνυν περὶ τὴν φυλακὴν τῶν ἐντολῶν διαγωνιζόμενον καὶ ἐν τῷ παραδείσῳ τῆς προσευχῆς διακαρτεροῦντα καὶ τῷ θεῷ προσεδρεύοντα διὰ τῆς συνεχοῦς μνήμης, ἐξιστᾷ ἀπὸ τῶν τῆς σαρκὸς φιληδόνων ἐνεργημάτων καὶ ἀπὸ πάντων τῶν κατ' αἴσθησιν κινη-
165 μάτων καὶ ἀπὸ τῶν κατὰ διάνοιαν σχημάτων, καὶ νεκρὸν τοῖς πάθεσι καὶ τῇ ἁμαρτίᾳ παρασκευάζων, τῆς θείας ζωῆς μέτοχόν σε καθίστησιν. ὡς γὰρ ὁ ὑπνώττων καὶ νεκρῷ παρεικάζεται καὶ ζῶν ὑπάρχει, τὸ μὲν τῇ ἐνεργείᾳ τοῦ σώματος, τὸ δὲ τῇ συναφείᾳ τῆς ψυχῆς, οὕτω καὶ ὁ πνεύματι παραμένων σαρκὶ μὲν καὶ κόσμῳ νεκροῦται, ζῇ δὲ τῷ
170 τοῦ πνεύματος φρονήματι.

22. Πρὸ τῆς δημιουργίας τῆς γυναικὸς ἔκστασις καὶ ὕπνος ἐν τῷ Ἀδάμ· καὶ πρὸ τῶν χαρισμάτων τοῦ πνεύματος ἔκστασις τῶν τοῦ κόσμου πραγμάτων καὶ νέκρωσις τοῦ σαρκικοῦ φρονήματος τῷ ἀσκητῇ.
175 **23.** Ἐν τῇ ξένῃ διαπλάσει τῆς Εὔας προκατεβάλετο ὁ θεὸς λόγος τὴν ἐς ὕστερον σοφὴν καὶ φιλάνθρωπον διὰ σταυροῦ ἀναζώωσιν τοῦ γένους ἡμῶν. τὴν ἐν τοῖς ἐσχάτοις χρόνοις τοῦ σωτῆρος ἐπὶ σωτηρίᾳ τῶν ἀνθρώπων διὰ σταυροῦ οἰκονομίαν καὶ τὴν ἐν ἀρχῇ τῶν αἰώνων ἐκ πλευρᾶς τοῦ Ἀδὰμ οἰκοδομὴν τῆς γυναικὸς ὁ Παῦλος τοῖς τοῦ
180 πνεύματος ὀφθαλμοῖς κατανοήσας καὶ τὰ ἐν ἀμφοτέροις μυστήρια κατοπτεύσας, *ἐμοί*, φησι, *κόσμος ἐσταύρωται κἀγὼ τῷ κόσμῳ·* τὴν ἐν τῷ παραδείσῳ ἔκστασιν καὶ τὸν ὕπνον τοῦ Ἀδὰμ ὑποσημαίνων. πάλιν δὲ προσειπών, *ζῶ δὲ ἐγὼ οὐκέτι, ζῇ δὲ ἐν ἐμοὶ Χριστός,* ὑπεδήλωσεν τὴν ἐκ τῆς κατὰ τὴν πλευρὰν οἰκοδομῆς τῆς γυναικὸς ἀνάληψιν,
185 δι' ἧς ἀπεκαλύφθη ὁ Ἀδὰμ τῶν ἐσομένων σωματικῶς καὶ πνευματικῶς τὴν ἔκβασιν.

24. Ἰδὼν γὰρ τὴν γυναῖκα καὶ τῇ ἀνοικοδομῇ τῆς γυναικὸς τὸ κατὰ Χριστὸν μυστήριον διαθροίσας ἐκ θείας ἀποκαλύψεως, ἔφησεν· *ἕνεκεν τούτου,* τοῦ κατὰ Χριστὸν δηλονότι μυστηρίου, *καταλείψει ὁ*
190 *ἄνθρωπος τὸν πατέρα καὶ τὴν μητέρα αὐτοῦ* – κόσμον φημὶ καὶ σάρκα,

---

167 παρεικάζεται OᵖᶜAM: παροικάζεται Oᵃᶜ   177 ἐσχάτοις OᵖᶜAM: αἰσχάτοις Oᵃᶜ

21.   Therefore, in your struggle to keep the commandments and in your perseverance in the paradise of prayer and as you attend upon God through continuous remembrance, he removes you from the pleasureful workings of the flesh, from all the movements of the senses and from the forms in the discursive mind; rendering you dead to the passions and to sin, he makes you a partaker in the divine life.[22] As the sleeper resembles one dead and yet is alive (in the first case with respect to the activity of the body and in the second with respect to the soul's attachment to it), so too the man who abides in the Spirit is dead to the flesh and the world, but lives in accord with the Spirit's way of thought.[23]

22.   Before the creation of woman an 'ecstasy' and sleep came over Adam and before the gifts of the Spirit are granted to the ascetic there must be an 'ecstasy' from the things of the world and a dying to the way of thinking that is bound to the flesh.[24]

23.   In the wondrous fashioning of Eve, God the Word laid the foundation for his wise and benevolent regeneration of our race that would take place in a later time through the Cross. With the eyes of the Spirit Paul considered the Economy of the Saviour on the Cross, effected in these latter times for the salvation of humanity, and the formation of woman from Adam's rib at the beginning of the ages. Seeing through to the mysteries in both events, he said, "The world has been crucified to me, and I to the world,"[25] alluding to the 'ecstasy' and sleep of Adam in paradise; then he added, "It is no longer I who live, but Christ who lives in me,"[26] so as to indicate the restoration that derives from the woman's formation from Adam's rib; through this means the outcome of the corporeal and spiritual events of the future was revealed in Adam.

24.   When he considered the woman and by divine revelation associated the mystery of Christ with the fashioning of woman, Paul said: "On account of this (namely, the mystery of Christ) a man shall leave his father and mother (that is, the world and the flesh, earthly

[22] Cf. 2 Pet 1:4.

[23] Cf. Rom 8:13.

[24] Here again 'ecstasy' refers to the abandonment of all attachment to the senses and to created things.

[25] Gal 6:14.

[26] Gal 2:20. In Gal 6:15 Paul insists that only 'a new creation' counts for anything, not circumcision or uncircumcision, but nowhere does he make any reference to the 'ecstasy' of Adam. Furthermore, the explanation that follows the quotation in Theoleptos' text is grammatically unclear.

πράγματα καὶ φρονήματα τῆς γῆς, θυμὸν καὶ ἐπιθυμίαν, ὕλην καὶ εἶδος ἐξ ὧν τὰ σώματα, θέλημα καὶ δικαίωμα – *καὶ προσκολληθήσεται τῇ γυναικί*, τῇ κατὰ Χριστὸν ζωῇ, *καὶ ἔσονται οἱ δύο ἓν πνεῦμα· ὁ γὰρ κολλώμενος τῷ κυρίῳ, φησὶν ὁ ἀπόστολος, ἓν πνεῦμά ἐστι.*

195 **25.** Τὸ παρὰ τοῦ Παύλου εἰρημένον ἰσοδυναμεῖ τῷ ὑπὸ τοῦ Ἀδὰμ προαγορευθέντι· τὸ γὰρ *ζῶ ἐγὼ οὐκέτι, ζῇ δὲ ἐν ἐμοὶ Χριστός* ταὐτὸν δύναται τῷ *ἕνεκεν τούτου καταλείψει ἄνθρωπος τὸν πατέρα καὶ τὴν μητέρα αὐτοῦ καὶ προσκολληθήσεται τῇ γυναικί*, τῇ κατὰ Χριστὸν ζωῇ. αὖθις τὸ *ἔσονται οἱ δύο εἰς σάρκα μίαν*, πνευματικῶς νοούμενον, συνᾴδει
200 τῷ *ὁ κολλώμενος τῷ κυρίῳ ἓν πνεῦμά ἐστιν.*

26. Ἐὰν γοῦν ἐκστῇς τῆς τῶν γηΐνων ἐπιθυμίας τῇ συνεχεῖ καὶ εἰλικρινεῖ προσευχῇ καὶ ἀντὶ ὕπνου καταπαύσῃς ἀπὸ πάσης ἐννοίας τῆς μετὰ θεὸν καὶ στηριχθῇς ὁλικῶς εἰς μόνην τὴν τοῦ θεοῦ μνήμην, ἀνοικοδομοθήσεται ἐν σοί, καθάπερ ἄλλη βοηθός, ἡ τοῦ θεοῦ ἀγάπη·
205 ἡ γὰρ ἐκ προσευχῆς κατὰ διάθεσιν βοὴ τὴν θείαν ἀγάπην ἀναδίδωσι καὶ ἡ θεία ἀγάπη διϋπνίζει τὸν νοῦν πρὸς φανέρωσιν τῶν ἀποκρύφων. τότε ὁ νοῦς τῇ ἀγάπῃ συναρμοσθεὶς τὴν σοφίαν καρποῦται καὶ διὰ τῆς σοφίας τὰ ἀπόρρητα καταγγέλλει· ὁ γὰρ θεὸς λόγος διὰ τῆς κατὰ τὴν προσευχὴν βοῆς κατὰ διάθεσιν ὀνομαζόμενος, λαμβάνων τὴν τοῦ
210 νοῦ νόησιν, καθάπερ πλευράν, τὴν γνῶσιν χαρίζεται καὶ ἀντ᾽ αὐτῆς ἀναπληρῶν τὴν ἀγαθὴν διάθεσιν δωρεῖται τὴν ἀρετήν.

27. Οὕτω τελειῶν τὴν ἀρετήν, οἰκοδομεῖ τὴν φωτοποιὸν ἀγάπην καὶ ἄγει παρὰ τὸν ἐξεστηκότα νοῦν καὶ ὑπνοῦντα καὶ ἀναπαυόμενον ἀπὸ πάσης γηΐνης ἐπιθυμίας. ἡ δὲ ἀγάπη ἄλλη βοηθὸς εὑρίσκεται
215 τοῦ καταπαύσαντος νοῦ ἀπὸ τῆς ἀλόγου τῶν αἰσθητῶν προσπαθείας· ὅθεν καὶ διϋπνίζει τὸν νοῦν ὡς καθαρὸν εἰς τὰ τῆς σοφίας ῥήματα. τότε πρὸς αὐτὴν ὁρῶν ὁ νοῦς καὶ καθηδυνόμενος, τὰς κρυπτὰς τῶν

---

197 τῷ corr.: τὸ OAM

things and thoughts, anger and desire, matter and form from which bodies are derived, self-will and self-justification) and he shall be joined to his wife (to life in Christ), and the two shall become one spirit,"[27] for the Apostle says, "He who clings to the Lord becomes one spirit with him."[28]

25. The statement made by Paul is equivalent to what Adam said in prophecy. The statement, "It is no longer I who live, but Christ who lives in me"[29] has the same meaning as the statement, "For this reason a man shall leave his father and mother and shall be joined to his wife"[30] (to life in Christ). Furthermore, the statement, "The two shall become one flesh,"[31] when it is taken in a spiritual sense, accords with the statement, "He who clings to the Lord becomes one spirit with him."[32]

26. Thus, if you withdraw from desire for earthly things by means of continuous and pure prayer and if, in place of Adam's sleep, you cease from all consideration of things posterior to God and if you are fixed firmly and entirely to the sole task of remembering God, the love of God will be fashioned within you, like another helpmate. For the habitual cry of prayer imparts divine love and divine love awakens the mind to the manifestation of hidden things. Then, when the mind has become assimilated to love, it bears the fruit of wisdom and through wisdom it announces ineffable truths. For when God the Word is habitually invoked in the cry of prayer, he takes the mind's conceptual faculty, like a rib, and grants knowledge, and in its place[33] he brings the good disposition to fulfilment and bestows virtue.

27. In thus perfecting virtue, God fashions a love that gives forth light and introduces it to the mind which has withdrawn into sleep and found rest from all earthly desire. Love is found to be another helpmate for the mind that has desisted from irrational attraction towards sensible things. Wherefore, God awakens the mind, now pure, to words of wisdom. Then, as the mind gazes upon wisdom and experiences delight, it makes known to others through the expressions

[27] Eph 5:31 (Gen 2:24).
[28] 1 Cor 6:17.
[29] Gal 2:20.
[30] Gen 2:24.
[31] Ibid.
[32] 1 Cor 6:17.
[33] Strictly speaking, ἀντ᾽ αὐτῆς should refer to γνῶσιν, which would make little sense. I assume that it was the author's intention to refer back to πλευράν – νόησιν.

ἀρετῶν διαθέσεις καὶ τὰς ἀθεάτους ἐνεργείας τῆς γνώσεως τοῖς ἄλλοις δημοσιεύει διὰ τῆς τῶν λόγων ἐκτάσεως.

220 **28.** Ἡ Εὔα καὶ τὴν ἀγάπην εἰκονίζει καὶ τὴν μετάνοιαν ὑποτυποῖ καὶ τὴν διάνοιαν σχηματίζει καὶ τὴν αἴσθησιν ὑπογράφει· τὴν μὲν ἀγάπην, ὡς φωτίζουσαν τὸν νοῦν καὶ νηφάλιον ἐργαζομένην· τὴν δὲ μετάνοιαν, ὡς ἀνιστῶσαν τοὺς πίπτοντας καὶ τὴν δημιουργίαν συντηροῦσαν, ἡ μὲν γὰρ δημιουργία ἐκ μὴ ὄντων παράγει, ἡ δὲ 225 μετάνοια τὸ συντριβὲν ἀναπλάττει· τὴν δὲ διάνοιαν πάλιν ὑπογράφει, ὡς τὰ κεκρυμμένα καὶ συνεσταλμένα τοῦ νοῦ νοήματα δεχομένην καὶ ἐγγυμνάζουσαν καὶ ἀνύουσαν τὸν δρόμον τοῦ λόγου· τὴν αἴσθησιν δὲ σχηματίζει ὅταν τῷ ὄφει προσομιλεῖ δεικνῦντι τὰ ἡδέα καὶ πρὸς τὴν ἡδονὴν τῶν αἰσθητῶν ὑποσύροντι.

230 **29.** Ὅταν ἀκούῃς, *ἔθετο ὁ θεὸς τὸν ἄνθρωπον ἐν τῷ παραδείσῳ ἐργάζεσθαι αὐτὸν καὶ φυλάσσειν,* διαβίβαζε καὶ πρὸς ἑαυτὴν τὸν λόγον· ἔθετο γὰρ καὶ τὸν σὸν νοῦν ἐν τῷ τῆς φύσεως λόγῳ πρὸς ἐργασίαν τῶν ἀγαθῶν ἔργων καὶ φυλακὴν τοῦ νοῦ, ἵνα μὴ συληθεὶς ὁ νοῦς ὡς ἀφύλακτος κατασυρῇ πρὸς τὰς ἀλόγους τῆς σαρκὸς πράξεις.

235 **30.** Ὅταν δὲ πάλιν ἀκούῃς, *ἤγαγεν ὁ θεὸς τὰ ζῷα πρὸς τὸν Ἀδὰμ καὶ τούτοις ἔθετο τὰ ὀνόματα,* ἐκλάμβανε καὶ περὶ σεαυτῆς τοῦτο καὶ τὰς ἀλόγους αἰσθήσεις ῥύθμιζε τῷ νῷ καὶ τοὺς νόμους τῆς φυσικῆς θεωρίας διέρχου.

31. Ἡνίκα δὲ πάλιν τὴν διάπλασιν τῆς γυναικὸς ἐκμανθάνῃς, 240 ἀνυψῶν τὸν νοῦν σου εἰς πνευματικὴν θεωρίαν, συνέτιζε τὴν διάνοιαν καὶ πνεύματι βάδιζε καὶ σαρκὸς ἡδονὰς οὐ μὴ τελέσῃς· ἡ γὰρ πνευματικὴ θεωρία τοῦ νοῦ καὶ ἡ μελέτη τῶν θείων λόγων τὸν νοητὸν ἀπελαύνουσιν ὄφιν ὡς ἀλλότριον τοῦ οὐρανίου φρονήματος.

32. Ἐν τούτοις ἀεὶ διατρίβων καὶ πρακτικὴν ἀρετὴν καὶ φυσικὴν 245 θεωρίαν καὶ πνευματικὴν ὁμιλίαν ἐκμανθάνεις καὶ ἐν τῷ ἀσφαλεῖ χωρίῳ τῆς θείας γνώσεως παραμένεις, ὡς σώματι καὶ ψυχῇ καὶ νοῒ καταρτιζόμενος. τότε καὶ γυμνὸς διατελεῖς καὶ τὴν αἰσχύνην ἐκφεύγεις· γυμνὸς ὑπάρχεις διὰ τὸ ἄμικτον τῆς τῶν γηΐνων ἐπιθυμίας·

227 ἐγγυμνάζουσαν conieci: ἐγγυμονοῦσαν ΟΜ, ἐγγυμονοῦσα Α   237 ῥύθμιζε corr.: ῥίθμιζε ΟΑΜ

of speech the hidden dispositions of the virtues and the unseen workings of knowledge.

28. Eve is also an image of love, a type of repentance, a form of the discursive intellect and an illustration of sense perception. She is an image of love, in that this bestows light upon the mind and renders it vigilant; of repentance, in that this raises up the fallen and preserves the created order, for creation is a bringing forth from nothing and repentance is a refashioning of what was crushed. In turn, she is an illustration of the discursive intellect, in that this receives the hidden and remote thoughts of the mind and exercises and sets in motion the course of speech; she represents sense perception, whenever this enters into converse with the serpent who displays pleasant things and drags it down to the pleasure to be found in sensible things.[34]

29. When you hear the scripture text, "God placed man in paradise to work it and keep it,"[35] apply the statement to yourself,[36] for he placed your mind within the faculty of natural reason to accomplish good works and to guard the mind so that the mind may not be carried away because it was left unguarded and drawn down to the irrational deeds of the flesh.

30. And again, when you hear the text, "God brought the animals to Adam and he gave them names,"[37] take it as applying to yourself: train the irrational senses with your mind and follow the laws of natural contemplation.

31. Furthermore, when you consider closely the fashioning of the woman, raising your mind to spiritual contemplation, instruct your discursive intellect, walk in the Spirit and do not gratify the pleasures of the flesh.[38] For the spiritual contemplation of the mind and meditation on the divine words drive away the spiritual serpent as one alien to a heavenly way of thought.

32. If you busy yourself always with these matters, you will learn the practice of virtue, natural contemplation and spiritual converse, and you will make your abode in the secure place of divine knowledge, since you are restored in body, soul and mind.[39] At that point you are naked and beyond shame. You are naked because you have nothing to do with desire for earthly things. You are free of shame because

---

[34] Gen 3:4-6.
[35] Gen 2:15.
[36] Note the change to the feminine pronoun, referring to Eulogia and Agathonike.
[37] Gen 2:19.
[38] Gal 5:16. Cf. MD 23.19.
[39] Note the Evagrian terminology. Cf. Evagrius, *Praktikos* 1 (SC 171:498).

αἰσχύνην οὐκ ἔχεις διὰ τὸ καθαρὸν τῆς διανοίας καὶ τὸ πεπαρρη-
250 σιασμένον τῆς συνειδήσεως πρὸς τὸν θεόν· ἐὰν γὰρ ἡ συνείδησις
ἡμῶν μὴ καταγινώσκῃ ἡμῶν, παρρησίαν ἔχομεν πρὸς τὸν θεόν.
   33. Ἡ ἐν γλώσσῃ ψαλμῳδία ἀναγκαίως ἐπιδέεται καὶ τῆς κατὰ
νοῦν ἐπιστασίας πρὸς τὸ μὴ διαφεύγειν τὴν θεωρίαν τῶν λεγομένων·
ψαλῶ, γάρ φησι ὁ ἀπόστολος, τῷ πνεύματι, ψαλῶ καὶ τῷ νοΐ. ἔργον
255 οὖν τέλειον καὶ ὀφειλόμενον τὸ ψάλλειν μετὰ καὶ τοῦ ἔχειν τὸν νοῦν
εἰς προσοχὴν τῶν σωτηρίων ῥημάτων, ὡς ἐξ ὅλης ψυχῆς καὶ σώματος
τῆς κατὰ τοὺς ὕμνους θυσίας ἐπιτελουμένης· ἥ τε γὰρ γλῶσσα
δοξάζεται διὰ τῆς τῶν λεγομένων προφορᾶς καὶ ὁ νοῦς ἁγιάζεται
ἐκ τῆς τῶν θείων λογίων γνώσεως. τότε τῆς διαθέσεως συναπτομένης
260 τῇ περὶ τὴν ἁγίαν γνῶσιν τῶν ψαλλομένων θεωρίᾳ, σύνεσις ἀκολουθεῖ,
κατὰ τὸν λέγοντα προφήτην, ψάλατε συνετῶς· τουτέστι, συνδιατίθεσθε
τῇ ψυχῇ πρὸς τὰ λεγόμενα καὶ μὴ ἀδιανοήτως καὶ ἀδιαθέτως τὰ διὰ
τοῦ στόματος ψαλλόμενα διέρχεσθε.

   34. Ἐντεῦθεν καὶ εἰς τὴν διὰ τοῦ σώματος πρᾶξιν τῶν καλῶν
265 ἡ ψυχὴ προκόπτει· ἀρχή, γάρ φησι, σοφίας φόβος κυρίου, σύνεσις δὲ
πᾶσι τοῖς ποιοῦσιν αὐτήν. ὁ μὲν φόβος ἀπωθεῖται τὰ φαῦλα· ἡ δὲ σύνεσις
περιποιεῖται τὰ κρείττω. ὁρᾷς ὅσον ἀγαθὸν προσξενεῖ τὸ
ἐπακολουθεῖν τὸν νοῦν γνησίως τοῖς λεγομένοις; εἰ γινώσκεις ἃ
ψάλλεις, λαμβάνεις καὶ ἐπίγνωσιν, ἐκ τῆς ἐπιγνώσεως κτᾶσαι σύνεσιν.
270 ἐκ τῆς συνέσεως ἡ πρᾶξις τῶν ἐγνωσμένων βλαστάνει, ἐκ τῆς πράξεως
τὴν καθέξιν γνῶσιν καρποῦσαι. ἡ δὲ ἐν πείρᾳ γνῶσις τὴν ἀληθῆ
θεωρίαν ἀναδίδωσιν. ἐκ ταύτης ἡ σοφία ἀνατέλλει, τῆς διὰ τῶν
φωτοβόλων λόγων χάριτος τὸν ἀέρα τῆς διανοίας πληροῦσα καὶ τοῖς
ἔξω διασαφοῦσα τὰ κεκρυμμένα.

275   **35.** Ὁ ψάλλων νηφόντως καί, ὡς εἰρήκαμεν, ἔοικεν ἀνθρώπῳ
τέχνην εὐφυῶς ἐπισταμένῳ καὶ διὰ τῶν ἀναχεῖρας ἐργαλείων ἔργον
ἐπιδεικνυμένῳ λυσιτελοῦν τῷ βίῳ καὶ κέρδος ὁμοῦ καὶ ἔπαινον
προξενοῦν τῷ τεχνίτῃ. ὁ δὲ γλώσσῃ μὲν ψάλλων, τὸν δὲ νοῦν
ῥεμβόμενον ἔχων γηΐναις φροντίσι καὶ πάθεσιν ἀλόγοις μετεωριζό-
280 μενον, ὁμοιοῦται ἀνδρί, ἐργαλεῖα μὲν περιφέροντι, τέχνην δὲ οὐκ
εἰδότι καὶ ἔργον οὐκ ἀνύοντι. οὗτος, εἰ συνήσει τὸ λεγόμενον ὑπὸ
τοῦ κυρίου διὰ τοῦ προφήτου καὶ τοῦ εὐαγγελίου, καὶ τὸν μετεωρισμὸν

of the purity of your discursive intellect and the freedom your conscience possesses before God, for if our conscience does not condemn us, we have freedom before God.

33.   Vocal psalmody necessarily requires the attention of the mind so as to prevent the distraction of contemplation from what is being said. The Apostle says, "I will sing with the spirit and I will sing with the mind also."[40] To be perfect and fitting, then, the task of singing the psalms requires that the mind focus its attention on the saving words so that the sacrifice of hymnody be made with the entire soul and body. The tongue is glorified in uttering the words and the mind is sanctified in knowing the divine scriptures. Then, when one's disposition is joined to the contemplation of the holy knowledge of the psalms being sung, understanding follows, according to the words of the Prophet, "Sing psalms with understanding";[41] that is, bring your soul into harmony with what is being said and do not mouth the words of the psalms mindlessly and without feeling.

34.   Then the soul makes progress in the practice of good works through the body. For scripture says, "The fear of the Lord is the beginning of wisdom: understanding belongs to all those who practise it."[42] Fear drives away what is bad and understanding acquires what is superior. Do you see how much good accrues when the mind really follows what is being said? If you know what you are singing, you acquire awareness and from awareness you procure understanding. From understanding springs the practice of what you know and from praxis you bear the fruit of habitual knowledge. Knowledge gained by experience ushers in true contemplation. From this there comes the dawning of wisdom, which fills the air of the discursive mind with the grace of its light-bearing words, revealing hidden things to those outside.

35.   As we have said, one who sings psalms with vigilance is like a man who is naturally skilled at a trade and with the tools at hand displays a work which has practical use and which brings both profit and praise to the craftsman. But one who sings the psalms with the tongue while leaving his mind to roam about in the midst of earthly thoughts and to be born up on the irrational passions is like a man who carries around tools but knows no trade and produces no work. If this man understands what the Lord is saying through the Prophet

[40] 1 Cor 14:15.
[41] Ps 46:8.
[42] Ps 110:10.

ἐκκόψει καὶ πρὸς τὴν γνῶσιν προκόψει τῶν λεγομένων· ὁ λαός, γάρ
φησιν οὗτος, τοῖς χείλεσί με τιμᾷ, ἡ δὲ καρδία αὐτῶν πόρρω ἀπέχει
285 ἀπ᾽ ἐμοῦ· καὶ οὐ πᾶς ὁ λέγων μοι, κύριε κύριε, εἰσελεύσεται εἰς τὴν
βασιλείαν τῶν οὐρανῶν, ἀλλ᾽ ὁ ποιῶν τὸ θέλημα τοῦ πατρός μου τοῦ
ἐν τοῖς οὐρανοῖς.

36. Ὁ τοιοῦτος πάλιν παραβάλλεται ἀνθρώπῳ οἰκοδεσπότῃ, ὃς
τὸν μὲν οἰκεῖον δοῦλον προεστήσατο περιέπειν τὸν οἶκον αὐτοῦ,
290 ἑαυτὸν δὲ τῇ ἐξουσίᾳ τῶν ἀθυρμάτων καὶ τῶν ματαιοτήτων
ἀπεμπολήσας ἐξέδωκεν.

37. Ἡ ψαλμῳδία ψυχῆς ἐστι διαλογὴ πρὸς τὸν θεόν. τίς εἰς
πρόσωπον ἑστὼς τοῦ βοηθεῖν δυναμένου, οὐ βλέπει τὴν ὄψιν τοῦ
εὐεργέτου καὶ μετὰ θερμῆς διαθέσεως καὶ ταπεινοῦ φρονήματος καὶ
295 τῆς κατὰ διάνοιαν ἐπιγνώσεως οὐ ποιεῖται τὴν πρὸς αὐτὸν δέησιν;

38. Λουκᾶς καὶ Κλεόπας μετὰ τὴν ἀνάστασιν τοῦ κυρίου πορευ-
όμενοι εἰς Ἐμμαούς, συνώδευον τῷ κυρίῳ καὶ ἔλεγον τὰ περὶ αὐτοῦ,
ἀλλ᾽ οὐκ ἐπεγίνωσκον αὐτόν. διὸ καὶ ὀνειδίζονται παρ᾽ αὐτοῦ, ὡς
μὴ νοοῦντες τὰς γραφὰς καὶ ὡς διστάζοντες ἐπ᾽ αὐταῖς. ὅτε δὲ
300 παρεβιάσαντο τὸν κύριον τοῦ μεῖναι σὺν αὐτοῖς, ὁ δὲ δυσωπηθεὶς
κατεκλίθη μετ᾽ αὐτῶν ἐν τῷ καταλύματι. τότε καὶ διηνοίχθησαν οἱ
ὀφθαλμοὶ αὐτῶν καὶ ἐπέγνωσαν τὸν ἀναστάντα Χριστὸν καὶ τοῖς
ἄλλοις ἐκήρυξαν μετὰ πίστεως εἰλικρινοῦς.

39. Καὶ σὺ τοίνυν ψάλλων καὶ στιχολογῶν, μὴ βλέπε πρὸς τὸν
305 ἦχον τῆς ἐν γλώσσῃ προφορᾶς, μηδὲ τὴν ποσότητα τῶν στίχων
ἐννόει, μηδὲ τὸ τέλος τῶν ὕμνων ἀποσκόπει, ἐπειγόμενος ὥσπερ τι
φορτίον ἀποθέσθαι τὴν ἀκολουθίαν ἐν τάχει. εἰ οὕτω διάκεισαι, οὔτε
γινώσκεις ἃ λέγεις καὶ ἀγνοεῖς τὸν συνόντα σοι καὶ διομιλούμενον
κύριον διὰ τῆς τῶν θείων λογίων ἀπαγγελίας.

310 **40.** Βίαζε δὲ σεαυτὴν ἀεὶ στρέφειν τὸν νοῦν ἐν τοῖς λεγομένοις
καὶ θησαυρίζειν τὴν γνῶσιν ἐν τῇ διανοίᾳ, ἵνα διὰ τῆς ἀγάπης καὶ
τῆς τῶν θείων μελέτης μονὴν ἑτοιμάσῃς τῷ κυρίῳ, καὶ λήψεται πέρας

---

297 συνώδευον corr.: συνόδευον OA

and the Gospel, he will eliminate his distractions and proceed towards the knowledge of what is said. For scripture says, "This people honours me with their lips, but their heart is far from me."[43] And, "Not everyone who says to me, 'Lord, Lord,' shall enter the kingdom of heaven, but he who does the will of my Father, who is in heaven."[44]

36. Such a man can further be compared to the master of a household who set his servant in charge of looking after his house but he sold out and surrendered himself to the power of playthings and vanities.[45]

37. Psalmody of the soul is conversation with God. Who is there who stands in the presence of one who has the power to offer help and does not look upon the face of his benefactor and make his petition to him with a fervent disposition, a humble attitude and mental awareness?

38. After the Lord's resurrection, Luke and Cleopas were on the way to Emmaus. They were journeying in the company of the Lord and were discussing the events that had happened concerning him but they failed to recognize him. And so they were reproached by him because they were not mindful of the scriptures and because they doubted them. When they constrained the Lord to stay with them, he was persuaded and sat down to table with them at the inn. Then, their eyes were opened and they recognized the risen Christ and told the others with a pure faith.[46]

39. Therefore, when you are singing psalms and hymns, do not give your attention to the melody you are chanting with the tongue, nor consider how many verses there are, nor look forward to the end of the hymns, quickly rushing through the office, as if you were laying aside some kind of burden. If that is your disposition, you do not know what you are saying and you are unaware of the Lord, who is accompanying you and conversing with you through the recital of the divine scriptures.

40. Force yourself to focus the mind on what is said and to treasure up knowledge in the discursive faculty, in order that through love and through meditation on divine things you may prepare an abode for the Lord, and in the end your petition will be received. For scripture

---

[43] Mt 15:8 (Is 29:13).
[44] Mt 7:21.
[45] Cf. Mt 21:33-41.
[46] Lk 24:13-35.

τὸ αἴτημά σου· ἐὰν γὰρ μείνητε, φησὶν, ἐν ἐμοὶ καὶ τὰ ῥήματά μου ἐν
ὑμῖν μείνῃ, ὃ ἐὰν θέλητε αἰτήσασθε καὶ γενήσεται ὑμῖν.

315   **41.** Διὰ τοῦ μὴ ἐπιγνωσθῆναι τὸν κύριον ἐν τῇ ὁδῷ μανθάνομεν
ὅτι οὐχ ἡ παροδικὴ καὶ μετὰ συγχύσεως γινομένη ψαλμῳδία καὶ
στιχολογία τὸν φωτισμὸν δίδωσιν, ὡς γνῶσιν καὶ διάθεσιν καὶ πρᾶξιν
μὴ ἔχουσα. διὰ δὲ τοῦ συγκατακλιθῆναι τὸν κύριον τοῖς μαθηταῖς
καὶ μεῖναι μετ᾽ αὐτῶν καὶ οὕτως ἐπιγνωσθῆναι, διδασκόμεθα ὅτι
320 ἀναγκαίως ὀφείλομεν ἐκτελεῖν σώματι, ἅπερ ἀπαγγέλλομεν στόματι,
καὶ διὰ τῆς κατὰ πρᾶξιν τῶν ἐντολῶν βίας δυσωπεῖν τὸν κύριον·
βιαστὴ γάρ ἐστιν ἡ βασιλεία τῶν οὐρανῶν, καὶ βιασταὶ ἁρπάζουσιν αὐτήν.
τοῦτο καὶ οἱ μαθηταὶ δεδηλώκασι, παραβιασάμενοι τὸν κύριον τοῦ
μεῖναι σὺν αὐτοῖς.

325   **42.** Ψάλλων, στιχολογῶν καὶ ἀναγινώσκων, βιάζου σεαυτὴν καὶ
περὶ τὴν τῶν ἐντολῶν τήρησιν καὶ τὴν τῶν ἀρετῶν ποίησιν, ἵνα
συνᾴδων τῷ εὐαγγελιστῇ λέγῃς, ὅτι *τὰς ἐντολὰς αὐτοῦ τηροῦμεν καὶ*
τὰ ἀρεστὰ ἐνώπιον αὐτοῦ ποιοῦμεν· οὕτω γὰρ δυσωπηθήσεται μονὴν
ἐν σοὶ ποιῆσαι. ὡς γὰρ βιασθεὶς ὑπὸ τῶν μαθητῶν εἰσῆλθε τοῦ μεῖναι
330 σὺν αὐτοῖς εἰς κώμην τὴν καλουμένην Ἐμμαοῦς, οὕτω καὶ παρὰ σοὶ
διαπονουμένῳ καὶ περὶ τὴν πρᾶξιν τῶν ἐντολῶν καὶ τῇ ἀκενοδόξῳ
μελέτῃ τῶν θείων λογίων ἐνασχολουμένῳ, μονὴν ποιεῖται ὁ κύριος.
ὁ τηρῶν, γάρ φησι, τὰς ἐντολὰς αὐτοῦ μένει ἐν τῷ θεῷ καὶ ὁ θεὸς ἐν
αὐτῷ.

335   **43.** Ἀπόδειξις τοῦ ἀγαπᾶν τὸν θεὸν ἡ φυλακὴ τῶν ἐντολῶν· *ὁ*
ἔχων, γάρ φησι, τὰς ἐντολάς μου καὶ τηρῶν αὐτὰς ἐκεῖνός ἐστιν ὁ ἀγαπῶν
με· ὁ δὲ ἀγαπῶν τὸν κύριον, ἀγαπᾶται ὑπ᾽ αὐτοῦ, καὶ ἐμφανίζεται αὐτῷ.
εἰ τηρεῖς τὰς ἐντολὰς, μένεις ἐν τῇ ἀγάπῃ τοῦ κυρίου· *ἐὰν τηρήσητε,*
φησί, τὰς ἐντολάς μου, μενεῖτε ἐν τῇ ἀγάπῃ μου, καθὼς ἐγὼ τετήρηκα
340 *τὰς ἐντολὰς τοῦ πατρός μου καὶ μένω αὐτοῦ ἐν τῇ ἀγάπῃ.*

   44. Ὁ οὕτω διακείμενος φθάνει καὶ εἰς τὴν κατανόησιν τῆς
ἀφάτου ταπεινώσεως τοῦ κυρίου, ἣν εἰργάσατο διὰ τῆς κατὰ τὴν
σωτήριον ἐνανθρώπησιν σοφῆς οἰκονομίας, καὶ ἀποκάλυψιν τῶν
μυστηρίων, τοῖς γὰρ ταπεινοῖς δίδοται χάρις. τότε γὰρ παρὰ σοὶ
345 μένων ὁ τοῦ θεοῦ λόγος διὰ τὴν ἐνδιάθετον καὶ ἐπίμονον μελέτην

---

337 ἀγαπᾶται corr. (M): ἀγαπᾶτε OA

says, "If you abide in me, and my words abide in you, ask whatever you will, and it shall be done for you."[47]

41. Through the failure to recognize the Lord on the road we learn that psalmody and hymnody performed in a perfunctory and distracted manner offer no illumination since they are devoid of knowledge, disposition and praxis. Through the Lord's sitting down to table with his disciples and remaining with them and thus being recognized we learn that we must necessarily complete with the body what we recite with the mouth and through the persuasion of practising the commandments importune the Lord. For "the kingdom of heaven is taken by force, and men seize it by force."[48] This have the disciples also shown in constraining the Lord to stay with them.

42. When you sing psalms and hymns or when you read, force yourself to keep the commandments and practise the virtues, in order that you may say in unison with the Evangelist, "We keep his commandments and practise what is pleasing in his sight."[49] For thus shall he be constrained to make his abode in you. As he was importuned by his disciples to go in and abide with them in a village called Emmaus, so too when you labour over the practice of the commandments and occupy yourself with humble meditation on the divine scriptures, the Lord makes his abode with you. For scripture says, "He who keeps my commandments abides in God and God in him."[50]

43. Keeping the commandments is proof of one's love for God. For scripture says, "He who has my commandments and keeps them, he it is who loves me; and he who loves the Lord will be loved by him and the Lord will manifest himself to him."[51] If you keep the commandments, you will abide in the love of the Lord, for scripture says, "If you keep my commandments, you will abide in my love, just as I have kept my Father's commandments and abide in his love."[52]

44. The person so disposed attains both the revelation of mysteries and the comprehension of the Lord's ineffable humility, which he wrought through the wise Economy of his saving incarnation, for grace is given to the humble.[53] Then, while the Word of God abides with you because of your interior and steadfast meditation on the divine

---

[47] Jn 15:7.
[48] Mt 11:12.
[49] 1 Jn 3:22.
[50] 1 Jn 3:24.
[51] Jn 14:21.
[52] Jn 15:10.
[53] Jas 4:6.

τῶν θείων λογίων λαμβάνει τὸν νοῦν σου καθάπερ ἄρτον ὡς τετε-
λειωμένον τῇ ἀγάπῃ καὶ τῇ ἀναπολήσει τῆς ἐνδόξου κενώσεως καὶ
πλουτοποιοῦ πτωχείας καὶ τῆς θαυμαστῆς πολιτείας καὶ τῶν θεοπρε-
πῶν σημείων καὶ τῶν ἰαματικῶν μωλώπων καὶ τοῦ διὰ σταυροῦ
350 ἐπονειδίστου θανάτου καὶ τῆς ζωοποιοῦ ταφῆς καὶ τῆς ἀναστάσεως·
καὶ διὰ τῆς ἐναργοῦς ἀναμνήσεως τῶν ταπεινῶν καὶ τῶν ὑψηλῶν,
τῶν ἀτίμων καὶ τῶν ἐνδόξων, κατακλῶν καὶ συντρίβων τὸν νοῦν,
διανοίγει τοὺς λογισμοὺς τῆς ψυχῆς καὶ διαδίδωσι τὴν ἐπίγνωσιν
τῶν σοφῶς καὶ ἀγαθοπρεπῶς οἰκονομηθέντων παρ' αὐτοῦ εἰς
355 ἀνάκλησιν καὶ δόξαν ἡμετέραν.

45. Ὁ τὴν τοῦ κυρίου ταπείνωσιν ἐν τῇ κατὰ τὸν κόσμον τοῦτον
ἀναστροφῇ κατανοήσας δύο ἐπιγνώσεται θαυμαστὰ πράγματα· ὅτι
ἐχθροὺς ἡμᾶς ὄντας θεοῦ καὶ πᾶσαν ἁμαρτίαν διαπραττομένους καὶ
διὰ ταῦτα κολάσεσιν ὑποκειμένους, οὐκ ἐβδελύξατο ὁ θεὸς λόγος,
360 ἀλλὰ καὶ κατεδέξατο τῆς σαρκὸς ἡμῶν κοινωνὸς χρηματίσαι διὰ τῆς
ἐνανθρωπήσεως· καὶ ὅτι μηδὲν ἀγαθὸν πεποιηκότας, κοινωνοὺς ἡμᾶς
τῆς αὐτοῦ θεότητος ἐποιήσατο.

46. Εἶδες πέλαγος ἀγαθότητος καὶ τῆς περὶ ἡμᾶς ἀγάπης ὑπερ-
βολήν; ἔγνως πλοῦτον χάριτος καὶ φιλανθρωπίας ἄβυσσον; ὑπὲρ τῶν
365 καταδίκων ὁ δίκαιος κατεδικάσθη καὶ ἡ ἄδικος καταδίκη τοῦ δικαίου
ἐδικαίωσε τοὺς καταδίκους. ἡμεῖς τῷ κέντρῳ τῆς ἁμαρτίας πληγέντες
ὑπεπέσαμεν τῷ θανάτῳ καὶ ὁ ἀναμάρτητος ὑπὲρ ἡμῶν ἐμωλωπίσθη
καὶ οἱ μώλωπες αὐτοῦ ἴαμα ἡμῖν γεγόνασι καὶ ὁ δι' ἡμᾶς αὐτοῦ
θάνατος ἐζωοποίησεν ἡμᾶς. ἡμεῖς πάθεσιν ἀτιμίας ὑπεκύψαμεν καὶ
370 ὁ τῆς δόξης κύριος ἀτιμίαν δι' ἡμᾶς ὑπέμεινε καὶ ἡ ἀτιμία αὐτοῦ
τιμὴν ἡμῖν περιεποιήσατο. ὁ πλούσιος κατὰ τὴν θεότητα ἐπτώχευσε
κατὰ τὴν ἐξ ἡμῶν σάρκα καὶ τῇ πτωχείᾳ αὐτοῦ ἡμεῖς οἱ πτωχοὶ
ἐπλουτίσθημεν, ἀδελφοὶ καὶ συγκληρονόμοι αὐτοῦ καὶ υἱοὶ θεοῦ
χρηματίσαντες.

375 **47.** Τούτων ἡ διηνεκὴς κατανόησις καὶ ἡ περὶ ταῦτα τριβὴ καὶ
συνεχὴς μελέτη, βρῶσις καὶ πόσις γίνεται τῇ μετὰ πόθου καὶ πίστεως
διαλογιζομένῃ ταῦτα ψυχῇ. καὶ ὥσπερ ὁ τὸν ἄρτον τοῦτον τὸν
αἰσθητὸν καὶ τὸν οἶνον ἐσθίων καὶ πίνων τοῦ σώματος συνιστᾷ τὴν
ζωήν, ἐπειδήπερ παραμένουσαν ἔχει τὴν ψυχὴν συγκρατοῦσαν αὐτοῦ

scriptures, he takes your mind like bread that has been consecrated by love and by the constant consideration of his glorious abasement, his wealth-bestowing poverty, his marvelous way of life, his divinely fitting signs, his healing bruises, his shameful death on the Cross and his life-giving tomb and resurrection; and breaking up and grinding the mind through the clear remembrance of things low and high, dishonourable and glorious, he opens the thoughts of the soul and bestows awareness of what he has wrought in his wisdom and goodness for our restoration and glory.

45.　The person who ponders the Lord's self-abasement during his life in this world will come to know two wondrous things: namely, that while we were enemies of God and involved in the practice of every kind of sin and on this account subject to punishment, God the Word did not treat us as an abomination, but rather accepted to be reckoned as a partaker of our flesh through the incarnation; and that he made us partakers of his own divinity[54] even though we have done nothing good.

46.　Do you see the ocean of his goodness and the abundance of his love for us? Do you understand the wealth of his grace and the abyss of his love for man? The just man was condemned for the sake of the guilty and the unjust judgement against the just man justified the guilty.[55] We have been struck by the sting of sin and have fallen victim to death[56] and the sinless one was bruised for our sake and his bruises have become a source of healing for us and his death on our account has brought us life.[57] We bent our necks under the yoke of dishonourable passions and the Lord of glory endured dishonour for our sake and his dishonour procured for us honour. He who is rich in divinity became poor in our flesh and by his poverty we who are poor were made rich and called brothers and co-inheritors with him and sons of God.[58]

47.　The perpetual pondering of these truths, our occupation with them and our continual meditation on them are food and drink for the soul that considers these truths with faith and longing. Just as one who eats and drinks this sensible bread and wine conserves the life of the body since he has the soul standing by to strengthen his

[54] Cf. 2 Pet 1:4.
[55] Cf. 1 Pet 3:18.
[56] Cf. 1 Cor 15:56.
[57] Cf. Is 53:5-8.
[58] Cf. 2 Cor 8:9, Rom 8:17.

380 τὴν ζωὴν διὰ τῆς τροφῆς, οὕτω καὶ ὁ μετὰ πίστεως καὶ πόθου μετέχων
τοῦ δεσποτικοῦ σώματος καὶ αἵματος τὴν ζωὴν τῆς ψυχῆς συντηρεῖ,
ἐπειδὴ καταμένον ἔχει τὸ πνεῦμα τὸ ἅγιον ἐν αὐτῷ, ζωογονοῦν τὴν
ψυχὴν καὶ πληροῦν αὐτὴν ἀγάπης καὶ εἰρήνης καὶ ἐπιεικείας καὶ
πάσης ἀγαθωσύνης. ὡς γὰρ ἀδύνατον σῶμα δίχα ψυχῆς ζῆν, οὕτω
385 καὶ ψυχὴν ἐκτὸς θεοῦ ζῆσαι ἀδύνατον.

48. Ἀλλὰ καὶ ὁ τοῖς θείοις λόγοις ἐμμελετῶν καὶ τὰ τῶν θείων
γραφῶν διανοούμενός τε καὶ διηγούμενος, ὡς ἀγγέλων ἄρτῳ διατρε-
φόμενός τε καὶ στηριζόμενος, ζῶσαν τὴν ἑαυτοῦ ψυχὴν συντηρεῖ,
ἐπειδὴ τὸν θεὸν λόγον διὰ τῆς κατὰ τὴν πρᾶξιν τῶν ἐντολῶν βίας
390 δυσωπεῖ καὶ διὰ τῆς κατὰ τὰς ἀρετὰς καθαρότητος εἰσοικίζει αὐτόν·
διὰ δὲ τῆς εἰλικρινοῦς ἀγάπης μονὴν αὐτῷ ἑτοιμάζει, ὃς κατακλι-
νόμενος ἐν τῇ καρδίᾳ εἰς συναίσθησιν ἄγει τὸν νοῦν τῆς ἀφάτου
ἑαυτοῦ ταπεινώσεως.

49. Ἐντεῦθεν καὶ πάσας τὰς ψυχικὰς δυνάμεις οἰκειούμενος ὁ
395 κύριος καὶ ἐπισπώμενος πρὸς ἑαυτὸν καὶ εὐλογῶν καὶ ἁγιάζων καὶ
μεταδιδοὺς αὐταῖς τοῦ παρ' ἑαυτοῦ φωτισμοῦ, διανοίγει τοὺς τῆς
ψυχῆς ὀφθαλμοὺς εἰς τὴν ἑαυτοῦ ἐπίγνωσιν, εὐφροσύνην ἀνα-
βλύζουσαν ἄρρητον. ὡς γὰρ ὁ ἀὴρ μὴ παρόντος ἡλίου ἀφώτιστος
μένει, οὕτω καὶ ψυχὴ θεὸν ἀγνοοῦσα, ἐσκοτισμένη καὶ νεκρὰ
400 χρηματίζει. καὶ ὁ μὲν αἰσθητὸς ἥλιος φωτίζει τὸν αἰσθητὸν κόσμον,
ὁ δὲ νοητὸς ἥλιος Χριστὸς τὸν νοητὸν καταυγάζει κόσμον. καὶ ὁ
μὲν τοῖς ἀνθρωπίνοις ὀφθαλμοῖς τὴν τέρψιν παρέχει, ὁ δὲ Χριστὸς
τοῖς νοεροῖς ὀφθαλμοῖς τὴν ἀπόλαυσιν τῶν νοουμένων χαρίζεται.

50. Ὁ θεὸς λόγος ἐνανθρωπήσας καὶ τὰ μυστήρια τῆς οὐρανίου
405 βασιλείας ἀπεκάλυψε καὶ τὰ τῆς σωτηρίας ἔργα καθυπέδειξεν ἐν τῷ
παναχράντῳ αὐτοῦ σώματι, ὅπως τοῖς ἴχνεσιν αὐτοῦ πολιτευσάμενοι
συνεισέλθωμεν αὐτῷ εἰς τὸν νυμφῶνα τῆς δόξης, συγκληρονόμοι
αὐτῷ γεγενημένοι κατὰ τὸν πλοῦτον τῆς περὶ ἡμᾶς χάριτος καὶ
ἀγαθότητος αὐτοῦ. ὅρα γοῦν τὰ διὰ σὲ παράδοξα πράγματα καὶ
410 πνευματικῶς ἀνακαινίζου, ἵνα μὴ τῆς χάριτος ἧς ἠξιώθης ἀποπέσῃς.

51. Ὁ Χριστὸς βαπτιζόμενος κατέβη ἐν τοῖς ὕδασι τοῦ Ἰορδάνου,
διδάσκων διὰ τῆς καταδύσεως νεκροὺς ἡμᾶς εἶναι τῇ ἁμαρτίᾳ εἰς
τὸ μηκέτι δουλεύειν τῇ ἁμαρτίᾳ, ἀκινήτους δὲ πρὸς τὸ κακὸν
χρηματίζειν. ἀνέβη Χριστὸς ἐκ τοῦ ὕδατος, τὴν κατὰ τὰ ἔργα τῶν
415 ἀρετῶν ἀνάστασιν καὶ τὴν ἐν δικαιοσύνῃ ζωὴν διὰ τῆς ἀναδύσεως

life through this nourishment, so too one who partakes of the Lord's body and blood with faith and longing preserves the life of the soul since he has the Holy Spirit dwelling within him, giving life to the soul and filling it with love, peace, forbearance and every kind of goodness. For as it is impossible for the body to live without the soul, so too the soul cannot live without God.

48.　Furthermore, the person who meditates on the divine words and gives careful thought and consideration to the divine scriptures, as though nourished and strengthened by the bread of angels, keeps his soul alive since he importunes God the Word by the persuasion of his practice of the commandments and has him abide within him through the purity of his virtuous life; through pure love he prepares an abode for the Lord who sits down to table in his heart and brings his mind to share the experience of his indescribable humility.

49.　Then, when the Lord has drawn all the powers of the soul to himself and made them his own, blessing and sanctifying them and granting them participation in the illumination that radiates from him, he opens the eyes of the soul to a knowledge of himself, which issues forth in ineffable joy. For as the air in the absence of the sun remains devoid of light, so too the soul that does not know God is reckoned to be dark and dead. The sensible sun gives light to the sensible world, but Christ, the intelligible sun, bestows radiance on the intelligible world. The former offers delight to the human eye, but Christ bestows the enjoyment of intelligible things on spiritual eyes.

50.　When God the Word became incarnate, he revealed the mysteries of the kingdom of heaven and manifested the works of salvation in his wholly undefiled body, so that we may follow in his footsteps and enter together with him into the bridal chamber of glory when we have become fellow heirs with him according to the wealth of his grace and goodness in our regard. Note, therefore, the extraordinary things done for you and renew yourself spiritually that you may not fall from the grace of which you have been deemed worthy.

51.　When Christ was baptized,[59] he went down into the waters of the Jordan, teaching us by his immersion that we are dead to sin so that we may no longer be slaves to sin but may be considered beyond the influence of evil. Christ came up out of the water, announcing to us by his emergence the resurrection wrought by the works of virtue and the life of righteousness. "When Christ came up

---

[59]　Mt 3:13-17, Mk 1:9-11, Lk 3:21-22.

κηρύττων ἡμῖν. *ἀναβαίνων ἀπὸ τοῦ ὕδατος ὁ Χριστὸς εἶδε σχιζομένους τοὺς οὐρανοὺς καὶ τὸ πνεῦμα ἐν εἴδει περιστερᾶς καταβαῖνον ἐπ᾽ αὐτόν· καὶ φωνὴ ἐγένετο ἐκ τῶν οὐρανῶν λέγουσα· οὗτός ἐστιν ὁ υἱός μου ὁ ἀγαπητὸς ἐν ᾧ ηὐδόκησα.*

420   **52.** Ὁ τὴν ῥοώδη τῶν παρόντων φύσιν ὑπερβαίνων καὶ τὴν ἐπιθυμίαν τῶν παρερχομένων παρατρέχων οὐ βλέπει ἐπὶ τὰ κάτω, οὐκ ἐπιποθεῖ τὰ ὡραῖα τῆς γῆς, ἀλλὰ τὰς ἄνω ὁράσεις ἀνοιγομένας ἔχει καὶ τὰ ἐν οὐρανοῖς κατοπτεύει κάλλη καὶ τὴν τῶν ἀκηράτων κατασκοπεύει μακαριότητα. ὡς γὰρ τῷ ἐπιχάσκοντι ταῖς ὕλαις τῆς
425 γῆς καὶ πρὸς τὰς ἡδονὰς τῆς σαρκὸς ἐγκύπτοντι κεκλεισμένοι εἰσὶν οἱ οὐρανοί, ὡς τοὺς νοεροὺς ὀφθαλμοὺς ἐσκοτισμένους φέροντι, οὕτως ὁ περιφρονῶν τὰ κάτω καὶ ἀποστρεφόμενος μετάρσιον ἔχει τὸν νοῦν καὶ τὴν τῶν ἀϊδίων ὁρᾷ δόξαν καὶ τὴν ἀποκειμένην τοῖς ἁγίοις κατανοεῖ λαμπρότητα. οὗτος καὶ τὴν τοῦ θεοῦ ἀγάπην ἄνωθεν
430 κατιοῦσαν ἐπ᾽ αὐτὸν δέχεται καὶ ναὸς τοῦ ἁγίου πνεύματος γίνεται καὶ τὰ θεῖα θελήματα ἐπιποθεῖ καὶ πνεύματι θεοῦ ἄγεται καὶ υἱοθεσίας καταξιοῦται καὶ τὸν θεὸν ἔχει εὐδοκοῦντα καὶ ἀρεσκόμενον ἐν αὐτῷ. *ὅσοι γὰρ πνεύματι θεοῦ ἄγονται, οὗτοι εἰσὶν υἱοὶ θεοῦ.*

   53. Ἐπίστησον τὸν νοῦν σου μετὰ ταπεινώσεως καὶ τῆς εἰς θεὸν
435 ἐλπίδος τοῖς τελεσθεῖσι παρὰ τοῦ σωτῆρος ἐν τῷ βαπτίσματι καὶ ὄψει τὸν θεάνθρωπον λόγον μυσταγωγοῦντά σοι τὰ μεγάλα· διὰ μὲν τῆς καταδύσεως καὶ ἀναδύσεως, τὴν ἠθικὴν ἀρετήν· διὰ τοῦ ἰδεῖν σχιζομένους τοὺς οὐρανούς, τὴν φυσικὴν θεωρίαν τῶν ὄντων· διὰ δὲ τοῦ ἐν εἴδει περιστερᾶς κατιόντος πνεύματος ἐπ᾽ αὐτὸν καὶ τῆς
440 πατερικῆς φωνῆς μαρτυρούσης τὴν υἱότητα τοῦ βαπτιζομένου, τὴν ἀκριβῆ θεολογίαν διδάσκοντα.

   54. Ἔχου τοιγαροῦν τῶν τοῦ σωτῆρος ἔργων καὶ λόγων καὶ συνήσεις τὸν θησαυρὸν τῆς ἀληθείας· αὐτὸς γάρ ἐστι καὶ ἡ τελείωσις τῆς ἀρετῆς, αὐτός ἐστι καὶ ὁ χορηγὸς τῆς τῶν ὄντων γνώσεως. αὐτός
445 ἐστι καὶ ὁ ἄριστος τῆς θεολογίας ἐξηγητής, *ὁ ὢν εἰς τὸν κόλπον τοῦ πατρὸς* καὶ *τὸν πατέρα γινώσκων καὶ ὑπὸ τοῦ πατρὸς γινωσκόμενος.*
   55. Ἡ ἄνωθεν τοῦ πνεύματος κατάβασις ἐπὶ τὸν υἱὸν καὶ τὴν ἐκ τοῦ πατρὸς ὑποστατικὴν πρόοδον τοῦ πνεύματος κατασημαίνει

---

423 κάλλη OᵖᶜM: καλλει OᵃᶜA

out of the water, he saw the heavens split asunder and the Spirit descending upon him in the form of a dove. And a voice came from the heavens saying,[60] 'This is my beloved son in whom I have been well pleased.' "[61]

52. When a person passes beyond the transitory nature of present things and leaves behind the desire for things that pass away, he does not look upon inferior things, he does not yearn for the beautiful things of earth, but keeps his gaze directed upwards, contemplates heavenly beauties and searches out the blessedness of things that are unfading. As the heavens are closed for the one who gapes greedily at the material things of earth and peeps in at the pleasures of the flesh because he possesses spiritual eyes which have been darkened, so the person who despises and flees from the things below keeps his mind held on high and beholds the glory of things eternal and perceives the radiance in store for the saints. This person also receives the love of God descending upon him from above, becomes a temple of the Holy Spirit, yearns for the will of God, is led by God's Spirit, is judged worthy of adoption, and God is well pleased and satisfied with him. "For all who are led by the Spirit of God are sons of God."[62]

53. With humility and hope in God set your mind on the mysteries effected by the Saviour in his Baptism and you will behold the theanthropic Word, who initiates you into mighty things. On the one hand, through his going down into the water and coming up again he teaches you moral virtue and through the vision of the heavens split asunder he teaches you the natural contemplation of beings. On the other hand, through the descent of the Spirit upon him in the form of a dove and through the Father's voice witnessing to the sonship of the one baptized, he teaches true Theology.

54. Therefore, hold to the deeds and words of the Saviour and you will understand the treasure of truth. For he himself is the perfection of virtue; he is the one who provides knowledge of beings; he is the supreme interpreter of Theology, "he who is in the bosom of the Father,"[63] who knows the Father and is known by the Father.[64]

55. The Spirit's descent from above upon the Son signifies the hypostatic procession of the Spirit from the Father, proclaims his

---

[60] Mk 1:10-11.
[61] Mt 3:17.
[62] Rom 8:14.
[63] Jn 1:18.
[64] Cf. Jn 10:15.

καὶ τὴν πρὸς τὸν υἱὸν οἰκειότητα φυσικὴν αὐτοῦ καταγγέλλει καὶ
450 τὸν πατέρα αἴτιον υἱοῦ καὶ πνεύματος ἀνακηρύττει· τοῦ μὲν υἱοῦ ὡς
γεννήτορα, τοῦ δὲ πνεύματος ὡς προβολέα.

56. Ταύτῃ τῇ μυσταγωγίᾳ τῇ ἐν τῷ βαπτίσματι τοῦ σωτῆρος
ἀναδειχθείσῃ καὶ ἡ ἐν τοῖς εὐαγγελίοις αὐτοῦ διδασκαλία συνᾴδει·
τὸ γὰρ πνεῦμα τῆς ἀληθείας, ἤτοι τοῦ υἱοῦ, ἐκπορεύεται ἐκ τοῦ
455 πατρός, ἀναπαύεται δὲ ἐν τῷ υἱῷ ὡς πνεῦμα αὐτοῦ, οὔτε τοῦ πατρὸς
ἐξ οὗ ἐκπορεύεται χωριζόμενον, οὔτε τοῦ υἱοῦ ἐν ᾧ ἀναπαύεται
διϊστάμενον, ἀλλὰ σύνεστιν αὐτῷ καὶ συμπαρομαρτεῖ ὡς ὁμοούσιον
καὶ οἰκειωμένον αὐτῷ κατὰ τὴν φύσιν. ἐκ τοῦ κατὰ τὴν θεολογίαν
ταύτην ὕδατος τοῦ ἐν Ἰορδάνῃ φανερωθέντος καὶ ἐκ τῆς πηγῆς τοῦ
460 εὐαγγελίου ἀναδοθέντος πίνε καὶ φωτίζου, καὶ πότιζε τοὺς διψῶντας
καὶ φώτιζε· τὴν δὲ ἰταλικὴν προσθήκην πάσῃ προθέσει καὶ ἰσχύϊ
περιΐστασο καὶ ἀποτρέπου, ὡς τὸ καθαρὸν νᾶμα τῆς θεολογίας
ἐπιταράττουσαν.

57. Ὥσπερ τι κάτοπτρον διαυγέστατον δέδωκεν ἡμῖν ὁ θεὸς τὸν
465 τῆς φύσεως λόγον, ὅπως ἀπὸ τῆς τοῦ κόσμου διαχύσεως πρὸς αὐτὸν
κεκαθαρμένον ὄντα ἐπιστρεφόμενοι, δι' αὐτοῦ πρὸς τὸν θεὸν
ἀναγόμεθα. *μακάριοι, γάρ φησι, οἱ καθαροὶ τῇ καρδίᾳ ὅτι αὐτοὶ τὸν*
θεὸν ὄψονται.

58. Πρῶτον ὁ νοῦς ζητεῖ καὶ εὑρίσκει, εἶτα ἑνοῦται τῷ εὑρεθέντι·
470 καὶ τὴν μὲν ζήτησιν ποιεῖται διὰ τοῦ λόγου, τὴν δὲ ἕνωσιν διὰ τῆς
ἀγάπης. καὶ ἡ μὲν διὰ τοῦ λόγου ζήτησις γίνεται διὰ τὴν ἀλήθειαν,
ἡ δὲ τῆς ἀγάπης ἕνωσις διὰ τὸ ἀγαθόν.

59. Τούτων τὴν ἀνάγνωσιν διέρχου, μὴ ἀργῶς ἀλλ' ἐναργῶς, μὴ
παροδικῶς ἀλλ' ἐπιστημονικῶς, μὴ ῥήματα ἐπισκεπτομένη διανοίας
475 ἐκτός, ἀλλὰ βαπτίζουσα τὸν νοῦν εἰς τὸ βάθος τῶν νοουμένων, ἵνα
ἐκεῖθεν ἑλκύσῃς πνεῦμα. εὑρήσεις γὰρ ἐν τοῖς γράμμασι τὰς τῆς
ψυχῆς δυνάμεις, τὴν διαφορὰν αὐτῶν, τὰς φυσικὰς κινήσεις, τὰς τοῦ
πνεύματος ἀναγωγὰς καὶ τὰς μυστικὰς ἐνεργείας, καὶ ἴδῃς καινοποιὸν
ἡμέραν ἣν ὁ προφήτης πανηγυρίζων λέγει· *αὕτη ἡ ἡμέρα, ἣν ἐποίησεν*
480 *ὁ κύριος· ἀγαλλιασώμεθα καὶ εὐφρανθῶμεν ἐν αὐτῇ.*

60. Οὕτως ἐπιμελομένη, δύνασαι μετὰ τοῦ καθηγητοῦ Χριστοῦ,
τὴν μὲν αἴσθησιν καὶ τὰ αἰσθητὰ πάντα παρελθεῖν καὶ ὑπερβῆναι,
ἐν τῇ χώρᾳ δὲ τῶν νοητῶν καὶ θείων κατασκηνῶσαι. ἔνθα ἐπιθυμία
σαρκὸς καὶ κόσμου ἐξόρισται, ἡ φωτοτόκος δὲ ἀγάπη τοῦ θεοῦ

---

478 ἴδῃς corr.: ἤδῃς OA

natural relationship to the Son, and also announces that the Father is cause of the Son and the Spirit, of the Son as begetter and of the Spirit as the one who sends forth.

56.   The teaching of the Saviour in the Gospels accords with this mystagogy manifested in his Baptism. For the Spirit of Truth (that is, of the Son) proceeds from the Father but rests in the Son as his Spirit without being separated from the Father, from whom he proceeds, nor being divided from the Son, in whom he rests. Rather, the Spirit coexists with and accompanies the Son since he is consubstantial with and proper to him by nature. Drink, receive illumination, satisfy the thirsty and illumine them from the water of this Theology made manifest in the Jordan and sent forth from the spring of the Gospel. But eschew and reject the Italian appendage with all your will and strength, for it troubles the pure stream of Theology.

57.   God has given to us the natural word as a very clear mirror so that when we turn away from the dissipation of the world towards that word in its purity we are led by it to God. For scripture says, "Blessed are the pure of heart for they shall see God."[65]

58.   First, the mind seeks and finds.[66] Then, it is united to the one it has found. The seeking is effected through the word and the union through love. The seeking through the word is for the sake of the truth and the union of love for the sake of the good.

59.   Read through these things carefully, not in idleness but with perspicacity, not cursorily but with understanding. Do not examine the words apart from their meaning, but rather baptize your mind in the depths of these considerations in order that you may draw the spirit from them. In these writings you will discover the powers of the soul, the differences between them, their natural movements, the leadings of the Spirit and his mystical workings, and you may see the new day of which the Prophet speaks in his rejoicing: "This is the day which the Lord has made. Let us be glad and rejoice in it."[67]

60.   Applying yourself in this way, may you be able, with Christ to guide you, to pass beyond and overcome the faculty of sense perception and all sensible things and make your abode in the land of things intelligible and divine. There the desires of the flesh and of

[65] Mt 5:8.
[66] Cf. Mt 7:7-8.
[67] Ps 117:24.

485 εἰσοικίζεται, καὶ ἁγνεία καὶ σεμνότης καὶ ἡ ἄρρητος εὐπρέπεια
ἐμπολιτεύονται, καὶ οἱ φωτισμοὶ τῶν γνώσεων τοῦ πνεύματος
ἀνατέλλουσιν. ὄψει τὴν ἐν κρυπτῷ κατὰ Χριστὸν ζωήν, ἀρραβῶνα
φέρουσαν τῆς κατὰ τὸ μέλλον δεδοξασμένης αἰωνίου ζωῆς, φανερ-
ωθησομένης ἡνίκα φανεροῦται Χριστὸς ἡ ζωὴ τῶν ζώντων μετὰ τῆς
490 ἀπορρήτου δόξης αὐτοῦ.

61. Εἰ τοίνυν πιστωθήσομαι ἐπιμελῶς μετιέναι ὑμᾶς ταῦτα, ὡς
γνώμῃ καὶ πράξει τὴν πρὸς ἀλλήλας ἀγάπην καὶ τὴν ὑπακοὴν καὶ
τὴν ταπείνωσιν καὶ τὴν ἐν τοῖς δεινοῖς καρτερίαν καὶ εὐχαριστίαν
ἐπιδείκνυσθαι, πρόθυμος ἔσομαι Χριστοῦ ἐμπνέοντος καὶ τὰ λοιπὰ
495 διατρανῶσαι καὶ ἐπιστεῖλαι ὑμῖν. εἰ δ᾽ οὔ, ἡ λύπη βάλλει με καὶ σιγὴν
τοῖς χείλεσι περιθήσει· ζῷον γὰρ λυπούμενον οὐκ ᾄδει κατὰ τὸ
ᾀδόμενον.

491 πιστωθήσομαι corr.: πιστοθήσομε OA

the world are banished; there the light-begetting love of God comes to dwell; sanctity and holiness and ineffable beauty are citizens there; and the rays of knowledge bestowed by the Spirit rise like the dawn. You will see the life hidden in Christ, bearing the pledge of the eternal life in glory to come, which will be revealed when Christ is revealed in his indescribable glory as the life of the living.

61. If, therefore, I am persuaded that you pursue these things diligently, as to display in will and in practice your love for one another, obedience, humility and perseverance and thanksgiving in the midst of trials, I will be eager, if Christ inspires me, to explain and send to you the rest. But if I am not so convinced, grief will overwhelm me and impose silence on my lips, for an animal overcome with grief does not sing its song.

Bibliography

Athanasius, Patriarch of Constantinople. *The Correspondence of Athanasius I, Patriarch of Constantinople*. Ed. and trans. by Alice-Mary Maffry Talbot. CFHB 7. Washington: Dumbarton Oaks Center for Byzantine Studies, 1975.

Balfour, David. "Saint Gregory the Sinaite: Discourse on the Transfiguration." *Θεολογία* 52 (1981) 631-681.

Barringer, Robert. "Ecclesiastical Penance in the Church of Constantinople: A Study of the Hagiographical Evidence to 983 A.D." D.Phil. dissertation, Oxford University, 1979.

Beyer, Hans-Veit. "Die Katechese des Theoleptos von Philadelpheia auf die Verklärung Christi." JÖB 34 (1984) 171-198.

Boissonade, Jean François. *Anecdota graeca*. 5 vols. Paris, 1829-1833; repr. Hildesheim: G. Olms, 1962.

——. *Anecdota nova*. Paris, 1844; repr. Hildesheim: G. Olms, 1962.

Choumnaina, Eirene (Eulogia). *A Woman's Quest for Spiritual Guidance. The Correspondence of Princess Irene Choumnaina Palaiologina*. Ed. and trans. by Angela Constantinides Hero. The Archbishop Iakovos Library of Ecclesiastical and Historical Sources 11. Brookline, MA: Hellenic College Press, 1986.

Constantelos, Demetrios J. "Mysticism and Social Involvement in the Later Byzantine Church: Theoleptos of Philadelphia — a Case Study." *Byzantine Studies/Études Byzantines* 6 (1979) 83-94.

Cupane, Carolina. "Una 'classe sociale' dimenticata: il basso clero metropolitano. Un tentativo di ricostruzione alla luce del Registro del Patriarcato Costantinopolitano (1315-1402)." In *Studien zum Patriarchatsregister von Konstantinopel I*, ed. Herbert Hunger, pp. 61-83. Österreichische Akademie der Wissenschaften, philosophisch-historische Klasse, Sitzungsberichte, 383. Band; Vienna, 1981.

Darrouzès, Jean. *Documents inédits d'ecclésiologie byzantine*. Archives de l'Orient chrétien 11. Paris: Institut Français des Études Byzantines, 1970.

——. *Les regestes des actes du patriarcat de Constantinople*. Vol. 1: *Les actes des patriarches*. Fasc. 5: *Les Regestes de 1310 à 1376*. Paris: Institut Français des Études Byzantines, 1977.

Denzinger, Heinrich and Adolf Schfnmetzer. *Enchiridion symbolorum definitionum et declarationum de rebus fidei et morum*. 32nd edition. Rome, 1965.

Failler, Albert. "Le séjour d'Athanase d'Alexandrie à Constantinople." REB 35 (1977) 43-71.

Galatariotou, Catia. "Byzantine Women's Monastic Communities. The Evidence of the Typika." JÖB 38 (1988) 263-290.

Garzya, Antonio. "Preghiere di un vescovo bizantino del XIII secolo." In *Convivium Dominicum, Studi sull'Eucarestia nei padri della Chiesa antica e miscellanea patristica*, pp. 331-336. Catania: Centro di Studi sull'Antico Cristianesimo, 1959.

Gouillard, Jean. "Après le schisme Arsénite. La correspondance inédite du Pseudo-Jean Chilas." *Académie roumaine, Bulletin de la section historique* 25 (1944) 194-211.

——. "Théolepte de Philadelphie." *Dictionnaire de théologie catholique* 15 (1943) 339-341.

Gregoras, Nikephoros. *Nicephori Gregorae Byzantina Historia*. Ed. by Ludovicus Schopen and Immanuel Bekker. 3 vols. Bonn, 1829-1845.

——. *Nicephori Gregorae Epistulae*. Ed. by Pietro A.M. Leone. 2 vols. Matino, 1982-1983.

——. *Nikephoras Gregoras, Rhomäische Geschichte*. Trans. by Jan Louis van Dieten. Bibliothek der griechischen Literatur 24. Stuttgart: A. Hiersemann, 1988.

Gregorios, Patriarch of Constantinople (Gregorios of Cyprus). Γρηγορίου τοῦ Κυπρίου οἰκουμενικοῦ πατριάρχου. Ἐπιστολαὶ καὶ Μῦθοι. Ed. by Sophronios Eustratiades. Alexandria, 1910.

Hausherr, Irénée. *Noms du Christ et voies d'oraison*. Orientalia Christiana Analecta 157. Rome, 1960.

Hero, Angela Constantinides. "Irene-Eulogia Choumnaina Palaiologina, Abbess of the Convent of Philanthropos Soter in Constantinople." *Byzantinische Forschungen* 9 (1985) 119-147.

——. "The Unpublished Letters of Theoleptos, Metropolitan of Philadelphia (1283-1322)." *Journal of Modern Hellenism* 3 (1986) 1-31; 4 (1987) 1-17.

Holl, Karl. *Enthusiasmus und Bussgewalt im griechischen Mönchtum*. Leipzig, 1896.

Ioannes Climacus. *John Climacus, The Ladder of Divine Ascent*. Trans. by Colm Luibheid and Norman Russell. New York: Paulist Press, 1982.

Janin, Raymond. *Les églises et les monastères des grands centres byzantins*. Géographie ecclésiastique de l'Empire byzantin, t. 2. Paris: Institut Français des Études Byzantines, 1975.

——. *Le siège de Constantinople et le patriarcat oecuménique. Les églises et les monastères*. 2nd ed. Géographie ecclésiastique de l'Empire byzantin, t. 3. Paris: Institut Français des Études Byzantines, 1969.

——. "Les monastères du Christ Philanthrope à Constantinople." REB 4 (1946) 135-162.

Kantakouzenos, Ioannes. *Ioannis Cantacuzeni eximperatoris Historiarum libri IV*. Ed. by Ludovicus Schopen. 3 vols. Bonn, 1828-1832.

——. *Johannes Kantakouzenos, Geschichte*. Trans. by Georgios Fatouros and

T. Krischer. Bibliothek der griechischen Literatur 17. Stuttgart: A. Hiersemann, 1982

Kirchmeyer, Jean. "Hésychie de Batos." DS 7 (1969) 408-410.

Kourouses, Stauros. *Μανουὴλ Γαβαλᾶς, εἶτα Ματθαῖος Μητροπολίτης Ἐφέσου (1271/2-1355/60)*. Athens: Epistemonike Hetaireia, 1972.

Lampe, G.W.H. *A Patristic Greek Lexicon*. Oxford: Clarendon Press, 1961.

Laurent, Vitalien. *Les regestes des actes du patriarcat de Constantinople*. Vol. 1: *Les actes des patriarches*. Fasc. 4: *Les regestes de 1208 à 1309*. Paris: Socii Assumptionistae Chalcedonenses, 1971.

—— and Jean Darrouzès. *Dossier grec de l'Union de Lyon (1273-1277)*. Archives de l'Orient chrétien 16. Paris: Institut Français des Études Byzantines, 1976.

——. "Les crises religieuses à Byzance. Le schisme anti-arsénite du métropolite de Philadelphie Théolepte († c. 1324)." REB 18 (1960) 45-54.

——. "La direction spirituelle à Byzance. La correspondance d'Irène-Eulogie Choumnaina Paléologine avec son second directeur." REB 14 (1956) 49-86.

——. "L'excommunication du patriarche Joseph Ier par son prédécesseur Arsène." BZ 30 (1929-1930) 489-496.

——. "Les grandes crises religieuses à Byzance: La fin du schisme arsénite." *Académie roumaine, Bulletin de la section historique* 26 (1945) 225-313.

——. "Une princesse byzantine au cloître, Irène Eulogie Choumnos Paléologine, fondatrice du couvent de femmes Philanthropos Soter." EO 29 (1930) 29-60.

——. "La question des Arsénites." *Ἑλληνικά* 3 (1930) 463-470.

——. "Les signataires du second synode des Blakhernes (été 1285)." EO 26 (1927) 129-149.

——. "Theoleptus." *Lexikon für Theologie und Kirche*. 2nd ed. 10:58. Freiburg: Herder, 1957-1965.

Leclercq, Jean. *The Love of Learning and the Desire for God. A Study of Monastic Culture*. 3rd ed. New York: Fordham University Press, 1985.

Menaion. *The Festal Menaion*. Trans. by Mother Mary and Kallistos Ware. London: Faber and Faber, 1969.

Meyendorff, John. *Introduction à l'étude de Grégoire Palamas*. Patristica sorbonensia 3. Paris: Éditions du Seuil, 1959.

Meyer, Ph. "Bruchstücke zweier τυπικὰ κτητορικά." BZ 4 (1895) 45-58.

Moncada, Francisco de. *Francisco de Moncada, Expedición de los Catalanes y Aragoneses contra Turcos y Griegos*. Ed. by Samuel Gili y Gaya. Clasicos castellanos 54. Madrid: Ediciones de "La Lectura," 1924.

——. *The Catalan Chronicle of Francisco de Moncada*. Trans. by F. Hermandez and J.M. Sharp. El Paso: Texas Western Press, 1975.

Moschonas, Th.D. "La correspondance de Théolepte de Philadelphie avec Irène Paléologue." *Ἀνάλεκτα* 7 (1958) 32-36 and 13 plates.

Oikonomides, Nicolas. *Hommes d'affaires grecs et latins à Constantinople*

(XIIIe-XVe siècles). Montreal: Institut des études médiévales Albert le Grand, 1979.

Pachymeres, Georgios. *Georgii Pachymeris de Michaele et Andronico Paleologis libri tredecim*. Ed. by Immanuel Bekker. 2 vols. Bonn, 1835.

——. *Georges Pachymérès, Relations historiques*. Ed. and trans. by Albert Failler. 2 vols. CFHB 24.1-2. Paris: Belles Lettres, 1984.

Palamas, Gregorios. *Grégoire Palamas. Défense des saints hésychastes. Introduction, texte critique, traduction et notes*. Ed. and trans. by John Meyendorff. Spicilegium sacrum lovaniense. Études et documents, fascs. 30-31. Louvain: Spicilegium sacrum lovaniense, 1959; repr. with revisions, 1973.

——. *Saint Gregory Palamas. The One Hundred and Fifty Chapters*. Ed. and trans. by Robert Edward Sinkewicz. Toronto: Pontifical Institute of Mediaeval Studies, 1988.

Papadakis, Aristeides. *Crisis in Byzantium. The 'Filioque' Controversy in the Patriarchate of Gregory II of Cyprus (1283-1289)*. New York: Fordham University Press, 1983.

Pargoire, Jules. "Les monastères doubles chez les Byzantins." EO 9 (1906) 21-25.

Philokalia. *Φιλοκαλία τῶν ἱερῶν νηπτικῶν*. 5 vols. Athens: Ekdotikos oikos Aster, 1957-1963.

Previale, L. "Due monodie inedite di Matteo di Efeso." BZ 41 (1941) 4-39.

Rigo, Antonio. "Le formule per la preghiera di Gesù nell' Esicasmo athonita." *Cristianesimo nella storia* 6 (1985) 1-18.

——. "Nota sulla dottrina ascetico-spirituale de Teoleptos Metropolita de Filadelfia (1250/51-1322)." RSBN 24 (1987) 165-200.

Romano, Roberto. "Un Canone inedito de Teolepto di Filadelfia sulla fine del mondo." *Bolletino della Badia Greca di Grottaferrata* 31 (1977) 15-29.

Salaville, Sévérien. "Deux documents inédits sur les dissensions religieuses byzantines entre 1275 et 1310." REB 5 (1947) 116-136.

——. "Un directeur spirituel à Byzance au debut du XIVe siècle: Théolepte de Philadelphie. Homélie sur Noël et la vie religieuse." In *Mélanges Joseph de Ghellinck*, 2:877-887. Museum lessianum. Section historique 14. Gembloux, 1951.

——. "Formes ou méthodes de prière d'après un Byzantin du XIVe siècle." EO 39 (1940) 1-25.

——. "Une lettre et un discours inédits de Théolepte de Philadelphie." REB 5 (1947) 101-115.

——. "La vie monastique grecque au debut du XIVe siècle d'après un discours inédit de Théolepte de Philadelphie,' REB 2 (1944) 119-125.

Ševčenko, Ihor. "The Palaeologan Renaissance." In *Renaissances before the Renaissance: Cultural Revivals of Late Antiquity and the Middle Ages*. Ed. by W. Treadgold. pp. 144-223. Stanford, CA: Stanford University Press, 1984.

——. "Le sens et la date du traité 'Anepigraphos' de Nicéphore Choumnos." *Académie royale de Belgique. Bulletin de la classe des lettres et des sciences morales et politiques*, 5ème serie, t. 35 (1949) 472-488.

——. "Society and Intellectual Life in the Fourteenth Century." *Actes du XIVᵉ Congrès international des études byzantines, Bucarest 1971*, 1:69-92. Bucharest, 1974.

Sinkewicz, Robert Edward. "Church and Society in Asia Minor in the Late 13th Century: the Case of Theoleptos of Philadelpheia." In *Conversion and Continuity: Indigenous Christian Communities in Islamic Lands, Eighth to the Eighteenth Centuries*, ed. by Michael Gervers and Ramzi Jibran Bikhazi, pp. 355-364. Toronto: Pontifical Institute of Mediaeval Studies, 1990.

——. "A Critical Edition of the Anti-Arsenite Discourses of Theoleptos of Philadelpheia." *Mediaeval Studies* 50 (1988) 46-95.

——. "An Early Byzantine Commentary on the Jesus Prayer: Introduction and Edition." *Mediaeval Studies* 49 (1987) 208-220.

——. "St. Gregory Palamas and the Doctrine of God's Image in Man According to the Capita 150." *Θεολογία* 57 (1986) 857-881.

Solignac, Aimé. "Philothée Kokkinos." DS 12 (1984) 1389-1392.

Stiernon, D. "Nicéphore l'Hésychaste." DS 11 (1982) 198-203.

Sykoutres, J. "Περὶ τοῦ σχίσματος τῶν Ἀρσενιατῶν." *Ἑλληνικά* 2 (1929) 257-332; 3 (1930) 15-44; 5 (1932) 107-126.

Symeon (Pseudo). *La méthode d'oraison hésychaste*. Ed. and trans. by Irénée Hausherr. Orientalia Christiana 9.2, no. 36. Rome: Pont. Institutum Orientalium Studiorum, 1927.

Theoktistos the Studite. *Faith Healing in Late Byzantium. The Posthumous Miracles of the Patriarch Athanasios I of Constantinople by Theoktistos the Studite*. Ed. and trans. by Alice-Mary Maffry Talbot. The Archbishop Iakovos Library of Ecclesiastical and Historical Sources 8. Brookline, MA: Hellenic College Press, 1983.

Trapp, Erich, Rainer Walther, and Hans-Veit Beyer. *Prosopographisches Lexikon der Palaiologenzeit*. Vienna: Verlag der Österreichischer Akademie der Wissenschaft, 1976-.

Triodion. *The Lenten Triodion*. Trans. by Mother Mary and Kallistos Ware. London: Faber and Faber, 1977.

Trone, Robert H. "A Constantinopolitan Double Monastery of the Fourteenth Century: the Philanthropic Saviour." *Byzantine Studies/Études Byzantines* 10 (1983) 81-87.

Velimirović, M. "The Musical Works of Theoleptos, Metropolitan of Philadelpheia." *Studies in Eastern Chant* 2 (1971) 155-165.

Verpeaux, Jean. *Nicéphore Choumnos, Homme d'état et humaniste byzantin (ca 1250/1255-1327)*. Paris: A. et J. Picard, 1959.

Ware, Kallistos Timothy. "The Jesus Prayer in St Gregory of Sinai." *Eastern Churches Review* 4 (1972) 3-22.

Index of Biblical Citations

Scriptural citations follow the Septuagint version of the Bible. References are made to the discourse number followed by the paragraph number. All references are to the *Monastic Discourses*, unless otherwise indicated. References to the *Philadelpheian Discourses* (PD) are to my edition published in *Mediaeval Studies* 50 (1988) 46-95.

OLD TESTAMENT

GENESIS

1:1-31 20.4
1:6 12.4
1:26 11.16
1:31 2.9
2:2 4.17
2:3 PD 1.4
2:7-3:24 11.13, 12.9
2:7 2.9, 20.5, 21.3, 23.12
2:15-17 2.11, 11.21
2:15 6.3, 23.29
2:16 PD 1.6, MD 6.5, 9.8
2:18 9.4
2:19 23.30
2:21 23.20
2:22 23.21
2:24 23.24, 23.25
2:25 6.8
3:1-7 20.4
3:4-6 23.28
3:6 12.1
3:7 PD 1.5
3:7, 21 11.17
3:24 2.30
4:1-16 PD 2.17, MD 7.8
4:9 7.8
12:1-3 3.2

14:13-20 PD 2.18
19 PD 2.18
22:1-19 2.33
28:10-22 2.23
28:11 2.23
28:12 2.24
37:34-36 2.41

EXODUS

4:2-5, 17 2.46
7:14-10:29 14.24
12:3 4.6
12:29-30 14.24
12:46 PD 2.8
14:15-21 14.13
14:15-29 3.1
14:15-31 2.47
14:16 2.46
14:21-22 2.48
14:22 14.19
14:26-28 14.19
14:26-29 3.7, 3.8
14:27-28 2.48
15:1 14.28
16:3 3.4
17:8-16 2.49
19:1-25 2.6

20:21 11.18
22:24 19.17
24:12-18 2.6
31:18 11.18
32:15 11.18
33:17-23 2.6
33:21-23 2.16
34:1 11.18
34:29-35 2.6

LEVITICUS

25:37 19.17

NUMBERS

9:12 PD 2.8
11:5 3.4
12 PD 2.19
14:23, 28-35 3.4
14:32-33 8.8
16 PD 2.19
16:5 1.24
20:7-13 2.46

DEUTERONOMY

6:5 1.18
8:2 PD 2.3
17:1 14.24
23:20-21 19.17
32:7 PD 1.8
32:39 10.5

1 KINGDOMS

2:6 4.23, 10.5
8:7 PD 1.8
16.14-23 2.45

2 KINGDOMS

2:11 14.10

4 KINGDOMS

19:28 10.1

2 CHRONICLES

26 PD 2.20
26:18 PD 2.20
26:19 PD 2.20

PSALMS

5:4 2.16
5:6 1.7
9:31 4.4
9:38 2.24
10:2 9.23
10:7 2.20
11:6 2.13
12:4 21.10
15:8 2.25, 23.8
16:4 10.4
16:15 PD 2.3, MD 23.2
17:10 21.5
21:7 21.6
21:26 2.49
21:28 2.49
22:19 PD 2.9
24:15 23.8
24:18 3.8, 18.8
25:8 PD 2.12
26:4 PD 2.12
26:10 13.3
29:6 5.8
33:11 14.1
33:13-14 10.1
33:15 1.5
33:20 PD 2.8
36:1-2 PD 2.19
37:10 23.8
38:4 1.27
39:10-11 2.52
41:2 20.2
44:15 23.8
44:18 EP 1.2, MD 2.49
45:2 2.25
46:8 23.33
48:15 6.2
50:19 PD 1.13, MD 1.17, 1.21

53:5 2.25
54:7 14.5
54:18 2.25
55:10 1.17, 1.24, 2.30
55:13 2.49
57:5-6 PD 1.12
57:11 14.9
62:7 PD 2.26
65:13-14 2.21
67:14 14.5, 15.3
72:27 2.26
72:28 2.25, 23.15
75:3-4 2.15
76:4 1.17, 2.49, 23.9
76:6-7 1.28
83:3-4 2.53
83:6 5.6
83:6, 8 22.1
83:8 3.17
84:8 8.6
84:9 10.4
84:13 4.24
85:11 2.20
88:3 4.1
89:17 6.9
90:7 3.6
90:9 1.7
90:9-10 2.53
90:10 1.7
90:14-15 1.9
100:2-3 2.25
100:2 2.25
100:4 2.25
101:7-8 3.17
103:15 PD 1.11
103:19-23 1.11
103:22-23 2.5
103:34 8.6, 23.8
104:2 2.21
104:3 1.19
105:2 21.1
106:16 9.24
110:10 23.34
114:6 3.9

114:7 1.5
115:7-8 3.3, 4.21
117:10 2.30, 6.6
117:24 2.32, 23.59
118:1 2.27
118:55 2.49
118:97 1.12
118:103 1.27
118:160 23.14
121:1 PD 2.1
123:7 14.5
132:1 PD 2.12, MD 9.4
138:6 4.13
140:3 2.58, 4.19, 10.3, 10.13
140:4 PD 2.11
140:5 11.7
140:10 EP 1.2
143:5 21.5
145:4 2.32

PROVERBS

3:34 3.10, 8.6
5:15 PD 1.9
9:1 8.4
9:5-6 2.26
9:8-9 9.10
13:3 10.3
13:4 6.2
16:5 8.6, 11.9
18:17 14.9
18:19 9.4, 9.7
21:23 10.3

ECCLESIASTES

4:10 9.4

CANTICLE OF CANTICLES

1:7 2.52
5:2 2.23

JOB

4:11 14.22

SIRACH

6:8-12 18.3
9:8 2.27
12:8 18.3

AMOS

4:12 2.24
8:11 PD 2.5

HABACUC

2:1 2.17
3:2 2.18
3:14 2.29
3:16 2.18

MALACHI

3:20 2.5, 21.1

ISAIAH

2:9 4.3
6:3 4.1
9:5 11.19

14:13-14 14.7
26:9 21.2
26:16 11.8
29:13 2.19, 23.35
37:29 1.6
40:3 2.20
43:26 14.9
45:4 23.11
53:5-8 23.46

JEREMIAH

9:2 7.8
9:20 4.19, 10.1
11:18 2.51
11:19 PD 2.8
15:19 PD 2.15

DANIEL

3:49-50 11.19
3:52-88 (Ode 8) 11.19
6:16-24 11.19
10:5 2.27
10:11-12 2.56

NEW TESTAMENT

MATTHEW

1:12 23.41
2:1-20 13.7
2:2-3 PD 1.10
2:13-15 13.10
2:20 13.11
3:13-17 23.51
3:17 23.51
4:1-11 11.20
4:4 PD 2.3
5:4 10.7
5:6 2.26
5:8 2.24, 8.4, 23.57
5:14, 16 5.6
5:16 11.20, 13.4, 13.8
5:17 PD 1.9

5:23-24 7.11
6:1 4.23
6:3 3.11
6:4, 6 14.28
6:14-21 11.0
6:23 4.3
6:33 2.17
7:7-8 23.2, 23.58
7:8 18.6
7:13-14 1.7
7:16 15.8
7:21 23.35
7:24-27 8.1
7:24-25 8.7
7:26-27 8.8
8:11 4.17
8:12 PD 2.14, MD 1.7

9:2 19.1
10:38 14.14
10:40 PD 1.8
11:28 4.8, 20.7
11:29 4.8, 8.6, 21.7
11:30 4.8
12:22-30 2.3
12:31-32 2.3
13:22 19.13
13:25 11.16
13:30 22.5
13:42 PD 2.14
13:44 2.29
13:46 1.4, 2.10
15:8 23.35
15:18 2.19
16:24 3.5
16:24 14.14
17:1-9 5
17:5 1.17
17:21 11.16
18:3 13.11
18:20 1.23
19:14 13.11
19:28 20.10
21:12 11.12
21:28-31 8.8
21:33-41 23.36
22:30 4.18
23:5 4.23
24:12 15.6
25:1-13 EP 1.3, MD 17.6
25:12 17.6
25:41 9.23
26:41 2.24, 6.3
27:35 PD 2.9
27:38, 44 PD 2.8
27:59 18.1
27:59-60 18.7
28:19 PD 1.7, MD 22.4

MARK

1:9-11 23.51
1:10-11 23.51

1:12-13 11.20
1:35 2.50
3:20-30 1.3
4:19 19.13
7:6 2.19
8:34 3.5, 14.14
9:29 11.16
9:35 14.4
11:15 11.12
12:30 1.18
14:38 2.24, 6.3
15:13 PD 2.8
15:24 PD 2.9
15:27 PD 2.8
15:43–16.8 18
15:43-45 18.6
15:43-46 18.1
15:43 18.2

LUKE

2:2-3 13.5
2:7 13.5, 13.7
2:8-12 13.8
3:21-22 23.51
4:1-13 11.20
4:4 PD 2.3
6:12 2.50
6:30 1.1
6:47-49 8.1
6:47-48 8.7
6:49 8.8
9:23 3.5, 14.14
9:28-36 5
10:25-37 15.2
11:10 18.6
11:14-23 1.3
11:52 2.6, 9.21
12:49 2.30, 15.6
13:3 1.7
13:10-17 4
13:10 4.7
13:12 4.5
13:13 4.5
13:14 4.9, 4.16

13:29 4.17
14:15-24 3.2
14:33 8.3
15:7 17.4
15:10 17.4
15:11-16 16.1
15:13-16 6.2
15:13 14.19
17:10 14.12
18:1-8 2.50
18:2-6 1.25
18:10-14 14.12
19:45 11.12
22:44 2.50
23:34 PD 2.9
23:52 18.6
23:53 18.1, 18.7
24:13-35 23.38

JOHN

1:9 5.4
1:18 23.54
2:14-16 11.12
4:5-42 20.T
4:6 20.1, 20.4, 20.10
4:7, 29-30, 39 20.1
4:7 20.2
4:10 20.5
4:13-14 20.1
4:14 20.5
4:25-26 20.5
4:28-30, 39-42 20.5
4:28 20.6
4:29-30 20.6
4:34 5.8
4:39-40 20.2
5:1-15 19.0
5:1 19.2, 19.3
5:2-4 19.4
5:4 19.11
5:5 19.7
5:7 19.1, 19.13
5:8 19.19
5:13 4.23

5:14 4.2
6:53-54, 56 PD 2.6
8:12 21.7
8:56 2.33
9:1-38 21
9:6-7 21.3
9:7 21.7
10:15 23.54
10:16 15.8
13:35 15.6
14:21 5.8, 6.4, 23.43
14:21, 23 8.2
15:5-6 2.30
15:5 2.30, 3.10, 4.2, 8.4
15:7 23.40
15:10 23.43
16:7 22.3
16:33 3.6, 9.24
17:3 2.44, 6.2, 23.16
17:10, 22 5.9
17:20 PD 1.7
19:12-15 PD 2.9
19:23 PD 2.10
19:23-24 15.3
19:24 PD 2.9
19:34 PD 2.8
19:36 PD 2.8
19:40 18.9
20:22-23 2.4

ACTS

1:10 22.2
2:1-4 22.3
2:3 22.2, 22.6
6:4 2.50
12:4 2.50
12:5 2.54

ROMANS

1:25 14.7
1:28 2.4, 2.6
6:4-6 3.7
6:6 8.2

8:2 2.5, 23.19
8:6-7 1.13
8:12-13 9.22
8:13 23.21
8:14 2.7, 2.28, 14.14, 23.52
8:17 2.26, 3.7, 23.46
9:3 15.6
9:31 4.15
11:33 20.2
11:36 2.55
12:1 2.9, 4.22, 6.9
12:2 PD 1.11, MD 5.5
12:17 21.4
13:10 PD 2.2
14:4 PD 2.24

1 CORINTHIANS

1:12-13 PD 2.9
1:20 13.9
3:11 8.4
3:16 8.2, 11.12
6:15 9.3, 18.5
6:17 2.30, 23.25
7:31 5.5, 10.12
8:1 2.42, 8.5, 23.13
9:27 4.18
12:27 9.3, 18.5
13:5 6.4
13:5, 7 14.3
13:8 13.9
13:12 1.24
13:15 9.27
14:15 23.33
15:20 12.1
15:56 23.46

2 CORINTHIANS

3:3 2.5
3:6 11.2
4:17 20.9
6:14-15 11.7
6:16 11.12, 11.12
8:9 4.4, 23.46

GALATIANS

1:4 5.5
2:2 1.19
2:19 3.7, 14.20
2:20 13.12, 14.14, 23.23, 23.25
3:27 1.4, 8.2
4:19 2.26
5:16 1.26, 4.19, 11.19, 23.19, 23.31
5:22 1.3, 14.26
5:23 2.29, 2.30
5:24 3.6, 4.24
6:14 23.23

EPHESIANS

1:21 2.9
2:14 22.3
4:7 1.1
4:13 7.12, 14.1
4:14 15.8
4:15 9.3
4:22 8.2, 13.11
4:24 5.6
5:30 18.5
5:31 23.24
6:10-13 3.3
6:11, 13 9.26
6:12 2.10
6:15 21.7
6:17 2.34

PHILIPPIANS

2:8 8.4
3:20 2.10, 22.1
4:7 3.16

COLOSSIANS

1:18 9.3
2:12-13 3.7
3:2 4.21, 6.8, 22.1
3:3 2.10, 13.12
3:5 4.22
3:9 8.2
4:2 2.50

1 Thessalonians

4:17 14.7
5:5 2.44
5:11 9.4
5:15 21.4

2 Thessalonians

3:10 6.1

1 Timothy

2:5 22.3
2:6 16.4

2 Timothy

2:12 1.33
2:19 1.24
3:6 PD 1.5

Hebrews

2:14 3.11
3:17 3.4
6:6 PD 2.8
6:20 22.2
7:27 4.6

10:10, 14 4.6
11:10 8.4

James

1:17 14.1
3:3 1.6
3:6, 8 10.1
3:9-10 10.2
4:6 3.10
4:6 8.6
4:6 23.44
5:13 2.30

1 Peter

1:19 15.8
3:9 21.4
3:18 23.46
5:5 8.6

2 Peter

1:4 23.21, 23.45
3:10 PD 2.14

1 John

3:22 23.42
3:24 23.42

Index of References to Classical,
Patristic and Byzantine Texts

All references are to the *Monastic Discourses*, unless otherwise indicated. References to the *Philadelpheian Discourses* (PD) are to my edition published in *Mediaeval Studies* 50 (1988) 46-95. References are made to the discourse number followed by the paragraph number.

APOPHTHEGMATA PATRUM
Macarius 3 (456) (PG 65:264B): 1.1
Poimen 130 (704) (PG 65:353): 8.1

ATHANASIUS
De virginitate 7 (PG 28:260): 11.6

BASIL OF CAESAREA
Ad adolescentes 5 (ed. Boulenger 46.8-47.13): 5.2

JOHN CHRYSOSTOM
Homilia 15 in Genesim (PG 53:124): 11.2
Homilia in Matthaeum 56.1 (PG 58:550): 5.3

PSEUDO-CHRYSOSTOM
Homilia in Samaritanam (PG 59:537): 20.4
Homilia de jejunio (PG 62:757): 11.9

JOHN DAMASCENE
Homilia in Transfigurationem 9 (PG 96:560CD): 5.3

DOROTHEUS OF GAZA
Instructions 6.70 (SC 92:270-272): 14.15
ibid. 7.89-90 (SC 92:306-319): 7.6

EUTHYMIOS ZIGABENOS
Commentarius in Lucam 13 (PG 129:1001C): 4.5
ibid. (PG 129:100CD): 4.3

EVAGRIUS PONTICUS
De oratione 3 (PG 79:1165): 1.17
Praktikos 1 (SC 171:498-499): 2.35
ibid. 15-33 (SC 171:536-577): 1.8
Rerum monachalium rationes 11 (PG 40:1264C): 1.22

GEORGIOS PACHYMERES
History 4.28: PD 1.3

GREGORIOS PALAMAS
Capita 150, c. 55: 11.15
ibid. cc. 34-35: 14.1

GREGORY NAZIANZEN
Oratio 45.1 (PG 36:624A): 2.17

GREGORY OF NYSSA
Contra Eunomium 2:84-95 (Jaeger 1:251-254): 3.2
Vita Moysi 2.217 (SC 1:254-256): 4
De perfectione christiana (PG 46:272AB): 23.13

PSEUDO-GREGORY OF NYSSA
Ad imaginem dei et ad similitudinem (PG 44:1328B): 11.18

HESIOD
Opera et dies 287-291: 5.2

HESYCHIOS OF BATOS
On Vigilance and Virtue 51 (*Philokalia* 1:149): 2.24
ibid. 169 (*Philokalia* 1:167): 17.5
ibid. 176 (*Philokalia* 1:169): 2.30

HOROLOGION
Mikron Apodeipnon: 2.24

IOANNES CLIMACUS
Scala paradisi 4 (PG 88:677-728): 9.12
ibid. 25.14 (PG 88:991): 3.9

IOANNES CHEILAS
Against the Arsenites 1.10 (357.25-28): PD 2.10
ibid. 1.11 (358.17-29): PD 1.3
ibid. 2.8 (364-365): PD 2.22
ibid. 3.2 (370.19-21): PD 2.9
ibid. 3.3 (370-371): PD 2.20
ibid. 4.1 (377.22-24): PD 1.10
ibid. 5.11 (398.16-17): PD 1.3

KALLISTOS
Letter to Manouel Disypatos 25.16-27 (ed. Sykoutres): PD 2.22

PSEUDO-MACARIUS
Homilia 43.4 (ed. Dörries-Klostermann 287): 17.3

MAXIMUS CONFESSOR
De caritate 2.62 (PG 90:1004C): 1.16

MENAION
December 24: Compline (*Festal Menaion,* 264, 266): 13.7, 13.5
December 25: Matins (*Festal Menaion,* 276): 13.6
December 26: Matins (*Festal Menaion,* 292): 13.3

METHODIOS
De schismate vitando 13 (PG 140:797C): PD 1.3
ibid. 14 (PG 140:797AB): PD 2.11

NILUS OF ANCYRA
De monastica exercitatione 73 (PG 79:805D): 19.17
Epistula 1:223 (PG 79:164D): 11.18

PENTECOSTARION
Easter 3rd Sunday: Synaxarion: 18 (title)
Easter 4th Sunday: Vespers: 19.13
Easter 5th Sunday: Vespers: 20.4

PSEUDO-SYMEON
Methodos (ed. Hausherr 164-165): 1.16

THEOPHYLAKTOS OF BULGARIA
Enarratio in Lucam 13 (PG 123:917C): 4.4

TRIODION
Tyrophagia Sunday: First Vespers Sticheron (*The Lenten Triodion* 168): 11.17
Monday, First Week of Lent: Matins 8th Ode (*The Lenten Triodion* 193): 11.20
Monday, First Week of Lent: Compline 9th Ode (*The Lenten Triodion* 208): 11.20
Tuesday, First Week of Lent: Matins 2nd Ode (*The Lenten Triodion* 213): 11.19
Tuesday, First Week of Lent: Matins 9th Ode (*The Lenten Triodion* 215): 11.18, 11.21
Monday in Holy Week: Matins Exaposteilarion (*The Lenten Triodion* 514): 15.4 Holy
Friday: Vespers (*The Lenten Triodion* 616, 622): 18.2

Index of Images of Daily Life

AGRICULTURE

PD 1.11   darnel mixed in with wheat
MD 1.15   bees sheltered in a beehive
PD 2.03   congealing cheese
MD 1.03   tall tree with roots, branches, fruit
MD 2.38   adverse weather and winter harvest
MD 6.06   farmer removing rocks from cornfield
MD 9.01   farmer plants variety of vines in one spot
MD 15.06   abundance of water causes seeds to rot
MD 22.04   plough, seed, sickle, granary

BIOLOGY

MD 1.20   pupil of the eye
MD 1.21   word uttered by tongue
MD 1.25   variety of foods rouses desire to eat
MD 1.27   food gives pleasure to taste when chewed by teeth

DAILY LIFE

PD 2.06   parents send children to school to learn to read and write
PD 1.09   wipe tablet clean so your teacher can write exercise for you
MD 1.13   footprints in the snow
MD 1.28   attention to eyes when talking to someone
MD 2.12   householder and a thief
MD 2.18   midwife assists in birthing
MD 2.45   man walking at night fears obstacles, getting lost, mugged
MD 5.02   travel on level ground on steep terrain
MD 6.03   vegetable garden or stand of fruit pilfered by passers-by
MD 7.01   man walking at night cannot see faces of passers-by
MD 14.01   hungry person looks for food
MD 14.06   treasure buried in ground and covered with garbage

MERCHANTS

PD 2.26   merchants and local fairs
MD 7.04   shopkeepers mix faulty goods in with quality merchandise

Natural Phenomena

MD 2.06   opposites in nature hot and cold
MD 2.21   incense prepared from many fragrant substances
MD 2.22   incense gives fragrance only when thrown on coals
MD 2.55   compass point stuck in centre describes circle
MD 5.07   wax melts in fire producing fuel and more light
MD 14.05   a bird with two wings
MD 14.27   leaf that drops off a tree in winter time
MD 15.07   candle wax burned in fire produces light
MD 23.49   air in absence of physical sun remains devoid of light
MD 2.14   crawling ants collecting things

Nautical

MD 1.12   wind stirs up waves of sea
MD 17.03   sailor stays close to harbours lest squalls arise
MD 17.04   sailor holds oars, cuts through water, boat moves forward
MD 17.05   helmsman falls asleep, squall comes, boat sinks, he drowns
MD 21.01   fisherman goes to sea, casts line to deep water, catches fish

Society

MD 1.22   conduct before earthly emperor
MD 17.04   offspring's social advancement honours family
MD 17.05   condemned man moved from prison to prison

Trades

MD 6.01   artisan involved in work has its reward as his goal
MD 8.01   process for building a house
MD 23.35   skilled craftsman uses tools of trade to produce practical works

Usury

MD 14.27   borrowing money from a rich man
MD 16.01   when rich become poor they resort to money-lenders

General Index to the Writings
of Theoleptos of Philadelpheia

The following is a general index to the text of the *Monastic Discourses*, the *Philadelpheian Discourses* and the *Letters* (including those not yet published). References are made to the discourse or letter number followed by the paragraph number. EP 1 is the introductory letter to the *Monastic Discourses*; EP 2 and 3 are the letters published by A. Hero. The reader can obtain the references for the two letters published by A. Hero by numbering the paragraphs in that edition. In order to render the index more useful to the reader, I have in some cases resorted to assembling a variety of references under a concept head-word (e.g., agriculture, light).

Aaron PD **2**.19, 20

Abel MD **7**.8; PD **2**.17

Abiram PD **2**.19

Abraham MD **2**.33; **3**.2, 3; PD **2**.18; EP **2**.20

abstinence (ἀποχή) MD **3**.15; **11**.2, 3, 6; **12**.3; **19**.5, 11; PD **2**.8; EP **2**.1

acedia (ἀκηδία) MD **1**.28, 29; **19**.10

action, activity (ἐνέργεια) MD **2**.2, 3, 9, 55; **3**.6, 12, 15; **4**.18; **5**.6; **9**.1, 6; **12**.5; **14**.21; **16**.4; **18**.9; **19**.6, 14, 15; **22**.6; **23**.4, 20, 21, 27, 59

Adam (Ἀδάμ, προπάτωρ) MD **6**.8; **9**.8; **11**.13, 21; **12**.1, 9; **23**.12, 19, 20, 22, 23, 25, 30; PD **1**.4, 7; EP **2**.5

adhere (προσκολλῶμαι) MD **1**.16, 20; **2**.25; **3**.18; **13**.3; **15**.3; **23**.8, 15, 24, 25; PD **2**.4, 5; EP **2**.19

adultery (μοιχεία) MD **19**.6, 8, 14; PD **2**.21

affliction (θλῖψις) MD **1**.1, 9, 12; **2**.11, 18, 19, 21, 26, 30, 57; **3**.12; **5**.2, 3; **7**.11; **8**.8; **11**.8, 14; **14**.2; **15**.7; EP **1**.3; **2**.5, 6, 12, 15; **3**.2, 3, 4, 5, 8, 10; **5**.2, 3, 4

Agathonike MD **23**.T; EP **2**.12, 22; **3**.1, 2, 3, 11, 12, 13

agriculture (ἀγρός, ἀμπελών, ἄροτρον, ἄσπαρτος, βότρυς, γεώργια, ζυγός, ζιζάνια, δρέπανον, ἔλαιον, θερίζω, καρπός, κηρός, κηρίον, κλάδος, κλῆμα, λάχανα, μύρμηκες, ὄσπριον, σιτίον, σῖτος, σπείρω, σπέρμα, στάχυς, συκῆς, φυτεία) MD **1**.3; **2**.9, 14, 29, 30, 37, 38; **3**.2; **4**.24; **5**.3, 6, 7, 8; **6**.2, 3, 5, 6; **7**.4; **8**.8; **9**.1, 9; **10**.11; **11**.1, 3, 7, 8, 12, 15, 16, 17, 21; **12**.3, 4, 9; **13**.4; **14**.1, 22; **15**.5, 7, 8; **17**.6; **21**.5, 8; **22**.4, 5, 6; **23**.26, 34, 44, 47, 48; PD **1**.5, 10, 11; **2**.3, 4, 5, 8, 7, 12, 15, 19; EP **1**.3; **2**.11, 12, 17; **3**.3, 5, 7, 9; **4**.4

Amalek MD **2**.49

Ammon MD **8**.8

angel (ἄγγελος) MD **2**.9, 13, 23, 33, 56, 58; **4**.18; **10**.7; **11**.19; **17**.4; **19**.4, 11; **23**.48; PD **2**.27; EP **1**.T; **2**.T

anger (θυμός, ὀργή) MD **1**.8; **2**.38, 42; **6**.10; **7**.2, 6, 8; **8**.8; **11**.9, 15, 19;

16.2, 4; **19**.7, 8, 9, 10; **20**.6, 7; **21**.4, 9; **23**.24; PD **1**.6; EP **2**.5, 9, 10, 12, 14; **3**.7, 8, 9; **4**.4

anxiety, care (μέριμνα) MD **2**.17, 27, 41; **4**.16; **6**.1; **10**.12; **17**.5, 6; **19**.3, 13, 14, 15; EP **3**.11

Apostle, apostolic (ἀπόστολος) MD **2**.50; **3**.6; **4**.19; **6**.1; **8**.4; **9**.22; **11**.2; **13**.12; **15**.6; **20**.5, 10; **21**.7; **22**.2, 3, 4, 6; **23**.19, 24, 33; PD **1**.1, 8, 11; EP **2**.4, 14, 19, 25 **3**.6, 7, 8; **5**.2

arrogance, pride (ὑπερηφανία) MD **2**.30, 34, 36, 38, 42, 43; **3**.6, 7, 8, 10, 11; **6**.10; **8**.6; **11**.9, 10; **14**.5, 9, 10, 13, 17, 19, 20, 21, 27, 28; **18**.7; **19**.10; **21**.6; **23**.3; PD **1**.12; **2**.15, 18; EP **2**.16; **4**.5; (ὑψηλοφροσύνη) MD **14**.21; **18**.7; (ὑψηλοκάρδιος) MD **8**.6; **11**.9; **14**.9

Arsenios EP **2**.6

artisan, *see* skill

Ascension (ἀνάληψις) MD **22**.2

asceticism, spiritual discipline (ἄσκησις) MD **1**.1, 2, 10, 29; **2**.23, 29, 38; **3**.1, 9; **5**.2; **6**.9; **7**.9; **8**.4, 6; **11**.3, 5, 9; **13**.10; **23**.22; EP **2**.6, 11, 24

assembly (σύναξις) MD **1**.22; **4**.11; **9**.7, 9, 12, 15; **11**.5; **17**.6; PD **1**.5; **2**.1, 3, 4, 6, 9, 15, 27

association, converse (ὁμιλία) MD **1**.7, 10, 12; **4**.23; **7**.2; **11**.19; **13**.1, 3; **20**.4, 8; **23**.32; PD **1**.5; EP **3**.7

attendance at church (σχολή) MD **18**.7; **19**.13; **20**.9; **21**.8; PD **1**.5; **2**.T, 2, 3, 4, 5, 6, 15, 20, 21, 26

attention (προσοχή) MD **1**.18; **2**.8, 11; **3**.12; **6**.4; **9**.14; **19**.1; **23**.33; PD **2**.3; EP **3**.9

attitude, way of thinking (φρόνημα) MD **1**.2, 6, 13; **2**.14, 32, 42, 46, 52, 53; **3**.2, 7, 10, 11, 14; **4**.19, 20; **5**.3, 5; **8**.3, 8; **9**.22; **11**.9; **12**.8; **13**.3, 12; **14**.10, 13, 14, 20, 21, 23; **18**.7, 8; **19**.12, 18; **21**.4, 6; **22**.1, 2, 5; **23**.21,

22, 24, 31, 37; PD **1**.3, 5, 6; **2**.2, 3, 4, 8, 9, 10, 12, 15, 18, 23; EP **2**.5, 6, 16, 23; **3**.3, 7, 9

avarice (φιλαργυρία) MD **3**.18; **19**.10; PD **1**.3; (φιλοχρηματία) MD **19**.17

baptism (βάπτισμα) MD **1**.4, 5; **4**.6; **8**.2; **19**.12; **21**.5; **22**.5; **23**.51, 53, 56, 59; PD **1**.5; **2**.9

Basil EP **5**.4

Beelzebub MD **2**.3

Beliar MD **9**.26; **11**.7

Bethlehem MD **13**.7

bishop (ἀρχιερεύς) PD **1**.T, 7, 8; **2**.9, 10; (ἱεράρχης) MD **2**.50

bitterness, remembrance of injuries (μνησικακία) MD **11**.7, 15; **19**.6; **20**.6, 7; PD **1**.2, 3; EP **3**.7, 8, 9

blessing (εὐλογία) MD **3**.12; **9**.9; **11**.19, 20; **13**.12; **23**.49; PD **2**.3, 14, 18; EP **1**.3; **5**.1

blind (τυφλός) MD **2**.35; **7**.1; **21**.T, 1, 3, 6, 7, 8, 9,

blood (αἷμα) MD **7**.8; **14**.9; **15**.8; **21**.5; **23**.47; PD **1**.3, 5, 7; **2**.6, 7, 8, 18; EP **2**.2

body, bodily (σῶμα) MD **1**.1, 3, 8, 10, 11, 12, 14, 20, 22, 29, 30, 31; **2**.8, 23, 27, 29, 30, 35, 37, 38, 40; **3**.4, 5, 11, 15; **4**.2, 3, 4, 5, 7, 8, 10, 11, 14, 15, 17, 18, 19, 20, 21, 22; **5**.2, 3, 4, 6; **6**.5, 9; **7**.6, 10, 11; **8**.3, 4, 5; **9**.3, 6, 12, 24; **10**.1, 6; **11**.2, 3, 5, 12, 18, 20; **12**.3, 5; **13**.1, 2, 3, 4; **14**.7, 25, 27, 28; **15**.2, 7; **16**.3, 4, 5; **17**.2, 4; **18**.1, 2, 5, 6, 7, 8, 9, 10; **19**.7, 9; **21**.1, 3; **23**.3, 4, 5, 6, 8, 21, 23, 24, 32, 33, 34, 41, 47, 50; PD **1**.3, 5, 6; **2**.3, 4, 5, 7, 8, 10, 14, 18, 27; EP **1**.2, 3; **2**.2, 14, 19, 23, 25; **3**.4, 5, 6, 7; **5**.3

bondage (δεσμεύω) MD **1**.11; **2**.19, 50, 54; **3**.2, 3, 5; **4**.5, 6, 21; **6**.4; **7**.1,

10; **10**.1, 3; **12**.9; **14**.2, 5; **17**.4; **18**.9;
EP 2.15; **3**.8

book, *see* reading

bread (ἄρτος) **PD 2**.7

bridegroom, bridal chamber (νύμφιος, νυμφών) **MD 1**.1, 2, 23; **11**.19; **15**.4, 15; **17**.6; **23**.50; **EP 1**.1, 3

brother (ἀδελφός) **MD 1**.7, 12, 22, 31, 31; **2**.41; **7**.6, 8, 11; **9**.2, 3, 4, 5, 7, 8, 10, 12, 13, 14, 16, 18, 19, 20, 21, 22, 25, 26; **10**.1, 2; **11**.7, 9, 10; **15**.6; **17**.T, 1, 6; **19**.9, 15, 16; **21**.4, 8, 9; **23**.46; **PD 1**.6; **2**.5, 8, 12, 13, 14, 15, 17, 25; **EP 2**.7, 9, 12; **3**.2, 5, 7, 8; **4**.4

Caesar **PD 2**.9

Cain **MD 7**.8; **PD 2**.17

calm, serenity (γαλήνη) **MD 1**.15; **2**.45; **8**.6; **11**.1, 11; **13**.9; **14**.20; **17**.3, 4; **EP 2**.12, 18, 22

canon, *see* rule

captivity, captive (αἰχμαλωσία) **MD 1**.7; **7**.5; **9**.23; **14**.13; **18**.4; **PD 2**.18; **EP 2**.15

cell (κελλίον) **MD 1**.12, 30, 31; **10**.7; **EP 1**.2; **2**.16, 22

chastity (ἁγνεία) **MD 2**.27; **12**.2; **23**.8, 60; (σωφροσύνη) **MD 2**.24; **11**.9; **14**.8; **17**.3; **18**.7; **19**.14, 15; **PD 1**.2; **2**.27; **EP 1**.3; **3**.3

cheese (τυρός) **MD 11**.T, 7; **PD 2**.3

Christian (χριστιανός) **MD 2**.T; **17**.3; **18**.5; **22**.1; **PD 1**.T, 3, 6; **2**.T, 1, 6, 10

church (ἐκκλησία) **MD 1**.22; **2**.50, 52, 54; **10**.1; **15**.8; **18**.5, 7; **19**.13; **20**.8, 9; **21**.8, 10; **22**.1, 4; **PD 1**.3, 5, 6, 7; **2**.T, 1, 2, 3, 4, 5, 6, 8, 9, 10, 11, 12, 13, 14, 15, 16, 18, 19, 20, 21, 22, 25, 26, 27; *see also* temple

clothing (ἔνδυμα, ἱμάτιον, στολή) **MD 2**.29, 39; **6**.8; **9**.7; **11**.17; **13**.6; **14**.26; **15**.2, 3, 4, 5; **19**.7; **21**.8; **23**.4; **PD 2**.8, 9, 10; **EP 2**.5

coenobium (κοινόβιον) **MD 7**.6, 8; **9**.T, 1, 2, 3, 5, 6

comforter, Holy Spirit (παράκλητος) **MD 22**.2, 3; **EP 2**.15

commandment, precept (ἐντολή, ἔνταλμα) **MD 2**.11, 24, 27; **3**.5, 12, 15; **4**.4, 8, 22; **5**.3, 8; **6**.1, 3, 4; **8**.2, 3, 7, 8; **9**.10; **10**.4; **11**.14, 21; **13**.4, 5; **14**.1, 7, 22, 24; **15**.2, 6; **16**.4; **17**.4; **18**.6; **19**.18, 19; **21**.5, 9; **23**.20, 21, 41, 42, 43, 48; **PD 1**.2, 4, 6, 7; **EP 1**.2; **2**.1, 5, 7, 19

community, *see* coenobium

compunction (κατάνυξις) **MD 1**.14, 17, 18, 19, 22, 23; **2**.26; **9**.12, 14, 21; **10**.7; **11**.14

conceit (οἴησις) **MD 2**.42, 43, 45; **14**.21, 27; **EP 2**.20

concord, harmony (ὁμόνοια) **MD 9**.1, 5; **PD 2**.2, 3, 9, 15; *see also* unanimity

condescension (συγκατάθεσις) **MD 2**.27, 29; **12**.6

confession (ἐξαγόρευσις) **MD 1**.29, 31, 32, 33; **6**.7; **9**.13; **11**.14; **14**.15; **17**.4; **19**.12; **EP 2**.13, 25; (ἐξομολόγησις) **MD 9**.14; **11**.14; **17**.3, 4, 6; **19**.5, 6, 7, 11, 12; **20**.7; **EP 2**.13, 25

confidence, boldness (παρρησία) **MD 1**.33; **3**.3; **4**.21; **11**.6, 17; **14**.28; **EP 2**.12, 19; **5**.5

conscience (συνείδησις) **MD 9**.17; **14**.17; **18**.8; **19**.13; **23**.32; **PD 1**.3; **2**.3; **EP 1**.1; **2**.8, 11, 17

consideration (ἐνθύμησις) **MD 2**.30, 38; **3**.17; **6**.8, 9; **18**.1; **19**.6; **21**.6; **EP 2**.8; *see also* theoria

contemplation, *see* theoria

conversation, *see* association

correction, amendment (διόρθωσις) **MD 2**.46; **4**.7; **9**.10, 21; **11**.11; **EP 2**.11, 13

covetousness, covet (πλεονεξία) **MD 14**.8, 9; **19**.15, 16; **PD 1**.2

creation (δημιουργία) MD 2.5, 8, 29;
4.17; 9.24; 20.4; 21.1, 3; 23.20, 22,
28
cross, crucifixion (σταυρός) MD 2.34,
57; 3.4, 5, 6, 7, 9, 11, 15; 4.6, 19;
6.10; 8.4; 9.2; 14.13, 14, 19, 21;
16.4; 20.10; 22.4; 23.23, 44; PD 1.5,
7; 2.8, 13; EP 2.5; 3.6, 7
custom, customary (συνήθεια) MD
1.7, 8, 10, 11, 12, 13, 14, 19; 3.2;
8.2, 3, 8; 9.11; 11.5; 13.8; 14.14;
18.5, 6; 19.1; 20.6; PD 1.3; EP 1.1;
2.16, 17; 3.2, 5, 7

Daniel MD 2.27, 56; 11.19
darkness (ἀφώτιστος, ζόφος, σκο-
τίζω, σκότος) MD 1.5, 7, 11, 32;
2.2, 5, 13, 25, 30, 41, 45, 48, 52;
4.3, 9, 14; 7.T, 1, 4, 9; 9.23; 11.7;
12.3; 14.7; 17.6; 23.16, 49, 52; PD
1.3, 13; 2.12, 14; EP 3.8
Dathan PD 2.19
David MD 1.7; 2.20, 21, 24, 25, 45,
49, 53; 4.4, 19; PD 2.1, 3
death (θάνατος) MD 1.6, 13, 31; 2.5,
11, 26, 43; 3.11; 4.19, 22, 23; 5.3;
6.2; 7.5; 8.4; 9.24; 10.1, 11; 11.21;
13.12; 14.7, 22; 16.4; 17.T, 1, 2, 4,
5, 6; 21.10 23.16, 44, 46; 23.46; PD
1.3, 13; 2.5, 8, 9, 13, 17; EP 1.1;
2.2, 7; 3.8; (νεκρός) MD 1.13; 2.10,
25, 31, 35; 3.6, 10; 4.8, 18, 23, 22;
6.5; 7.6, 9; 10.7; 11.3; 19.6; 20.2;
23.21, 22, 49, 51; PD 2.8; EP 3.7,
8; see also going forth
demon, demonic (δαίμων) MD 2.3, 9,
12, 13, 18, 26, 29, 36, 45, 53, 58;
3.7, 15; 4.23; 7.4; 9.23; 11.15, 16
14.9, 21, 23, 28; 16.3; 19.2, 9; PD
1.3, 12; EP 2.15
desire (ἐπιθυμία) MD 1.8, 26, 31; 2.2,
7, 9, 10, 11, 14, 15, 22, 27, 30, 37,
43, 44, 46, 49, 56, 57; 3.4, 6, 15,
17; 4.2, 7, 10, 19, 21; 5.5, 7; 6.2,

10; 8.2, 8; 10.7; 11.9, 19; 12.7, 9,
10; 13.3, 5, 11; 14.7, 26; 15.3, 5;
16.2; 19.7, 8, 19; 20.2; 22.5; 23.3,
4, 5, 8, 10, 11, 17, 19, 24, 26, 27,
32, 52, 60; PD 1.2, 3; EP 2.5; 3.7,
6, 8, 9; 4.4; (ὄρεξις) MD 1.25; 2.10,
25, 48, 53; 9.23; 15.3, 7; 23.2; PD
2.6, 15, 27; (πόθος) MD 3.18; 9.12;
11.18; 14.1; 20.2; 23.13, 47; PD 2.1,
2, 3, 16
detachment from desires/passions
(ἀπροσπάθεια) MD 1.3; 2.25; 10.11
devil, diabolic (διάβολος) MD 2.6, 18;
9.19; 10.1, 2; 14.19, 21, 22, 23; 15.3,
5, 6; 16.3, 4; PD 1.3; EP 2.21;
(Σατᾶν) MD 2.12, 24; 3.15; 4.4, 5
discernment (διάκρισις) MD 2.11, 12,
13, 14, 18, 34, 47, 48; 3.16; 7.T, 1;
11.6, 16; 14.25, 27; 22.6; 23.2, 4;
EP 2.6, 11, 13; 3.8
disciple (μαθητής) MD 2.4, 7; 3.5; 5.3;
6.3; 8.311.7; 15.6; 18.6; 22.4; 23.41,
42; PD 1.7
dioratic, clear-sighted (διορατικός)
MD 11.6, 11, 19; EP 2.11
discursive mind (διάνοια) MD 1.5, 7,
10, 11, 13, 14, 17, 18, 19, 20, 21,
22, 23, 25, 26, 27, 28, 29, 30, 31,
32, 33; 2.2, 5, 7, 8, 9, 16, 17, 24,
25, 26, 27, 34, 35, 40, 41, 46, 54;
3.2, 4, 17; 4.2, 5, 10, 15, 16, 19,
20, 21, 22, 23; 5.3, 5; 6.1, 2, 3, 5,
7, 9; 7.1, 8; 9.1; 11.2, 3, 6, 9, 12,
15, 18, 19, 20; 12.7, 8; 13.5 14.3,
24; 15.2, 5; 18.1, 9; 19.1; 20.8; 23.4,
5, 7, 8, 10, 11, 12, 18, 19, 21, 28,
31, 32, 34, 37, 40, 59; PD 2.1, 2,
4, 5, 8, 10, 22, 27; EP 1.2; 2.6, 12,
18, 19; 3.9; 4.2; 5.2
dispassion (ἀπάθεια) MD 3.5, 6, 16;
7.1; 14.20, 23; 19.3; EP 3.8; see also
detachment
disposition (διάθεσις) MD 1.13, 16, 19,
20; 2.2, 5, 6, 8, 9, 13; 3.14, 18; 4.13;

6.5; 7.T; 8.2, 5, 8; 9.5; 14.4, 26, 27; 15.7; 16.3; 20.7; 21.1; 23.5, 7, 12, 16, 26, 27, 33, 37, 41; PD 2.1; EP 2.2, 7, 11, 13, 19; 3.8

distraction (περισπασμός) MD 1.5, 10; 3.4; 4.1; 9.6; 14.24; 21.8; EP 2.16

divinization (θεοποιῶ) MD 1.3; 2.16; 13.4; 21.5; 23.12; EP 2.1

doctrine (δόγμα) MD 2.5; 10.2; PD 1.6; 2.2, 3, 8, 25

earth, earthly (γῆ, γήϊνος) MD 1.22, 30; 2.9, 15, 38, 40, 49, 57; 3.2, 4, 9; 4.1, 2, 3, 6; 5.2, 7; 6.6; 8.8; 9.4; 10.1; 11.4, 12, 18; 12.9; 13.5, 11, 12; 14.3, 6, 7, 14, 19, 20, 26; 15.3, 5, 6; 17.2; 18.10; 20.5, 8; 21.2, 3, 4, 5, 6; 22.1, 2, 4, 5; 23.8, 24, 26, 27, 32, 35, 52; PD 2.3, 14, 27; EP 3.9

eating (ἐσθίω, ἑστίασις) MD 2.11; 6.11; 9.5, 15, 16; 11.7, 14, 17; 13.7; 23.47; PD 1.2, 4, 5; EP 3.2

ecstasy (ἔκστασις) MD 2.18; 7.6; 23.20, 22, 23

Egypt, Egyptian (Αἴγυπτος, αἰγύπτιος) MD 2.47; 3.T, 3, 4, 7, 8, 11, 12, 13, 15; 8.8; 13.10; 14.19, 23, 24

Eirene (Εἰρήνη) EP 1.T; 2.T

elder (γέρας) MD 9.6, 13, 14, 15, 16

emperor, ruler (βασιλεύς) MD 1.22; 2.9, 13, 20; 6.8; 20.8; 23.8

enemy (ἐχθρός) MD 2.18, 19, 25, 26, 27, 30, 48; 3.3, 8, 10, 12; 6.6, 10; 7.2, 4, 5, 7; 9.3, 5, 22, 23, 24, 25; 11.7, 21; 14.13, 17, 22, 28; 22.2, 3; 23.45; PD 1.3, 10; 2.5, 10, 18; EP 2.7, 9, 10; (πολέμιος) MD 1.32, 33; 3.14; 7.4; 9.5, 25; 10.2; 14.17, 20, 24; PD 2.4, 10; EP 2.9; 3.11

enslavement, slavery (δουλεία) MD 2.5, 19, 27, 41, 43, 58; 3.12, 13, 14, 15; 4.18; 7.4; 8.2; 9.16, 17; 11.7, 10, 16; 14.12, 19, 24; 16.5; 18.4, 6, 18;

19.8, 13; 20.8; 23.26, 51; PD 2.18, 23; EP 2.4

error (πλάνη) MD 2.2, 3, 7, 45; 7.5; 22.5; PD 1.3, 5; 2.3, 4 Eulogia MD 23.T; EP 1.T; 2.T, 1, 6; 5.1

Eve MD 11.13; 20.4; 23.20, 23, 28

evening (ἑσπέρα) MD 1.11; 2.14, 25; 19.13; EP 2.14

experience (πεῖρα) MD 1.20, 28; 2.6, 25; 15.1, 8; 23.34; EP 2.19

eye (ὀφθαλμός) MD 1.20, 22, 28, 30; 2.1, 25, 27, 30, 41, 52; 7.9; 10.6, 12; 11.9, 15, 16; 12.7; 14.27; 17.2; 21.1, 3, 6, 8, 9, 10; 23.8, 20, 23, 38, 49, 52; PD 1.11; 2.3, 21; EP 2.19

faction (σχίσμα) MD 9.3, 5; 23.51, 53; PD 1.3, 5; 2.2, 4, 9, 19

faith (πίστις) MD 1.15; 2.16, 23, 27, 30; 4.12, 19; 9.12, 26; 18.2, 3; 19.2; 20.1, 2, 6; 22.4, 5; 23.38, 47; PD 1.5; 2.1, 3, 4, 17, 19, 21, 22, 25; EP 1.3; 2.25

faith, lack of (ἀπιστία) MD 22.4, 5; PD 1.5, 9; 2.22; EP 3.9

family relations (συγγένεια) MD 1.7, 10, 12; 2.6; 3.2; 8.3; 11.7; 13.3; 15.6; 17.4; 18.3; 22.5; EP 3.2, 5, 7

fasting (νηστεία) MD 2.37, 57; 7.10; 9.9; 11.T, 1, 2, 3, 4, 5, 7, 8, 11, 12, 13, 16, 17, 18, 19, 20, 21; 12.T, 1, 2, 3, 4, 9, 10; 18.7; EP 2.5, 14; 4.4

fault, failing (πλημμέλημα) MD 9.17, 18, 19; 11.9, 10, 12; 14.5; 18.8; EP 2.11

feast, festival (ἑορτή) MD 2.58; 4.6; 5.T, 1, 6; 7.5; 19.2, 3; 22.1, 2, 3; EP 2.4; (πανήγυρις) MD 1.12; 19.2, 3; 22.2; 23.59; PD 2.25, 26, 27

flesh, fleshly, carnal (σάρξ) MD 1.4, 11, 13, 23, 26, 32, 33; 2.15, 19, 25, 26, 30, 31, 36, 46, 53; 3.2, 5, 6, 7, 10, 12, 15, 17, 18 4.2, 3, 4, 5, 6,

7, 14, 16, 18, 19, 20; **5**.2, 3; **6**.8, 10; **8**.2, 5, 8; **9**.22; **10**.10; **11**.1, 4, 7, 9, 12, 15, 19 **13**.2, 3, 4, 6, 10, 11, 12; **14**.2, 3, 7, 13, 14, 15, 21, 23, 24; **15**.3, 6, 7; **16**.5; **18**.6; **21**.1, 4, 5, 6; **22**.3; **23**.3, 4, 6, 8, 16, 17, 19, 21, 22, 24, 25, 29, 31, 45, 46, 52, 60; PD **1**.2; **2**.6, 8, 25; EP **1**.3; **2**.5; **3**.7, 8; **4**.5; **5**.3

flock (ποίμνη, ποίμνιον) MD **15**.8; PD **2**.27

forgetfulness (λήθη) MD **2**.15, 25; **6**.3; **12**.1; **23**.16; EP **2**.18

forgiveness (ἄφεσις) MD **2**.4; **3**.8; **13**.11; **14**.19; **17**.5; **18**.8; **20**.6, 7; PD **1**.7

fornication (πορνεία) MD **11**.9; **19**.6, 8, 10, 14, 15; PD **1**.2; EP **2**.11

founder, foundress (κτήτωρ) MD **2**.51; EP **1**.T

free choice (προαίρεσις) MD **1**.31; **4**.2; **7**.7; **11**.16; **14**.1; **17**.3; **18**.1, 3, 8; **21**.4; **23**.3; PD **2**.13, 14, 23, 27; EP **2**.5; **3**.2, 8

free, freedom (ἐλεύθερος) MD **1**.11, 32, 33; **2**.4, 5, 19; **3**.11; **7**.5; **14**.24; **16**.4, 5; **18**.3, 6, 8; **19**.12; PD **2**.18; EP **3**.8

freedom from anxiety, tranquillity (ἀμεριμνία) MD **2**.9, 37

gangrene, *see* sickness
Gehenna MD **9**.23; **13**.10; PD **1**.2; EP **4**.4

gentle (πρᾶος) MD **2**.16, 26, 30, 43; **4**.8; **8**.6; **9**.18; **16**.4; **21**.4, 7; PD **1**.9; EP **2**.12, 14; **3**.4, 13

genuflection (γονυκλισία) MD **1**.29; **2**.37; **3**.12; **11**.9; EP **2**.14

gift, charism (χάρισμα) MD **2**.16, 30, 40; **4**.10, 18; **10**.4; **12**.9; **14**.1, 26, 27; **20**.7; **23**.22; PD **1**.1

gluttony (ἀδδηφαγία, γαστριμαργία) MD **9**.16, 17, 19; **11**.5; **19**.10; PD **1**.3

going forth (ἔξοδος) MD **1**.11, 33; **9**.22; **10**.12, 13; **17**.1, 5; **19**.17; EP **2**.24; **5**.3

gospel (εὐαγγέλιον) MD **1**.28; **4**.2, 8, 18; **5**.3; **13**.9; **19**.18, 19; **20**.10; **21**.7; **22**.4; **23**.35, 42, 56; PD **1**.9; **2**.6; EP **4**.4

governing faculty (ἡγεμονικόν) MD **2**.23; **11**.18

grace (χάρις) MD **1**.1, 4, 5, 6; **2**.4, 47, 51; **3**.15, 16; **4**.16, 22; **5**.1, 9; **8**.6; **9**.5, 6, 10, 24; **11**.7, 21; **12**.4; **14**.27; **15**.8; **16**.5; **19**.19; **20**.2, 5; **23**.34, 44, 46, 50; PD **1**.1, 7, 9; **2**.10, 22, 23, 24, 25, 27; EP **2**.15, 16, 21; **3**.1, 2; **5**.2

Gregorios MD **2**.17

grief, grievance, wrong (λύπη) MD **1**.8; **2**.36; **7**.3, 5, 6, 7, 8, 12; **8**.7; **9**.7, 8, 25, 26; **10**.10; **13**.8; **14**.3; **17**.2; **19**.10, 13; **23**.61; PD **1**.2; **2**.17; EP **2**.4, 7, 8, 9, 10, 11, 12, 13, 18; **3**.7, 8, 9, 10, 12

Habakkuk MD **2**.17

habit (ἕξις) MD **2**.22; **14**.24; **18**.5; EP **2**.19

habit, monastic (σχῆμα) MD **1**.10; **8**.8; **13**.3, 6; PD **1**.3; EP **1**.T; **2**.T

healing (θεραπεία, θεράπευω) MD **4**.1, 5, 7, 8, 9, 11, 13, 15, 16; **7**.6; **9**.25; **11**.1, 5; **16**.5, **18**.4; **17**.6 **19**.3, 11, 13, 14, 15, 17; **21**.1; PD **1**.7; EP **2**.2, 13, 17; **3**.8

health (ὑγιεία) MD **4**.12; **17**.3, 4, 5; **18**.4; **19**.4, 6, 7, 12; PD **2**.13, 21; EP **2**.2, 6, 23; **5**.1

heart (καρδία) MD **1**.2, 8, 13, 14, 16, 18, 19, 21, 22, 31, 33; **2**.3, 5, 12, 13, 16, 17, 18, 19, 20, 22, 23, 24, 25, 26, 30, 34, 36, 38, 39, 40, 41, 43, 45, 46, 53, 55, 56, 57, 58; **4**.1, 8; **6**.1, 4, 5, 6, 9 **7**.1, 5, 6, 7, 8; **8**.4, 5, 6; **9**.13; **10**.1, 3, 4, 11; **11**.12, 19;

13.4; **14**.1, 3, 9, 6, 13; **15**.1, 2, 3, 5, 7; **17**.1; **18**.1, 7, 8, 9, 10, 11; **19**.1, 9, 12, 14, 18; **20**.2, 6, 10; **21**.4, 6, 7; **22**.1, 4, 8; **23**.35, 48, 57; PD **1**.3, 5, 7, 8, 9, 11, 12, 13; **2**.14, 17, 22, 26, 27; EP **1**.2; **2**.12, 15; **3**.2, 4, 8, 9, 11, 13; **4**.4

heaven, heavenly (οὐρανός) MD **1**.33; **2**.9, 10, 15; **4**.1, 14, 22; **5**.8; **6**.8; **8**.4; **11**.18, 20; **13**.2, 5, 8, 11; **14**.5, 7, 16, 20; **17**.4, 5; **19**.19; **20**.9, 10; **21**.5; **22**.1, 2, 3, 4; **23**.31, 35, 41, 50, 51, 52, 53; PD **1**.13; **2**.5, 27; EP **2**.21; **3**.5, 7, 13

heresy, faction (αἵρεσις) MD **2**.6; PD **2**.18, 25

Herod MD **13**.10

holy (ἅγιος) MD **1**.24, 25; **2**.2, 4, 50, 58; **3**.16, 18; **8**.2, 8; **9**.11; **10**.3; **14**.2, 28; **15**.6, 8; **16**.4; **18**.1; **19**.2, 3; **20**.7; **21**.5; **22**.4, 5, 6; **23**.33, 47, 52; PD **1**.1, 5, 8; **2**.4, 5, 7, 8, 10, 12, 13, 21, 22, 27; EP **1**.3; **2**.1, 6, 7, 11, 12, 25; **5**.2, 5

homoousion, of the same substance (ὁμοούσιον) MD **23**.56

hope (ἐλπίς) MD **1**.1, 9, 33; **2**.16, 25, 30, 38, 40; **5**.7; **9**.26; **10**.1; **11**.6; **23**.15, 53; PD **1**.5; **2**.3, 25; EP **2**.4, 12, 18; **3**.7

hostile, *see* enemy

Hosea PD **2**.20

humble, humility (ταπεινός, ταπείνωσις) MD **1**.21, 25; **2**.23, 24, 30, 36, 39, 34, 42, 44, 46, 53, 57 **3**.7, 8, 9, 10, 11, 14, 16, 18; **4**.8; **6**.10; **7**.8; **8**.6; **9**.7, 12, 20, 21; **11**.9, 14; **12**.8; **13**.8; **14**.T, 4, 3, 5, 7, 8, 9, 10, 11, 12, 13, 14, 15, 16, 17, 20, 24, 26, 27; **17**.4; **18**.7, 8; **21**.4, 6, 7, 9; **23**.T, 37, 44, 45, 61; PD **1**.13; **2**.18, 20, 22; EP **2**.1, 5, 9, 13, 14, 16, 23; **3**.3

hypocrisy (ὑπόκρισις) MD **3**.8; **4**.13, 23; **7**.4; **11**.7; **13**.6; **14**.17, 21; **23**.3; PD **1**.3

idiorrhythmy (ἰδιορρυθμία) MD **8**.2

ignorance (ἄγνοια, ἀγνωσία) MD **1**.16; **2**.5, 15, 25, 35, 48; **4**.9, 23; **6**.2, 5; **7**.4, 6; **9**.10; **20**.6; **21**.1; **23**.16, 39, 49; PD **1**.5; EP **2**.6

image (εἰκών) MD **1**.4, 20, 24, 29; **2**.27, 47, 48; **3**.17, 18; **4**.5; **5**.2; **11**.16; **14**.19; **19**.5; **21**.4; **23**.13, 14, 18, 28

imagination, phantasy (φαντασία) MD **1**.1, 12, 19; **2**.9, 24, 27, 28, 29, 34, 35; **4**.20; **11**.5; **12**.8; **14**.3; **23**.4, 5, 10, 11

imitation (μίμησις) MD **1**.15, 25; **5**.3, 6; **9**.8, 9, 14; **11**.19; **13**.7; **14**.13; **16**.4, 5; **18**.1, 3, 5; **19**.3; **21**.7; **23**.13; PD **1**.7; **2**.27; EP **2**.11, 15, 19; **3**.5

immovable (ἀκίνητος) MD **2**.15; **4**.22; **10**.1; **19**.7; **23**.51; EP **3**.7

imperial, royal (βασιλικός) MD **1**.22, 25; **3**.5; EP **1**.T

impure (ἀκάθαρτος) MD **2**.30; **8**.6; **11**.9; **14**.9; **19**.7; PD **2**.20

incarnation (ἐνανθρώπησις) MD **2**.19, 20, 47; **23**.44, 45, 50; (θεάνθρωπος) MD **4**.5; **23**.53

incontinent (ἀκρασία) MD **1**.7; **14**.8; **16**.2

indifference, neglect (ἀμέλεια) MD **1**.6, 12; **2**.13, 25, 37; **4**.6, 21; **6**.2, 7, 8; **7**.7; **8**.8; **9**.10, 19; **14**.4; **17**.3, 6; PD **1**.10, 11; **2**.24; EP **2**.19

injustice, wrong (ἀδικία) MD **2**.12, 50; **14**.8; **16**.2, 4; **19**.6, 8, 15, 16; **23**.46; PD **1**.2, 9; **2**.8; EP **2**.15; **3**.8

insolence, injury (ὕβρις) MD **2**.27; **7**.5, 6, 8, 9; **10**.1, 2; **11**.7; **13**.7; PD **1**.2, 3; **2**.9, 12, 19; EP **3**.8

instruction, teaching (διδασκαλία) MD **2**.19, 20, 30, 50, 52; **3**.12; **4**.9; **9**.T, 13; **11**.17, 21; **12**.9; **13**.T, 2, 6; **14**.4; **19**.1, 2; **20**.5; **21**.2, 4, 8; **23**.19, 41, 51, 53, 56; PD **1**.3, 5, 6, 9, 10, 12; **2**.2, 3, 4, 5, 6, 18; EP **2**.14, 19; (κατήχησις) MD **5**.T; **13**.2; **17**.1; **19**.1; EP **2**.19

intellectual, spiritual (νοερός) MD 1.9, 29; 2.4, 34; 23.18, 49, 52

intelligible (νοητός) MD 1.4, 11, 15; 2.9, 25; 4.8; 6.5; 10.3, 6; 14.20; 20.2; 23.11, 18, 31, 49, 60

invocation (ἐπίκλησις) MD 1.17, 18, 29; 2.9, 32, 45; 23.12; PD 2.8; EP 1.2

irrational (ἄλογος) MD 1.8, 22, 13; 2.14, 18, 19, 31, 34, 44, 46, 48; 3.4, 11, 14; 6.8; 8.2, 3; 9.11; 11.3, 9, 12; 13.7; 19.12; 23.3, 4, 27, 29, 30, 35; EP 2.15; 3.8, 9; 4.4

Isaac MD 2.33

Isaiah MD 2.20; 4.3

Israel, Israelite MD 2.24, 47, 48; 3.4, 7, 8, 12, 13, 15; 4.6, 14; 11.18; 13.11; 14.19, 20, 21, 23, 24

Italian (ἰταλικὴν) MD 23.56

Jacob MD 2.23, 41; 5.3

Jeremiah MD 4.19

Jerusalem MD 19.2, 3, 4, 11; PD 2.13

Jesus MD 2.25, 31, 44, 45, 49, 50; 3.14; 4.23; 5.T, 9; 6.2, 10; 11.19; 12.10; 18.1, 5, 6, 11; 19.2, 3, 19; 20.1, 2, 4, 5, 6, 9, 10; 21.1, 10; 23.16; PD 1.1; 2.27; EP 2.12, 14, 21

Jew MD 2.3, 37; 4.5, 9, 11, 13, 19; 11.3; 18.2; 19.2; 21.9; PD 1.1; 2.7, 8, 9, 10, 11

John MD 5.3; EP 2.25

John Climacus MD 3.9

Jordan MD 23.51, 56

Joseph MD 2.41; 18.T, 1, 2, 3, 5, 6, 7, 10

joy, gladness (ἀγαλλιῶμαι) MD 2.32, 33, 52, 53, 58; 3.8; 8.6; 23.59; PD 2.1, 2; (εὐφραίνομαι) MD 1.3, 17, 19, 23, 27, 33; 2.16, 32, 49, 58; 6.5; 8.6; 12.9; 14.3, 9; 18.1; 20.2; 22.1; 23.8, 9, 49, 59; PD 2.1, 14; EP 2.8, 12; 3.2, 6; 4.2; 5.3, 4

Karbones EP 2.4; 3.1

kingdom, empire (βασιλεία) MD 2.17; 9.21; 13.11; 17.5, 6; 19.19; 23.35, 41, 50; PD 2.5, 9

knowledge (γνῶσις) MD 1.9, 17, 19, 20, 22, 24, 26, 27; 2.2, 9, 11, 12, 14, 17, 18, 22, 24, 30, 39, 40, 41, 42, 43, 44, 45, 48, 51, 54, 55; 4.13, 19, 24; 5.4, 7; 6.2, 3, 4, 5; 7.1; 8.5; 9.11; 10.3, 5, 6, 7, 8, 9, 10, 11, 12, 13; 11.16, 18; 12.7; 13.12; 14.1, 2, 5, 25; 16.5; 19.1, 12, 15, 16; 20.2, 4, 9; 21.3; 23.2, 7, 14, 15, 17, 26, 32, 33, 34, 35, 40, 41, 54, 60; PD 1.2, 5, 9, 18; 2.1, 4, 5, 6, 8; EP 2.10, 19; 3.2, 4, 9

knowledge of God (θεογνωσία) MD 4.8; 22.4; 23.1; PD 1.9

Kydonates EP 2.4; 3.1

labour, see work

Lazarus EP 2.20

law (νόμος, νομοθεσία) MD 1.11, 12; 2.5, 6, 8, 49; 4.5, 6, 7, 9, 10, 11, 12, 13, 14, 16, 18, 20; 5.7; 11.2, 3, 20, 21; 13.3; 14.24; 17.3, 4; 19.2; 23.3, 19, 30; PD 1.9; 2.2, 11, 16

laziness, sloth (ῥαθυμία) MD 1.29; 2.5, 15, 25, 35, 58; 3.3; 6.2, 3, 8; 9.7, 23; 14.5; 17.1, 6; 20.2; PD 2.25; EP 2.18, 20

Lent (τεσσαρακοστής) MD 11.1

Leo MD 17.T, 1

letter (ἐπιστολή) MD 13.1; EP 1.T; 2.T, 21, 22, 25; 3.T, 1, 11; 4.T, 2; 5.T

licentiousness (ἀκολασία) MD 2.27; 14.8; PD 2.23; EP 3.9

light (ἀκτίς, διαυγάζω, διαφωτίζω, λάμπω, ἐκλάμπω, ἐλλάμπω, ἐπιλάμπω, καταυγάζω, καταφωτίζω, λαμπρός, περιαυγάζω, φαιδρότης, φῶς) MD 1.2, 4, 10, 12, 13, 14, 15, 16, 17, 20, 32; 2.1, 2, 5, 6, 8, 9, 11, 12, 13, 14, 22, 23, 26, 32, 35,

39, 40, 41, 42, 43, 45, 51, 52, 54, 58; **3**.9; **4**.1, 3, 6, 14, 16; **5**.1, 3, 4, 6, 7, 8; **6**.4, 5; **7**.T, 1, 4, 11; **9**.9, 12; **11**.7, 11, 19, 20; **12**.3, 7; **13**.4, 7, 8, 9; **14**.1, 3, 26, 27; **15**.2, 3, 4, 5, 7; **17**.T; **19**.2; **21**.1, 2, 3, 6, 7, 10; **22**.2, 6; **23**.2, 20, 27, 28, 34, 41, 49, 52, 57, 56, 60; PD **1**.2, 3, 13; **2**.3, 7, 12, 14; EP **2**.6, 16, 19; **3**.4

lion (λέων) MD **1**.8; **11**.19

literal sense, of scripture (ἱστορία, γράμμα) MD **4**.14, 15, 16; **11**.2; **23**.59; PD **1**.4; **2**.20

liturgy, ministry, service (λειτουργία) MD **1**.18, 26; **2**.9, 10, 27; **19**.13; PD **1**.T, 9

long-suffering (μακροθυμία) MD **8**.7; **9**.26; EP **2**.13; 3.9

Lot PD **2**.18

love (ἀγάπη) MD **1**.3, 4, 8, 12, 16, 17, 18, 19, 22, 25, 26, 33; **2**.9, 16, 21, 22, 25, 27, 35, 37, 39, 41, 43, 44, 48, 52, 53, 57; **3**.15; **4**.14; **5**.1, 3, 7, 8; **6**.4, 5, 7, 8; **7**.2, 3, 5, 11, 12; **8**.2, 5, 8; **9**.1, 8, 9, 10, 12, 20, 25, 26, 27; **10**.10; **11**.14, 16, 19; **12**.9, 10; **13**.1, 2, 8; **14**.3, 12, 14, 21, 24, 26, 28; **15**.T, 1, 2, 3, 4, 5, 6, 7, 8; **16**.2, 4; **17**.1, 17; **18**.2, 3, 6, 7, 11; **19**.4, 14, 15, 18; **20**.2, 6, 7; **21**.1, 7, 9; **23**.2, 7, 8, 9, 12, 14, 15, 16, 17, 26, 27, 28, 40, 43, 44, 46, 47, 48, 51, 52, 58, 60, 61; PD **1**.2; **2**.1, 2, 6, 12, 14, 15; EP **1**.3; **2**.5, 6, 8, 9, 12, 13, 15, 16, 23, 25; **3**.4, 5, 6, 7, 9, 10, 13; (ἔρως) MD **1**.5, 7, 16, 20; **2**.T, 8, 9, 14, 21, 25, 30; **4**.4, 20, 21; **5**.7; **6**.5; **12**.2; **15**.1; **19**.9; **23**.1, 2, 13; PD **2**.1

Luke MD **23**.38

magic (μαγγανεία, μαγεία) MD **7**.5; **19**.8

market (ἀγορά, ἀγοράζω) MD **7**.4, 11; **11**.12; **18**.2, 7; **20**.1, 5; PD **2**.5, 25

matter (ὕλη) MD **2**.10; **3**.2, 12, 17; **8**.1; **9**.6; **14**.6; **15**.3; **19**.19; **22**.4, 5; **23**.24, 52; PD **1**.2; EP **3**.6

medicine (φάρμακον) MD **11**.5; **14**.7, 15; EP **2**.2; **3**.10

meditation, study (μελέτη) MD **1**.8, 10, 11, 12, 27, 28, 33; **2**.13, 27, 37, 38, 52, 56, 57; **3**.14; **4**.10, 20; **5**.3; **6**.4; **9**.11; **11**.14; **12**.8; **13**.4; **14**.3; **15**.2; **16**.4, 5; **21**.3, 4; **23**.31, 40, 42, 44, 47; PD **2**.3, 5, 27; EP **2**.11; **3**.9

mercy, compassion (ἐλεημοσύνη, ἔλεος) MD **2**.38, 58; **4**., 1, 12; **11**.7, 8; **15**.3, 4; **16**.1, 5; **17**.5; **18**.7; **19**.17, 18; **21**.8; PD **2**.2, 6, 14, 27; EP **1**.3; **2**.11; **4**.4

mind (νοῦς) MD **1**.7, 10, 11, 16, 17, 18, 19, 20, 21, 22, 23, 25, 26, 27, 28, 28, 29, 29, 31; **2**.5, 6, 9, 11, 12, 13, 15, 16, 17, 18, 19, 21, 24, 25, 28, 29, 31, 34, 36, 39, 46, 49, 53, 54, 55, 56, 58; **3**.14, 15, 16, 17; **4**.1, 3, 4, 13, 14, 18, 19, 21; **5**.3, 4; **6**.3, 4, 5, 9, 10; **7**.4, 10, 11; **10**.3, 5, 7, 9, 13; **11**.2, 5, 8, 11, 18, 19; **12**.3, 7, 9; **13**.11, 12; **14**.2, 3, 7, 24; **15**.2; **23**.1, 2, 3, 4, 5, 6, 7, 10, 11, 12, 13, 15, 17, 18, 26, 27, 28, 29, 31, 32, 33, 34, 35, 40, 44, 48, 52, 53, 5 8, 59; PD **1**.7, 12; **2**.18, 26; EP **1**.2; **2**.5, 6, 19, 22; **3**.4; **4**.2; *see also* discursive mind; governing faculty

ministry, *see* liturgy

mixed, monks (μιγάς) MD **9**.2, 6

monastery (μοναστήριον, μονή) MD **1**.6; **13**.5; EP **5**.5; (φροντιστήριον) MD **1**.6; **3**.3

monk, monastic, nun (μοναχός, μοναδικός) MD **1**.T, 2, 3, 12, 14, 30; **3**.1, 17; **6**.1, 3, 6, 9; **7**.9; **8**.8; **9**.T, 2, 6, 21; **13**.T, 3, 6, 8; **23**.T; PD **2**.10;

EP 1.T; 2.T, 1, 14, 17, 23; 3.1, 3, 12, 13; 5.1, 5

monologic (μονολόγιστον) MD 2.21

mortification, *see* death (νεκρός)

Moses, Mosaic MD 2.6, 16, 46, 47, 49; 3.T, 6, 7, 15; 4.15; 14.13, 19; 20.4; PD 1.10; 2.19

mother (μήτηρ) MD 1.23; 2.T, 22; 3.8; 7.1, 12; 8.1, 8; 13.1, 3, 4; 15.1; 16.1; 17.1; 18.1; 19.1; 20.1; 21.1; 22.1; 23.24, 25; PD 1.3; 2.3, 13, 14; EP 3.2, 8; 5.5

mourning, sorrow (πένθος) MD 2.26; 15.4; 10.7; 19.5; PD 2.14; EP 1.1

mystagogy (μυσταγωγία) MD 4.T; 11.10; 23.53, 56

mystery (μυστήριον, μυστικός) MD 1.26; 2.2, 9, 11, 17, 20, 28, 33, 34; 3.6, 8, 15; 4.7, 13, 16; 5.1, 6; 13.T, 2; 18.1; 20.2; 21.4; 22.3; 23.23, 24, 44, 50, 59; PD 2.T, 3, 6, 8, 10, 17

nature (φύσις) MD 1.28; 2.9, 22, 24, 34, 40, 46, 47, 48, 55; 4.5, 12, 22, 24; 5.3, 7; 11.15, 21; 12.1; 14.1; 16.3; 17.3, 4; 19.5; 21.1, 4, 5; 22.2, 3; 23.2, 7, 13, 18, 29, 30, 32, 52, 53, 55, 56, 57, 59; EP 2.2

Neilos EP 2.12

obedience (ὑπακοή) MD 1.1; 2.26, 34; 3.15; 6.7; 8.4, 5, 6; 9.2; 13.4, 8; 19.18, 19; 23.61; PD 2.23; EP 2.15

ordination, imposition of hands (χειροτονία) MD 20.5; PD 1.6, 8

orthodoxy (εὐσέβεια) MD 1.6; 2.46; 4.18; 5.6; 14.11, 26; PD 1.5, 6, 9, 10; 2.1, 7, 9, 10, 11, 17; (ὀρθοδοξία) PD 1.T, 6, 8; 2.T, 2, 7, 8, 10, 17, 18, 22

paradise (παράδεισος) MD 2.11; 6.3, 5; 9.8; 11.13, 14; 12.9; 23.20, 21, 23, 29; PD 1.4, 5, 6; EP 2.5

partaking, communion (μετάληψις) MD 1.25; 6.5; 9.15; 11.5, 17; 12.4; PD 13, 9; 2.7, 8, 10, 18, 19; EP 4.1

passion (πάθος) MD 1.1, 5, 11, 19, 24, 31, 32; 2.1, 5, 9, 14, 15, 18, 19, 22, 25, 26, 27, 29, 31, 36, 37, 38, 45, 49, 50, 53, 57, 58; 3.5, 6, 7, 10, 11, 14, 16; 4.8, 10, 18, 19, 20, 23; 6.5, 8; 7.T, 1, 5; 8.2, 5, 6; 9.8, 17, 22, 24; 10.4, 10; 11.2, 3, 6, 7, 8, 11, 12, 15, 19; 13.10; 14.7, 20, 22, 24, 25; 16.4, 5; 18.7, 8; 19.3, 5, 6, 7, 8, 9, 10, 12; 21.4; 23.21, 35, 46; PD 1.12; EP 2.5, 10, 11, 25; 3.4, 8, 9; (ἐμπάθεια, εὐπάθεια, ἡδυπάθεια, προσπάθεια) MD 1.4, 8, 23, 31; 2.19, 22, 25, 54; 3.2, 14; 4.19, 22; 8.7, 9.13; 11.1, 3; 12.6; 13.4, 11; 14.3; 23.10, 11, 27; PD 1.5; EP 3.2, 9

passover (πάσχα) MD 4.6

patient endurance (ὑπομονή) MD 1.33; 2.30; 3.12; 5.2; 7.11; 8.7; 9.8, 25; 11.14; 13.7, 8; 14.2, 8; 21.8; EP 1.3; 2.5, 7, 8, 9, 10, 12, 13, 20; 3.2, 4, 5, 9, 13; 5.2, 4

patriarch (πατριάρχης) PD 2.9

peace (εἰρήνη) MD 1.3, 5, 15, 22, 32, 33; 2.15, 16, 18, 26, 39; 3.7, 16; 7.2; 10.4; 14.26; 16.2; 19.3; 21.9; 22.2, 3; 23.47; PD 2.9, 15; EP 2.12, 16; 3.9

Pentecost MD 19.2; 22.T, 3

perseverance (καρτερία) MD 8.8; 9.9; 13.8; 21.8; 23.61; EP 2.8; 3.1, 8

Persia MD 13.7

Peter MD 2.50, 54; 5.3

Pharaoh MD 2.48; 3.15; 14.19, 20

Pharisee MD 4.9; 14.15, 16, 17

Philadelpheia MD 23.T; PD 2.T; EP 2.T

philanthropy, human concern (φιλανθρωπία) MD 1.21; 2.48; 4.5, 8; 15.8; 19.19; 23.23, 46; PD 2.26, 27; EP 1.T; 2.1

philosophy (φιλοσοφία) MD 1.1; EP 2.10

Pilate MD **18**.2, 5

pleasure, pleasureful (ἐνήδονος, ἡ-δονή, φιληδονία, καθηδυπαθῶ, καθήδονος) MD **1**.8, 12, 13, 22; **2**.11, 19, 26, 30, 38, 41; **3**.10, 11, 12, 14, 18; **4**.2, 3, 15, 23; **5**.2, 3; **6**.3, 5; **7**.12; **8**.2, 8; **9**.17; **10**.10; **11**.1, 3, 7, 8, 15; **12**.2, 5; **13**.3, 6; **14**.2, 3, 7, 17, 20, 24, 25, 28; **16**.4; **19**.7 **20**.2; **23**.3, 4, 5, 6, 8, 10, 11, 21, 28, 31, 52; PD **1**.1, 2, 3; **2**.14; EP **2**.5; **3**.4, 5, 8, 9; **4**.1, 5; **5**.3

pollution, filth (ῥύπος, ῥυπαρός, ῥύπασμα, μολυσμός) MD **1**.4; **4**.20; **6**.7; **11**.14; **14**.15; **18**.8; **19**.7

poverty (ἀκτημοσύνη, ἀκτησία, πένης, πτωχεία) MD **1**.1; **2**.13, 26, 37, 38, 42, 51; **3**.5, 12, 18; **4**.4; **13**.1; **14**.26; **16**.1; **18**.7; **19**.17; **21**.6, 8; **23**.44, 46; PD **1**.2, 3; EP **1**.3; **2**.6; **3**.6

power (δύναμις) MD **1**.1, 6, 24; **2**.8, 16, 20, 22, 25, 28, 30, 40, 41, 48, 50, 54; **3**.5, 7, 17; **4**.1, 9, 13, 22, 24; **5**.1; **6**.10; **7**.12; **8**.5; **9**.23, 26; **11**.15; **14**.8, 10, 27, 28; **15**.3; **16**.1; **17**.4; **19**.7, 8, 11; **20**.1; **21**.1; **22**.1; **23**.1, 2, 3, 7, 13, 17, 49, 59; PD **1**.4; **2**.18; EP **1**.2; **2**.4, 14, 21; **3**.1, 11

praxis (πρᾶξις, πρακτικός) MD **1**.10, 13, 14; **2**.15, 40, 54; **4**.4, 19, 21, 22; **5**.4, **6**.5, 9; **7**.11; **9**.12; **11**.3, 11, 14; **12**.5; **13**.3, 4; **14**.24, 25, 28; **16**.3, 5; **17**.3, 4; **18**.1; **19**.7, 14; **23**.4, 13, 29, 32, 34, 41, 42, 48, 61; PD **1**.11; **2**.27; EP **1**.1; **2**.9, 19

prayer (εὔχομαι, προσευχή) MD **1**.11, 12, 13, 14, 17, 19, 20, 21, 22, 23, 24, 25, 26, 27, 28, 29, 30, 31, 32, 33; **2**.T, 5, 8, 11, 14, 15, 16, 18, 19, 20, 21, 24, 25, 28, 29, 30, 38, 49, 50, 53, 54, 55, 56, 57, 58; **3**.8, 12; **4**.11, 20, 21; **5**.3, 4; **6**.T, 3, 4, 6, 7, 9; **7**.5; **8**.6; **9**.8, 9, 19; **11**.12, 14,

16, 18, 19; **12**.8; **13**.1, 2, 12; **14**.3, 8, 13, 16; **23**.7, 8, 9, 21, 26; PD **1**.7; **2**.8, 19, 26; EP **1**.2; **2**.1, 9, 10, 12, 13, 14, 16, 23; **3**.9; **4**.2; **5**.5

priest (ἱερεύς) MD **2**.55; PD **1**.5, 6, 7, 8, 9, 10; **2**.7, 8, 10, 16, 17, 18, 19, 20, 21, 22, 24, 25

princess (βασίλισσα) MD **1**.1; **23**.T; EP **1**.T; **2**.T,

progress (προκοπή) MD **3**.4; **5**.1; **8**.6; **9**.9; **11**.10; **14**.1 **17**.4; **19**.3; **23**.3; PD **2**.4

promise (ὑπόσχεσις) MD **1**.7; **22**.3; PD **1**.5, 7

prophet (προφήτης) MD **1**.12; **2**.15, 17, 18, 21, 24, 32, 51, 56; **3**.6, 8, 17; **4**.4, 7, 15, 19; **5**.8; **6**.9; **10**.1, 4; **14**.9; **21**.2, 6; **23**.33, 35, 59; PD **1**.5, 9; **2**.1, 3, 8, 13; EP **2**.3; **4**.5; **5**.4

providence (πρόνοια) MD **2**.55, 57; **4**.16; **9**.26; **14**.7

psalmody (ψαλμῳδία) MD **1**.19, 22, 28, 30; **2**.19, 25, 30, 32, 45, 49; **3**.12; **4**.8, 21; **7**.10; **8**.6; **9**.7, 15; **10**.4; **11**.5, 7, 14; **13**.3; **14**.3; **15**.4; **19**.3, 13; **23**.8, 33, 34, 35, 37, 39, 41, 42; PD **1**.3; **2**.1, 3

punishment (κόλασις) MD **13**.11, 12; **14**.7, 17; **17**.5; **19**.12; **23**.45; PD **2**.5, 13, 17, 23; EP **2**.1, 14; **3**.9; **4**.3

purity (καθαρότης) MD **1**.2, 12, 17, 19, 20, 22, 24, 25; **2**.2, 15, 19, 24, 29, 30, 34, 45, 55, 57, 58; **3**.18; **5**.3; **6**.4, 6, 10; **7**.4, 11; **8**.2, 4, 5, 6; **11**.2, 5, 8, 12; **12**.3; **13**.4, 5, 12; **14**.2, 3, 9, 24; **18**.8, 9; **19**.7; **23**.6, 8, 12, 18, 27, 32, 48, 56, 57; PD **1**.9; **2**.2, 3, 20, 21, 25; EP **3**.9

rational (λογικός) MD **2**.2, 9, 19, 44, 43, 46; **4**.5, 22; **6**.8, 9; **23**.1, 2, 5, 13, 18; PD **2**.5; EP **1**.1

reading (ἀνάγνωσις, βιβλίον, βίβλος) MD **1**.27, 28, 31; **2**.5; **3**.12; **4**.11, 15;

9.13, 15; **11**.T, 14; **13**.9; **14**.3; **20**.4; **23**.42, 59; PD **1**.3, 9; **2**.3, 5, 6, 8, 27; EP **3**.1, 9, 11, 12; **4**.2

relation, relationship, association (σχέσις) MD **1**.3; **2**.22, 23, 36, 46; **3**.11, 15; **4**.3; **6**.8; **10**.10; **11**.11; **14**.3, 24, 25

remembrance (ἀνάμνησις, μνήμη, μνεία) MD **1**.8, 12, 13, 14, 16, 17, 20, 26, 28, 30, 31, 33; **2**.11, 15, 16, 26, 49, 57, 58; **3**.4, 14; **4**.11; **5**.4; **6**.3, 10; **7**.2, 5, 11; **9**.4, 13; **10**.1, 7; **12**.1, 6; **13**.4, 10, 12; **14**.3, 4, 21; **17**.1; **18**.1, 7, 10; **19**.5, 11, 12, 18; **20**.9; **23**.9, 11, 15, 17, 21, 26, 44; PD **1**.6; **2**.17, 26, 27; EP **1**.1; **2**.6, 7, 9, 20; **3**.1, 9

renunciation (ἀποταγή) MD **1**.8; **8**.3; **13**.4, 5, 8

repentance (μετάνοια) MD **1**.6, 7, 29, 31; **2**.30; **4**.7; **7**.2, 6, 8, 9; **9**.13, 14, 15, 18, 20, 21; **10**.11; **14**.9, 12, 15; **17**.4, 5, 6; **18**.10; **19**.4, 5, 6, 11, 12; **20**.6, 7; **23**.28; PD **1**.3; **2**.18; EP **2**.10, 11, 20

Resurrection (ἀνάστασις) MD **2**.31, 33; **4**.18; **9**.8; **17**.1; **23**.38, 44, 51; PD **1**.1, 2; EP **2**.14

riches, wealth (πλοῦτος) MD **1**.1, 9, 16, 21, 51; **2**.10, 20, 42; **4**.4; **13**.1; **14**.9, 10, 26, 27; **16**.1; **18**.2, 11; **19**.10; **20**.2; **23**.44, 46, 50; PD **2**.9; EP **2**.15; **3**.6, 10

righteousness, righteous, just, justify (δικαιοσύνη, δίκαιος, δικαιῶ) MD **1**.31, 32; **2**.5, 17, 26, 50, 52, 57, 58; **3**.7; **9**.10, 11; **10**.2; **11**.7, 9, 20; **13**.9; **14**.8, 9, 10, 12, 13, 15, 16, 17; **16**.2, 4; **18**.7; **19**.3, 15, 16; **23**.24, 46, 51; PD **1**.2, 9, 12; **2**.3, 8, 10, 11, 16, 20, 27; EP **2**.10; **3**.3, 7

rigidity, rigid adherence (ἀκρίβεια) MD **1**.16, 17; **2**.8, 17, 54; **7**.12; **9**.14; **15**.1; **23**.13, 53; PD **2**.2, 8, 10, 11, 25; EP **2**.5; **4**.3

rule, canon (κανών) MD **1**.30, 32; PD **2**.8; EP **2**.1, 19

sabbath (σάββατον) MD **4**.7, 8, 9, 11, 12, 13, 15, 16, 17, 18, 19, 21, 23

sacrifice (θυσία) MD **1**.17; **2**.21, 55; **3**.3; **4**.6, 21, 22; **6**.9; **7**.11; **14**.24; **23**.33; PD **2**.7, 17, 20, 21; EP **2**.14

Samaria, Samaritan MD **20**.T, 1, 2, 4, 5, 8

Samuel PD **1**.8

sanctification (ἁγιασμός, ἁγιάζω) MD **8**.5; **23**.33, 49; PD **1**.3, 7, 9, 10; **2**.10, 18, 19, 22, 25

Satan, *see* devil

Saul MD **2**.45

sea (θάλασσα) MD **1**.12; **2**.47; **3**.T, 5, 7, 8, 11, 12, 15; **7**.10; **14**.19, 20, 23, 28; **15**.7; **17**.2, 3, 4; **20**.1; EP **3**.3

seal (σφραγίς) MD **2**.35; **23**.11; PD **2**.21

self-discipline (ἐγκράτεια) MD **2**.30, 37; **3**.12; **5**.2, 3; **9**.9; **10**.4; **11**.1, 11, 13, 17, 18; **12**.2, 4; **13**.12; **14**.2, 8; **16**.2; EP **2**.5; **3**.8, 9

self-love (φιλαυτία) EP **2**.10

senses, sense perception, sensible (αἴσθησις) MD **1**.4, 7, 11, 13, 20; **2**.1, 8, 9, 14, 22, 23, 29, 34, 35, 37, 40, 41, 52, 54, 55; **3**.10, 11, 12, 13, 14; **4**.2, 20, 21, 22, 23; **5**.4, 8; **6**.5; **7**.2, 5, 6; **8**.3; **9**.8; **10**.1, 5, 10; **11**.3, 8, 11; **16**.5; **18**.6, 10; **20**.2, 3; **21**.1, 3; **23**.3, 4, 5, 6, 8, 10, 11, 16, 18, 19, 20, 21, 27, 28, 30, 47, 49, 60; PD **1**.3, 12; **2**.1, 2, 5, 18, 26; EP **1**.2; **3**.2, 3; **5**.3

serpent (ὄφις) MD **2**.43; **7**.2; **20**.4; **23**.31; PD **1**.3, 4; **2**.12

service (διακονία, διακόνημα) MD **1**.8, 31; **2**.9, 11, 23, 27, 50; **5**.4; **6**.5; **9**.6, 7, 12, 16, 17, 20, 21; **11**.5; **23**.17; EP **2**.8, 18, 24

shame (αἶσχος, αἰσχρός, αἰσχύνη, ἀσχημοσύνη) MD **1**.24, 32; **2**.16, 27, 58; **6**.8; **7**.2; **9**.7, 14; **11**.6, 12,

17; **14**.10, 12, 16, 27; **15**.2, 3; **16**.2;
19.7; **20**.8; **23**.5, 32; PD **1**.9; **2**.13,
14; EP **4**.5
sheep (πρόβατα) MD **4**.6; **14**.24; **19**.4;
PD **1**.3
shepherd (ποιμαίνω, ποιμήν) MD **2**.52,
53; **6**.2; **13**.8; PD **1**.3, 6, 7, 8, 9, 10,
13; **2**.18; EP **2**.11
sickness (νόσος, ἀρρωστία, γάγγραι-
να) MD **2**.1, 14; **4**.2; **6**.2; **7**.6, 10, 12;
9.25; **10**.1; **17**.4; **19**.6, 8, 9, 11, 12;
PD **1**.13; **2**.13, 18; EP **2**.2, 3, 23, 25
silence (σιγή, σιωπή) MD **1**.20, 25, 31;
2.25, 30; **3**.12; **6**.5; **7**.7; **9**.9, 15, 19,
20; **10**.T, 3, 5, 6, 7, 8, 9, 10, 11,
12; **11**.9; **13**.7; **14**.5; **23**.61; EP **2**.10,
15
Siloam MD **21**.3, 7
simplicity (ἁπλότης) MD **1**.20; **2**.8, 17,
23; **9**.9; **11**.5; **13**.9; **16**.5; **23**.11; PD
1.8; **2**.13
sin, sinner (ἁμαρτία, ἁμαρτωλός,
ἁμάρτημα) MD **1**.24, 29; **2**.1, 4, 5,
18, 19, 29, 45, 58; **3**.1, 8, 11, 12,
15; **4**.2, 6, 8, 22, 23; **7**.9; **8**.3; **10**.1,
13; **11**.7, 8, 14; **14**.5, 9, 10, 12, 13,
15, 16, 17, 19, 24; **15**.6; **16**.4; **17**.3,
4, 5; **18**.5, 6, 7, 8, 9, 10; **19**.3, 4,
5, 6, 11, 12; **20**.8; **21**.2, 5, 10; **22**.4,
6; **23**.21, 46, 45, 46, 51; PD **1**.2, 3,
5, 12; **2**.11, 22, 25; EP **3**.3, 7; *see
also* fault; transgression
Sion MD **2**.15
sister (ἀδελφή) MD **7**.1, 2, 3, 5, 6, 7,
8, 9; **8**.1, 5, 7; **13**.1; **15**.1, 2; **16**.1;
17.1, 2, 7; **18**.1, 3, 5, 11; **19**.1, 18;
20.1, 9; **21**.1; **22**.1; PD **2**.7, 19; EP
2.6, 7, 8, 9, 10, 11, 12, 13, 24; **3**.13
skill, art (τέχνη) MD **2**.6; **4**.10; **8**.1, 4;
23.35
sleeping on the ground (ξηροκοιτία)
MD **2**.37
soul (ψυχή) MD **1**.1, 3, 4, 5, 8, 10, 11,
12, 14, 15, 17, 18, 19, 21, 23, 24,
27, 29, 31; **2**.1, 2, 4, 5, 6, 8, 9, 10,

11, 12, 13, 14, 15, 16, 17, 18, 19,
20, 21, 22, 23, 25, 27, 28, 29, 30,
31, 33, 32, 35, 36, 38, 39, 40, 41,
43, 44, 45, 46, 48, 51, 52, 53, 54,
55, 57; **3**.2, 4, 5, 10, 11, 12, 14, 15,
16, 17, 18; **4**.1, 2, 3, 5, 6, 8, 10,
11, 14, 16, 18, 20, 21, 22; **5**.3, 4;
6.1, 4, 5, 6; **7**.1, 2, 3, 4, 5, 6, 7,
8, 9, 10, 11, 12; **8**.3, 5, 6, 7, 8; **9**.12,
18, 22; **10**.1, 4, 6; **11**.1, 2, 3, 6, 7,
12, 14, 18, 19; **12**.5, 6; **13**.3, 4, 5,
11, 12; **14**.2, 3, 7, 17, 23, 24, 25,
26, 27, 28; **15**.2, 3, 4, 5, 6, 7, 8;
16.1, 3, 4, 5; **17**.1, 2, 4, 5, 6; **18**.1,
7, 8, 9, 10, 11; **19**.1, 3, 4, 5, 6, 7,
8, 9, 11, 12, 13, 14, 15, 17; **20**.2,
5, 6, 7, 9; **21**.1, 2, 3, 4, 6, 7, 8, 9,
10; **22**.1, 4, 6; **23**.3, 4, 8, 9, 10, 12,
13, 16, 17, 21, 32, 33, 34, 37, 44,
47, 48, 49, 59; PD **1**.1, 5, 9, 12, 13;
2.1, 2, 3, 4, 5, 8, 9, 13, 14, 16, 18,
22, 23, 26, 27; EP **1**.1, 2, 3; **2**.1, 5,
6, 12, 15, 17, 18, 19, 22, 23, 24, 25;
3.2, 4, 7, 8, 9; **4**.1, 2, 4; **5**.2, 3
spirit (πνεῦμα) MD **1**.3, 10, 12, 17, 18,
22, 25, 26, 31, 33; **2**.3, 4, 5, 6, 7,
10, 13, 18, 28, 29, 30, 31, 34, 37,
38, 39, 44, 45, 58; **3**.3, 6, 16; **4**.5,
6, 7, 13, 14, 16, 18, 19, 20, 22; **5**.6,
9; **6**.10; **7**.8; **8**.2, 4, 7; **9**.2, 12; **10**.7,
13; **11**.2, 4, 19; **13**.1, 3; **14**.10, 14,
15, 26, 28; **15**.8; **18**.11; **20**.7; **21**.2,
10; **22**.T, 2, 3, 4, 5, 6; **23**.19, 21,
22, 23, 24, 25, 31, 33, 47, 51, 52,
53, 55, 56, 59, 60; PD **1**.1, 8; **2**.1,
3, 7, 8, 10, 22; EP **1**.1, 2, 3; **2**.1,
2, 23; **3**.7, 8, 9
spiritual (πνευματικός) MD **1**.4, 8, 11;
2.2, 5, 6, 7, 8, 9, 16, 27, 40, 55;
3.T, 15; **4**.7, 10, 11, 14, 17, 18; **7**.2;
11.2, 3; **13**.5, 8, 12; **14**.28; **15**.T;
19.3, 18; **20**.2, 5; **22**.1; **23**.23, 25,
31, 32, 50; PD **2**.1, 4; EP **1**.T; **2**.T,
16, 18, 20; *see also* intellectual
stillness, quiet (ἡσυχία) MD **1**.5, 28;

2.6, 17, 22, 30; **3.**4; **6.**T; **9.**4, 15; **14.**3, 8; **EP 2.**16

stranger, foreigner (ξένος) **MD 1.**10; **2.**9, 13, 23, 36; **3.**2, 7; **6.**8; **14.**10, 19; **16.**3; **22.**3

strife, contention (φιλονεικία) **MD 2.**6; 7.10; **8.**2, 6; **9.**5; **14.**17; **21.**4; **PD 2.**1, 9, 12; **EP 2.**10, 15

struggle (ἀγών, ἀγωνία, ἀγωνίζομαι, ἀγωνιστής) **MD 1.**8, 10, 29, 32, 33; **2.**18, 38 **3.**T, 3, 6, 8, 11; **4.**8, 17, 18; **5.**6; **6.**10; **7.**4; **9.**4, 8, 11; **11.**5; **12.**2, 3, 4, 5, 6, 7, 8; **14.**4, 7, 11; **PD 1.**5, 7; **2.**6, 11, 13, 18, 26; **EP 2.**6, 8, 20, 24; **3.**4

submission (ὑποταγή) **MD 2.**7; **4.**8; **8.**T, 3, 4, 5, 6; **9.**12; **13.**4; **PD 1.**3, 7, 12; **2.**15, 22; **EP 2.**16

supplication, petition (δέησις) **MD 1.**17, 18, 25; **2.**57; **6.**10; **14.**27; **23.**37; **PD 1.**7; **EP 2.**19

suspicion, opinion, estimation (ὑπόνοια) **MD 1.**31, 33; **6.**10; **7.**7; **8.**8; **9.**22, 25; **11.**15; **PD 1.**5, 10; **EP 2.**7, 18

sweetness (γλυκύτης, ἡδύς) **MD 1.**12, 19, 27; **2.**25; **5.**5; **6.**5; **11.**19; **14.**3; **20.**2; **23.**2, 10, 11, 28; **PD 1.**1, 5; **2.**5; **EP 3.**2

synagogue (συναγωγή) **MD 2.**50; **4.**9, 20; **PD 2.**9

table (τράπεζα) **MD 1.**31; **2.**55; **9.**5, 12, 15, 21; **12.**9; **PD 2.**5

teaching, *see* instruction

tears (δάκρυα) **MD 1.**13; **2.**1; **6.**7; **19.**4, 6; **20.**6; **PD 2.**14, 18, 26

temple, church (ναός) **MD 1.**22, 26, 30; **2.**55; **8.**2; **9.**7, 21; **11.**5, 12; **17.**6; **19.**3; **23.**52; **PD 1.**T; **2.**12; **EP 2.**2

temptation (πειρασμός) **MD 2.**30; **8.**7; **9.**9; **13.**7; **15.**7; **18.**3; **PD 1.**2; **EP 2.**12; **3.**2, 3, 4, 10

thanksgiving (εὐχαριστία) **MD 7.**5;

9.20; **10.**1; **11.**14, 19; **14.**27; **17.**4; **21.**8, 9; **23.**61; **PD 1.**2, 7; **EP 2.**20

Theodote **EP 2.**17; **5.**5

Theoleptos **MD 23.**T; **EP 2.**T

theology (θεολογία) **MD 23.**53, 54, 56; **EP 2.**25

Theophany (θεοφανεία) **MD 2.**6

theoria (θεωρία) **MD 1.**16, 20, 22, 26; **2.**9, 30, 31, 35, 39, 40, 53, 55, 58; **4.**14; **6.**4, 5; **9.**12; **13.**9; **14.**3; **23.**2, 15, 17, 30, 31, 32, 33, 34, 53; **PD 2.**5

thought(s) (λογισμοί) **MD 1.**4, 5, 7, 10, 12, 13, 23, 26, 31, 32, 33; **2.**2, 9, 10, 11, 12, 13, 14, 15, 17, 21, 22, 24, 25, 26, 27, 28, 30, 31, 34, 35, 36, 39, 40, 41, 45, 46, 48, 49, 53, 54, 55, 57, 58; **3.**7, 11; **4.**19, 20, 23; **5.**3; **6.**2, 4, 10; **7.**7, 10; **8.**7, 8; **9.**13, 18; **10.**1, 3, 11, 13; **11.**6, 7, 9, 14, 20; **12.**6; **13.**3, 4, 11; **14.**3, 9, 10, 25; **16.**2, 4; **18.**6, 9; **19.**4, 7, 8, 11, 12, 13, 14, 15, 16, 17, 19; **21.**6, 7; **22.**1; **23.**3, 4, 5, 10, 11, 20, 44; **PD 1.**5, 7, 13; **2.**8, 12, 13, 14, 18, 19, 20, 22, 26, 27; **EP 1.**1; **2.**8, 9, 12, 14, 17, 18, 19, 22; **3.**10, 11; **4.**3; *see also* attitude

thought, care, solicitude (φροντίς) **MD 2.**9, 12, 17, 26, 31, 37; **4.**4, 10, 20; **6.**1; **12.**9; **13.**4; **19.**1; **20.**8; **22.**1; **23.**35; **EP 3.**11

tongue (γλῶσσα) **MD 1.**12, 19, 20, 21, 22, 30; **2.**T, 6, 19; **4.**20; **7.**8; **8.**3; **9.**21; **10.**1, 2, 3, 4, 13; **11.**15, 19, 20; **12.**5; **13.**7; **22.**3, 6; **23.**33, 35, 39; **PD 1.**5; **2.**8, 13; **EP 1.**2; **3.**7

Transfiguration (μεταμόρφωσις) **MD 5.**T, 1, 5, 6

transgression (παράβασις) **MD 2.**46; **8.**3; **12.**1; **20.**8; **21.**5; **PD 1.**4; **EP 2.**7

tree(s) of paradise (ξύλον) **MD 6.**5; **9.**8; **11.**13, 14, 15, 21; **12.**9; **PD 1.**4, 6

trinity (τριάς, τρισυπόστατος) **MD 1.**25; **2.**T; **3.**18; **9.**26; **14.**28

troparion (τροπάριν) MD 15.4
truth (ἀλήθεια) MD 1.1, 4, 16, 19, 23;
2.2, 6, 16, 20, 32, 33, 34, 42, 44,
52; 4.1, 6, 8, 13, 14, 16, 18, 21, 24;
5.3, 4; 6.2; 7.1; 10.12; 11.2, 10, 13,
14, 18; 12.2; 13.3, 12; 14.15, 16, 17,
18, 26; 19.5; 20.1; 21.3, 8; 23.1, 14,
15, 16, 34, 54, 56, 58; PD 1.5, 9, 11;
2.1, 2, 5, 6, 7, 12, 13; EP 3.5, 6

unanimity, agreement (ὁμοφροσύνη)
MD 9.3, 5; PD 2.9
union (ἕνωσις) MD 1.23; 2.47, 48; 6.5,
8; 7.2; 9.27; 13.1; 14.3, 20, 21, 26;
23.2, 15, 58; PD 2.3, 9, 13; EP 2.16
usury (δάνειον) MD 2.17; 7.4; 14.27;
16.1, 2, 3; 19.17

vainglory (κενοδοξία) MD 1.32; 2.42;
3.2, 7, 8, 11, 17, 18; 4.23; 6.9; 8.7,
8; 9.16, 17; 11.3, 10; 14.3, 5, 8, 9,
18, 19, 21; 18.7; 19.10; 21.6; 23.3,
42; PD 1.3; 2.18; EP 2.5; 3.8; 4.3,
4, 5
vigil, watchfulness (ἀγρυπνία) MD
2.23, 37; 3.9, 12, 17; 7.10; 9.12;
11.5; 14.3; 19.3; PD 1.7
vigilance (νῆψις, νηφάλιος, νήφω)
MD 1.22; 2.T, 5, 12, 14, 15, 16, 17,
18, 20, 21, 23, 24, 25, 34, 46, 48,
53, 54, 57; 4.22; 6.3, 6; 11.3, 5, 19;
12.8; 23.28, 35
virgin, virginity (παρθένος) MD 4.18;
13.3, 4, 5; 17.6; 21.5; 23.8; EP 2.25
virtue (ἀρετή) MD 1.1, 2, 3, 10, 14, 23,
24, 25, 29, 31; 2.T, 5, 9, 17, 18, 21,
22, 24, 26, 29, 35, 37, 46, 49, 52;
3.3, 5, 6, 7, 8, 9, 10, 11, 14, 17;
4.8, 17, 18, 20, 21; 5.3, 4, 5, 7, 8;
6.5; 7.4, 11; 8.4, 5, 6; 9.9, 12, 26;
10.3; 11.8, 12, 14, 17, 18; 12.5; 13.4,
7; 14.T, 1, 2, 3, 4, 5, 6, 7, 8, 13,
17, 19, 20, 23, 25, 26, 27, 28; 15.1,
4; 16.1, 4; 18.7; 19.3, 5, 19; 21.1,

4; 22.4; 23.1, 12, 13, 14, 17, 26, 27,
32, 42, 48, 51, 53, 54; PD 1.5, 13;
2.3, 18, 27; EP 1.3; 2.1, 5, 11, 19,
20, 22; 3.3, 4; 4.3; 5.2, 3, 4
vision (ὅρασις) MD 1.16, 20; 23.52

wakeful (γρηγορῶ, ἐγρήγορσις) MD
2.13, 15, 23, 24; 6.3; 9.7; 17.3, 6;
21.7
warfare (πόλεμος) MD 2.6, 15, 18; PD
2.9; EP 3.10
warmth (θέρμη) MD 1.14, 18, 21; 2.5,
6; 5.3, 7; 7.11; 9.18; 15.2; 19.27, 29;
23.2, 12, 37; EP 2.6
weakness (ἀσθένεια) MD 2.1, 7, 24,
36; 4.1, 2, 5, 6, 7; 9.7, 25; 17.4, 5;
18.4; 19.4, 6, 7, 9, 11, 13, 14, 15,
17; 21.4; PD 2.13, 18, 22; EP 2.8,
16, 24; 3.2
will (θέλημα, θέλησις) MD 1.21, 31;
2.9, 34; 3.5, 7, 10, 11, 14, 15, 16;
4.18, 22; 5.8; 8.2, 3, 6, 8; 9.1, 2,
5, 22; 11.16; 13.8; 14.23, 28; 16.3,
5; 21.4; 23.24, 35, 52; PD 1.1, 9, 13;
2.13, 14; EP 2.5, 16, 17; 3.4, 7, 8,
11
wine (οἶνον) MD 2.26; 11.7, 9, 12;
23.47; PD 2.7, 8, 18; EP 2.12
wisdom (σοφία) MD 1.2, 8, 15, 22; 2.9,
39, 41, 42, 44; 8.4; 11.18; 13.9;
14.10; 20.2, 4; 23.26, 27, 34; PD 1.9;
EP 2.1
withdrawal (ἀναχώρησις) MD 1.2, 33;
2.50; 4.23; PD 2.26; EP 2.6, 11
woman (γυνή) MD 2.27; 3.2; 4.1, 2,
4, 5; 6.8; 11.9; 20.2, 5, 7; 23.20, 24,
22, 23, 24, 25, 31; PD 1.2, 5; EP
2.11; 4.4
wood gong (ξύλον) MD 1.30; 9.7
work (κόπος) MD 1.12; 2.26, 29, 30,
37, 38; 3.6, 8; 4.3, 8, 17; 5.2; 6.1,
6, 7; 7.10; 8.8; 9.6; 11.9; 13.10; 15.7;
16.4; 17.4; 18.8; 20.7, 9, 10; EP 2.2,
7, 14, 20, 22; 3.11, 13; 4.3; (πόνος)

MD 1.2, 33; 2.14, 24, 26, 28, 29; 3.17; 5.4, 8, 9; 7.3; 14.1, 2, 7; 19.1; PD 2.4; EP 1.3; 2.4; 3.3, 4; 4.3

world, worldly (κόσμος) MD 1.1, 2, 4, 5, 8, 11, 12, 13, 14, 15, 19, 23, 26, 32; 2.8, 9, 12, 22, 25, 29, 30, 32, 35, 36, 39, 41, 44, 58; 3.2, 3, 4, 6, 15, 17; 4.6; 5.3, 4, 5; 6.8; 7.9; 8.2, 3, 4, 8; 9.24; 10.9, 12; 13.3, 5, 6, 8, 9; 14.2, 3, 26; 15.3, 5; 16.4; 17.3, 4; 18.5; 19.2, 7, 9, 13, 18, 19; 21.3, 7; 22.5; 23.17, 18, 19, 21, 22,

23, 24, 45, 49, 57, 60; PD 2.17, 26, 27; EP 1.1; 2.6, 6, 11; 3.5, 6, 7, 8

worship (λατρεία, προσκύνησις) MD 1.33; 2.9, 19, 58; 3.18; 4.22; 5.9; 6.10; 10.13; 11.7; 14.7, 28; 15.8; 18.11; 19.19; 21.10; PD 1.13

wound (τραῦμα) MD 3.12; 18.4; PD 2.13; EP 2.9; 3.5

wrong, see grief

yoke (ζυγός) MD 4.8; PD 2.13, 15